# Canadian Social Welfare

GENERAL EDITORS

**JOANNE C. TURNER**
PROFESSOR EMERITA, RENISON COLLEGE,
UNIVERSITY OF WATERLOO

**FRANCIS J. TURNER**
PROFESSOR EMERITUS,
WILFRID LAURIER UNIVERSITY

SIXTH EDITION

PEARSON

and

Toronto

**Library and Archives Canada Cataloguing in Publication**

Canadian social welfare / general editors, Joanne C. Turner, Francis J. Turner.—6th ed.

Includes bibliographical references and index.
ISBN 978-0-205-53665-8

       1. Public welfare—Canada. 2. Social service—Canada. 3. Canada—Social policy.
I. Turner, Joanne C. II. Turner, Francis J. (Francis Joseph)

HV105.C28 2008     361.971     C2007-906452-3

ISBN-13: 978-0-205-53665-8
ISBN-10: 0-205-53665-4

Vice-President, Editorial Director: Gary Bennett
Senior Acquisitions Editor: Laura Forbes
Marketing Manager: Sally Aspinall
Developmental Editor: Charlotte Morrison-Reed
Production Editor: Söğüt Y. Güleç
Copy Editor: Erica Fyvie
Proofreader: Lenore Latta
Production Coordinator: Janis Raisen
Composition: Laserwords
Permissions: Glen Herbert
Art Director: Julia Hall
Cover Design: Jennifer Stimson
Cover Image: Ron Alston/GettyImages

Statistics Canada information is used with the permission of the Minister of Industry, as Minister responsible for Statistics Canada. Information on the availability of the wide range of data from Statistics Canada can be obtained from Statistics Canada's Regional Offices, its World Wide Web site at http://www.statcan.ca, and its toll-free access number 1-800-263-1136.

1 2 3 4 5     12 11 10 09 08

Printed and bound in USA.

We dedicate this book to the memory of Dr. Bev Antle and Mrs. Marilyn Parsons, two colleagues who had begun work on chapters for this edition but who met untimely deaths before completing their respective contributions: one through an accident and the other through illness.

Both of these colleagues were from Newfoundland, both had graduated from Memorial University, both had been friends, both were committed colleagues of stature, both contributed much to the profession and served with distinction.

They shall be missed.

# Contents

# Foreword

As in so many countries, Canada's commitment to social welfare has shifted from the charitable and voluntary efforts of the past to the much more complex systems of today. Understanding how all the parts of the system fit together, and how they can be improved, begins with the knowledge that is at the heart of this well-known textbook. Our deepest ethical obligations are to seek justice—and we do that not simply by being generous and thoughtful in our own lives, but by making better public policy.

Our economy produces wealth, but it does not necessarily produce fairness. For a long time many social reformers believed that it was by "eradicating capitalism" that justice would be found. Today the debate on public policy focuses on a different set of questions, not the "capitalism versus socialism" debate that dominated politics in so many countries for over a hundred years, but rather a different question—"what kind of capitalism?"—and the practical issues that arise from an effort to understand the relationship between our economy, how we produce wealth, and how we take care of each other. Profound differences in ability and circumstance, in history, in how groups have been treated, in access to education, to mention just a few, inevitably affect outcomes. This book helps us better understand where politics meets policy—whether in health care, housing, disability issues, or the world of welfare and work.

Each generation faces the challenge of creating a sustainable economy and a just society. And the Turners have been there each step of the way, detailing the policy issues and debates that lie at the heart of what we call "social welfare." But behind all the debates lie the fundamental questions "what do we owe each other?" and "how can we make real progress in improving the circumstances of all Canadians?" These issues will continue to be argued out—but the arguments are better if informed by a knowledge of history, and an understanding of the inevitable tensions in making good policy. Read on!

Hon. Bob Rae

# Preface

We are pleased that *Canadian Social Welfare* has matured to the point of a sixth edition. The choice of the word "matured" is not to suggest that earlier editions reflected an immaturity but rather that it is the field itself that has matured. As the table of Contents indicates, the choice of topics viewed as essential in presenting a comprehensive picture of the complex structure known as our welfare system has been modified since the publication of the fifth edition. Much has changed in our social network. Much more than in earlier editions. We are aware that although our system is a factor distinct to our Canadian mosaic, it is one much more influenced by world events than in an earlier day. Thus, to look at the system as it exists in the country, we need to be aware of the nature and thrust of these influencing external factors. In earlier editions there were chapters that addressed Canada's role in international social welfare matters. Now we are writing about the influence of global matters much broader than social welfare and their influence on Canadian social welfare.

So too has the roster of authors changed as new topics are selected for attention and as changes take place in our cadre of colleagues with current expertise in the areas addressed. Indeed, not one of the authors in this present edition, apart from Joanne and me, was among the authors of the first edition.

We are pleased as well that, as with each edition, the cadre of authors who participated represents well our coast-to-coast reality. We are most grateful and appreciative of the contributions of these colleagues. As yet the book still exists in English only, a factor that remains a challenge to us and to the field in general.

In this edition, a chapter has been added on oppression in view of its importance in current social work. As well, in looking at the section on the structure of the social welfare system, we have added a chapter on social service workers.

A new section has been added that deals with quality control in which several societal systems are discussed. These are systems that affect in various ways how quality control is maintained in our complex milieu where many different groups influence the direction of our social welfare policies and services.

It is clear that social welfare remains an important component of the country's fibre and structure. It is one, which needs to be studied in all its aspects. It is an area that requires constant evaluation supported by quality research.

Overall our perspective is that we have a system that needs to be viewed from a positive perspective but since we live in a changing world, it is a system that still has flaws, limitations, and weaknesses. These need to be recognized, addressed, and corrected from the perspectives of an informed citizenry and a quality, dedicated, and research-oriented body of professionals.

## Supplements

*Canadian Social Welfare*, Sixth Edition, will be supplemented with a **Test Item File** and **PowerPoint Presentations**. Both supplements can be downloaded by instructors from a password-protected location on Pearson Education Canada's online catalogue (**vig.pearsoned.ca**). Simply search for the text, then click on "Instructor" under "Resources" in the left-hand menu. Contact your local sales representative for further information.

## Acknowledgments

Once again we have come to the end of the process of organizing a further edition of *Canadian Social Welfare*. Although there is much that is similar in the task of preparing further manuscripts of an edited book, there is also much that is unique about each edition.

This edition was marked by the death of two of our originally selected contributors and the serious injury of another, at different times during the process of the book's preparation. Each of these sad events required our searching for new authors and alterations in the original table of contents. We are most appreciative of the assistance of our colleagues in making the requisite adjustments.

We also wish to acknowledge the collegial cooperation of everyone involved in the process in meeting the various deadlines. Our research assistant Mr. Carlos Pereria was once again of stellar assistance in the planning and carrying out the organizational, technical, and logistic components of the process.

In preparing the previous edition, we commented on the extent to which the use of email, fax, and phone had been an important adjunct to postal and courier services. In this edition, we have seen a complete reversal, with a total shift to these resources. Apart from our original letter of invitation, which was sent by Canada Post, the entire process was completed by these technical resources. (Ironically, this last phase of the process is being written by hand.)

As mentioned before, our family, now geographically widespread, keeps a watchful and supportive eye on these projects. The staff at Pearson Canada and the freelance editors have been most helpful and patient, well aware of their need to understand various interpretations of concepts, such as deadlines and manuscript lengths.

We are of course appreciative of those persons across the land who have and, hopefully, will continue to find the book useful.

In particular, we wish to thank the Honourable Bob Rae for his willingness to prepare the Foreword for the volume.

To all we are thankful!

Joanne and Francis Turner
Toronto, Ontario
March 2008

# Contributors

**Dr. Dan Andreae,** MSW, RSW, Ed.D., is President of the Ontario Association of Social Workers (OASW). He previously served as President from 1993–2000 making him the longest serving president in the history of the profession. During the 1990s he led the profession's successful campaign for statutory regulation. He was also former director of agencies including the Alzheimer Society for Metropolitan Toronto. Dan teaches at the University of Waterloo, where in 2005 he was presented the Distinguished Teaching Award, as well as teaching in Toronto, Ontario. In 2006, he was awarded the Canadian Association of Social Work (CASW) Award for Outstanding National Service presented to one Canadian social worker every two years. In 2007, Dr. Andreae was given an honorary doctorate of laws from Assumption University in Windsor, Ontario, for contributions to social work, health care, education, and public policy.

**Dr. G. Brent Angell,** PhD, RSW, is Professor and Director of the School of Social Work at the University of Windsor. Since joining the University of Windsor in 2003, Dr. Angell has continued to build his research interests focused on social justice and anti-oppressive practice with a particular emphasis on First Nations and at-risk youth. He is renowned for his direct practice research and publications, which concentrate on critical perspectives on therapy and cross-cultural practice. He also serves as a consultant and trainer to a broad constituency on topics-related effective practices, organizational development, and institutional leadership. Of note, Dr. Angell is Chair of the Canadian Association of Deans and Directors of Schools of Social Work (CADDSSW), a member of the Board of Directors of the Canadian Association for Social Work Education (CASWE), and is the Editor of the online periodical *Critical Social Work: An Interdisciplinary Journal Dedicated to Social Justice*.

**Dr. Ken Barter** received his BA degree from Memorial University, Newfoundland and Labrador, his MSW from the University of Calgary, and his PhD from Wilfrid Laurier University, Waterloo, Ontario. He is currently a full professor in the School of Social Work, Memorial University. From September 1998 to April 2004 he held the Research Chair in Child Protection position at Memorial University. Ken spent over 30 years working in child protection systems in several provinces. His many years of experience, combined with his academic research and scholarly activities over the past 12 years support his belief that fundamental paradigm shifts are necessary within public child welfare systems in order to realize more positive outcomes for children and families. Ken is a board member with the Child Welfare League of Canada and also with the Canadian Association for Social Work Education.

**Dr. Rachel Birnbaum,** Ph.D, RSW, is an Associate Professor at King's University College, at the University of Western Ontario, where she teaches children and families, ethics and the law, and research methods. Dr. Birnbaum has both practice experience in working with children and families of separation and/or divorce, has published in this area, and has presented both nationally and internationally. She is presently completing her Master of Law degree, specializing in family law. At the time of this writing she has been the President of the Ontario College of Social Workers and Social Service Workers since 2006.

**Dr. Ralph Bodor** has extensive experience in the delivery of human services, research, and social work education in rural, remote, and Aboriginal communities in Alberta and northern Canada. Using a hermeneutic approach, Dr. Bodor has explored in depth the experiences of professional social workers with nonsexual dual/multiple relationships in rural and remote communities. Dr. Bodor is a member of the Faculty of Social Work, University of Calgary and, since 1999, has been heavily involved in the development and delivery of accredited social work courses in various communities throughout Alberta. Most of his current research is in partnership with various First Nations communities in northern Alberta and he has spent the last four years learning to speak Woodland Cree. Dr. Bodor lives by a lake in rural Alberta with his family—and his co-dependent cat, Max.

**Dr. Tom Brenner** received his MSW and PhD from Wilfrid Laurier University. He has held positions in direct practice, program planning and evaluation, and policy development with municipal social services and the social resources council. He has taught at the community college and university levels joining the faculty at Renison College, University of Waterloo, in 1988. Currently, he is involved in a variety of community agencies, including the Community Safety and the Crime Prevention Council of Waterloo Region and the SUNDANCE group that attempts to advance academic opportunities for First Nations people.

**Cathy and John Brothers** met as graduate students in the social work program at Wilfrid Laurier University. Both have their Masters degree in social work. In addition, John received an M.B.A. from Wilfrid Laurier University. Cathy and John have each enjoyed 40 years of broadly based social work practice. Both have been long-term sessional lecturers in social work practice and social issues and policy at both Wilfrid Laurier University and University of Guelph. Both have extensive service on a variety of boards of directors for social services, associations of social services, hospital and health care systems, and community service organizations, including Rotary. Presently, John is a social work therapist in private practice in Kitchener, Ontario. He also is an adjudicator throughout Ontario with the Criminal Injuries Compensation Board for the Province of Ontario. Since 1992, Cathy has been the Executive Director of Catholic Family Counselling Centre (Region of Waterloo). CFCC provides Employee Assistance Programs both locally and through its affiliates throughout North America. CFCC is a pioneer in hosting an innovative "under one roof" multi-sector approach to helping women and children who are victims of domestic violence.

**Dr. Carole Pigler Christensen** is Professor Emeritus and a former Director of the University of British Columbia School of Social Work and Family Studies. Prior to her UBC appointment she was on the faculty of the McGill University School of Social Work for 21 years. She chaired the Task Force on Multicultural and Multiracial Issues in Social Work Education (1988–1991) of the Canadian Association of Schools of Social Work. This led to accreditation standards that take these issues into account. She has initiated and serves as Program Director of the Vancouver-based Multicultural Family Centre, and she has published extensively in multicultural and anti-racist social work, the focus of her research, practice, and teaching for many years.

**Melanie Cohen** earned her BSW from York University. Her professional interests are clinical practice in the area of psychosocial adjustments, child welfare, and social policy. She actively volunteers with a group of psychiatrically disabled people.

**John Cossom** is Professor Emeritus, School of Social Work at the University of Victoria. He has also taught at Regina, Saskatchewan, and at Waterloo and Wilfrid Laurier universities in Ontario. He practised in child welfare, family services, and corrections. John is a long-suffering supporter of Gillingham Football Club.

**Dr. Roger Delaney** is a professor of social work at Lakehead University with over 30 years of teaching and research experience. Roger is a co-author of *Canadian Social Policy: an Introduction* as well as a co-editor of five books on northern and rural social work. Roger's main interests are social work/welfare philosophy and ethics, social policy and social welfare, rural and northern social work, poverty, organizational and community development, family violence, child welfare, and young offenders.

**Sabra Desai,** MSW, RSW, is a faculty member in the Social Service Worker Program at the Humber Institute of Technology and Advanced Learning (Humber College) in Toronto, Ontario. In addition to her teaching responsibilities, she is seconded to the Human Resources Department as Manager Diversity Initiatives to advance equity issues within Humber College. While grounded in theory, she is far more of a practitioner than a theorist as clearly revealed by her commitment to civic responsibility and volunteerism. Sabra has over 20 years of experience in teaching and consulting on issues of racism, equity, access and organizational development, and change both in Canada and abroad in countries like Ethiopia, Guyana, South Africa, and the U.S.

**Dr. Glenn Drover** is retired. Formerly, he was director of the Schools of Social Work at Dalhousie University, Carleton University, and the University of British Columbia. He was also chair professor in the Department of Applied Social Studies at the City University of Hong Kong. He remains an active member of the eastern branch of the Ontario Association of Social Workers and is a policy consultant with the Canadian Association of Social Workers. He also participates in many community activities.

**Donald Evans,** BA, BSW, is the President of the Board of the Canadian Training Institute, a nonprofit organization providing training and technical assistance to both correctional and social service agencies. Mr. Evans served as Assistant Deputy Minister, Policing Services Division in the Ministry of the Solicitor General and Correctional Services, Ontario, until leaving the government. Prior to this appointment, he served as Executive Director Community Corrections in the Ministry of Correctional Services, Ontario, Executive Coordinator of Justice Policy, Cabinet Office, Ontario, and Executive Director Executive Development Institute, Human Resources Secretariat, Ontario. Mr. Evans has been an adjunct professor at Woodsworth College, University of Toronto, in Penology and Policing from 1975 to 2006. He is currently the executive editor of the *Journal of Community Corrections* and on the editorial board of the *Journal of*

*Offender Monitoring*, and the National Association of Probation Executives' *Executive Exchange Journal*. Mr. Evans is a past president of the International Community Corrections Association, a past president of the American Probation and Parole Association, and a past president and life member of the Probation Officers Association of Ontario. Mr. Evans serves on the executive of APPA. Mr. Evans is the Chair of the American Correctional Association's International Relations Committee. He has served on a number of community agency boards. Currently, he is on the board of the Toronto St. Leonard's Society and is Chair of the Citizen's Advisory Committee for the Downtown Toronto Parole Office (CSC), and also serves as cluster Chair for the Central District (Ontario) CAC.

**Margaret (Maggie) Fietz** is a retired social worker, recent CEO of Family Service Canada (1994–2006). She has extensive expertise in the areas of family services, strengths-based practices, home support, HIV/AIDS, information technology in the voluntary sector, and employee assistance program national management. She is a skilled workshop and meeting facilitator and social policy analyst. Maggie has a MSW from Carleton University (1974) and is a member of the Ontario College of Professional Social Workers and of the Ontario Association of Social Workers. She has authored and edited quarterly newsletters (*Let's Talk Families*), articles on child and family matters, social policy briefs, and is reviewer of articles and books for Canadian Association of Social Workers. She has made numerous presentations and speeches throughout her 40 year social work career. Maggie is a Site Reviewer for the Canadian Family Services Accreditation Program.

**Kerri-Ann Fitzgerald** received her MSW from McMaster University. She has a variety of research interests including the care that grandparents provide to grandchildren who receive services from child welfare agencies as well as children's health. She has conducted research on Canadian child nutrition and plays an advocacy role for healthy nutrition policies and programs in school settings. Her clinical experience also includes counselling with older adults and their families in hospital settings.

**Dr. James Gladstone** is a professor in the School of Social Work at McMaster University. His research has concentrated on family relationships and the way that relationships are negotiated within families and between families, and other systems. His research, for example, has focused on grandparenting, adoption reunions, the relationships between elderly married couples, relocation to long-term care, and the relationships between formal and informal caregivers.

**Dr. John R. Graham** is the Murray Fraser Professor at the Faculty of Social Work, University of Calgary. He has published in the areas of spirituality and social work, international development in the Arab Middle East, and Canadian social policy. His co-authored *Canadian Social Policy: An Introduction* (3rd edition) appears in 2008, and his co-edited *Canadian Social Work and Spirituality: Current Readings and Approaches* was published in 2007. His co-authored *Helping Professional Practice with Indigenous Peoples: The Bedouin-Arab case* is upcoming.

**Sheila Hardy, Anishinaabe-Kwe** from Northern Ontario, is director of Academic Native Affairs and an Associate Professor in the Bachelor of Social Work: Native Human Services program at Laurentian University. Her current doctoral research focuses on intergenerational trauma, historical witness, and Aboriginal pedagogy.

**Linda Hill** is a professor in the Social Service Worker Program at Humber College, Ontario. She has a passion for education and is strongly committed to supporting the important role of social service workers in the helping profession. Linda has spent over 20 years working in the social services sector in front-line and management positions focusing on counselling, case management, and supportive services for older adults and persons with disabilities. She also works on a consulting basis with community groups in the areas of funding proposal development, needs assessment, and project development and evaluation. Linda has a Masters of Arts Degree from the University of Toronto in community development and is a registered social worker.

**Dr. Marion E. Jones** received her Ph.D. in economics from the School of Oriental and African Studies, University of London, and is associate professor of economics at the University of Regina. She has 14 years of experience teaching and researching in the field of social welfare economics in developing countries, particularly China, but also India, Nepal, and Costa Rica. She is the Vice-President of the Chinese Economists Society, and the President of the Justice Emmett Hall Foundation—fostering excellence in Canadian Health Policy Research. She has also been active in social welfare and social cohesion research in rural Saskatchewan and on the labour market attachment needs of vulnerable groups in Regina and Calgary. This research is currently being expanded to examine social welfare services for the employed homeless in western Canada, and the social welfare implications of housing policy in North Central Regina.

**Katka Hrncic-Lipovic,** M.S.W., R.S.W., immigrated to Canada in 1997 from an ethnically divided, war-torn Bosnia-Herzegovina. As a newcomer, she has started a new life in Canada where cultural diversity is embraced and welcomed. Ms. Hrncic-Lipovic's interests include social justice as it relates to issues of immigration and the refugee determination process in Canada. Currently, she is a research assistant exploring social exclusion and incidences of racially-motivated hate crimes in public housing. Ms. Hrncic-Lipovic's practice focus is on elder abuse and the vulnerability of seniors.

**Teri Kay,** MSW, RSW, is the former director of Family and Community Service at Jewish Family and Child Service in Toronto. She was also a board member of Family Service Ontario and an accreditor and member of the accrediting committee of that body.

**Dr. Dennis Kimberley** received his M.S.W. from McGill University and his Ph.D. from the University of Toronto. Since 1985 he has been a professor at Memorial University in Newfoundland and Labrador. Earlier in his career he was the Executive Director of the Canadian Association of Schools of Social Work and was a director with the Addiction Research Foundation of Ontario. He has been an educator, consultant, and trainer provincially, nationally, and internationally and has been on numerous boards including those of CASW and IASSW. His areas of expertise include children's protection and addictions. He has an active private practice and has a special interest in child sexual abuse, sexual exploitation, sexual deviation, sex offending, parental capacity of mentally ill and addicted parents, and addictions and concurrent disorder. He has appeared as an expert witness on numerous occasions before courts and government inquiries.

**Dr. Brigitte Kitchen** received her PhD from the School of Social Administration (today the School of Social Policy) at the London School of Economics. The major focus of her research and publications has been on the distribution of income for families raising children in or outside the labour market in terms of questioning who gets what size of the income pie and why. From 1990 to 1993, she served as a commissioner of the Ontario Fair Tax Commission where she represented the popular sector. She is active in the community; a former chair and co-founder of the Child Poverty Action Group and the Centre for Social Justice and currently a co-editor of the *Canadian Social Policy Review*, the only academic social policy journal in Canada.

**Dr. Iara Lessa** is an associate professor at the School of Social Work at Ryerson University in Toronto where she teaches social policy and social work practice. Her fields of study include feminist theory, single motherhood, social policy and social welfare, gender and women, and food security. On these subjects she has been developing knowledge, which has been disseminated through various national and international publications, conferences, and other forums, and also applied in a variety of community projects and partnerships. Iara holds a PhD in Social Work and she supports international projects as a consultant on gender issues.

**Dr. Grant Macdonald** received his MSW and PhD from the University of Toronto's Faculty of Social Work. He has 30 years of teaching experience and is currently an associate professor at York University. His current research interests include the measurement of social support and qualitative research methodologies.

**Dr. Anne-Marie Mawhiney** is Dean of the Faculty of Professional Schools and professor of social work at Laurentian University in Sudbury, Ontario. She is a former director of the school and of the Institute for Northern Ontario Research and Development.

**Dr. Ted McNeill,** Ph.D., R.S.W., is the Director of Social Work and Child Life at The Hospital for Sick Children in Toronto and is an associate professor in the Faculty of Social Work at the University of Toronto. Working in a health-care setting, he understands the institutional context of social work practice within the health-care field and is knowledgeable about interprofessional approaches to care. His academic interests include child and family adaptation to chronic health conditions, positive father involvement, evidence-based practice, diversity, and the social determinants of health. These foci are part of his continuing interest in families, health, and social justice.

**Dr. David Nicholas** is Clinical and Academic Specialist, Social Work; Associate Scientist, Research Institute, The Hospital for Sick Children; and Associate Professor, Faculty of Social Work, University of Toronto. He brings research leadership in multiple funded studies addressing psychosocial adaptation to paediatric health conditions. Dr. Nicholas holds multiple research awards and is widely published. Examples of research initiated by Dr. Nicholas include trajectories of autism-based parental care, social support needs of fathers of children with spina bifida, and quality of life among mothers of children with chronic kidney disease. Dr. Nicholas brings a strong research grounding in qualitative and mixed method approaches, demonstrated by substantial graduate teaching in qualitative and mixed method research design. Based on his strong research and clinical background, Dr. Nicholas is well-versed in the complex impacts of chronic illness and disability, and he is a sought-after speaker nationally and internationally.

**Louise Osmond,** MSW, RSW, received her BSW and MSW from Memorial University. She has directed her own private practice since 1993. Louise has presented nationally and internationally and has taught, as a sessional lecturer, child abuse assessment and intervention as well as social work in addictions. Her areas of expertise include sexualized and traumatized children and youth, services for victims of violence and trauma, sibling incest, victims of domestic violence, treatment of concurrent disordered persons, and integrated foster care treatment.

**Dr. Barbara Decker Pierce** is the Director of the School of Social Work at King's University College at the University of Western Ontario. She has her PhD degree in general management from the Ivey Business School. Before entering academia she worked in program design and delivery for the Ontario Ministry of Community and Social Services and has practised as a strategy consultant for human service organizations. She focuses her management research on leadership and organizational structure and is currently involved in program evaluation with a range of social service organizations.

**Dr. Linda Snyder** is an associate professor at Renison College's School of Social Work at the University of Waterloo. Her Doctorate and Master's degrees are from Wilfrid Laurier Univeristy. She has done research on social mobilization in women's collective endeavours in Canada, Chile, and Mexico and she has accompanied student groups on field trips in Mexico. She is currently the Chair of the CASSW Standing Committee on International Affairs and represents Canada on the board of the IASSW.

**Dr. Tracy Swan** is an assistant professor with the School of Social Work, Memorial University. Before moving to Memorial, she was with the School of Social Work, McMaster University, where she taught a variety of courses that related to direct practice. While residing in Ontario, Dr. Swan also provided training throughout the province in the field of child welfare and children's mental health. Her writing and research focuses on pedagogical issues related to teaching critical social work and anti-oppressive practice, as well as policy and practice in child welfare, with a specific focus on foster care.

**Dr. Francis Turner** is a Professor Emeritus and former Dean of the Faculty of Social Work at Wilfrid Laurier University, Waterloo, Ontario. He has written and edited several books on theory and practice, including *Social Work Practice: A Canadian Perspective*, 2nd Edition, and *Social Work Treatment: Interlocking Theoretical Perspectives*, 4th Edition. He is also editor of the *Canadian Encyclopedia of Social Work*. He earned his Master's degree from the University of Ottawa and his doctorate from Columbia University, New York.

**Dr. Joanne Turner** is a Professor Emerita and former director of Social Work, Renison College, University of Waterloo, Ontario. She has extensive experience in clinical practice, teaching, supervision, research, and policy initiatives. She served as past chair of the Ontario College of Certified Social Workers and chairs the Finance Committee of the Ontario College of Social Workers and Social Service Workers. She is currently the Board President of the Catholic Children's Aid Society of Toronto.

**Dr. Linda Turner** is an Associate Professor in the Department of Social Work at St. Thomas University in Fredericton, New Brunswick. She completed her PhD in social work at Memorial University and her MSW at Université de Moncton. Her writing and research focus on forms of creativity in social work practice, linguistic respect, and the challenges and benefits of practising in an officially bilingual context.

**Dr. Doreen Winkler** received her Ph.D. in social work from the University of Toronto and taught social work courses at York University, Toronto, and at King's University College, London, Ontario. She held social work positions in mental health and rehabilitation settings in Toronto and served on the provincial board and is completing her second term on the Toronto Central Branch Board of OASW. She served ten years as a member of the Immigration and Refugee Board of Canada and is now serving a five-year appointment on the Ontario Review Board. Currently, she is the Acting Chair of the Accessibility for Ontarians with Disabilities Act Alliance.

**Dr. Kim Zapf** received his MSW from the University of British Columbia and his PhD from the University of Toronto. Following years of practice in the Yukon, he has been with the Faculty of Social Work at the University of Calgary since 1986 where he is a full professor. Dr. Zapf has published some 50 journal articles and book chapters on social work practice and education in rural, remote, and Aboriginal communities. He has presented his work at conferences across North America as well as in Hawaii, Australia, Sweden, Denmark, Finland, and South Korea. Teaching primarily in the undergraduate program, he has been active in the development of new curriculum, team teaching, and course integration.

# CHAPTER 1

# The Socio-Cultural Base of Canadian Social Welfare

*Francis J. Turner*

## INTRODUCTION

> *Brother, can you spare a dime?*
> *They used to tell me*
> *I was building a dream,*
> *With peace and glory ahead.*
> *Why should I be standing in line,*
> *Just waiting for bread?*
> *Brother, can you spare a dime?*

The above words are from a now long forgotten song of the Great Depression of the 1930s: the era in the last century known as the "Dirty Thirties." This was a period in our history that had significant impact on the development and shape of that critical facet of contemporary Canadian fabric which we call social welfare, the topic of this volume.

The words of this song reflect several themes of import in understanding social welfare as it now exists in the first decade of the twenty-first century, themes that will be discussed in more detail in subsequent chapters. First, the song expresses the reality that there were then, as there are now, people in Canadian society lacking the basic necessities of life. The song also reflects a perception (or hope) that we are all part of a common family in which a stranger could comfortably address another stranger as "brother" with some expectation of a positive response. Finally, one can see in these words a sense of cynicism and futility that in a country with such vast resources people could still go hungry. The breadlines of the thirties still exist in the food banks of the new century.

## DEFINITION

What then do we mean by *social welfare*? Social welfare is the term used in contemporary society to describe the structure and network of policies, services, legislation, institutions, and personnel that have developed over the almost 150 years of our country's history. The system exists to provide the psychosocial needs of all. That is, it seeks to enable us to achieve and maintain a position in a just society that fosters the development of each person's potential.

For many reasons the structure of Canadian social welfare has been and remains highly intricate, reflecting the complexities of our country and our times. Thus, to understand, assess, and contribute to its ongoing development in a professional manner requires that we understand its complexities, the reason for its complexities, the diversity of needs addressed or not addressed by the systems, and how these various systems interact.

## SOME QUESTIONS

As we begin our discussion of social welfare we are faced with a group of questions that need to be addressed. *Who should be helped? Why should they be helped? How much should they be helped? How should they be helped? What kinds of help are appropriate? Who should decide what is appropriate and who should help them?* In various segments of society there are a variety of strongly held responses to each of these questions. This variety creates unevenness in the structure of welfare that has emerged in our country.

In addition to a range of views about forms and targets of help, there is a variety of need in a country as large and geographically diverse as Canada. As well, we live in an ever-changing world that means the needs of individuals and groups change as does the variety of ways of providing needed assistance.

## THE RECIPIENTS OF SOCIAL WELFARE

In beginning our discussion it is important to remind ourselves of a frequently overlooked reality in our society directly associated with the present structure of social welfare. That is, that every citizen of Canada, whether newly arrived, or descended from families living here for generations or families here for several millennia, is a recipient of social welfare. Each one of us, from the young street person to the prime minister, directly benefits from one or more municipal, provincial, or federal programs that are a part of the Canadian welfare structure. Many as well will benefit from some part of the informal network known as the voluntary section. In one way or another, we are all recipients of social welfare.

Further, every adult citizen contributes to the financing of this important component of our society. We do so indirectly through the municipal, provincial, and federal systems of taxation, including the various types of wage deductions that finance this system. To an increasing extent, many citizens also contribute directly to the system through voluntary donations to the myriad causes that solicit our support. We do this whether it be by giving a loonie directly to a street person, or by donating to highly visible organizations such as the United Way or an international body such as the Red Cross.

This point about the universality of the system is mentioned early in our discussion to help us internalize this fact. It is a reality that reflects one of many attitudinal changes that have taken place in regard to the questions mentioned above as to who should be helped, how, and why.

## WHY SUPPORT SOCIAL WELFARE?

In order to understand the complexity of our welfare system, we need to answer an important question: *Why should we Canadians choose to help each other at all?* This is not a simple question.

What are some possible responses?

For many Canadians, the commitment or willingness to help each other arises from a religious perspective and the exigencies of the virtue of charity in the word's proper theological meaning. In this way, one still refers to some aspects of social welfare as charity. Some social agencies and institutions include the word "charity" in their names, for example, "the Catholic Charities." From this perspective, persons deemed to be blessed by divine providence are seen as having a responsibility to help those less fortunate than they. They do this either directly or by supporting groups and organizations that provide various kinds of help.

Others in our society view the concept of social welfare as a form of charity, but in a pejorative sense of the word. Over the decades there has been and still is a work-oriented ethic that strongly frowns on the idea of persons receiving "charity." This is viewed as having access to the goods and services of society without "working" for them or "deserving" them. This idea was manifested in the term "welfare bum" of a few years ago, a term which suggested that there were people who were taking from society rather than contributing to it. For some, this perception of persons being dependent on society was viewed as a cause of many of our economic problems.

From another perspective, some advocate a responsibility to help each other from a philosophical base. It is posited that as intelligent members of the human race, each of us has a social responsibility to ensure that all people have access to what is needed to achieve their full human potential.

A tenet of this latter value is that each and every citizen has a right to society's assistance when needed. This concept of individual citizen rights has developed over centuries of thought and varies within and between various political systems.

It is this perception of a common societal responsibility that motivates individuals and groups to lobby for, sponsor, and support a vast range of philanthropical endeavours across the country. In addition, this view of societal responsibility promotes advocating and lobbying for more just, effective, and universal social policies, programs, and legislation at all levels of society.

For many, but not all, Canadians, our rights and duties to each other in meeting social welfare needs extends to people in other parts of the world who may be in need of help that we can provide. Although there is not full consensus on this to date, Canada has an excellent track record of providing help to other countries.

Another approach to social welfare argues that whether we have a right to such services or not, it is sound economic practice for a country to have a system that ensures the distribution of that country's resources and services to everyone. This attention to individual and group needs ensures the smooth running of a country and assists in harmony between countries.

From an economic perspective, others hold that it makes good economic and business sense to enable all people to participate in the commerce of a country and to help them use their individual strengths by contributing to society. Such a position avoids the question of who should and should not be helped and focuses rather on the public and economic benefits of a fully functioning citizenry.

Finally, some believe, but rarely express openly, the idea that a strong, equitable, fairly administered social welfare system functions as a method of social control, and hence should be encouraged and supported. Without such a system, persons in need could become upset, angry, and liable to commit violent acts. Thus, effective political policy ensures peace, order, and maintenance of the status quo.

## DIVERSITY OF SOCIAL WELFARE

Policies, methods, programs, goals, structures, and the extent of social welfare vary from country to country and indeed within countries. Thus, to understand a particular social welfare system we need to understand something of the society in which it has developed, especially its values and history. Because of our diversity in values, the system that has emerged is diverse. Diversity in a system is neither good nor bad. On the positive side, a highly diverse system can insure that a wide range of needs is being met. However, a diverse system can also be highly uneven so that different needs are met in an unequal way.

## VALUES

As such, in looking at Canada we need to take into consideration the various values that influence a welfare system. These values differ across the country and from individual to individual. They incorporate such things as self-sufficiency, individual and group responsibilities to others, and the perceived responsibilities of communities, families, churches, businesses, and governments in our lives.

Our values also differ according to ideological, political, cultural, and professional positions about collective duties and responsibilities to various individuals and groups. These values in turn shape the structures and extent of policies and services that our country has developed and supported.

Although we all participate to some extent in the system, for many people today there is still a strong we/they aspect to understanding welfare and, thus, a perceived rationalization for distancing ourselves from discussions of social responsibility. This attitude is a carry-over from the ideologies that drove the early days of social welfare in Canada.

## HISTORICAL ISSUES

Prior to the First World War, what social welfare existed was an uneven combination of the traditions of the English *Poor Law* with its stress on the deserving and undeserving categorization of people in need and a disconnected structure of voluntary services. These were provided through the private sector, principally the various denominations of churches. The aftermath of WWI, which saw thousands of veterans return with a broad range of needs, stirred the guilt of the nation and helped sow the seeds for the understanding of society's responsibilities to those in need.

This beginning sense of a social responsibility for persons in need regardless of cause was further emphasized in the latter stages of the Great Depression. In the early years of this calamity the reality of the need was greatly minimized by the body politic, followed by a period of blame that those in need were there by their own doing. Only slowly did some political confirmation develop. As the reality of the situation clarified and social responsibility emerged, the little assistance that was available was difficult to receive as the various levels of government strove to project upon each other the responsibility to help.

Eventually, however, a system of public assistance, though inadequate, was put into place. It was on this base that a more permanent structure was built.

Nevertheless, it took the ravages of the Second World War and the millions of persons who were in need through no cause of their own to clarify for the Canadian public the universality of need and national responsibility of responding to need. This established a broad range of social programs that serve as the basis for our contemporary network.

# THE PRESENT

World events always help to shape societal attitudes to welfare. Today there is a much broader acceptance of the need for a strong countrywide social net. This is built on the realization and assumption that our social welfare structure is a critical part of contemporary society. Differing views are about the content and shape of such a structure.

For any number of reasons, be it the transferring of some industry to another part of the world or the increasing need for programs for the elderly, at some time in our lives we are going to need help from others in society. In an interesting way, the dramatic climatic disasters of recent years, which have left whole populations in need, have helped shaped the acceptance of the fact that at any time the former "they" could be "we." We learned this lesson after the events of 9/11; we are all at risk of being tomorrow's victims.

There has also been a shift in attitude about how society views single parents, addicts, or persons infected with various diseases, such as AIDS. Although not universal, there is a growing acceptance that much individual need comes from systemic faults rather than individual failings.

One limiting aspect of the acceptance of the need for a strong social welfare network is a sense that our system is a good one and does not need to be changed. What is being overlooked with this assumption are two realities. First, in spite of the appearance of a supposedly comprehensive network, many of the benefits provided are inadequate. In the nineties, a highly supported move on the part of governments was to cut social spending. This was based on a rationale that the level of benefits was more than enough and that there was considerable abuse in the system. Both of these premises have been refuted and yet the resources cut at that time have not been restored. In fact, the gap between the haves and the have-nots is growing even though the reality of this gap is not always accepted and understood.

Second, what is also overlooked is that in our efforts to develop plans and programs for all needs on an equitable basis, many citizens of Canada fall between the cracks and suffer considerable deprivation because of this. That is, many needs are very idiosyncratic and do not fit the requirements of various groups without a change in policy or legislation. The population of our working poor best demonstrates this.

Some of the visual cues that the system is lacking include the emergence of childhood poverty, the existence of food banks in most cities, the increasing number of street people, and the lack of adequate low-level housing. Although there is still a tendency, as there has been over the centuries, to blame the persons in need, this is no longer as firm a position. Over and over again it has been shown that real need exists, that poverty is a huge problem in our affluent country, and that the causes are complex and systemic.

One of the further challenges facing a broader understanding of social welfare in society is the "warp and woof patterns." In other words, because much of the public concept of social welfare revolves around essential yet mundane things like food, clothing, money, and housing, as well as the essential area of child welfare, many believe they understand the dimensions of need in these areas. In this way, there is a tendency for a significant component of society to view themselves as quasi experts in matters of social welfare.

Hence, many decisions about needed programs, the regulations surrounding such programs, and the ability to assess need get debated and settled by the body politic, the media, and the citizenry at large rather than by experts in the disciplines. It is this attitude of quasi expertise that leads to criticisms and journalistic attacks on persons and groups perceived by society to be abusing the system for their perceived deficits. The usual criticism of social welfare programs argues that they are too generous with "taxpayer money."

This perceived expertise is still tainted by the centuries-old concept of deserving and undeserving. Such an attitude often carries with it a belief that programs of assistance should be minimal, lest persons choose to rely on them rather than seek employment. The skill, of course, that makes a program effective is in knowing what is needed, why it is needed, and how best to meet an identified need in a way that facilitates growth and development while avoiding undue dependence.

One of the problems related to this needed skill in assessing need is also related to the warp and woof pattern. Many of the skills and resources for addressing social welfare problems touch on the skilful use of components of the daily life of clients. Thus, a shared cup of coffee with a client at Tim Hortons may well have as much or more positive effect on a problem-laden client than several weeks of intensive interviews. Yet this might be viewed by many as possibly spoili`ng someone and creating dependency.

Scientific knowledge is based on tangible fact and, as such, is not questioned in the same way that social or arts programs would be. In this way, an individual would be unlikely to question an expensive medical prescription for some identified problem, yet have strong views of the appropriateness of giving a client $25.00 in cash to purchase some food for the family. The client's anxiety about this need could well be the cause of the medical problem for which medical help is given.

## ATTITUDINAL CHANGES

However, attitudinal changes are taking place; views are changing, shaped by more recent trends and events. Although, of course, there are still some who focus on particular societal groups and question their receipt of various benefits, for the most part there is a country-wide acceptance of the necessity of a strong social net. With this is a growing understanding that the majority of social need stems from systemic causes over which individuals have little or no influence. The fact that many of these requests for assistance are for needs in other parts of the world reflects another aspect of our growing attitudinal change in that psychosocial need does not exist only in Canada but everywhere. A further part of this, one only now being generally realized, is that as we provide aid to other parts of the world we are also in the long run helping our own country and ourselves.

The growing acceptance of the need for a strong social welfare structure is an interesting one because of its extent. Programs such as pensions, Employment Insurance, Old Age Assistance, and child care are now understood as a necessary part of any country's socio-cultural structure. Many of these programs that we regard as basic rights were seen as revolutionary in our grandparents' time. Interested parties espousing these views were seen as communists and radicals, persons who needed to be put down by force if necessary.

## LIMITATIONS

Our social welfare system is both comprehensive and flawed.

We are deluged with mail and telemarketing requests from dozens of organizations seeking our financial assistance for some urgent social welfare need. These organizations need to spend an inordinate amount of time and energy seeking funds rather than devoting their efforts to the needs of their identified target groups.

One of the real challenges of building a system that fairly and efficiently responds to the needs of all citizens stems from our geography and our climate. Although the majority of our population is clustered in a coast to coast ribbon on our southern border, there is still a significant number who live in more remote areas away from the border in very isolated situations challenged by weather. Persons in these areas often have different needs. Thus, for some families the provision of a snowmobile as a social welfare benefit could be a life-protecting resource, while in another part of the country the same snowmobile would be viewed as a political scandal with demands for a parliamentary investigation.

Social welfare is sometimes viewed as a solely financial network, a system of input and output. As such, citizens can deem themselves as worthy judges of how that money is spent. There is still a fear of social welfare programs' just being "handouts." If we look at health care, though, therein lies a hypocritical dilemma. Our citizens will each require thousands of dollars of health care, regardless of lifestyle choices that may contribute to a greater share of need. Yet we question whether we should give a loonie to a street person in considerable need lest he "misuse" it. Since we all need some economic skills to survive in a society such as ours, we like to think of ourselves as experts regarding the needs of others. But since we are not all medically trained we dare not question the costs of medical care. In this way, we support the right and necessity of a physician to dispense medications, but would probably question whether social workers should be allowed to dispense money to persons in need.

At times we may question whether we should help people in need or not. For the homeless, we spend considerable amounts of money looking for ways to hide homeless citizens rather than helping with affordable housing. We might find ourselves irritated by the request for a quarter while we would quite comfortably write a cheque for $50.00 to aid the victims of some natural disaster far from home.

Canadians have been dependent for decades on universal programs (i.e., programs in which everyone in a particular category receives the benefits of the program, like children or the elderly). Social welfare's voluntary sector can best serve those who fall between the cracks. The main problem with the voluntary sector is the fact that it must raise its own funds and the competition for the private dollar is intense. This mandates that organizations spend a considerable amount of time fundraising, which can detract from the social issues at hand.

The social issues raised in this introduction will be studied more closely in subsequent chapters. The book as a whole represents the complex and thought-provoking Canadian social welfare structure. Since the structure is one aspect of our society that personally touches us, as responsible citizens in a democratic society we ought to insure we are well-informed about it. This is true if our goal is to become a social worker, a social service worker, a member of another profession in the human services, a better informed recipient of services, a volunteer, an advocate for social change, or an inquiring, responsible citizen.

A system as personal as our social welfare network ought not to be taken for granted. Each of us needs to hold accountable those who are responsible for its maintenance, evaluation, and development. To do so requires a level of understanding of its structure and functioning. It is our hope that the contents of this book will contribute to the requisite knowledge base.

# CHAPTER 2

# The Philosophical and Value Base of Canadian Social Welfare

*Roger Delaney*

*Most real progress occurs when individuals take hold of the idea that there is a better, more humane, or more just way. They assert that our capacity for excellence, in ourselves and in our affairs with one another, matters and that acting on that capacity is as much a choice as is rejecting it. They are just not willing to settle for mediocrity or meanness. These people are idealists.*

*Homan, 1994, p. 32*

## INTRODUCTION

As Turner notes in Chapter 1, widely divergent views on the nature of social welfare exist within each society, and between different societies. These views are based on competing perspectives and values, each with its own definition of human nature, society, and the relationship of people and society. In many ways, social welfare becomes each society's definition "of the good and the desirable which in turn are embedded in societal values" (Frederico, 1984, 20). Advocates of social welfare essentially believe that equality reflects both the public interest and the common good.

As the twentieth century progressed, Canada's governments began to take a greater role in social welfare, and social programs began to expand. However, the positive gains achieved by the Canadian social welfare system from the 1940s to the 1970s were slowly eroded during the 1980s and the 1990s.

One major factor in the decline of Canada's social programs and its concomitant decrease in its citizens' physical and emotional resources is the "globalization" social movement. Driven by multinational companies and neo-conservative governments, free trade agreements are eroding the ability of governments to govern and to control the economic forces within their own territories (Clarke, 1997). Included with these free trade agreements sanctioned by neo-conservative and right-wing liberal governments is also a sinister and malevolent effort to destroy the Canadian social welfare system:

> Their [neo-conservatives'/free trade advocates'] remarkably successful demonization of the public sector has turned much of the citizenry against their own [*sic*] mechanisms. Many of us have been enrolled in the cause of interests that have no particular concern for the citizen's welfare, our welfare. Instead, the citizen is reduced to the status of a subject at the throne of the marketplace (Saul, 1995).

This new thrust, known as *corporatism*, is entering the lifeblood of social programs and is being driven by a desire to alter the very culture of Canadian social welfare. Because social programs depend on the government or the public for funding, governments' social and economic policies have the power to determine not only the nature of services, but also, equally importantly, how these services will be delivered:

> Well, corporatism with its market- and technology-led delusions is profoundly tied to a mechanistic view of the human race. This is not an ideology with any interest in or commitment to the shape of society or the individual as citizen. It is fixed upon a rush to use machinery inanimate or human while these are still at full value, before they suffer any depreciation (Saul, 1995, 162).

## What Does an Advocate of Social Welfare Look Like?

Social welfare advocates believe that all human beings are equal based on the very essence of what it means to be a human. This perspective views all human beings as transformative, that is, as beings capable of continuous development and evolution. Freire (1968) refers to this transformation process as the "ontological and historic vocation to become more fully human" (48).

In very simple terms, equality promotes the view that all human beings are equal and human attributes, such as gender, race, colour, sexual orientation, wealth, health, ability, talents, and religious preference *describe* humans but do not *define* humans. Violence, power, and oppression begin the moment one group asserts the greater value of their attribute over different attributes that other human

beings have. This manifests itself in the concept of ascendancy (Graham, Swift, and Delaney, 2003, 90–91) where being white or heterosexual or Canadian or male or rich or tall or young is given higher importance than its counterpart.

Social welfare advocates recognize that humans create the societies in which they live and that when societies are created or evolve based on privilege for some and disadvantage for others, systemic inequalities exist which maintain this inequality. Advocates believe that a primary function of society is to provide every citizen with sufficient physical, emotional, and spiritual resources required to manage physical, emotional, and spiritual life tasks. Social justice and social contracts are major themes promoted by social welfare advocates.

With a powerful rhetoric (language), propaganda (self-serving information), and dialect (use of corporate language), corporatism is trying to gain global control of the economy and ascendancy of that economy over social policy (Saul, 1995). Moreover, because of the international infiltration by the multinational companies and other economic interest groups, it is very difficult to find the "enemy" with whom to be angry. How does a citizen confront what is global? Moreover, the ideas driving the neo-conservative agenda are not new ideas at all; they have been hotly debated for centuries. What is new is the advancement of technology and communications, which have permitted globalization access to the entire world.

This chapter examines the philosophical base that underlies different views Canadians have about social welfare. *Philosophy* is the search for wisdom and truth based on an understanding of the rational principles on which our notions of reality are founded. In our modern era, we use applied philosophy to help people understand the meaning of the concepts we use when describing our social welfare values (Plant, 1974). All social welfare programs are based on societal approval. This approval, in turn, represents society's dominant values—the intrinsic worth of the individual, the responsibility of society for the welfare of its members, and what constitutes individuals' and society's shared responsibility for the common good. Therefore, depending on how each society defines these beliefs, distinct variations will exist in each society's social welfare programs.

## THE NATURE OF SOCIETY

In Canada, we strive for a pluralist society: that is, a society that benefits from the many world views that contribute to our societal definition of the common good. We value bilingualism, multiculturalism, and a multi-party political system, among other elements of our national life.

Two major issues that arise from pluralism have particular implications for social welfare. First, pluralism encourages competition for political dominance among these different world views. Depending on which view dominates, the social welfare system in Canada looks very different. Second, some of these world views do not accept that social welfare should even exist as a social institution. In fact, some people do not accept pluralism as a valued social goal. The current constitutional debate in Canada and the creation of new political parties that would dismantle existing structures that support pluralism are examples of these different priorities.

While much of Canadian philosophy does not directly address the issue of social welfare, distinct philosophical views influence our thinking about the nature of society. The *accommodationist perspective* asserts that all theories contain part of the truth within them. The philosopher is the one to seek the common ground in all theories in order to find closer approximations of truth (Rabb, 1989; Armour and Trott, 1981).

From the accommodationist perspective evolved the *polycentric perspective*. This supports pluralism by arguing that the common-ground approach leaves out those features of a world view that differ from it, so this view limits what could be considered truth. The polycentric perspective argues that radically different world views reveal not only something about culture and language but also about reality itself and the ways different people come to know it. Therefore, each world view reveals something about the total picture, which can never be fully known. We can achieve an accurate picture of reality only by attempting to accommodate and reconcile as many world views as possible (McPherson and Rabb, 1993). This perspective supports social work's emphasis on maintaining the individuality, dignity, and freedom of choice of all people through self-determination.

Another major philosophical perspective is *communitarianism*, which places an intrinsic and instrumental value on both the community and the individual (Cragg, 1986; Grant, 1959). In *Canadian Identity*, Robin Mathews defined communitarians as "the seekers of means to anchor values in human worth" (Mathews, 1988, 32). In communitarianism, individual rights arise from community rights; thus, the community rights can override individual rights. The same right that the community has to survive translates into limited consideration given to the rights of individuals to benefit from that community or indeed to the distribution of power, status, privilege, or resource allocation within that community. Therefore, the poor or individuals having difficulty in functioning socially could very well be seen as detrimental to the community's well-being. Social workers tend to resist this perspective and support the worth and dignity of the individual.

Ramsay Cook, a Canadian historian, provides further insight into the Canadian perspective on social welfare with his concept of *regeneration*. He suggests that the crisis of faith that affected Canadian Protestants in the late nineteenth century resulted from the social impact of early industrialization and that it subsequently required that society dramatically change its focus. This change shifted the meaning of regeneration from a spiritual rebirth that individuals experienced to a "rebirth" through social salvation. This drastic change in thinking gave rise to the Social Gospel Movement and the Liberalism Movement from which many of our current attitudes about Canadian social welfare derive today.

These different perspectives on Canadian philosophical thought support Rein's (1974) perspective that social policy is the product of competing values and their associated world views. Therefore, the social policies that govern the social welfare system can result from one value's perspective gaining dominance over all others. Similarly, political parties, when they win majority government status, may very well follow their own value-based agendas regardless of their impact on society.

## THE NATURE OF HUMAN VALUES

Since the term "values" is important in our understanding the philosophical base of Canadian social welfare, we must take care to understand just what values are. Milton Rokeach (1973, 5) defines a value as an enduring belief that "a specific mode of conduct or end state of existence is personally or socially preferable to an opposite mode of conduct or end state of existence." All individuals have beliefs about what is true about themselves, about the meaning of life, about God, about appropriate behaviour, and about other people, other cultures, and other societies. The social work profession espouses a social welfare system in which all members of its society come together to determine social policies. For example, citizen participation is a means by which members from different groups in society experience each other and integrate their different beliefs. Universal social welfare programs prevent one group from being identified as different (isolated) from other groups.

According to Rokeach, there are three types of beliefs. *Descriptive* or *existential beliefs* define what is true and what is false. For example, I might believe that my notion of God is the only true definition and so reject all other notions of God as false. I might also believe that all people are born good and reject the notion that any people are born evil.

*Evaluative beliefs* define what is good and what is bad. Again, I might believe that pleasure is good and reject the notion that pleasure is bad. I might believe that doing good things for people makes them lazy and dependent and reject the notion that doing good things for them is good.

Finally, *prescriptive beliefs* define what means or ends of action we judge desirable or undesirable. In this case, I might believe that hitting anyone is an undesirable act or that being cruel is appropriate in the work world but not at home. Obviously, when there is congruence between these three types of beliefs, then the bonds between them are stronger, which increases that system of beliefs' resistance to change. For example, if I believe that every individual is responsible for his or her own success, then achieving my own success makes me feel good about myself and, at the same time, I need not worry about what I had to do to become successful.

This discussion suggests that human beings have a complex system of values and beliefs. Together, these give each person a unique world view. However, in today's society, there is often such an abundance of information that the world, once comprehensible, seems increasingly complex and confusing. To handle this information overload, people often feel compelled to clarify and simplify the world by applying their own world views in accepting or rejecting new information. Harvey (1967) defines this way of organizing our experiences, our knowledge, and our values in order to comprehend the world around us as a *conceptual system*.

Conceptual systems help explain why so many Canadians continue to believe that many people who receive social assistance are really just being lazy or trying to cheat the public. This mistrust continues to exist despite the evidence from social science research and from several public inquiries that shows this is not what is really happening (Macarov, 1995, 1978). These data suggest that individuals can translate elements of their values in order to comply with a dominant social value system. For example, Judeo-Christian believers can translate "Thou shalt not kill" and the aspiration of unconditional love to allow them to kill when certain conditions are met, such as in self-defence and for national security.

Erich Fromm (1955, 13) casts more light on this phenomenon. He posits his notion of the pathology of normalcy, which suggests that a "collective value when held by the majority becomes the normative basis for determining appropriate social actions." In essence, this means that no matter how pathological a behaviour is, as long as the majority believe it is not pathological, those people will behave as if this behaviour is normal. This helps explain why people continue to discipline their children (and each other) with violence, for example, despite the abundance of literature that indicates that violence is a dehumanizing and ineffective problem-solving tool and, in fact, an act of oppression and power.

# DIVERSE PERSPECTIVES AND VALUES

This section of the chapter began with a statement that there are diverse perspectives and values on the nature of social welfare. These competing perspectives are based on values that support various views on what human beings are and what responsibility society and its members have for each other. In addition, each individual possesses a unique world view to which he or she adapts an array of individual values. When the majority of a society shares a world view, it becomes the dominant and prescriptive norm. The following section will explore and define these competing values as they relate to social welfare.

# COMPETING VALUES ON THE NATURE OF SOCIAL WELFARE

Many social welfare theorists apply the residual and institutional perspectives to social welfare to delineate the differences between a restrictive and a supportive approach to social welfare as a social institution (Wilensky and Lebeaux, 1958). This chapter is concerned with the values and theories that underlie these approaches. One of the major goals of social welfare advocates (and of the social work profession) is to establish a societal environment that promotes and enhances the human potential of all members of that society, each in accordance with his or her own potential.

## Institutional Perspective

The institutional concept views social welfare as a necessary social institution that essentially meets the needs of people in industrial societies. To explain these needs we can consider that human beings are required to perform a vast array of life tasks that are both developmental (life-cycle tasks) and instrumental (skill-acquisition tasks). To accomplish these, humans require resources that are material, emotional, and spiritual. If a person faces a discrepancy between the life tasks he needs to perform and the appropriate array of resources that would allow him to do so, then that person will find his ability to perform personal and social tasks proportionately limited. Society's members are interdependent, and thus value-sharing resources are means to ensure that all can equally and uniquely contribute to the common good.

In other words, if each member of a society is constantly improving his or her social functioning, then this improvement, in turn, benefits all other members of that society. Advocates of social welfare tend to support the notions of mutual aid, social justice, equality, altruism, common human needs, socialized individualism, and humanization. We will discuss these concepts later in this chapter.

## Residual Perspective

The residual perspective essentially sees social welfare as a limited and temporary societal response to human problems that affect families or the marketplace when normal functioning fails. Opponents of social welfare argue that each person or family is responsible for its own growth and will acquire the resources necessary to maximize that growth, if the person or family values such growth. Therefore, what each individual or family acquires by its own merit, gained by hard work and personal/financial risks, is justifiably that party's property. From this perspective, human freedom becomes essentially non-societal interference, and the social hierarchy establishes itself by superior talent and/or the superior ability to acquire resources.

This perspective supports this notion of independence through the belief that if people can survive and even surmount the challenges of surviving in a society, then the whole of society will benefit by having those stronger individuals. Those who become dependent, then, are the weaker elements of a society and weaken the society as a whole. Those who oppose social welfare tend to support the corporatism, globalization, earned access, possessive individualism, existentialism, utilitarianism, Protestant work ethic, laissez-faire economics, general mistrust, social Darwinism, and the Malthusian theory of population.

## THE CONCEPT OF HUMAN NATURE

Perhaps one of the most difficult and unanswerable questions that confronts humanity is: *What is a human being?* Social welfare tries to address this eternal problem by focusing on the notion of human nature itself rather than debating definitions of human. Some common beliefs about human nature support the view that social welfare is a social institution:

- Humans are rational, emotive, and social beings (Aristotle, Aquinas, Kant).
- Humans are in a constant state of "becoming"; not only can humans transcend physical nature, but also they share an ontological vocation to become more fully human (Kierkegaard, Marx, Teilhard de Chardin, Freire).
- This human potential for development responds to and affects the physical and social environments; the environment influences the human potential for development and the human potential for development influences the environment.
- The basis for understanding this reciprocity with the physical environment is commonality; the physical environment is the common place to sustain all of the world's life forms. A further balance exists that allows all life forms to co-exist in an interdependent state.

- The basis for understanding our reciprocity with the social environment is mutuality; humans cannot fulfill their potential if that fulfillment restricts or denies any other human being's opportunity to fulfill his or her potential. In this sense, equality is the shared journey of all humans to fulfill their potential to become more fully human, and mutuality is the fundamental predisposition for survival and developmental co-existence.

- The end state of human potential is a transformed human state that every human being can achieve. It is characterized by such terms as love, knowledge, harmony, peace, and beauty (Fromm, Rousseau).

As Frankl (1969, 18–19) notes, "Man transcends himself either toward another human being or toward meaning. Love, I would say, is that which enables him to grasp the other human being in his very uniqueness. Conscience is that capacity which empowers him to seize the meaning of a situation in its very uniqueness, and in the final analysis meaning is something unique."

Social welfare advocates tend to operationalize these propositions in terms of society's obligation to provide people with the "means" and "opportunities" in an environment that supports every person's right to develop. Conversely, social welfare advocates tend to criticize social arrangements and conditions that promote the potential development of one set of people at the expense of another set of people (elitism), that suggest that one set of people has greater human potential than another set (through gender or racial inequality), or that deny that one or more sets of people have human potential (through oppression or slavery).

These beliefs also suggest that our observations in the real world (*experiential reality*) are subject to interpretation. Our interpretation draws on the array of values, knowledge, and experience that constitutes each person's world view about what is true, what is good, and what are appropriate actions (*conceptual system*). We share these interpretations with those whose opinions we deem valuable, producing an *agreement reality* that allows each of us to interpret an external event or behaviour according to the symbolic meaning the event or behaviour has in relation to our individual conceptual system (*symbolic interactionalism*). When a large number of people shares this agreement reality, that common interpretation becomes self-reinforcing; each member who agrees with it supports the continuation of that agreement with all other members (Babbie, 1986, 1977).

This collective association of agreements, then, defines truth. It also shapes and defines how the social arrangement between people (social structure) should look according to those people who are part of the symbolic interactionalism. Because these agreements simplify reality by denying that other truths could co-exist, they also reduce personal and social anxiety by stabilizing the environment and limiting the scope for change (Schon, 1971; Fromm, 1955). Frankl (1969) states that we find this association of agreement realities in such entities as social values, social mores, and political ideologies. As this association of agreement realities consists of shared individual agreement realities, it itself becomes a unique perception of reality, or *gestalt*—one that is consistent with, but different from, any one member's individual agreement reality.

In an ideal pluralist society, agreement realities from a *polycentric perspective* would be open systems that constantly accept, interpret, and adapt information the society gains from other agreement realities. They would, therefore, be in a constant state of flux and reorganization (Hegel, 1907). In a society where one dominant agreement reality defines the social order, the agreement reality is a closed system; it values the stability held through law and order. When this dominant agreement reality reflects the view of a minority group but is politically imposed upon the majority, it produces a state of oppression. The minority prescribe to the majority an agreement reality that imposes one group's choice upon another, transforming the consciousness of the majority group into one that conforms with that of the minority group (Freire, 1985, 1969). Accordingly, social welfare advocates are very concerned with the ways power, privilege, status, and wealth are distributed within society and tend to promote "power-with" strategies of "openness, trust, vulnerability, creativity, risk, emotional expression, honesty, [and] giving before receiving" (Bishop, 1994, 46).

## VIEWS OF SOCIAL WELFARE

Those who oppose social welfare tend to view human nature as essentially evil or neutral (Kluckholn and Strodbeck, 1961). They believe that humans are motivated essentially by desires for power, happiness (pleasure/pain), and security. The *economic view* of social welfare is based on the principles of *utilitarianism*, *laissez-faire economics*, and *possessive individualism* (MacPherson, 1962; Bentham, 1967; Smith, 1937).

Figure 2.1 presents a visual arrangement of beliefs that support and oppose social welfare and the resulting societal views that are compatible with each set of beliefs. In other words, one would expect that people who express beliefs that support social welfare would also support commonality, mutuality, and equality and that those who express beliefs that oppose social welfare would also support societal arrangements that tolerate elitism, class, gender, racial inequality, and oppression and slavery. However, the degree to which one espouses these beliefs also reflects the degree to which these societal views are held.

Adam Smith (1937) believed that no one should be allowed to interfere in any way with the free operation of supply and demand, self-interest, and competition. He used the term *laissez-faire* to describe a "hands-off" approach to the marketplace. In essence, supply and demand will regulate the marketplace and determine the incomes of those who produce the goods. Thus, efficiency and effectiveness, free from any government influence, would determine economic survival based on the producers' ability to meet the demands of the market.

MacPherson (1962) uses the term *possessive individualism* to describe the consequences of an economic view of people. Because people essentially are responsible for themselves based on their own capacities, they are not responsible for society as a whole nor for any of its members. Human freedom is seen as independent from the wills of other people, except those whom one agrees to befriend, based on self-interest. Each person, therefore, owns him- or herself and thus enjoys all the freedoms associated with ownership, including a laissez-faire approach to social freedom.

*Utilitarianism* was the first set of principles that gave rise to the concept of "the economic human." In this view (Bentham, 1967), all questions regarding society must be reduced to questions regarding individuals, all questions regarding individuals must be reduced to questions regarding their happiness, and all questions regarding happiness must be reduced to questions regarding measurable pain and pleasure (*felicific calculus*).

For example, if we are considering a particular social or economic policy, we must examine it according to whether it will increase (pleasure) or decrease (pain) the happiness (or self-identified well-being) of individuals. Only those changes that measurably bring

| FIGURE 2.1 | Beliefs and Their Impact on Canadian Social Welfare |
| --- | --- |

**Beliefs Supporting Social Welfare**

Mutual Aid

Social Justice

Participatory Democracy

Political, Social, & Economic Equality & Freedoms

Entitlement to Life-Supporting & Life-Enhancing Resources

Common Good

Community

**Beliefs Opposing Social Welfare**

Utilitarianism

Rugged Individualism

Globalization & Corporatism

Social Darwinism

Earned Access

Theory of Population

Protestant Work Ethic

Domination

**Societal Views**

**Commonality**
(The physical environment that sustains all life forms in balance)

**Mutuality**
(Human potential that cannot be fulfilled if it restricts, denies, or alters others' opportunity to maximize their human potential)

**Equality**
(The shared journey of all humans to fulfill their potential)

**Societal Views**

**Elitism**
(Social conditions that promote the potential development of one set of people at the expense of another)

**Class, Gender, & Racial Inequality**
(Suggestion that one set of people has greater human potential than another set of people)

**Oppression & Slavery**
(The denial that one or more set(s) of people have human potential)

more pleasure than pain to the majority of people should be approved by government. Since all humans are basically lazy and selfish, according to these philosophers, the only way we can motivate people is to allow them to have as much pleasure as they can earn. Government should, therefore, act in the least intrusive way possible in the affairs of business and personal property of people, including their spouses and children.

John Stuart Mill's (1806–1873) notion of *individualism* countered this notion of utilitarianism. Mill's theory emphasized the reality and importance of human liberty and spontaneity and interpreted pleasure not in terms of the greatest amount possible, but in the attainment of the highest pleasures humans could achieve. To Mill, the mature human being is free to determine the meaning of experience in her or his own way, rather than to try to imitate others. Each human being is unique and, therefore, capable of making a unique and creative contribution to society as a whole.

In the modern economic view, human beings are economic beings who work for economic gain and whose behaviour is economically determined. *Individualism* has come to be associated with independence and looking solely after oneself (*rugged individualism*). This is the "dog-eat-dog" view of society in which the individuals' best-developed talents increase their personal advantages. Other members of society are opponents attempting to gain control over social power and resources. Winning and surviving on one's own merits are highly valued. Dependent people are seen as morally inferior and less worthy than independent people. Material possessions become an indicator of social power, privilege, status, and worth. People are valued for what they own and not for who they are; "to have" becomes a primary motivation for human existence (*possessive individualism*). Fromm (1967) identified the outcome of these beliefs as the creation of *homo consumens*, the human being whose primary purpose in society is to consume goods; therefore, being a consumer of goods is perceived as an attribute of human nature.

Two views that support the neutral view of human beings are *social biology* and *technological determinism*. The first suggests that human behaviour is instinctual and endemic to the human species. A human's potential is predetermined genetically, and people act according to these genetic predispositions (Lorenz, 1968). The technological determinists argue that, over time, human society will reach such a disastrous state that knowledge and technology alone will solve the world crisis (Mishra, 1981).

Jacques Ellul (1964) sees a world driven only by knowledge and technology as one in which modern people are sterile and living in hopeless and endless irrelevance. Both of these views succumb to the *is–ought fallacy*: although both describe what exists (is), this description in itself does not limit what could be (ought). For example, social biology correctly identifies that all humans have genetic maps that unfold over their lifespans (truth that exists). However, to imply that these maps determine human potential denies that any other human factors can influence human development, such as human spirituality, conscience, and self-actualization.

Opponents of social welfare accept a "power-over" mentality, which Bishop (1994, 36) describes as "a world of systems designed to keep people in unjust and unequal positions [which] is held in place by several interrelated expressions of 'power-over': political power, economic power, physical force, and ideological power."

Both advocates and opponents of social welfare disagree on what human nature is and also on the relationship between human beings and society (the environmental context within which people live) as well.

## PERSPECTIVES ON HUMAN BEINGS IN SOCIETY

One approach to understanding the relationship between society and its people can be summarized by considering the following statements:

- "Society is what people make it." Every member of society has the power to shape society in accordance with his or her own belief about what society should look like.
- "It is society's well-being, not the individual's well-being, that is important." Therefore, each member of society must be prepared to sacrifice his own self-interest if and when it benefits society as a whole to do so.
- "Society's well-being and the individual's well-being are mutually interdependent." Therefore, what benefits society also benefits its members and what benefits its members

also benefits society. Conversely, what diminishes society diminishes its members and what diminishes its members diminishes society.

Within the realm of these statements the different concepts of human nature come into play. Social welfare advocates tend to accept the last statement as true, and social welfare opponents tend to accept the first two statements as true. Each perspective is based on a set of beliefs about people in society, and these beliefs shape the thinking of both advocates and opponents of social welfare.

The following is a summary of the sets of beliefs and major theoretical perspectives that support each of these perspectives. The student of social welfare should understand that these sets of beliefs do not influence a perspective individually but collectively. However, how much each belief contributes to one's perspective depends on the value one puts on it. One belief can certainly have more influence on one's thinking than another. This helps explain why there are not only differences in perspectives between advocates and opponents of social welfare, but also among advocates and opponents of social welfare. Nor are these two categories of beliefs mutually exclusive; a person who promotes social welfare might accept one or more of the sets of beliefs that some social welfare opponents do, and vice versa.

Canadian advocates of social welfare generally support the following principles and beliefs about people in society:

- Mutual aid is the very essence of human relationships as well as the basis for individual and societal existence (Macarov, 1978). This view supports Kropotkin's (1925) conclusion that the species that have survived evolution have not been those that could dominate or destroy others but those most able to co-operate with one another.

- A system of social justice that ensures each individual maximum freedom to the extent that an individual's pursuit of freedoms does not impinge on, restrict, or deny another individual's pursuit of freedoms must prevail (Rawls, 1973).

- Democracy, whether participatory or representative, is a preferred social arrangement. However, all citizens must have equal rights and opportunities so they can participate in social decisions or elect representatives to do so on their behalf.

- Political, social, and economic equality must govern all aspects of society. Equality and freedom are fundamental human rights and necessary prerequisites for humanization (Freire, 1994, 1968; Teilhard de Chardin, 1955). These include the right of all citizens to work and to be equitably reimbursed for that work.

- Society is obliged to ensure that all citizens have sufficient life-sustaining and life-enhancing resources to perform their life tasks (Gil, 1992).

- All citizens are socially responsible for maximizing their own potential and respecting the similar striving of other citizens. Thus, each citizen has a dual moral responsibility to help other citizens reach their goals and to help society reach its goals (Siporin, 1975).

- The common good as a major social goal is concerned with the well-being of the community, which includes the integrity and preservation of its basic institutions, practices, core values, and human growth and development. Social workers with a common-good perspective tend to focus on individual well-being, community intervention, organizational change, legislative lobbying, and other forms of social work intervention (Reamer, 1993).

Opponents of social welfare tend to espouse the following set of beliefs:

- Self-help, economic freedoms, and social liberty are the prerequisites for all societal arrangements. Except in exceptional circumstances, society must not interfere in the private or business life of its citizens (Armitage, 1996; Mencher, 1967).

- Access to society's resources must be earned and society, according to this thought system, must never limit a person's ability to make money. This is the laissez-faire philosophy in the extreme. Competition for limited resources acts as a stimulant to citizens to maximize their growth and human potential.

- The theory of population as articulated by Thomas Malthus (1766–1834) still applies in our world today. Malthus stated that human populations grow geometrically (2, 4, 8, 16, 32 . . . ) whereas food production grows only arithmetically (1, 2, 3, 4. . . ). Therefore, because people need food to survive and human sexual passion (especially among the poor) will not decrease, eventually population must outstrip food resources (Dismal Theorem). Increasing the food supply arithmetically and, therefore, improving health and survival temporarily will only lead to more people being born, thus increasing the number of those who will eventually die of starvation (Utterly Dismal Theorem). Irresponsible people who have more children than they can afford to feed, then, should not be protected by the state, and the poor should practise moral restraint (Macarov, 1978).

- The Protestant work ethic is the principle underlying and shaping social responsibility. First articulated by Martin Luther (1483–1546), work was viewed as a vocation—that is, a calling to do God's work in all things. John Calvin (1509–1564) extended the work ethic to define work as a divine vocation, and, therefore, work in the marketplace as a religious experience. As such, the material rewards from work are less important than the act of working. For many endorsing this work ethic, material success became proof of God's personal favour. One's failure to succeed demonstrated personal immorality or moral inferiority. The concept of the deserving and the undeserving stems from the work ethic (Macarov, 1995; Nisbet, 1932).

- Since all citizens must take personal responsibility for their own behaviour and life choices, society is responsible only for assisting these individuals to return to the marketplace where they can earn back their pride and self-esteem.

- Society has the right to protect itself from those who would seem to radically change it or from those who illegally seek to benefit from it.

- Charity (philanthropy) is an individual choice a citizen makes or that the state makes on behalf of its citizens. In other words, society values humanitarian acts over state responsibility.

While these sets of beliefs are not inclusive, they do orient the value systems of advocates and opponents and their view of people within society.

These sets of beliefs form the basis from which Canadians determine the cause of a particular social problem and the steps required to resolve the problem. For example, the marked rise in unemployment and social assistance that the economic recession in the first half of the 1990s created was viewed by some (advocates) as caused by the North American Free Trade Agreement (Canada/United States) and the Goods and Services Tax. They claimed that this accord unjustly affected Canadians whose jobs or income were vulnerable to these political decisions. This group saw the solution in the political arena and the resolution in the restoration of employment and economic security to those adversely affected. Others (opponents) saw the same situation as a lesson for Canada about the way our social programs and unionized labour force had eroded Canada's economic competitiveness with other countries. For this group, the solution was to dismantle universal programs and redirect social benefits to those most in need; they prescribed that society suffer through the difficult period until the economy recovered.

Advocates tend to favour political and collectivist resolutions to social problems. The advocate believes that society is responsible for ensuring that all citizens have the means to meet common human needs, particularly at physiological, safety, and security levels. Opponents tend to favour a functionalist and individual approach, which suggests that the existing society is the best there is, and that only incremental adjustments are necessary when problems arise.

A further issue arises from these sets of beliefs about people in society: some people claim that they reflect the English Canadian experience. French Canada, on the other hand, has been greatly influenced by other factors—existentialism, Roman Catholicism, social freedoms, and the belief in the family as a distinct unit. These influential factors also shape how French Canadians view social problems and their resolutions. One obvious resolution for the people of Quebec would be to design social programs that are compatible with that province's value systems. However, social welfare advocates with a *polycentric perspective* would hope that Quebec would not resolve its social problems through isolationism but would contribute to developing Canada's world view on social programs. The same argument would apply to other members of Canada's multicultural communities.

## CONCLUSION

Modern Canadian thinking is being influenced by globalization, and also by postmodernism. According to this latter theory, meta-theories and professionalism are "oppressive function(s) in society, perpetuating the capitalist/liberal social order to the advantage of the few over the many" (McKay, 1999, 13). Postmodernists call for new mechanisms to allow the voices of the many to be heard and demand "the acknowledgement and celebration of diversity in cultures, sexualities, abilities, ages, and other human characteristics" (Leonard, 1997, xiii).

For some social workers, postmodernism constitutes a call "to integrate a social justice orientation into everyday practice" (Gil, 1998, 126) and to take political action (Carniol, 1987). For other social workers, it is a call to return to neighbourhood and community (McKnight, 1995), where we can replace the deconstruction of oppressive community narratives with one that incorporates many voices and many meanings. These would take into account those that are discordant or unpleasant, and that can awaken people to an alternative and more hopeful view of their communities.

Key here for the social workers who are trying to understand the community's ways of interpreting its own history is their ability to hear multiple layers of stories, even conflicting stories, of the same event, without silencing or suppressing discordant voices. Social workers can understand the full meaning of an event only when they take the time to really listen to the forgotten stories and the marginalized voices (Delaney, Brownlee, and Sellick, 1999). Harmonizing social work values and postmodern thinking challenges social work to "ground its interventive practices in a clearly articulated, revitalized expression of identity and purpose" (McKay, 1999, 20).

This chapter presents the competing values that exist in Canada regarding beliefs about the intrinsic worth of the individual, society's responsibility for its members, and the responsibility of those members for the common good. It is imperative that those people advocating social welfare as a vital and necessary social institution possess a clear and concise understanding of these values. Such clarity allows them to interpret more precisely various efforts at social change and enable the systematic analysis of current events and their potential impact on the social and personal well-being of Canada's citizens. A fundamental governing principle for both social welfare advocates and the social work profession is the belief that all human beings have potential and that this potential is best nurtured in an environmental context governed by mutuality and respect.

# References

Armitage, A. 1996. *Social welfare in Canada revisited*. 3d. edn. Don Mills, ON: Oxford University Press.

Armour, L., & Trott, E. 1981. *The faces of reason: An essay on philosophy and culture in English Canada, 1850–1950*. Waterloo, ON: Wilfrid Laurier Press.

Babbie, E. 1977. *Society by agreement*. Belmont, CA: Wadsworth.

Babbie, E. 1986. *Observing ourselves: Essays in social research*. Belmont, CA: Wadsworth.

Bentham, J. 1967. *A fragment of government and an introduction to the principles of morals and legislation*. Oxford: Basil Blackwell.

Bishop, A. 2002. *Becoming an ally: Breaking the cycle of oppression in people*. Halifax: Fernwood.

Bishop, A. 2005. *Beyond token change: Breaking the cycle of oppression in institutions*. Halifax: Fernwood.

Carniol, B. 1987. *Case critical: The dilemma of social work in Canada*. Toronto: Between the Lines.

Clarke, Tony. 1997. *Silent coup*. Toronto: CCPA and James Lorimer.

Cragg, W. 1986. Two concepts of community or moral theory and Canadian culture. *Dialogue, XXV.* 31–52.

Delaney, R., Brownlee, K., & Sellick, M. 1999. Communities. In R. Delaney, K. Brownlee, & M. Sellick (Eds.), *Social work with rural and northern communities* (pp. 1–13). Thunder Bay: Lakehead University Centre for Northern Studies.

Douglas, J. (Ed.). 1970. *Freedom and tyranny: Social problems in a technological society*. New York: Alfred A. Knopf.

Ellul, J. 1964. *The technological society*. New York: Alfred A. Knopf.

Federico, R. 1984. *The social welfare institution*. 4th edn. Toronto: D. C. Heath and Company.

Frankl, V. 1969. *The will to meaning*. Scarborough, ON: Plume.

Freire, P. 1968. *Pedagogy of the oppressed*. New York: Seabury Press.

Freire, P. 1985. *The politics of education: Culture, power and liberation*. South Hadley, MA: Bergin and Garvey.

Freire, P. 1994. *Pedagogy of hope*. New York: Continuum.

Fromm, E. 1955. *The sane society*. Greenwich: Fawcett.

Fromm, E. 1967. The psychological aspects of the guaranteed income. In R. Theobald (Ed.), *The guaranteed income* (pp. 183–193). Garden City, NY: Anchor.

Gil, D. 1992. *Unravelling social policy.* Rev. 5th edn. Rochester: Schenkman Books.

Gil, D. 1998. *Confronting injustice and oppression: Concepts and strategies for social workers*. New York: Columbia University Press.

Graham, J., Swift, K., & Delaney, R. 2003. *Canadian social policy: An introduction.* 2nd edn. Toronto: Prentice Hall.

Grant, G. P. 1959. *Philosophy in the mass age.* Toronto: Copp Clark.

Harvey, O. J. 1967. Conceptual systems and attitude change. In C. Sherif & M. Sherif (Eds.), *Attitude, ego involvement, and change*. New York: Wiley.

Hegel, G. W. 1907. *Theologische Jugendschriften.* H. Nohl, Ed. Tübingen: Mohr.

Homan, M. 1994. *Promoting community change: Making it happen in the real world*. Pacific Grove, CA: Brooks/Cole Publishing Co.

Kluckholn, F., & Strodbeck, F. 1961. *Variation in value orientations.* Evanston, IL: Row Peterson.

Kropotkin, P. 1925. *Mutual aid: A factor of evolution*. New York: Alfred A. Knopf.

Leonard, P. 1997. *Postmodern welfare: Reconstructing an emancipatory project*. London: Sage.

Lerner, M. 1997. *The politics of meaning: Restoring hope and possibility in an age of cynicism*. Don Mills, ON: Addison-Wesley.

Lorenz, K. 1968. *On aggression.* London: Methuen.

Macarov, D. 1995. *Social welfare: Structure and practice*. Thousand Oaks, CA: Sage.

Macarov, D. 2003. *What the market does to people: Privatization, globalization and poverty*. London: Zed Books.

MacPherson, C. B. 1962. *The political theory of possessive individualism*. Oxford: Clarendon Press.

Mathews, R. 1988. *Canadian identity.* Ottawa: Steel Rail Publishing.

McKay, S. 1999. Postmodernism, social well-being, and the mainstream/progressive debate. In F. Turner (Ed.), *Social work practice: A Canadian perspective* (pp. 10–22). Scarborough, ON: Prentice Hall/Allyn and Bacon Canada.

McKnight, J. 1995. *The careless society.* New York: Basic.

McPherson, D., & Rabb, J. D. 1993. *Indian from the inside: A study in ethno-metaphysics*. Occasional Paper 14. Thunder Bay: Lakehead University Centre for Northern Studies.

Mencher, S. 1967. *Poor law to poverty program.* Pittsburgh: University of Pittsburgh Press.

Mishra, R. 1981. *Society and social policy.* 2d edn. London: Macmillan.

Mullaly, B. 1993. *Structural social work: Ideology, theory and practice*. Toronto: McClelland & Stewart.

Nisbet, R. 1932. *The contribution of religion to social work*. New York: Columbia University Press.

Plant, R. 1974. *Community and ideology: An essay in applied social philosophy.* London: Routledge and Kegan Paul.

Rabb, J. D. 1989. The polycentric perspective: A Canadian alternative to Rorty. *Dialogue, XXVIII.* 107–115.

Rawls, J. 1973. *A theory of justice.* London: Oxford University Press.

Reamer, F. 1993. *The philosophical foundations of social work.* New York: Columbia University Press.

Rein, M. September 1974. Social policy analysis as the interpretation of beliefs. *Journal of the American Institute of Planners.* 297–298.

Rokeach, M. 1973. *The nature of human values.* New York: Free Press.

Saul, J. R. 1995. *The unconscious civilization.* Concord, ON: Anansi.

Schon, D. 1971. *Beyond the stable state.* Toronto: George McLeod Limited.

Siporin, M. 1975. *Introduction to social work practice.* New York: Macmillan.

Smith, A. 1937. *The wealth of nations.* New York: Modern Library.

Teilhard de Chardin, P. 1955. *The phenomenon of man.* New York: Harper and Brothers.

Wilensky, H., & Lebeaux, C. 1958. *Industrial society and social welfare.* New York: Russell Sage Foundation.

# CHAPTER 3

# The Political Base of Canadian Social Welfare

*Thomas Brenner*

The rise and subsequent decline of social welfare in Canada can be observed through a variety of lenses. It has been examined through political, economic, and social perspectives. The impact of events, such as the World Wars and the Great Depression, has been considered. As well, the influences of gender, race, and class have been evaluated. Policy analysts have examined the Canadian social welfare system from many angles in an effort to understand the forces that have shaped various programs and services in Canada. These programs and services include, but are not limited to, the areas of health, housing, child care, income security, education, immigration, and human rights. Social welfare programs are derived from public policy, and, therefore, politics at all levels of government in Canada is a reasonable place to begin our discussion. It is the political process that generates the terms and conditions under which social workers operate. Among other things, the political process initiates or eliminates programs, establishes eligibility criteria, and ultimately determines the level of service to vulnerable populations. Hick (2007) notes that there are both public and private systems of social welfare, but as the current debate on health care suggests, politics determines even the extent to which the social welfare system is provided in the public or private sector.

The political bases of social welfare in Canada are vast. Local, provincial, federal, and even global politics play a part in shaping Canada's social welfare system. It is a rather cumbersome perspective, but some have argued that politics are everywhere and in all social interactions. Like Brooks (2007), a more limited perspective on what constitutes politics has been adopted for the purposes of this chapter, one that "separates the public and private realms" (p. 5). It is recognized, however, that in a pluralistic society such as Canada's there are many competing interests, and some groups in the private realm have tremendous influence on the political process.

Newman (1998), Hurtig (2002), and McQuaig (1996) are among those who have highlighted the strong influence that organizations such as the Business Council on National Issues (BCNI)[1] and the C. D. Howe and Fraser Institutes have had on shaping the public agenda in favour of the business community. In fact, Tom d'Aquino, the president and chief executive officer of the BCNI, was quoted as saying

> If you ask yourself, in which period since 1900 has Canada's business community had the most influence on public policy, I would say it was in the last twenty years. Look at what we stand for and look at what all the governments, all the major parties including the Reform have done and what they want to do. They have adopted the agendas we've been fighting for in the past two decades (Newman, 1998, p. 159).

The Canadian Council on Social Development (CCSD), the Council of Canadians, and the National Action Committee on the Status of Women (NAC) are also examples of groups in this pluralistic society who attempt to influence public policy. In her book *Imagine Democracy*, Judy

---

1 Presently known as the Canadian Council of Chief Executives (CCCE).

Rebick (2000) describes a time during the 1970s and 1980s when NAC had its greatest impact on government policy. It was a time when the federal government offered financial support to a variety of advocacy groups representing, among others, women, children, older people, and people with disabilities. NAC was a strong voice for women, and like the CCSD and the Council of Canadians, a defender of social programs. In her explanation of how and why things changed, Rebick talks about "right wing forces" attacking the public funding of advocacy groups and a "neo-liberal" assault on social programs; she uses terminology that describes political identities and ideologies that differ from those she sees as defenders of social welfare. This chapter will elaborate on the identities and ideologies of the political process and examine a swathe of political activity during the development and subsequent decline of social welfare in Canada. Three phases will be considered: a period of growth and development (1949–1973), a period of stalled growth (1974–1982), and a period of decline (1983–2007). This chapter will focus primarily on the public arena and the federal level of government. However, social welfare reforms by the parties in power will also be discussed within a social and economic context. The social context provides a sense of some important events and groups that have influenced the parties in power. The economic data considered will include public debt and deficit as well as the unemployment rate. Some political parties have argued they were not in a position to act on their political priorities because of higher than expected deficits and a poorly performing economy. In contrast, political parties who do not advance the social welfare agenda during good economic times and times of budgetary surpluses also articulate a particular political stance.

## PROCESS, IDENTITIES, AND IDEOLOGIES

Democracy is commonly described as a system of government whereby people express themselves and exercise power through free elections. Also linked to democracy is the notion of social and political equality. Brooks (2007) considers the concept of democracy and the wide range of countries who all claim to be democratic. Clearly, Canada has a system of free elections, but when the question of equality is considered, a debate emerges. To what degree do all Canadians experience political and social equality? Given that certain groups have greater political influence than others, just how democratic is Canada? "A respect for rights and freedoms is generally considered a distinguishing feature of democratic government" (Brooks, 2007, p. 16). However, in this era of globalization, the question seems to be: whose rights and freedoms?

> Libertarians, many economists, and conservative philosophers argue that [the] government that levies heavy taxes on citizens is undemocratic. Their reasoning is that individual choice is reduced when government, representing the collectivity, decides how a large share of people's income will be spent. Others argue that the same levels of taxation actually promote freedom by paying for policies that give less advantaged groups opportunities that they would not have in a "free" market (Brooks, 2007, p. 17).

Despite apparent inequalities, Canada, according to Freedom House's World Democracy Audit, is considered to be one of the most democratic countries in the world (ranked 8th out of 150 countries, August 2007).

All groups competing for political influence take on a political identity that can be related to issues, values, ideas, or financial interest. Groups organized around issues, such as right to life or drinking and driving, are not likely motivated by financial interests when contrasted with groups organized around privatizations of public services or lowering taxes. As one can imagine, there are numerous groups attempting to get the attention of government officials and parliamentarians, and a growing number are hiring professional lobbyists. According to McMenemy (2006), professional lobbying had "increased significantly following the election of Brian Mulroney's Progressive Conservative government in 1984" (p. 201).[2] Elected to the House of Commons in Ottawa as of January 2006 were representatives of the Conservative Party, the Liberal Party, the Bloc Québécois, and the New Democratic Party. The Conservative Party, the result of a merger in 2003 of the Progressive Conservatives and the Canadian Alliance (formerly the Reform Party), won enough seats to form a minority government. McMenemy's assessment was that

> While it was apparent that the Conservatives—whether former Alliance or Progressive Conservative activists—were solidly in agreement in their opposition to the Liberals, the electorate seemed uncertain whether the merged party was fundamentally a populist, social conservative party of protest or a moderate and pragmatic party with policies and organizational cohesion that would lead to electoral victory. In the party's first policy convention in 2005, the latter appeared to prevail. Populist direct democracy proposals for legislative initiative and recall were rejected, official bilingualism was supported, and the less direct Progressive Conservative method of leadership review was approved. Social conservatism is still evident, however, in the party's strenuous objection in the debate that year to the inclusion of same-sex couples in the legal definition of marriage (McMenemy, 2006, p. 77).

Each of the political parties embraces an ideology that is, at times, simply described as being more "right wing" or "left wing," with the former capturing more of a conservative ideology and the latter capturing more of a social democratic or socialist ideology. Policy positions and ideologies of a political party can shift over time. The Conservatives, for example, became the Progressive Conservatives when John Bracken assumed the leadership of the party in the mid-1940s; when Brian Mulroney and the Progressive Conservatives formed the government in 1984 they were labelled as part of the "neo-conservative" movement; and when Stephen Harper assumed leadership of the newly merged party they once again became the Conservatives. The party has, at times, adopted more of a fiscally conservative agenda and at times more of a socially conservative agenda. There is also evidence to support Tom d'Aquino's claims of a strong pro-business influence exerting pressure on all major political parties to shift to the right, to become more ideologically conservative. "Right wing" politics, since the mid-1980s, has been described as "neo-conservative," or as Judy Rebick stated, "neo-liberal." McMenemy (2006) notes that in Canada the term "conservatism" was, in the past, linked with British Toryism or European conservatism, but since the 1960s it has been confused with the American usage which "is a manifestation of early liberalism, in which individualism, self reliance, and antipathy to the state are stressed" (p. 76). Much has been written about the similarities and differences between the terms neo-conservatism and neo-liberalism. Wiseman's (2006) perspective is that

---

2  Lobbyists are required to register with the government, so more can be learned about their activity by searching for the "Lobbyists Registration System" at: https://www.strategis.ic.gc.ca or by contacting the Advocacy Research Centre at: http://www.arcpub.com/ARCPUBLICATIONS.htm.

The new conservatism is a modern variant of the old liberalism. The new conservatism or neo-liberalism gives priority to the individual over the community in the economic sphere. Immense business corporations are seen as individuals. . . . [and] the new conservatism, unlike the old conservatism, is loath to use the state to protect the public good or broad community interest at the expense of the private freedom (p. 64).

Brooks (2007) points out a limitation of the left and right categorization of politics, saying that social conservatives and libertarians are both at the right end of the political spectrum sharing a similar disregard for aspects of social welfare. However, there are some significant philosophical differences. Social conservatives tend to be against abortion and same-sex marriage, and tend to support capital punishment, while libertarians believe in the greatest degree of individual freedom in all aspects of life including matters of morality (p. 34). In his description of political ideologies, Brooks, like McMenemy (2006), notes a shift over time in the three ideologies that most pertain to politics in Canada: liberalism, conservatism, and socialism (Tables 3.1 and 3.2).

| TABLE 3.1 | Classical Ideologies | | |
|---|---|---|---|
| | **Liberalism** | **Conservatism** | **Socialism** |
| Characteristics of the Good Society | Individual freedom is maximized; politics and economics are free and competitive; achievements and recognition are due to personal merit and effort; a capitalist economy will produce the greatest happiness for society and maximize welfare; personal dignity depends on the individual's own actions. | The traditional social order is preserved; individuals are members of social groups that are linked together by a web of rights and obligations; those born in privileged circumstances have an obligation to those below them on the social ladder; there is a natural social hierarchy based on inherited status; personal dignity depends on one's conformity to the norms and behaviour of the social group. | Social and economic equality are maximized; private ownership of property is replaced by its collective ownership and management; competition is replaced by co-operation; the welfare of society is maximized through economic and social planning; personal dignity depends on work and one's solidarity with the working class. |
| Chief Supporters | Industrialists, merchants, property-owning individuals. | Landed aristocracy, established church and military officers, and agents of the Crown whose status and income depended on maintenance of the traditional social hierarchy. | Organized workers; intellectuals. |

*Source:* From *Canadian Democracy: An Introduction,* 5th ed., by Stephen Brooks. © Oxford University Press, 2007, pp. 40–41. Adapted with permission of the publisher.

| TABLE 3.2 | Contemporary Ideologies | | |
|---|---|---|---|
| | Liberalism | Conservatism | Socialism |
| Characteristics of the Good Society | Individual freedom is balanced by protection for disadvantaged elements in society and recognition of group rights; capitalism must be regulated by the state to ensure the social and economic well-being of the majority; social diversity should be recognized and promoted through public education, hiring, and the policies of governments; social entitlements are respected, including a certain standard of living and access to decent education, health care, and accommodation; personal dignity is based on freedom and social equality. | Individual freedom is more important than social equality and should not be sacrificed to the latter; state regulation of capitalism should be kept to a minimum and should not be used to promote any but economic goals; social diversity is a fact, but is not something that should be actively promoted by government; individuals should be responsible for their own lives, and policies that encourage dependency on the state should be avoided; personal dignity depends on one's own efforts and is undermined by collectivists' policies and too much emphasis on promoting social and economic equality. | Social and economic equality are the most important values; individual rights must be subordinated to collective goals; small-scale capitalism has its place, but state economic planning and active participation in the economy are still necessary to promote both economic competitiveness and social fairness; the environmental consequences of all public and private actions must be considered; systemic discrimination based on gender, race, and ethnicity is eliminated through government policies; personal dignity depends on social and economic equality. |
| Chief Supporters | Many middle-of-the-road advocacy groups within the feminist, environmental, and multicultural movements; middle-class intellectuals in the universities and the media; the national Liberal Party and the Bloc Québécois; think-tanks, including Canadian Policy Research Networks, the Institute for Research on Public policy, and the Canada West Foundation. | Business groups; middle-class workers in the private sector; the mainstream of the Conservative Party of Canada; the Alberta and Ontario Conservative parties; think-tanks, including the Fraser Institute, the Atlantic Institute for Market Studies, and the C.D. Howe Institute. | More extreme advocacy groups within the feminist, environmental, and multicultural movements; some elements in the NDP and within the organized labour movement; think-tanks, including the Canadian Centre for Policy Alternatives, the Caledon Institute of Social Policy, and the Canadian Council on Social Development. |

*Source:* From *Canadian Democracy: An Introduction*, 5th ed., by Stephen Brooks. © Oxford University Press, 2007, pp. 40–41. Adapted with permission of the publisher.

# PERIOD OF GROWTH AND DEVELOPMENT: 1949–1973

The twin crucibles of the Great Depression and the Second World War, not to mention the First World War, were significant factors in the development of the Canadian social welfare system. The arrival of the Second World War on the heels of the Great Depression threatened people's sense of security, and the Canadian political scene was forced to respond. Socialism and communism were the politics of choice in a number of countries during the post-war period, and in Canada the political agenda shifted to the left. The two main political parties were adjusting to the political will of the Canadian electorate, and also to the articulations of the newly created party known as the Co-operative Commonwealth Federation (CCF). Finkel (1997) states, "both the Liberals and the Conservatives, wishing to stem the growth in support for socialism, began to advocate extensive programs of social insurance, labour rights, and job creation" (p. 7). They were policies that resonated in parts of Canada and caused the Conservatives to become "progressive," and the Liberals to shift to the left. Mackenzie King asked Leonard Marsh to produce a report on social security in Canada—a report that contained ideas similar to those in the Beveridge report presented to the British parliament.

On an economic basis, the ideas of the British economist John Maynard Keynes were in vogue. The hardships people experienced, especially through the Great Depression, had shaken their confidence in the capitalist system, and the ideas that Keynes advanced in his book *The General Theory of Employment, Interest and Money* (1936) had general appeal. This book provided the theoretical justification for state intervention within modern capitalism. In basic terms, McQuaig (1998) points out that "Keynes essentially supported the notion that government should play a role in ensuring full employment and delivering strong social programs" (p. 68). His approach "was able to steer the capitalistic state clear of both 'the political shoals of conservative *laissez-faire*' and the massive state ownership that socialism would bring" (Wolfe 1985, p. 128, as cited in McBride & Shields, 1997, p. 36). He successfully challenged the ideas of economists such as Adam Smith who extolled the virtues of the free market system and self-interest as the path to social good (Stiglitz & Broadway, 1994, pp. 175–176).

The social policy developments during this period were significant, as Table 3.3 demonstrates. In the 1950s, there was a collective response to the needs of the elderly, people with disabilities, and victims of the War. In 1951, the *Old Age Security Act* was passed, which provided $40 per month to all Canadians at the age of seventy (Guest, 1997). It was Canada's second piece of social welfare that was universal in nature, the first being the *Family Allowance Act* of 1944. In the 1960s, the focus was on the development of programs for youth, women, and the elderly, as well as health coverage for the general population. Two signature pieces of social policy legislation were enacted: the Canada Assistance Plan (CAP), and the Federal-Provincial Fiscal Arrangements and *Federal Post-Secondary Education and Health Contributions Act*, more commonly referred to as the Established Program Financing (EPF). Under CAP, the federal government provided 50 percent of what it cost the provinces to provide welfare and social services, and under EPF, the government provided a per capita grant to help with the cost of post-secondary education and for hospital and personal health care (Moscovitch, 1997). In addition to assisting the provinces with the cost of vital services, the government also provided some national standards with respect to the terms and conditions under which these programs and services were delivered. Another remarkable thing about the 1960s was that the government acknowledged poverty as a problem and appointed a committee of the Senate to study and make recommendations on how to eliminate it.

**TABLE 3.3**    Period of Growth and Development: 1949–1973

| Political Party | Social Welfare Initiatives | Year | Net Public Debt (Millions of Dollars) | Economic Indicators — Budgetary Surplus or Deficit (-) | Unemployment Rate (%) |
|---|---|---|---|---|---|
| **1949** Liberal Majority (St. Laurent) | **1951** <br>• Old Age Security Act <br>• Old Age Assistance Act <br>• Blind Persons Act <br>• Revision of Indian Act <br><br>**1952** <br>• War Veterans' Allowance Act | **1949** <br>1950 <br>1951 <br>1952 | 11 029 <br>10 751 <br>10 414 <br>10 790 | 166 <br>278 <br>337 <br>-377 | 2.8 <br>3.6 <br>2.4 <br>2.9 |
| **1953** Liberal Majority (St. Laurent) | **1953** <br>• Children of the War Dead Act <br><br>**1954** <br>• Disabled Persons Act <br>• National Housing Act <br><br>**1956** <br>• Unemployment Assistance Act | **1953** <br>1954 <br>1955 <br>1956 | 11 189 <br>11 780 <br>11 819 <br>11 502 | -399 <br>-591 <br>-40 <br>317 | 3.0 <br>4.6 <br>4.4 <br>3.4 |
| **1957** Progressive Conservative (PC) Minority (Diefenbaker) | **1957** <br>• Hospital Insurance and Diagnostic Services Act <br><br>**1960** <br>• Bill of Rights | **1957** <br>**1958** <br>1959 <br>1960 | 11 703 <br>12 580 <br>13 247 <br>13 831 | -201 <br>-876 <br>-668 <br>-584 | 4.6   Recession <br>7.0   " <br>6.0   " <br>7.0   " |
| **1958** PC Majority (Diefenbaker) | **1961** <br>• Vocational Rehabilitation Act <br>• Royal Commission on Health | 1961 <br>1962 | 14 825 <br>15 673 | -994 <br>-848 | 7.1   " <br>5.9 |

| Political Party | Social Welfare Initiatives | Economic Indicators | | | |
|---|---|---|---|---|---|
| | | Year | Net Public Debt (Millions of Dollars) | Budgetary Surplus or Deficit (-) | Unemployment Rate (%) |
| **1963** <br> Liberal Minority (Pearson) | **1964–65** <br> ● *Established Programs (Interim Arrangements) Act* <br> ● *Youth Allowance Act* <br> ● *Canada Student Loans Act* | **1963** <br> 1964 <br> 1965 | 16 871 <br> 17 243 <br> 17 223 | -1198 <br> -372 <br> 21 | 5.5 <br> 4.7 <br> 3.9   Auto-Pact |
| **1965** <br> Liberal Minority (Pearson) | ● *Canada Pension Plan* <br> **1966–67** <br> ● *Medical Care Act* <br> ● *Health Resources Fund Act* <br> ● *Training Allowance Act* <br> ● Company of Young Canadians (CYC) <br> ● Guaranteed Income Supplement <br> ● Canada Assistance Plan <br> ● Royal Commission on the Status of Women | 1966 <br> 1967 | 17 708 <br> 18 750 | -486 <br> -1042 | 3.6 <br> 4.1 |
| **1968** <br> Liberal Majority (Trudeau) | **1968** <br> ● Senate Committee on Poverty <br> ● Divorce Act | **1968** <br> 1969 | 19 417 <br> 19 277 | -666 <br> 139 | 4.8 <br> 4.7 |
| **1970** <br> Liberal Minority (Trudeau) | **1970** <br> ● Opportunity for Youth (OFY) replaces (CYC) <br> **1971** <br> ● *Unemployment Insurance Act amended to include Maternity Benefits* <br> ● Local Initiatives Program (L.I.P.) <br> **1973** <br> ● Working Paper on Social Security in Canada <br> ● OAS/GIS fully indexed to CPI (inflation) | 1970 <br> 1971 <br> **1972** <br> 1973 | 20 293 <br> 22 079 <br> 23 980 <br> 26 191 | -1016 <br> -1786 <br> -1901 <br> -2211 | 5.9 <br> 6.4 <br> 6.3 <br> 5.6   Energy Crisis |

*Source:* Economic data from Statistics Canada (CANSIM). Political party data from *Canada Votes 1935–1986* by Frank B. Feigert (1989), Duke University Press. Federal response from *The Emergence of Social Security in Canada*, 3rd Edition by Dennis Guest (1997), UBC Press.

# PERIOD OF STALLED GROWTH: 1974–1982

As the Great Depression of the 1930s turned people's attention to Keynesian ideas, an economic condition known as "stagflation" provided an opportunity for the expression of ideas advanced by the economist Milton Friedman. It was the 1970s, and the economy was faltering in an unusual fashion, with high unemployment and high inflation. This condition came to be known as "stagflation." The decade after 1973 was one of the most challenging in Canada's political and economic history. Norrie and Owran (1996) note that "many of Canada's difficulties in this period stemmed from the international economy . . . [and] the growth slowdown and stagflation that were gripping the industrial world" (p. 437). McBride and Shields (1997) point to the energy crisis of 1973, an event they describe as "the first shock wave of an economic earthquake that rocked the international economy" (p. 47). Multinational corporations were moving their operations to maximize profit, often to Third World countries where labour costs were substantially less. The traditional labour-intensive manufacturing jobs rapidly declined. Across the country "employment in goods-producing industries fell from 34.8 percent of the labour force in 1951 to 26.7 percent in 1981" (McBride & Shields, 1997, p. 47). As manufacturing jobs declined, technology advanced quickly, and corporations modernized to remain competitive, which also resulted in reduced labour costs.

Whereas Keynes advocated government spending to stimulate full employment, Friedman's aim was to drive down inflation by reducing government spending. McQuaig (1998) described Friedman as an "articulate advocate for the classical school of 'laissez-faire' economics" (p. 38). Friedman was able to convince policy-makers that there was a "natural rate of unemployment" necessary to curb inflation, at a time when Cecile Vickery was receiving his Nobel Prize in Economics and stating otherwise. Friedman's idea is based on the notion that full employment is never good for the economy. Full employment is advantageous for workers, because it increases their bargaining power and drives up the cost of production. Classical economics puts the workers at a disadvantage and Teeple (1995) saw it as "the very basis of inequity and class definition in capitalist society" (p. 76).

Politically, the 1970s saw a shift to the "right," to the neo-conservative ideas introduced by Prime Minister Margaret Thatcher in Britain. Paul Leduc Browne (1997) described Thatcher's eleven-year term from 1979 to 1990 as "a potent neo-conservative brew of neo-liberal economics and 'authoritarian populist' social policy" (p. 37). According to Leduc Browne

> The Thatcher government could not have implemented its neo-conservative agenda in such a matter without translating it into a 'populist idiom,' without 'hard faced economics' being converted 'into language of compulsive moralism' by what Stuart Hall dubbed 'authoritarian populism.' Entrenched feelings of class identity had to be broken and replaced with an individualistic, consumerist mentality oriented towards personal gain and private family life (p. 40).

Social policy developments stalled during this period, as can be seen in Table 3.4. The Local Initiatives Program, which helped establish a number of important social service programs at the municipal level, experienced severe cuts. Family Allowance ceased to be indexed to the cost of living for a year. Trudeau reluctantly introduced a program of wage and price controls to fight off inflationary pressures. The Unemployment Insurance Program no longer provided coverage to workers over the age of sixty-five and eliminated the differential for beneficiaries with dependants (Guest, 1997, p. 181). The Opportunities for Youth, the Company of Young Canadians, and Information Canada were eliminated. A new

**TABLE 3.4**     Period of Stalled Growth: 1974–1982

| Political Party | Social Welfare Initiatives |
|---|---|
| **1974** | **1974** |
| Liberal Majority (Trudeau) | • C/QPP fully indexed to CPI (inflation) |
| | **1975** |
| (1976 Parti Québécois elected) | • Wage and price controls |
| | • Family Allowance indexing frozen for one year |
| | • Opportunities for Youth, Company of Young Canadians, and Information Canada were abolished |
| | • Local Initiatives Program drastically reduced |
| | • *Unemployment Insurance Act* resulted in tightened eligibility |
| | **1977** |
| | • Bill C57 (New Social Services Act) introduced, but withdrawn |
| | • Federal-Provincial Fiscal Arrangements |
| | • *Established Programs Financing Act* |
| | **1978** |
| | • Refundable Child Tax Credit |
| **1979** | **1979** |
| Progressive Conservative Minority (Clark) | • Mortgage Interest and Property Tax Credit |
| | • Refundable Energy Tax Credit |
| **1980** | |
| Liberal Majority (Trudeau/Turner) | |

**Economic Indicators**

| Year | Net Public Debt (Millions of Dollars) | Budgetary Surplus or Deficit (-) (Millions of Dollars) | Unemployment Rate (%) | Recession |
|---|---|---|---|---|
| **1974** | 28 416 | -2225 | 5.4 | Recession |
| 1975 | 34 620 | -6205 | 7.1 | " |
| 1976 | 41 517 | -6896 | 7.0 | |
| 1977 | 52 396 | -10 879 | 8.0 | |
| 1978 | 65 425 | -13 029 | 8.3 | |
| **1979** | 77 392 | -11 967 | 7.5 | |
| **1980** | 91 948 | -14 557 | 7.5 | |
| 1981 | 107 622 | -15 674 | 7.6 | Recession |
| 1982 | 136 671 | -29 049 | 11.1 | " |

*Source:* Economic data from Statistics Canada (CANSIM). Political party data from *Canada Votes 1935–1986* by Frank B. Feigert (1989), Duke University Press. Federal response from *The Emergence of Social Security in Canada, 3rd Edition* by Dennis Guest (1997), UBC Press.

social services act and a companion piece that would have provided a guaranteed annual income (GAI) were also withdrawn. The 1960s war on poverty that began in the United States was about to be implemented in Canada; however, it got only as far as an experimental project in Manitoba. The federal government picked Dauphin, Manitoba, for its experiment with a negative taxation form of GAI to determine if such a program would decrease work effort (Armitage, 1996, p. 166). The experiment was implemented, but the progressive reforms were not.

## PERIOD OF DECLINE: 1983–2007

Margaret Thatcher in the United Kingdom, Ronald Reagan in the United States, and Brian Mulroney in Canada ushered in the neo-conservative era. Brian Mulroney and the Progressive Conservatives took office in 1984 and remained there for nine years, but the neo-conservative agenda lived on in Canada as it did in the other countries. In the United States, the Reagan administration used a number of legislative tools to roll back social programs, reduce government intervention, and empower the private sector. George Bush Sr. continued this agenda with his concept 1000 Points of Light. It was a concept that "rests on the belief that the private sector will pick up the social responsibilities of a declining public sector" (Fisher & Karger, 1997, p. 19). Private charities, such as the United Way and voluntary food banks, became the primary providers of care and assistance to the poor and disadvantaged members of society. Fisher and Karger note that even the Clinton administration eventually bowed to the pressure of the neo-conservative agenda and allowed the shift of responsibility to state officials for the Aid to Families with Dependent Children program.

In Canada, there were some parallels to what was going on in the United States. Mulroney, like Reagan, adopted a policy agenda that ultimately favoured the interests of business. On the campaign trail leading up to the 1984 election, Mulroney acted like an old conservative saying that social programs were a "sacred trust" not to be violated. However, within a year of taking office he announced that old age security and family allowances would no longer be fully indexed to the cost of living. Family allowance was eventually folded into the income tax system, and tax reform was used as a less obvious means of clawing back social security. Government spending on unemployment insurance was reduced, as were the grants to the National Action Committee on the Status of Women. In 1989, Canada signed a Free Trade Agreement with the United States, and many Canadians perceived this agreement as a threat to social security. Despite assurances to the contrary, unemployment insurance received further cuts, and transfer payments to the provinces for health, post-secondary education, welfare, and social services were reduced.

Mulroney's brand of neo-conservative policies, McGilly (1998) argues, were not of the order pursued by Thatcher in Britain or Reagan in the United States, but there is no denying Mulroney and the Progressive Conservatives set Canada on a different course. In discussing Mulroney's policy direction, Johnson and Stritch (1997) describe the trade arrangements as "the beginning of a very slippery slope towards greater dependence on the United States" (p. 218). They also note that "the Conservatives had set the stage for major changes to social security immediately prior to the 1993 election" and that "business interest groups were claiming they had not gone far enough in reducing social security expenditure" (p. 174). During Mulroney's time in office, the business lobby was well organized and able to express itself through the "right wing" think-tanks of the Fraser and the C.D. Howe Institutes. Both institutes were founded in their present form a decade earlier, at the twilight of the Keynesian era. Linda McQuaig (1995) notes that the C.D. Howe was "funded entirely by its members, which includes the country's five big banks, major corporations, investment houses, life insurance and trust companies, as well as law and accounting firms" (p. 18). She also identifies the pivotal role it plays in bringing deficit reduction and social spending cuts to the top of the policy agenda. On another front, Mulroney attempted, through the Meech Lake and Charlottetown accords, to make Canada's constitution acceptable to Québec. His failure to do so and his struggles with the economy no doubt contributed to his resignation as prime minister in June of 1993. Kim Campbell became the next leader of the Progressive Conservatives and the first woman prime minister of Canada, and within five months a national election was held.

Jean Chrétien and the Liberals campaigned for that election on promises to invest in job creation, eliminate the Goods and Services Tax (GST), and renegotiate the North American Free Trade Agreement that had been approved by the previous government in May of 1993. The Liberals managed to win the election, but the results were unusual in that the Bloc Québécois, a party set on separating Québec from Canada, captured enough seats to form the official opposition. In Western Canada, the Liberals were also challenged by the new Reform Party who won seats in British Columbia, Alberta, Saskatchewan, and Manitoba. Once in office, Chrétien and the Liberals faced regional differences, a budget deficit of approximately $40 billion, and a trade agreement with the United States and Mexico that they felt was disadvantageous for the Canadian economy. On an international basis, a group of six nations (France, United States, Britain, Germany, Japan, and Italy) had been meeting on an annual basis to address major economic and political issues facing their domestic and international communities. It was known as the G6, and when Canada joined in 1977 it became the group of seven, or G7. In 1994, the G7 began meeting with Russia and four years later Russia joined, making it the G8. The General Agreement on Tariffs and Trade (GATT) that had been negotiated after WWII was under review and eventually replaced in 1994 with the World Trade Organization (WTO). The economy was globalizing and there was a process of global governance. The circumstances were clearly different from the days when the Liberals last had a majority government. For the Canadian electorate who thought there would be a return to the policy agenda of Lester Pearson, Pierre Trudeau, and the earlier Liberals, surprises lay ahead. The pressure to balance the budget and to hold with the direction started by the Progressive Conservatives was too strong. From a policy perspective, the critics argued the Liberals were behaving more like neo-conservatives while the supporters would counter by saying they were being pragmatic, taking the necessary steps to balance the budget and protect social welfare programs in the long term.

Nevertheless, the Unemployment Insurance Program was converted to the Employment Insurance Program in 1996 with cuts in the level and duration of benefits. In the same year, the Canada Assistance Plan (CAP) and the Established Programs Financing (EPF) were phased out and replaced with the Canada Health and Social Transfer (CHST). Both were cost-saving measures and the latter gave more autonomy, but less cash, to the provinces for the delivery of health, post-secondary education, welfare, and social services. By eliminating CAP and EPF, Allan Moscovitch commented that

> Far from accomplishing the renewal of social programs as they promised, the federal government . . . created the condition for the dismemberment of what was once a national income program. Until the 1990s, and while social welfare remained popular with business and the public, the

Liberal Party has repeatedly presented itself as the party that created the welfare state. Will they be so proud to present themselves as the party that did more to dismantle it than any other since the 1960s (Moscovitch, 1997, p. 118)?

Under the Liberals, much of the pro-business agenda was accomplished (see Table 3.5). The budget deficit was eliminated, going from a high of slightly more than $39 billion in 1993 to a budget surplus of about $20 billion by 2001. The rate of inflation, which was driven down by the Progressive Conservatives, came under further attack by the Liberals and went from a high of 12.5 percent in 1981 to a low of 0.2 percent in the late 1990s. Under the Liberals with Jean Chrétien as prime minister and Paul Martin Jr. as finance minister, the economic state of the country improved, but not the social welfare state. Unlike his father who had been an important member of the Liberal Party during the growth and development of social welfare, Paul Martin Jr. presided over the dismantling of social welfare programs. Despite the cutbacks, Chrétien and the Liberals were re-elected in 2000 with an even larger majority than in the previous election. Politically, the parties on the right (the Progressive Conservatives and Alliance) and the NDP on the left did not provide much of a challenge on a national basis. The Alliance Party, with a strong base of support in Alberta, attempted to broaden its national appeal, but Stockwell Day, the leader of the party, was viewed as a born-again Christian and social conservative with little appeal in central and Eastern Canada.

The Progressive Conservative Party had a base of support in Atlantic Canada with a policy platform that might have positioned them left of the Liberals, while the Bloc Québécois continued to appeal only to the voters in Québec. In the 2000 election, the NDP captured less than ten percent of the vote. Brooks (2007) suggests there was a "long-simmering debate over whether the way out of marginal status in national politics could be found in moving the party further to the left, or in recapturing the centrist orientation it had under former leaders Ed Broadbent and David Lewis" (p. 298).

As noted in Table 3.5, the Liberals, with back-to-back majority governments in 1997 and 2000, and with a fairly healthy budgetary surplus, made minor enhancements to social welfare. A National Child Benefit Supplement (NCBS) was introduced in 1998 to provide low-income working families with monthly payments and services, such as child care and extended health care benefits. The NCBS was created to promote participation in the workforce, and to overcome "the welfare wall." Also that year, steps were taken to ensure the future viability of the Canada Pension Plan by increasing the contribution rates from 5.85 percent of earnings to 9.9 percent. Following the discontinuation of CAP and the implementation of the CHST, relations between levels of government were strained. In 1999, the Liberals introduced the Social Union Framework Agreement (SUFA) as a way to improve relations and to assist levels of government in working together. The SUFA includes direction for funding, administration, and delivery of health care, social services, and education. The *Employment Insurance Act* was amended in 2000 to increase parental leave benefits in the event of a newborn or an adoption, allowing thirty-five weeks of benefits to be taken by one parent or split between two parents. Women can also claim benefits for up to fifteen weeks and when these benefits are combined, parents can receive up to one year of paid leave (at 55% of average insured earnings) to care for their infants. In the same year, Old Age Security and Canada Pension Plan were extended to include same-sex and common law couples. In 2003, a five-year initiative on Income Security Reform for First Nations people on reserves came to an end. It was an initiative designed to break

| TABLE 3.5 | Period of Decline: 1983–2007 |
| --- | --- |

| Political Party | Social Welfare Initiatives | Economic Indicators | | | |
| --- | --- | --- | --- | --- | --- |
| | | Year | Net Public Debt (Millions of dollars) | Budgetary Surplus or Deficit (-) | Unemployment Rate (%) |
| **1980**<br>Liberal Majority (Turner) | | 1983 | 136 671 | -29 049 | 11.9 |
| **1984**<br>Progressive Conservative Majority (Mulroney) | **1984**<br>● Regulatory approach-focus on the private pensions<br>● G.I.S. increased by $50 per month<br>● *Canada Health Act* (April 1984)<br><br>**1985**<br>● CPP Spouse's Allowance extended<br>● Macdonald Commission<br>● Child benefits and personal income tax system reduction<br>● Forget Commission<br><br>**1986**<br>● De-indexing of Pensions (OAS & FA) announced, but followed through only on FA<br>● Refundable Child Tax Credit increase announced<br>● EPF reduction<br><br>**1987**<br>● White Paper on Tax Reform<br>● National Strategy on Child Care | 1984<br>1985<br>1986<br>1987 | 169 549<br>207 986<br>242 581<br>273 323 | -32 363<br>-37 167<br>-33 389<br>-29 842 | 11.3<br>10.6<br>9.6<br>8.8 |

*(continued)*

**TABLE 3.5** (continued)

| Political Party | Social Welfare Initiatives | Economic Indicators | | | |
|---|---|---|---|---|---|
| | | Year | Net Public Debt (Millions of Dollars) | Budgetary Surplus or Deficit (-) | Unemployment Rate (%) |
| **1988** | | **1988** | 301 117 | -29 017 | 7.8 (FTA) |
| Progressive Conservative Majority (Mulroney/Campbell) | **1989**<br>• Tax Reform—OAS and FA to be repaid by individuals with net incomes over $50,000<br>• Bill introduced to overhaul UI | 1989 | 329 890 | -27 947 | 7.5 |
| | **1990**<br>• UI cutbacks<br>• CAP limited to 5% increases for "have" provinces<br>• EPF cut again by reducing the GNP escalator one point | 1990 | 358 820 | -29 143 | 8.1 |
| | | 1991 | 390 820 | -33 899 | 10.3 Recession |
| | **1992**<br>• Elimination of Family Allowance<br>• Child Tax Credit<br>• $500 million, five-year program to help children "at risk because of poverty" | 1992 | 425 177 | -32 319 | 11.2 |
| **1993**<br>Liberal Majority (Chrétien) | **1996**<br>• Elimination of CAP and EPF<br>• Canada Health and Social Transfer (CHST)<br>• *Employment Insurance Act (EI)* | **1993** | 466 198 | -39 019 | 11.4 (NAFTA) |
| | | 1994 | 508 210 | -38 530 | 10.4 |
| | | 1995 | 545 672 | -36 632 | 9.5 |
| | | 1996 | 574 289 | -30 006 | 9.6 |
| **1997**<br>Liberal Majority (Chrétien) | **1998**<br>• Canada Child Tax Benefit (CCTB) and National Child Benefit Supplement (NCBS)<br>• NCB clawback for Social Assistance recipients<br>• Contribution rates increase for CPP with a change in financing | **1997** | 583 186 | -8719 | 9.1 |
| | | 1998 | 579 708 | 2959 | 8.3 |
| | **1999**<br>• Social Union Framework Agreement (SUFA)—designed to improve relations and better coordinate services between levels of government | 1999 | 576 824 | 5779 | 7.6 |

| Political Party | Social Welfare Initiatives | | Economic Indicators | | |
|---|---|---|---|---|---|
| | | Year | Net Public Debt (Millions of Dollars) | Budgetary Surplus or Deficit (-) | Unemployment Rate (%) |
| **2000** | **2000** | **2000** | 564 526 | 14 258 | 6.8 |
| Liberal Majority (Chrétien/Turner) | • Increased parental leave benefits in the *Employment Insurance Act* | 2001 | 547 378 | 19 891 | 7.2 |
| | • OAS and CPP benefits extended to include same-sex and common law couples | 2002 | 536 489 | 8048 | 7.7 |
| | **2003** | 2003 | 510 576 | 6621 | 7.6 |
| | • Income Security Reform (ISR) applicable to First Nations, a five-year initiative came to an end | | | | |
| **2004** | **2004** | **2004** | 501 493 | 9145 | 7.2 |
| Liberal Minority (Martin) | • CHST divided into Canada Health Transfer (CHT) and Canada Social Transfer | 2005 | 499 863 | 1463 | 6.8 |
| | • Compassionate Care Benefits (CCB) introduced as part of EI | | | | |
| **2006** | **2006** | **2006** | 481 499 | 13 218 | 6.3 |
| Conservative Minority (Harper) | • CCTB's young child supplement abolished | | | | |
| | • Universal Child Care Benefit introduced, taxable to the spouse with the lowest net income—low income, single parent families are hardest hit by this taxation | | | | |
| | **2007** | | | | |
| | • Funding for child care and early learning cut | | | | |
| | • Proposed tax credits for businesses who create work-place child care spaces | | | | |
| | • Working Income Tax Benefit (WITE) | | | | |

*Source:* Political party data from *Canada Votes 1935–1986* by Frank B. Feigert (1989), Duke University Press; Elections Canada. Social welfare initiatives from *The Emergence of Social Security in Canada, 3rd Edition* by Dennis Guest (1997), UBC Press; *Social Welfare in Canada: Understanding Income Security, 2nd Edition* by Steven Hick (2007), Thompson Educational Publishing; *Budget 2C07*, Canada Revenue Agency (2007). Economic data from Statistics Canada (CANSIM & Fiscal Reference Table 2006); *Federal Deficit: Changing Trends* by Marion G. Wrobel & Jean Soucy (2000), Parliamentary Research Branch.

welfare dependency and promote greater self-sufficiency through training programs and employment opportunities.

In December of 2003, Jean Chrétien stepped down as prime minister and Paul Martin Jr. became leader of the party and the next prime minister. Approximately six months later an election was held and the Liberals won, but it was a minority government, the first in twenty-five years. Prior to the 2004 election, the Auditor General had just released her annual report highlighting what appeared to be inappropriate spending of public funds on advertising in Québec. As the details of what came to be known as the "AdScam" or "sponsorship scandal" unfolded, Liberal support in Québec dropped precipitously. The Liberals also had to contend with a new unified party on the right under the leadership of Stephen Harper and the NDP's new leader, Jack Layton. With public opinion polls showing the possibility of a Conservative minority government, the Liberals responded with campaign ads suggesting the Conservatives had a "hidden agenda" to privatize health care, neglect efforts to protect the environment, reconsider abortion and same-sex legislation, and establish closer relations with the United States. The strategy worked in June of 2004, but not in January of 2006 when the Conservatives took enough seats to form a minority government. By 2006, the results of a public inquiry on the AdScam scandal were released and this inquiry was quite damaging to the Liberals. The Conservatives ran a campaign that featured promises of government accountability, reductions in the Goods and Services Tax (GST), and a child care allowance for parents with young children.

While in office, Paul Martin Jr. and the Liberal minority government introduced Compassionate Care Benefits as a feature of Employment Insurance. This is a benefit available to people requiring time away from work to provide care and support to a seriously ill family member at risk of dying within six months. In 2005, the Liberals enacted the *Civil Marriage Act* recognizing same-sex marriages and they proposed a Universal Child Care program. The Conservatives countered with a less generous Universal Child Care Benefit (UCCB), which they eventually implemented. Under the Conservative program, families receive a taxable benefit of one hundred dollars per month for each child under the age of six. The spouse with the lowest net income is taxed, which makes it possible for a one-earner couple making $250 000 to keep more of the benefit than a single parent making $20 000. Also, to create the UCCB, the Canada Child Tax Benefit's young child supplement was eliminated, resulting in a loss of $249 annually for each child under the age of seven. In 2007, the Conservatives cut one billion dollars previously committed to early learning and child care and replaced it with tax credits for businesses interested in creating workplace child care spaces. They also proposed a Working Income Tax Benefit that would provide families earning less than $21 167 a year with a maximum tax credit of $1000.

## CONCLUSION

Social policy developments in Canada experienced two dramatic shifts: one in the post-World War II era, and the other following the energy crisis and period of stagflation in the early 1970s. Following the twin crucibles of the World War and the Great Depression, there was a collective will to create a social safety net not only in Canada, but also in Britain and the United States. Communism and politics to the left of centre were popular in the inter-war era, and this popularity helped to moderate the free-market enthusiasts. In Canada, a social democratic party, the CCF, had arrived on the scene in the 1930s and it caught the attention of the voters at the beginning of this period of growth and development. The economic ideas of John Maynard Keynes were popular, and Canada took steps towards building an institutional system of social welfare.

What back-to-back crises set in motion in the 1940s was reversed by back-to-back crises in the 1970s. However, the transition did not occur overnight. A faltering economy gave way to new economic theories, and Milton Friedman's persuasiveness paved the way, once again, for the free-market perspective. In 1984, Brian Mulroney followed the scripts of Thatcher in Britain and Reagan in the United States, and introduced the neo-conservative agenda to Canadians. In an era of globalization and unfettered capitalism, the Liberals under Jean Chrétien gave greater priority to balanced budgets than to the social safety net. After 2000, there were some minor enhancements in social welfare and a promise of a universal child care program. However, the new merged Conservative Party under Stephen Harper signalled a possible policy direction away from concern for children, especially those in poverty, by replacing the universal child care proposal with a far less generous initiative.

The future of Canada's social welfare system is unclear. The current trend of minority governments has led to little real progress in social welfare. The voting preferences of the Canadian public, the positions of influential groups and businesses, and social and economic contexts will continue to play a role in shaping social welfare policies. As globalization increases rapidly, many new pressures and considerations will enter into the social policy arena in Canada. Canadians must remember the legacy of social welfare this country has had, and continue to push for improvement. As it is the political process that generates the terms and conditions under which social workers operate, we must be strong political advocates, and as stated in the professional code of ethics, "uphold the right of people to have access to resources to meet basic human needs, ensure fair and equitable access to public services and benefits for equal treatment and protection under the law, to challenge injustices, especially those affecting the vulnerable and disadvantaged, and to promote social development and environmental management in the interest of all people" (Canadian Association of Social Workers, Code of Ethics, 2005, p. 5).

# References

Armitage, A. (2003). *Social welfare in Canada* (4th ed.). Toronto: Oxford University Press.

Barlow, M. (1990). *Parcel of rogues: How free trade is failing Canada*. Toronto: Key Porter.

Barlow, M., & Campbell, B. (1995). *Straight through the heart: How the Liberals abandoned the just society*. Toronto: Harper-Collins Publishers Ltd.

Bothwell, R., Drummond, I., & English, J. (1981). *Canada since 1945: Power politics and provincialism*. Toronto: University of Toronto Press.

Brooks, S. (2007). *Public policy in Canada: An introduction* (5th ed.). Toronto: Oxford University Press.

Canadian Association of Social Workers. (2005). *Code of ethics*. Online at http://www.casw-acts.ca.

Finkel, A. (1997). *Our lives: Canada after 1945*. Toronto: James Lorimer & Company Ltd.

Finkel, A., & Conrad, M. (2002). *History of the Canadian peoples: 1867 to the present*. Toronto: Addison Wesley Longman.

Fisher, R., & Karger, H. (1997). *Social work and community in a private world: Getting out in public*. New York: Longman.

Frank, T. (2000). *One market under God.* New York: Anchor Books.

Guest, D. (1997). *The emergence of social security in Canada* (3rd ed.). Vancouver: UBC Press.

Hick, S. (2007). *Social welfare in Canada: Understanding income security* (2nd ed.). Toronto: Thompson Educational Publishing, Inc.

Hurtig, M. (2002). *The vanishing country: Is it too late to save Canada?* Toronto: McClelland & Stewart Ltd.

Leduc Browne, P. (1997). Déjà Vu: Thatcherism in Ontario. In D. Ralph, A. Regimald, & N. St. Amand (Eds.), *Mike Harris's Ontario* (pp. 37–44). Halifax: Fernwood Publishing.

McBride, S., & Shields, J. (1997). *Dismantling a nation: The transition to corporate rule in Canada* (2nd ed.). Halifax: Fernwood Publishing.

McMenemy, J. (2006). *The language of Canadian politics: A guide to important terms and concepts* (4th ed.). Waterloo: Wilfrid Laurier University Press.

McQuaig, L. (1995). *Shooting the hippo.* Toronto: Penguin Books.

McQuaig, L. (1998). *The cult of impotence: Selling the myth of powerlessness in the global economy.* Toronto: Penguin Books.

Moscovitch, A. (1997). The Canadian Health and Social Transfer. In R. Blake, P. Bryden, and J.F. Strains (Eds.), *The welfare state in Canada: Past, present, and future* (pp. 105–119). Concord, Ontario: Irwin Publishing.

Moscovitch, A., & Drover, G. (1987). Social Expenditures and the Welfare State: The Canadian Experience in Historical Perspective. In A. Moscovitch & J. Albert (Eds.), *The benevolent state: The growth of welfare in Canada* (pp. 13–45). Toronto: Garamond Press.

Norrie, K., & Owran, D. (1996). *A history of the Canadian economy.* Toronto: Harcourt Brace Canada.

Teeple, G. (1995). *Globalization and the decline of social reform.* Toronto: Garamond Press.

Rice, J., & Prince, M. (2000). *Changing politics of Canadian social policy.* Toronto: University of Toronto Press.

Wiseman, N. (2006). Going Nowhere: Conservatism and the Conservative Party. In M. Charlton & P. Barker (Eds.), *Contemporary and political issues (5th ed.),* (pp. 57–69). Publisher unavailable.

# CHAPTER 4

# The Economics Base of Canadian Social Welfare

*Marion E. Jones*

This chapter provides economic theoretical and philosophical perspectives on social welfare more generally, with some specific reference to the Canadian context. As social welfare is holistic both in study and practice, material discussed in detail elsewhere in this volume will be trespassed upon here.

## SCARCITY, CHOICE, AND OPPORTUNITY COSTS—ECONOMIC DECISION MAKING

Fundamental to the field of economics and to economic perspectives on any subject is the idea of scarcity. If the world were full of unlimited resources, there would be no need for this textbook, because all people would have all of the goods and services they wanted and needed without recourse from state or private provision. This surely is the socialist utopia of many people's dreams. Unfortunately, the resources of this world are finite—and the daily constraints of climate change contribute to their rapid decline. As a result, we, as both individuals and societies, must make choices, and every choice made means that some other option is given up—the opportunity cost is the lost benefit of the other option or choice. The three central questions of choice arising from scarcity in economics are: *What gets produced? How is this output best produced? Who gets to consume the output?* The optimization problem quickly becomes: *How do we get more stuff for more people?* Market widening and deepening in more formal language is the measure of economic success and the engine of economic growth. Little wonder that when psychologists measure the impact of undergraduate education they discover that four years of economic study makes people increasingly selfish. However, this chapter will set out to demonstrate that a selfish end does not always have to be the case.

As individuals and as a society, we have to make some fundamental choices about how to use the money, votes, or income that we command. The first choice is: *How much do we save and how much do we consume?* In Canada, we see that savings is actually a significant priority (although often hidden), because we have tax laws that promote pension savings to the tune of twenty percent of income, and foster investment in Canadian equities through reduced tax rates on these capital gains. Some people are also fortunate enough to "save" through paying a mortgage on a house—another common form of savings and accumulating net worth. People save for a number of reasons: to hedge against risk and spread income over their life cycle as with pension savings, to cover unforeseen expenses, or to protect against lost income. The opportunity cost of these savings equals the benefits of the current consumption that has been forgone. The best tool to illustrate this is the production possibility frontier (PPF)—a graph that shows the trade-off between savings and consumption within an economy (see Figure 4.1). Points inside the PPF represent unemployment productive factors (labour, capital, and/or land and natural resources), and points outside the PPF represent points unattainable with the productive factors currently available within the economy. The PPF itself shows the options and trade-offs of production and consumption at full employment of all productive factors. The slope of the PPF shows the trade-off between the two alternatives, or the opportunity cost of one with respect to the other at any given point—in this case, the trade-off

| FIGURE 4.1 | Savings vs. Consumption |
|---|---|

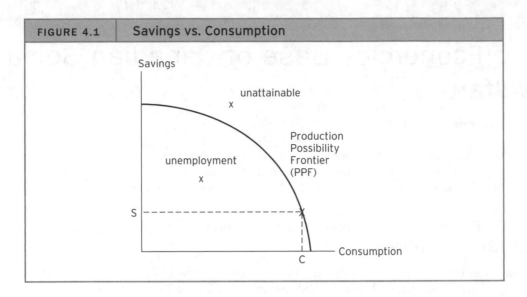

between savings and consumption. The reason that the PPF is convex to the origin is scarcity, and the law of diminishing returns—some productive factors are better suited to one use over another. The existence of various rates of social welfare systems will influence the amount of savings as a hedge against risk in any society.

The second choice that we make is how much of our current consumption goes to goods and services provided by the private sector and how much goes to goods and services from the public sector. This decision is strongly influenced by ideology (fought with positively religious zeal), and also principles of social justice and moral philosophy. Public goods and services are provided to Canadian residents, citizens of the provinces, and residents of municipalities by the three levels of government, respectively. They range from the Canadian Armed Forces to traffic lights to the social welfare system. There are two things to remember about a public good: first, the social benefit derived from consuming an additional unit of the good (the marginal benefit) is greater than the private marginal benefit; and second, this arises from the fact that it is very hard to keep people from benefiting from the good without paying for it—the "free rider" principle. We can also use a production possibility frontier diagram to illustrate the public–private goods trade-off (Figure 4.2).

There is a wide range of social welfare public goods that take the form of risk spreading or life cycle expenditure spreading. The most important ones are the Canada Pension Plan (CPP), the Guaranteed Income Supplement (GIS), and the Old Age Pension (OAP) to reduce poverty among the elderly; Employment Insurance (EI), Maternity Leave, Disability Benefits, and Worker's Compensation Insurance to reduce risk for those in the labour force; welfare programs, Canadian Child Tax Benefit (CCTB), and minimum wage legislation to reduce poverty; and medicare to spread medical expense risks across people (well and sick) in any one time period, and over the course of a life in the long-run. There are several excellent chapters later in the book that will illustrate in great detail the threats and transformations of these programs under neo-liberalism over the past two decades.

Some of these programs are funded directly through overt contributions, as we see for EI and the CPP, and others are funded through general tax revenues by various levels of

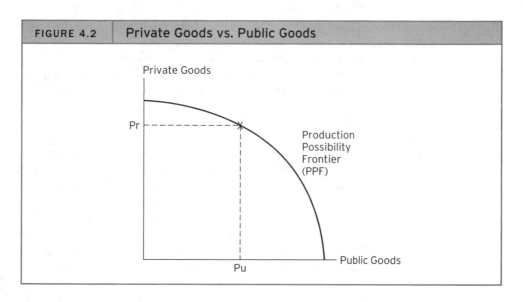

FIGURE 4.2 | **Private Goods vs. Public Goods**

governments. As a result, the rate of income tax, as imposed by the government in power, is a reflection of the dollar votes of Canadian society for the consumption and provision of these public goods. As such, it is very difficult to get a proper sense of the support of the Canadian public for any given social program, particularly for the programs funded through general revenues. What we have seen over the better part of two decades has been a strong shift away from support for public expenditures (with the possible exception of health care), and in favour of increased private consumption. This is most notably apparent in the persistent use of government budget surpluses to reduce income tax burdens and to increase corporate tax credits—yet another social choice.

## GOVERNMENT BUDGET SURPLUSES

Elsewhere in this volume there is much discussion of the use of federal and provincial government budget surpluses to pay down the debt at the cost of social program spending, particularly outside of the health care sector. This is an area that requires some careful discussion and examination, particularly since it is an emotionally and ideologically charged topic. Underlying this issue is a debate that turned the macroeconomics' sections of economics departments into armed camps for more than two decades. It all started with two star economists during World War II. John Maynard Keynes was at the height of his game—*The General Theory* and *How to Pay for the War* were highly influential in driving both Great Depression recovery efforts and the war effort in London, Ottawa, and Washington, and he was soon to be instrumental in setting up the World Bank and the IMF at Bretton Woods in 1944. Friedrich von Hayek, formerly of Austria, was somewhat less fortunate with his book, *The Road to Serfdom*, on the perils of unbridled government expenditures and the monetization of the debt (funded by printing money), which was inspired by the hyperinflation of Weimar Germany. Von Hayek has become the darling of the Chicago and Austrian Schools in economics, who are the champions—on a highly ideologically charged basis—of small government, price stability, and the superiority of personal choice and free markets. These are the prime movers of the Washington Consensus and neo-liberalism that is causing such destruction to social programs and economic development around the world. Von Hayek's personal experience of hyperinflation in 1930s Germany meant that, in this monetarist's view of the world, price stability was paramount, and anything that governments might do to stimulate the economy would only cause inflation. Keynes took a rather different view of the world, emphasizing the importance of stability in employment as a result of his experiences during the Great Depression. As explored in Chapter 3, Keynes observed that the economy moves in cycles, where there are periods of up-turns where inflation picks up, and down-turns in the economy where more people become unemployed. Keynes further observed that if there is a crisis of confidence in the economy during a recession, this can lead to a sustained downward spiral in the economy without the intervention of governments. Indeed, Keynes posited that it is the role of government both to take the economy off the boil when it is in an inflationary boom, and to kick-start the economy during a recession. To that end, part of the modern welfare state functions as built-in automatic stabilizers which aim to smooth out the extremes of the business cycle. Examples of this include employment insurance and social welfare payments that rise and pump money into an economy during a recession because more people need them, and fall during an inflationary period because fewer people will need them through increased employment. The tax system functions in a similar manner, where the total value of taxes collected, both income and excise, will rise as the economy takes off and grow quickly, and the total value of taxes collected will fall as the economy drifts into recession.

The result of this is that when the economy is performing well, and unemployment is low, governments will have total tax revenues (T) in excess of total government expenditures (G), and thereby run a surplus, merely as a function of the level of economic activity and not due to any changes in the marginal tax or benefit rates. This surplus should be used to pay down debt incurred through deficits in previous recessions. During a recession, total tax revenues will fall, while total government expenditures will rise, again with no change in the marginal tax or benefit rates, producing a government budget deficit where T is less than G. There are other reasons why governments should borrow money and incur debts, such as long-term capital investment in infrastructure like roads, schools, and hospitals, and in support of the money supply and low-risk mandatory investment instruments for regulated pension funds, but that is another story. However, it does sharply illustrate what we stand to lose as a result of balanced budget legislation that seeks to eliminate budget deficits.

As a result of this, it should become clear that it is important to make a distinction between the relatively neutral policy of paying down government debt from budget surpluses in a period of robust economic growth in preparation for the next recession, compared to the fundamental choice of reducing taxes instead of increasing social welfare spending outside of the health care system, which absorbs about ninety cents out of every additional dollar of government expenditure these days.

One of the most important differences between the Keynesian and Monetarist (von Hayek) vision of the work comes from whether or not there is a trade-off between inflation and unemployment in the economy. It all comes down to what their ideas and models have to say about the shape of the short-term aggregate supply curve—a line that shows the relationships between price level and total output for all producers in an economy. Please see Figures 4.3 and 4.4 below. In Figure 4.3, we have the Keynesian model, where the short-run

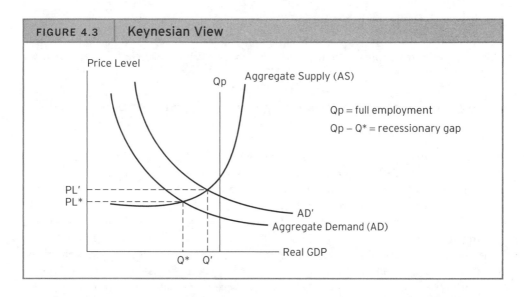

FIGURE 4.3    Keynesian View

aggregate supply has a very flat section where output in the economy is low, and a recession would be quite severe, and where an increase in output would yield an increase in employment without inflation. The inclined section is closer to full employment, where more output yields both increased employment and inflation. The vertical section is where increased output would yield only inflation, because we are at or beyond full employment. In Figure 4.4, we have the Monetarist vision, where an economy is always at full employment, so the aggregate supply curve is vertical and equal to potential GDP. As a result, any change in aggregate demand here will always yield pure inflation with no scope for generating further employment. Here, if you are unemployed, then it is no fault of the labour markets! From these two pictures or diagrams, it is easy to understand why when the economy is in a recession the Keynesians are in favour of government intervention to prime the pump in the

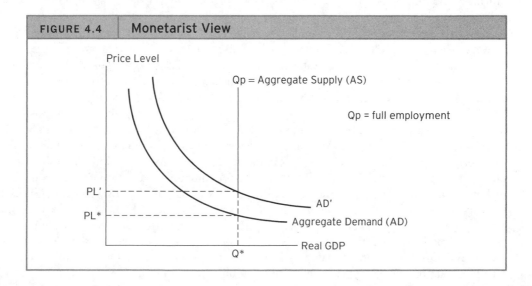

FIGURE 4.4    Monetarist View

economy and help push things back towards full employment, while the Monetarists are set against it, because it will only end in inflation. It is easy to see how this would yield a "blame the victim" approach to difficulties in labour market attachment and the need for welfare support.

## CANADIAN SOCIAL WELFARE EXPENDITURES AND TAX REVENUES

Now that you understand something about the theoretical ideas around business cycles and why some people are in favour of government intervention in the economy and others are not, it is time to turn our attention in more detail to the composition of those tax revenues and government expenditures and what they mean for Canadian society.

There are a number of ways that governments can collect taxes, and the Canadian and provincial governments use a combination of these. One type of tax is excise taxes—taxes levied on consumption. The Goods and Services Tax (GST) is an excise tax, as are provincial sales taxes. Taxes on cigarettes, tobacco and alcohol, and customs' duties are all different types of excise taxes. Another type of tax is income tax. In Canada, we have income taxes on private incomes and also on corporate incomes. These are taxes paid (net of deductions) on income earned for private incomes and on corporate earnings for corporate taxes. EI and CPP payments made by both workers and employers are really just another form of income tax, but are collected for a special purpose. This is also true of the separate health care payments in Alberta. Property taxes and Capital Investment taxes are two types of taxes levied on property owned. There are also flat taxes, head taxes, or poll taxes. All of these are a flat tax rate levied on an individual. In Britain, under Margaret Thatcher, there were poll taxes (and riots against them) brought in to provide additional government revenue. In Canada, the most infamous flat tax was the head tax imposed on Chinese immigrants in the late 1800s and early 1900s for which compensation has recently been paid and a government apology issued.

These different types of taxes impact people in different ways. If the burden of the tax falls most heavily on those most able to pay, then it is said to be progressive. In Canada, and in most provinces, the income tax system is progressive because below a certain threshold, no tax is paid, but as incomes get higher, higher percentages of tax are paid. Property taxes are often also thought to be progressive taxes—where the burden is falling on those with greater resources. However, even people who rent accommodation are also responsible for paying property taxes through their rent, and farmers in rural Saskatchewan with large tracts of land, but little income, feel their property taxes to support local school boards are highly regressive compared to non-farmers living in rural areas (who often have significant cash income and little land).

If a tax is not progressive, then it is regressive—when the burden of the tax falls most heavily on those with the least ability to pay. Head taxes or poll taxes are said to be mildly regressive, because the burden for people who have low income is proportionately higher than for people with high incomes. For example, a $200 head tax is vastly different in its burden for someone working two part-time jobs for minimum wage than for someone making $100 000 per year. The Alberta health care fees would fall into this category also. Excise taxes are seen as being strongly regressive, because people with low incomes spend a higher portion of their incomes than people with high incomes (they have no or negative savings). This is why, for instance, there is no GST on most groceries and children's clothing, and no GST on children's diapers, while there is GST on geriatric diapers and feminine hygiene products, to try and reduce the worst of the regressive nature of the tax.

With the advent of the GST, and also the period in the 1990s when income tax brackets were removed from indexation for inflation, there has been a shift in Canada from a taxation system that was modestly progressive through neutrality to a system that is modestly regressive. This is particularly true in Alberta, where the 11 percent provincial flat tax on income and health insurance payments more than makes up for the lack of a PST.

So much for the revenue side of the equation; now we need to turn our attention to the patterns of and changes to government expenditure on social welfare in Canada. In the 2005–06 fiscal year (Table 4.1), total government spending (all levels) was $515 billion. Of this, $131 billion was spent on income security programs (25 percent), $102 billion (20 percent) on health and $82.7 billion (16 percent) on education (Statistics Canada).

From the data in Tables 4.1 and 4.2 we can see there has been a steady growth in both GDP and government expenditure in real terms over the last fifteen years, with government expenditures—led by growth in health care expenditures—growing a little faster. The shares of social welfare spending have varied only a little over the last decade and a half, with the only significant change in sectoral shares coming from health, where the cutbacks of the early 1990s, and then the more recent increased expenditure, are evident. The counter cyclical increase in social services spending during the recession of the 1990s is also evident. Business cycle effects were dominant in determining social service expenditures during the entire period, as policies of "fostering independence" and reducing the opportunity cost of seeking work were prevalent in social service policies starting with the

| TABLE 4.1 | Consolidated Canadian Federal, Provincial, Territorial, and Local Government Revenue and Expenditures, for Fiscal Year Ending March 31 | | | |
|---|---|---|---|---|
| Year | Total Expenditures Millions $ | Health | Social Services | Education |
| 1989 | 278 421 | 13% | 25% | 14% |
| 1990 | 304 509 | 13% | 24% | 14% |
| 1991 | 330 500 | 14% | 25% | 14% |
| 1992 | 356 372 | 14% | 26% | 14% |
| 1993 | 365 336 | 14% | 27% | 15% |
| 1994 | 368 752 | 14% | 27% | 15% |
| 1995 | 373 760 | 14% | 26% | 15% |
| 1996 | 381 158 | 14% | 26% | 15% |
| 1997 | 371 693 | 14% | 26% | 15% |
| 1998 | 372 695 | 15% | 27% | 15% |
| 1999 | 387 438 | 15% | 26% | 15% |
| 2000 | 401 520 | 16% | 26% | 15% |
| 2001 | 424 557 | 17% | 26% | 15% |
| 2002 | 437 568 | 18% | 26% | 15% |
| 2003 | 455 442 | 18% | 26% | 15% |
| 2004 | 476 284 | 19% | 25% | 16% |
| 2005 | 496 111 | 20% | 25% | 16% |
| 2006 | 515 019 | 20% | 25% | 16% |

*Source:* Statistics Canada. N.d. Table 385-0001 *Consolidated federal, provincial, territorial, and local government revenue and expenditures for fiscal year ending March 31, annual (dollars)* (table). CANSIM (database). Using E-STAT (distributor). Accessed March 16, 2007. http://estat.statcan.ca.libproxy.uregina.ca:2048/cgi-win/CNSMCGI.EXE

| TABLE 4.2 | Real per Capita GDP and Government Expenditures, 1990–2005 | | | |
|---|---|---|---|---|
| Year | PC GDP | PC Gov't Exp | PC Health | PC Social Serv | PC Educ'n |
| 1990 | 25 385 | 10 923 | 1474 | 2652 | 1524 |
| 1991 | 24 771 | 11 737 | 1590 | 2892 | 1652 |
| 1992 | 24 732 | 12 529 | 1723 | 3259 | 1800 |
| 1993 | 25 084 | 12 716 | 1771 | 3405 | 1884 |
| 1994 | 25 950 | 12 706 | 1778 | 3484 | 1870 |
| 1995 | 26 364 | 12 750 | 1765 | 3320 | 1898 |
| 1996 | 26 470 | 12 872 | 1793 | 3283 | 1878 |
| 1997 | 27 310 | 12 428 | 1786 | 3290 | 1815 |
| 1998 | 28 151 | 12 358 | 1882 | 3294 | 1837 |
| 1999 | 29 390 | 12 743 | 1953 | 3368 | 1907 |
| 2000 | 30 826 | 13 084 | 2096 | 3423 | 1970 |
| 2001 | 30 968 | 13 686 | 2272 | 3551 | 2048 |
| 2002 | 31 535 | 13 947 | 2452 | 3658 | 2122 |
| 2003 | 31 980 | 14 381 | 2631 | 3695 | 2227 |
| 2004 | 33 691 | 15 344 | 2896 | 3898 | 2420 |
| 2005 | 34 422 | 15 824 | 3126 | 4020 | 2546 |
| % growth | 2.05% | 2.50% | 5.14% | 2.81% | 3.48% |

*Source:* Statistics Canada. N.d. Table 385-0001 *Consolidated federal, provincial, territorial, and local government revenue and expenditures for fiscal year ending March 31, annual (dollars)* (table). CANSIM (database). Using E-STAT (distributor). Accessed March 16, 2007. http://estat.statcan.ca.libproxy.uregina.ca:2048/cgi-win/CNSMCGI.EXE

Ontario and Alberta "common sense" revolutions brought in by Progressive Conservatives Mike Harris and Ralph Klein.

According to Figure 4.5, the counter cyclical patterns of per capita GDP and per capita government expenditure are obvious, with per capita GDP falling back during the recessions,

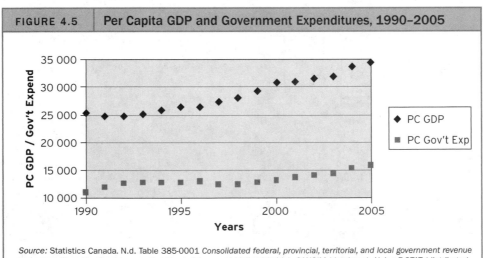

FIGURE 4.5 | Per Capita GDP and Government Expenditures, 1990–2005

*Source:* Statistics Canada. N.d. Table 385-0001 *Consolidated federal, provincial, territorial, and local government revenue and expenditures for fiscal year ending March 31, annual (dollars)* (table). CANSIM (database). Using E-STAT (distributor). Accessed March 16, 2007. http://estat.statcan.ca.libproxy.uregina.ca:2048/cgi-win/CNSMCGI.EXE

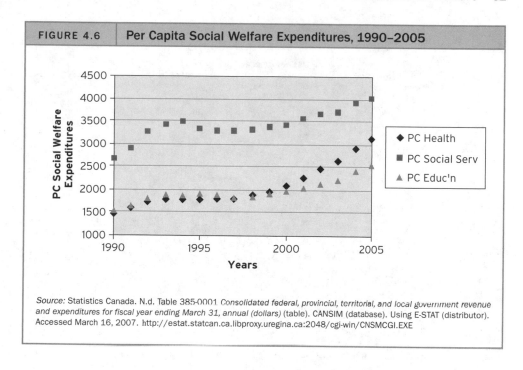

FIGURE 4.6    **Per Capita Social Welfare Expenditures, 1990–2005**

Source: Statistics Canada. N.d. Table 385-0001 *Consolidated federal, provincial, territorial, and local government revenue and expenditures for fiscal year ending March 31, annual (dollars)* (table). CANSIM (database). Using E-STAT (distributor). Accessed March 16, 2007. http://estat.statcan.ca.libproxy.uregina.ca:2048/cgi-win/CNSMCGI.EXE

and per capita social welfare expenditures rising. This also reflects the relatively large size or importance of social service expenditures in total social welfare expenditures. Towards the end of the time period, the more rapid increase in health expenditures and their rising importance in total social welfare expenditures dominates the faster rise in per capita social welfare expenditure over per capita GDP.

In Figure 4.6, we see the time series trends for per capita expenditures on health, social services, and education. The dominance of social service expenditure and the impact of the mid-1990s recession are very clear here. Also very clear is the rapid increase in health expenditure per capita since 2000, making education and social service expenditures appear positively stagnant by comparison. This is somewhat misleading given that per capita health expenditures grew by 5.1 percent over the fifteen years, compared to 3.5 percent for education and 2.8 percent for social services.

In 1996–97, corporate taxes accounted for 7.6 percent of all taxes paid, while personal income taxes accounted for 32 percent and excise taxes accounted for 20 percent out of a total tax bill of $351 billion (Lightman, 2003: 170–171). By 2006, the total tax bill had increased to $532 billion, and personal income tax was 31 percent, excise taxes were 20 percent, and corporate taxes were 9 percent. The data in Table 4.3 show that there have been significant year-over-year changes in the contributions of the various components of government revenue. The relative stability in shares of government revenue in the late 1990s and early 2000s is a product of the steady growth in the economy, and the relatively stable tax systems in successive minority governments. The rather more chaotic patterns for much of the 1990s were a product of both the recession, which affected corporate taxes first and personal taxes and excise taxes later, and the shift to fiscal conservatism under Jean Chrétien and his finance minister, Paul Martin.

| TABLE 4.3 | Government Revenue by Source | | | |
|---|---|---|---|---|
| Year | Total Revenue | Personal Income Taxes | Corporate Income Taxes | Excise Taxes |
| 1989 | 24 203 | 32% | 7% | 22% |
| 1990 | 273 006 | 33% | 7% | 22% |
| 1991 | 289 202 | 34% | 6% | 20% |
| 1992 | 293 731 | 35% | 5% | 20% |
| 1993 | 299 232 | 33% | 4% | 20% |
| 1994 | 305 105 | 32% | 5% | 21% |
| 1995 | 321 073 | 32% | 6% | 20% |
| 1996 | 337 869 | 32% | 7% | 20% |
| 1997 | 351 459 | 32% | 8% | 20% |
| 1998 | 373 531 | 33% | 9% | 20% |
| 1999 | 385 460 | 33% | 9% | 20% |
| 2000 | 414 170 | 33% | 9% | 19% |
| 2001 | 446 959 | 32% | 10% | 20% |
| 2002 | 437 288 | 33% | 9% | 20% |
| 2003 | 447 861 | 31% | 8% | 22% |
| 2004 | 468 040 | 31% | 8% | 21% |
| 2005 | 500 411 | 31% | 9% | 21% |
| 2006 | 532 183 | 31% | 9% | 20% |

*Source:* Statistics Canada. N.d. Table 385-0001 *Consolidated federal, provincial, territorial and local government revenue and expenditures for fiscal year ending March 31, annual (dollars)* (table). CANSIM (database). Using E-STAT (distributor). Accessed March 16, 2007. http://estat.statcan.ca.libproxy.uregina.ca:2048/cgi-win/CNSMCGI.EXE

## FUNDAMENTAL CHANGES IN WAGES AND INCOMES—CHALLENGES AND SOLUTIONS

There are several long-term trends that have been challenging the provision of social welfare services in Canada since the oil crises of 1973 and 1979–81. To these long-term trends, we have the additional challenges of globalization, free trade, and neo-liberalism, all of which came to the forefront during the recession and federal and provincial budget crises of the mid- to late 1990s. The story is well documented elsewhere (for example, Yalnizyan, 2007; Caledon Institute, 1995; Stanford, 1999), but deserves summary here (Table 4.4). Real wages have been falling for Canadian workers since the late 1970s. In the 1990s alone, after-tax real incomes declined by seven percent, while the decline was three percent for gross real earnings (Stanford, 1999). This means that families in Canada were able to afford seven percent fewer goods and services than they did at the beginning of the decade. Simultaneously, the last two decades have seen soaring corporate profits and manager remuneration (Clarke, 1997) and cuts in government expenditures on social welfare (Yalnizyan, 2007). The net impact of this reality is that the number of working poor has been growing, the number of families that need two working adults to support them has increased, and the number of people working multiple jobs, often part-time jobs, has increased also. So, in addition to the headline numbers on unemployment, we need to add the hidden unemployed who are working outside their area of expertise, those who are working in part-time employment when they would like a full-time job, and discouraged workers who are no longer actively seeking employment because they feel it is impossible to obtain.

At the same time there has been a general shift in the tax burden away from corporate taxes and towards personal income tax and excise taxes on personal consumption. The net result of all of these shifts has been a marked shift in the returns to the factors of production, and one that cannot be explained adequately through capital investment and human capital investment to yield productivity gains. Indeed, a serious problem in the Canadian economy has been the signal failure of Canadian business to invest in productivity with their record profits, instead relying on a combination of anti-inflationary policies (Stanford, 2007) and loose monetary policy (a low Canadian dollar) to maintain their competitiveness.

There are a number of important distortions in the labour market that contribute to irrational or inefficient outcomes, including welfare dependency and these trends in real wages and returns on capital investment. At a provincial level, we have minimum wage legislation. Minimum wage legislation is often justified on the grounds of subsistence wages.

| TABLE 4.4 | Canadian Gross Domestic Product (GDP) by Factor Shares | | | | |
|---|---|---|---|---|---|
| Year | Gross Domestic Product Millions $ | Labour Wages | Capital Interest | Land and Natural Resources Rent | Profits | Taxes |
| 1980 | 314 390 | 54% | 9% | 5% | 14% | 9% |
| 1981 | 360 471 | 55% | 9% | 5% | 11% | 11% |
| 1982 | 379 859 | 55% | 10% | 5% | 8% | 11% |
| 1983 | 411 386 | 54% | 9% | 6% | 10% | 10% |
| 1984 | 449 582 | 53% | 9% | 6% | 11% | 10% |
| 1985 | 485 714 | 53% | 8% | 6% | 11% | 10% |
| 1986 | 512 541 | 53% | 8% | 6% | 10% | 11% |
| 1987 | 558 949 | 53% | 7% | 6% | 11% | 11% |
| 1988 | 613 094 | 53% | 7% | 6% | 12% | 12% |
| 1989 | 657 728 | 53% | 7% | 6% | 10% | 12% |
| 1990 | 679 921 | 54% | 8% | 6% | 8% | 12% |
| 1991 | 685 367 | 55% | 8% | 6% | 6% | 13% |
| 1992 | 700 480 | 55% | 8% | 6% | 6% | 13% |
| 1993 | 727 184 | 54% | 7% | 6% | 6% | 13% |
| 1994 | 770 873 | 53% | 7% | 6% | 9% | 13% |
| 1995 | 810 426 | 52% | 6% | 6% | 10% | 13% |
| 1996 | 836 864 | 51% | 6% | 6% | 10% | 13% |
| 1997 | 882 733 | 51% | 6% | 6% | 11% | 13% |
| 1998 | 914 973 | 52% | 5% | 7% | 10% | 13% |
| 1999 | 982 441 | 51% | 5% | 6% | 12% | 13% |
| 2000 | 1 076 577 | 51% | 5% | 6% | 14% | 12% |
| 2001 | 1 108 048 | 51% | 5% | 6% | 12% | 12% |
| 2002 | 1 152 905 | 51% | 4% | 7% | 13% | 12% |
| 2003 | 1 213 408 | 51% | 4% | 6% | 13% | 12% |
| 2004 | 1 290 788 | 51% | 4% | 7% | 14% | 12% |
| 2005 | 1 371 425 | 50% | 4% | 6% | 15% | 11% |

*Source:* Statistics Canada. N.d. Table 380-0016. Accessed March 28, 2007. http://estat.statcan.ca.libproxy .uregina.ca:2048/cgi-win/CNSMCGI.EXE

However, here we have an odd situation, because the minimum wage is universally below the living wage (calculated as the wage needed based on a 40-hour work week, to afford shelter, transportation, groceries, utilities, and a modest set of clothing and entertainment). Before the boom in Alberta, the minimum wage lagged some $4.00 per hour behind the living wage ($10.00 and $6.00, respectively, at the time of the study—and this gap has widened as the cost of living has outpaced wage increases, according to the Alberta Federation of Labour). In Saskatchewan, the living wage is still more than $3.00 above the recently increased minimum wage. On the other side of the equation, small businesses are complaining that they cannot afford to hire workers at this new higher minimum wage. In Alberta, the shortage of labour has meant that the minimum wage is virtually an irrelevance, with burger joints in Red Deer offering $18.00 per hour. All of these distortions push the labour market into disequilibrium for people with limited human capital and limited job experience, or who for health or disability reasons no longer can make use of their human capital.

What does all of this mean for our social choices as citizens of Canada? Well, it means that we have seen a significant shift away from social welfare systems, risk spreading, and mutual aid, and towards a system of individualism and self-reliance. Part of this arises from the tenuous political situation over the last 15 years, and the constant need to worry about seeking and maintaining a political mandate. As a result, interest group politics has been dominating our fiscal policy, with the result that the tax cut bone has been thrown out to the centre-right, and what is left of the Canadian upper-middle class and the balanced budget/surplus bone has been thrown out to the corporate sector along with considerable corporate tax cuts and credits. The bone of increased health expenditure has been thrown out to the aged, those with aging family members, and the people working in the health care sector, while the vulnerable underclass in Canadian society has largely been ignored as a disenfranchised community with little political clout, such as the working poor or those on social assistance or employment insurance.

The solution to these problems is to have a stable democracy where a party is certain of power for four to five years, and where a more comprehensive and holistic approach can be taken to revenue generation (taxation) and expenditures, particularly to reinvigorate our social welfare system, and to ensure productivity of Canadian industry into the future. One element in such a plan, which would benefit welfare recipients and working poor alike, would be a *negative income tax system*. A negative income tax system would set a minimum income value below which people would receive a payment from the government. So, for example, if the tax neutral/living wage was set at $15 000 per year, then someone earning $12 000 in income from a minimum wage job would receive an additional $3000 credit from the tax system to top them up. This would be a genuine means of providing social assistance and support for stay-at-home parents, the elderly, the working poor, and people with disabilities, without the overarching bureaucracy and stigma of the welfare system. Above the $15 000 income mark, people would pay taxes just as they do today.

This contrasts enormously with the move towards "workfare," where firms are effectively given a subsidy for the employment of labour by the government so that these "employees" can be removed from the welfare roles. First, it is amazing that such a program would not produce a problem for Canada (or the US) under the World Trade Organization (WTO) or the North American Free Trade Agreement (NAFTA), as this represents unfair labour practices. It certainly is unfair to the other companies who hire labour and pay their full wage bill without this government subsidy. Finally, it also produces distortions in the economy, by providing subsidies for firms and industries, which are otherwise not profitable. The only place where such behaviour is excusable is in a sheltered workshop for people with severe disabilities. Otherwise, training, education, and equipment should be made available so that people can obtain full employment at a market wage in businesses and industries where they are making a productive contribution to the economy. Anything else is in complete violation of the rules of economic (allocative) efficiency.

## POVERTY AND INEQUALITY

There are a number of reasons why we should care about poverty and inequality in our society. The first is that high levels of inequality and poverty lead to social unrest and instability. These are not good for the functioning of an economy or the practice of democracy (mob rule being decidedly undemocratic), and it leads to considerable anxiety on the part of citizens. The second is that significant amounts of poverty and income inequality within a society are an affront against principles of social justice. The best way to think about this is to imagine the type of society you would wish to live in if you had no clue whether you were going to be homeless on the streets of Toronto, Calgary, or Vancouver, or you were going to be a Weston or an Asper or another of Canada's wealthiest people. This is what John Rawls called the "veil of ignorance"—an important tool for determining what is socially just and desirable. Finally, large amounts of inequality and poverty lead to too little savings in the economy and too much expenditure on luxury goods. A simple numerical example will illustrate this. Imagine a simple economy with ten people in it. In the first instance, everyone is poor except one person, so that the national income of $300 000 is divided up in the following manner: nine people have $10 000 income, and one person has $210 000 income. In the second instance, all ten people have an equal income of $30 000,

| TABLE 4.5 | Savings and Consumptions Patterns from Different Income Distributions | | | | | | |

**Scenario 1 – Income Polarization**

| Poor - 9 people, $10 000 income each | | | | Rich - 1 person, $210 000 income | | | |
|---|---|---|---|---|---|---|---|
| Income | Savings | Consum-N | Consum-L | Income | Savings | Consum-N | Consum-L |
| $90 000 | $4500 | $81 000 | $4500 | $210 000 | $31 500 | $31 500 | $147 000 |
| 100% | 5% | 90% | 5% | 100% | 15% | 15% | 70% |

| Total | | | |
|---|---|---|---|
| Income | Savings | Consum-N | Consum-L |
| $300 000 | $36 000 | $112 500 | $151 500 |
| 100% | 12% | 38% | 51% |

**Scenario 2 - Income Equality**

| Middle - 10 people, $30 000 income each | | | |
|---|---|---|---|
| Income | Savings | Consum-N | Consum-L |
| $300 000 | $60 000 | $150 000 | $90 000 |
| 100% | 20% | 50% | 30% |

for a total national income of $300 000. Table 4.5 shows the savings and consumptions of luxuries and necessities that results from these two scenarios. Savings are crucial fuel for capital investment and growth within an economy. Necessity goods tend to be dominated by domestic production, thereby fueling the domestic economy, while luxury goods are much more likely to be produced offshore and, therefore, need to be imported.

## LOW INCOME CUT-OFFS AND MEASURING POVERTY

Measuring poverty is a subject of some considerable controversy. The first controversy surrounds the establishment of the poverty line, particularly whether it is absolute or relative poverty that is the reference point. Absolute poverty is measured through the direct means necessary to sustain life—such as 2200 kilocalories per day, divided with a ratio of 1:2.2:5.4 for fat, protein, and carbohydrate, respectively, although obviously these amounts vary by age, sex, occupation, and level of physical activity. Absolute poverty by this measure is often converted into the money amount that is necessary to secure these food stuffs, which is the origin of the less than $1 US per day and less than $2 US per day employed by the United Nations Development Program (UNDP) and the millennium development goals. This measure of poverty is rather more meaningful in developing nations. Relative poverty is measured with respect to social norms. For example, it is often measured as 40 or 50 percent of average income. It is such measures of relative poverty that are most often employed in the wealthy industrialized nations, such as Canada. Table 4.6 provides the recent low income cut-offs (LICOs) before tax as calculated by Statistics Canada for different household (HH) sizes and rural and urban locations. These measures in themselves are highly controversial, due to the bundle of goods and services that are included, or that such an income could command. Another interesting fact is how far below the LICOs most social welfare assistance amounts are, although the LICOs correspond quite well to the living wage figures for medium or large cities based on data from Regina and Calgary ($17 000 and $20 000, respectively).

There are further controversies about how best to measure the incidence of poverty. The simplest measure is the head count index, where the number of people whose income falls below the poverty line is divided by the total population to give the proportion of the

| TABLE 4.6 | LICOs for Canada, 2005 (in Dollars) | | | | |
|---|---|---|---|---|---|
| 2005 | Before Tax | | | | |
| # in HH | Rural | Small Town | Small City | Med. City | Big City |
| 1 | 14 303 | 16 273 | 17 784 | 17 895 | 20 778 |
| 2 | 17 807 | 20 257 | 22 139 | 22 276 | 25 867 |
| 3 | 21 891 | 24 904 | 27 217 | 27 386 | 31 801 |
| 4 | 26 579 | 30 238 | 33 046 | 33 251 | 38 610 |
| 5 | 30 145 | 34 295 | 37 480 | 37 711 | 43 791 |
| 6 | 33 999 | 38 679 | 42 271 | 42 533 | 49 389 |
| 7 | 37 853 | 43 063 | 47 063 | 47 354 | 54 987 |

Source: Canadian Council on Social Development: (http://www.ccsd.ca/factsheets/fs_lico05_bt.htm). Accessed on April 2, 2007.

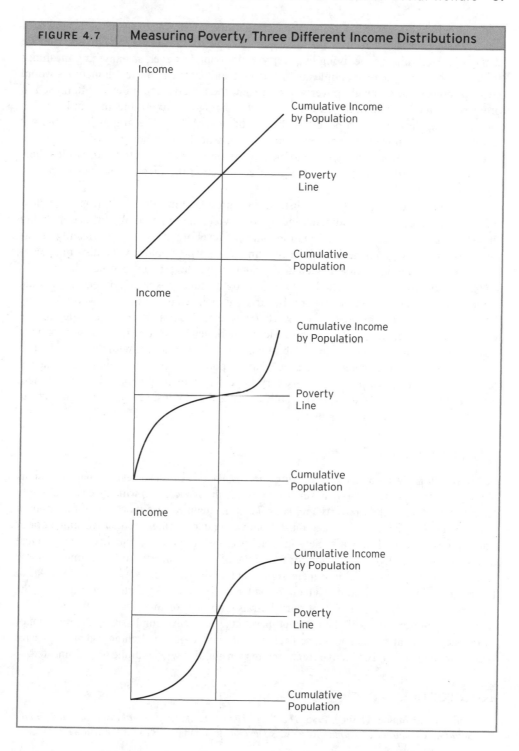

**FIGURE 4.7**  **Measuring Poverty, Three Different Income Distributions**

population living in poverty. This is a very straightforward, simple measure of the extent of poverty, and is at the heart of the headline data on poverty in Canada, such as the statistic that one in five children are living in poverty. It does not, however, say anything meaningful about how poor the poor people are, or to put it another way, how much incomes would need to increase to eliminate poverty. As a result, the poverty gap index is often used to provide a fuller measure of the extent of poverty—being the sum of the amount by which the income of those living in poverty is below the poverty line. The graphs in Figure 4.7 illustrate why the poverty gap index is superior—particularly in being sensitive to situations where a few people living close to the poverty line escape poverty status while others are made worse off. The index is also good at reflecting the income changes of people below the poverty line.

From the three different income distributions presented in Figure 4.7, it is quite clear that in all three cases, the head count index would yield the same number of people living in poverty, but the actual distribution of income and level of poverty is significantly different by the poverty gap measure. In formulating anti-poverty policies, we also must consider these distributions. In the second distribution we have many people who are just under the poverty line and a small number of people who are exceedingly poor; we could make great gains in alleviating poverty by targeting policies towards those who need only a small increase in income to escape poverty (such as with a minimum wage policy for the working poor) to great political acclaim. Here economics lets us down, because economic efficiency criteria are blind to the distributional effects. By contrast, with the third distribution, a policy that is targeted towards helping the poorest of the poor might be the sensible priority because the poverty gap is very large for so many people. The remedy here might be access to guaranteed food supplies at subsidized rates, or direct income supplements—a guaranteed income policy.

## CONCLUSION

Public policy is always a matter of making choices. We need, as a society, to make decisions about the type of society in which we wish to live. Is this a society in which we are willing to tolerate widespread child poverty and significant inequalities of opportunities for children from financially viable families and those from vulnerable families—either working poor or on social assistance? Is this a society in which we wish to promote equality through equal access to early childhood education for the future of society, and at the same time facilitate work for single parents, yielding them significant self-esteem and social inclusion? All of these choices have implications both on the patterns of social and private consumption in the country, and also the revenues that must be raised to pay for them. As the forces of neo-liberalism gain strength, with their strong libertarian perspective emphasizing the importance of choice, personal freedoms, and self-reliance, the range of social choices that emphasize greater social good and collective rights and responsibilities will continue to be truncated.

# References

Caledon Institute of Social Policy, 1995, *The Comprehensive Reform of Social Programs: Brief to the Standing Committee on Human Resources Development*. Ottawa: Renouf Publishing.

Graham, J.R., K.J. Swift, and R. Delaney, 2003, *Canadian Social Policy*. Toronto: Pearson Education/ Prentice Hall.

Hick, S., 2004, *Social Welfare in Canada*. Toronto: Thompson Educational.

Keynes, John Maynard, 1936, *The General Theory*. Cambridge: Cambridge University Press.

Keynes, John Maynard, 1940, *How to Pay for the War*. London: MacMillan and Co.

Lightman, E., 2003, *Social Policy in Canada*. Don Mills, ON: Oxford University Press.

Stanford, Jim, 1999, "Facts from the Fringe No.13," *Canadian Autoworkers Union and The Globe and Mail*. September 1999.

Stanford, Jim, 2007, "Facts from the Fringe No.138," *Canadian Autoworkers Union and The Globe and Mail*. February 2007.

Statistics Canada – data from various CANSIM tables accessed online.

Von Hayek, Friedrich, 1944, *The Road to Serfdom*. Chicago: University of Chicago Press.

Yalnizyan, Armine, 2007, *The Rich and the Rest of Us: The Changing Face of Canada's Growing Gap*. Ottawa: Canadian Centre for Policy Alternatives. http://www.policyalternatives.ca/index.cfm

# CHAPTER 5

# The Geographic Base of Canadian Social Welfare

*Michael Kim Zapf and Ralph Bodor*

*Humans possess a strong sense of place—that is, a feeling for the features that contribute to the distinctiveness of a particular spot on Earth.*

*Rubenstein, 2005, p. 15*

*Land is not a metaphor of our mother. Land is our mother.*

*Leroy Little Bear, Blackfoot (Meyer, 2005)*

## INTRODUCTION

Recognition of a geographic base for Canadian social welfare has been a relatively recent addition to the literature. The first two editions of *Canadian Social Welfare* (Turner and Turner, 1981, 1986) identified a philosophical base, a knowledge base, an historical base, and a base in the sense of individual pioneers in the field. The third edition (1995) then added a political base. Armitage's *Social Welfare in Canada Revisited* (1996) presented a foundation that included features of industrialism and affluence, politics, economics, and societal values. Chappell's *Social Welfare in Canadian Society* (1997) confirmed the conventional list of foundation influences. None of these explorations of Canadian social welfare accorded geography the status of a base. It was not until the fourth edition of *Canadian Social Welfare* (Turner and Turner, 2001) that geography was recognized as a base for Canadian social welfare. We are not suggesting that geography has been ignored completely in discussions of social welfare in Canada. The first three editions of *Canadian Social Welfare* contained material on demographics, location, isolation, climate, and physical characteristics in chapters entitled "Canadian Realities" (Woodsworth, 1981, 1986; Watt, 1995), but these discussions appeared as part of the context rather than the base of Canadian social welfare.

Certainly context is important. Canada is a huge country with a small ribbon of population concentrated along its southern border. Much of the country is wilderness with tiny communities scattered over vast regions. These simple facts of physical and demographic geography have influenced the development of social welfare across this country. Most of the legislation and policy that define our social welfare system have been designed in urban centres in the south. Professional social workers, trained in these same centres, deliver programs and services through urban institutions with urban world views. Can we expect the resulting range of goods and services to be appropriate for persons trying to achieve their full human potential in regions outside urban southern Canada?

Far from trivial, the distinction between a base and a context is crucial to understanding the impact and potential of geography as an influence on social welfare in this country. The difference between a core element (base) and a background or milieu (context) is key to understanding geography's importance to the Canadian social welfare system. To consider geography as simply a context for Canadian social welfare is to explore how features such as topography, climate, population distribution, and transportation routes affect the practical design and delivery of social welfare services. To consider geography as a base, on the other hand, is to explore the importance of geographic concepts and issues for the theoretical foundation of Canadian social welfare. That is the aim of this chapter.

Considering the mutual focus on person/environment interaction, we find it strange that geography was absent for so long from the acknowledged foundations for social work. The knowledge base for social work incorporates material from other disciplines including psychology, sociology, economics, anthropology, political science, and history (Chappell, 2006; Kirst-Ashman, 2007; Zastrow, 2004). When Norton (2004) identifies the disciplines in which human geography is grounded, the list is the same! From the perspective of geography, Pile (1997, 430) made a useful distinction between *peopled places* and *placed people*. Using this terminology as a framework, we have explored parallel activities in geography and social work as both seek to understand the complex relationships between person and environment, and we found areas of convergence between the two disciplines, particularly around the notion of *place*.

Implications of place for human identity and environmental responsibility have been expressed in traditional knowledge systems for centuries, but they are relatively new to the disciplines of geography and social work. Environmental concerns are now at the top of the Canadian public's agenda (Laghi, 2007; Neuman, 2007), and we are witnessing a flurry of political responses at all levels of government. This may be a crucial time for social work to understand and clearly articulate its geographic base. Can full human potential even be considered any longer as separate from the health of the physical environment, the natural world? Does it make sense any more to tackle issues of social welfare without environmental welfare? Our outdated and limited notion of *person-in-environment* may be hindering our ability to contribute in a meaningful way to the urgent discussions about what it means to *live well in this place*. We may need to let go of the dualistic notion of person-in-environment and explore new understandings of environment, sustainability, and stewardship.

## DISCONNECT FROM THE NATURAL WORLD

As we begin to explore these new notions of the person/environment relationship, it may be useful to consider some recent concrete examples from the environmental sciences that challenge us to think differently about the interconnections between the health of the physical environment and the species that inhabit a particular place. Reimchen (2001) has examined the manner in which spawning salmon, bears, and the coastal forest interact in a complex relationship that serves to ensure the survival of each component of the process. As thousands of salmon swim up shallow streams to spawn, they provide an easily accessible food source for wildlife such as eagles, bears, and crows. To avoid the frantic competition over food, bears will take the salmon into the woods so they can devour their catch in relative peace and quiet (except for the crows). The salmon carcasses left by the bears provide nutrition for a number of species including crows, ravens, and insects. The salmon skeletons that are left provide massive amounts of nitrogen, phosphorus, and calcium—nutrients that are vital to the sustainable growth of the coastal forest. As the forest continuously develops alongside the spawning stream, additional habitat is created that supports the spawning salmon. If any one element in the process is removed or neglected, the entire system begins to fail.

Another example of complexity and interdependence in the natural world illustrates the unintended consequences of intervention by outside forces on one component of a working system. Early conservationists advocated for the wholesale killing of wolves in areas such as Yellowstone Park in order to improve hunting for game animals such as elk, moose, and deer. However, once the wolf population was decimated, wildlife observers began to notice specific negative—and unexpected—changes in the environment. Fish populations in the streams dropped, streams began to change course, and wetland vegetation, such as willow and aspen, was disappearing. Studies soon proved that the demise of the wolf population had initiated a negative cascading effect on the environment. Researchers determined that elk, deer, and moose, no longer threatened with predation by wolves, had changed their grazing and ranging habits in ways that were causing severe damage to the ecosystem. Allowed more time to graze in larger groups, the herds had overgrazed on wetland vegetation and reduced the ability of the vegetation to clean and purify runoff waters. These waters were, in turn, silting up the stream beds and decreasing the viability of the fish population. In addition, the lack of streamside vegetation allowed greater erosion and more extensive channelling of the streambeds—all as a consequence of wolf extirpation in the surrounding areas (Beschta & Ripple, 2006; Ripple & Beschta, 2005, 2006).

When the interconnections between species and place are ignored or violated, the effects are long-term and often unforeseen. As we come to better understandings of the complex web of relationships in nature, we wonder if the achievement of full human potential also requires the same deep and intimate connection with our natural environments. While it may seem obvious to suggest that we need to emulate nature, it is possible that we have lost our understanding of a sustainable, dialectical relationship to our environment—except for the one very notable exception of connection through exploitation. We have arrived at this place of separation between ourselves and our environment via the cumulative effects of our prevailing beliefs, values, and ethics about the places we inhabit.

The Enlightenment emphasized the belief that logical, empirical thinking was the means to determine what was really true in the world. We think we can reduce complexity into smaller and smaller truths until we arrive at a place where we believe we have control and the ability to predict a course of events—the ultimate goal of empirical research. The need to reduce human complexity to such simple factors is similar to, as Jardine (1998, 9) suggests, the empirical response that requires us to "disconnect ourselves from it [life] and then reconnect with it only in those ways that render it our predictable and manageable object." With regard to social work, Heineman (1981, 377) observes that "the belief that social work models can and should be reduced to simplified, quantified, time-limited, experimentally 'testable' models without any loss of valuable information is an example of the influence of the logical empiricist belief in reductionism on social work research" (377).

We construct our identity in relationship with those around us who are members of our community. The intertwining of these co-created realities is at the essence of life-as-lived. In "stark contrast to the Cartesian mode" is the "sacred narrative which coordinates the living person with the cycle of his own life, with the environment in which he is living, and with the society which itself has already been integrated in the environment" (Vest, 2005, 576). To separate our relationships into concepts of duality allows us to take a stance of subject/object that separates us from the lived world. Separating our relationships into concepts of duality creates a subject/object stance that disconnects us from the lived world.

## PERSON/ENVIRONMENT AND SOCIAL WORK: PLACED PEOPLE

A perspective of person-in-situation or person-in-environment, borrowed from ecology, has been a popular starting point in the discussions of Canadian social work for over two decades. Yet there is a common but subtle and generally unacknowledged pattern in the presentation of this metaphor in the social work literature. A clear and early example can be seen in this excerpt from Yelaja's (1985, 29) discussion of the dominant concepts that influence Canadian social work: "The use of the ecology metaphor accentuates the reciprocal relationships between the individual and the environment and the continuous adaptation of both person and environment to each other. . . . Within the ecological perspective, human growth and development constantly change in relation to the social environment— and the social environment changes in response to the human factors."

What happened here? Within one paragraph, "the environment" has become "the social environment"!

This pattern appears frequently in the social work literature. Many examples, from both the Canadian and American literature, were discussed in an earlier edition of this book (Zapf, 2005a). As with the example from Yelaja (1985), the broad notion of *environment* is most often transformed into the much narrower *social environment* within a few sentences, with no explanation given to justify the change.

Even following the declared focus on person-in-environment, both practice and education in social work have tended to concentrate on the personal side of the duality at the expense of the environmental side (McKay, 2002; Zapf, 2002). Social work has long been satisfied with a simple categorization of environments into urban, rural, and, more recently, remote (Collier, 2006; Zapf, 2001, 2002). Our knowledge base for Canadian social welfare appears to provide many more categories for understanding people than environments. One partial explanation may be found in David Suzuki's (1999, 45) observation that "most people now live in the human-created environment of big cities where it's easy to believe the illusion that we have escaped our biological dependence on the natural world."

The limiting of environment to social environment appears to be entrenched in the social work literature, a pattern that continues even in the most recent practice textbooks. Heinonen and Spearman (2006, 182) present the primary focus of social work as "the interface or relationship between the person and the social environment." Kirst-Ashman (2007) bases her model on human coping behaviour, which is defined as social coping, effective interaction with social systems. Johnson and Yanca (2007) begin by defining the ecosystems approach as including the physical environment (9), but later limit the concept to "human systems" (128). Maybe the only progress is that it now takes more than 100 pages rather than a few sentences to abandon the physical environment in favour of the social environment!

Although rare, there are some calls in the Canadian social work literature for integration of the social and physical environments. Delaney's (2005, 81) recognition that "the physical environment is the common place to sustain all of the world's life forms" is central to his articulation of the philosophy and value base for Canadian social welfare. Graham, Swift, and Delaney (2003, 89) warn that "social policies have scarcely begun to integrate issues of social justice for people with the imperative of physical ecology." They argue that relevant social policy for the twenty-first century may require "a new world view that equates spiritual growth and self-realization with stewardship of the earth" (90). An entry in the new *Encyclopedia of Canadian Social Work* makes similar reference to the need for "an underlying world view that emphasizes stewardship rather than exploitation" (Zapf, 2005b, 322).

These challenging notions of environmental responsibility and stewardship may be difficult for the profession to incorporate when we have neglected the geographic reality of our physical environment for so long. Returning to the terminology introduced earlier by Pile (1997), we could say that social work's development of the person/environment inter-action has shifted social work's focus to *placed people*. The individual person or group has been the subject, the main concern, while the environment has been presented as mere modifier or context.

## PERSON/ENVIRONMENT AND GEOGRAPHY: PEOPLED PLACES

Perhaps one reason why social work has ignored geography can be found in the often less than satisfying introduction to the subject in high school. Long lists to be committed to memory (capital cities, annual precipitation, etc.) were accompanied by intimidating tests involving the placement of memorized labels on blank maps. All of this contributed to the common stereotype of geography as a subject "steadfastly committed to long factual inventories and rote memorization" (Taaffe, Gauthier, & O'Kelly 1996, 3). Many of us were left in a state of "geographic illiteracy" (deBlij & Murphy, 2003, 6) with no real understanding of human settlement patterns or regional interaction. The standard map of Canada in the high school classroom depicted the provinces in different colours and no neighbours on three sides, only our firm attachment to the United States to the south. To the north, east, and west, there was nothing but a thin strip of ocean giving way to the noth-ingness of the bare wall supporting the map. This particular representation of Canada inhibited our ability to perceive the regional nature of the country and the core/periphery relationships that have shaped us (Bone, 2002).

Modern geography is a very different discipline, concerned with "how, why, and where human and natural activities occur and how these activities are interconnected" (Strahler & Strahler, 2005, 6). Geography bridges the physical sciences and the social sciences, although the two have often been divided into separate streams of physical geography (landforms, climates, coastlines, vegetation, soils, animals) and human geography (culture, language, spatial patterns of human activities, meanings). This distinction between physi-cal and human geography, however, has been explained as more a matter of emphasis than complete separation (Norton, 2004; Rubenstein, 2005).

Two major projects designed to clarify the foundations of geography (Geography Edu-cation National Implementation Project, 1986; National Research Council, 1997) both identified the concept of *place* as a major point of intersection between physical and human geography. In his textbook on human geography, Norton (2004, 509) affirms that "space and place are constantly being reinforced as our key concepts." Just what is this geographic notion of *place*? From a geographic perspective, every point on the Earth's sur-face can be uniquely described in terms of location (mathematical representation using meridians and parallels), site (physical characteristics, landforms), situation (relative to other points), space (physical intervals or gaps between points), and maybe even a name (Rubenstein, 2005). Essentially, these descriptors identify aspects of physical location. Moving beyond location, Rubenstein (2005, 5) clarifies that "to geographers, a *place* is a specific point on Earth distinguished by a particular character." Place then involves loca-tion plus meaning associated with the location.

Other geographers clearly support this notion of place as location plus meaning. Nor-ton (2004, 56) presents place as location "plus the values that we associate with that loca-tion . . . a location that has a particular identity." Tuan (1974, 213) explains how, in addition to simple location, place is "also a reality to be clarified and understood from the perspectives of the people who have given it meaning." Agnew and Duncan (1989) present the concept of place as the integration of "geographical and sociological imaginations." To Entrikin (1997, 299), *place* refers to "the areal context of events . . . that includes natural elements and human constructions, both material and ideal." Thus, the built environment is a feature of place, not just ascribed meanings in the abstract.

The geography literature also identifies a related notion of *sense of place*, or "the attachment that we have to locations with personal significance" (Norton, 2004, 56). This sense of place appears to be a phenomenological concept, a consideration of the meanings that places hold for people, an acknowledgment of identification with place. Some have added a sense of time to this sense of place in order to incorporate heritage, or the development of a place identity over time (Ashworth & Graham, 2005). From the perspective of phenomenological geography, the essence of this sense of place can be found in "the experience of an 'inside' that is distinct from an 'outside'; more than anything else this is what sets places apart in space and defines a particular system of physical features, activities, and meaning. To be inside a place is to belong to it and to identify with it, and the more profoundly inside you are the stronger is the identity with the place" (Relph, 1976, 49).

The incorporation of self with place and place with self reaches its ultimate expression in the context of personal, communal, and spatial identity. As we build our personal and communal identities that paradoxically and simultaneously bind us together and set us apart we are engaged in shaping our landscape—even as the landscape is engaged in shaping us. As we are faced with the changes imposed by modern life, the "old certainties of class, of culture, of a stable identity, of belonging to a community, of a sense of one's life being rooted and grounded in the past (and in place) have long since vanished" (Tilley, 2006, 10).

As a multi-modal, highly mobile, and virtual society with instantaneous connections around the world, we are at risk of eroding even further our relationships between person and place. We are increasingly spending much of our time in what the sociologist Augé (1995, 125) refers to as the self-contained "non-places of super-modernity" such as airports, hotels, supermarkets, and motorways. Identity becomes "non-placed"—identity and community that are no longer embedded within a spatial or geographic context have become shared by "people who may never meet each other" (Tilley, 2006, 13). Identity and connection with others becomes, in the context of modernity, something not linked with place and, while electronic modes of connection such as the Internet "may play an important role in sustaining certain diasporic communities [it] cannot provide a substitute for the sense of belonging achieved through actual contact, meeting in a homeland" (13). It may be, in the final expression of this process, that we have only exchanged the impersonality of the map on the bare wall with the non-placed pseudo-intimacy of the electronic computer screen.

## ABORIGINAL SOCIAL WORK AND THE LAND

The developing literature on Aboriginal social work features a strong spiritual foundation and a keen emphasis on the land. Connection to the land "suffuses the tribal world" (Coates, 2004, 47). Aboriginal knowledge systems have been described as "contextual and relational" (Cajete, 2000, 98), based on experiences and observations from the land and the natural world. Aboriginal societies identified themselves with specific places, or home-lands. Since the entire natural order is believed to be reflected in each geographic place or region, people come to find their place in the cosmos by coming to understand their place in a given local system.

When a group of people inhabit a region for many generations, their identity incorpo-rates the place and their relationship to it. McCormack (1998, 28) explains how this process ties Aboriginal cultural identity "directly to the land and concepts of place." Cajete (2000, 187) called this link "geopsyche" whereby people assume traits of their homeland, and the place assumes human traits, in a continual process of co-creation. Aboriginal heal-ing practices derive from this profound connection with the land, a living physical environ-ment, a partner.

In contrast, Western traditions have tended to separate humans from the natural world. Mainstream understandings of land involve boundaried parcels subject to individual or collective ownership. We view the physical environment as separate from ourselves, as an objective commodity to be developed or wasted or traded, as an economic unit, as prop-erty. On the other hand, traditional Aboriginal land use "was typically understood in terms of stewardship and responsibility, rather than ownership" (Coates, 2004, 50). When the people and the land are perceived as different expressions of the same creation, as part-ners in the ongoing process of that creation, then social work's *person-in-environment* approach has very little meaning because it assumes the fundamental separation of person and environment—or that the environment exists to serve and provide for the person.

A poster created by the Canadian National Railway's Colonization Department in the 1930s serves to illustrate clearly this subordination of environment to person. Copies of the large poster were originally posted in London, Liverpool, Belfast, and Glasgow to encour-age potential European settlers to create "A Farm in Canada." Extolling "life in the open country" with the potential for "fine dairy herds" and "sport-fishing," the posters include an assertion that "sheep do well and cattle are profitable." A huge grain farm is depicted, stretching back to a horizon of towering, snow-capped mountains. Connections to the land were limited to a world view that encouraged settlers to clear the existing forests, remove indigenous wildlife and populations, grow grain, and raise imported cattle and sheep.

This Western world view that North America was an untouched wilderness allowed the process of colonization and assimilation to completely ignore the connection between the land and the Aboriginal inhabitants. In their multi-generational stewardship of the land, place was deeply interconnected with person—a dialectical relationship of inter-dependence. "The traditional Native world view is cosmotheistic, holistic, and transcen-dent. The secular is not separated from the sacred. Hence, place and the 'other than human beings' who reside there—plants, animals, rocks, minerals, water, and other tran-scendent beings—are viewed as part of, and associated with, each other. All are one, and all are interdependent on each other for the continued well-being of each, as well as the whole" (Reeves, 2007, 42).

Any argument that place shapes or influences identity still assumes that identity and place can be separated from one another. According to Wilson (2003, 88), such a separa-tion may have little meaning from an Aboriginal perspective: "The relationship Anishin-abek have with the land cannot be captured by the simplified notion of being 'close to nature.' The land is not just seen as shaping or influencing identity, but being an actual part of it." The foundation metaphor of Aboriginal knowledge has been characterized as a per-spective of "I am I and the environment (Ortega y Gasset, 1985). Suopajarvi (1998, 3) asserts: "I'm not in the place but the place is in me," very similar to Cajete's (2000, 60) observation that "we are the universe and the universe is us." These Aboriginal expressions of *world-image* identity contrast sharply with the *self-image* concepts of Western culture (Stairs & Wenzel, 1992).

From an Aboriginal perspective, human experience cannot be understood except through an understanding of place. Place and sense of place are vital to human health and development in fundamental areas such as a sense of security, control, feelings of attachment, self-identity, trans-generational memories, and shared experiences and history. Conversely, loss of place and sense of place can result in a loss of identity, destruction of inter-personal relationships, and even the loss of memory of a place. Windsor and Mcvey (2005, 159) observed that "throughout Canada's history, governments and industry have continued to apply pressure to Native peoples to sever their ties to the land." Arguably, social work has been one of the industries that supported policies and procedures to create disconnect from the land and community.

"Understanding the various ways people organized themselves on the landscape . . . reveals settlement and subsistence practices as well as glimpses into their social and political organization" (Nicholas, 2006, 352) while "sacred geography provides a deep sense of place, identity, and continuity with past generations" (Reeves, 2007, 43). For example, ceremonies like Potlatch or Give-aways serve to determine social status and social structure while providing a shared system of accountability for the use of environmental and human resources. The public re-distribution of resources ensured, as much as possible, the overall success of the group—and provided a means and a process to achieve that goal while still maintaining high levels of individual respect and caring. Western approaches to land and resource ownership have moved these systems from "the principle of sustainability to one of competitive resource use" (Richmond, Elliott, Matthews, & Elliott, 2004, 355), as well as the purposeful exploitation of resources.

## SOCIAL WORK, GEOGRAPHY, AND LIVING WELL IN PLACE

Through this overview, we have observed many similar interests, perspectives, and activities between social work and geography. As discussed earlier, their knowledge bases are rooted in the same disciplines. An ecosystems perspective appears fundamental to both human geography and social work. Both disciplines apply their frameworks on three interdependent scales or levels: local, regional, and global in geography; micro, mezzo, and macro in social work. Feminist geography links the oppression of women to the patriarchal domination of nature (Nesmith & Radcliffe, 1997; Wilson, 2005); feminist social work links oppression of women to patriarchal social structures and attitudes (Heinonen & Spearman, 2006; Valentich, 1996). Issues of human suffering are a concern in human geography (deBlij & Murphy, 2003); issues of damage to the physical environment are beginning to appear in the international social work literature addressing global social justice (Wilson & Whitmore, 2000).

Yet geography appears to be moving in some directions that we see only on the margins of mainstream social work at this time. Incorporation of place and sense of place has become central in the discipline of geography. Human and natural activities are interconnected. Personal attachment to places leads towards a sense of responsibility and of stewardship for environments local and global. Social work recognizes the interconnections between individual and larger social enterprises, but we still have done little to incorporate the natural environment in our frameworks. It may be difficult for mainstream social work to move to a world view supporting a sustainable planet while we cling to our limiting focus on the social environment.

To illustrate the shift to a world view of stewardship and respect, Cheney and Hester (2000) offer an intriguing example of two persons from different world views confronted with a two-pound rock. For you and me to agree that this rock weighs two pounds, we would have to agree on a process of weighing the rock. Suppose, however, that from within your world view an obvious question arises: "Why weigh this rock? I would no more do that than I would simply grab a human being off the street and place her on a scale. It is a matter of courtesy" (Cheney & Hester, 2000, 84). We would find ourselves unable to reach an agreement on the weight of the rock because "you will not, for what you take to be good reason, agree to perform the relevant action" (84) of weighing the rock (relevant from my perspective, irrelevant from yours). The neutral act of measurement within my world view is different than yours. My world view does not consider the experience of the rock. To approach the task with the inclusion of a sense of courtesy and respect for the rock may save it from a potentially exploitive and humiliating experience.

In the context of our overall discussion, we are suggesting that this same sense of courtesy, respect, and ceremony be awarded to place and our relationship to place. If we expand the rock metaphor to the size of the planet, we begin to appreciate the notions of stewardship and respect fundamental to an Aboriginal perspective but lacking in most mainstream social work approaches. Through its attention to place and sense of place, geography appears to be moving towards these notions of place identity and environmental responsibility, while social work remains stuck with its restricted scope on the social environment. Our ultimate goal, our mission, must move beyond social welfare or the fulfilling of individual human potential to a broader vision of learning to live well in place.

This notion of *living well in place* (Orr, 1992) is a very different concept from the conventional idea of welfare to which the profession of social work has been committed. Welfare, or "faring well," refers more to a state of well-being and freedom from oppression, regardless of context; it is a quality of the individual or family. *Living well in place*, on the other hand, involves the building of sustainable communities and living in tune with the rhythms of nature (Morito, 2002). Tall (1996) describes the process with terms such as *dwelling* or *placemaking* as distinct from merely residing in a location. Others have extended the concept of inhabiting one's place to introduce the possibility of *re-inhabiting* the places where we already reside (Kemmis, 1992; Spretnak, 1991) through processes of *human homecoming* (Grange, 1977) or learning to *live attentively in place* (Spretnak, 1991), eventually becoming *people of place* (Cajete, 1994).

In the third edition of *Our Environment: A Canadian Perspective*, Draper and Reed (2005, 91) offer this perspective: "Humans could learn to live sustainably if they understood and mimicked how nature perpetuates itself. Learning to live sustainably begins with recognizing the following: humans are a part of, and not separate from, the dynamic web of life on Earth; human economies, lifestyles, and ultimate survival depend totally on the Sun and the Earth; and everything is connected to everything else, although some connections are stronger and more important than others."

Western geography appears to be converging with an Aboriginal world view to meet the challenges of current environmental threats. Any relevant expression of the geographic base of Canadian social welfare may require moving beyond our historic focus on person-in-environment towards a more inclusive notion of living well in place.

# References

Agnew, J.A., & Duncan, J.S. 1989. Introduction. In J.A. Agnew & J.S. Duncan (Eds.), *The power of place: Bringing together geographical and sociological imaginations* (pp. 1–8). Boston: Unwin Hyman.

Anderson, R.B., Dana, L.P., & Dana, T.E. 2005. Indigenous land rights, entrepreneurship, and economic development in Canada: "Opting-in" to the global economy. *Journal of World Business, 41.* 45–55.

Armitage, A. 1996. *Social welfare in Canada revisited.* Don Mills: Oxford University Press.

Ashworth, G.J., & Graham, B. (Eds.). 2005. *Senses of place: Senses of time.* Aldershot: Ashgate.

Augé, M. 1995. *Non-places. Introduction to an anthropology of supermodernity.* London: Verso.

Beschta, R.L., & Ripple., W.J. 2006. River channel dynamics following extirpation of wolves in northwestern Yellowstone National Park, USA. *Earth Surface Processes and Landforms, 31.* 1525–1539. Published online in Wiley InterScience.

Bone, R.M. 2002. *The regional geography of Canada.* 2d edn. Don Mills: Oxford University Press.

Cajete, G. 1994. *Look to the mountain: An ecology of indigenous education.* Durango: Kivaki Press.

Cajete, G. 2000. *Native science: Natural laws of interdependence.* Santa Fe: Clear Light Publishers.

Chappell, R. 1997. *Social welfare in Canadian society.* Scarborough: ITP Nelson.

Chappell, R. 2006. *Social welfare in Canadian society.* 3d edn. Toronto: Nelson (Thomson Canada).

Cheney, J., & Hester, L. 2000. Ceremonial worlds and environmental sanity. *Strategies, 13.1.* 77–87.

Coates, K.S. 2004. *A global history of Indigenous peoples: Struggle and survival.* New York: Palgrave Macmillan.

Collier, K. 2006. *Social work with rural peoples: Theory and practice.* 3d edn. Vancouver: New Star Books.

de Blij, H.J., & Murphy., A.B. 2003. *Human geography: Culture, society, and space.* 7th edn. New York: John Wiley and Sons.

Delaney, R. 2005. The philosophical and value base of Canadian social welfare. In J.C. Turner & F.J. Turner (Eds.), *Canadian social welfare.* 5th edn. (pp. 13–27). Toronto: Pearson Education Canada.

Draper, D., & Reed, M.G. 2005. *Our environment: A Canadian perspective,* 3d edn. Toronto: Nelson (Thomson Canada).

Entrikin, J.N. 1997. The betweenness of place. In T. Barnes & D. Gregory (Eds.), *Reading human geography: The poetics and politics of inquiry* (pp. 299–314). London: Arnold.

Geography Education National Implementation Project. 1986. *Maps, the landscape, and fundamental themes in geography.* Washington: National Geographic Society.

Graham, J. R., Swift, K. J., & Delaney, R. 2003. *Canadian social policy: An introduction.* 2d edn. Toronto: Pearson Education Canada.

Grange, J. 1977. On the way towards foundational ecology. *Soundings: An Interdisciplinary Journal, 60* (2). 135–149.

Heineman, M. 1981. The obsolete scientific imperative in social work research. *Social Service Review, 55.3.* 371–392.

Heinonen, T., & Spearman, L. 2006. *Social work practice: Problem-solving and beyond.* 2d edn. Toronto: Irwin Publishing.

Jardine, D. 1998. *To dwell with a boundless heart: On curriculum theory, hermeneutics and the ecological imagination.* New York: Peter Lang Publishing.

Johnson, L.C., & Yanca, S.J. 2007. *Social work practice: A generalist approach.* 9th edn. Boston: Allyn & Bacon (Pearson Education).

Kemmis, D. 1992. *Community and the politics of place.* Norman: University of Oklahoma Press.

Kirst-Ashman, K.K. 2007. *Introduction to social work and social welfare: Critical thinking perspectives.* 2d edn. Belmont: Thomson Brooks/Cole.

Laghi, B. 2007, January 26. Climate concerns now top security and health. *Globe & Mail*, p. A1, A4.

Mackenzie, A., & Fiona, D. 2004. Place and the art of belonging. *Cultural Geographies, 11.* 115–137.

McCormack, P. 1998. Native homelands as cultural landscape: Decentering the wilderness paradigm. In J. Oakes, R. Riewe, K. Kinew, & E. Maloney (Eds.), *Sacred lands: Aboriginal world views, claims, and conflicts* (pp. 25–32). Edmonton: Canadian Circumpolar Institute (University of Alberta).

McKay, S. 2002. Postmodernism, social well-being, and the mainstream/progressive debate. In F. J. Turner (Ed.), *Social work practice: A Canadian perspective.* 2d edn. (pp. 20–32). Toronto: Pearson Education Canada.

Meyer, M. 2005. *Remembering our future: Higher education quality assurance and indigenous epistemology.* University of Hawaii: World Indigenous Nations Higher Education Consortium.

Morito, B. 2002. *Thinking ecologically: Environmental thought, values and policy.* Halifax: Fernwood.

National Research Council. 1997. *Rediscovering geography: New relevance for science and society.* Washington: National Academy Press.

Nesmith, C., & Radcliffe, S. A. 1997. (Re)mapping Mother Earth: A geographical perspective on environmental feminisms. In T. Barnes & D. Gregory (Eds.), *Reading human geography: The poetics and politics of inquiry* (pp. 195–210). London: Arnold.

Neuman, K. 2007. Topping the chart: Canadian priorities. *Alternatives: Canadian Environmental Ideas & Action, 33.1.* 15.

Nicholas, G. 2006. Decolonizing the archaeological landscape. *American Indian Quarterly, Summer & Fall 30.3 & 4.* 350–380.

Norton, W. 2004. *Human geography.* 5th edn. Don Mills: Oxford University Press.

Orr, D.W. 1992. *Ecological literacy: Education and the transition to a postmodern world.* Albany: State University of New York Press.

Ortega y Gasset, J. 1985. *Meditations on hunting.* New York: Scribners.

Pile, S. 1997. Human agency and human geography revisited: A critique of "new models" of the self. In T. Barnes & D. Gregory (Eds.), *Reading human geography: The poetics and politics of inquiry* (pp. 407–434). London: Arnold.

Reeves, B. 2007. Sacred geography: First Nations of the Yellowstone to Yukon. *Human Influences and Trends,* 31–50. Retrieved May 1, 2007 from http://www.y2y.net/science/conservation/humany2y.pdf

Reimchen, T.E. 2001. Salmon nutrients, nitrogen isotopes and coastal forests. *Ecoforestry 16.* 13–17. pdf version: http://web.uvic.ca/~reimlab/reimchen_ecoforestry.pdf

Relph, E. 1976. *Place and placelessness.* London: Pion.

Richmond, C., Elliott, S.J., Matthews, R., & Elliott, B. 2004. The political ecology of health: Perceptions of environment, economy, health and well-being among 'Namgis First Nation, *Health & Place, 11.* 349–365.

Ripple, W., & Beschta, R. 2005. Linking wolves and plants: Aldo Leopold on trophic cascades. *BioScience, 55.7.* 613–621.

Ripple, W., & Beschta, R. 2006. Linking wolves to willows via risk-sensitive foraging by ungulates in the northern Yellowstone ecosystem. *Forest Ecology and Management, 230.* 96–106.

Rubenstein, J.M. 2005. *An introduction to human geography: The cultural landscape.* 8th edn. Upper Saddle River: Pearson Prentice Hall.

Spretnak, C. 1991. *States of grace: The recovery of meaning in the postmodern age.* New York: Harper Collins.

Stairs, A., & Wenzel, G. 1992. "I am I and the environment": Inuit hunting, community, and identity. *Journal of Indigenous Studies, 3.1.* 1–12.

Strahler, A., & Strahler, A. 2005. *Physical geography: Science and systems of the human environment (Canadian version).* 3d edn. Hoboken: John Wiley & Sons.

Suopajarvi, L. 1998. *Regional identity in Finnish Lapland.* Paper presented at the Third International Congress of Arctic Social Sciences, Copenhagen, Denmark.

Suzuki, D. T. 1999, June 14. Saving the Earth. (Essays on the Millenium series). *Maclean's, 112.24.* 42–45.

Taaffe, E.J., Gauthier, H.L., & O'Kelly, M.E. 1996. *Geography of transportation.* Upper Saddle River, NJ: Prentice-Hall.

Tall, D. 1996. Dwelling: Making peace with space and place. In W. Vitek & W. Jackson (Eds.), *Rooted in the land: Essays on community and place.* New Haven: Yale University Press.

Tilley, C. 2006. Identity, place, landscape, and heritage. *Journal of Material Culture, 11, 1/2.* 7–32.

Tuan, Y.F. 1974. Space and place: Humanistic perspectives. *Progress in Geography, 6.* 213–252.

Turner, J. C., & Turner, F. J. (Eds.). 1981, 1986. *Canadian social welfare.* 1st & 2d edns. Don Mills, ON: Collier Macmillan Canada.

Turner, J. C., & Turner, F. J. (Eds.). 1995. *Canadian social welfare.* 3d edn. Scarborough, ON: Allyn and Bacon Canada.

Turner, J. C., & Turner, F. J. (Eds.). 2001. *Canadian social welfare.* 4th edn. Toronto: Pearson Education Canada.

Valentich, M. 1996. Feminist Theory and Social Work Practice. In F. Turner (Ed.), *Social work treatment,* 4th edn. New York: Free Press.

Vest, J. 2005. The Oldman river and the sacred: A mediation upon aputosi pii'kani tradition and environmental ethics. *The Canadian Journal of Native Studies, 25.2.* 571–607.

Warner, L.S. 2006. Native ways of knowing: Let me count the ways. *Canadian Journal of Native Education, 29.2.* 149–164.

Watt, S. 1995. Canadian realities. In J. C. Turner & F. J. Turner (Eds.), *Canadian social welfare.* 3d edn. (pp. 120–129). Scarborough, ON: Allyn and Bacon Canada.

Wilson, K. 2003. Therapeutic landscapes and First Nations people: An exploration of culture, health and place. *Health & Place, 9.* 83–93.

Wilson, K. 2005. Ecofeminism and First Nations peoples in Canada: Linking culture, gender and nature. *Gender, Place and Culture, 1.3.* 333–355.

Wilson, M. G., & Whitmore, E. 2000. *Seeds of fire: Social development in an era of globalism.* Halifax: Fernwood; and Ottawa: Canadian Consortium for International Social Development.

Windsor, J. E., & Mcvey, J. A. 2005. Annihilation of both place and sense of place: The experience of the Cheslatta T'En Canadian First Nation within the context of large-scale environmental projects. *The Geographical Journal, 171.2.* 146–165.

Wood, P. 2003. A road runs through it: Aboriginal citizenship at the edge of urban development. *Citizenship Studies, 7.4.* 463–479.

Woodsworth, D. 1981. Canadian realities. In J. C. Turner & F. J. Turner (Eds.), *Canadian social welfare* (pp. 59–72). Don Mills, ON: Collier Macmillan Canada.

Woodsworth, D. 1986. Canadian realities. In J. C. Turner & F. J. Turner (Eds.), *Canadian social welfare* (2d edn., pp. 61–76). Don Mills, ON: Collier Macmillan Canada.

Yelaja, S.A. 1985. Concepts of social work practice. In S. A. Yelaja (Ed.), *An introduction to social work practice in Canada.* Scarborough, ON: Prentice-Hall Canada.

Zapf, M.K. 2001. Notions of rurality. *Rural Social Work, 6(3).* 12–27.

Zapf, M.K. 2002. Geography and Canadian social work practice. In F. J. Turner, *Social work practice: A Canadian perspective.* 2d edn. (pp. 69–83). Toronto: Pearson Education Canada.

Zapf, M.K. 2005a. The geographic base of Canadian social welfare. In J. C. Turner & F. J. Turner (Eds.), *Canadian social welfare.* 5th edn. (pp. 60–74). Toronto: Pearson Education Canada.

Zapf, M.K. 2005b. Remote practice. In F.J. Turner (Ed.), *Encyclopedia of Canadian social work* (pp. 322–323). Waterloo: Wilfrid Laurier University Press.

Zastrow, C. 2004. *Introduction to social work and social welfare: Empowering people.* 8th edn. Belmont: Brooks/Cole-Thomson Learning.

# CHAPTER 6

# The Historical Base of Canadian Social Welfare

*Joanne C. Turner*

History, of course, has much to teach us about present society and perhaps most of all about human complexities. We can and thankfully sometimes do learn from both the successes and failures of history. The most profitable lessons often come out of the frustrations of failure.

Over the centuries, all societies have had to come to terms with social problems, especially poverty and disease, through charity or alms-giving.[1] To understand contemporary Canadian social welfare, we must know something of these earlier events. In Canada, the development of social welfare has been influenced by a range of factors. However, the early principal shaping influences come from developments in Western Europe, as does much of our culture.

To set the stage for our discussion, let us review the advantages and disadvantages of the feudal system, which began in Western Europe as early as the fifth century and flourished until the fourteenth century. This system was a form of land tenure based on a lord's delegation of property to a subordinate servant or serf to cultivate. This agricultural agreement provided "a social, political, military, and economic structure to the society of that time."[2] Among many negative aspects of this arrangement was the fact that the serfs did not own the land but worked it for their lords. On the positive side, the system did meet most of the serfs' basic needs. It provided a home, food, fuel, community, some independence, and usually someone to take care of them when they were unable to work because of sickness, accident, or old age. Often care was provided by the lord's household or by the local parish. Of course, the serfs paid a price for this security, for they were bound to serve their lords in whatever way the latter saw fit, sometimes as soldiers, though more often as farmers. Serfs were also forbidden to leave their villages without permission, and such permission was hard to obtain.

Under the feudal system, then, life for the serfs offered limited stability. The decline of the system resulted in the dislocation of the labourers from the land, which brought them more freedom but less security. Ever since the breakdown of the feudal system, individuals, groups, and governments have been trying to create a system of social welfare that gives people both freedom and security. To date, no attempt has been entirely successful.

## BRITISH ROOTS

For centuries, the Christian Church bore the major responsibility for the organization of charity in Western society. The state supported, or at least tolerated, that arrangement. The tradition changed dramatically in England in response to the onset of the bubonic plague, which wiped out two-thirds of the

---

1  Although the early church praised charity and helping one's neighbour, often the state did not. In 800 A.D., under the statutes of Charlemagne, citizens who gave alms to able-bodied beggars were fined. In sixteenth-century Germany, Martin Luther tried to organize relief at a parish level and implored the princes, who refused to take any responsibility for the poor, to forbid begging. In the same century, the Spanish philosopher Juan Luis Vives proposed a program of relief for the poor of the city of Bruges in Flanders, which was not adopted until 2.5 centuries later in Hamburg in 1788.

2  *Funk and Wagnalls New Encyclopedia*, vol. 9 (New York, 1973), p. 436.

English population within two years (1348–1349). The resulting shortage of labour and the simultaneous rise in wages compelled Edward III to issue the Statute of Labourers of 1349. The law required able-bodied labourers to accept employment from any masters willing to hire them, and it forbade them to leave their parishes. Furthermore, citizens were prohibited from giving alms to able-bodied beggars. Evidently, the law was intended to prevent begging and to force the serfs to stay on the land.

In the sixteenth century, Henry VIII broke with the Pope and the Roman Catholic Church. This schism further weakened the church's tradition of caring for the poor for, in closing monasteries and confiscating their properties and wealth, Henry made it almost impossible for the church to continue as the principal reliever of economic distress. This lent urgency to a long process, begun in 1349, in which the state slowly and reluctantly assumed responsibility for those who could not care for themselves. In the end, public money collected through taxation was allocated to solving the problem. As Karl de Schweinitz explains it: "The experience of the years between 1349 and 1601 had convinced the rulers of England of the presence of a destitution among the poor that punishment could not abolish and that could be relieved only by the application of public resources to individual need."[3]

This realization led to a long series of measures known as the *Poor Laws*, many of which were formalized by legislation under Elizabeth I (1533–1603), and eventually, over four more centuries and through a lengthy series of modifications, led to Britain's *National Insurance Act* and the Beveridge Report of 1943. The latter serves as the basis of the modern system of social security in the United Kingdom today.

Although these historical events are both interesting and enlightening, they are documented in detail elsewhere.[4] This chapter will examine two significant factors with long-term implications for the development of social welfare systems in Britain and then in Canada. These are the principles of less eligibility and the perception of need.

The principle of less eligibility can be traced to the *Report of the Royal Commission for Inquiring into the Administration and Practical Operations of the Poor Laws* in 1834.[5] It laid out that "the assistance provided for people in need must be such as to cause their condition to be less desirable, less satisfactory . . . less eligible than the condition of the lowest-paid labourer who was not in receipt of welfare."[6] This concept arose from the fear that more than minimal assistance would encourage people to seek welfare rather than work. This concept still underlies the attitudes of some policy-makers today.

Able-bodied or employable men who wished to obtain relief, along with their wives and children, were obliged to move into workhouses. There the men were housed in one section, women in another, and children in still another. Thus, families were broken up, and all members, including children over the age of seven, were obliged to work in return for their bed and board. It is no wonder that Benjamin Disraeli, the great British prime minister (1868 and 1878–1880), felt compelled to say of this system, "It announces to the world that in England, poverty is a crime!"[7]

---

3   Karl de Schweinitz, *England's Road to Social Security* (New York: Barnes, 1943), p. 29.

4   Ibid. See particularly chapters 1, 3, 4, 7, & 21.

5   Ibid., p. 117.

6   Ibid., p. 124.

7   William F. Monypenny, *The Life and Times of Benjamin Disraeli, Earl of Beaconsfield*, vol. 1 (New York: Macmillan, 1910), p. 374.

The practice of relegating those in need to a second-class existence strongly influenced the development of social welfare in Britain, the United States, and Canada. Evidence of this practice will be given in the discussion of early events in Canadian history.

The second principle, perception of need, concerns how people view other people who are in need. There are two ways of looking at need: people are impoverished because of their own personal failures or because of the failures of society and its economic system. The first position suited the individualism fashionable in eighteenth- and nineteenth-century England. As Wilensky and Lebeaux comment: "As doctrine, individualism states that the good of all will best be served if each individual pursues his self-interest with minimal interference."[8]

The concepts of capitalism and a market economy usually co-exist with the belief that people are in need because of their own failures. A leading proponent of the concepts of capitalism and a market economy was Adam Smith, an eighteenth-century economist and philosopher from Scotland. His *Wealth of Nations*, published in 1766, is a thorough analysis of the process by which economic wealth is produced and distributed. The work details rent, wages, and profits, the key points of the capitalist system. For our purposes, Smith states most significantly that individuals pursuing their own good work toward achieving the good of all. Any interference by government in business would most certainly be harmful, writes Smith. This philosophy came to be known as *laissez-faire*, and it strongly influenced thinking in Britain about welfare matters in the eighteenth and nineteenth centuries.

Laissez-faire as a concept profoundly influenced Britain, and it provoked some strong opposition as well as support. Leading social reformers of the nineteenth and early twentieth centuries, such as Robert Owen[9] and Beatrice and Sidney Webb, pushed theories of humanitarianism that redefined certain persons as needy owing to circumstances outside their control. Based on this philosophy, the social reformers fought for better wages, housing, and working conditions. They often debated with proponents of laissez-faire.

## THE CANADIAN APPROACH

### The 1700s

A review of early events in Canada reveals that these ideological differences spread beyond Britain and Europe. Before Confederation, proponents of laissez-faire and the principle of less eligibility often clashed with those who held more humanitarian views of the obligation to their neighbours.

The traditional leader in the arena of social welfare was the church, and the Catholic Church in particular continued to pioneer in the lands that would eventually become Canada. Its long experience in Europe in ministering to the suffering, its strong administrative organization, its personnel and wealthy patrons, and its abundant resources equipped the church as an institution to meet the temporal as well as the spiritual needs of the people newly arrived to this land.

Marguerite Bourgeoys founded the Sisters of the Congregation of Notre Dame in New France in the mid-seventeenth century, who taught and cared for the children of New

---

8    Harold L. Wilensky and Charles N. Lebeaux, *Industrial Society and Social Welfare* (New York: Free Press, 1968), p. 34.

9    *Columbia Encyclopedia*, 3rd ed. (New York: Columbia University Press, 1963), p. 338.

France, especially young girls sent by the mother country to the colony. The influence of the religious orders, in particular of these sisters and the Jesuit fathers, spread beyond the boundaries of New France to develop into a vast network of institutions in the new world.

The church humanitarian groups in Quebec in the mid-eighteenth century established centres for poor relief in three urban communities as well, which demonstrates a growing social responsibility on the part of colonial society toward the worthy poor.[10]

Atlantic Canada strongly felt the British philosophy of less eligibility. The government of Nova Scotia adopted the *English Poor Laws* in 1763, complete with such institutions as public workhouses and orphanages. One public workhouse for both adults and children in that province dealt out whippings, shacklings, starvation, and other punishments for many years to correct the behaviour of its reluctant or vagrant inmates.[11] The *Poor Laws* also operated in New Brunswick, although not in Prince Edward Island.

When government social-welfare programs began to appear in Upper Canada, they aimed to protect society from undesirables, such as criminals, delinquents, the poor, and the mentally ill. In general, they were intended to reinforce the responsibility of individuals for their own welfare through negative and punitive measures.

Upper Canada led all the territories in the development of child welfare legislation, again reflecting the earlier concept of the worthy and the unworthy poor. An act to provide for the education and support of orphaned children was passed in 1799. This first Canadian child welfare legislation provided that two justices of the peace could bind an orphaned child to an apprenticeship until she or he reached the age of 21.[12] Almost 50 years later, two other acts were passed in Ontario, both concerned with the protection of children whose parents could not provide for them.

## The 1800s

In 1867, the *British North America Act* (*BNA Act*) assigned welfare provisions to the provincial governments. This assignment of responsibility to the provinces greatly influenced the development of a variety of approaches to welfare services across the country. At that time welfare was not seen as a major function of governments. In the early years following Confederation, public welfare fell under the provision of the *Poor Law*, which was almost wholly the responsibility of the municipalities. Following this British precedent, municipalities found themselves obliged to provide for the poor, while the provincial governments did little beyond operating jails or insane asylums.[13] Toward the end of the nineteenth century, people began to realize that this decision made in 1867 would create many problems for the quickly growing young country.

---

10   Robert Owen, *A New View of Society* (London, 1813), pp. 9, 23.

11   Donald Bellamy, "Social Welfare in Canada," *Encyclopedia of Social Work* (New York: National Association of Social Workers, 1965), pp. 36–37. For a fuller account of this period, see also Allana G. Reid, "First Poor Relief System of Canada," *Canadian Historical Review* 27.4 (December 1946): 424–31.

12   Bellamy, "Social Welfare in Canada," p. 37.

13   John Melichercik, *The Development of Social Welfare Programmes in Canada: A Chronology of Significant Events at the National and Ontario Levels* (Waterloo, ON: Wilfrid Laurier University Press, 1975), p. 2.

Between 1867 and 1900, social welfare legislation was enacted more and more frequently as Canada began to appreciate the complexity of need among many societal groups. Most provisions concerned the protection of neglected and delinquent children. Two important events took place in Toronto, owing in large measure to the work of J. J. Kelso, a Toronto journalist who had become concerned about children's welfare. In 1891, the Children's Aid Society of Toronto was organized in recognition of society's responsibility to care for neglected children. And, in 1893, the first piece of child welfare legislation was passed in Ontario, an *Act for the Prevention of Cruelty to and Better Protection of Children*. It was intended to encourage the founding of additional children's aid societies in Ontario. The act gave the new societies the power to apprehend and bring before a judge any child that the act classified as neglected. Mr. Kelso was appointed Ontario's first superintendent of neglected and dependent children in 1893.[14] Clearly, needy children were classified as members of the worthy poor. Overall, however, the principles of "laissez-faire" dominated the emergence of a social welfare system for the country. Welfare was not considered an urgent matter and for the most part was left to local governments.

## The 1900s

In the early twentieth century, it became obvious that the constitutional decision to allocate responsibility for welfare to the provinces did not fit either the complexities of a modern welfare state or the need for strong central planning in welfare matters. During the 1920s and 1930s, World War I veterans and their families pressured the federal government more and more with their staggering needs. Yet, under law, that level of government did not have the power to assume responsibility for health and welfare matters.

In 1926, Parliament tried to find a way around the Constitution. It passed enabling legislation that allowed the federal government and the provincial government to cost-share the funding provided by the *Old Age Pension Act*.[15] This set the precedent for legislative initiative for the federal government in the field of social welfare.

In 1932, the federal government set up relief camps for single men under the supervision of the Department of National Defence. Refused assistance by municipal authorities, most men had no alternative but to work in the camps for 20 cents a day. By spring 1935, 4000 angry, restless camp workers in Vancouver organized a march (although they travelled by freight car) to Ottawa to meet directly with the federal government. The authorities stopped them in Regina and encouraged them to send delegates to Ottawa instead to confer with Prime Minister R. B. Bennett. The applicants achieved nothing at the meeting with Bennett, and when the men attempted to continue their symbolic march the police arrested several truckloads of them. The discontent finally erupted in the Regina Riot of July 1, 1935, in which one man was killed, more than 100 injured, and more than 80 people arrested.[16] Confusion, anger, and dismay were found at every level of government, and it was obvious that provincial revenues were no longer adequate to meet society's needs.

---

14   Harry M. Cassidy, *Public Health and Welfare Reorganization* (Toronto: Ryerson Press, 1945), p. 7.

15   John Melichercik, *The Development of Social Welfare Programmes*, p. 5.

16   John Melichercik, *Constitutional Factors Affecting the Development of Social Welfare Legislation in Canada* (Waterloo, ON: Wilfrid Laurier University Press, 1975), p. 6.

By 1933, the effects of the Depression had intensified. Fifteen to 20 percent of the population was dependent on municipal social assistance, and the local municipalities were quickly going bankrupt under the strain. "Twenty-five percent of the normal male working force was unemployed; and most of the young men had not found their first jobs after leaving school."[17]

Out of this turmoil, the government of the day made its first timid attempts at welfare state legislation. In 1935, Bennett's Conservative government introduced an unemployment insurance scheme, which ignored the provisions of the Constitution. In 1937, it was declared unconstitutional, and the Liberals under Mackenzie King eventually had to reintroduce the measure in 1940 as an *Unemployment Insurance Bill*, which was safely passed with an amendment to the *BNA Act*.[18]

The Royal Commission on Dominion-Provincial Relations (the Rowell-Sirois Commission) was appointed in 1937 to propose new fiscal agreements and legislation between the federal and provincial governments. Its principal recommendation was that the federal government relieve the provinces of their constitutional responsibility for the unemployed and any debts that had accumulated. The commission also proposed that the federal government in turn be given exclusive rights to levy necessary duties and taxes on personal and corporate incomes.[19]

The outbreak of World War II in 1939 overshadowed the commission's work, and its report was never implemented. The two federal–provincial conferences that followed both collapsed. Kenneth McNaught writes: "To implement the Rowell-Sirois Plan would have required a combination of *BNA Act* amendments and policy agreements between Ottawa and at least a majority of the provinces. Such agreement was never reached. Throughout the Commission's period of research it was virtually boycotted by the premiers of Ontario, Quebec, and Alberta."[20]

## World War II to the 1970s

The war nearly eradicated unemployment, yet world events were moving Canadians closer to accepting that their society needed broad-based social security legislation. The citizen's right to social security was formulated in the Atlantic Charter of 1941, one result of the historic meeting between Winston Churchill and Franklin Delano Roosevelt during World War II. An agreement was also reached that provision must be made in the post-war world to cover those risks and contingencies of family life that lie beyond the capacity of the average person. Further, there was a general agreement that the greatest need in a social security program was adequate provision for the unemployed. The necessity of legislating for particular categories of need, such as permanent pensions for disabled war veterans, was also recognized. For Canada, a country still strongly bound by a traditional approach to social welfare, a laissez-faire philosophy and a belief in the worthy and the unworthy poor, all of these developments represented a dramatic change in thinking.

---

17  Jack Williams, *The Story of Unions in Canada* (Toronto: Dent, 1975), pp. 148–50.

18  Leonard Marsh, *Report on Social Security for Canada 1943* (Toronto: University of Toronto Press, 1974), pp. 14, 19.

19  L. Marsh, *Report on Social Security for Canada*, pp. 14–15.

20  Canada, *Report of the Royal Commission on Dominion–Provincial Relations* ("The Rowell–Sirois Report"), 3 vols. (Ottawa: King's Printer, 1939).

A greater public recognition of these needs also lent strong endorsement to a report the federal government commissioned on present and anticipated needs in social welfare in the early 1940s. Leonard Marsh, then director of social research at McGill University, prepared *The Report on Social Security for Canada*, which was presented to the House of Commons Special Committee on Social Security in 1943. It has been hailed as a "pivotal document in the development of war and post-war social security programs, the equivalent in Canada of the Beveridge Report in Great Britain."[21]

Marsh and his commission produced a lengthy and complicated document. He began by describing the universal risks against which individuals cannot protect themselves, then outlined a comprehensive scheme of social security that he believed would protect society from those risks. He also proposed a system of social insurance and taxation to pay for the proposed plan.

Two important themes emerge from this historic document. First, it stated that provisions for unemployment are the greatest priority in any social security program for a modern industrial society. Second, universal risks, which apply to all persons, and employment risks, which apply to wage earners only, must be clearly distinguished. The report declares that society must provide for those needs that individuals cannot fill; it rejects the concepts of laissez-faire and of the worthy and unworthy poor and signals a growing recognition that many problems of individuals originate in the economic system, not personal ones.

Marsh's proposals gave impetus to the concept of a national minimum or a guaranteed annual income, which the federal Department of Health and Welfare has been advocating ever since.[22] To date, the provinces, especially Ontario and Alberta, have not supported the idea of a guaranteed annual income.

On January 28, 1944, the *Vancouver Sun* reported that the federal government had promised "a comprehensive scheme of social insurance which will constitute a charter of social security for the whole of Canada." By the following summer, Parliament had enacted legislation to authorize both a national Family Allowance scheme and the establishment of the federal Department of Health and Welfare.

At the Dominion–Provincial Conference of 1945, the federal government submitted proposals to the provinces for developing a comprehensive welfare program, a "rearrangement of fiscal resources, economic policies and health and welfare services."[23] The conference, however, did not succeed in its goals, and Liberal hopes for a complete package deal for health and welfare services were disappointed.

Instead, the federal government proceeded to add piecemeal to welfare services, as quickly as rapidly rising expectations and a developing sense of social justice allowed. In the first two decades following the war, an impressive, if at times unco-ordinated, series of social

---

21  Kenneth McNaught, *The Pelican History of Canada* (Markham, ON: Penguin, 1969).

22  Michel Bliss, in *Preface* to Marsh, *Report on Social Security for Canada*, p. 9.

23  For some background material regarding the many attempts of the federal Department of Health and Welfare to introduce a guaranteed annual income, see *The Report of the Special Senate Committee on Poverty* (Ottawa, 1971); *The Working Paper on Social Security in Canada* (Ottawa: Department of Health and Welfare, 1973); *Income Security for Canadians* (Ottawa: Department of Health and Welfare, 1970); and the proposed New Social Service Bill (Ottawa: Department of Health and Welfare, 1977).

welfare laws and improved social services was established. Parliament passed at least eight major pieces of social legislation in the 1950s and 1960s,[24] the most significant being the Canada Assistance Plan (CAP) of 1966. This plan brought together and consolidated previous cost-sharing programs, unemployment assistance, blind and disabled persons' assistance, child welfare measures, and administrative costs. It also extended the federal cost-sharing presence in provincial social welfare programs.[25] According to Melchers, "CAP is the largest single source of funding for social services in Canada, accounting for an average of 38.5 percent of provincial spending."[26] Costs were to be shared 50-50 with the provinces.

During the 1970s, the emphasis in social welfare shifted from developing new social welfare programs to an evaluation and reorganization of programs already established. This evaluation process produced the tabling of several White Papers. The first, *Income Security for Canadians*, appeared in 1970. *Unemployment Insurance in the Seventies* and *The Report of the Royal Commission on the Status of Women* were also tabled that year, and, in 1973, the federal government published the *Working Paper on Social Security in Canada*.[27] This particular working paper constituted the federal government's contribution to a joint federal–provincial review of the total social security system of the country. It examined what each government had done individually and what the governments had done collectively in the field of social welfare. The federal government made a number of changes in its social welfare programs as a result. Benefits under the Family Allowance program tripled, for example.

In February 1976, the federal and provincial ministers of welfare legislation gathered at a conference to discuss sharing the costs of developing and delivering social services, based on strategies developed during the federal–provincial social security review. Under the proposed legislation, the social services were recognized as a miniature collective force in their own right, or, as Marc Lalonde, then minister of health and welfare, described them, a linchpin, rather than a residual role.[28] This marked recognition of an important distinction: society would have to build in provisions for social services in certain high-risk areas, such as loss of income owing to accident or high unemployment, rather than hustle to provide these services in the middle of a crisis.

Thirty-three years after the release of Marsh's report, it seemed that social welfare was finally accepted as a necessary institution of Canadian society and would be taken into account in all future planning.

On June 20, 1977, Lalonde introduced a new social services bill in the House of Commons. It was one of the main outcomes of the social security review he had launched in April 1973 and of the negotiations that followed between the federal and provincial governments. At the time, the new act was described as one that "would allow the federal government to share with the provinces in the cost of a wider range of social services than is possible at present. This includes cost-sharing of the provision, development, extension,

---

24    John S. Morgan, "Social Welfare Services," in *Social Purpose for Canada*, ed. Michael Oliver (Toronto: University of Toronto Press, 1961), pp. 138–39.

25    John Melichercik, *The Development of Social Welfare Programmes,* pp. 14–17.

26    Andrew Armitage, *Social Welfare in Canada* (Toronto: McClelland and Stewart, 1975), p. 277.

27    Ronald Melchers, "The Cap on CAP," *Perception* 14.4 (Autumn 1990): p. 19.

28    Canada, Department of Health and Welfare, *Working Paper on Social Security in Canada* (Ottawa, 1973), pp. 1–3.

and improvement of social services throughout Canada in order to ensure that adequate services are available. These additional services are required to meet the current needs of society, which have changed since the previous legislation was implemented."[29]

The government accepted the bill, but it was never given final reading. Although two subsequent ministers, Monique Bégin and David Crombie, adopted parts of the proposed legislation, to date no further comprehensive plan has been introduced by the federal government.

## Social Policy in the 1980s and 1990s

Since the mid-1980s, with the election of Brian Mulroney and a Progressive Conservative federal government, social policy-making has shifted away from liberalism and toward neo-conservatism. Fundamental values have shifted in ways that, along with the poor economic climate of the early 1990s, have affected social welfare policies and governments' willingness to intervene.

Conservative philosophy holds that employment should naturally flow with the economy and that government intervention in creating full employment only creates more economic problems. As Mishra (1989) writes, "Neo-conservatives believe that unemployment is an unavoidable feature of market economies, a price to be paid for freedom of enterprise and growth."[30]

In addition, neo-conservatives generally believe that welfare dependency is a consequence of people's reluctance to accept low-wage jobs. Indeed, welfare payment levels in Ontario did provide most claimants with an income higher than minimum wage earnings until the early 1990s. On the principle that claimants should not be better off on social assistance than they would be employed, governments devoted attention to devising ways to ensure that assistance to the working poor continued to motivate them to work instead.[31]

Generally, neo-conservatism aims to reduce government spending on social welfare. The move away from universality toward selectivity in social policy development has affected employment, child poverty, health, and education in far-reaching ways.

The following pieces of legislation are examples of this shift in direction:

**Bill C-21** *Bill C-21* is an act to amend the *Unemployment Insurance Act* and the *Employment and Immigration Department and Commission Act*. It came into effect in November 1990. According to the Canadian Council on Social Development, "Nineteen-ninety will be remembered as the year Canada discarded universality in two established income programs and terminated its funding of a major income security program—Unemployment Insurance. . . . " The bill altered provisions of the act to conform with the Canadian Charter of Rights and Freedoms. It also ended the federal government's contribution to the fund, ending a 50-year association with the program.[32]

---

29  Notes from an address by Marc Lalonde to the Social Planning Council of Metropolitan Toronto Seminar on "Family Income Security Issues," 1976, p. 16.

30  Health and Welfare Canada, *News Release*, June 20, 1977, p. 2.

31  Ramesh Mishra, "Riding the New Wave: Social Work and the Neo-Conservative Challenge," *International Social Work* 32.3 (July 1989): 174.

32  M. Loney, "Pricing the Poor Back to Work," *Policy Options* 13.10 (December 1992): 21–23.

**Bill C-69** *Bill C-69* (1991) capped the federal contribution to the Canada Assistance Program, which had been a federal–provincial, equally shared program paying for social assistance, child care subsidies, homemaking programs, and child welfare. The program also reduced the federal government's funding for post-secondary education and health care. This cap on transfer payments was applied to the three wealthiest provinces: Ontario, British Columbia, and Alberta.[33]

Withdrawal of federal support for the Canadian safety net changed the original cost-sharing agreement between the federal and provincial governments regarding social assistance and social services. One commentator has claimed that "it is thereby fundamentally changing the CAP in a way inconsistent with its purpose as adopted by the Parliament of Canada."[34]

**Bill C-80** In 1993, *Bill C-80* set out to amend the *Income Tax Act*, to enact the *Children's Special Allowances Act*, amend certain other acts affected by these changes, and repeal the *Family Allowances Act*.[35] *Bill C-80* became effective in January 1993 and was perceived as a landmark that ended the universality of services in Canada.

The Child Tax Benefit proposed in the White Paper and in the 1992 budget was intended to replace family allowances, as well as refundable and non-refundable child tax credits. The poorest families on welfare, then, did not benefit at all. The working poor received a 41 percent increase, lower-middle-income families received a 38 percent increase, those in the upper-middle-income bracket received 7 percent less, and high-income families received 17 percent less.[36]

The social, political, and economic changes of the 1990s placed a great deal of stress on the social welfare system. As government funding was cut back, new problems emerged that demanded attention. For example, immigration policies increased the need for the greater integration of minorities into Canadian life. According to Bracken and Walmsley, "Ensuring full participation of minorities in Canadian society as well as equal access to and treatment by social service systems are emerging challenges for Canadian social welfare."[37] The family structure was also changing, and higher divorce rates led to a greater number of single-parent families and blended families. There are now more teenaged single parents and fewer teen marriages, thanks to lowered social expectation that parents marry. In addition, in 1992, one of every five children in Canada was living in poverty.[38] Finally, the stresses of modern-day life led to a myriad

---

33   Canadian Council on Social Development, "Constitutional Reform and Social Policy," *Social Development* 1 (Fall 1991).

34   Canadian Council on Social Development, "Constitutional Reform and Social Policy," *Social Development* 1 (Fall 1991).

35   Melchers, "The Cap on CAP," p. 19.

36   House of Commons, *Statutes of Canada*, 1993.

37   Ken Battle, "White Paper Whitewash: The New Child Benefit," *Perception* 16.2 (Spring/Summer 1992): 3.

38   Dennis Bracken and Christopher Walmsley, "The Canadian Welfare State: Implication for the Continuing Education of Canadian Social Workers," *The Social Worker* 60.1 (Spring 1992): 23.

of problems, not the least of which was that both sexes were absent from work more often between 1977 and 1991.[39]

In 1993, the Liberal government under Jean Chrétien replaced the federal Progressive Conservative government. Ideologically, when the Liberals were elected in 1993 they declared their ongoing commitment to traditional Liberal values. These included concern for individual welfare, faith in humanity, recognition of people's potential to change and grow, the value of equity (i.e., eliminating discrepancies in the treatment of different groups within Canadian society), general issues of inequality as well as the ongoing dilemma of child poverty in Canada specifically, the importance of community as a structure and a system in which most Canadians grow up, diversity (i.e., the need to recognize and appreciate differences between individuals and groups within society), and, finally, a faith in democracy. In reality, this last point translates into the concept that the elected representatives of all parties debate and vote on changes and developments in the policies and laws of a nation and these are carried out through the political processes of the party in power. Philosophically, the newly elected Liberal government of 1993 still embraced a social welfare system that provided security for all citizens and freedom of lifestyle choice based on personal values and economic opportunity.

Brian Mulroney's legacy is quite another matter. The McDonald Commission of 1985—formally the Royal Commission on the Economic Union and Development Prospects for Canada—had submitted its report, recommending as its third major proposal changes to the Canadian Income Security System. The commission called "for a universal income security program [to replace the guaranteed income supplement, family allowances, child tax credits, married exemptions, child exemptions, federal contributions to social assistance payments, and federal social housing programs]. The central features of the UISP would be a universal minimum guaranteed rate of income, federally funded and administered. Payment of UISP would be reduced with receipt of other income at a rate that would maintain work incentives and integrate with income tax rates. Although the commission made specific proposals for guarantee and tax back rates, it also made plain that these features should be flexible."[40]

The commission recommendations suffered the same fate as earlier counterparts had in that none of them were adopted by the Conservative government. One of the major problems the Liberals inherited in 1993 was a social security system that had been partly unravelled by the neo-conservative philosophy of the former Conservative government and by the economic recession of the early 1990s.

Social policy scholars (Evans, Armitage) define the social welfare system in 1993 as one seriously damaged by the country's fiscal problems in the industrial recession of 1990 to 1992. The weak economy had reduced government revenues in central Canada and raised social security expenditures. As Dr. Evans notes, "The Canadian experience in targeting child benefits, and the slow death of Family Allowance, indicates the dilemmas of maintaining universal benefits in a climate of fiscal restraint."[41] In addition to these fiscal problems, the new Liberal government took over Canada's tradition of humanitarian social

---

**39**   Ibid.

**40**   "Employee Absenteeism Changing, Study Says," *The Globe and Mail,* March 25, 1993, p. B1.

**41**   Andrew Armitage, *Social Welfare in Canada Revisited: Facing Up to the Future*, 3d ed. (Don Mills, ON: Oxford University Press, 1996), p. 206.

welfare. A significant percentage of its citizens believed universal programs such as health care, Old Age pensions, and the former Family Allowance benefits were their rights, regardless of the country's economic climate.

The fledgling Chrétien government faced a further challenge: the state of the Canada Assistance Plan, as described earlier in the chapter. The Conservatives had slated the plan for demolition and had already surrendered a large share of the federal transfer payments to the provinces. As Armitage recounts, "Lloyd Axworthy, then Minister of Human Resources Development, held a series of consultations on the future of our social security and our safety net and a discussion paper, 'Improving Social Security in Canada,' was developed in 1994. Concurrently, the Minister of Finance, Paul Martin, released a report entitled 'Creating a Healthy Fiscal Climate' and held a series of consultations based on that report. The result of these two consultations and reports was the passing of the *Canada Health and Social Transfer Act* (CHST) in 1995, which replaced the Canada Assistance Plan."[42]

The CHST that came into being in the 1997 fiscal year is a block-funding method. It has decreased, then stabilized, transfers for health, post-secondary education, and social assistance.[43] Today this has translated into a major change in federal transfers to the provinces for the programs mentioned above, and it continues to affect relations between the two levels of government.

Implementation of the *Canada Health and Social Transfer Act* (*Bill C-76*) redefined the nature of the federal government presence in social welfare. As Chenier notes, "This single funding mechanism replaced both Established Program Financing (EPF) transfers covering health and post-secondary education and Canada Assistance Plan (CAP) transfers covering social assistance and services."[44] This major change gave the provinces greater power in deciding the redistribution of funding to these three key areas.

Its proponents at the time argued that the CHST would allow the provinces more leverage to meet their regional needs; its critics worried that less federal presence in provincial decisions would result in a patchwork of programs across the country.

## IDEOLOGICAL PERSPECTIVE IN THE TWENTY-FIRST CENTURY

In the twenty-first century, the challenge for social democracies such as Canada "consists of being able to reconcile the demands of a popular agenda with those of a capitalist market."[45] In this country over the last 20 years, Mishra has pointed out that both ruling parties have demonstrated "a tendency to be more pragmatic than ideological in their approach . . . and to follow pro-market and pro-business policies." He also cautions that globalization in the

---

42   Patricia Evans, "Eroding Canadian Social Welfare: The Mulroney Legacy, 1984–1993," *Social Policy and Administration* 28(2) (June 1994): p. 110.

43   Andrew Armitage, 1996, p. 204.

44   O. Madore and C. Blanchette, *The Canada Health and Social Transfer* (Ottawa: Government of Canada, 1997).

45   Nancy Chenier, *The CHST: The Debate over Outcomes* (Ottawa: Parliamentary Library, 1997), p. 1.

economic sector has helped strengthen the influence of corporate business interests and widened "the influence of domestic politics and party ideology on social policy."[46]

As government support and funding shrink, governments are encouraging communities to take on more responsibility to maintain needed social services. In such countries as Canada, the voluntary sector has had to step into this breach. Communities committed to maintaining the quality of life people had enjoyed since the 1950s now find themselves relying heavily on the volunteers in every area of the "non-profit" sector. While the voluntary sector employs more than one million workers, 6.5 million volunteers working within 180 000 organizations across the country support its unofficial network. In tightknit cities like Oakville, Ontario, volunteers comprise the largest workforce in their communities.

One new model in community development is called "the social economy," which is defined as economic activity with social goals. It represents community partnerships between voluntary and non-voluntary sectors. Such organizations subscribe to such values as sustainable development, equal opportunity for all, the inclusion of disadvantaged people and people with disabilities, and enhancing the civil society.[47] The recent Liberal government, which supports such initiatives, promised financial resources through Canada's small-business program. It is to be hoped that the current government will implement similar commitments as their social policies emerge.

## CHILD WELFARE AND CHILD POVERTY IN THE NEW CENTURY

Canada's child welfare policy and practice have come under intense and very noticeable public scrutiny for the past several years. A disturbing number of Canadian children in the care of a provincial child welfare system have died, and this fact has fuelled the public perception that these services are crumbling. During the past 25 years, child welfare practice has shifted away from out-of-home care and toward bringing the services to children in their own homes. As Nico Trocmé noted in 1997, the number of children in care in Ontario dropped from close to 18 000 in the early 1970s to an average of 10 000 in the 1990s. Simultaneously, the same agencies are serving a greater number of families, more than 80 000, the number having risen from slightly fewer than 30 000.

Actually, experienced front-line workers were the first to request more home-based services. They concluded that removing children at risk from their own homes was not itself a solution. Too many of these workers know first-hand of many children who drift through the foster care system from one home to another and end up at age 16 essentially on their own and with few supports. Conversely, there is little evidence to date that the return to home-based services has caused unforeseen damage if sufficient support systems are indeed in place. However, during the 1970s and 1980s, a number of innovative programs designed to teach parenting and homemaking skills in high-risk neighbourhoods were introduced. Other community initiatives were attempted as well, most with positive results. Then, during the recession of the late 1980s, governments

---

**46**   Ramesh Mishra, "The Political Bases of Canadian Social Welfare," in *Canadian Social Welfare*, 5th ed., eds. J. C. Turner and F. J. Turner. Toronto: Pearson Education, Chapter 4, p. 7.

**47**   Ibid.; Bonnie Brown, *Oakville Report* (Oakville, ON: 2004), pp. 1–4.

made major cuts to child welfare agencies and many of these new preventive programs were discontinued. These changes, of course, hurt the programs' former clients, especially disadvantaged youths who have demonstrated serious negative effects in their own neighbourhoods.

Over the past two decades, however, child welfare experts and forward-thinking agencies across the country have continued to develop innovative new programs and services that offer a greater range of options to meet the very complex and compelling needs of children and their families. As Trocmé notes, "We must ensure that we do not lose the momentum towards a diverse and community-based child welfare system."[48]

Stuart Alcock conducted an excellent review of the major changes to child welfare in British Columbia, published in 1997, and the province's ongoing efforts to resolve the issue of child protection successfully by means that he described as "being mirrored in Ontario and other provinces across the country."[49]

While neither social scientists, economists, nor politicians deny the negative relationship between poverty and children's healthy development, we still cannot agree on a general definition of poverty for both families and children.

On one side of the debate stands the Fraser Institute, a major representative of neoconservative thinking. The institute has suggested that "child poverty is really only a problem among those who live in families where incomes are so low that the parents cannot even afford adequate food and shelter."[50] On the other side, people like David Ross of the Canadian Council on Social Development, a proponent of more liberal thinking, reminds us that Canada is not a have-not country. He describes our country as a "socially complex economically advanced and democratic society,"[51] in which adult success requires far more than physical survival; it demands of each person a complex set of social, cultural, and moral norms. People learn these foundations at home within their families. Ross urges us to consider the real consequences of economic hardship as it affects the development of these basic values.

Social scientists, economists, and informed citizens in general share the worry that our quality of life is declining. As Canadians, we value "our level of safety, cohesion, civility, our generally high standard of health, and our economic and cultural prosperity. Few among us would want to create a large underclass of desperate people who are unable to attain and help maintain these societal goals."[52]

Some significant statistical evidence indicates that family income dramatically affects children's well-being. Two large national surveys have published data that show that children's chances of developing to their full potential increase steadily as their families' incomes rise.[53]

---

**48**  Nicol Trocmé, "Staying on Track While the Pendulum Swings: Commentary on Canadian Child Welfare Policy Trends," *OASW News Magazine* 24.4 (Winter 1997): p. 13.

**49**  Ibid., p. 14.

**50**  *OASW News Magazine* 24.4 (Winter 1997): p. 18.

**51**  David P. Ross, "Rethinking Child Poverty." *Insight: An Information Series* (Ottawa: The Canadian Council on Social Development, 1998), p. 1.

**52**  Ibid., p. 1.

**53**  Ibid., p. 2.

It was to be hoped that the federal Liberal government's commitment to attack child poverty and support healthy early development (1999) would include provisions to reduce what Ross dubs "the poverty of opportunity." This situation prevents too many of our children from reaching adulthood in possession of the four main ingredients they need to live as successful adults: good health, good social skills, good learning skills, and economically sustainable skills.[54]

Indeed, the Liberal government considered this commitment a major policy initiative for almost five years. Since 2002, with the establishment of the Early Childhood Development Agreement, the federal government promised $2.2 billion over a five-year period (2001–2006) to the provinces and territories to improve and expand their programs and services in early childhood development. The agreement targeted four areas: healthy pregnancy, birth and infancy, parenting, and family support.[55]

The federal budget of 2003 set aside an additional $900 million over five years specifically to improve access to affordable high-quality, regulated early-learning and child care programs and services in the provinces and territories. Under the agreement, additional funding was to be available for early childhood development and early-learning and child care programs for First Nations children living on reserves.

Within that funding allocation, early learning and child care under the Canada Social Transfer would amount to $150 million in 2004–2005 and $225 million in 2005–2006, to rise to $350 million annually in 2007–2008.[56] While the debate continues over the amount of funding needed, such substantial fiscal supports should at least reduce the number of children caught in the "poverty of opportunity" cycle that Ross describes above.

It is unfortunate that the current federal Conservative government announced the termination of these bi-lateral agreements as of March 2007. Instead of funding child care services in communities, the current federal government has introduced a taxable family allowance and announced an incentive-based child care space initiative that they promise will be "flexible enough to meet the needs of all families" and "will work for all sizes and types of employers."[57] While the federal government has allocated a financial commitment of $250 million each year for the next five years, the reality is that the $250 million annual budget replaces previously committed and dedicated funds for child care of $1.2 billion, for a net loss of $550 million. With this large reduction in available funding, the federal government in the 2007 budget announced that it would: 1) meet the needs of all families regardless of their hours of work or whether they live in cities, small towns, or rural areas; 2) work with business, community, and non-profit organizations and with provinces and territories to make the initiative work with all sizes and types of employers; 3) work with the provincial and territorial governments to ensure the initiative complements are already in place; and 4) create up to 25 000 new child care spaces each year beginning in 2007.[58] This seems a very ambitious agenda given the sizable reduction in funding allocated to

---

54  Ibid.

55  Ibid., p. 4.

56  Department of Finance, Federal Transfer to Provinces, www.fin.gc.ca

57  Government of Canada, Market Child Care Spaces Initiative: Frequently asked questions (Ottawa: June 26, 2006).

58  Government of Canada. Federal Budget (Ottawa: 2006).

carry out all of these commitments. According to the Child Care Advocacy Association of Canada, the net result of these changes will play out in that next year (2007–2008) communities will face a 79% reduction in the level of funding committed to improving family access to quality affordable child care services.[59] It has been well documented that a credible approach to expanding child care services across this country requires adequate resources, public standards, and provincial and territorial plans. So far, according to the Child Care Advocacy Association of Canada, the current federal government's special initiative lacks all of these, and to quote their conclusion, "the words and the numbers simply don't add up."[60]

In Ontario, in October of 2003 with a change in government, a new Ministry of Children and Youth Services was introduced as responsible for the province's child welfare system, which it operates on a transfer payment basis for 53 Children's Aid Societies within the province. Shortly after, a program evaluation was undertaken to "examine Ontario's child welfare system to identify and recommend further improvements in the design, delivery, and management of services across the province."[61]

A major conclusion of the study was that "the present child welfare program is not sustainable without modifications to the funding framework, to government policy, and to CAS approaches to service delivery."[62]

The evaluation recommended changes in a number of areas including integration of services—especially in the area of children's mental health services—accountability, efficiency, and sustainability in order to prepare for "the introduction and ongoing management of a multi-years funding approach in the child welfare sector."[63] The anticipated results of this evaluation and the implementation of its recommendations include an improvement in the overall quality of life for children through evidence-based practice and specific outcomes, increasing the efficient use of public resources through changes in service delivery patterns and changes to the funding framework, and strengthening the integration of child welfare services with an array of child and family services through shared outcomes and formal partnerships.[64] It was anticipated that a positive outcome in these areas over the next three years could have a major impact on social policy development in child welfare not only in Ontario but across the country.

A Child Welfare Secretariat, also known as the Transformation Secretariat, was established in March 2004 to study the recommendation from the Child Welfare Program Evaluation, to develop new policies and models of service delivery, to implement the recommendations of the program evaluation, and to incorporate the new multi-year funding approach. The new ministry developed this child welfare funding model, known as the Multi-Years Results Based Plan (MYRBP), as recommended in the earlier program evaluation. Annually, each society prepares a budget and a management plan,

59   Child Care Advocacy Association of Canada Bulletin (Ottawa: 2006).

60   Child Care Advocacy Association of Canada Bulletin (Ottawa: 2006).

61   *Child Welfare Programme Evaluation Report* (Toronto: Ontario Ministry of Children's Services, 2003), pp. 1–56.

62   Ibid., p. 2.

63   Ibid., p. 5.

64   Ibid., p. 3.

which, following ratification by the Board, is filed with the Ministry of Children and Youth Services for approval by the ministry. The ministry also provides the agencies with planning amounts for Years II and III in a three-year cycle. The financial statements of each agency are audited annually, and quarterly service and financial data reports are submitted to the ministry. Based on these case volume reports, the financial allocation is adjusted by the ministry. All of these changes reflect the contents of *Bill 210*, an important new legislation which amended the *Child and Family Services Act* and became the law in October 2006. Time will tell whether this new child welfare legislation passed recently in Ontario, and implementation of its Transformation Agenda, will continue to nurture ongoing improvements in the funding and delivery of services in the child welfare sector.

## THE 1999 BUDGET: A FISCAL RESPONSE TO POVERTY AND HEALTH

The recent Liberal government revealed its first real response to the poverty issue in its budgets of 1998 and 1999. As early as the 1998 budget, the government announced the elimination of the federal deficit that would allow the government to introduce tax relief. The budget of 1999 built on the measures that made this possible, and together the two budgets provided $16.5 billion in tax relief over three years. While this sounds like a huge amount, the individual Canadian taxpayer felt little effect. The 1998 budget raised by $500 the amount of income low-income taxpayers could receive tax-free. The 1999 budget increased that amount to $675 and extended it to all taxpayers. As a result of both of these budgets, 600 000 lower-income Canadians were taken off the tax rolls altogether. As well, the 1998 budget began the process of eliminating the three percent surtax for taxpayers with incomes up to $50 000, and reducing the surtax for those with incomes between $50 000 and $65 000. The 1999 budget completed that process by wiping out the three percent surtax for all taxpayers. As a result, single taxpayers earning $20 000 or less each year saw their federal income tax shrink by at least 10 percent. Further, families with an annual income of $45 000 or less also had their federal income tax reduced by at least 10 percent. Families with two children and an annual income of $30 000 or less paid no federal income tax.

The 1999 federal budget provided additional assistance for families with children through the Canadian Child Tax Benefit (CCTB). This benefit increased total federal support for families by $2 billion, and by July 2000 it had reached an annual level of close to $7 billion. This measure ensured that most taxpayers with children pay less tax than individuals with similar incomes and no children. The 1999 budget committed an additional $300 million to CCTB payments, which increased child benefits to two million low- and middle-income families.[65]

Perhaps the most important component of the March 1999 budget was the government's promise to enhance Canadians' quality of life, particularly their health care. In fact, the 1999 budget made health the focus of the largest single investment that a Liberal government had ever made. Over a five-year period, the provinces and territories would receive an additional $11.5 billion specifically for health care costs. In addition, the government

---

**65**  *CAS/UAW Collaboration Agreement for Toronto* (Toronto, April 2004), pp. 29–81.

pledged to invest close to $1.4 billion in health information systems research, First Nations and Inuit health services, prevention efforts, and other initiatives to improve the lives and health of Canadians.

Of the $11.5 billion dedicated to health care over the next five years, $8 billion was allocated to future increases in the *Canada Health and Social Transfer Act* (CHST), the successor of CAP (Canada Assistance Plan). Over the next three years, the provinces would receive $6.5 billion. For the 1999 fiscal year, the budget allocated $3 billion as an immediate one-time cash injection into the CHST. The provinces and territories could draw on these funds in ways that best suited their most pressing needs in their individual health care systems. A further budget item allocated $240 million for two years to carry out the proposal of a national task force that represented the health research community, the Canadian Institute of Health Research (CIHR). The institute would bring together the best researchers from across Canada to study aging, arthritis, women's health, cancer, heart disease, and other subjects. It constituted a major step toward bringing Canada back into the mainstream of health-related research.[66]

In 2004, health-related issues continued to dominate the concerns of many Canadians, and hence, the federal government. As noted, the government continued to allocate large amounts of money to the provinces for their health care systems. In the 2003–2004 budget, the federal government allocated a total of $36.8 billion to health care over a five-year period. Priorities cited health research, First Nations, children's programs (such as early learning and child care), and a new public health ministry among other areas in this major investment in our health care system.[67]

Also in 2004, *Bill C-6*, an *Act Respecting Assisted Human Reproduction and Related Research*, became law. An all-party committee drafted this significant piece of legislation over three years, following a lengthy consultation process with experts in this field. It gives Canada one of the most comprehensive legislative frameworks in the world regarding assisted human reproduction.[68] In spite of the significant progress made in health care over a five-year period, both federal and provincial governments continue to grapple with developing a model of health care that provides access for all citizens in a timely and effective manner, while being financially sustainable now and in future, unknown economic climates.[69]

## POVERTY AND HOMELESSNESS

The primary source of information for this introductory section comes from the report of the task force on homelessness commissioned by the City of Toronto in 1998 and chaired by Ann Golden. Its contents exemplify the very similar situations about which members of the task force learned during visits to Vancouver, Calgary, Winnipeg, and Montreal.[70]

---

66   Summarized from the *Liberal Times*, March 1999.

67   Ibid.

68   *Bill C-6, An Act Respecting Assisted Human Reproduction and Related Research* (Ottawa, Government of Canada, 2004).

69   *Key Highlights: The Liberal Record on Women, 1993–2004* (Ottawa: Liberal Party of Canada).

70   Ann Golden, "Speech to the Canadian Club of Toronto" (Toronto, September 28, 1998), pp. 3, 9.

The task force encountered difficulties conceptualizing a common definition of "homelessness" that all its members could accept. This proved a major obstacle as the Toronto group began its work in 1998. Data from an earlier longitudinal study conducted between 1987 and 1996 revealed that 170 000 different persons had been homeless within that period in the city of Toronto; in 1996, 26 000 persons used the available shelters and of that number, 5300, or one in five, were children. This group breaks down further into the chronic users, who constitute about 14 percent of those studied. Chronic users tend to stay in the hostel system for more than a year on average and to move from shelter to shelter. They consume almost 50 percent of the resources available in Toronto. If homelessness for the chronic users could be resolved, it would reduce the demand for scarce resources by almost half. Persons suffering from mental illness, addiction, and substance abuse characterized the chronic group.

A second significant variable that quickly emerged involved the link between the causes of homelessness and poverty, at a time in Ontario when the economy was prospering and poverty was increasing. The commission found that the poverty trends coincided with all levels of governments' withdrawal from affordable and subsidized housing programs. The number of rooming houses continued to decline steadily; at the same time, the province reduced by 21.6 percent the social assistance it contributed to many families who depended on it to make their rent payments. Particularly hard hit were single-mother families, and the severity of the housing situation worsened.

"One of the most significant pieces of work done by this task force was the identification of systemic problems in our communities which result in homelessness and add to the poverty of individuals," the report states.[71] Three of these problems are worth noting: a housing market that does not supply an adequate amount of affordable housing, a changing job market that leaves people poorly paid or unemployed, and a weakening social safety net that does not provide what the vulnerable groups need to exist day to day. The task force confirmed the cycle of homelessness triggered by eviction, loss of jobs, personal crises, and premature releases from mental health institutions. The report's recommendations pertain not only to Toronto but to urban centres across the country. These include a multi-pronged strategy that would involve all three levels of government. Together they would provide more supportive housing for vulnerable people unable to compete in the normal housing market, more affordable housing for low-income groups, rental assistance to the working poor at risk of losing their current homes, and, finally, improved co-ordination of all the relevant systems. This excellent report provides the groundwork for action at all levels of government.

One important change in the overall housing situation since the publication of the Golden report was that, although housing remained the responsibility of the provincial and municipal governments, a growing understanding of the immensity and complexity of the problem compelled senior ministers at the federal level to provide assistance in this area.

One good example of new federal support for affordable housing was the Supporting Communities Partnership Initiative, known as SCPI, which was the core program of the National Homelessness Initiatives launched in 1999 by the federal government in an attempt to create a more integrative and inclusive approach to homelessness in Canada.

---

71   Ibid.

The National Homelessness Initiatives, or NHI as it is called, began in December of 1999 and was a three-year, $753-million initiative. Their goal was to engage all levels of government as well as the non-profit and private sectors to begin to develop effective approaches to help homeless people in Canada make the transition from living in the streets and emergency shelters to a more secure life and more adequate housing. The Supporting Communities Partnership Initiative (SCPI), along with providing financial support to various communities, also encouraged the NHI to work together with all levels of government and the private sector to identify major issues and gaps in existing capacity and develop new responses to homelessness. Communities were allocated a maximum funding level to be matched from other community sources such as fundraising, local sponsors, etc. The communities were required to explain how these activities would continue once the funding ended from the SCPI. Projects funded were done so on the basis of priority areas identified through community planning processes.

In a report released by the Government of Canada in December 2002, the Hon. Claudette Bradshaw, then Minister of Labour and Federal Coordinator on Homelessness, gave her rationale for this program. She explained the face of homelessness varied from person to person and community to community. This is why "we have implemented the SCPI, a program which allows local groups and all levels of government to come together to find the approaches that work best for them in their unique circumstances. Every Canadian should have access to a safe place to live that they can call home." She continued: "there is still work to do before we can accomplish this" but noted that "the report makes it clear that progress is being made, much of it due to the perseverance and vision of the communities who have responded to the challenge and whose groups and organizations have been working tirelessly to combat homelessness."[72] Eighty percent of the SCPI funds were allocated to the 10 cities seen as most affected by the problems of homelessness. These were Vancouver, Calgary, Edmonton, Winnipeg, Toronto, Ottawa, Hamilton, Montreal, Quebec City, and Halifax. The remaining 20% of the budget was allocated to the provinces and territories in accord with an agreed-upon funding formula, which provided for a minimum base of $200 000 per community. An initial allocation to the SCPI of $305 million was made by the federal government, to cover the first three years of the project in December of 1999. Five broad objectives were identified within which the program was to operate. The first was to ensure that no individuals were involuntarily on the streets by insuring that sufficient shelters and adequate support systems were available. The second was to significantly reduce the number of individuals requiring emergency shelters and transition and supportive housing. The third was to help individuals move from homelessness through to self-sufficiency where possible; the fourth, to help communities strengthen their capacity to address the needs of their homeless; and the fifth, to improve the social health and economic well-being of people who are homeless. These comprehensive objectives were developed on a broad scale to fund initiatives based on the communities' ability to address a wide range of homeless issues, which might differ from community to community.

The document released by Minister Bradshaw in 2002 involved reports on community responses to homelessness in 10 Canadian communities, which are identified above, and covered the period from 1999 to 2002. These 10 cities were selected as a

---

72  Honourable Claudette Bradshaw, *Government of Canada Report on Homelessness* (Victoria, British Columbia, 2002).

sample set from 61 communities, all of which were involved in the project to report on their particular experience under the initiative and on the challenges and successes experienced during the planning phase of those initiatives. The report summarized these communities' views and experiences with SCPI and provided examples of some of the lessons learned. As a result of the positive report on the first phase of this project, the government made a commitment to continue the SCPI for another three years and it was extended to 2006. However, following the federal election in 2005 and the return to power of the Conservative Party, a new Homelessness Partnering Strategy (HPS) was announced by the federal government on December 19, 2006. This program replaced the National Homelessness Initiative, which expired on March 31, 2007. This new strategy, which began on April 1, 2007, provides $269.6 million over two years to prevent and reduce homelessness by helping to establish the structures needed to move homeless and at-risk individuals toward self-sufficiency and full participation in Canadian society. Under this new initiative, the federal government will offer the provinces and territories an opportunity to enter into bi-lateral partnerships, improve collaboration, and develop linkages between the federal homelessness programs and provincial and territorial social services to help communities make strategic investments that will best serve their homeless population.[73]

In summary, since 1999, the Liberal government and latterly, the Conservative government, have both moved quite strongly back into the arena of housing the homeless and have committed significant allocations of money and programs to further that end. It will be interesting to watch the unfolding of this new program developed by the Conservative Party over the next few years and to hope that the initiative being put forward will have a substantial impact on the thousands of people who still lack affordable, adequate housing across the country.

## IMMIGRATION

Over the decades immigration has played an important role in the history of Canadian social welfare. The structure of our immigration policies has varied over the years, shaped by world events, the perceived needs of the country, and various ideological positions of the policy-makers of the day. The significance of immigration in the new millennium continues.

A federal–provincial meeting of the ministers responsible for immigration in Victoria, British Columbia, early in 2004, best expressed the nation's current policy regarding the importance of attracting skilled and knowledgeable immigrants to Canada: "Immigration is critical to building our economy and society," stated the Honourable Judy Sgro, Minister of Citizenship and Immigration, and "we need to ensure that newcomers have every chance to succeed whether they come to Canada as skilled immigrants, to join family members, for business reasons, or as refugees fleeing persecution."[74]

Flowing from this statement, the various programs and procedures stress several themes. Among these are increased efforts to provide higher levels of training in Canada's two official languages, and a related emphasis on work placements and mentoring opportunities.

---

73   Government of Canada, The New Homelessness Partnership Strategy (Ottawa: December, 2006).

74   Canadian Intergovernmental Conference Secretariat, www.scics.gc.ca.

A significant new focus in this area is group processing for refugees. This means process-ing would seek to identify entire refugee populations and resettle them together in the same community, satisfying the human need for safety and encouraging permanence as a step in helping the groups better integrate into Canadian culture.

In the twenty-first century, amid the new realities of terrorism, unrelenting warfare, and a shifting global economy, all levels of government in Canada face challenges to maintain the social welfare system within a healthy economy and environment that pro-vides security and freedom for all Canadians, all based on personal values and economic opportunity.

# CHAPTER 7

# Aboriginal Peoples in Canada

*Anne-Marie Mawhiney and Sheila Hardy*

## INTRODUCTION

Many Canadians remain perplexed about Aboriginal peoples' demands for recognition of their inherent right of self-government and self-determination. For many Canadians, part of the problem is a lack of knowledge about the historical, socio-political, and economic context for Aboriginal assertions. Government policies have had far-reaching and negative consequences for the welfare of Aboriginal peoples in Canada, so it is particularly important that social workers understand the historical context for the development of culturally appropriate social services provided to Aboriginal communities. It is for this reason that this chapter is included in a book on Canadian social welfare.

Before examining the history of relations between Aboriginal peoples and the government of Canada, it may be helpful to include some background information about Aboriginal peoples. The term "Aboriginal peoples" refers to organic political and cultural entities that originate from the first peoples of North America (Royal Commission on Aboriginal Peoples, 1997). Here "Aboriginal peoples" is used as a term that encompasses all Aboriginal people in Canada, including Status and Non-Status Indians, Métis, and Inuit.

Great diversity exists amongst Aboriginal peoples and is reflected in the many languages, cultures, traditions, and philosophical beliefs. For example, the Assembly of First Nations, a national political organization, represents 592 000 people from 633 First Nations across Canada. The Inuit Tapirisat of Canada represents 30 000 Arctic Inuit (Foster, 1982). Each Aboriginal nation also has a distinct culture and tradition. For example, there are 11 separate Aboriginal language groups and 53 distinct Aboriginal languages spoken in Canada (Foster, 1982).

*Inuit* are those Aboriginal peoples who live in the far northern regions of Canada; they are distinct, culturally and legally, from First Nations peoples and Métis. In 1939, the Supreme Court of Canada determined the federal government was responsible for the Inuit, but they were not legally Indians (Brinski, 1989). By early 1999, however, some Inuit communities were starting to challenge the court decision and were seeking First Nations status.

*Métis* people are those of mixed Aboriginal and non-Aboriginal heritage (Brizinski, 1989). For generations, Métis people have struggled to be recognized as distinct Aboriginal peoples in Canada. After generations of fighting for constitutional recognition, the *Constitution Act* of 1982 acknowledges existing Aboriginal and treaty rights of Canada's Aboriginal peoples under Section 35. This section provides that: (1) The existing Aboriginal and treaty rights of the Aboriginal peoples of Canada are hereby recognized and affirmed. (2) In this act, "Aboriginal Peoples of Canada" includes the Indian, Inuit, and Métis peoples of Canada. However, only in September 2003 did the Supreme Court recognize the distinctiveness of the Métis Nation. The Powley decision recognizes and protects Métis people's existing Aboriginal rights.

It is well documented that living conditions in Aboriginal communities have been compared with living conditions in Third World countries. Studies undertaken over the last 30 years (Hawthorne, 1967; Social Conditions, 1982; Assembly of First Nations, 1988; RCAP, 1997) have shown time and again that social and health indicators of Aboriginal peoples in Canada fall far below those of Canadians in mainstream society. First Nations people are admitted to hospital at more than twice the rate of the national population; the infant mortality rates among First Nations people are 60 percent higher than the national rate; Aboriginal people have a life expectancy 10 years shorter than the national average; and the death rate of First Nations is two to four times that of other Canadians (Assembly of First Nations, 1988). These grim statistics highlight the correlation between health and living conditions: First Nations peoples' average income is half to two-thirds of the national average, and their unemployment rate ranges from 35 to 90 percent (Royal Commission on Aboriginal Peoples, 1997; Assembly of First Nations, 1988).

Until recently, a piecemeal, band-aid approach has been taken to address the social and health conditions among Aboriginal peoples. These statistics tell a compelling story. First Nations people in Canada live in difficult and impoverished conditions unimaginable to the average person in Canada. Virtually all Aboriginal peoples experience these realities and know very well the impact of poor economic and social conditions on themselves, on family members, and on their communities.

The horrific living conditions of Aboriginal peoples in Canada are difficult for many people to acknowledge. Yet it is impossible to ignore the impact that colonization has had in creating structural inequities experienced by Aboriginal peoples, as individuals and as communities. The conflicts between Aboriginal peoples and the federal and provincial governments are best understood by connecting the realities of everyday experiences of Aboriginal communities with the colonial social policies and programs instituted by Euro-Westerners since the early days of contact.

## HISTORICAL BACKGROUND

To understand the historical relationship between Aboriginal nations and Euro-Westerners, in this section we look at traditional lifestyles before contact with Europeans, during early contact and the formation of Canada in the nineteenth century, to the circumstances of the 1990s. We are concerned here with understanding the ways that Aboriginal peoples' relationships with various groups of non-Aboriginal peoples have affected the well-being of generations of Aboriginal peoples living in and outside Aboriginal nations. We are also concerned with ways that Aboriginal peoples have preserved, or in some cases reclaimed, their traditional values, practices, and lifestyles that supported the well-being of Aboriginal peoples for centuries before contact.[1]

### Pre-Contact and Early Contact

Aboriginal traditional lifestyles were complex and differed from one community to the next. A complete description of traditional lifestyles would far exceed the scope of this chapter. However, a brief sketch of the social structure of some Aboriginal peoples may help to explain the political, economic, and social clashes that occurred after contact.

Each Aboriginal community has its own unique social structure, traditions, culture, language, and ways of living, thinking, and viewing the world. The following describes some Anishnabe Nations near Lake Huron. Even within this geographic area, traditions

---

1    For a thorough analysis of this history, readers are encouraged to read Volume 1 of the Royal Commission on Aboriginal Peoples, *Looking Forward, Looking Back* (1991).

and ways of living differ from one location to another; however, a discussion of their experiences may be useful as background for the rest of the chapter.[2]

Before contact, the Anishnabe peoples operated on the basis of community welfare; the value placed on the best interests of the community or group was more crucial than the interests of individuals. Survival of the group was the primary concern. Young children were taught the value of co-operating for the benefit of the community rather than focusing on individual interests. Through role modelling and various other socialization techniques, they learned the importance of "wisdom, love, respect, bravery, honesty, humility, and truth" (Odjig-White, 1992).

Before European contact, the social structure of the Anishnabe community was egalitarian; all members were equal, and no individual, with the exception of the elders—who were revered—stood apart as special or above anyone else. All members received their fair and equitable shares of any goods that were provided. Survival depended on a balance of labour between women and men who contributed equally to the survival of the community and whose work was seen as equally important. For example, women were responsible for caring for children, gathering and preparing food supplies, and providing shelter and clothing. Men were responsible for harvesting game and ensuring the safety and security of the community. Elders were revered and largely responsible for ensuring that children learned the values, beliefs, and ways of living of the people.

In contrast, European social structures were based on individualism and independence. Gender roles were based on a patriarchal model. When they set out to colonize various regions throughout the world, Europeans brought with them a belief in the superiority of their race and cultures. Their ethnocentric views were based on an assumption that in all things they were superior, the most able, and the most civilized.

To the Europeans, Christianity was fundamental to civilization, so converting Aboriginal people to Christianity became the first attempt to make over the Aboriginal peoples that the missionaries encountered. It was generally believed by the colonizers that if these conversions could be accomplished, Aboriginal peoples might eventually be integrated into European civilized society and perhaps even become worthy citizens (Frideres, 1983). Of course, conversion required that Aboriginal peoples reject their own spiritual beliefs and practices and accept Christian philosophical and moral principles.

Well aware that economic self-sufficiency did not serve their own commercial interests, the newcomers set out to convince original inhabitants to give up their valued items and practices in exchange for "better" things and "better" ways. Fur traders in North America learned to promote and exploit Aboriginal peoples in order to obtain valuable goods and services. Through their economic relations with European traders, Aboriginal peoples became less and less self-sufficient. These economic relations, combined with changes in spiritual practices, had a tremendous impact on their values, on family and community relations, and on their traditional ways of meeting human needs.

The Europeans did recognize they had much to learn from Aboriginal peoples about surviving in North America, yet they were, for the most part, blind to the wisdom of Aboriginal values and practices. It did not occur to them that Aboriginal cultures had achieved integrated systems for ensuring the physical, mental, emotional, and spiritual well-being of all community members.

---

2   The author acknowledges with gratitude feedback on an earlier version of this chapter by Arthur Solomon, Carol Nadjiwan, and Jennifer Keck.

For a time, conciliation and diplomacy characterized the Europeans' treatment of Aboriginal peoples. Aboriginal peoples were valuable partners in the fur trade and later, when that trade began to dwindle, formidable allies in the French–British struggle for supremacy in North America. Neither the French nor the British recognized the sovereign powers of Aboriginal nations. Furthermore, since the land Aboriginal people occupied was perceived as belonging to the French or British Crowns, neither the French nor the British were willing to legally recognize Aboriginal land rights. However, to the extent that it served their purposes, Euro-Canadian governments were prepared to enter into nation-to-nation relations with Aboriginal groups.

French Aboriginal policy aimed to assimilate the Aboriginal peoples (Tobias, 1983). This goal had nothing to do with mutual assimilation, whereby each group would take on some of the characteristics of the other. Instead, the French set out to achieve one-sided assimilation—making "them" like "us." They wanted to convert the Aboriginal peoples into servants of both the Christian God and the French king through convincing them to accept the values and practices of Roman Catholicism and French economic interests as well as the language, the laws, and the political authority of France.

As we move beyond the period of early contact, we see that the problems that characterized relations between Europeans and Aboriginal peoples were compounded when the state, to protect colonial interests, began to impose its authority on Aboriginal nations. In the nineteenth century, policy-makers and legislators took up the task of assimilation, establishing patterns of disruption with new and greater significance.

## From Self-Government to State Control

The Royal Proclamation of 1763 was the first significant legislation in Canada that concerned Aboriginal peoples. The proclamation re-established friendly relations with some Aboriginal groups, who had been dissatisfied with their earlier contacts with Euro-Christian missionaries (Nazar, unpublished), and ensured Aboriginal control of their own lands. Under the proclamation, and until 1857, tribal councils still made decisions about their own people.

Self-government was starting to erode as the government of the United Canadas assumed more responsibility for decisions about Aboriginal peoples. In 1857, the British government passed the *Gradual Civilization Act*, which proposed moving smaller groups of Aboriginal peoples onto reserves. The legislation provoked a serious crisis. Tribal councils, seeing its danger, rejected it. They demonstrated this rejection in a variety of ways: some councils removed their children from schools, others refused to participate in surveys and the census, and others stopped providing financial support for schools (Milloy, 1983). The Crown responded by centralizing responsibility for Aboriginal peoples with the United Canada.

Enfranchisement—from the French word, *franchiser*, "to cloak"—was one of the means used to promote assimilation from 1857 into the early twentieth century. To become Canadian citizens, and thereby acquire certain rights such as voting, property ownership, and advanced education, Aboriginal peoples had to prove their readiness to be absorbed into Euro-Canadian society. To become a citizen of Canada, an Aboriginal person was required to demonstrate an adequate level of "civilization," as defined from the European perspective.

A rigorous means test was applied to determine this. It included a demonstration that the candidate was able "to read and write either in the French or English language, was free of debt, and of good moral character" (Tobias, 1977). This criterion, as Tobias suggests, was paradoxical in that many Euro-Canadians, who were illiterate and in debt, were unable to meet the same standards of civilization. Nevertheless, Euro-Western leaders rationalized the double standard out of a belief that Aboriginal peoples were inherently inferior and in need of civilizing.

From a present-day perspective, these assumptions are obviously racist, but in the late nineteenth century, however, all parts of Euro-Western society endorsed them. As a result, Europeans accepted the double standard as an appropriate way of dealing with Aboriginal peoples.

## The *Indian Act* of 1876

Shortly after the *British North America Act* (*BNA Act*, 1867) came into effect, several pieces of legislation were passed that resulted in the *Indian Act* of 1876. Such legislation eroded Aboriginal peoples' control over their own lives in several ways. The *BNA Act* established the Canadian federal government and gave it jurisdiction over Indian affairs. At that point, federal control officially replaced Indian self-government. The *Indian Act* of 1876 established the Canadian government's complete control over the cultural, social, economic, and political activities of those persons defined in the act as Indian. In doing so, the federal government redefined who was Indian; the act defined Indian as

- Any male person of Indian blood reputed to belong to a particular band
- Any child of such person, or
- Any woman who is or was lawfully married to such a person (Venne 1981, 24)

By 1876, the government definition was limited to male persons, their children, and spouses. Obviously, these changes reflected increasing restrictions on who the government would define legally as an Indian person and, consequently, on who would be eligible to receive health, education, and social services, as well as tax exemptions available to Indians living in the reserve communities that were negotiated during the treaties in exchange for land for Europeans settlers.

In the post-Confederation period, education and Christianity were the key methods for assimilating Aboriginal peoples. In the late nineteenth and early twentieth centuries, Aboriginal children were removed from their families and communities for extraordinarily long periods of times. In some instances they were removed for their elementary school years and placed in residential schools to instill proper work habits. This measure was consistent with the civilization mission established by the humanitarians for poor children in Europe during the same time. Aboriginal children attended schools that taught them no more than rudimentary skills, with emphasis on the Euro-Western values of hard work. Taught by religious clerics, Aboriginal children were forbidden to speak their languages and subjected to racist curriculum delivered through force and domination (AFN, 1994; Mecredi & Turpel, 1993; Miller, 1997; Milloy, 1999; RCAP, 1996). Documented accounts of emotional, mental, spiritual, and physical abuse, including sexual abuse (AFN, 1994; Read, 1999), during the residential school era have resulted in profound and long-lasting effects for Aboriginal individuals, their families, and communities.

Some Aboriginal leaders resisted the government policy that required Aboriginal children to attend residential schools. It took threats of military intervention and starvation to force leaders to send the children to school (Kellough, 1980). As a consequence of the separation from their communities, many Aboriginal children lost access to their elders and, hence, to their traditions and values. By the 1950s, Aboriginal peoples were "caught between two cultures" (Shkilnyk, 1985, 81), and alcoholism, suicide, and violence in reserve communities began to replace many of the traditional ways.

In 1951, the *Indian Act* was amended again. Throughout the twentieth century, several amendments were made to the *Indian Act* in an attempt to increase the federal government's control over Status Indians. With the amendments to the *Indian Act* in 1951, under Section 87, provincial laws applied to Status Indians. As a consequence, Status Indian children were encouraged to attend provincial schools, and provincial child-welfare policies were enforced in reserve communities. The 1951 revisions also changed the legal definition of Indian: "Indian means a person who pursuant to this act is registered as an Indian or is entitled to be registered as an Indian" (Venne, 1981, 315).With these amendments, the provinces started to wield their new authority over First Nations in the area of child welfare. Aboriginal children were removed from their homes and placed in Euro-American homes and adoptive homes, and decisions about which children would be placed into Euro-American homes were based on Euro-Western, middle-class standards of child care. The traditional child-rearing practices of Aboriginal families were not considered appropriate. In addition, the many years of oppression experienced by Aboriginal peoples—through the residential schools, for example—meant that some had not developed appropriate parenting skills, according to the ways of either culture. Policy-makers decided that adoption by Euro-American families was the best way to assimilate Aboriginal children into mainstream society. As a result, Aboriginal children were again separated from their families and cultures, and many were sent to the United States, Europe, and other parts of Canada.

Removing large numbers of Aboriginal children from their culture by provincial legislation—in some communities as many as 77 percent of the children were removed (Johnson, 1983)—had adverse effects on the First Nations. Certain communities lost a whole generation of their children. The families' and communities' trauma resulting from this loss has begun to be understood only recently by Euro-Canadian policy-makers and social workers (RCAP, 1997).

Adopted children also suffered trauma; they found themselves surrounded by dominant ideologies and values reflected in schools, health care facilities, social service systems, the media, peers, and by Christian denominations. Values and ideas esteemed in their own cultures were not introduced or reinforced, and many of them did not fully fit in with the Euro-Canadian society. They often experienced discrimination and racism. Many children suffered serious deprivation and abuse at the hands of their adoptive families; others felt that they did not fit into their own culture or their adopted culture.

The 1951 amendments in the *Indian Act* occurred as our Euro-Canadian society's views shifted as a result of the events of World War II. The world's horror at Nazi Germany's policies of genocide generated a condemnation of racist practices in democratic societies—including Canada. Social equality, justice, and humanitarianism became important concepts. At the same time, treaty and Status Indians and other Aboriginal groups were becoming more vocal about their rights to education and health and social services. They also argued for the right to work, for adequate housing, and for equitable treatment within Canada.

The federal government suggested improving the terrible living conditions of Aboriginal peoples, probably motivated in part by the active participation in the war effort by thousands of Aboriginal people (Tobias, 1983). As well, government was shifting its laissez-faire approach to social programs to that of a welfare state. This shift in government function supported the ideological concepts of equality and humanitarianism. As the provinces developed social policy measures for dependent groups within their Euro-Western populations, they found the gaps between the slightly more generous provincial benefits for those people and the less generous federal benefits for Status Indians more difficult to justify (Getty & Lussier, 1983).

## The White Paper, 1969

The Hawthorn Report (1967), a study of social and economic conditions on reserves, revealed the large divide between the ideal of social equality and the deplorable circumstances in which Canada's Status Indians were living. It was obvious that the ways the federal authorities had addressed issues related to Aboriginal peoples had had negative results. Alternate approaches to improving social and economic conditions were needed. In 1969, the government responded to this challenge with its *Statement of the Government of Canada on Indian Policy*, also known as the White Paper.

Before writing their statement, government officials consulted various Aboriginal groups across Canada in meetings held between July 1968 and May 1969. The process raised expectations among Status Indians and other Aboriginal groups that the government was considering their priorities in formulating its policy changes relating to them. The prioritics Aboriginal groups cited included recognition of their special rights as the original inhabitants in Canada, and land-claim settlements to redress their historical grievances, particularly about agreements that were made with the Crown during treaty negotiations. Equally important, they wanted to participate directly and meaningfully in the development and implementation of policies that would affect their own future. However, the White Paper, released in June 1969, proved the government's consultative process had been a facade and had not influenced the intentions of Euro-Western policy-makers (Chiefs of Alberta, 1970).

Prime Minister Pierre Trudeau held strong views of Quebec's place in federalism and he rejected special status for Franco-Québécois during the early 1970s. These issues also had a significant impact on the framework for this policy on Aboriginal peoples across Canada. Trudeau rejected consideration of special status for any people. Rather, he believed in individualism, freedom, and competition—trademarks of liberal ideology— not only for individuals but also for cultural groups (Weaver, 1981). The White Paper policy was intended to create an equal society for all; Aboriginal peoples would not enjoy any special relationship with the federal government or any special status as original peoples of this land. In effect, this policy made the white settler society the new rightful and equal owners of the country. In response to the White Paper, Aboriginal peoples mounted a concerted effort to resist continued colonial oppression, regain control over their lives, and maintain their status as original peoples of this land (Erasmus, 1989; NIB, 1972).

Because the recommendations in the White Paper removed their entitlements to land and services, the chiefs of Alberta, in a document called *Citizens Plus*, asserted their collective cultural rights. They considered themselves legally and culturally separated and distinct from Euro-Canadians. In contrast to a policy of integration, Status Indians were advocating cultural pluralism with a goal of self-sufficiency that would free them from their political and economic dependence on the Canadian state. They could also maintain their own traditions and social practices. The message that the chiefs gave in *Citizens Plus* was clear: they were prepared to assume responsibility for the welfare of their own peoples. The institutions to handle this responsibility, they said, would be developed based on the idea of self-determination rather than on integration.

In contrast, the White Paper suggested that the institution providing services to Status Indian peoples should remain under Euro-Canadian control, but should be shifted from federal to provincial jurisdiction. This transfer of jurisdiction implied the integration of Status Indians and would effectively eliminate the federal government's fiduciary responsibility to them.

During the late 1970s, Aboriginal peoples came to see the repatriation of Canada's Constitution as a critical issue. They feared that the proposed Charter of Rights and Freedoms, which was to be included in the amended Constitution, would override their Aboriginal rights. Various Aboriginal groups, including Status and Non-Status Indians, Métis, and Inuit, insisted on their participation in the process of constitutional reform (Hawkes, 1985). After the Supreme Court of Canada prevented unilateral repatriation of the Constitution in 1981, Aboriginal leaders lobbied to ensure that Section 25—which recognizes existing Aboriginal and treaty rights—would be included in the charter. They wanted a guarantee that the equity rights of Section 15 would not challenge their rights. Since the *Royal Proclamation Act* of 1763 and various land-claim settlements, the Constitution had confirmed protection of all Aboriginal or treaty rights.

Aboriginal groups further pressed to have Section 35 of the Constitution entrenched. That section recognized the treaty and Aboriginal rights of Indian, Inuit, and Métis peoples, regardless of gender (*Constitution Act*, 1982). The identification and definition of the specific Aboriginal rights were left to a series of first ministers' conferences that ended in 1987 without accomplishing this task. Aboriginal peoples' insistence that the concept of self-government be included in the definition remained a major point of contention.

Until Aboriginal rights are identified and defined, the Constitution's protection of these rights remains ambiguous and weak. On the other hand, because of the Aboriginal peoples' powerful pressure on the issues of self-government and their rights, the federal government has not successfully formulated and imposed any unilateral modifications to Indian policy since 1982; the government needs the agreement of the Aboriginal peoples before implementing any new policy.

From the release of the White Paper in 1969 until the early 1980s, Status Indians and other Aboriginal groups demanded more control over decisions that affected them. During the mid-1970s (1974 until 1978), the National Indian Brotherhood and the Joint National Brotherhood Cabinet Committee strengthened Status Indians' political ability to influence decisions. At the same time, the demand presented in *Citizens Plus*—that the government consult with Status Indians before formulating policy—transformed into demands for self-government with the repatriation of the Constitution in 1982 and the implications of Section 35 for the rights of all Aboriginal peoples (Gibbins, 1986).

Repatriating the Constitution had serious ramifications for Aboriginal rights and self-government. To understand these questions from the Aboriginal perspective, the House of Commons established a committee (chaired by Keith Penner) to review these and related questions. The committee consisted of members of Parliament from the three major political parties in constituencies with significant numbers of Aboriginal peoples. Therefore, they were viewed as having some knowledge of the issues as the First Nations perceived them (Tennant, 1985). In addition to the MPs, three national Aboriginal organizations, the Assembly of First Nations, the Native Council of Canada, and the Native Women's Association, were all invited to work with the committee as ex officio members.

The committee released its *Report of the Special Committee*, also known as the Penner Report, in 1983. It came out in support of special and distinct status for Indian First Nations. The committee also recommended that self-government be entrenched in the Constitution (Penner et al., 1983). Instead of recommending details of any new legislation, the committee proposed general principles to allow all parties to reach consensus with enough flexibility to accommodate different arrangements for each First Nation. The committee proposed that Aboriginal and treaty rights be taken into account in any new legislation to conform to constitutional standards.

The government responded to the Penner Report by advocating increased powers for First Nations. However, the Liberals specified that decisions defining the new powers should be controlled by and subject to the approval of the federal government. In other words, a limited level of self-government was proposed. In contrast, Aboriginal peoples saw self-government as a control over all decisions that affected their lives. They would require the federal government to relinquish its control, particularly in the areas of health, social services, education, and economic development. The government, accordingly, accepted the principle of self-government in very broad terms, as it was later to do in the constitutional conferences; however, the federal government would continue to control the services for Aboriginal peoples. By the mid-1980s, Euro-Canadian policy-makers' ideas about Aboriginal peoples had started to favour ideas of special status and self-government, a shift away from the Liberal notion of social equality.

However, events in the 1990s overshadowed the actions of the various governments.

## The 1991 Royal Commission on Aboriginal Peoples

The Royal Commission on Aboriginal Peoples (RCAP) was established in August 1991 by an Order in Council of Parliament. In part it was an answer to the Oka Crisis of the previous summer. The commission's mandate is outlined in the following passage: "The Commission of Inquiry should investigate the evolution of the relationship among Aboriginal peoples (Indian, Inuit, and Métis), the Canadian government, and Canadian society as a whole. It should propose specific solutions, rooted in domestic and international experience, to the problems which have plagued those relationships and which confront Aboriginal peoples today. The Commission should examine all issues which it deems to be relevant to any or all of the Aboriginal peoples of Canada . . ." (RCAP, 1997, 2).

The commission consulted with Aboriginal peoples and recorded a large number of Aboriginal testimonials and traditional teachings to help shape their final recommendations. RCAP publications are voluminous and should be required reading for all social work and other students as they convey a comprehensive understanding of relations between Aboriginal peoples and the Canadian government. The publications point out the differences in the ways of thinking and living between the Aboriginal and non-Aboriginal groups. They also recount the oppression and dominance of Aboriginal peoples by Euro-Canadians and trace the drastic ramifications for Aboriginal peoples. The RCAP proposes that the Canadian government return to its original nation-to-nation relationship with Aboriginal governments, and spells out the ways that the transition to this re-established relationship might best be accomplished. The principles of this renewed relationship would be mutual recognition, mutual respect, mutual sharing, and mutual responsibility (RCAP, 1991). To date, the federal government has endorsed few of these recommendations, with one limited exception. The former Minister of Indian Affairs has apologized publicly for the treatment of Aboriginal children in residential schools and allocated funds for healing these former students. Currently, the federal government has approved a settlement for students who attended residential schools.

## The 1997 Delgamuukw Decision of the Supreme Court of Canada

Another significant event in December 1997, the handing down of the Delgamuukw decision by the Supreme Court of Canada, has offered direct legal support to Aboriginal peoples' demand for a new relationship between them and Canadians. In this decision, the justices of the Supreme Court of Canada set down the basis for decision making regarding the traditional lands of Aboriginal peoples; the locus of decision shifts from Euro-Canadian hegemony in decisions about Aboriginal peoples' lands and other entitlements to one where Aboriginal peoples have more involvement and say in the use of their traditional lands.

The 1997 Supreme Court decision on Delgamuukw lends support for the Aboriginal perspective on their relationship with the government of Canada. Some Aboriginal leaders take exception to having to accept a Euro-Canadian institution validation of what Aboriginal leaders have asserted all along: if Euro-Canadian governments would recognize and respect the inherent rights of Aboriginal peoples then the latter could regain control of their own lives. Aboriginal criticisms of the need for Delgamuukw are fair, in light of governments and resource industries in Canada having refused, until now, to recognize Aboriginal rights. Delgamuukw at least requires other parties to take the inherent rights of Aboriginal peoples into account in decisions that affect their lives. Any parties contemplating new resource developments that impinge on Aboriginal lands, whether under land claims or actually held by Aboriginal peoples, must enter into a new contract with those peoples and involve them in the development process. This marks a fundamental shift in government and business practice.

What is evident from events in the late 1990s—including the 1997 Delgamuukw decision, the establishment of Nunavut in 1999, and the May 1999 Nisga'a Treaty in British Columbia—is the shifting relations among Aboriginal and Canadian peoples. Whereas in the past federal and provincial governments made binding decisions about Aboriginal peoples and their territories, now Delgamuukw signals that such unilateral decisions by outside governments are no longer possible.

## Aboriginal Women

We would be remiss if we did not speak to some of the unique issues of Aboriginal women.[3] Egalitarian relationships structured the roles and responsibilities of the sexes in traditional Aboriginal societies. Aboriginal women participated actively in community decision making and contributed to overall family and community maintenance and survival. With Euro-Western contact and colonization, patriarchal and racist ideologies led to the subjugation of Aboriginal women. As a result, they found their roles and status in many communities were minimized and traditional forms of self-government replaced by male-dominated, hierarchical systems (Voyageur, 1996). No longer could they participate in decision making (Alfred, 1999; Stevenson, 1999).

The *Indian Act* evinces a clear example of gender discrimination: "The patriarchal provisions of the *Indian Act* removed Native women from their roles as decision-makers and teachers and robbed them of their voice in community affairs" (Anderson, 2000, 70). Until the act was amended in 1985, Aboriginal women who married non-Indians also lost their Aboriginal status. This completely denied them as well as their children any legal recognition as members of their home communities. They lost eligibility for any services or programs provided to those with "status" (Stevenson, 1999; Russell, 2000). However, when Aboriginal men who had "status" under the *Indian Act* married non-Indians, they retained their status. In fact, until 1985, non-Indian women who married an Indian man gained "status" and for all purposes were regarded as Indians, and so were their children by such marriages. The 1985 amendments to the *Indian Act, Bill C-31*, restored their legal status as Indians to women and their children. The amendments also allowed the women who had lost their status to have it reinstated (Stevenson, 1999; Russell, 2000).

Aboriginal communities have steadfastly resisted the extreme pressures to assimilate and integrate into Euro-Western society and have survived. This resistance finds its source partly in the many aspects of traditional Aboriginal women's roles. As Anderson (2000) points out, "underneath all the oppression and confusion, there has always been a part of them [Aboriginal women] that knew the strength and vitality of being a Native woman. Uncovering this part is an act of recognition, a physical, spiritual, and emotional remembering that can link us back to our ancestors and to a time when Native women were uniformly honoured and respected" (Preface). Many Aboriginal women still adhere to their traditional responsibilities for maintaining family and culture, ensuring a strong sense of community, and caring for future generations, including the land (Anderson, 2000; Voyageur, 1996).

## IMPLICATIONS FOR SOCIAL WORK

Aboriginal leaders argue convincingly that the deplorable economic and social conditions of their peoples over generations can be attributed to social policy-makers, social workers, and other agents of the government. They blame the Eurocentric interventions that have eroded Aboriginal cultural traditions and ways of living and thinking. According to those

---

3   It is important to note that this does not represent a comprehensive overview of the unique issues and challenges experienced by Aboriginal women in Canada. The reader is encouraged to seek out additional writings, including those listed in the References in this chapter.

who work with Aboriginal peoples, the high rates of incarceration, suicide, and violent death, as well as physical and sexual abuse, can be found in the experiences of several generations of children placed in residential schools and then in non-Native foster and adoptive homes. Some Aboriginal communities have watched their values and spiritual base erode through this lack of continuity from one generation to the next.

As part of an ongoing decolonization process, Aboriginal peoples are claiming and reaffirming their history, stories, and traditional beliefs. They are declaring their right to educate their own people and to have control over how their health and social services are provided. They are involved in the education of their own social work professionals in Canadian colleges and universities and are educating non-Natives as well, who can learn from them about helping others.

What are the implications of this history for social work practice as we move further into this millennium? Presumably, Aboriginal peoples' assertions about self-determination and self-government are goals that social workers can and should support, as these are consistent with the profession's ideological position of respecting self-determination and cultural diversity, advocating against oppression and inequity, and promoting non-discriminatory practice. These are all critical elements in our practice. However, some changes are needed in the ways that we practice if we are to act on these ideals.

First, we must acknowledge the extent to which learning in mainstream social work education programs is still predominantly middle-class, patriarchal, and white in its values, traditions, assumptions, and ways of thinking—qualities that are limited in their application to Aboriginal peoples and communities. Part of addressing these limitations must be building on an understanding of the colonial history and context of Aboriginal and of Euro-Canadian relations. We cannot expect relationships to improve unless we face up to ongoing colonial systems of practice, racism and oppression. While we have made some progress in the ways that we educate social workers about gender, race, and class, these issues are still mainly being taught in Canada by Euro-Canadian academics who are, for the most part, teaching Euro-Canadian students. We need to make structural shifts in how we prepare social workers for practice. Indeed, in some Canadian schools these shifts have begun.

In Canada, some Aboriginal human and social services courses and programs have been developed, controlled, and taught by Aboriginal faculty members and elders. The curricula in these programs reflect the Aboriginal beliefs, values, traditions, and ways of life and break down the barriers Aboriginal students in mainstream programs have had to overcome. More Aboriginal students stay in the programs, and, most important, the graduates are prepared to work in both Aboriginal communities and in mainstream settings on behalf of their people.

To ensure meaningful participation in Aboriginal human services programs, Aboriginal faculty members need greater representation in schools of social work to influence curriculum development, research, and publications. They need appropriate support so they can articulate fundamental Aboriginal values, traditions, assumptions, and ways of thinking, upon which to formulate and teach new social work theory and practice to all students. In this area, Euro-Canadian faculty members should follow, rather than lead.

There is another shift in the interactions between Aboriginal and non-Aboriginal students and faculty. Non-Aboriginal students and faculty need to learn other ways of living. In some schools, Aboriginal professors and students are beginning to guide this process. They are working to pull the concept of cultural diversity out of the abstract, creating an environment in which students and faculty can start to confront the limitations of their own belief systems. They can then examine how these beliefs influence their own practice and can thus learn other ways of thinking for working across cultures without appropriating others' traditions and cultures. This is a difficult, and at times painful, fine and crucial line to walk.

This shift in social work education would have obvious benefits in the education of mainstream students and faculty. It would have significant benefits for Aboriginal faculty and students. Mainstream students and faculty are learning that self-determination for Aboriginal peoples means that the same students and faculty will develop their own services and ways of helping their own peoples. When invited to become involved, mainstream social workers should provide the support requested and not interfere otherwise.

Recent shifts in social work education parallel the development of culturally appropriate social services within Aboriginal communities, rural and urban. These services draw on traditional ways of helping guided by community elders. They also operate along the lines of some Western European helping traditions that Aboriginal workers have adapted to fit within their own values and beliefs. Some Aboriginal peoples who have lost touch with some of their traditions are now learning more about these and seeking advice from their elders on how to bring traditional ceremonies into contemporary life.

The ways of helping promoted in many communities share a community-based approach. While individuals and families are assisted in their healing processes, ways of helping are integrally linked to the historical, social, economic, political, and spiritual context. The social work profession also recognizes that we need to make major structural changes to improve the economic and social conditions in which Aboriginal peoples live.

## CONCLUSION

In spite of the various studies and projects undertaken in the last three decades, there still remain two very different perspectives about the nature of relations among Aboriginal peoples and the governments of Canada. The Canadian federal and provincial governments still hold the view that all Aboriginal peoples are citizens of Canada and subject to all government policies and legislation, whether or not Aboriginal peoples agree to those policies, even when government decisions are unilateral ones.

Many Aboriginal leaders see the relationship as one between two nations, a relationship that flows from the treaties between governments: Canada (or the Crown, prior to Confederation) on the one hand and the various Aboriginal governments on the other. They assert their right to be part of any decision about their communities and to have a veto over policies and legislation that affect their peoples (RCAP, 1997).

The historical interactions between social workers and Aboriginal peoples have paralleled the differences at the political level. Many social workers, working in front-line, research, and policy agencies, have operated from ethnocentric and Eurocentric values and belief systems, imposing these on Aboriginal peoples.

In the last decade, the ramifications of past interventions by non-Aboriginal social workers have become evident, and some social workers are starting to support Aboriginal social workers in their mission to establish services and policies that are consistent with Aboriginal peoples' own values and beliefs.

However, it is difficult for many non-Aboriginal social workers to give up control in setting policies and in working across cultures. Doing so requires that they accept the role of learner and create space for Aboriginal social workers to work in their own ways. Just as feminist theory has changed the ways that we, as a profession, view our society and the people living in it, so too are theories and practices advocated by Aboriginal social work educators and practitioners revolutionizing the profession's understanding of race and culture, particularly regarding Aboriginal peoples in Canada. The question for all new social workers is whether they will become allies or a barrier to the establishment of Aboriginal services and ways of working.

# References

Anderson, Kim. 2000. *A Recognition of Being: Reconstructing Native Womanhood*. Toronto: Second Story Press.

Brizinski, Peggy. 1989. *Knots on a String: An Introduction to Native Studies in Canada*. Saskatoon: University of Saskatchewan.

Chiefs of Alberta. 1970. *Citizens Plus*. Edmonton: The Indian Association of Alberta.

Culhane, Dara. 1998. *The Pleasure of the Crown*. Vancouver: Talon Press.

Foster, Michael. 1982. *Canada's First Language*. Ottawa: Commissioner of Official Languages.

Frideres, James. 1983. *Native People in Canada: Contemporary Conflicts*. Scarborough, ON: Prentice-Hall Canada Inc.

Gibbins, Roger. 1986. Canadian Indians and the Canadian Constitution: A Difficult Passage Toward an Uncertain Destination. In *Arduous Journey: Canadian Indians and Decolonization*, ed. J. Rick Ponting. Toronto: McClelland & Stewart.

Government of Canada. 1969. *The Statement of the Government of Canada on Indian Policy*. Ottawa: Minister of Supply and Services.

Haig-Brown, Celia. 1988. *Resistance and Renewal: Surviving the Indian Residential School*. Vancouver: Tillacum Library.

Hawkes, David. 1985. *Negotiating Aboriginal Self-Government*. Kingston, ON: Queen's University Institute of Intergovernmental Relations.

Hawthorn, H.B. 1967. *A Survey of the Contemporary Indians of Canada*. Ottawa: Indian Affairs Branch.

Johnson, Patrick. 1983. *Native Children and the Child Welfare System*. Toronto: James Lorimer and Company.

Kellough, Gail. 1980. From Colonialism to Imperialism: The Experience of Canadian Indians. In *Structured Inequality in Canada*, ed. John Harp and John R. Hofley. Scarborough: Prentice-Hall Canada.

Knox, R.H. 1982. *Indian Conditions: A Survey. Government of Canada*. Ottawa: Ministry of Indian Affairs and Northern Development.

Milloy, John. 1983. The Early *Indian Act*: Developmental Strategy and Constitutional Change. In *As Long as the Sun Shines and the Water Flows*, ed. Ian A.L. Getty and Antoine S. Lussier. Vancouver: University of British Columbia Press.

National Indian Brotherhood, Assembly of First Nations. 1988. *The MacPherson Report on Tradition and Education: Towards a Vision of Our Future*. Ottawa: Department of Indian Affairs and Northern Development.

Odjig-White. 1992. *Nishnaabe Kinoomaspwin Naadmaadwin Field Manual for SWRK 3605* EN. Sudbury, ON: Laurentian University Press.

Penner, Keith, et al. 1983. *Report of the Special Committee on Indian Self-Government.* Ottawa: House of Commons Issue #40.

Royal Commission on Aboriginal Peoples. 1997. *Looking Forward, Looking Back.* Ottawa: Canada Communications Group Publishing.

Royal Commission on Aboriginal Peoples. 1997. *For Seven Generations: An Information Legacy of the Royal Commission on Aboriginal Peoples.* Ottawa: Libraxus Inc.

Russell, Dan. 2000. *A People's Dream: Aboriginal Self-government in Canada.* Vancouver: UBC Press.

Shkilnyk, Anastasia. 1985. *A Poison Stronger than Love.* New Haven: Yale University Press.

Stevenson, Winona. 1999. Colonialism and First Nations Women in Canada. In *Scratching the Surface: Canadian Anti-racist Feminist Thought,* eds. Enakshi Dua and Angela Robertson. Toronto: Women's Press.

Tennant, Paul. 1985. Aboriginal Rights and the Penner Report on Indian Self-government. In *The Quest for Justice*, ed. M. Boldt and A. Long. Toronto: The University of Toronto Press.

Tobias, John. 1976. Protection, Civilization, Assimilation: An Outline History of Canada's Indian Policy. In *The Western Canadian Journal of Anthropology* 6 (2).

Tobias, John. 1983. Protection, Civilization, Assimilation: An Outline History of Canada's Indian Policy. In *As Long as the Sun Shines and the Water Flows*, ed. Ian A.L. Getty and Antoine S. Lussier. Vancouver: University of British Columbia Press.

Venne, Sharon Helen. 1981. *Indian Act and Amendments, 1868–1975: An Indexed Collection.* Saskatchewan: University of Saskatchewan, Native Law Centre.

Voyageur, Cora J. 1996. Contemporary Indian. In *Women in Visions of the Heart: Canadian Aboriginal Issues,* ed. David Alan Long and Olive Patricia Dickason. Toronto: Harcourt Brace Canada.

Weaver, Sally. 1981. *Making Canadian Indian Policy.* Toronto: University of Toronto Press.

# CHAPTER 8

# Our Bilingual Heritage: The Context of Official Languages Policy

*Linda Turner*

Social welfare programs and policies reflect and reinforce the cultural norms and established practices of governing powers. Canadian social welfare as it appears today was shaped by the cultures of the linguistically different colonizing forces of France and Britain. Struggles with one another and with First Nations peoples who found themselves invaded by oppressive European forces would eventually determine whose norms would prevail and who would maintain ruling status. In this chapter, we examine how Canada came to be referred to today as a French- and English-speaking bilingual nation, and the implications for social welfare policies and practices.

If the history of Canada had not been what it was, and if First Nations societies had been granted founding nation status, "official languages" in Canada might refer to a multitude of languages. Even today, authors such as Vaz and Foucher (2004) note

> To date, it seems that the federal government has failed to provide a mechanism by which to ensure the recognition of Aboriginal language rights. However, the implementation of such rights may require the government to provide the necessary financial and human resources for ensuring that these rights are respected. . . . It seems to us that there is at least some duty on the part of the federal government to ensure that Aboriginal languages are preserved (p. 311).

Having a national policy of French and English bilingualism is of great importance and significance to individuals and communities who use French to communicate in their personal and business lives. As Isajiw (1999) observes,

> The policy of bilingualism in Canada gave the French a certain recognition of equality with the British. It also gave them an opportunity to gain entry and more influence in the civil service of the federal government (p. 120).

While official recognition at the national level provides assurances in the delivery of federal programs, many social welfare programs are administered by the provincial government, a fact that poses some limitations: "It is important to note that the majority of services provided to the public are provided by provincial institutions. It thus seems unfortunate that only New Brunswick has agreed to be bound by sections 16 and 20 of the Charter. Any true policy of bilingualism in Canada must have provincial participation as a necessary component" (Vaz & Foucher, 2004, p. 278).

This chapter begins with reflections on reasons why language issues, in this case French and English, are important when discussing social welfare concerns. That section is followed by a demographical linguistic portrait of Canada today. A brief historical summary is then provided, followed by consideration of aspects of bilingualism in political and legislative realms, in health, in education, and in employment. The chapter concludes with references to initiatives that have contributed to competence in and respect for French–English bilingualism among Canadians, and areas where further commitments are required.

# WHY LANGUAGE IS IMPORTANT

Why is Canada's policy of official bilingualism worthy of contemplation? References to anglophone and francophone realities or to bilingualism are often absent in the indexes of major works on Canadian social welfare (Armitage, 2003; Hick, 2007; Chappell, 2006). Yet Bishop (1994), when explaining the terms *anglophone* and *francophone* in her glossary, notes that while many people outside Canada lack an awareness of the fact, "The struggles between these two groups, dating from the English conquest of New France in the eighteenth century, is a major feature of the Canadian political landscape" (p. 127).

The power and significance of language is likely understood more profoundly by individuals who do not have the everyday privilege of communicating in their first language. Part of the centrality of language is explained by Breton (1999), who proposes that "the fact that a person's identity is acquired, to a degree at least, through a particular language easily leads to the conviction that language and identity are inseparable—that one's identity would be hurt by a change of language" (p. 104). Thompson (2003) claims that while issues linking power and language are recognized in identifying oppressive use of words, for example, consideration of power issues in the selection of one language over another still needs further development and exploration.

Granting official language status to French and English provides much to both linguistic groups, for it "means that official language groups will enjoy protections going far beyond tolerance. The purpose behind the adoption of an official language is in fact to encourage the flourishing of official language groups as a component of the democratic ideal" (Bastarache, 2004, p. 6).

He continues: "Language rights serve to define the values of the nation in regard to participation in public affairs, fair treatment, cultural diversity, and recognition of the will of the language community to flourish. They speak persuasively of the conditions for the existence of a language community" (p. 10).

This message is echoed by Graham Fraser, author of *Sorry, I Don't Speak French* and Commissioner of Official Languages in Canada at the time of writing this chapter, when he states

> We often tend to forget that in Canada there are four million unilingual francophones and 20 million unilingual anglophones. The *Official Languages Act* (OLA) is not there to force Canadians to learn the other official language; it's there to protect the rights of people who speak only one of the languages, so that they have access to services of the same quality as those of unilingual people speaking the other language. The OLA must be seen from the perspective of a service having an impact on quality of life (p. 5).

While it may be tempting to pay only cursory attention to contextual aspects of the historical developments in language policy, there are issues in the interplay between these two dominant forces which hold importance for other cultural groups. As Isajiw (1999) writes, "Ever since the conquest, French Candians have struggled to preserve their own identity and to gain a measure of equality vis-à-vis the British. This struggle, however, has had implications beyond the French-English relationship. The Canadian government's policies in relation to other ethnic groups have been affected by this struggle" (p. 45). He goes on to explain that the *Quebec Act* of 1774 and the *BNA Act* of 1867 officially recognized the principle of ethnic pluralism in this country, in its offering control of civil rights and education to Quebec and, in so doing, to the other provinces.

Social welfare includes a multitude of programs for Canadians, thus the opportunity to be served at an equivalent level of service in French or English is an institutionalized demonstration of respect and a commitment to social justice in a central facet of everyday life.

## TERMINOLOGY AND DEMOGRAPHICS

Stebbins (2000) indicates that those who "routinely speak French or English are known in linguistics as francophones or anglophones" (p. 20). An additional clarification sometimes necessary is differentiating between first-language and second-language francophones and anglophones. He also notes that when a linguistic group is said to be a minority society, most of their day-to-day activities take place in another language, whether when seeking medical treatment, working, using government services, or conducting business transactions. The state of living in a majority society for French-speaking people indicates the language used in day-to-day interactions with institutions is French. The same author asserts that Quebec is the only majority francophone society within Canada; however, he identifies Caraquet and the Acadian Peninsula of New Brunswick and the cities Hearst and Kapuskasing in Ontario, where numbers of francophones are proportionally very high, as some regions where the "majority" status for francophone societies can also be claimed.

Statistical information available from Statistics Canada reveals that 17 352 315 Canadians identified English as their mother tongue (defined as the language first learned at home as a child and still understood) in 2001; 6 703 325 citizens identified French as their mother tongue. The next five mother tongue languages include Chinese, which is applied as a broad category including Cantonese, Mandarin, Hakka, and others, with 853 745 speakers; Italian with 469 485; German with 438 080; Punjabi with 271 220, and Spanish with 245 000 (Statistics Canada, 2001). Shifts in the ethnic diversity of the Canadian population are important. Armitage (2003) points out that "until the 1970s, the assumption of Canadian Social Policy was that immigrants (and Aboriginal peoples) would assimilate to either the English or French majorities. This is clearly no longer the case" (p. 16).

Regarding languages used, 18% of Canadians, or one in every five, speaks both English and French, while 13% speak only French and 67% speak only English, according to 2001 census information (Pendakus, Hedges, & King, 2003). Great variation among Canadian cities exists: while in Halifax only 12% of the population can speak both languages, more than half of Montreal's residents (53%) are bilingual, with 38% being able to speak only French and 8% able to speak only English. Toronto and Vancouver, on the other hand, reveal nine out of ten people who speak English only of the two official languages, and 8% who speak both French and English.

Of languages spoken in the home, 66.7% of Canadians identify English, 21.8% French, less than one percent both English and French, and nearly 10% only speak a non-official language at home.

Reference to French-speaking communities requires respect for the diversity of those communities. In francophone Ontario, for example, stability is more evident in the east, which boasts higher numbers, a strong youth population, the highest rates of educational achievement in Franco-Ontario, and a mobile and dynamic francophone population. Meanwhile in the north, the past few decades have witnessed a decline in the francophone population, in part attributable to the exodus of young people from the area (Pendakus, Hedges, & King, 2003).

Some of the socio-economic variations among francophone minority populations can be found when comparing income also: Franco-Ontarians have the highest incomes, averaging $32 300, followed by Western Francophones coming in at $29 700, and Acadians at the lowest level of $23 000. Levels of schooling are similar for the first two groups, while Acadian populations have lower than average formal education in comparison. Another variation is a continuing homogeneity among francophones of Atlantic Canada in terms of ethnic and religious affiliations, while francophones living in the West and Ontario have seen stronger trends of diversity thanks to greater immigration from French-speaking countries (Floch & Frenette, 2005)

## HISTORICAL SUMMARY

Historical accounts of French–English relations vary in the degree to which they describe the conflicts, tensions, and injustices that have been part of the development. Investigative journalist Normand Lester (2002) shares disturbing evidence of cruelty and disrespect in areas such as the Acadian deportation (which some authors now refer to as a genocide), the Louis Riel hanging, and the widespread anti-Catholic and anti-French Orange Lodge movement that pervaded the Canadian landscape in the 1800s and 1900s.

Bastarache (2004) maintains that if one wishes to attempt to fully understand the context in which language rights and linguistic policies have developed, it is necessary to gain an appreciation of the colonial and more recent historical occurrences, including the agreements inherent in the constitutional agreements of 1867 and of 1982. He maintains that today's "language guarantees reflect political reality and ideals rather than the desirability of language maintenance for its own sake" (p. 6).

Some major landmarks during the historical journey of the past few centuries include the Treaty of Utrecht of 1713, when Acadia was ceded to England and no provision was made for the use of the French language in spite of its being virtually the only language in use in the region (Bastarache, 2004); the Seven Years' War, which signalled the beginning of the deportation of Acadian settlers in the 1750s for failing to swear allegiance to the British Crown; the battle of the Plains of Abraham in 1759; and the Treaty of Paris of 1763 in which Quebec was transferred into English hands (Denis, 1999).

With the 1791 creation of an Upper and Lower Canada, a blanket of bilingualism remained in Lower Canada but disappeared in Upper Canada, where a policy of official unilingualism was imposed in 1839 (Bastarache, 2004).

History also reveals the adoption of the 1840 *Act of Union,* an act that would have done away with French language use in its intent to combine the two regions into one province. Only a year later, however, French was reintroduced in the legislative process and the judicial system continued to operate bilingually (Bastarache, 2004).

A list of major pieces of legislation pertaining to language rights would include the *Constitution Act*, 1867, which allowed for limited bilingualism in legislation and courts through Section 133, applicable to Quebec and federal Parliament; Ontario's reconfirmation of unilingualism (1897); and the *Manitoba Act* of 1870,which originally provided constitutional language rights for French (Bastarache, 2004). Only 20 years later, Manitobans would see English become the only official language proclaimed in legislation and the courts, and despite rulings late in the 1800s and early in the 1900s that the declaration was unconstitutional, it was ninety-one years before the government would see fit to respect those decisions (Denis, 1999).

Much more recently, hugely significant legislation was born in the form of the adoption of the *Official Languages Act* by the federal government in 1969 following recommendations of the Laurendeau-Dunton Commission. The same year saw New Brunswick pass the *Official Languages of New Brunswick Act* while Quebec's *Act for the Promotion of the French Language Bill 63* saw the light of day. While not conferring official language status, Bastarache (2004) indicates its intent was to promote French. It was in 1974 that Quebec adopted its own first official language act, *Bill 22*. Currently, Quebec language legislation consists of the Charter of the French Language (*Bill 101*) and its amendments (Bastarache, 2004).

A summary of the implications of the Canadian Charter of Rights and Freedoms (1982) and its guarantees with regard to languages are described by Bastarache (2004). He writes that the new sections contained in this legislation

> . . . have added New Brunswick to the provinces providing for institutional bilingualism and have bolstered the rights prescribed by section 133 in a significant way. Section 23 in particular has established a right to education in the minority language in each of the provinces and territories. Section 20 has created the right to government services at the federal level and in New Brunswick. That province is also, since 1993, subject to section 16.1, a provision providing for the equality of its official language communities and their right to distinct cultural and educational institutions (p. 24).

Historically significant issues during the 20th century in the relationship between Canada and Quebec merit concentrated consideration and reflection which are beyond the scope of this chapter. Topics such as the Quiet Revolution, le Parti Québécois, Quebec's *Official Languages Act* (*Bill 22*), the FLQ Crisis, "Distinct Society" status, Referendums in 1980 and 1995, and defeat of the Meech Lake and Charlottetown Accords are all worthy of closer examination. Harrison and Friesen (2004) sum up essential questions about relationships between Quebec and the rest of Canada: "is it possible for English-speaking Canada to acknowledge Quebec's distinctiveness in a meaningful way, to grant recognition and respect for Québecois identity, and to give Quebec sufficient power for its survival within Canada's existing state structures?" (p. 77).

An error often made by English-speaking Canadians, and even more often by citizens of other countries, is the assumption that French-speaking Canada exists only in Quebec. Francophone populations can be found, in varying sizes, in all provinces and territories. A few comprehensive descriptions of French-speaking populations in every region in Canada are available. They are helpful to increase awareness of current issues faced by linguistic minorities in communities outside of Quebec (Allaire, 1999; Stebbins, 2000; Thériault, 1999).

As the first established francophone community in what we now know as Canada, Acadia deserves a special place in this historical overview. The story of the ravaging upheaval and exile imposed on the non-arms-bearing society by British authorities in the mid-1700s gained recognition thanks to Longfellow's poem *Evangeline*, but recently several books have appeared discussing Acadian origins and the deportation as the 250th anniversary of the deportation was acknowledged in 2005 (Arsenault, 1994; Pitre, 2003; Reid, Basque, Mancke, Moody, Plank & Wicken, 2004). Dubois and Boudreau (1996) offer a valuable collection of writings regarding Acadians and their language in a minority context.

Moss (2004), in an article entitled "The Drama of Identity in Canada's Francophone West," examines how through plays and performance, the preoccupations of French-speaking people in those regions are shared. Moss (2004) recognizes that establishing a francophone identity in Ontario, Manitoba, Alberta, and British Columbia continues to require persever- ance and commitment, to counteract the forces of assimilation.

## ASPECTS OF BILINGUALISM IN CANADIAN SOCIETY

### Policies and Legislation

Within the past 40 years, French and English bilingualism in Canada has stepped onto solid footing because of two key pieces of federal legislation: The Charter of Rights and Freedoms, written into the *Constitution Act* (1982), and the *Official Languages Act* (1969). The former decrees that English and French are the two official languages of the nation, and, therefore, ensures access to and use of either language in parliamentary activities, courts of law, and federal public services (Stebbins, 2000).

The *Official Languages Act* (1969) represents the country's federal bilingualism policy, and its focus is the maintenance and transmission of language and culture by anglophones and francophones living in a minority linguistic status. The work was assigned to the Department of the Secretary of State while the position of Commis- sioner of Official Languages provided a "watchdog" to observe progress in promoting bilingualism. In 1988, an additional *Official Languages Law* expanded the responsibil- ities of the department to include community development wherever either linguistic group was a minority. Thus, support for clubs, community radio stations, festivals, net- works, and various other events was institutionalized (Stebbins, 2000), while the ombudsman role was also strengthened through the creation of the Office of the Com- missioner of Official Languages.

Hayday (2005) notes that critics of the Government of Canada's Official Languages efforts view them as "failing to stem the tide of Quebec separatism, failing to foster sub- stantial growth in the size of official-language minority communities elsewhere in the country, [and] failing to produce a nation of fluently bilingual citizens" (p. 179). His study documents Canadian language policy development in education and also explores Cana- dian federalism. The author challenges the criticisms mentioned as not being founded on solid analysis and insists that it is a mistake to attempt to draw conclusions prematurely about the impact of initiatives such as the Official Languages Policy in Education Pro- grams, which will demonstrate results only after an established period of time. He cites French immersion programs, second-language teacher training, and minority-language learning as resounding examples of success given their taken-for-granted presence and durability in Canadian society today.

### Language in the Courts

Courtroom environments can be perceived as both intimidating and formidable. If one must understand proceedings and defend one's self in another language, there is a real dan- ger of misrepresentation. Bastarache (2004) points out that "language laws can promote equal access to the courts for members of an official language minority, irrespective of their personal language skills" (p. 8). He goes on to say that provisions found in Section 133 of the *Constitution Act,* 1867, and Section 16 of the Canadian Charter of Rights and Freedoms of 1982

> . . . establish rights available in Quebec and New Brunswick, as well as in federal institutions. As they can be exercised by any person, these rights do not reflect a desire to privilege the two official languages only to the extent that they are the mother tongues of individuals. For instance, by virtue of subsection 19(2) of the Canadian Charter of Rights and Freedoms, an Anglophone can ask for a trial in French in New Brunswick. Someone whose first language is neither English nor French can, similarly, enforce the right to choose either official language (p. 19).

## Health

There are great variations among the issues and contexts depending on which region of which province one is examining. When people are unable to access services in their first language, the quality of their care is at risk. While in New Brunswick the right to health care services in French or English is entrenched, in the neighbouring province of Nova Scotia the challenge of obtaining services in French presents the same scenario described for unilingual English people in Quebec:

> . . . in times of crisis, or when people have something important to express, they tend to revert to the language they know best. Canadian citizens needing health care or social services may find themselves in situations where expression in a second language, regardless of their level of bilingualism, impedes communication. This issue, then, is critical for the hundreds of thousands of English-speaking Quebeckers who prefer to express themselves in English when seeking health services (Vaz & Foucher, 2004, p. 328).

## Education

Martel (2001) describes the significance of a legislated right to education in an official language for minorities, which puts the onus on provincial or territorial governments to pay for instruction and provide facilities "where numbers warrant":

> . . . section 23 was one of the most important milestones in this history of francophone and Acadian communities in Canada . . . court judgments, including three from the Supreme Court of Canada . . . have confirmed that the Canadian duality is a part of the political landscape and affirmed the right of francophone and Acadian communities' language schools . . . unconvinced governments have been obliged to recognize the rights and needs of francophone and Acadian communities; the communities themselves have taken control of their future by creating community structures . . . this section has contributed to the increase in the number of French-language schools (+47 schools) and in student populations (+2.3%) since 1986 (p. 34).

As much as the accomplishments in obtaining French-language education throughout Canada are worthy of praise, there is also a consciousness of the influences of globalization as a threat to culture and language, and leaders where French has a minority existence in particular have been vocal with their calls for strategies to strengthen use of the French language and identification of roles of communities in supporting that development (Landry & Rousselle, 2003; Martel, 2001).

## Employment

Bilingualism requirements for jobs represent a site where the personal issue—finding employment—intersects with the political issue—ensuring the public has access to service in their language. An important clarification is offered by Vaz and Foucher (2004): ". . . for institutions affected, section 16 does not require that all employees be bilingual. Instead, this guarantee is satisfied by the employment of a sufficient number of bilingual agents who work in federal or New Brunswick institutions that provide services to and deal directly with the public" (p. 294). The more often individual employees are in frequent direct contact with the public or directly involved in delivering a service, the more essential it is for that individual to be capable of communicating competently in either official language (Vaz & Foucher, 2004).

The same authors also comment on the issue of adequacy of translation and the standard of provision of service in the language of choice of the client:

> Recourse to translation, (however), cannot become a permanent substitute for the recruitment or training of qualified bilingual personnel where necessary. If it is necessary to establish personal contact between the public servant and the public, not only will translation be inadequate, but considerations arise with regard to the quality of service. If a government specialist cannot assure precise and complete service unless he is working in his mother tongue, or if he must delegate his responsibilities to an assistant or other replacement that is less qualified or less familiar with the file, we must conclude that service has not been received in the language of choice of the client. While we appreciate that federal institutions may not yet have secured completely bilingual resources, 'services' cannot reasonably mean 'partial services' or 'inferior services' (Vaz & Foucher, 2004, p. 267).

Another common focus of discussion is whether insisting on bilingual employees is required or, if not, how work units can be maintained with linguistic needs in mind, to which Vaz and Foucher (2004) offer this opinion:

> Each government organization must attempt to strike a balance by taking into account the nature of the service offered, the frequency of contacts with the public, the linguistic composition of the region to be served, and the importance of the position in the delivery of services. The more frequently contact with the public is required and the more often the office holder participates directly in the delivery of services, the more necessary it is for him or her to be able to serve the public directly in either official language (p. 267).

## EFFECTIVE INITIATIVES AND STRATEGIES REGARDING BILINGUALISM

A recent study examining factors influencing favourable attitudes toward Canada's officially bilingual reality (Adsett & Morin, 2004) notes positive associations with bilingualism are more likely when there is "contact with the other linguistic community (whether personal or through travel), the ability to understand the other language, and a good opportunity to learn the other official language" (p. 147).

There are numerous programs that promote increased linguistic and cultural appreciation along with skill competence. One example is the six-week summer immersion programs housed at universities and available to both native French and native English speakers. Social and cultural activities are combined with academic offerings, and bursaries for accommodations, food, and tuition provide access to participants unable to cover those expenses.

Many younger students have the chance to connect with youth from other official language communities through letter-writing programs and group exchanges with schools. In New Brunswick, an organization known as Dialogue New Brunswick facilitates such exchanges. The organization, Parents for French, has also been highly effective in achieving recognition for the value of anglophone children becoming bilingual.

Katimavik, a federally funded voluntary community service program for youth aged 17–21, which began in 1976, also maintains second language learning as one of its highest priorities. Groups reflect the country's diversity among their 11 members. As they live together in one household and have brief billeting periods with families in the three communities they travel to during the nine months, many participants achieve functional if not fluent bilingualism by the program's conclusion.

Numerous federal employees have benefited from opportunities for brief or extended immersion training programs with English or French language learning institutes. Newcomers to the country have also had some access to this essential service, although there have been criticisms that financial support to ensure availability and access is too limited.

Leadership, co-operation, and persistence are evident in initiatives that prove to be most successful, as the French Language Services Committee established by the Social Planning Council of Ottawa-Carleton in 1976 demonstrates (Bilodeau & Dugas, 2001). The accomplishments of that particular group include Ontario's first francophone alcohol and drug addiction residential treatment facility, a study of services for French-speaking older adults, a report on needs for additional French-speaking professionals for the health and social services sector in that province, and contributions toward the creation of Université d'Ottawa's MSW program in French. In 2006, a new organization was launched, the Assemblée de la francophonie de l'Ontario, which offers a collective voice for the 549 000 residents of that province whose mother tongue is English (http://afo.franco.ca).

In a 2007 communiqué by Josée Verner, the minister responsible for La Francophonie and Official Languages, there was a listing of federal government initiatives and supported projects that include such things as consultative meetings with minority official-language representatives, $1 billion in four-year bilateral education agreements with all provinces and territories, support for the *Sommet des communautés francophones et acadienne* (http://www.fcfa.ca/home/index.cfm) of 2007, funding of combined community-school centres, launching of a strategic plan related to encouraging immigration in French-language minority communities, and *Bill C-23*, a piece of legislation related to ensuring individuals who have had charges laid against them are aware of the right to communicate in the language of their choice.

Private agencies and non-profit community resources may struggle to create bilingual environments when resources are stretched and funding is uncertain. It is important to note that a major site for assimilation is in one's workplace. Canadian Heritage currently offers a guide entitled "Making Your Organization Bilingual" (http://www.

pch.gc.ca/guide/postes_bilingues_e.html), which takes readers through steps and lived experiences of successful organizations. Bilingualism in professional social work associations in New Brunswick and Ontario reflect commitments to respecting French and English in service to membership.

## AREAS NEEDING DEVELOPMENT

Morf (1976) proposed that "harmony and mutual understanding are possible on condition that both linguistic groups are willing to learn and use both languages and to consider each other as equal" (p. 90). Certainly unilingualism can obstruct the construction of the highest quality of social welfare programs, services, and policies for the simple reason that scholars and others engaging in research are not able to access reports and studies in other languages. If one takes the case of social work education, how can unilingual anglophone students and professors integrate, utilize, and replicate creative and successful accomplishments or ideas of their fellow Canadians if they cannot read or understand French? They would need to rely on the generosity of the French-speaking authors and presenters, willing to bear the expense and to donate the time required to translate their findings and insights. If one cannot read in French, one will not benefit from the body of literature in academic journals such as *Reflets, Revue ontaroise d'intervention sociale et communautaire*, or from *Nouvelles pratiques sociales*, written by fellow Canadians. It is ironic that literature reviews often contain references from American, British, Australian, or other national journals yet may not contain a single reference written in Canada by a francophone. The same limitation also exists for unilingual francophones who also are unable to integrate knowledge or consider ideas contained in materials available only in English. How much richer and more beneficial might the policies and programs become if bilingual and multilingual communication among more Canadians allowed advanced exchanges of knowledge and practices?

If supporting and expanding bilingualism in this country is a priority, what then can be done? Statistics reveal that francophones are more likely than anglophones to become bilingual, thus worth exploring are factors interfering with second language fluency among anglophones. Dunn (2002), in his doctoral dissertation entitled "Effects of power and identity on access to participation in second language communities," uncovers the complexity of attempting to practise using French as a second language in New Brunswick:

> With respect to power, anglophones in the province are in a difficult situation when it comes to accessing francophone communities. On the one hand, they are in a powerful position due to the dominance of English in the province. Because of the difference in status between the two languages, English is automatically imposed as the language of communication. Its use as the default language is a firmly entrenched social norm in New Brunswick, and one which can override the competing norm of using French in francophone spaces. . . . Learners have little control over the linguistic resources of the communities to which they seek access, and in many cases, they feel powerless to establish French as the language of interaction. The power to do so is considered to be held primarily by the native speaker (p. 202).

It follows that in addition to summoning up the personal courage to take risks when attempting to practise a second language, sociological dynamics need to be examined and overcome so it becomes more common and comfortable for individuals to utilize a second language during daily communication exchanges.

Social workers from the officially bilingual province of New Brunswick mention numerous approaches and actions that affirm linguistic respect for clients and co-workers, including advocating for translation at meetings, contributing to minority language institutional and organizational development, articulating and affirming the right to be served in one's first language, and facilitating same-language formal and informal support services (Turner, 2005).

Whether or not professional programs should assign a higher value to official bilingualism among applicants and during graduate preparation merits consideration. Doing so would expand the eventual capacity to serve individuals and client groups in both official languages wherever services are offered, and would demonstrate appreciation for the significance of language and for official bilingualism as a principle. In turn, that increased understanding of the importance of having access to service in one's first language may generate a commitment to greater social welfare provision in other languages.

## CONCLUSION

In this chapter, Canada's status as a French and English officially bilingual nation is considered through a historical lens. Implications of official bilingualism in the legal realm, in health, in education, and in employment are considered. Beneficial initiatives and strategies are offered along with suggestions of where additional development is required. As Canada's cultural, ethnic, and linguistic diversity expands, issues related to language use and social welfare service delivery and administration become more pronounced. Achievements gained through official bilingualism policies may provide valuable reference points for new regional or national policies that respond to other linguistic realities throughout Canada.

## References

Adsett, M. & Morin, M. (2004). Contact and regional variation in attitudes towards linguistic duality in Canada. *Journal of Canadian Studies,* 38(2):129–150.

Allaire, G. (1999). *La francophonie canadienne: Portraits.* Sainte-Foy (QC): CIDEF-AFI.

Armitage, A. (2003). *Social welfare in Canada* (4th ed.), Don Mills, ON: Oxford University Press.

Arsenault, B. (1994). *History of the Acadians.* Saint-Laurent, QC: Editions Fides.

Bastarache, M. (Ed.) (2004). *Language rights in Canada* (2nd ed.), Cowansville (QC): Les Éditions Yvon Blais Inc.

Bilodeau, F. H. & Dugas, Y. (2001). French language services: An integral part of our bilingual heritage. In J. C. Turner & F. J. Turner, *Canadian social welfare* (104–117). Toronto: Pearson.

Breton, A. (Ed.) (1999). The cultural yield on languages and linguistic assimilation. In A. Breton, *Exploring the economics of languages* (89–109).

Chappell, R. (2006). *Social welfare in Canadian society* (3rd ed.), Toronto: Thomson Nelson.

Denis, W. (1999). Language policy in Canada. In Peter S. Li, *Race and ethnic relations in Canada* (2nd ed.) (178–216). Don Mills, ON: Oxford University Press Canada.

Dubois, L. & A. Boudreau (1996). *Les Acadiens et leur(s) langue(s): quand le français est minoritaire*; Actes du colloque. Moncton, NB: Centre de recherche en linguistique appliquée, Université de Moncton.

Dunn, W. E. (2002). *Effects of power and identity on access to participation in second language communities*. Unpublished doctoral dissertation. Cornell University.

Floch, W. & Frenette, Y. (2005). *New Canadian perspectives: Community vitality, community confidence: Official Languages Research Forum. Analysis and discussion of the GPC International Survey on Attitudes and Perceptions of Official Languages.* Canadian Heritage.

Harrison, T. W. & Friesen, J. W. (2004). *Canadian society in the twenty-first century: A historical sociological approach*. Toronto: Pearson/Prentice Hall.

Hayday, M. (2005). *Bilingual today, united tomorrow: Official languages in education and Canadian federalism*. Montreal & Kingston: McGill-Queen's University Press.

Hick, S. (2007). *Social welfare in Canada: Understanding income security* (2nd ed.), Toronto: Thompson Educational Publishing, Inc.

Isajiw, W. W. (1999). *Understanding diversity: Ethnicity and race in the Canadian context.* Toronto: Thompson Educational Publishing, Inc.

Landry, R. & Rousselle, S. (2003). *Education et droits collectifs; Au-del de l'article 23 de la Charte.* Moncton, NB: Les Editions de la Francophonie.

Lester, N. (2002). *The Black book of English Canada.* Toronto: McClelland & Stewart Ltd.

Martel, A. (2001). *Droits, écoles et communautés en milieu minoritaire: 1986–2002. Analyse pour un aménagement du français par l'éducation*. Ottawa: Commissariat aux langues officielles.

Morf, G. (1976). Ethnic groups and developmental models: The case of Quebec. In A. Said and L.R. Simmons, *Ethnicity in an international context* (76–91). New Brunswick, NJ: Transaction Books.

Moss, J. (2004). The drama of identity in Canada's francophone west. *The American Review of Canadian Studies* (Spring 2004): 81–97.

Pendakus, R., Hedges, J., & King, E. (2003). *Canada: A demographic overview 2001*. Canadian Heritage.

Pitre, M.-C. (2003). *La déportation des Acadiens.* Grand-Pré, NS: Société promotion Grand-Pré.

Reid, J., Basque, M., Mancke, E., Moody, B., Plank, G. & Wicken, W. (2004). *The 'Conquest' of Acadia, 1710: Imperial, colonial and aboriginal constructions*. Toronto: University of Toronto Press.

Stebbins, R. A. (2000). *The French enigma: Survival and development in Canada's Francophone societies.* Calgary, AB: Detselig Enterprises Ltd.

Thériault, J. Y. (1999). *Francophonies minoritaires au Canada: L'état des lieux.* Moncton, NB: Les Editions d'Acadie.

Thompson, N. (2003). *Promoting equality: Challenging discrimination and oppression.* New York: Palgrave.

Trahan, L. (2007). *Official languages: Community development and linguistic duality bulletin.* Canadian Heritage, 41–42.

Turner, L. (2005). Social work practice in Canada's officially bilingual province: Challenges and opportunities. *Canadian Social Work Review*, 22(2): 131–154.

Vaz, N. & Foucher, P. (2004). The right to receive public services in either official language. In M. Bastarache, *Language rights in Canada* (2nd ed.), (251–364). Cowansville, QC: Editions Yvon Blais.

# CHAPTER 9

# The Changing Status of Women: From Poverty to Precarious Work

*Iara Lessa*

## INTRODUCTION

The World Economic Forum, an independent international organization under the supervision of the Swiss Federal Government, released its Global Gender Gap Report in December 2006. Providing insight into the economic, legal, and social aspects of the inequality between men and women, the report measured indicators in four critical areas—economic participation and opportunity; educational attainment; political empowerment; health and survival—for 115 countries covering 90% of the world's population. Canada was ranked 14th, lagging well behind the Nordic countries (Sweden, 1; Norway, 2; Finland, 3; and Iceland, 4), some European countries (Germany, 5; Denmark, 8; UK, 9; Ireland, 10; Spain, 11; Netherlands, 12); as well as the Philippines (6); New Zealand (7); and Sri Lanka (13) (Hausmann et al., 2006). Similar to issues of child poverty and the environment, which were also objects of unfavourable international comparison, Canada finds itself wanting in equity for women. This is a particularly hard realization, especially considering that 2007 is the 40th anniversary of the establishment of the Royal Commission on the Status of Women (1970). The Commission put women's issues firmly onto the federal government agenda in Canada, encouraged by a recharged women's movement of the 1960s (Begin, 1997; Eicheler & Luxton, 2006, p. 79). Aided by a booming economy and a political discourse around a just society, the problematic situation of women, as shown in the following examples, was seen as in need of state action:

- A married woman lacked legal identity, capacity, and entitlement. She was under the legal control and authority of her husband in common law and Civil Code.
- Women could not testify against their husband or have a separate domicile.
- A widow had no automatic legal right to share equitably in her husband's wealth.
- An Indian [*sic*] woman who married a non-Indian or non-registered Indian, together with her children, lost all rights and privileges of an Indian, while an Indian man could confer Indian status on his non-Indian wife.
- Wife assault was regarded as a private, intimate matter between husband and wife (Paltier, 1997, p. 30).

In these last 40 years, equity has remained a constant theme for women. Without managing to reverse the feminization of poverty—the concentration of poverty among women noticed in the 1960s—Canada is now embarking on discussions around the feminization of the labour market. This new focus calls attention to the conditions under which women are forced into the labour market and the consequences of these new demands for them, their families, and society. Understanding these brings new hopes of redefining roles and ways of life that are equitable, flexible, diverse, and capable of guiding us through the anxieties and changes of the contemporary world.

In the following sections, we will first explore the grounds under which the position of women in Canada continues to deserve special attention (i.e., issues of equity). Then we will examine how this position has changed in situations of paid employment and work; in the family and domestic life; and in terms of resources to support women's full participation in society. Finally, in the last section, I will discuss current paths and challenges in the pursuit of equity for all.

## MAKING WOMEN VISIBLE: EQUITY

Women constitute slightly more than half of the Canadian population—50.4% in 2004—with a much higher proportion in older age groups—69% among persons aged 89 or older (Statistics Canada, 2006a, p. 11). Their participation in the total wealth of the country, however, is much less representative: they generally have a lower income than men and make up a disproportionate share of the people with low income (p. 143). Women's access to decent employment is restricted (Vosko, 2000), and their unequal load of domestic work severely limits their ability to be economically self-sufficient (Lochhead & Scott, 2000, p. 2). Today in Canada, women are not only much more at risk of being poor than men—a risk that is much higher for certain groups of women—but also the lives of large numbers of women include domestic violence, systemic discrimination, and exclusion from society's benefits. Women in Canada are less likely than men to have a university degree, although they are gradually increasing their ratio: 15% in 2001, up from just 3% in 1971 (Statistics Canada 2006a, p. 13). While they have a higher life expectancy than men, their gains since 1981 have only been about half those experienced by men (p. 12). Furthermore, this profile of inequality deepens considerably when we consider different groups of women, such as those characterized by race, as Aboriginal, as recent immigrants, as disabled women, and as lone mothers (Steinsky-Schwartz et al., 2005). Canada is not unique in these disparities. As the Global Gender Gap Report illustrates, women are in a position of disadvantage worldwide.

What accounts for such social disparity?

Gender inequity has deep roots in the way society is organized, and constructs men as opposite to women. Understanding men and women as a binary, social organization produces and reproduces power differentials and determines gender roles. As a group, men have superiority and control that are defined and enforced through all social systems and institutions, and, as well, through everyday attitudes and behaviours. They benefit in terms of opportunities, authority, and privileged positions in paid work. Women are confined to subordinate positions in society where their lack of power affects every sphere of their lives (Baines, Evans & Neysmith, 1998; Baker, 2001).

Rights and equity, consequently, have become the banner of the women's movement worldwide, encompassing campaigns for education, equality of opportunity, pay and conditions of work, welfare rights, and social provision of child care. The movement is against poverty and violence against women like rape and sexual objectification. It is also concerned with the right to choose freely whether and when to have a child. In some of these issues, worldwide and in Canada, the indicators show remarkable change since the 1970s, but many groups of women continue to find themselves in poverty, discriminated against, without rights, geographically and personally isolated, and locked in pre-determined devalued roles lacking recognition and economic or social status. Canada is signatory of the 1995 UN Beijing Platform for Action, which states: "The advancement of women and the achievement of equality between women and men are . . . the only ways to build a sustainable, just and developed society. [ . . . ] Empowerment of women and gender equality are prerequisites for achieving political, social, economic, cultural, and environmental security

## The Expert Panel on Accountability Mechanisms for Gender Equality

The phrase "strengthening gender equality" means acting to achieve substantive equality for women. "Gender equality" means that women have the conditions for realizing their full human rights and potential to contribute to national, political, economic, social, and cultural development, and to benefit from the results. In the past, it was believed that equality could be achieved by giving women the same opportunities as men, on the assumption that this would bring sameness of results. However, same treatment, also referred to as "formal equality," was found to not necessarily yield the expected results.

Today, the concept of equality acknowledges that different treatment of women and men may sometimes be required to achieve comparable results, given their similarities and differences,

and their varying histories, roles, and life conditions. It is this notion of substantive equality, equality in the results, that is embedded in the Canadian Charter of Rights and Freedoms. The panel notes that achievement of substantive equality for women must reflect not just the differences between men and women, but the different situations in which different groups of women live and the interaction of different forms of discrimination. This is sometimes referred to as "intersectionality." In any specific context, equality for immigrant women may have very different meanings than equality for women with disabilities, or for Inuit women in a small, northern community (Steinsky-Schwartz et al., 2005, p. 15).

*Source:* Status of Women Canada. www.swc-cfc.gc.ca/resources/panel/report/report_6_e.html

among all peoples" (Reaffirmed at the 49th session of the UN Commission on the Status of Women, March 2005, as well as Canada's International Policy Statement, 2005).

The word "women" encompasses a variety of groups that find themselves in very different locations in society. Various other socially structuring factors such as race, ethnicity, sexuality, class, education, age, geographic location, and physical ability/disability, among others, contribute to differentiation among women. For example, a rapidly growing number of women in Canada (25% increase between 1996 and 2001) belong to visible minorities, corresponding, in 2001, to 14% of all women living in Canada being visible minorities (Statistics Canada, 2006a, p. 246). This is a relatively well-educated group of women (21% had a university degree compared with 14% of other women [p. 239]), which, despite the large variance among different communities, in general, are less likely to be employed than other Canadian women (p. 249), earn less at their jobs, and are twice as likely as other women in Canada to have low incomes (p. 252). Another group, Aboriginal women, is growing much more rapidly than the rest of the female population in Canada. A majority are living off reserves (pp. 181–2), and a relatively high proportion live with the immediate or extended family. They are much more likely to be lone parents than non-Aboriginal women, and have larger families than those headed by their non-Aboriginal counterparts (p. 189). Their life expectancy is well below that of non-Aboriginal women (p. 190), and 4 in 10 Aboriginal women have not completed high school (p. 196).

In this section we reflected that women as a group of people understood in opposition to men experience several inequities in society. Women, however, are not a uniform category of people—different groups experience inequalities differently. The following sections examine several aspects of the lives of women in Canada, bearing in mind the diversity among them and the significant changes occurring in Canadian society.

## TRANSFORMATIONS IN THE WORLD OF PAID WORK

One of the most remarkable contemporary trends is commonly described as the feminization of the labour market. This refers to the large numbers of women, worldwide, who are joining the labour force, that is, women entering into formal paid employment relations (Armstrong, 1996; Vosko, 2000).

> In fact, there were 7.5 million Canadian women with jobs in 2004, twice the figure in the mid-1970s. Overall, 58% of all women aged 15 and over currently are part of the paid workforce, up from 42% in 1976. In contrast, the proportion of men who were employed fell during this period from 73% to 68%. As a result, women accounted for 47% of the employed workforce in 2004, up from 37% in 1976 (Statistics Canada, 2006a, p. 103).

Some very significant aspects must be understood as we examine this trend. First, it is important to remark that the majority of women have always worked and worked very hard in activities not included in statistics about the labour market: unpaid domestic work and in the informal economy. While men were expected to work outside the family home in goods-producing industries, women were defined as wives and mothers, essential figures to the private space of the home. They were assigned the roles described as biologically determined, which include bearing, rearing, and caring for family members. This is called "reproductive labour" since it helps to replenish and renew labour power, which is the capacity to perform productive work (Graham, 1991; Lister, 1990). Many women have also worked out of the home in the formal or informal market as domestics, nannies, teachers, and nurses, using similar skills to those they perform in their unpaid domestic roles. This work was invisible and considered temporary or peripheral, or, at best, secondary to that of men. In the post-industrial era, changes in attitudes, different needs of life, and the nature of the economy of the late 1990s provide the contexts in which a large number of women were forced into formal paid labour (McDaniel, 2002).

Second, unlike what may be suggested by "the substitution hypothesis" (Standing, 1999), women's entry into the workforce is not at the expense of men's jobs. Vosko (2000) has shown that, rather than assuming formerly occupied male jobs, women have been joining the labour market in newly created jobs in the service industries, which traditionally rely on female labour. The growth in jobs in these industries has been followed by a marked decline in manufacturing jobs, which have been highly dominated by men. The feminization of the labour market, hence, reflects the traditional gender segregation of occupations that has kept as a privilege of men the jobs that are secure, full-time, unionized, and entitled to work benefits. Despite the drop in full-time permanent employment for men, they are still more likely than women to hold this form of employment (66% versus 54% for women in 2002), as documented by Cranford et al. (2003, p. 12). In contrast, in 2004, 27% of the total female workforce was in part-time employment, compared with just 11% of employed men (Statistics Canada, 2006a, p. 14).

## Women's Employment

"In 2004, 67% of all employed women were working in teaching, nursing, and related health occupations, clerical or other administrative positions, and sales and service occupations. This compared with just 30% of employed men." Women remain very much a minority among professionals employed in the natural sciences, engineering, and mathematics (21% in 2004) and also among those employed in most goods-producing occupations. Women have, however, increased their representation in several professional fields in recent years, coming to constitute "half those employed in diagnostic and treating positions in medicine and related health professions. In 2004, 55% of all doctors and dentists in Canada were female, up from 43% in 1987." In 2004, they also represented 51% of those employed as business and financial professionals, and 72% of professionals employed in social science or religious occupations. While women have been increasing their representation in managerial positions, they tend to be better represented in lower-level positions as opposed to those at more senior levels showing even a decline among the latter: "In 2004, women made up 22% of senior managers in Canada, whereas in 1996, the figure had been 27%" (Statistics Canada, 2006a, p. 113).

*Source:* Statistics Canada. Women in Canada (2006) (cat 3 89-503-XIE).

A third angle for understanding the feminization of labour is that women's engagement in the labour force is done under devalued and precarious conditions. Similar to the caring or reproductive work they do within the family, which although essential, is neither valued nor supported, the jobs women do in the world of paid labour are usually low pay, unskilled, and part time. When women join the labour market, they often perform jobs that require their devalued knowledge about caring for the young, the old, and the dependent; cleaning, cooking, and preparing food for consumption; sewing clothing and looking after the health of people, and so forth. "These jobs are characterized by high levels of insecurity and, consequently, the service industry jobs created in the current period reflect these conditions of precariousness" (Armstrong, 1996, Vosko, 2000).

A fourth aspect to examine in the feminization of labour is pay inequality. "Canada has the 5th largest wage gap between women and men full-time workers out of the world's 29 most developed countries. Only Spain, Portugal, Japan, and Korea have larger wage gaps" (CRIAW, 2006, p. 2). In general, employed women earn substantially less than men even when employed full-time, working side by side with men, or when in the same occupational category or level of education as men. Further, the gap between the earnings of women and men has not changed substantially in the past decade. In 2003, the full-year average earnings of women working full-time were 71% those of men in the same circumstances, a figure slightly lower than the 72% recorded in the mid 1990s. When all employed women in 2003 are considered, this ratio drops to 64%, reflecting the precariousness of women's employment (Statistics Canada, 2006a, pp. 138–9). While the continuum of unstable wage work varies with age—the young are more concentrated in part-time, both temporary and permanent, work—women in each age group are more likely than men to hold precarious employment (Cranford et al., 2003, pp. 18–19).

Finally, for all sectors and occupations, insecure jobs are not only sex segregated but also racialized (Tran, 2004). Some dimensions of racialization can be illustrated using the characterization of visible minority, although there are large variances among the different groups of visible minority women. Similar to other women but unlike men, the majority of employed visible minority women work on non-standard schedules. Their wages, when employed on a full-time, full-year basis, however, are lower—about 10% less than their non-visible minority counterparts in 2000 (Statistics Canada, 2006a, p. 250, 252). Furthermore, the workplace is a site of discrimination and unfair treatment for visible minority women with 13% reporting in 2002 having experienced some form of discrimination in the previous five years. These incidents were related to their ethnicity, culture, race, skin colour, language, accent, or religion and occurred over five times more often than for women in the overall population. In addition, visible minority women experience a slightly higher percent of these incidents than their male counterparts (Statistics Canada, 2003).

In this section, we examined several aspects of what is commonly referred to as the feminization of the labour market. In fact, this trend reflects the growth in the service industries, which are traditionally dominated by female labour. Trends to de-industrialization, which generated predominantly low-paid, temporary, part-time, or contract jobs, marked the conditions under which women have joined the labour force. This precariousness has been reflected in all aspects of women's lives and has affected the various groups of women differently.

## UNPAID WORK AND THE PRIVATE WORLD OF THE FAMILY

Although women's entry into the public arena of paid employment has been remarkable, the responsibility for reproductive work at home continues to rest primarily with them: on average they spent 4.3 hours per day in unpaid work in 2005 compared to 2.5 for men (Marshall, 2006, p. 26). In heterosexual households where both partners worked full-time, 80% percent of the women were still expected to do all or most of the daily housework, while the chores were shared equally in only 10% of them, and in another 10%, men were responsible for housework. While in all types of families women's rates of participation in housework are higher than men's, there is some indication that the gap is narrowing with the participation rate among married men with children changing from 54% in 1986 to 71% in 2005 (Statistics Canada, 2006b).

The consequences of this imbalance in unpaid work are that "women are expected to cut down on their paid work, quit their jobs, take emergency leave from work, or refuse promotions, in order to care for children, elderly parents or in-laws, or disabled relatives. Men are not" (CRIAW, 2005, p. 3). These expectations have life-long impacts on women's wages, accumulation of pension benefits, stress, and career paths. Both men and women have added to their overall workday (including paid and unpaid work) since 1986. As Marshall (2006, p. 7) documents, women have added 0.7 hour to their workday despite a half-hour drop in unpaid work, while men have added 0.6 hour to their workday from unpaid work. Overall, in 2005, workers were spending 45 minutes less with their home activities during workdays than they did two decades earlier (Statistics Canada, 2007).

Another aspect of the changes in dual earner families is that employment among women with children in the past two decades has increased sharply, in particular among women with children under age 3—from 28% in 1976 to 65% in 2004. Employment has also risen among single mothers although, reflecting the challenges of undertaking alone the roles of breadwinning and caring in the absence of social supports, they are less likely than mothers in two-parent families to be employed. One in five families with children in 2001 was headed by a female lone parent. The absolute numbers of families led by single mothers have almost doubled in the last 20 years. While most of today's single mothers are either divorced or separated from a spouse, a growing proportion of them are single, never-married women raising children on their own. The latter tend to be older, on average, than their counterparts were in the past, and the proportion of single, never-married female lone parents in the 15 to 24 age group dropped from 38% to 20% in the last 20 years (Statistics Canada, 2006a, p. 38). The rights of single mothers represent a long struggle of women's groups to legalize divorce and change the strict morality that regulated the lives of women. The lives of these women continue to be challenging and are often marked by poverty (Evans, 1996; Little, 1999; Lessa, 2004). As many as "37% of lone mothers with paid employment must raise a family on less than $10 per hour" (CRIAW, 2006, p. 2). For many women, having a job is not a path out of poverty.

The private world of the family and domesticity also harbours considerable threats for women. According to Mosher (1998, p. 139), one-third of Canadian women have been physically or sexually assaulted by their marital or common law partner, with many of them enduring multiple assaults and injuries. Women experience a greater likelihood of being injured, fearing for their lives, enduring repeated and more serious forms of violence, and seeking medical help due to spousal violence than men (Statistics Canada, 2006a, pp. 160–62). In addition, Steinsky-Schwartz et al. (2005, p. 44) report that in the period from 1974 to 2003, the female spousal homicide rate has been four to five times higher than the rate of male spousal homicide. Girls were the victims in eight out of ten family-related sexual assaults committed against children and youth in 2003. Further, elderly women are more likely than their male counterparts to be victims of family violence (25% and 20% respectively).

While gender is important to understanding the prevalence of domestic violence in society, it is imperative to point out that many other intersecting oppressions combine to make the experience of violence a complex and multifaceted occurrence, which cannot be traced to a single cause. The binary constructs of men and women—women are not only constructed as nurturing, caring, dependent, and submissive but also as property of independent, aggressive, and rational men—interact with other forms of oppression to produce unique experiences of violence (Mosher, 1998, pp. 142–47). For example, an examination of the literature on family violence experiences of Aboriginal women shows that intersecting factors have to be considered. In 2004, "24% of Aboriginal women, three times the figure among their non-Aboriginal counterparts (8%), experienced spousal violence from either a current or previous marital or common-law partner in the five-year period prior to the survey" (Statistics Canada, 2006a, p. 195). To understand such data and to search for solutions to this situation, it is necessary to place its distinctive features, among other factors, in the deliberate disruption of Aboriginal life and family functioning caused by state interventions, the persistent racist environment of Canadian society and its demeaning stereotypes of Aboriginal peoples, and the poverty and lack of resources in which Aboriginal peoples live. In this sense, the Royal Commission on Aboriginal Peoples (1996, vol. 4, p. 66) recognizes the relevance of sexism as it exists in the rest of Canada, but points to colonialism as the central cause of domination in the lives of Aboriginal women.

The previous sections provided an overview of the lives of women in Canada, in their diversity, and in the context of structural changes and continuities. We examined the transformations in a post-industrial economy and the consequent push for large numbers of women to join the labour market. We also discussed how this happened in conditions of precariousness and how it affected different groups of women differently. These changes had many effects in the family form and the roles its members are expected to perform. An unacceptable continuity has been the prevalence of experiences of domestic violence in the lives of women. Our understanding of these issues has deepened to incorporate the complexities of interlocking social oppressions for different groups of women.

## SOCIAL SUPPORTS AND SERVICES

The multiple and conflicting demands being placed on women accompanied by changes in the roles of the welfare state have profoundly eroded women's individual and collective entitlements and opportunities (Benoit, 2000). Women continue to figure disproportionately among the poor in Canada, and particularly overrepresented are Aboriginal women, single mothers, elderly women, women with disabilities, racialized and immigrant women, and women living in rural areas (CRIAW, 2006, p. 4). Unattached women and single mothers constitute the highest incidence of poverty among women, with respectively 42% and 49% of all women in these groups being poor (NCW, 2006, p. 2). The reasons for this poverty concentration are multiple and complex. As we discussed above, they can be found in women's relationship with paid employment and the market, structured by discrimination and devaluation of women's work, and, as well, the reality that women carry an unequal share of unpaid work.

Considering their precarious position in the labour market, government transfers constitute an important source of support for women and their families. Although earnings from employment corresponded to 70% of women's income in 2003, government income transfer benefits represented an important share of their total income (17%), including 5% from Old Age Security and Guaranteed Income Supplements, 4% on Canada and Quebec Pension Plans (CPP and QPP), 3% on Child Tax Benefits, 2% on social assistance benefits, and 2% on employment insurance payouts (EI) (Statistics Canada, 2006a, pp. 135–36). The design of the welfare system reflects an embedded gender bias (Boyd & McDaniel, 1996) as can be demonstrated in the functioning of the CPP and QPP. As these are based on earnings, women's historically low earnings are reflected in what they receive from these plans—on average, women aged 65 to 69 are paid 56% of the payments men receive in the same age group (CRIAW, 2006, p. 3).

Canada, in sync with other major economies in the Western world, has adopted a neo-liberal economic model which has implied intense privatization of public services and institutions, reduction of social spending and market regulation and, importantly, a transformation in the discourse around social programs from that of a safety net to that of a springboard to paid employment (Rice & Prince, 2000). The reforms and cuts have profoundly affected women's lives and entitlements. For example, in 1997, many changes were implemented in employment insurance: an increase in the number of hours required for qualification, changes in the way the benefits are calculated, and, of particular importance for women, modifications to maternity leave which extended the time of coverage, but restricted eligibility and capped the benefit level. As a result, the number of unemployed women qualifying for EI fell from 70% to 32% between 1989 and 1999, and today it is easier for fathers than mothers to qualify for parental benefits (Townson, 2005).

Single mothers provide a good case to further illustrate the importance of income support programs (Evans, 1996). With sole responsibility for both family care and financial support, 60% of single mothers relied on social assistance at some point in 2001 (NCW, 2004, p. 86). Social assistance or welfare is provided by the provinces and territories to individuals and families whose resources are inadequate to meet their needs and who have exhausted all other avenues of support. However, the rates of this support for single parent families, most of which are headed by women, range from a low of only 48% of the poverty line in Alberta, to a high of 70% of the poverty line in Newfoundland and Labrador (Townson, 2005). In 2004, social assistance benefits were at their lowest level since the 1980s, and most provinces even clawed back the National Child Benefit Supplement from families receiving social assistance. As a result, these benefits do not provide enough for mothers to afford the basic necessities of life such as food, clothing, and shelter. In addition, since the mid-1990s, social assistance in Canada has become conditional upon participation in the workforce through various workfare programs (Snyder, 2006). Most poor mothers are forced into the workforce earning minimum wage, in precarious contract employment, and with the unstable cyclical pattern of employment–unemployment identified above. Attempting to juggle multiple responsibilities, single mothers feel stigmatized and stereotyped by societal judgments and attitudes (Lessa, 2006).

Other groups of women are also faced with high poverty rates. For example, 26% of women with disabilities lived in poverty in 2001, and the more severe the disability, the lower the income. In 2001, 29% of visible minority women were living in poverty, and the rate of poverty for recent immigrant women was 35% (Townson, 2005). In addition, the exclusion and marginalization that accompany poverty are compounded by substantial cuts to social services and supports including health care, child care, housing, mental health care, substance abuse treatment, employment training, recreation, family supports and others.

Central to women's presence in the labour force is the issue of adequacy of child care arrangements. Canada has no universal child care, and most families have to rely on the market or informal arrangements for the care of their children. In many cases, the lack of child care forces women into cycles of paid employment and unemployment, locking them into unstable and low-paid jobs as well as leaving them unable to develop a career path (Bakker, 1998, p. 21). It is estimated (Timpson, 2001) that about 80% of the day care provision remains informal or unregulated. The lack of affordable, good quality child care keeps many women from finding full-time, well-paying work. Another important basic need, housing, has become increasingly unaffordable and inadequate, contributing, as argued by Mosher et al. (2004), to maintaining many women in unsafe, isolated, and unhealthy conditions which can be said to be forms of hidden homelessness (Neal, 2004, p. 27).

Cuts to transfer programs and social services have further affected women since they are expected to fill the gaps left by these either as primary caregivers of their families or as the majority of paid workers in the caring sectors. In balancing between work and care giving need or assuming the burden of understaffed social services, women bear unequally the effects of social welfare reforms. Land and Rose (1985) point out that women's activities have a character of "compulsory altruism," that is, most women do not have the choice not to do it without damaging those whom they care about or their own self-esteem. They consistently feel stressed and time-crunched. As documented by Statistics Canada (2006b), the longer workdays and the need to care for children affect women more than men: 52% of women with children in couples in contrast to 71% of their male counterparts felt satisfied with their work-life balance.

Women's opportunities in society are also strongly shaped by legislations and political participation. Modelled on the Canadian Charter of Rights and Freedoms, the Royal Commission on Employment Equity produced a report in 1984 encouraging affirmative action for employment discrimination, which is implemented through contract compliance and the courts (Timpson, 2001). Examples of other important legislation for women is the legal recognition of same-sex couples, which grants them the same rules as heterosexual couples around child support, adoption, and pension benefits, and provides further equality, including rights of being considered next of kin and rights around inheritance, succession, and so forth. Women are, however, under-represented in the positions of power responsible for proposing and passing legislation within federal, provincial, and territorial governments, creating the circumstance that "both women's presence and women's issues are missing from the political and legal agenda" (CRIAW, 2006, p. 10). Women accounted in 2003 for 21% of the Members of the House of Commons, 35% of the Senate, 21% of federal Deputy Ministers, 26% of federally appointed judges, and 20% of members of provincial and territorial legislatures (Steinsky-Schwartz et al., 2005, p. 43).

In summary, women's changing relations to the state have been the focus of much attention. The cuts to programs of income support and to social services have affected women disproportionately, eroding their entitlements and changing the way they see themselves in society. The results have been devastating for many poor women, placing them in levels of impoverishment and marginalization unprecedented in the contemporary history of Canada. Increased pressures to join the labour market without the adequate supports to balance work and family life have generated increased stress and caring responsibilities for all women, which place not only them and their families but society as a whole in a very vulnerable position.

## CHALLENGES AND OPPORTUNITIES AHEAD

This chapter has examined central themes around the current status of women in Canada using concrete data to illustrate its main points. It has shown that while the position, roles, and social expectations of women are changing substantially, much has remained the same in regard to Canada's relatively poor performance in gender issues. Women in Canada have made many inroads in terms of educational achievements and have also gained representation in some high status professions previously dominated by men. The gaps in wages and in responsibility for housework are slowly diminishing, though there is much ground still to be crossed. While some women are benefiting from these modest gains, others sink further into disadvantage and exclusion.

Rapid economic and technological changes and expanded movements of capital, goods, and labour have imposed shifts in socio-economic relations and structures, forcing women to join the labour market in large numbers. Contradictions between the gendered dismantling of welfare states and women's dramatic rate of entry into the labour market generate the urgent need to develop new ways of combining paid and unpaid work at home and in communities. However, a significant erosion of women's social rights and entitlements has become evident in the cutting and re-shaping of social programs, the loss of state investment in services and redistributive justice, and the diminished funding for women's social action, with serious consequences for families, individuals, and society as a whole. As a result, women in Canada continue to be more at risk of living in poverty than men, a risk that is much higher for specific groups of women. Violence and systemic discrimination mark the lives of many groups of women. Affordable, decent child daycare and housing, crucial for women's equitable participation in society, remain a distant dream.

The goal of equality for women has been importantly advanced by the federal government, but legislation and the courts alone cannot bring this much-wanted advancement. It is necessary to reinvest in the well-being of women while recognizing the new social contexts and the important role women play in every sphere of social life. Women's economic security and ability to contribute to society operate at several interconnected levels—individual, community, and society—and require that women feel valued and recognized, that they experience neither individual nor systemic discrimination, that they have access to programs and services, meaningful and decent employment, education and training, and that their lives are free from violence and marginalization.

# References

Armstrong, P. (1996). Feminization of the labour force: Harmonizing down in a global economy, in I. Bakker (Ed.) *Rethinking restructuring: Gender and change in Canada* (pp. 29–54). Toronto: University of Toronto Press.

Baines, C., Evans, P. & Neysmith, S. (1998). *Women's caring: Feminist perspective on social welfare* (2nd ed). Don Mills, ON: Oxford University Press.

Baker, M. (2001). *Families, labour and love.* Vancouver: University of British Columbia Press.

Bakker, I. (1998). *Unpaid work and macroeconomics: New discussions, new tools for action* (Cat. # SW21–33/1998). Ottawa: Status of Women Canada.

Begin, M. (1997). The Canadian government and the Commission's report, in C. Andrews & S. Rogers (Eds.), *Women and the Canadian state* (pp. 12–26). Montreal & Kingston: McGill-Queen's University Press.

Benoit, C. M. (2000). *Women, work and social rights: Canada in historical and comparative perspective.* Scarborough, ON: Prentice Hall.

Boyd, M. & McDaniel, S. A. (1996). Gender inequality in Canadian policy contexts: A mosaic of approaches. *The World Review of Sociology,* 3, 25–50.

Canadian Research Institute for the Advancement of Women (2006). *Disentangling the web of women's poverty and exclusion.* Ottawa: CRIAW.

Canadian Research Institute for the Advancement of Women (2005). *Women and poverty fact sheet* (3rd ed.). Ottawa: CRIAW.

Cranford, C. J., Vosko, L. F. & Zukerwich, N. (2003). Precarious employment in Canadian labour market: A statistical profile. *Just Labour,* 3 (Fall), 6–22.

Eicheler, M. & Luxton, M. (2006). Women's studies in focus. Atlantis, *A Women's Studies Journal,* 31(1), 76–83.

Evans, P. (1996). Single mothers and Ontario's welfare policy: Restructuring the debate, in J. Brodie (Ed.), *Women and public policy* (pp. 151–171). Toronto: Harcourt.

Graham, H. (1991). The concept of caring in feminist research: The case of domestic service. *Sociology,* 25(1), 61–78.

Hausmann, R., Tyson, L. D., & Zahidi, S. (2006). *The global gender gap, Report 2006* (Ref. 112006). Geneva, Switzerland: World Economic Forum. http://www.weforum.org/gendergap

Land, H. & Rose, H. (1985). Compulsory altruism for some or an altruistic society for all, in P. Bean, J. Ferris, & D.K. Whynes (Eds.), *In Defence of Welfare* (pp. 74–96). London: Tavistock.

Lessa, I. (2006). Single motherhood in the Canadian landscape: Postcards from a subject, in A. Westhues (Ed.), *Canadian Social Policy* (4th ed.). Waterloo, Canada: Wilfrid Laurier Press.

Lessa, I. (2004). Just don't call her a single mother: Shifting identities of women raising children alone. *Atlantis: A Women's Studies Journal*, 29 (1), 43–51.

Lister, R. (1990). Women, economic dependency, and citizenship. *Journal of Social Policy*, 19(4), 445–67.

Little, M. H. (1999). Limits of Canadian democracy: The citizenship rights of poor women. *Canadian Review of Social Policy*, 42, 59–76.

Lochhead, C. and Scott, K. (2000). *The dynamics of women's poverty in Canada*. Ottawa: Status of Women Canada.

Marshall, K. (2006). Converging gender roles. *Perspectives on Labour and Income* (cat.75-001-XIE), 7(7), 5–17.

McDaniel, S. (2002). Women's changing relations to the state and citizenship. *Canadian Review of Sociology and Anthropology*, 39(2), 125–150.

Mosher, J. (1998). Caught in the tangled web of care: Women abuse in intimate relationships, in C. Baines, P. Evans & S. Neysmith, (Eds.), *Women's caring: Feminist perspective on social welfare* (2nd ed., pp. 139–159). Don Mills, ON: Oxford University Press.

Mosher, J., Evans, P., Little, M., Morrow, E., Boulding, J., & VanderPlatts, N. (2004). *Walking on eggshells: Abused women's experiences of Ontario's welfare system*. http://dawn.thot.net/walking-on-eggshells.htm

National Council of Welfare (2006). *Poverty facts, 2003*. www.ncwcnbes.net.

National Council of Welfare (2004). *Poverty profile 2001*. Ottawa: NCW.

Neal, R. (2004). *Voices: Women, poverty and homelessness in Canada*. Ottawa: National Anti-poverty Organization.

Paltiel, F. L. (1997). State initiatives: Impetus and effects, in C. Andrews & S. Rogers (Eds.), *Women and the Canadian state* (pp. 27–51). Montreal & Kingston: McGill-Queen's University Press.

Rice, J. J. & Prince, M. J. (2000). *Changing politics of Canadian social policy*. Toronto: University of Toronto Press.

Royal Commission on Aboriginal Peoples (1996). *The Royal Commission on Aboriginal Peoples Report*, vol. 4. North Bay, ON: Union of Ontario Indians.

Royal Commission on the Status of Women in Canada (1970). *Report of the Royal Commission on the Status of Women in Canada*. Ottawa: Information Canada.

Snyder, L. (2006) Workfare: Ten years of pickin' on the poor, in A. Westhues, *Canadian social policy: Issues and perspectives* (4th ed., pp. 309–330). Waterloo, ON: Wilfrid Laurier Press.

Standing, G. (1999). Global feminization through flexible labour: A theme revisited. *World Development*, 27(3), 583–602.

Statistics Canada (2007). Study: Time with the family, in *The Daily*, Tuesday, February 13, 2007. Ottawa: Statistics Canada.

Statistics Canada (2006a). *Women in Canada* (cat # 89-503-XIE). Ottawa: Statistics Canada.

Statistics Canada (2006b). General survey of unpaid work, in *The Daily*, Wednesday, July 19, 2006. Ottawa: Statistics Canada.

Statistics Canada (2003). *Ethnic diversity survey: Portrait of a multicultural society* (cat # 89-593-XIE). Ottawa: Statistics Canada.

Steinsky-Schwartz, G., Rowan-Campbell, D., & Langevin, L. (2005). *Equality for women beyond the illusion*. Ottawa: Status of Women Canada.

Timpson, A. M. (2001). *Driven apart: Women's employment equality and child care in Canadian public policy*. Vancouver: University of British Columbia Press.

Townson, M. (2005). *Poverty issues for Canadian women*. Ottawa, ON: Status of Women Canada. http://www.swc-cfc.gc.ca/cgi-bin/printview.pl?file=/resources/consultations/ges09-2005/poverty_e.html

Tran, K. (2004). Visible minorities in the labour force: 20 years of change (cat # 11-008-XPE). *Canadian Social Trends*, 73 (Summer). Ottawa: Statistics Canada.

Vosko, L. (2000). *Temporary work: The gendered rise of a precarious employment relationship*. Toronto: University of Toronto Press.

# CHAPTER 10

# Immigrants: History and Current Issues

*Carole Pigler Christensen*

## INTRODUCTION

Among the world's industrialized countries, Canada has one of the most diverse populations in terms of ethnicity, culture, and race. Thirty-nine percent of the population was born outside of Canada (Statistics Canada, 2001a). This percentage will likely increase, and will continue to be reflected in the clientele that social workers are called upon to serve. Social work is the sole profession charged with the responsibility of offering services to individuals, groups, families, and communities in the context of the environment. Ethical practice demands that practitioners be cognizant of the complex social, economic, and political forces that enhance, or limit, clients' life chances, and affect their social service needs.

This chapter examines the effects of immigration regulations, formal and informal social policies, human rights, and access to services and resources on immigrant groups. Recent studies documenting the impact of racial, cultural, and ethnic factors, seldom addressed in the social welfare literature, are considered.

The chapter begins with an overview of the motivations underlying immigration and the major changes in patterns of immigration over time. Also discussed is the process by which immigrants from Europe and other parts of the world have assumed majority or minority status within the Canadian system of stratification, the major effects of immigration and refugee policies on individuals and population groups, and Canada's responses to multicultural realities. To illustrate, the experiences of three immigrant groups are briefly examined, noting the extent to which their social welfare needs have been met or impeded by conditions in Canada, and by governmental and voluntary efforts. The chapter ends with examples of programs assisting immigrants and identifies implications for social work practice.

## WHY DO PEOPLE IMMIGRATE?

Migration was recently referred to as humanity's "great genetic commonality," having been practised worldwide from time immemorial (*Vancouver Sun*, January 22, 2007a, p. A7). People of all origins leave their home countries seeking greater economic opportunities, improved living standards, and greater social, religious, or political freedom and stability. Sparsely populated and rich in natural resources, Canada has sought immigrants to fill specific needs. Migration is a global phenomenon best understood in terms of *push factors* that cause people to leave a country and *pull factors* that attract immigrants to receiving countries.

During the colonial era, European explorers migrated to the Americas in search of land and raw materials to enrich their mother countries. Later, Canada attracted permanent European settlers, as surplus labourers from densely populated cities and depressed rural areas sought opportunities in the "new world." Migration peaked between 1845 and 1924, when some 50 million people travelled to North America and South America, the greatest migration in recorded history. Canada's need for unskilled labour again became a pull factor during the post–World War II abundance economy. As Western Europe continued to prosper, migration was tied to war and political upheaval, resulting in displaced persons or refugees.

Currently, great migrations are taking place in Third World post-colonial countries in Asia, Africa, and Latin America, where independent countries are caught up in a global system of social and economic stratification. Increasingly, pressures are being placed on relatively wealthy post-colonial Western countries such as Canada to accept more immigrants and refugees. Due to population growth and limited opportunities for upward mobility, people in Third World countries are likely to continue to wish to emigrate, as the Europeans did before them, in search of better lives. Moreover, geographic changes in Europe's Eastern bloc countries, the ensuing unrest after, and the dissolution of the former Soviet Union, have led to increasing emigration demands from countries experiencing unrest and uncertainty.

## Formulation of Immigration Policy

Canada established its Department of Citizenship and Immigration in 1950 and passed its *Immigration Act* of 1952. Before this time the government had no coherent policy regarding the many categories of people who wished to enter the country, such as independent immigrants, family members of immigrants, and refugees. Popular myth suggests that Canada has always had an open-door immigration policy, allowing almost anyone to enter. In fact, immigration policies have been devised with consideration of the national and racial origins of prospective immigrants; Canada's economic conditions and labour needs; international conditions of poverty; political unrest, war, or natural disaster; people in Canada wishing to sponsor relatives; and the anticipated short- and long-term effects of specific immigrant groups on the French and English communities.

## Who Is an Immigrant?

Canada is often referred to as a nation of immigrants. With the exception of the First Nations populations, all Canadians are descendants of immigrants.

**The Earliest European Immigrants: The Charter Groups** From 1667 to 1763, French settlers consolidated their control of the political, economic, and religious spheres in New France, as the colony was then called. The economy was based mainly on the fur trade and extracting natural resources. French immigration slowed considerably after the British conquest of 1759. By the time of Confederation in 1867, British nationals had become the largest single source of immigration, a status they maintained, albeit in declining proportions, through most of the twentieth century. The British government promoted migration to Canada, often paying immigrants' transportation costs. In the decade immediately following Confederation, 60 percent of the population was British and 35 percent was French. The Catholic Church's encouragement of high birth rates enabled French Canadians to maintain a relatively stable percentage within the population.

The second European immigration phase began around 1880, when land was made available in the Prairies, attracting those from outside the British Isles and France. At that time only 8 percent of the population was of ethnic origin other than British or French: 70 percent were German and 10 percent were Dutch. As the dominant cultural group outside Quebec, the British assumed control of immigration and major economic, social, and political decisions. They determined which groups to allow into the country, which jobs they could fill, and what social ranking would be accorded them. From the time of Confederation until 1902, fewer than 100 000 immigrants arrived annually.

**Other European Immigrants** During a third phase of European immigration, between the turn of the century and World War I, more than 200 000 people arrived every year. A record number of immigrants (400 870) arrived in 1913, fleeing poor socio-economic conditions or religious and political persecution. Pluralism came to Western Canada with the arrival of settlers who were Scandinavian, Slavic, or Russian including Mennonites, Hutterites, Ukrainians, Poles, and Doukhobors. Most spoke neither English nor French, and were poorly educated. Language differences led to regional enclaves with these ethno-cultural groups.

The fourth immigration phase occurred between World Wars I and II when the Depression greatly reduced the flow. Most immigrants were skilled technicians who settled in urban areas. Restrictions continued for those speaking "enemy" languages and for those not of European ancestry, who were considered near impossible to assimilate owing to their cultural, linguistic, religious, or climatic backgrounds (Christensen, 2003). A 1923 order-in-council gave "most favoured" immigrant status to those from Britain and the United States followed by Northern and Western Europeans. Southern, Central, and Eastern Europeans were accepted only if no one else was available for specific employment categories. A "Euro-Canadian" flavour (rather exclusively British and French) prevailed, and newcomers were expected to conform to Anglo-Saxon norms.

The last immigration phase that began after World War II has extended to the present. Numbers again increased, as did the diversity of the immigrants. By 1941, the British had become a statistical minority (44 percent of the population). About half of the unskilled immigrants in the 1950s came from Italy, Portugal, and Greece. A "third force" was emerging, too, composed of immigrants neither British nor French in origin. While each ethnic group comprised less than five percent of the population, together they had become a quarter of the total population of Canada.

**Immigrants from Outside Europe** Until the 1960s, only whites were considered "suitable" immigrants. This made Canada almost inaccessible to those of other racial backgrounds and prevented immigration from sources outside Europe. Racist ideologies remained that prevailed during the colonial era, based on the principles of Manifest Destiny or Social Darwinism. These ethno-centric theories fostered the belief that Europeans had proven themselves fittest to survive by conquering the "uncivilized" peoples on the North and South American, Asian, and African continents, and were superior to yellow, black, brown, and red "races." This belief system was used to implement policies of oppression and extermination to claim the land and to justify the enslavement of First Nations people and Blacks. Although the concept of "race" is indeed a social construct—there being but one human species—the ideology of white supremacy played a major role in shaping Canada's immigration policies. It formed the basis of majority–minority relations as we know them today (Christensen, 2003).

In 1947, Prime Minister Mackenzie King stated that Canadians did not wish to alter the character of the population in the interests of growth, and immigration should be restricted to people who could be advantageously absorbed into the economy (Henry, 2005). The *Immigration Act* of 1952 prohibited or limited prospective immigrants' admission for reasons of nationality or ethnic group, peculiar customs or modes of life, climatic and socio-economic unsuitability, and probable inability to become readily assimilated or to assume the responsibilities of Canadian citizenship. The official ranking of preferred immigrants was strikingly similar to the ranking of the "superior" white race and "inferior" races (people of colour) postulated in Europe two centuries earlier. Only Europeans could sponsor relatives without difficulty. Third World families were separated, with devastating effects, when only one member managed to immigrate (such as domestic workers). Vestiges of such policies survive today.

The ideology of Britain's Elizabethan Poor Law formed the basis for early Canadian social welfare legislation, citing the "able-bodied poor" as "sturdy beggars" who should be forced to work under distasteful conditions (Christensen, 1996). Policies that ignored the plight of immigrant groups experiencing systemic racism reflected this laissez-faire attitude. These immigrants were blamed for being unwilling to work hard owing to their "cultural attributes." This thinking fostered racial prejudice. Until the mid-twentieth century, discriminatory legislation on the basis of race was introduced periodically to sanction and promote negative, stereotypical attitudes toward racialized groups.

## RISING IMMIGRATION FROM THE THIRD WORLD

In response to the contradictions of a racially restrictive immigration policy and Canada's desired reputation as a country fostering equality and human rights, the federal government passed the *Immigration Act of 1962*, removing obvious restrictions based on race. The Points System was introduced in 1967, evaluating potential entrants on the basis of their probable short-term independence, and long-term "adjustment" to Canadian life. Subsequently, the number of immigrants from European sources has declined while greater numbers have arrived from Third World countries. Also, for the first time, residents whose origins were other than European could nominate or sponsor relatives wishing to immigrate.

Although hailed as a racially non-discriminatory merit system, forms of discrimination have remained despite the implementation of the Points System. Immigration officers exercise considerable discretionary powers in the allocation of points for "personal potential"; a disproportionate number of immigration offices are located in predominantly white countries, with fewer in the Third World; and only those with high levels of education and skill, or the wealthy, easily qualify as economic immigrants. Because of the points allocated for educational attainment, immigrants arriving since the 1970s have generally been better educated than the Canadian-born white population (Fleras & Elliott, 2002). If held to today's selection standards, most forefathers of Euro-Canadians would not have qualified as immigrants.

Protests from some quarters followed the unprecedented rise in the number of Third World immigrants, resulting in the restrictive *Immigration Act of 1978* that halved the immigration quota and allowed deportation of immigrants considered a security risk and those unable to support sponsored family members. The "nominated" immigrant category was abolished and the Points System made more stringent. Still, European immigration dropped from 90 percent in 1961 to 25 percent from 1981 to 1991. By 1986, more than one million Canadians or permanent residents were born in, or emigrated from, Asia, Africa, South and Central America, and the Caribbean.

## RECENT TRENDS

Projections suggest that immigration will continue to be the main source of growth at the national level through 2031, due to the aging "baby boomers" and projected below-average replacement fertility rates (Statistics Canada, The Daily, Thursday, December 15, 2005).

Labour needs and concerns about competing internationally in coming decades have continued to provide an incentive for governments to maintain rising immigration levels. However, despite several years of promises of an immigration intake equal to one percent of Canada's population, this target has not once been met in the past 13 years (Citizenship and Immigration Canada, 2006a).

Canadian governments have often held public hearings to ascertain the national attitudes about labour and immigration. Concern is also expressed about the number of Third World migrants Canada can "absorb" without threatening social cohesiveness and the dominant Euro-Canadian cultural identity. Discourse in the media has been considerable in this regard.

There is an emerging trend to tie global warming to anticipated immigration pressures and refugee issues of *climate refugees*, particularly since the tsunami in Indonesia and earthquakes in Asia displaced large numbers of people. A September 2005 internal RCMP report entitled *External Trends Influencing Policing in BC*, obtained by the *Vancouver Sun*, warns of potential security challenges posed by an influx of those forced to flee their homelands due to rising sea levels. Experts suggest that over 100 million climate refugees could exist by 2100, and, as the main producers of greenhouse gases, Western countries would have a moral obligation to assist them (*Vancouver Sun*, January 30, 2007c, pp. A1 and A7). Also, the United Nations estimates that by 2025, two-thirds of the world's population will be afflicted by water stress, particularly those in North Africa, the Middle East, and West Asia (United Nations Environment Network [in press, for April 2007]). It remains to be seen how Canada will respond to these emerging global circumstances that may produce increased demands for immigration.

## CURRENT IMMIGRATION PROFILE

Canada's current population is an estimated 31 700 000 (Statistics Canada, 2006), assisted by the third consecutive increase in new permanent residents since 2001–2002. Table 10.1 depicts immigration during the years 2004 and 2005, and indicates continuation of the trend that began in 2001. The four highest-ranking numbers of immigrants are from Asia, with noteworthy percentage differences over a two-year period.

In 2005, the 262 236 new permanent residents came from over 200 countries. Overall, 60 percent were in the economic class and 40 percent were in the non-economic classes. As to gender, 51.27 percent of the newcomers were female, and there were more women (60 percent) than men (40 percent) in the family class. Genders were fairly evenly split among economic class immigrants (51.8 percent male, 48.2 percent female), although the majority of primary applicants were male (68.6 percent). Sixty-four percent spoke English, French, or both official languages. The most popular immigrant destinations were: Ontario, 54 percent; British Columbia, 17 percent; and Quebec, 16.5 percent (Citizenship and Immigration, 2006a).

Most visible minorities live in Toronto, Montreal, and Vancouver, the urban areas where they are most likely to find employment and may have family or friends. Of the three Prairie provinces, Alberta receives the highest proportion of immigrants, due to its positive economic growth. About 13.4 percent of the Canadian population are "visible" minorities, with the largest groups being Chinese (3.4 percent), South Asians (3.1 percent), and Blacks (2.2 percent) (Statistics Canada, 2001a).

| TABLE 10.1 | Immigration by Top Source Countries (Principal Applicants, Spouses, and Dependants) | | | | | | |
|---|---|---|---|---|---|---|---|
| Country of Last Permanent Residence | 2004 Total | 2004 Rank | 2004 Percent of Total | 2005 Total | 2005 Rank | 2005 Percent of Total | Percentage Difference 2005/ 2004 |
| People's Republic of China | 36 429 | 1 | 15.5% | 42 291 | 1 | 16.1% | 16% |
| India | 25 576 | 2 | 10.9% | 33 146 | 2 | 12.6% | 30% |
| Philippines | 13 303 | 3 | 5.6% | 17 525 | 3 | 6.7% | 32% |
| Pakistan | 12 795 | 4 | 5.4% | 13 576 | 4 | 5.2% | 6% |
| United States | 7507 | 5 | 3.2% | 9262 | 5 | 3.5% | 23% |
| Colombia | 4438 | 11 | 1.9% | 6031 | 6 | 2.3% | 36% |
| United Kingdom | 6062 | 7 | 2.6% | 5865 | 7 | 2.2% | -3% |
| South Korea | 5337 | 9 | 2.3% | 5819 | 8 | 2.2% | 9% |
| Iran | 6063 | 6 | 2.6% | 5502 | 9 | 2.1% | -9% |
| France | 5028 | 10 | 2.1% | 5430 | 10 | 2.1% | 8% |
| Total – YTD Top Ten Only | 122 538 | | 52.0% | 144 447 | | 55.1% | 18% |
| Total – Other Countries | 113 286 | | 48.0% | 117 789 | | 44.9% | 4% |
| Total | 235 824 | | 100.0% | 262 236 | | 100.0% | 11% |

Source: Citizenship and Immigration Canada, 2005. *Facts and Figures 2005, Immigration Overview: Permanent Residents*, Table: Canada, Permanent Residents by Top Source Countries. Retrieved January 22, 2008, from http://www.cic.gc.ca/ENGLISH/resources/statistics/facts2005/permanent/12.asp.

# MAJORITY AND MINORITY GROUP IMMIGRANT STATUS

## Majority Group Immigrant Status

The terms "majority" or "dominant" group must take into account not only numerical considerations but also the dimensions of power, privilege, and prestige. Even when small in numbers, the majority group occupies the highest social, economic, and political positions, and is the group from which the societal elite is drawn. This group's culture and values are transmitted through society's formal institutions—the schools, the media, and the social welfare agencies. The social welfare needs of this dominant group receive the greatest attention and sanction from official sources.

The British have occupied the majority group position in all provinces except Quebec. Until recently, even in Quebec, they have tended to occupy the highest positions in corporate structures. Historically, white immigrants of British descent have automatically become part of the majority group and have moved into society's mainstream institutions. The preferred categories of British, Northwest Europeans, and white Americans have traditionally been encouraged to immigrate freely, followed by Eastern and Southern Europeans. The same has been true for many "white ethnics" who have been absorbed into the dominant group through assimilation, including intermarriage. Although prejudice and ethno-centrism was experienced at times by some Europeans (for example, the Irish, Italians, and Germans), white skin functions as a kind of "affirmative action," benefiting majority group immigrants and those so identified. Some European immigrant groups retain a collective national, ethnic, or religious identity and voluntarily remain somewhat apart from the Anglo or French ideal type—for example, the Hutterites. Canada's bilingual status has meant that immigrants must attempt to integrate into the English or French linguistic communities in order to participate fully in the wider society.

## Minority Group Immigrant Status

All immigrants not British or French in origin are, by definition, minority Canadians. These immigrants will have entered the country in response to specific pull factors—for example, to fill certain employment categories—and will generally have been assigned an entry status below that of British and French immigrants. These groups are minorities in more than numbers; they are also minorities in terms of the amount of power, prestige, and privilege they enjoy. These immigrants have historical backgrounds, cultures, and current concerns to which Canadian public schools, the media, and other formal institutions pay little or no attention. They are also underrepresented in decision-making bodies. Most important, they are aware of their subordinate status in the social, economic, and political spheres of life. It is estimated that by the year 2017, minority groups will be the numerical majority of the residents in both Toronto and Vancouver (Statistics Canada, 2005).

Some groups occupy minority status in several categories, such as language, religion, or racial origin. However, one category becomes the *master status*, or the most salient feature, in the eyes of the majority group, along a continuum of acceptance or rejection. Perceived racial origin has been the major distinguishing precondition of minority status in Canada, reinforced by common stereotypes and menial positions in the job market (Christensen, 2003). The limited number of racial minorities who were initially allowed to enter Canada tended to come as transient labour through Canada's international agreements with poor Third World countries, including the Caribbean, Mexico, and the Philippines. Even today, Canada continues to invite people from poor countries as migrant workers and live-in caregivers, many of whom have long been exploited.

Racialized minorities have suffered "not occasional insults or prejudice to some of their members, but blatant, prolonged, and persistent discrimination" (Krauter & Davis, 1978, p. 2). Results from a study based on Statistics Canada's 2002 Ethnic Diversity Survey involving 3000 racialized minority immigrants living in Toronto, Vancouver, and Montreal are revealing. Over a five-year period, discrimination was experienced at some point by 52 percent of Blacks, 45 percent of Chinese, 38 percent of Hispanics, 37 percent of South Asians, and 36 percent of West Asians/Arabs. Among these groups, all but the Chinese said that the media presents negative stereotypes of them. Only 22 percent of white-skinned Italians reported experiencing discrimination (Reitz & Banerjee, 2007). It is hardly coincidental that groups currently perceiving the highest levels of racism are those that were the most unwelcome in Canada prior to the 1960s.

Even if having generations of Canadian ancestors (as is true for nearly half of Blacks, and for many Chinese, Japanese, and Indo-Canadians), and being without foreign accents, citizens of colour continue to be asked, "Where are you *really* from?" Considered "new-comers" indefinitely, and challenged to prove one's legitimacy as truly Canadian, it is no wonder that recent studies indicate that second generation people of colour feel less Cana-dian than their white counterparts (Reitz & Banerjee, 2007).

## Minority/Majority Group Relations Today

In his classic work, *The Vertical Mosaic*, John Porter indicated that, in 1965, immigrant groups in Canada constituted a ladder-like hierarchy, based on ethnic ranking or stratifica-tion and, implicitly, on race (Porter, 1965). At the top were the British and immigrants from Northern and Western Europe, the middle ranks included Eastern and Southern Europeans and a small number of individuals from racial minorities, and at the bottom of the hierar-chy in the greatest numbers were racialized minorities (or people of colour) and the First Nations. Recent studies indicate that this general pattern of stratification has persisted, documenting racism in most important areas of daily life—employment, housing, educa-tion, social services, the justice system, and the media (Christensen, 2003; Fleras & Kuhz, 2001; Henry,Tator, Mattis & Rees, 2005; Reitz & Banerjee, 2007). Those exposed to a con-tinuous cycle of unequal access suffer the cumulative effects, from birth to old age. New immigrants may not recognize Canadian forms of "subtle" racism; other minority individ-uals may find it too painful to acknowledge.

Today, *culture* is no longer a major issue for the vast majority of European immigrants whose cultures are generally accepted in Canada. However, people considered to be of dif-ferent *races* are still viewed less likely to "fit in." As long as race remains a potent concept in Canadians' everyday perceptions, the degree of minority people's societal participation will continue to depend not only on their motivation, but also on the extent to which the majority group instigates barriers to limit their full participation.

"Visible minorities" is a uniquely Canadian term, first used in official government doc-uments. The *Employment Equity Act* defines visible minorities as "persons, other than Aboriginal peoples, who are non-Caucasian in race or non-white in colour" (Daily, 2003). Groups specified include Chinese, South Asians, Blacks, Arabs, West Asians, Filipinos, Southeast Asians, Latin Americans, Japanese, Koreans, and Pacific Islanders (Statistics Canada, 2001b). Labelling particular minority groups as "visible" could be interpreted as state-initiated racialization (Christensen, 2003, p. 723). Whatever the original intention behind applying this term, these disparate groups did not choose the term "visible minori-ties" themselves. They have nothing in common with each other save for their not being white and, therefore, facing discriminatory treatment.

A report by the United Nations' Committee on the Elimination of Racial Discrimina-tion indicated that identifying people susceptible to racial discrimination as "visible minorities" might contravene the aims and objectives of the International Convention on the Elimination of All Forms of Racial Discrimination, to which Canada is a signatory. On March 7, 2007, a Canadian Heritage–led delegation appeared before this committee and asked it to "reflect further" on the implications of using the term "visible minorities." Concerns were also raised about the term "ethno-cultural communities," and about racial profiling (*Vancouver Sun*, March 8, 2007e, p. A6). Many who are not white prefer the term "people of colour," or "racialized minorities," that are used interchangeably in this chapter, according to context. Racialized groups find meanings are attributed to their identifiable features connoting special, negative, or exotic significance and justifying their treatment as less deserving "others" with respect to societal benefits. Those suffering this common experience may eventually unite to defend their human rights and to gain a sense of belonging.

Displeasure with the growing racial diversity of the population is expressed overtly by the activities of organized hate groups such as the Heritage Front and neo-Nazis advocating white supremacy (Laquian & Laquian, 1997, p. 11) and, most recently, by use of the Internet.

## The Persistence of Inequality

Canada professes to adhere to equality and multiculturalism, so it is often difficult for students of social welfare to understand why some immigrant groups maintain a minority status over time while others seem to be upwardly mobile and are eventually absorbed into the dominant culture. In fact, from the earliest times in Canadian history until the present, some immigrant groups have been barred from equal access and life chances more than others in their dealings with major social institutions and other decision makers with cumulative effects. Racial minorities have suffered "not occasional insults or prejudice to some of their members, but blatant, prolonged, and persistent discrimination" (Krauter & Davis, 1978).

Majority-group Canadians have employed a number of techniques of domination and control that ensure that, once in Canada, immigrant groups are likely to retain a particular position in the racially and ethnically stratified society. Table 10.2 demonstrates the degree to which these techniques have been applied to immigrants of European and racial minority backgrounds. Racialized immigrants and their descendants have had to face the greatest number of restrictions. Skin colour and other racialized features make them identifiable targets for discriminatory treatment. Recent studies conclude that generalizations about assimilation and integration over time are apparently not applicable for "visible minorities" (Reitz & Banerjee, 2007). Moreover, all the individuals within a particular ethno-racial category do not experience the same degree of discriminatory treatment, either objectively or subjectively. Because of the hierarchy of racism in Canada, some racialized groups more than others find themselves accepted by Euro-Canadians and find some degree of change possible over time. For example, Japanese Canadians, considered "enemy aliens" during World War II, are now viewed as a "model minority." Domination and control techniques may be expressed in the form of covert and systemic racism rather than overt, individual discrimination. Institutional discrimination is rooted in racism that is so ingrained in the fabric of society's systems that it perpetuates itself.

Attitude studies suggest that 12 to 16 percent of Canadians admit to holding bigoted, intolerant attitudes, but these responses may be skewed by a desire to give "liberal" responses (Henry, Tator, Matthis, & Rees, 2005). Racism persists because ever since colonialism spread throughout the world, the concept of race and its attendant stereotypes has been deeply embedded in the value system and the discourse of European cultures. Moreover, racism supports a capitalist economic system that maintains oppression in the context of liberal "democracies," while providing personal, group, and social satisfaction by protecting privileges that few whites acknowledge or would wish to share (Christensen, 1999).

| TABLE 10.2 | European and Non-European Immigrants' Overall Experience of Techniques of Domination | | |
|---|---|---|---|
| Techniques of Domination | British and North/West European Immigrants | East/South European Immigrants | Non-European/ and Non-White Immigrants |
| 1. Immigrant restrictions | Low | Medium | High |
| 2. Persecution and expulsion | Low | Medium | High |
| 3. Land ownership restrictions | None | None | Medium to High |
| 4. Denial of civil liberties | Low | Medium | High |
| 5. Voting restrictions | Low | Low | Medium |
| 6. Arbitrary search and seizure | Low | Low | High |
| 7. Employment and promotion restrictions | Low | Low | High |
| 8. Housing restrictions | None | Low | High |
| 9. Public accommodation restrictions | None | None | High |
| 10. Education restrictions | None | None | Low to High |
| 11. Formally sanctioned negative racial myths and stereotypes | None | Medium | High |
| 12. Mass media restrictions | Low | Low | High |
| 13. Differential treatment by financial institutions | None | Low | Medium to High |
| 14. Social welfare/social service restrictions | None | Low | Medium to High |

# DOCUMENTING THE RACIAL DIVIDE

It is noteworthy that since the 1980s when a number of Canada-wide investigations documented the existence of racism affecting immigrants of colour (*Equality Now*, 1984), issues relating to racism have all but disappeared from the public arena, receiving little or no attention from politicians and other decision makers.

Recent studies have documented disturbing trends indicating that visible minority immigrants, whether recent or of long standing, are having a different experience of life in Canada than experienced by their counterparts of European origin (Kazemipur & Halli, 2000; Ornstein, 2000). Given Canada's colonial past with First Nations, Black slavery, and a history of blatant racist policies toward Asians, this has undoubtedly been the case since the founding of Canada. However, research is now exploring the root causes of the racial divide and underlying differences in the perceived life experiences and actual life chances of Canadians of various racial backgrounds (Christensen, 2003). Important findings relating to the economic status of racialized minorities include: reduced employment success for new immigrants, although their educational levels are at an all-time high (Reitz & Banerjee, 2007); men and women with university degrees earn less than 50 percent of that earned by their Canadian-born counterparts (Canadian Race Relations Foundation, 2005) due to the devaluing of foreign credentials (Aydemir & Skuterud, 2005); low career satisfaction among those with 20 years work experience (Catalyst Canada and the Diversity Institute in Management and Technology, 2007); and a racial dimension to economic inequality, resulting in rising poverty rates and reduced living standards (Picot & Sweetman, 2005). In some communities, the second generation is accomplishing less than their parents did in terms of education and employment (Orenstein, 2000). The economic situation of new immigrants showed no improvement after the turn of the millennium, despite reports of gains in the Canadian economy. The term "racial apartheid" has been used in a study concluding that poverty is on the rise only for some, not all, Canadians (Galabuzi, 2005). Several studies call for an in-depth investigation of regulatory bodies and government agencies to identify and remove obvious barriers to equality of opportunity and outcome (Canadian Race Relations Foundation, 2005). It is estimated that the cost of employment discrimination is $5 billion yearly.

Recent research findings in the psychosocial area are equally disturbing. When compared with white immigrants, racial minorities are less likely to vote, to become citizens, and to feel "Canadian." Moreover, perceptions of discrimination were found to increase the longer visible minorities remained in Canada. Perceived discrimination was greatest for the children of immigrants, who felt excluded and vulnerable, in part due to their experience of discrimination in school (Burrell & Christensen, 1987), but also because of observing the negative experiences of parents and role models. Integration is clearly hampered by racialized minorities' perceiving discrimination as a part of their daily lives (Reitz & Banerjee, 2006). Overall, obstacles to immigrant success have *increased* in recent decades while, at the same time, government funding for social services to assist immigrant settlement and integration has been reduced, and costs for credential upgrading and retraining have risen (Wayland, 2006).

Somewhat in contradiction to the above research results, other studies indicate that in recent decades, a majority of Canadians have supported maintaining, or increasing, emphasis on immigration (Reitz & Banerjee, 2006). Also, a recent report found that Canadians are the lowest among 23 Western industrialized nations on a number of indices of bigotry, with fewer than five percent stating that they would not wish to have a neighbour who was Muslim, Jewish, or an immigrant of a different race (Borooah & Mangan, in press). Nonetheless, studies suggest that most Euro-Canadians maintain social distance between themselves and racialized minorities. The anti-immigrant policies adopted by most European countries cause some to question how Canada too could be impacted.

## Islamophobia

Since September 11, 2001, there has been evidence of increasing intolerance against Muslims, and those identified as *likely* to be adherents of the Muslim faith. Although seldom discussed in the broader context of race, as opposed to religious affiliation, *racial profiling*, or undue harassment of individuals seeming to fit a predetermined set of visual characteristics, has become a national issue. Those assumed to "look like" Muslims, including those of South Asian and Arab/West Asian backgrounds, often experience delays at border crossings. In the worst case scenario, some have been arrested and subsequently tortured, on foreign soil, as has happened in several now-notorious cases. Controversy has also arisen from unsuccessful efforts by some male leaders in Toronto's Muslim community to introduce Sharia law in personal disputes, from the wearing of Islamic headdresses by some females, and from the June 2006 arrest of 17 individuals in Toronto suspected of planning terrorist activities. As of November 6, 2006, guidelines issued by Canada's immigration ministry

stipulate that, for security purposes, facial features must be visible for passport pho-
tographs, permanent residence cards, and temporary resident visas (*Vancouver Sun*, 2007b).

## Limits to Accommodation?

Prompted by government and by the media, the pros and cons of immigration are often discussed, especially when the economy slows down. Although recognizing certain advantages to high levels of immigration, some question whether there should be limits to
accommodating racial and cultural differences. A rural Quebec town, Herouxville, recently
issued and posted on the Internet a "declaration of norms," apparently aimed at potential
Muslims and Sikh immigrants. Some of the "norms" include not stoning women to death
and allowing women to drive, dance, own property, choose what they want to wear, sign
cheques, and make decisions (*Vancouver Sun*, January 31, 2007d, p. A5). At the time, Herouxville had one immigrant family, but claimed willingness to accept others as long as
they followed the rules of the majority. Several Muslim leaders are considering lodging a
complaint to the Quebec Human Rights Commission.

## CURRENT IMMIGRATION AND REFUGEE POLICY

Students of social work may be unsure of how immigrants differ from refugees and other
types of residents. Yet these distinctions are significant in residents' daily lives. Under the
direction of the Minister of Citizenship and Immigration (currently Diane Finley), the
Department of Citizenship and Immigration Canada (CIC) plays a crucial role in all matters pertaining to immigrants and refugees and presents an Annual Report to Parliament. In
selecting foreign nationals, the CIC states that Canada's immigration program is based on
non-discriminatory principles—foreign nationals are assessed without regard to race,
nationality, ethnic origin, colour, religion, or gender.

The current *Immigration and Refugee Protection Act* (IRPA) came into effect on June
28, 2002, and aimed to modernize Canada's immigration policy; facilitate the entry of
adaptable workers with flexible skills, rather than specific occupations; and provide new
security measures to prevent the entry of those deemed a threat to "safety and security"
(Annual Report to Parliament on Immigration, 2005a).

Notably, Security Certificates may be issued by the IRPA to non-citizens suspected of
being a threat to national security, leading to their indefinite detention with no right to legal
counsel. A judge has the right to withhold from the detainee any information considered
injurious to national security. If judged a threat to national security, a removal (from
Canada) order is issued. The judge's decision is final, with no right of appeal.

## Anti-Terrorism Legislation

Events of September 11, 2001 ("9/11") led to greater emphasis being placed on security
measures. In December 2001, the Canadian Parliament passed the *Anti-terrorism Act*
(formerly *Bill C-36*) to improve the screening of prospective refugees and immigrants,
and to secure borders in close co-operation with the United States. Through "tough
anti-terrorism measures, the act seeks to combat terrorism and terrorist activities at
home and abroad, while protecting Canadian values of respect and fairness" (Department of Justice, Canada, 2007). Controversial measures expanded powers given to the

security establishment in efforts to "identify, remove, detain, or prosecute, convict, and punish terrorists, and address the root causes of such hatred" (Citizenship and Immigration Canada, 2001). Such provisions, perceived as incompatible with the Charter of Rights and Freedoms, expired on March 21 and, against the wishes of the Conservative government, were not renewed. Checks and balances have been proposed when targeting, listing, or prosecuting those suspected or accused of terrorist activity, placing the burden of proof on the state.

Countless law-abiding immigrants and Canadians now find themselves under suspicion and at risk of discrimination from authorities and the general public. The much publicized case of Maher Arar, a 36-year-old Syrian-born Canadian, indicates the danger of racial profiling. It indicates the need for Canadian law enforcement agencies such as the Royal Canadian Mounted Police (RCMP) and the Canadian Security Intelligence Service (CSIS) to exercise extreme caution when implementing policies under the *Anti-terrorism Act*. A costly inquiry found the RCMP culpable, as Mr. Arar suspected, in having passed false information to the U.S. in 2002 that led to his airport arrest and deportation to Syria. He suffered 11 months of torture and was forced to make false confessions about links to al-Qaeda terrorists. Mr. Arar recently received a public apology from Prime Minister Stephen Harper, and $12.5 million for hardship and legal fees. Had Mr. Arar's wife not kept the situation before the public, the outcome could well have been different. Several other Arab men have claimed RCMP complicity in their arrest and torture when visiting Syria and have requested independent reviews.

## Immigrant Selection

CIC is responsible for ensuring that entrants to Canada contribute to the country's social and economic interests, whether as permanent or temporary residents wishing to work, study, or visit. The categories for permanent residents are: (1) economic class (skilled workers, business immigrants, provincial nominees, and live-in caregivers); (2) family (spouses, partners, children under age 22, parents, and grandparents of the sponsors); (3) refugees in need of protection, or asylum (see "Refugees" later in the chapter); and (4) exceptionally, those who do not meet the usual criteria may be accepted on humanitarian, compassionate, or public policy grounds.

The points system of "selection factors" below, adopted in June 2002, remains in effect for those seeking economic class immigrant status, with the exception of business applicants. However, the selection criteria for business class (formerly "independent") immigrants excludes language, and the maximum for experience is 35 points. Adaptability for business class is awarded only 6 points. The necessary pass mark is 35 points, subject to change at the direction of the Minister of Immigration.

## Selection Grid

1. Education: 5 to 25 points maximum (from high school to a Master's degree or Ph.D. and at least 13 years of full-time or equivalent study);

2. Language: 0 (neither official language) to 24 points maximum (for fluency in both English and French);

3. Experience: 15 to 21 points maximum (for 1 to 4 years of work experience);

4.  Age: 10 points maximum (if 21 to 49 years of age) less 2 points for each year older than 49 or younger than 21;

5.  Arranged employment: 10 points maximum (for confirmed job offer or a temporary work permit);

6.  Adaptability: 3 to 10 points maximum (including point awarded for education level of spouse or common law/same-sex partner).

An applicant requires a minimum of 67 points to "pass" (Citizenship and Immigration Canada, 2006c).

Recently modified selection criteria for skilled workers requires that work experience (criteria 3 above) during the last 10 years must have been managerial and requiring university, college, or technical training. As of December 2003, "transitional measures" allowed economic class immigrants to be assessed according to criteria that were in effect prior to the adoption of the current IRPA. Notably, category 6, adaptability, is a subjective judgment made by an immigration officer.

As of May 2006, the non-refundable Permanent Residence fee was reduced by 50 percent, to $490 for the principal applicant, and to $475 for any accompanying spouses or common law partners. This fee is not required for dependent children, orphaned family members, or protected persons, including Convention refugees. Adopted children need no longer be declared Permanent Residents before becoming citizens (Citizenship and Immigration Canada, 2006a). Selection criteria and application fees are subject to change without notice.

In 2007, Canada aims to attract 240 000 to 265 000 newcomers, the highest number in 25 years (Citizenship and Immigration Canada, 2006b). The target for economic class immigrants has increased by 15 000 since 2006. Emphasis is again being placed on attracting business immigrants meeting the following criteria: investors need business experience, a net worth of at least CAN$800 000, and $400 000 invested for job creation and economic development before obtaining a visa; entrepreneurs must have a net worth of at least CAN$300 000 and be able to own and manage a business that creates jobs for Canadians or permanent residents; and self-employed persons must demonstrate their intentions to contribute significantly to Canadian culture, athletics, or farm management.

## Bilateral Agreements

Bilateral collaboration between the CIC and certain provinces has been formalized by comprehensive framework agreements on immigration with British Columbia, Saskatchewan, Manitoba, Ontario, Quebec, Prince Edward Island, and the Yukon, and provincial delivery of settlement services is included for British Columbia, Manitoba, and Quebec. With the exception of refugees and members of the family class, Quebec sets its own annual immigration targets and selects its own immigrants and refugees abroad, most of whom come from French-speaking Third World regions such as francophone Africa. The agreements between the federal government and Saskatchewan, Manitoba, Quebec, and New Brunswick are "indefinite." All others are time-limited (Citizenship and Immigration Canada, 2006). CIC is working with francophone minority communities in provinces and territories to attract and retain French-speaking immigrants. The Provincial Nominees Program (PNP) works exclusively to allow provinces and territories to identify and designate an agreed-upon number of nominees for immigration who meet their specific labour market and economic needs. New Brunswick, Newfoundland and Labrador, Alberta, Manitoba, and Nova Scotia participate in this program, viewed as potentially encouraging for immigrants to settle outside Canada's three largest cities. The provinces' nominees bypass the federal Points System, but must meet health and security requirements (Citizenship and Immigration Canada, 2006a).

## Citizenship and Residency

Non-citizens cannot vote in federal and provincial elections. Landed immigrants may apply for citizenship after living three years in Canada, within a five-year period. The citizenship oath demonstrates ability in an official language and allegiance to Canada, as well as the Queen of England. Providing they meet the residency requirements, pass a citizenship test, and have no criminal record, landed immigrants are granted full rights and privileges of citizenship. Permanent residents and citizens 18 years or older may sponsor relatives who want to become permanent residents or family class immigrants.

As of February 15, 2005, a controversial retention of citizenship aspect of the 1998 *Citizenship Act* came into full effect for second and third generations of children born to Canadian parents abroad who had not lived in Canada. Since 1977, the law requires that such persons take action before their 28th birthday, or they automatically cease to be citizens (Citizenship and Immigration Canada, 1998). As of January 1, 2007, citizenship certificates of those subject to retention will expire when they reach the age of 28. People who lost their citizenship as adults can apply to resume citizenship, but must meet certain conditions. In the case of "obvious error," citizenship officers, not judges, can make decisions that only the Minister of Immigration can reverse, rather than an appeal board (Canadian Bar Association, 2003a). Under the *Access to Information Act*, CBC found that 4000 Canadians had lost their citizenship in seven years (*CBC News*, 2007). It is believed that thousands more are similarly at risk (for example, war brides, those living abroad who never registered as Canadians, and those born "out of wedlock"). A House of Commons Committee is reviewing the citizenship retention law and related procedures with senior staff of CIC. Critics have suggested that the act be amended temporarily to allow Canadians stripped of citizenship to be repatriated, and that the entire act be overhauled to prevent current problems (*CBC News*, 2007).

Controversy also surrounds the requirement that all "permanent residents"—landed immigrants who are not citizens—carry a Permanent Resident Card (PRC), which took effect on January 1, 2004. The card generally expires after five years and a resident who is abroad cannot return without it. Permanent residents must remain in Canada for a cumulative period of two years for every five working years, unless they are working for a Canadian company abroad or accompanying someone doing so. A breach of any of these requirements, misuse of a prior card, a removal order, a criminal conviction, or being suspected of being a security risk are all reasons for non-renewal. The Canadian Bar Association has questioned why, since permanent resident status is good for life, a PRC is required and must be renewed by a CIC officer by a specific date—a power that is open to abuse, with no process of appeal (Canadian Bar Association, 2003).

## Refugees

Social workers often serve refugees whose life experiences, before and after arrival in Canada, differ significantly from those of immigrants. Refugees seek resettlement in foreign countries for reasons other than voluntary immigration, and Canada will undoubtedly face increasing requests to accept refugees. Worldwide, there are 8.4 million refugees (UNHCR, 2006). Refugees enter Canada through several routes and must undergo security and criminal record checks.

The current *Immigration and Refugee Protection Act* (IRPA) came into effect in June 2002, covering all aspects of immigration to Canada and the granting of refugee protection. The act contains provisions for a Refugee Appeal Division that has yet to be implemented. The reigning government considered the system in place fair, generous, and fully in accord with the Canadian Charter of Rights and Freedoms and international legal obligations (Citizen and Immigration Canada, 2005b). The Immigration and Refugee Board (IRB), created by Parliament in 1989, is an independent, quasi-judicial tribunal, reporting to Parliament through the Minister of Citizenship and Immigration. The IRB is responsible for applying the IRPA and makes decisions on immigration and refugee claims and appeals pertaining to who needs protection among the thousands of claimants who apply yearly while in Canada.

In February 2007, the chair of the IRB, Jean-Guy Fleury, resigned, along with five members of the seven-member panel that selects new members, over a report calling for half of the panel to be appointed by the Minister, Diane Finley. Several organizations concerned with immigrants and refugees expressed concern about a return to patronage appointments based on ideology, rather than merit. Moreover, many fear that a Conservative government may stem the flow of refugees by adopting restrictive policies (*Toronto Star*, March 3, 2007). At the time of this writing, 52 of the 156 IRB positions are vacant, adding to the problem of growing backlogs.

Through the Humanitarian Resettlement Program, Canada extends protection to Convention refugees. As a signatory to the United Nations Convention and Protocol, Canada has declared its international responsibility to protect Convention refugees from being returned to countries where these people fear persecution. Convention refugees "are individuals who, because of a well-founded fear of persecution for reasons of race, religion, nationality, membership in a particular social group, or political opinion, are outside their country of nationality or habitual residence, and are unable or unwilling by reason of that fear to return to that country" (Citizenship and Immigration Canada, 2005, p. 34). Convention refugees are selected abroad, assisted by the United Nations High Commissioner for Refugees (UNHCR), and receive government assistance to enter Canada. The definition of a "protected person" is extended to individuals in similar circumstances (that is, those who are seriously and personally affected by armed conflict, civil war, or massive human rights violations), but who do not qualify as Convention refugees.

Group processing of Convention refugees occurred, for the third time in Canada, when 800 Karen refugees (of Burmese ancestry) from Thailand were brought to Canada late in 2006 and early in 2007, following the tsunami. Attention was given to risk factors, including trauma and settlement issues facing single female-headed households.

The Immigrant Loans Program allows refugees from abroad to cover required costs of pre-entry medical examination, transportation to Canada, and initial resettlement. Currently, 91 percent of loans are repaid (Citizenship and Immigration Canada, 2006, p. 29). Under the Resettlement Assistance Program, CIC provides essential services (such as accommodation, temporary health care, income support) to the refugees selected abroad for one year after they arrive in Canada. These costs too must be repaid. Unless for reason of disability, refugees receiving social welfare assistance are ineligible to sponsor family members for reunification purposes, and must apply to the Immigration Appeals Division for humanitarian and compassionate consideration, adding at least two years to the process. Debt repayment is required before sponsorship of relatives can proceed, making financial interests appear to be placed above human rights by the state (Canadian Council for Refugees, 2006).

The Private Sponsorship of Refugees program allows the government to collect social assistance costs should the sponsor (who may be an individual or organization) not provide its own financial support. In 2004, innovative partnerships began with CIC, the Hebrew Immigrant Aid Society, and the United Church, facilitating private sponsorship.

## Asylum and Protection

A second category defined by the IRPA is persons in need of protection who are already in Canada. "Asylum" seekers arrive as visitors, or illegally, and apply for refugee status through the IRB. Negative decisions usually lead to extremely lengthy waiting times for review by the Immigration Appeal Division. A "pre-removal assessment" assesses the risks that a person might be removed from Canada and returned to a dangerous or changing political situation in another country. Risk of persecution, torture, cruel and unusual punishment, or risk to life are assessed. If accepted, "protected" refugees, including their family members, may then apply for permanent residence status. It is a little known fact that those in this category must pay cost recovery fees of $550 per adult and $150 per child to apply for permanent residency and include their family members. Refugee children who have been separated from their parents are treated as principal applicants, and each child must pay the $550 processing fee. This requirement has been criticized as a significant barrier to family reunification. Charitable organizations wishing to sponsor refugees may find such fees prohibitive (Canadian Council for Refugees, 2006).

Freedom of movement does not necessarily apply to refugees. They may be questioned, arrested, detained, or deported while awaiting examination at ports of entry or immigration inquiries. Removal orders may be executed if they are considered security risks or a public danger. Those unable to confirm their identity may also be detained, although obtaining passports and other documentation is often impossible for refugees.

In 2005, Canada accepted 35 768 refugees. Those accepted while in Canada (and their families) accounted for 70 percent, and those accepted while abroad as government-assisted refugees (many directly from refugee camps) accounted for the remaining 30 percent. The leading refugee source countries were Colombia, Afghanistan, Pakistan, China, and Sri Lanka (Citizenship and Immigration Canada, 2006d). Canada's response to overseas refugees and claimants from certain countries is fraught with political overtones in the international arena.

## Foreign Workers and Temporary Residents

Temporary residents play a vital, if unrecognized, role in filling gaps in the Canadian labour market. Visa requirements are determined on a country by country basis. Generally required is a valid passport, a work permit specifying the prospective job and the employer, the duration of employment, and an assessment by Human Resources and Development

Canada, ensuring that there will be no adverse affects on citizens or permanent residents. Prospective workers must be in good health, not have a criminal record, and pose no security risk. As of 2004, foreigners may apply for a work permit at ports of entry in visa-exempt countries. In 2005, Canada admitted a total of 99 146 foreign workers for whom employment was authorized (Centre for Research and Information on Canada, 2005).

To facilitate the entry of temporary foreign workers, CIC negotiated revisions to the North American Free Trade Agreement with the United States and Mexico, expanding the list of professionals eligible to work in each other's countries. In 2006, the Canadian government announced the piloting of temporary foreign worker units in Calgary and Vancouver. In addition to legal immigrants and temporary workers, Third World people of colour constitute a majority of the underground economy in, for example, Toronto's construction industry, British Columbia's farm and fruit market, and among female domestic workers.

The Live-in Caregiver Program falls under the jurisdiction of special agreements Canada has signed with Third World countries—for example, the Philippines. To receive a work permit, participants must have completed the equivalent of Canadian secondary school education; have six months of full-time training in a field related to their work; speak, read, and understand English or French; and sign a contract with the future employer. Caregivers can apply for permanent residence after two years and within three years of their arrival (Citizenship and Immigration Canada, 2005a, p. 54). Critics note that although often well-educated, caregivers are also often exploited, working long hours and facing threats or harassment. Given the source countries, the live-in requirement, and the female gender of most participants, many see racist, classist, and sexist components in this policy.

The Seasonal Agricultural Workers Program allows the import of temporary labourers, mostly from Mexico and the Caribbean, ensuring that Canada's crops are planted and harvested at the best times. They fall outside the regulations and benefits that apply to other Canadian workers, such as being able to form unions, and often live and work under extremely poor conditions. Accidents and even deaths are occasionally publicized by the media, but far more are unreported.

Foreign students are temporary residents and pay the highest tuition fees, often easing their entry into Canada. They seek a quality education, but in recent years problems in the education industry and occasional attacks on females have caused China to take a somewhat jaundiced view of Canadian colleges and universities. Those who register in programs lasting six months or less no longer require study permits. In 2006, the Minister announced the national "roll-out permit program" allowing foreign students, viewed as potential skilled immigrants, to work off-campus.

Critics of the current IRPA fault the act for lack of transparency of its framework legislation. It leaves operational details outside the domain of the House of Commons and thus avoids public scrutiny. It also gives greater powers to immigration officers and the Minister of Immigration, and limits opportunities for appeal. Although increasing attention has been given to gender issues recently, the impact of CIC's policies, programs, and settlement initiatives have yet to be systematically analyzed.

## NEW CIC INITIATIVES

In 2005, CIC introduced the *Strategic Framework for Gender-Based Analysis* (GBA, 2005–2010), focusing on the differential impact on men and women of existing and proposed CIC immigration and refugee policies and programs over the life cycle. This analysis was used in the group processing and resettlement of the Karen refugees from Thailand following the tsunami between the fall of 2006 and early 2007, and included, for example, factors relating to women at risk, single female-headed households, and age-related issues. The framework also suggests simply continuing to follow 1993 guidelines on women refugee claimants fearing gender-related persecution, which includes domestic violence. In fact, there is a pressing need to update these guidelines given the rise in global wars using violence against women as a strategic weapon.

In May 2006, the Minister announced measures allowing the issuance of fee-exempt 120-day temporary resident permits to victims of the human rights violation of human trafficking. Recognizing that a method of control used by traffickers is confiscation of identification papers, bona fide victims are offered time-limited health care benefits and recovery opportunities (Citizenship and Immigration Canada, 2006a, p. 24).

A new initiative facilitates immigrant integration into the labour market. A major frustration for immigrants is finding only menial jobs despite having received high selection points for education. Acknowledging immigrants' difficulties finding jobs commensurate with their skills, the Internationally Trained Workers Initiative focuses on foreign credential assessment and recognition, enhanced language skills, information, research, bridge-to-work initiatives, and workplace discrimination.

Led by the Department of Canadian Heritage, A Canada for All: Canada's Action Plan Against Racism is a multi-dimensional initiative aimed at building "a true sense of belonging and shared citizenship for immigrants" (Citizenship and Immigration Canada, 2006a, p. 35). However, the plan simply suggests co-ordinating existing ineffective broad policies and has few specifics.

# CANADA'S RESPONSE TO MULTICULTURAL REALITIES

## The Multiculturalism and Equality Measures

The report of the 1969 Royal Commission on Bilingualism and Biculturalism documented concerns by those of non-French and non-British heritage that their contributions to Canada had been ignored (Royal Commission on Bilingualism and Biculturalism, 1970). Consequently, Prime Minister Pierre Trudeau announced the 1971 policy of "multiculturalism within a bilingual framework." Multiculturalism remains the underlying philosophy of programs promoting intergroup understanding and harmony, given Canada's increasing diversity, not least of all in Quebec. The multiculturalism policy recognized the cultural and racial diversity of Canadian society as a fundamental characteristic of Canadian heritage and identity, and requested the removal of barriers to equitable participation, service access, and protection under the law. The policy called on federal institutions, in particular, to ensure equal opportunity in employment and advancement.

The earliest phase of multiculturalism (1971–1980) emphasized the preservation of cultural traditions and ancestral folkways, but failed to respond to systemic causes of inequality. In 1977, the Canadian Human Rights Commission was established and empowered by the *Human Rights Act* to settle complaints of discrimination in employment and federal government services. Its focus has been on information, prevention, and investigation of systemic issues impacting specific groups or human rights as a whole. Human rights commissions at the federal level and in various provinces have had disappointing results in combatting racial discrimination and structural inequality, and are often criticized for being slow to act and lacking in public accountability and enforcement provisions. Moreover, governments in power have disbanded some provincial commissions on a whim, as happened in Ontario and, most recently, in British Columbia under the government of Gordon Campbell.

Twenty-five years ago, the Canadian Charter of Rights and Freedoms was enacted as part of the Canadian Constitution. Aspects of the Charter are still being debated. Critics feared that unelected judges could override Parliament's decisions. Section 15 (1) specifies equality before the law, the right to equal protection and benefit of the law without discrimination and, "in particular, without discrimination on the basis of race, national and ethnic origin, colour, religion, sex, age or mental or physical disability." Critics fault the "notwithstanding clause," for allowing provinces, for a period of time, to opt out of adhering to specific sections of the Charter protecting "targeted groups"—that is, women, racial minorities, Aboriginal peoples, and the disabled. To date, women from majority-group backgrounds are the only targeted group that has benefited from the Charter's equity clauses affecting hiring and promotion. Racialized minorities are testing the equality clause of the Charter in courts and in the human rights commission.

The period from 1980 through 1988 was the phase of "institutional multiculturalism," prompted by reports of pervasive inequality in the hiring and promotion of visible minorities, women, First Nations people, and disabled persons (for example, Abella, 1984, *Equality Now*). The *Multiculturalism Act* of 1988 made Canada the first country ever with an official multiculturalism law and a Multiculturalism Ministry promoting cultural pluralism. Subsequent employment equity legislation produced some improvement in the private sector for racialized minorities, but only limited progress in the government public services, the primary focus of the legislation. Women made considerable progress in both sectors.

A final phase of "instrumental multiculturalism," capitalizing on the economic benefits of a culturally diverse workforce, began in the 1990s and continues today. This phase emphasizes attracting economic class investors and entrepreneurs as immigrants. Under the Department of Canadian Heritage, multiculturalism and citizenship focuses more on integrating racial minorities than on dealing with racism and correcting its negative societal effects.

Official multiculturalism has come under attack by majority-group Canadians as supporting "special interest groups," and some racialized groups fear developing separate and unequal stratified enclaves. Euro-Canadians speak of "backlash" and "reverse discrimination," as some white males, oblivious to racial discrimination and white privilege, view employment equity provisions as discriminating against them. Some minority individuals consider multiculturalism a form of social control aimed at co-opting oppressed groups through the rhetoric of equality without alleviating structural inequalities. Multiculturalism policies are simultaneously viewed as threatening and enhancing national unity. Governments and the media devote little attention to multicultural and racial issues during elections and constitutional debates, perhaps because the racialized minorities most affected by inequities and injustice have yet to organize an effective, united response. Most important, the conclusion drawn by current researchers is that multiculturalism is not working well for visible minorities (Galabuzi, 2005; Pico & Sweetman, 2003; Reitz & Banerjee, 2007; Statistics Canada, 2003; Wayland, 2006).

In 1997, the establishment of the Canadian Race Relations Foundation (CRRF) was announced by Canadian Heritage. CRRF is a charitable organization operating at "arm's length" from government that aims to document the nature and extent of racism and discrimination, develop policies and programs to counteract it, and empower targeted groups through advocacy, education, and persuasive information (Canadian Race Relations Foundation, 2004). The effectiveness of this organization to influence meaningful and lasting change in the status of racialized minorities has yet to be determined.

## A SUMMARY OF THE SOCIAL WELFARE EXPERIENCE OF THREE IMMIGRANT GROUPS

Social workers must be able to recognize the subtle and overt inequalities that various immigrant groups have endured historically, and which continue to influence majority group perceptions of racialized groups, affecting their life chances and sense of belonging. For purposes of illustration, the past and present social welfare experience of three immigrant groups is highlighted here.

### Jewish Immigrants

The early Jewish settlers entered Canada under British rule, when restrictions against non-Catholic settlers were lifted (Weinfeld, Shaffir, & Cotler, 1981). Montreal had a very small Jewish population by 1760 (Sloame, 2007). Most of the 107 Jewish settlers listed in the 1831 census were relatively wealthy emigrants from the thirteen colonies of what would become the United States. They settled in Montreal with little difficulty. These Sephardic Jews, with ancestry in North Africa, Portugal, and Spain, established the congregation of the Remnants of Israel as early as 1768, and helped new immigrants adjust to Canadian socio-economic conditions.

From 1840 to 1900, Jews from Germany, Poland, and the Russian Empire came as colonists. Most of the 2000 residents in the 1889 census resided in Ontario and Quebec—a closely knit, unified community of European or Ashkenazi immigrants having survived poverty. As their religious customs differed somewhat from those of the earlier Sephardic congregation, they founded Montreal's Congregation Shaar Hashomayim. Jews are considered both an ethnic and a religious community.

From 1870 to 1914, religious persecution in Russia drove 15 000 refugees to seek better living standards and religious freedom in Canada. They settled in Winnipeg, having accepted homestead grants or work on the Canadian Pacific Railway. By 1915, Jewish congregations existed in Winnipeg, Calgary, Regina, and Saskatoon, and the community in Canada was 125 000 strong (Tulchinsky, 1992).

Jewish immigration fluctuated according to economic conditions and religious persecution in their countries of origin. During World War I, the number of Jews from Eastern Europe increased. The Jewish Immigrant Aid Services (JIAS), established in 1919, formulated a response to Canadian immigration policy, a role that it continues to play. In 1934, the Canadian Jewish Congress lobbied on behalf of Jewish refugees hoping to escape the Nazi regime, when Canada considered them a "less preferred" group. Despite protest from some quarters, Jewish immigration peaked between 1930 and 1940, when 11 005 were admitted. In the 1950s, displaced persons from the Hungarian uprising and the Jewish expulsion from Egypt arrived.

The late 1950s saw the arrival of Israeli and North African French-speaking Jews from Morocco who were darker in appearance, and whose religious customs made their integration into the older Euro-Canadian Jewish community challenging. During the 1970s, some 35 000 Jews (3500 yearly) immigrated to Canada. Currently the Canadian Jewish population numbers 370 505 (Statistics Canada, 2005), 99 percent of whom live in Montreal, Toronto, Winnipeg, Vancouver, and Ottawa.

Practising acculturation without assimilation, the Jewish community is among Canada's most institutionally complete. In major cities, Jewish organizations cater to the cultural and social welfare needs of their community—with hospitals, Jewish Family Services, and Jewish Vocational Services. Altruistic charity is highly valued, encouraged by a sense of responsibility for other Jews (Klein & Mirsky, 2003). Holocaust studies conducted over a 30-year period indicate that, along with the British, Canadian Jews are over-represented at the highest economic, educational, and occupational levels, and are well-integrated into the social, economic, and political fabric of the wider society. The Jewish community is well-organized, with advocacy organizations such as B'nai Brith Canada and the Canadian Jewish Congress. Communication is fostered through some twenty newspapers and journals, and children have opportunities to maintain their cultural and religious heritage by attending day schools and synagogue-affiliated after-school programs (Sloame, 2007).

Although socially accepted and allowed opportunities for upward mobility, anti-Semitism exists in forms of covert discrimination, hate propaganda, the occasional desecration of gravesites, and Holocaust denial (The Stephen Roth Institute, 2005). Issues in the Middle East continue to be a major focus for the community, as is the pursuance of Nazi war criminals at home and abroad. Such ongoing issues both unify and divide the Jewish people, given the diverse attitudes toward such emotionally laden subjects.

## Black Immigrants

Most Canadians seem unaware that people of African descent have been in Canada for 400 years. In the 1600s, Matthieu da Costa was a Black navigator who interpreted the Micmac language for Samuel de Champlain when he reached Canadian shores (Canadian Heritage, 2005). Such facts, coupled with the myth that legalized slavery never existed in Canada, has contributed to Canadians of African ancestry being the oldest, but most invisible, racialized minority in Canadian history (Christensen, 2005). Blacks are the only Canadians whose ancestors suffered enslavement for some 200 years under French and British rule. The legacy of slavery for the colonists was to normalize the perception of Blacks as "other," and as being oppressed.

In 1628, Oliver de Jeune was the first slave recorded sold in New France. In 1689, King Louis XIV legalized slavery, providing unpaid African labour for fisheries, mines, agriculture, and households in Montreal, Quebec City, and Trois-Rivières. By 1759, there were some 4000 slaves in New France. The *Code Noire* protected Europeans from slave revolt, theft, and escape in Quebec, where marriage to a French man freed a slave woman. Elsewhere, slaves gained freedom only by "gift or purchase" (Winks, 1997). From the time of the "founding" of present-day Quebec, New Brunswick, Nova Scotia, and Ontario, until the early nineteenth century, Blacks endured unspeakable inhumane treatment, and were sold on livestock markets as chattel (Walker, 1995). Escape attempts were diagnosed as "drapetomania," a supposed mental illness that caused slaves to flee their enslavement.

In 1776, 3000 Blacks who served segregated Loyalist armies during the American Revolution seldom received the land promised (Walker, 1995). Subjected to assaults, mob violence in Shelburne and Birchtown, and three hangings for food theft during the 1789 Nova Scotia famine, hundreds of disillusioned Blacks left for Sierre Leone, Africa, some in 1792, and others in 1800 (Winks, 1997). During the War of 1812, ancestors of many Black Nova Scotians arrived, deserters from the American colonies. If not returned to their masters, slaves who sought freedom through the Underground Railroad faced severe forms of prejudice and discrimination in Canada, contrary to popular myth. By 1860, Canada had a population of 60 000 Blacks. Many returned to the United States when the Civil War ended. The first official Canadian census, in 1871, recorded 21 496 Blacks.

Until the 1960s, in both Ontario and Nova Scotia, land ownership was restricted and schools were segregated, as were social services in Nova Scotia. Nova Scotia's ghetto-like Black areas were without water or sewage services, similar to conditions in the south of the United States at that time. City officials ordered a Black church bulldozed at night when Blacks refused to leave their Africville homes, considered too close to downtown Halifax. Unwelcome in the Prairies, Blacks settled on Salt Spring Island and opened businesses on Vancouver Island. Other than the 3000 Caribbean female domestic servants, Black immigration was restricted between 1955 and 1965. In the late 1960s, when racially restrictive immigration regulations were removed, most Blacks came from the West Indies (Christensen & Weinfeld, 1993). Although 95 percent were skilled labourers, work as railway porters and waiters was the only occupation readily available for men.

Since the 1960s, Haitians, now numbering about 90 000, have settled mostly in Montreal, resulting in two "black solitudes," one speaking Creole/French and the other English, but having the experience of racism in common. The 1960s immigrants were mostly professionals, while the backgrounds of later arrivals varied. Under the general amnesty of 1973, many Haitian "visitors" became legal residents, while 1500 were deported and "illegals" were exploited in the job market (Jean-Baptiste, 1979).

Blacks have responded to marginalization by establishing Black churches, self-help movements, lobby groups, social services, and the Black press. Education is highly valued, contrary to the mainstream media portrayals of Blacks involved almost exclusively in sports, entertainment, and crime (Fleras & Kuhz, 2001).

The 662 210 Blacks living in Canada are ethnically, culturally, and religiously diverse (Statistics Canada, 2001). Almost half of the recent Black immigrants are from Africa. Blacks are the third largest immigrant group in Canada, and nearly half are Canadian-born and are as likely to be university educated as others born in Canada. Research indicates that, among racialized minorities, systemic racism appears to affect Blacks most severely, whether in education, employment and promotion, or criminal justice (Galabuzi, 2005; Reitz & Banerjee, 2007), limiting their opportunities for integration and upward mobility. The incidence of family poverty is 44.6 percent, due to cumulative effects of racism and the fact that 46 percent of Black children live in single-parent households (Milan & Tran, 2004). Owing to racial profiling and police harassment and brutality toward Black males, in particular, a number have been killed, though unarmed. Frustration and hopelessness among alienated males has also led to self-destructive behaviours. Conflict in poverty-stricken areas has resulted in many highly publicized deaths. Blacks are now overrepresented in Ontario prisons (Henry et al., 2005).

For the first time ever, and urged to do so by many of African ancestry, the government of Canada commemorated the anniversary of the abolition of the slave trade on March 25, 2007 (Canadian Heritage, 2007). The 1807 *Abolition of the Slave Trade Act* prohibited the traffic of slaves, but it was in 1833 that debates about the profitability and morality of slavery led to its abolishment in British colonies. Any discussion of an apology or compensation by the government for Canadian-born descendants of slaves, similar to action taken on behalf of Japanese and Chinese Canadians, is averted by politicians.

Blacks have made, and continue to make, significant contributions to all walks of life in Canada, but their racial identity is seldom associated with these achievements. James Douglas, the first governor of the colony of British Columbia, was of African and European ancestry. The current Governor General of Canada, Michaëlle Jean, of Haitian origin, speaks proudly of being of African descent. Black Canadians will undoubtedly continue to press for the enforcement of their human rights and for fair and equal opportunity, hoping to soon enjoy full participation and a sense of belonging in Canada.

## The Chinese

The Chinese first came to Canada during the Fraser River gold rush of the 1850s, hoping to escape the economic hardships caused by imperialist invasions and peasant revolts in China (Li, 1998; Nguyen, 1982). Referred to as "the yellow peril," many intended to return one day to China, as expected by governing officials. Unable to amass sufficient wealth for transport to China, most remained in British Columbia and were viewed as casual cheap labour.

About 17 000 Chinese came to help build the Canadian Pacific Railroad in the mid-1800s. They experienced extreme forms of harassment and oppression from the general public, and also as a result of government policies. Prevented from bringing their wives and children to Canada, Chinese "bachelors" faced social sanctions for "lusting after" white women. When the railroad was completed, an unknown number did return to China. Those who remained worked in laundries, clearing forests, gardening, and domestic service, for low wages. Even such employment was perceived as unfair competition by white workers whose Workingman's Protective Association in Victoria, British Columbia, charged the Chinese licence fees of $30 to work and $500 for the use of opium. Considered inferior and unsuitable for assimilation, the Chinese were barred from receiving welfare benefits, owning Crown lands, holding public works jobs, and owning liquor licences. Chinese self-help groups were opposed by the Anti-Mongolian League, claiming concern about Chinese morals (Li, 1998).

In Alberta, the Chinese were blamed for spreading smallpox during the 1892 epidemic. The RCMP often had to respond to anti-Chinese violence and threats of mob lynchings. An 1884 Royal Commission on Chinese Immigration reported that residents of British Columbia desired legislation reserving the province "for people of the European race." Head taxes ranging from $100 to $500 were imposed on all Chinese entering Canada between 1885 and 1903, and the *Chinese Immigration Act* of 1923 barred the entry of people from China altogether. Until the act was repealed in 1947, wives could not enter Canada, delaying the growth of a second generation and separating families most of their lives.

The "Oriental problem" was debated and racist treatment of the Chinese continued in the twentieth century, severely affecting their social welfare experience (Anderson, 1991). In both World Wars, Chinese men were barred from military service until Canada desperately needed more soldiers, when Chinese recruits served in segregated units. Until 1947, the Chinese were legally barred from many professions, such as law and dentistry, but could become physicians.

Vietnamese people arrived in two large groupings as "boat people," between 1975 and 1980 during a wave of sympathy toward refugees created by the Vietnam War. Although the first to arrive were urban, middle class, and settled mostly in Quebec as French speakers, the second group had none of these attributes and were settled by government agents in the Canadian north (the Yukon and Northwest Territories). A study of the overall adjustment indicated that the boat people had done well, overall, in terms of finding employment, and had overcome mental health issues with little assistance from social services. Racism had been experienced most when they had integrated sufficiently to wish to move from menial jobs to better paying work (Beiser, 1999).

The 2001 census indicates that the 1 094 700 Chinese in Canada today are among the most highly educated groups. They are also well-represented in higher occupation categories, no doubt enhanced by business-class immigrants entering Canada. Chinese people are found in considerable numbers in affluent suburbs such as Markham, Ontario, and Richmond, British Columbia. Many give generously to Chinese agencies and mainstream institutions, the latter providing a measure of acceptance in the wider community. Major cities have Chinese hospitals, seniors' homes, language and cultural schools, newspapers, and social services, but the community is neither homogeneous nor institutionally complete. Social welfare institutions, such as the United Chinese Community Enrichment Services (S.U.C.C.E.S.S.), serve immigrants from Hong Kong, Taiwan, and Mainland China, and other parts of the world, including Vietnam.

Daily needs cannot be totally met independent of the institutions of the wider society. Although overt forms of prejudice and discrimination against the Chinese have decreased, resentment is expressed in complaints about monster houses, Asian malls, "astronaut" parents leaving teens alone while in Asia on business, and the cost of English as a Second Language (ESL) courses in public schools. Media reports of gang activity are considered by many Chinese to be exaggerated. Despite evidence of affluence for some, research indicates that the incidence of family poverty is 34.6 percent among East and Southeast Asians, twice as high as for Euro-Canadian families (Reitz & Banerjee, 2007).

Measures of achievement for today's Chinese population may be found in the former Governor General of Canada, Adrienne Clarkson, who is of Chinese ancestry, and in recognition of historical racist acts, after years of advocacy by Chinese community leaders. In December 2006, the new Conservative Government apologized for the "grave injustice" of the head tax, compensating survivors or their spouses $20 000 each. Another acknowledgement of past wrongs occurred in February 2007, when the Secretary of State (Multiculturalism and Canadian Identity) expressed regret and "solidarity with the Chinese Canadians in Vancouver" on the 120th anniversary of the Anti-Chinese Riot of 1887. Given the government's awareness of China's international standing as an emerging global economic force, one can expect that attention will continue to be paid to the concerns of the Chinese community.

## PROVIDING FOR THE SOCIAL WELFARE NEEDS OF IMMIGRANTS

Elsewhere, the influence of the governing party's ideology on the extent to which support is given to policies and programs advantageous to immigrants and racialized minorities has been discussed (Christensen, 2003). As a country depending on immigrants to maintain its population growth and fill labour force requirements, all Canadian governments must consider their immediate and longer term needs. This section provides a brief overview of major government programs and services offered by the voluntary sector.

## Government Programs

CIC acknowledges that successful settlement and integration of immigrants maximizes the economic, social, and cultural benefits of immigration. Thus, the stated aim of IRPA is that immigrants be enabled to participate fully in Canadian society, and have the same quality of life that Canadians enjoy (Citizenship and Immigration Canada, 2005a, p. 31). Currently, the federal government operates three core programs.

Immigrant Settlement and Adaptation Program (ISAP) services are two-fold. For "pre-arrivals," the Canadian Orientation Abroad (COA) program is available in only 35 countries. Various modules provide orientation to life in Canada including education, employment, housing, and rights and responsibilities. For those already in Canada, ISAP funds organizations to deliver direct, essential immigrant services in the form of translation and interpretation, referral to community services, and counselling that emphasizes labour market adaptation. In May 2006, the federal government committed $307 million to immigration settlement funding. However, as is true of funds transferred to provinces under the Settlement Renewal Initiative, exactly how these funds will be allocated is generally left to the provinces.

The HOST program matches new immigrants with Canadian volunteers who help them to practice speaking one of the official languages, learn about services available in their community, and understand the labour market. Other goals are to promote cross-cultural understanding and to reduce racial stereotyping.

The Language Instruction for Newcomers to Canada (LINC) program provides language training in one of Canada's official languages for adult newcomers to facilitate economic, social, and cultural integration.

**Problems in Government-Sponsored Programs** Lack of funding remains the major problem in government-sponsored services. Programs are often inadequate and not guaranteed for the long term. Structural problems include regional disparity and discrepancies in ethno-racial groups' access to government decision-makers and to ethnic and mainstream social services. The generally unrecognized culture of bureaucratic structures is itself problematic. Government bureaucracies too often lack the personnel to offer culturally appropriate services to immigrants from various ethnic and racial backgrounds, including systemic barriers. Professional social workers seldom choose the area of immigrant integration. Service delivery is further hampered by immigrants' lack of knowledge about rights and services, insufficient availability of translation and interpretation services, and lack of co-ordination between mainstream government agencies and non-governmental immigrant service agencies. Despite recent increases in federal–provincial agreements concerning immigrants' recruitment and admission, problems of jurisdiction and joint planning to fully address settlement needs remain, often leaving needed immigrant services in a twilight zone. It would behoove official government planners to incorporate the results of the many recent studies delineating specific problem areas, as experienced by immigrants themselves.

**Issues in Voluntary and Non-Government Sectors** Once immigrants have dealt with initial settlement needs, they are expected to use services available to other Canadians residents. A major cultural expectation embedded in Canadian social welfare philosophy is that people should not remain dependent on the state. Many government settlement programs, such as language courses (LINC), impose time limits. Thus, the responsibility for immigrant integration is often left to the voluntary or non-governmental sector by default, to fill the gaps not covered by governments. In 2004, a voluntary sector initiative led to the establishment of the Settlement and Integration Joint Policy and Program Council for the purpose of facilitating collaboration and planning between the government and the settlement sector. The several hundred voluntary services involved in immigrant social welfare are extremely varied and are summarized briefly under several major categories. Detailed listings of specific services are available on the Internet.

Well-established religious groups, such as those of the Catholic, Protestant, and Jewish faiths, offer sectarian-based services (for example, Jewish Immigrant Aid Services). Long-standing Canadian communities, such as the Chinese, Japanese, Ukrainians, and, to some extent, Black Canadians, operate ethno-specific community organizations, some of which hire professional social work staff and specialize in assisting immigrants. Popular stereotypes suggest that some ethnic and racial groups "take care of their own," but some important needs of these populations—especially those of women, children, and the elderly—are simply not being met. Immigrant groups that have difficulty accessing the opportunity structure are unable to raise sufficient funds internally; the range of services that they can offer is limited, as are the salaries they can offer staff. Dependent on mainstream social service supported by governments (for example, child welfare agencies), these immigrant groups often experience discrimination or poor service due to providers' lack of cultural knowledge and understanding of the minority's life experience. Miscellaneous charitable and non-governmental organizations, alliances, and committees often operate with precarious or time-limited funding. Competition for scarce dollars limits the types of programs they can offer and they must accord with societal priorities. This makes long-term planning difficult, unless an organization attracts wealthy patrons or is supported, to some extent, by local, provincial, or federal governments. Since voluntary organizations choose which causes are deemed worthy, the very groups that are most in need may not be considered.

From the viewpoint of equal access, the extent to which various ethnic and racialized groups have been able to supply the needs of their members varies greatly. Factors range from their internal financial resources, cohesiveness and organization, to access to society's economic structure and major decision makers.

## CONCLUSION AND IMPLICATIONS FOR PROFESSIONAL SOCIAL WORK

Historically, schools of social work have not viewed the preparation of their students to work with immigrants and racialized groups as a high priority, assuming that social work values of acceptance and client self-determination would suffice for interventions with all clients, regardless of ethnic or racial background (Christensen, 1996). In the 1980s, when the need for cross-cultural training of social workers was first recognized, well-documented research exposing the differential plight of second-generation immigrants and long-standing minorities was not available (Canadian Association of Schools of Social Work, 1991). This is clearly no longer the case. During the last decade, numerous authors have provided disturbing evidence of the growing economic gap between European and racialized immigrant groups, and the divergence in their sense of having a place in the Canadian mosaic. Racialized minorities have tended to come to mainstream social services as a last resort, most often as involuntary, vulnerable clients.

The social work practice literature abounds with concerns about Eurocentric practice methods that view problems with systemic causes as being rooted in the individual, family, or "foreign" culture. When working with immigrants and racialized minorities, social workers have a critical need to return to methods of advocacy and community development approaches (Christensen, 1999).

Based on the current literature, there is now ample evidence suggesting what needs to be done:

- There is an urgent need to encourage people from immigrant and racialized minority backgrounds to enter the social work profession, so that it eventually represents the entire spectrum of Canadian society.
- Schools of social work must take up their ethical responsibility to ensure that all graduates are competent to work effectively across cultures and with racialized minorities.
- Agency policies must assure that impediments to retention and promotion of staff from ethnoracial backgrounds are removed.
- Social welfare personnel, at all levels, must act to remedy the effects of ethnocentrism and racism in existing policies and practices, however subtle and informal, on the social welfare of immigrant and racialized minority clients.
- Outreach, information, and education programs must be developed to involve under-served and underrepresented minorities in all aspects of social welfare, from policy and planning to direct service and evaluation.
- Leadership opportunities must be offered to qualified persons from racialized minorities so that their understanding of the needs of these groups will be included in program and service planning.
- Mainstream and ethnic agencies must undertake joint efforts to bring minority immigrants' needs before governments and the public through advocacy and research documenting their concerns that affect the well-being of individuals, families, and society as a whole.

Canada will continue to be a country of immigrants, and the colour of clients seeking social work services will likewise continue to change. By 2011, most new immigrants will come from racialized groups (Canadian Race Relations Foundation, 2004). Studies clearly indicate that racial diversity will affect Canada positively only if all people are committed to values of fairness and equality because these values are integral to everyone's experience. Now that the research evidence is available, social workers have no excuse for being unaware of the extraordinary pressures faced by a majority of immigrants, leading many to feel unable to participate fully in Canadian society. Social workers are trained to understand how individual, family, and societal problems are often rooted in such feelings. Social work educators have an ethical responsibility to ensure that graduates are prepared to provide caring, knowledgeable, and appropriate interventions to immigrants and all generations of their descendants. Offering clients anything less would be a betrayal of the very values for which the profession stands.

# References

Abella, R. (1984). *Report of the Commission on Equality in Employment*. Ottawa: Supply and Services Canada.

Anderson, K. J. (1991). *Vancouver's Chinatown: Racial discourse in Canada, 1875–1980*. Montreal: McGill-Queen's University Press.

Aydemir, A. & Skuterud, M. (2005). Explaining the deteriorating entry earnings of Canada's immigrant cohorts. *Canadian Journal of Economics/Revue Canadienne d'economique*, 38, (2), 641–672.

Beiser, M. (1999). *Strangers at the gate: The Boat People's first ten years in Canada*. Toronto: University of Toronto Press.

Borooah, V. & Mangan, J. (In press). Love thy neighbour: How much bigotry is there in Western countries? *Kyklos, International Review for Social Sciences*.

Burrell, L. F. & Christensen, C. P. (1987). Minority students' perceptions of high school: Implications for Canadian school personnel. *Journal of Multicultural Counseling and Development*, 15, 3–15.

Canadian Association of Schools of Social Work (CASSW). (1991). *Social work education at the crossroads: Report of the Task Force on Multicultural and Multiracial Issues in Social Work Education*. Ottawa: CASSW.

Canadian Bar Association. (2003a). *Permanent Residency Cards. Canadian Bar Association and Immigration Law Section Issue Paper*.

Canadian Bar Association. (2003b). *Submission on Immigration and Refugee Protection Regulations Part s 1–17 [02–03]*. National Citizenship and Immigration Law Section, Canadian Bar Association.

Canadian Council for Refugees. (2006). *Non-citizens in Canada: Equally human, equally entitled to rights. Report to the UN Committee on Economic, Social and Cultural Rights on Canada's compliance with the International Covenant on Economic, Social and Cultural Rights. Background Information*.

Canadian Heritage. (2005). *Who was Mathieu Da Costa?* www.pch.gc.ca/special/mdc/dacosta/index_e.cfm

Canadian Heritage. (2007). Canada's new government commemorates 200th Anniversary of the 1807 *Act for the Abolition of the Slave Trade*.

Canadian Race Relations Foundation (CRRF). (2004). *Initiatives against racism*. www.crr.ca

Canadian Race Relations Foundation (CRRF). (2005). *News Release. New CRRF report confirms significant barriers to fair employment for racialized groups and immigrants*. Toronto: May 17, 2005.

Catalyst Canada and the Diversity Institute in Management and Technology. (2007). *Career advancement in corporate Canada: a focus on visible minorities, an early preview.* www.catalystwomen.org

*CBC News*. (2007). *Liberals call for new Citizenship Act for 'lost Canadians.'* Updated: Tuesday, March 27, 2007.

Centre for Research and Information on Canada. (2005). *Diversity Survey, Backgrounder.*

Christensen, C. P. (1990). Toward a framework for social work education in a multicultural and multiracial Canada. In S. A. Yelaja (Ed.), *The settlement and integration of new immigrants to Canada* (pp. 103–124). Waterloo, ON: Faculty of Social Work, Wilfrid Laurier University & Centre for Social Welfare Services.

Christensen, C. P. (1996). The impact of racism on the education of social service workers. In C. James (Ed.), *Perspectives on racism and the human service sector: A case for change* (pp. 140–151). Toronto: University of Toronto Press.

Christensen, C. P. (1998). Chapter 5, Social welfare and social work in Canada: Aspects of the black experience. In V. D'Oyley & C. James (Eds.), *Re-visioning: Canadian perspectives on the education of Africans in the late 20th century* (pp. 36–57). Concord, ON: Captus Press.

Christensen, C. P. (1999). Multiculturalism, racism and social work: An exploration of issues in the Canadian context. In G. Yong-Li & D. Este (Eds.), *Professional social service delivery in a multicultural world* (pp. 293–310). Toronto: Canadian Scholars' Press.

Christensen, C. P. (2003). Canadian society: Social policy and ethno-racial diversity. In A. Al-krenawi & G. J. R. Graham (Eds.), *Multicultural social work in Canada: Working with diverse ethno-racial communities* (pp. 70–97). Don Mills, ON: Oxford University Press.

Christensen, C.P. (2005). Black Canadians. In F.J. Turner (Ed.), *The encyclopedia of Canadian social work.* Waterloo, Ontario: Wilfrid Laurier University Press.

Christensen, C. P. & Weinfeld, M. (1993). The black family in Canada: A preliminary exploration of family patterns and inequality. *Canadian Ethnic Studies,* XXV, 26–44.

Citizenship and Immigration Canada. (1998). Citizenship and Immigration Canada. (December 7, 1998). *News Release 98-59: A new Citizenship Act.*

Citizenship and Immigration Canada. (2005a). *Annual report to Parliament on immigration 2005.* Ottawa: Minister of Public Works and Government of Canada. Retrieved January 22, 2008, from http://www.cic.gc.ca/English/pdf/pub/immigration2005_e.pdf

Citizenship and Immigration Canada. (2005b). *The refugee appeal division: Backgrounder.*

Citizenship and Immigration Canada. (2006a). *Annual report to Parliament on immigration 2006.* Ottawa: Minister of Public Works and Government of Canada.

Citizenship and Immigration Canada. (2006b-17). NEWS RELEASE, Citizenship and Immigration Canada Minister Tables the 2006 *Annual Report to Parliament on Immigration,* Backgrounder.

Citizenship and Immigration Canada. (2006c). *Skilled workers: Six selection factors and pass mark.*

Citizenship and Immigration Canada. (2006d). *2005 immigration overview.* The Monitor, 2006, Issue 1.

*The Daily.* (2003). www.statcan.ca

*The Daily.* (2005). Statistics Canada, Thursday, December 15, 2005.

*The Daily.* (2007). www.statcan.ca

Department of Justice Canada. (2001). *Highlights of the Anti-terrorism Act.* News Room Backgrounder.

Department of Justice Canada. (2003). *Focus group report: Minority views on the Canadian Anti-terrorism Act (formerly Bill C-36). A qualitative study.* PRO3-4e Prepared for Department of Justice Canada, Research Division.

*Equality Now: Report of the Parliamentary task force on the participation of visible minorities in Canada.* (1984). Ottawa: Queen's Printer.

Fleras, A. & Elliott, J. L. (2006). *Unequal relations: An introduction to race, ethnic and Aboriginal dynamics in Canada.* Scarborough, ON: Prentice Hall Canada.

Fleras, A. & Kuhz, J. L. (2001). *Media and minorities: Representing diversity in a multicultural Canada.* Thompson Educational.

Galabuzi, Grace-E. (2005). *Canada's economic apartheid: The social exclusion of racialized groups in the new century.* Toronto: Canadian Scholars' Press Inc.

Henry, F., Tator, C., Mattis, W. & Rees, T. (2005). *The colour of democracy: Racism in Canadian society* (3rd ed.). Toronto: Thompson Nelson.

Jean-Baptiste, J. (1979). *Haitians in Canada*. Hull, QC: Ministry of Supply and Services Canada.

Kazemipur, A. & Halli, S.S (2000). *Perspectives on ethnicity in Canada.* Toronto: Harcourt.

Klein, R. & Mirsky, J. (2003). Social work with Canadians of Jewish background: Guidelines for direct practice. *Multicultural social work in Canada: Working with diverse ethno-racial communities* (pp. 70–97). Don Mills, ON: Oxford University Press.

Laquian, E. & Laquian, A. (1997). Asian immigration and racism in Canada—A search for policy options. In E. Laquian, A. Laquian, & T. McGee (Eds.), *The silent debate: Asian immigration & racism in Canada* (pp. 3–28). Vancouver: Institute of Asian Research, University of British Columbia.

Li, P. S. (1998). *The Chinese in Canada*. Don Mills, Ontario: Oxford University Press.

Milan, A. & Kelly, T. (2004). *Blacks in Canada: A long history.* Canadian Social Trends. Statistics Canada, Catalogue No. 11–808.

Ornstein, M. (2000). *Ethno-racial inequality in Metropolitan Toronto: Analysis of the 1996 Census*. Toronto: Institute for Social Research, York University.

Picot, G. & Sweetman, A. (2005). *The deteriorating economic welfare of immigrants and possible causes: Update 2005.* Analytical Studies Branch Research Paper Series. Cat. No. 11F0019MIE B no. 262. Ottawa: Statistics Canada.

Porter, J. (1965). *The vertical mosaic*. Toronto: University of Toronto Press.

Reitz, J. G. & Banerjee, R. (2007). Racial inequality, social cohesion, and policy issues in Canada. In K. Banting, T. J. Courchene, & L. Seidle (Eds.), *Belonging, diversity, recognition and shared citizenship in Canada*. Montreal: Institute for Research on Public Policy.

Royal Commission on Bilingualism and Biculturalism. (1970). *The cultural contributions of the other ethnic groups: Report book IV.* Ottawa: Queen's Printer.

Sloame, J. (2007). *The virtual Jewish history tour Canada.* Jewish Virtual Library. A Division of the American-Israeli Cooperative Enterprise.

Statistics Canada. (2001a). *2001 Census of Population*. Ottawa: Ministry of Supply and Services.

Statistics Canada. (2001b). Population by religion, by province and territory (2001 census).

Statistics Canada. (2001c). *Visible minority population: census metropolitan areas*. www.statcan.ca

Statistics Canada. (2005). *Population, projection of visible minority groups, Canada, provinces and regions, 2001 to 2017*. Cat. No. 91–541-X1E.

Statistics Canada. (2006). *Portrait of the Canadian population: Findings.*

The Stephen Roth Institute for the Study of Contemporary Anti-Semitism and Racism, Tel Aviv University. (2005).

*Toronto Star*. (2006). What it's like being an ethnic minority in Canada. *Toronto Star,* September 25, 2006.

*Toronto Star. (2007).* Board changes spark worries about refugees. www.thestar.com/article/187770

Tulchinsky, G. (1992). *The origins of the Canadian Jewish community*. Toronto: Lester Publishing.

United Nations Environment Network. (In press). 2nd UN World Water Development Report, International Panel on Climate Change, IPCC World Water Council.

United Nations High Commissioner on Refugees. (2006). *Basic facts, Refugees by numbers 2006 edition.*

*Vancouver Sun.* (2007a). Tides of immigration, issues and ideas. January 22, 2007, p. A7.

*Vancouver Sun.* (2007b). Canada said to have no clear policy on Muslim women's veils. Thursday, January 25, 2007, A5.

*Vancouver Sun.* (2007c). B.C. faces future flood of 'climate refugees': RCMP. Tuesday, January 30, 2007, A1 and A4.

*Vancouver Sun.* (2007d). Rural Quebec town welcomes immigrants, but only if they conform to certain 'norms.' Wednesday, January 31, 2007, A5.

*Vancouver Sun.* (2007e). UN criticizes Canada over racism: A committee says the term 'visible minorities' used by Ottawa may contravene a treaty. Thursday, March 8, 2007, p. A6.

Walker, J. St. G. (1995). African Canadians. In P. Magocsi (Ed.), *Encyclopaedia of Canada's Peoples* (pp. 139–76). Toronto: University of Toronto Press.

Wayland, S. (2006). *Unsettled: Legal and policy barriers for newcomers to Canada.* Community Foundations of Canada. www.cfc-fcc.ca

Williams, C. (2004). *Policy responses for groups at risk of long-term poverty.* Queen's International Institute on Social Policy.

Winks, R. (1997). *The blacks in Canada: A history* (2nd ed.). Montreal: McGill-Queen's University Press.

# CHAPTER 11

# What Is Happening to the Living Standards of Working Age Canadians?

*Brigitte Kitchen*

## FRAMING THE ISSUES

Canada is among the world's wealthiest nations and a member of the Group of Eight (G8), the privileged club of the eight most powerful economies in the world. Together they represent about 65% of the global economy. Through the Free Trade Agreement (FTA) with the United States, and later the North American Free Trade Agreement (NAFTA) with the U.S. and Mexico, Canada entered into the competitive, entrepreneurial, fast-moving, and flexible climate of open trade and global integration. The notion that increased trade would eventually benefit all countries and all peoples (Ellwood, 2003) drove Canada's expansion in international trade and was readily embraced by governments at all levels and political stripes.

Fundamental structural adjustments to the Canadian economy were required and implemented very quickly. The changes significantly increased the prospects for the accumulation of capital, but were decidedly not positive for working people (Teeple, 2000: 143). Indeed, a long trail of unemployment and underemployment followed in some parts of the economy. Thousands of workers lost their jobs. Others saw their jobs "restructured" into part-time, casual, and contingent employment and self-employment. Pushed to the periphery of the labour market, working people become part of the working poor; others joining them are new entrants or re-entrants into the labour market.

Canada is among the major players in the global economy of export-led capital accumulation. Per capita GDP gauges the collective value of the goods and services in a country but not the distribution of that value among the population. It is not a measure of the actual distribution of income in a population. This is most likely skewed among class, race, ethnicity, gender, disability, age, and other social divisions. However, if GDP were divided equally, a family household of three would have had an income of $102 819, 14% more than the actual average total income of $90 400 for a two-earner household with children in 2004 (Statistics Canada, 2006a).

Trade liberalization has been widely associated with job and income insecurities. A public opinion poll conducted with 2021 randomly selected adults for the Canadian Centre for Policy Alternatives (Nov. 20, 2005) found that many Canadians felt they were living close to the financial edge.

- Almost half of Canadians (49%) reported that they are always just one or two missed paycheques away from being poor.
- About two-thirds of Canadians (65%) believe most people have not benefited from Canada's economic growth and that benefits have mostly gone to the very rich.
- Three-quarters of Canadians (76%) worry that a growing gap will lead to more crime and, if left unchecked, will also cause Canada to end up like the U.S. in terms of violence.

The chapter begins with a profile of the labour market income disparities Canadians have come to feel increasingly uneasy about. This is followed by an examination of the reconfiguration of Canada's social welfare system and its failure to protect the new income needs generated as a result of economic restructuring.

In a modern economy, money operates as a symbol of value as opposed to a thing of value (Rowe, 2005). Money income is used as a proxy to reflect levels and trends in living standards. While these may not tell the real story of people's positions in the economy, they are nonetheless powerful indicators of the extent to which some individuals and families have surged ahead or fallen behind in terms of income and the level of material well-being it buys.

## THE GROWING SOCIAL DIVIDE

In 2001 and 2002, Canada was downgraded on the annual United Nations Human Development Index (HDI) as the most desirable country in the world to live in (Human Development Index, 2000, 1999, 1998, 1997, 1996) to third place and further downgraded to eighth place in 2003 (United Nations, 2003). Encouragingly, in the recent 2006 annual report, Canada moved up into sixth place among the UN's 177 member states (United Nations, 2006).

HDI rankings are based on three crucial aspects of human development: (1) opportunity for a long and healthy life in terms of life expectancy at birth; (2) educational attainment, through gauging adult literacy (two-third weights) and the combined gross enrolment ratio in primary, secondary, and tertiary education (one-third weight); and (3) standard of living by GDP per capita at US$PPP. This last measure denotes the purchasing power parity of currencies (United Nations, 2006, Technical Note 1 p. 393). By averaging these three components, the final tabulation, or world ranking, is calculated.

That Canada's ranking among the top eight nations on the HDI has more to do with forward-looking social spending and public investment decisions by previous governments in earlier decades than with the present strength of the economy. The complex interaction between corporate restructuring and cutbacks in governmental activities to their lowest level in 50 years has made Canada the first among G8 countries to solve its budgetary deficit problem and reduce its debt load (Canadian Centre for Policy Alternatives, 1999). The slashing of federal social spending was so drastic that an annual federal budget deficit of about $40 billion was turned around within four years to a $2.1 surplus in 1998, the first surplus in 27 years. The federal government has been awash in surpluses ever since. Its surplus in the first nine months of the fiscal year 2006–07 was $7.3 billion. In December alone, $1.2 billion was added to the total (*Toronto Star*, Feb. 22, 2007).

## THE GROWTH IN INEQUALITY

A disturbing reality in Canada, as in many other industrially developed countries, is that the distribution of income is becoming increasingly unequal (Evans, 2006). If the economy is left on its own, as John Kenneth Galbraith once poignantly observed, it works wonderfully well for the already well-to-do but not so well for the rest of society. Many consider inequality as "a given—a product of the deep and impersonal machinery of the free market" (Lardner, 2005: 23). For Picot and Myles, trends in low income and the level of income inequality are two of the more closely watched economic indicators of living standards in Canada (2004). The reason for this interest is that the rich–poor divide does not just signal the siphoning off of monetary rewards by the rich. It also leaves the rest of society with less.

## THE GINI INDEX

The most widely used international measure of income inequality is the *Gini Index*. It gauges the share of total income within a country by income percentile. If incomes were equally distributed, every 10% of the population would receive 10% of the total income.

Table 11.1 indicates that although income equality in Canada is not nearly as horrific as in the U.S. and the UK, it is not anything as good as in the Scandinavian countries. In 1997, Canadian family incomes in the top 90th percentile were four times higher than in the bottom 10th percentile, compared to over five times in the U.S. and almost five times in the UK. By contrast, in Finland and Sweden, the ratio was only about three-to-one. The gap between middle income groups and the top percentile was less accentuated than the ratio between the highest and the lowest income earners in all eight of the selected countries. Canada found itself wedged in the middle between the United States, the UK, and the continental and Northern European countries.

Further data from the Survey of Consumer Finances (SCF), now replaced by the Survey of Labour and Income Dynamics (SLID), led Frenette, Green, and Picot (2004) to conclude that the Gini index for families, based on disposable income (after tax and transfer income) increased in the decade from 1990 to 2000 by what they considered a modest increase of 6%. However, in a later study, Picot and Myles conceded that depending on the data source used, the increase in family income inequality in Canada was indeed substantial (2005: 26).

The rise in income inequality has primarily been attributed to faster increasing incomes at the upper end of the income scale. Neo-liberal economic logic insists on high rewards for individual entrepreneurial initiatives to legitimate their importance for economic growth and social well-being. It is, therefore, hardly surprising that in an era of unrestrained

| TABLE 11.1 | Measures of Family Income Inequality: An International Comparison | | | |
|---|---|---|---|---|
| Country | Gini Index | Ratio of High to Low Income (P90/P10) | Ratio of Low to Middle Income (P10/P50) | Ratio of High to Middle Income (P90/P50) |
| United States (2000) | 0.37 | 5.43 | 0.39 | 2.10 |
| UK (1999) | 0.35 | 4.54 | 0.47 | 2.14 |
| Canada (1997) | 0.29 | 3.99 | 0.47 | 1.86 |
| Netherlands (1999) | 0.25 | 3.27 | 0.53 | 1.75 |
| Germany (2000) | 0.25 | 3.17 | 0.55 | 1.73 |
| Belgium (1997) | 0.25 | 3.19 | 0.53 | 1.70 |
| Sweden (2000) | 0.25 | 2.95 | 0.57 | 1.68 |
| Finland (2000) | 0.25 | 2.90 | 0.57 | 1.64 |

*Source:* Garnett Picot & John Myles, Income Inequality and Low Income in Canada, Poverty and Exclusion, Dec. 2004, Vol. 7, No. 2, Table 1. http://www.statcan.ca/english/research/11F0019MIE/11F0019MIE2005240.pdf.

market forces, salary increases were headed by the highest paid CEOs. Nonetheless, the staggering level of their remuneration, ranging among the top 100 CEOs from a low of $2 870 118 to a high of $74 824 355 in 2005 is surprising (Mackenzie, 2007). According to calculations by McMaster University economist Michael Veall, the top-earning 1% of Canadians almost doubled their share of national income—from 7.6% in 1980 to 13.6% in 2000. Top-earning Canadians have not enjoyed such a large share of Canada's national income since the 1920s and 1930s (McQuaig, Dec. 12, 2006: A17).

By comparison, average income earners are hardly well-paid. The 2006 weekly average wage for all industrial sectors in the provinces and territories was $728.17. In a work week of 37 hours this amounts to $19.68 an hour or $37 865 a year. Over a five-year period, 2001–2006, the average weekly wage increased by 9%. This translates into a modest annual increase of 1.8%. In 2004, 47.3% of the employed aged 25–64 earned $10 to $19.99 an hour and only 11% were paid $30 or more (*The Daily*, Jan. 26, 2005).

To earn $30 000 without overtime requires an hourly wage of $15.59 an hour, and to earn $20 000 a year a worker would have to be paid $9.50 an hour working 40 hours a week for 52 weeks a year. That the average CEO, working from 9 a.m. to 5 p.m. reaches average full-time minimum wage earnings in less than a full day of work illustrates not only the enormity of the income gap that exists between the highest and the lowest paid but also between top and average earners (Mackenzie, 2007). CEOs, who may be responsible for the laying off of thousands of workers, can earn in a few hours what it takes the average minimum worker to earn in a whole year.

## THE LOW-WAGED TREND

Among OECD countries, Canada has with 21%, after the U.S. with 26%, the second highest incidence of low-waged employment (Morissette & Picot, April 2005). The proportion of workers aged 25–64 earning less than $8 per hour fell from 9% to 7% over the period 1981–2004, despite a substantial increase in the percentage of adult workers with a university degree (*The Daily*, April 25, 2005). The downward pressure on Canadian wages has been associated with the competition for jobs in the global economy. Production and new investment can be easily shifted to regions within and between countries that offer lower production costs, including lower wages. The competitive "race to the bottom" in wage levels hollows out the living standards of wage earners in industrialized countries and at the same time prevents the rise of better living conditions in developing countries.

In Canada, growth in low-wage employment has occurred mainly in the precarious job market typically paying the provincial minimum wage or just slightly above it, with no benefits or access to training and development. These jobs have gone mainly to new entrants in the labour market, such as recent immigrants and young, visible minority men (Table 11.2).

While there has been some reduction in the proportion of low-waged workers, those in jobs paying less than $10.00 an hour (in 2001 dollars) dropped by a mere one percentage point—from 17% to 16%—between 1981 and 2004 (Morissette & Picot, April 2005). About 567 000 couple families had incomes under $20 000 in 2004 (Statistics Canada, b). Low-waged service industries, such as hotels, restaurants, fast food outlets, retailers, theatres, and agriculture offer more temporary or part-time employment opportunities for women than for men. Statistics more than doubled, as 23% of newly employed women held time-limited jobs

| TABLE 11.2 | Proportion of Low-Paid Workers in Low-Income Families, Canada, 1980–2000 | | | | | |
|---|---|---|---|---|---|---|
| | 1980 | 2000 | Men 1980 | 2000 | Women 1980 | 2000 |
| All Earners | 29.6 | 30.0 | 39.3 | 36.4 | 24.1 | 25.3 |
| Recent Immigrant | 37.9 | 43.7 | 53.5 | 54.0 | 30.9 | 36.3 |
| Visible Min | 40.7 | 39.4 | 51.9 | 45.1 | 35.1 | 35.0 |
| Can. Born Visible Min | 29.8 | 31.3 | 32.5 | 33.2 | 27.8 | 29.3 |
| Can. Born Non-Visible Min | 29.2 | 28.1 | 37.7 | 34.2 | 24.1 | 23.8 |

Source: Statistics Canada. Low-paid Work and Economically Vulnerable Families by René Morissette and Garnett Picot; Catalogue no. 11F0019MIE—No. 248; http://www.statcan.ca/english/research/11F0019MIE/11F0019MIE2005248.pdf

in 2004 compared to 11% in 1989. Twenty percent of men also found only temporary jobs in 2004, compared to 12% in 1989 (*The Daily*, Jan. 26, 2005).

Some men are now economically dependent on their wives or partners. An estimated 11% of women in spousal relationships earned more than their male partners in 1967. The proportion nearly tripled to 29% by 2003. Average earnings of primary earner wives are, however, substantially lower than those of their male counterparts, $41 200 compared to $57 800 (*The Daily*, Aug. 23, 2006).

## THE MINIMUM WAGE

For many, employment is no guarantee for wages that pay for a decent standard of living. British Columbia's staggering child poverty rate of 23.5%, which is 5.8% above the national rate of 17.7%, has been attributed to the great number of working poor families unable to find jobs with adequate pay, hours, and benefits to lift them above the poverty line (Campaign 2000, 2006). The logic of the market economy requires that low-waged earners be paid the smallest amount that will ensure that their work gets done (Jencks, 2005: 130). This may partly explain why minimum wages have been kept at a level where they barely meet the basic consumption requirements of a single person.

Minimum wages vary widely, from a high of $8.50 in Nunavut to a low of $6.75 in Newfoundland. Working for the minimum wage means living below the subsistence level in terms of the LICOs (low income cut-offs) of $20 337, Statistics Canada's unofficial poverty level for an individual living in a large urban centre (National Council of Welfare, Spring 2005). Individuals or families are considered poor when they spend more than 54.7% of their income on basic necessities. In a workforce of 16 484.3 people, about 923 000 (5.6%) were working for minimum wages in June 2006. Their percentage share varies from a high of 10.4% in Newfoundland and Labrador to a low of 2.9% in Alberta (Alberta Human Resources and Development, 2006).

A motion to reinstate the federal minimum wage (abolished in 1996) at $10 an hour, and to periodically increase it in accordance with the rise in the consumer price index, was defeated in the federal Parliament on Feb. 20, 2007. In the past, the federal minimum wage acted as a trend-setter for minimum wage levels in the provinces and territories. Working at $10 an hour for 40 hours over 52 weeks for $20 800 a year would barely lift an individual above the LICO. Yet there is considerable opposition to raising the minimum wage.

Three counter-arguments are consistently put forward. Firstly, raising the minimum wage would kill jobs and cause unemployment. Secondly, it is unnecessary because a number of minimum wage earners such as teenagers, adult students, and adult women may not be living in poor families. Thirdly, wages would increase throughout the economy, driving up production costs and pricing workers out of the job market.

Economists are by no means unanimous in their assessment of the minimum wage as a job killer. Ron Saunders from the Canadian Policy Research Network concluded that existing research would support any position one might want to take on the issue (*Toronto Star*, Feb. 7, 2007: A17). Most minimum-waged jobs are not found in small businesses but with retail giants, fast food chains, or temporary employment agencies. Those who work in them are mainly lone parents (the majority of them women), unattached individuals, recent immigrants (10 years or less in Canada), and individuals without a high school diploma (Kunz & Frank, 2004). Collectively, they make up more than one-third (37%) of all full-time workers and accounted for 71% of all employees who were both in low-paying jobs and members of a low-income family (*The Daily*, April 25, 2005). Their insufficient earnings should be enough of an argument to prove that a living wage would also benefit those not living in poor families. Besides, nobody should be expected to work for poverty wages just to maintain a job.

Making people work for poverty wages makes a travesty of the work ethic. In market societies it is assumed that work is rewarded at a fair price. The social value of this assumption is that it holds out regular work as a morally superior way of life, eradicates poverty, and assures social peace (Bauman, 1998: 2, 21).

## THE PERSISTENCE OF POVERTY

"Canadians don't know what to make of poverty," wrote Thomas Walkom in the *Toronto Star* (Jan. 27, 2007: F4). Poverty is the most extreme form of income inequality at the bottom. A snapshot approach to poverty gives us numbers but tells us little about the economic, social, and familial circumstances that influence and shape an individual's or a family's descent into poverty. Job loss or downsizing as part of labour market restructuring, inadequate social transfers, rising rates in family breakups, and lone parenting are all risks that have been associated with poverty.

While the number of poor people in Canada is decreasing, the decline is stubbornly slow. On the UN's Human Poverty Index (HPI) of 2003, Canada ranked a disappointing 12th among 17 selected rich OECD countries with 12.8% of its population having incomes below 50% of median income. On the 2006 HPI, based on 2004 income data, with 11.4% of the population living below 50% of median income, Canada moved into 8th place. The shift, while a welcome improvement, still compares poorly with 5.4% in Finland, 6.4% in Norway, and 6.5% in Sweden.

When markets fail people, the welfare state, with its social transfer systems, is designed to step in to protect against loss or reduction of income. Since the beginning of the new millennium, social transfers in the form of tax credits or direct cash benefits have done little to lift poor Canadians out of poverty. A mere 262 000, or 7%, fewer people were living in poverty in 2004 than in 2000 (Table 11.3; Statistics Canada, c).

Poverty has remained to a large extent a gender issue. Lone mothers and their children continue to lead the poverty march with 40.0%, closely followed by single women under

| TABLE 11.3 | Persons in Low Income after Tax, by Number (2000–2004) | | | | |
| --- | --- | --- | --- | --- | --- |
| | Numbers in Thousands 2000 | Percentages 2000 | Numbers in Thousands 2004 | Percentages 2004 | Ranking |
| All persons | 3741 | 12.5 | 3479 | 11.2 | |
| Persons in economic families | 2396 | 9.3 | 2159 | 8.1 | |
| Children -18 | 955 | 13.8 | 865 | 12.8 | 6 |
| With 2 parents | 540 | 9.5 | 450 | 8.1 | 8 |
| With lone parents | 372 | 40.1 | 367 | 40.0 | 1 |
| Other eco. families | 43 | 14.4 | 48 | 14.8 | 5 |
| Unattached men -65 | 554 | 32.1 | 617 | 31.5 | 3 |
| Unattached women -65 | 568 | 44.4 | 530 | 38.4 | 2 |
| Unattached men +65 | 51 | 17.6 | 36 | 11.6 | 7 |
| Unattached women +65 | 172 | 21.6 | 137 | 17.3 | 4 |
| Couples +65 | 52 | 2.1 | 45 | 1.6 | 9 |

Source: Statistics Canada (c).

65 with 38.4%. The much lower poverty incidence of 31.5% for working age single men speaks to the persistence of the gender gap in earnings. Women still do not match the earning power of men although they work in almost the same percentages as men, they are commonly the household breadwinners, and they are more likely to live on their own as families represent a decreasing share of households.

Besides women, other high poverty risk groups that have been identified are people with disabilities that impact on their ability to work and immigrants—in particular, most recent immigrants and Aboriginal peoples. The child poverty rate among these groups is startling (Table 11.4). Child poverty casts a gloomy shadow over the future of children in these families. Higher parental income is almost always associated with better outcomes for children's futures. Lethbridge and Phipps (May 2006) concluded from an extensive literature review that regardless of the child's age or how household income is measured,

| TABLE 11.4 | Child Poverty Rates among Selected Social Groups in 2001 | | | | |
| --- | --- | --- | --- | --- | --- |
| All Children | With Disability | Visible Minority | Aboriginal Identity | All Immigrants | Immigrated in 1996–2001 |
| 18.4% | 27.7% | 33.6% | 40.0% | 40.4% | 49.0% |

Source: Campaign 2000. Oh Canada! Too Many Children in Poverty for Too Long. 2006 National Report Card on Child and Family Poverty in Canada. Retrieved from http://www.campaign2000.ca/rc/rc06/06_c2000NationalReportcard.pdf

| TABLE 11.5 | Average After-Tax Income of Economic Families, Two Persons or More by After-Tax Quintiles (in 2004 Constant Dollars) | | |
|---|---|---|---|
| Economic Families | Year 1995 | Year 2004 | % Change |
| 1st Quintile (Poor) | $19 800 | $22 300 | 12.6% |
| 2nd Quintile (Vulnerable) | $34 500 | $39 100 | 13.3% |
| 3rd Quintile (Mainstream) | $47 000 | $54 200 | 15.3% |
| 4th Quintile (Advantaged) | $62 100 | $72 700 | 17.0% |
| 5th Quintile (Affluent) | $90 400 | $125 000 | 38.3% |
| Source: Statistics Canada (d). | | | |

higher income tends to be related to better physical, social/emotional, cognitive, and behavioural well-being among children.

As a strong indicator of diminishing social mobility, child poverty affects Canadian society as a whole. There is every reason to be concerned that limiting social mobility may inculcate a sense of social exclusion and alienation among those who come to believe that there is no place for them in Canada.

## IMPACT OF TAX AND SOCIAL TRANSFERS

Tax and social transfers no longer effectively bridge differences in living standards. The after-tax income gap is not only widening between the two extremes of the income pyramid, the poor and the affluent, whose average after-tax income quintile income is almost 6 times that of the poor, but also most dramatically between advantaged and affluent economic families. The income differential between these two groups in dollar terms widened to a staggering $52 300 in 2004 compared to $28 300 in 1995. Over the same time period, the size of the income gap between advantaged and mainstream families grew by $3400, compared to $2100 between poor and vulnerable families (author's calculations based on Table 11.5).

## STRUCTURE OF THE LABOUR MARKET

Paid employment is the primary source of income for almost 80% of Canadians (Census 2001). The availability of employment as a source of income and the purchasing power of wage levels are, therefore, crucial determinants of living standards.

However, the demands of businesses to lower production costs shape the structure of the labour market. In the broader context of labour market restructuring, the segmentation of the labour market into core (good) and contingent (precarious) jobs (Heisz, 1996) and unemployment have become national problems. Jobs may be insecure because they are short-term although well-paid or stable, or long-term but precarious when they do not pay enough to support a wage earner and her/his dependants (Cranford, Vosko, & Zukewitch, 2003).

As wages and salaries make up the largest share of productions costs, cutting jobs has become one of the fastest and most readily accessible ways of cutting costs (Kitchen,

2005). To increase the profitability of their production of goods or delivery of services employers look at new technologies to raise labour productivity. This is the measure of how efficiently an economy is transforming labour inputs (hours worked) into outputs (goods and services produced). An increase in labour productivity through technological change has meant that banking machines replaced bank tellers, factories speeded up assembly line jobs, and in self-service restaurants and stores customers do some of the work formerly carried out by employees, like serving their own food or bagging their own groceries.

Canadians not only work harder on the job but are also putting in longer hours. Data from the General Social Survey (GSS) on time use in 2005 found that the typical workday had increased by 45 minutes over a twenty-year period. While this may not seem like much, it adds up to five more work weeks over a year. A ten-hour workday was reported by 25% of workers participating in the survey, an increase from 17% in 1986. More time at work means, of course, less time with the family (Turcotte, Feb. 2007).

On the positive side, employment prospects are improving. This is a welcome change from the years of economic recession in the early 1990s when unemployment peaked at 11.3% in 1993. With the increasing upswing of the economy in the later half of the 1990s, unemployment fell slowly but steadily from a high of 8.3% in 1998 to 7.2% in 2001, 7.7% in 2002, and 7.6% in 2003 to reach a 30-year low of 6.1% in December 2006 (Canadian Social Trends, 2006; Statistics Canada, Jan. 5, 2007). Other statistics include

- The proportion of the working-age population aged 15 and over holding a job rose to an all-time high in December 2006 and labour force participation rate reached a record level of 67.7%.
- 1 173.9 million more people had jobs in 2006 compared to 2002.
- Almost two-thirds of the employment gains went to adult women aged 25 and over, making the unemployment rate of women lower than that of men.
- More full-time jobs—8.6%—were created, compared to 3.6% in part-time employment from 2002–2006.

Strong economic growth, coupled with increasing employment and low interest rates, generally pushes up wages and salaries. Indeed, with the strength in employment, average hourly wages rose by 2.6% from the year before to an estimated $20.00 in December 2006. Loss of jobs in the manufacturing sector (8% in three-and-half years) in Ontario meant that for the first time the highest hourly wage was paid not in Ontario but in Alberta where it rose to $21.60, an increase of 5.9% from the previous year (Department of Finance, 2006). Also for the first time ever, families in Alberta had the highest median income in the country, while Ontario, where more than half of Canada's manufacturing capability is located, is losing jobs because of the decline in its automotive industry. Alberta's oil industry is driving its economic growth and opening up job opportunities.

## DIFFERENT SOCIAL WELFARE SYSTEMS

Article 25 of the Universal Declaration of Human Rights in 1948, which Canada signed, gave everyone the right "to a standard of living adequate for the health and well-being of himself and his family, including food, clothing, housing and medical care, and necessary social services." Adam Smith suggested in his monumental work, *An Inquiry into the Wealth of Nations,* in 1776 that everyone should share in the kind of comforts "the custom of the country renders indecent for creditable people, even of the lowest order, to be without." Working people expect to support themselves and their families at a reasonably decent level of material well-being in the labour market. But they also want their governments to assist them with social welfare provision should they not be able to earn a living as the result of circumstances beyond their control.

The Organisation for Economic Co-operation and Development (OECD) identified three major social welfare systems that define the different ways in which governments provide income protection: a liberal-residual system, a corporatist statist regime, and a social-democratic solidaristic and universalistic system (Esping-Anderson, 1989).

The liberal-residual system is primarily oriented toward market-based provisions of individual welfare and focused on limiting the extent to which social programs replace or interfere with market forces and their impact on individuals and families. Corporatist statism systems are less concerned with free-market dogmatism, but their social welfare provisions are dominated by the preservation of status differentials and families' responsibility to help their members in financial need.

By contrast, social-democratic solidaristic and universalistic systems largely socialize the cost of "familyhood." They take direct responsibility for children, the aged, and the helpless by providing much higher levels of publicly financed social services (Esping-Anderson, 1989). With its emphasis on a fusion of social welfare and employment, this last model promotes the equality of adequate living standards. This goal differs from the two other social welfare systems; they aim to meet only the minimal consumption needs of those whom the market economy has failed and whose families are not able to support them (Olson, 2002).

Up to the mid-1980s, the Canadian welfare state could be categorized as an example of the liberal-residual system. However, it did contain features of the solidaristic-universalistic systems as defined by Esping-Anderson. In modern industrial nations like Canada, market and life-related contingencies link individuals and families to the state through social transfers and social service provisions. Without public education, health services, and income transfers, living standards would be far more precarious. Transfers through the social welfare system play an important role in contributing to the standard of living of all Canadians and permanent residents, not only to those at the lower end of the income scale.

Federal transfer payments to the provinces for health care, post-secondary education, the Canada Assistance Plan, and federal equalization payments ensured that social programs and services were roughly equivalent across the country. Old Age Security benefits, the Canada/Quebec Pension Plan, and universal family allowances pointed in the direction of the socialization of the costs of "familyhood." These programs assumed an intergenerational contract between the income needs of seniors and the financial responsibility of parents raising children.

## THE NEO-LIBERAL SOCIAL WELFARE SYSTEM

Trade integration and the rise in the international mobility of capital prompted the reconfiguration of the Canadian "mixed" social welfare system in accordance with free market principles. The result was the hollowing out of the solid foundation of the Canadian welfare state built on a compromise between the profit interests of business and labour's concern for decent living standards in the decades immediately following World War II. As long as economic growth ensured that social welfare provisions did not interfere with the accumulation of capital, this class compromise remained unchallenged. With the economic recession of 1973 and 1981–82, however, fundamental cracks became apparent. Political neo-liberals and most professional economists claimed that "Canadians [were] supporting one of the world's most over-governed and foolishly generous welfare states" (Francis, 1991).

Corporate welfare state reforms require that governments not regulate market forces or mitigate the effects of these forces with social transfer programs (Boyer & Drache, 1996). The placing of corporate over public interests meant the effective abrogation of government responsibilities for the social and economic well-being of Canadian society (Teeple, 2000: 107). The *Budget Implementation Act* of February 1995 with its drastic expenditure cuts in education, health, and, above all, transfers to the provinces·and territories sent Canadian social welfare policy in a new direction. Maintaining that high interest payments on public debts were crippling their ability to fund social programs, governments insisted they had no choice but to cut public expenditures.

As a result, work- and family-related risks are no longer shared but confronted individually. Three key principles of the neo-liberal approach to social welfare—individual economic self-sufficiency, fiscal responsibility, and the ethic of paid work—have played a crucial role in squeezing money out of tax and social benefits that previously protected living standards. De-universalizing Old Age Security benefits and family allowances amounted to outright spending cuts. The partial de-indexation of tax credits and tax brackets (re-indexed again in 2001) translated into an automatic tax hike. Combined with the tightening of eligibility criteria and cuts in benefit levels for such key income support programs as Employment Insurance and Social Assistance, the neo-liberal restructuring of Canada's social welfare system was put in place (details below).

A mixture of market liberalism and moral authoritarianism concerned with the presumed behavioural dysfunctioning of poor people fuelled the new policy orientation. Employment Insurance and Social Assistance in particular were singled out as encouraging recipients to depend on social transfers instead of moving them into employment. Social transfers were even questioned for jobless lone parents and persons with long-term disabilities, two groups that up to that point had a special claim for public income support in the eyes of society. The realization that some individuals and families were better off on social benefits gave rise to the notion of a "fairness gap" between those on welfare and the working poor. Accordingly, social transfer scales were slashed drastically to match minimum wage levels to ensure that people were always better off holding down a job.

## SOCIAL UNION FRAMEWORK: NEW GROUND RULES FOR SOCIAL POLICY

With the signing of the Social Union Framework Agreement (SUFA) in 1999, the federal and provincial/territorial governments committed themselves to work more closely together to meet the needs of Canadians. There was agreement that Canadians should not face unreasonable residency-based barriers to crucial social services in whatever province or territory they moved to. Residence requirements were removed for student loans, social housing, youth training programs, basic education and skills development, health and persons with disabilities programs (Federal/Provincial/Territorial Ministerial Council on Social Policy Renewal, 2003: 5). Certain barriers for non-residents considered reasonable and consistent with the principles of the Social Union framework were, however, maintained. One such example is the residency requirement for specialized post-secondary education programs.

An important aspect of the SUFA was its confirmation of the essential role of the federal government in ensuring the funding security of social programs and services. The Canada Health and Social Transfer replaced federal–provincial cost-shared arrangements for social assistance, social services, health care, and post-secondary with a lump sum of cash transfers. This gave the provinces the flexibility they had asked for to decide their own social priorities in funding decisions, but it also diminished the role of the federal government in setting national standards for social programs and services. The result has been a balkanization of services by province/territory of residence.

Furthermore, the federal government's ability to initiate new social programs has been limited. Support from a majority of provinces, representing 50% of the Canadian population, is now required to introduce new initiatives, for instance, a national child care program. Prior notice of at least 12 months has to be given before the federal government can introduce a new social policy initiative, and it has to consult with other governments to avoid duplication and overlap. Each province or territorial government can design specific details of new programs to fit their own interests as long as they meet agreed objectives.

## The National Child Benefit

An important outcome of the SUFA was a consensus reached by all governments that child poverty should be one of the first priorities of Social Union initiatives. In January 1993, the three then existing child benefits—the non-refundable and refundable child tax credits and universal family allowances—were integrated into one income-tested program, the Canada Child Tax Benefit (CCTB). It was restructured again as the Canadian Child Tax Benefit in 1998, consisting of a basic benefit and a supplement for working families, the National Child Benefit Supplement (NCBS). The supplement was specifically to address the "fairness gap" between parents in and out of paid work. As a work incentive, it was to ensure that parents in the labour market were always better off than on social assistance. It was, however, just as likely a response to the fast job growth in the low-paid sector of the economy and the need to fill these jobs.

The NCBS for parents with low earnings in the workforce effectively transformed the CCTB from a child benefit into a parental work incentive program. This is unfortunate. Work incentives have no place in child benefit programs. Families with net employment income below $20 435 in 2005 qualify for the maximum base benefit of the CCTB and maximum NCB Supplement, as well as the supplement for each additional child in the July 2006/2007 benefit year:

- $266.67 per month ($3 200 per year) for the first child,
- $247.97 per month ($2 975 per year) for the second child, and
- $243.33 per month ($2 980 per year) for all other children in the family, along with any supplements for children under seven that are applicable.

A child benefit of $6175 for a lone mother with two school-aged children, working at the minimum wage of $8 an hour in British Columbia or Ontario, will raise her earned income of $16 640 a year by 37% to a total of $22 815. Families with net incomes between $20 435 and $36 378 receive the maximum basic CCTB and part of the NCB Supplement. The CCTB base is reduced by 2.5% for every $1000 of additional net income over $36 378 up to approximately $99 128 for families with one child; with two or more children benefits are cut back by 5%. This has given rise to speculations that the government may be encouraging one-child families.

In 2001–2004, the base benefit of the CCTB was paid to 3.1 million families with 5.6 million children, or approximately 82% of Canadian families with children. The NCB Supplement went to 1.5 million families with 2.7 million children, or 40% of all Canadian families with children. An additional supplement of $232 was added in 2003–2004 for each child under the age of 7 for whom no child care expenses were claimed. The supplement was slated to go up to $249 in July 2006. Instead, it was eliminated and rolled into the new Universal Child Care Benefit (UCCB) of $1200 a year introduced by the Conservative government in Ottawa. This reduces the real value of that new initiative to $951 a year (National Council of Welfare, Oct. 2006: 98).

A particular quirk of the NCBS is its integration with the child portion of provincial/territorial social assistance programs. The intention was to remove children from social assistance because of its psychological damage on their self-esteem. While this is undoubtedly a laudable objective, it seems hardly plausible as long as the significant adult(s) in their life still has to rely on social assistance. Ample empirical evidence suggests that low-income families pool their income to pay for the necessities of life. It seems unlikely that splitting between the income support for children and their parents will convince children that they have escaped from the embarrassment of provincial social assistance and that their shattered self-esteem has been miraculously restored.

The integration, however, allows the provinces and territories to offset their social assistance payments by the amount of the supplement. In accordance with an intergovernmental agreement reached in 1997, they were to use the money they saved on other provincial or territorial programming for high-risk children. These are, however, not necessarily the children whose families lost the money in the first place.

## Employment Insurance (EI)

Despite the increase in precarious jobs, the number of laid-off workers eligible for benefits fell from 80% in the early 1990s to just over 40% today. While EI benefits have been cut, contributions have been substantially increased from 5% in the 1970s to 14% in 1996, and the fund is now showing a healthy $51 billion surplus (*Toronto Star*, Feb. 25, 2007: A12). For the last 12 years, contributions from both workers and employers far exceeded benefits paid out, in contradiction to sections 65.3 and 66.6 of the *Employment Insurance Act*, which explicitly stipulates that premiums should generate just enough revenue to cover payments to be made.

Eligibility under EI is now conditional upon a minimum number of hours worked. Even those who can find work only for a couple of hours a week and who were previously exempted from contributions are now required to pay into the fund. Almost 17% of these people do not qualify for benefits should they become unemployed because they failed to accumulate the required working hours, ranging from 420 to 700 hours, depending on the unemployment rate in their area of residency. New entrants to the labour market and repeat recipients have to have worked 910 hours to qualify. Benefits can be paid from 14 to a maximum of 45 weeks. The exact benefit period is based on the unemployment rate in the region and the amount of insurable hours applicants have accumulated in the qualifying period (Service Canada, 2007). Today, benefits replace 55% of previous earnings, down from 60% in the 1980s and 57% in the 1990s.

In November 2006, close to half a million Canadians (483 980), of whom 226 090 were initial or renewal claims, received regular Employment Insurance benefits. This is a decline of 3.6% from November 2005 (*The Daily*, Jan. 23, 2007). The maximum taxable benefit for those whose application was completed by December 2006 is $423 a week or $21 150 a year, barely above the poverty level for an individual. Low-income families with children who qualify for the Canada Child Tax Benefit (CCTB) and the NCB Supplement receive a Family Supplement under section 16 of the *EI Act*. With a net family income of under $20 921, they are paid the full benefit which is scaled back at that point to peter out at $25 921. Recipients with a family can receive up to 80% (55% plus 25%) of their weekly insurable earnings, depending on the number of children they have to support.

Canadians have repeatedly expressed support for social welfare policies that support families through the life cycle. A welcome initiative in January 2004 was the expansion of Employment Insurance by a Compassionate Care benefit. It allows a leave of up to six weeks to care for a family member likely to die within 26 weeks. Regulatory changes as of June 15, 2006, extended access to the program to anyone who the gravely ill person considers to be like a family member. As important as this new policy initiative is, it fails to address the plight of some families. There are families taking care of a severely incapacitated person who is unable to live independently and who is not terminally ill. Compassionate care benefits should be extended to these families for as long as they need them.

## PROVINCIAL SOCIAL ASSISTANCE REFORM

People whose employment insurance coverage has been exhausted, who are unable to find re-employment and who have no financial means or other source of income generally end up on provincial/territorial social assistance. It is today the primary income support for working age unemployed. In March 2005, 1 679 800 persons, not including First Nations peoples of an estimated 150 000, were living on social assistance. Almost half a million were children (National Council of Welfare, Oct. 2006).

Under the neo-liberal market model of social welfare reconfiguration, it is harder to apply and stay on social assistance. Complex and intrusive application requirements are to deter applicants. They are required to demonstrate that they are financially destitute and have no alternate source of income. To promote self-sufficiency, recipients have to seek employment or volunteer in business or community service agencies for a prescribed minimum number of hours. The difficulty of finding affordable, accessible, and high-quality child care for parents does not remove this requirement.

Block funding under the Canada Social Transfer gives the provinces and territories a financial incentive to cut the costs of social assistance. Most chose to spend funds on health care or aid to students and universities, which are more popular with the general public than social assistance. Social assistance benefits were either reduced or allowed to erode with inflation so that recipients are now deprived of the most basic human requirements for food, shelter, clothing, and other essentials. To survive many have to rely on food banks while others, unable to pay their rent, end up in homeless shelters.

Families with children on social assistance are the poorest among the poor. Their poverty, however, does not prevent the majority of the provinces/territories from deducting the NCBS from social assistance cheques. This is known as the "NCBS clawback." Most provinces/territories claw back all or some of the federal money, with the notable exceptions of New Brunswick, Nova Scotia, Newfoundland and Labrador, and Manitoba. The National Council of Welfare (1998), a citizen body that advises the HRDC Minister, estimated that about 64% of poor children and 83% of poor single-parent children do not receive any increased income support from the child benefit.

## CONCLUSION

Structural adjustments in the global forms of capital accumulation, alongside the neoliberal reconfiguration of Canada's social welfare system, created a disturbing nexus between increasing economic insecurity and social inequality. As the disenchantment with precarious employment and low wages remains high, values such as collective responsibility and the common good may be beginning to regain their former support (Piven & Ehrenreich, 2006: 89). For all but the extremely wealthy, the social welfare system remains essential for the protection of living standards and to ensure that economic prosperity is more equally shared.

# References

Alberta Human Resources and Employment, *Alberta Minimum Wage Profile*. Released July 2006. http://www.hre.gov.ab.ca/documents/LMI/LMI-WSI_minwageprofile.pdf

Bauman, Zygmunt. 1998, reprinted 2001. *Work, Consumerism and the New Poor*. Buckingham: Open University Press.

Boyer, Robert, and Drache, Daniel, eds. 1996. *States Against Markets: The Limits of Globalization*. London: Routledge.

Campaign 2000. Nov. 2001. *Family Security in Insecure Times: Tackling Canada's Social Deficit*. Toronto: Family Services Association.

Campaign 2000. Nov. 2006. *Oh Canada! Too Many Children in Poverty for Too Long*. 2006 National Report Card on Child and Family Poverty in Canada. Toronto: Family Services Association.

Canadian Centre for Policy Alternatives, Alternative federal budget. 1999. Ottawa.

Canadian Centre for Policy Alternatives, Nov. 20, 2006. *Growing Gap, Growing Concerns: Poll*. Press Release, http://policyalternatives.ca/index.cfm?act=news&call=1487&pa=BB736455&do=Article

Canadian Social Trends. Summer 2006, No. 81. *Social Indicators*, Ottawa: Statistics Canada.

Census 2001. Overview. University education experience payoff in higher earnings. Ottawa: Statistics Canada.

Community Legal Education Ontario (CleoNet). Feb. 2006. *Employment Insurance*. http://www.cleonet.ca/items/482

Cranford, Cynthia, Le. J. Vosko & Nancy Zukewich. 2003. "Precarious Employment in the Canadian Labour Market: A Statistical Portrait." *Just Labour, A Canadian Journal on Work and Society*. Special Forum on Precarious Employment, Vol. 3 (Fall).

*The Daily*. January 26, 2005. *Are Good Jobs Disappearing in Canada?* http://www.news.gc.ca/cfmx/view/en/index.jsp?articleid=123299&keyword=agriculture&keyword=agriculture&

*The Daily*. April 25, 2005. Study: *Low-Paid Work and Economically Vulnerable Families*. http://www.statcan.ca/Daily/English/050425/d050425a.htm

*The Daily*. August 23, 2006. Study: *Wives as Primary Breadwinners*. http://www.statcan.ca/Daily/English/060823/d060823b.htm

*The Daily*. January 23, 2007. *Employment Insurance*. http://www.statcan.ca/Daily/English/070123/d070123d.htm

*The Daily*. Feb. 13, 2007. *Time with the Family*. http://www.statcan.ca/Daily/English/070213/d070213b.htm

Department of Finance, *2006 Budget*. Chapter 3. "Building a Better Canada." http://www.fin.gc.ca/budget06/bp/bpc3e.htm#Introduction

Ellwood, Wayne. 2003 (reprinted). *The No-Nonsense Guide to Globalization*. London: Verso.

Esping-Anderson, Gosta. 1989. "The three political economies of the welfare state."*Canadian Review of Sociology and Anthropology*, 26 (1).

Evans, Robert. "From World War to Class War: The Rebound of the Rich." *Health Policy*, Vol. 2, No. 1, 2006.

Federal/Provincial/Territorial Ministerial Council on Social Policy Renewal. June 2003. *Three Year Review of Social Union Framework Agreement (SUFA)*. http://www.gov.bc.ca/igra/down/FPT_SUFA_E.pdf

Frenette, M., D. Green & G. Picot. 2004. *Rising Income Inequality in the 1990s: An Exploration of Three Data Sources*. Ottawa: Statistics Canada-Analytical Studies Branch.

Heisz, A. 1996. *Changes in Job Tenure and Job Stability in Canada*. Statistics Canada-Analytical Studies Branch. No. 95.

Institute for Competitiveness and Prosperity. Nov. 2006. *Agenda for Our Prosperity*. Task Force on Competitiveness, Productivity and Economic Progress.

Jencks, Christopher. 2005. "Why do so many jobs pay so badly?" In *Inequality Matters: The Growing Divide in America and Its Poisonous Consequences*. Edited by James Lardner and David A. Smith. New York: The New Press.

Kitchen, Brigitte. 2005. *Life-Chance Guarantees: A New Agenda for Social Policy*. Toronto: Centre for Social Justice.

Kunz, Jean Lock and Jeff Frank. Dec. 2004. "Poverty Thy Name is Hydra." Government of Canada: *Horizons, Poverty Exclusion*. Vol. 7, No. 2.

Lardner, James. 2005. "What's the Problem?" In *Inequality Matters: The Growing Divide in America and Its Poisonous Consequences*. Edited by James Lardner and David A. Smith. New York: The New Press.

Lethbridge, Lynn and Shelley Phipps. May 2006. *Income and the Outcomes of Children*. Ottawa: Statistics Canada-Analytical Studies Branch: Research Paper Series. http://www.statcan.ca/english/research/11F0019MIE/11F0019MIE2006281.pdf

Mackenzie, Hugh. 2007. *Timing Is Everything: Comparing the Earnings of Canada's Highest CEOs with the Rest of Us*. Ottawa: Centre for Policy Alternatives.

McQuaig, Linda. Dec. 12, 2006. "The rich walk ever taller." *Toronto Star.*

Morissette, Rene & Anick Johnson. Jan. 2005. *Are Good Jobs Disappearing in Canada?* Statistics Canada-Business and Labour Market Analysis Division. http://www.statcan.ca/english/research/11F0019MIE/11F0019MIE2005239.pdf

Morissette, Rene and Garnett Picot. April 2005. *Low Paid Work and Economically Vulnerable Families over the Last Two Decades*. Analytical Studies-Research Paper Series. Ottawa: Statistics Canada Cat. # 11F0019 No. 248.

National Council of Welfare. 1998. *Poverty Profiles*. Ottawa.

National Council of Welfare, Poverty Lines 2004 from *Welfare Incomes 2004*, Spring 2005. Ottawa.

National Council of Welfare. Revised Oct. 2006. *Welfare Incomes 2005*. Ottawa.

Olson, G. 20002. *The Politics of the Welfare State: Canada, Sweden and the United States*. Don Mills, ON: Oxford University Press.

Picot, Garnett and John Myles. 2004. "Income Inequality and Low Income in Canada," in *Poverty and Exclusion*, Vol. 7, No. 2, Table 1.

Picot, Garnett and John Myles. 2005. *Income Inequality and Low-Income in Canada: An International Perspective*. Ottawa: Statistics Canada-Business Division and Labour Market Analysis Division.

Piven, Frances and Barbara Ehrenreich. 2006. "The Truth about Welfare Reform," in *Socialist Register* 2006, Edited by Leo Panich and Colin Leys. London: The Merlin Press, New York: Monthly Review Press, Halifax: Fernwood Publishing.

Rowe, Jonathan. 2005. "The Vanishing Commons," in *Inequality Matters: The Growing Divide in America and Its Poisonous Consequences*. Edited by James Lardner and David A. Smith. New York: The New Press.

Saunders, Ron. Feb. 7, 2007. "Should we jack up minimum wage?" *Toronto Star*.

Service Canada. *Employment Insurance (EI) and Regular Benefits*. http://www1.service-canada.gc.ca/en/ei/types/regular.shtml#top

Teeple, Gary. 2000. *Globalization and the Decline of Social Reform: Into the Twenty-First Century*. Aurora, ON: Garamond Press.

Statistics Canada (a). *Economic Families*, Table 202-0202. Cat. # 75-202XIE (last modified, 2006-03-28). http://www40.statcan.ca/l01/cst01/famil22a.htm?sdi=market%20income%20family%20type

Statistics Canada (b). *Family Income, by Family Type* (couple families) CANSIM, table 111-0012 (last modified 2006-07-25). http://www40.statcan.ca/l01/cst01/famil106a.htm?sdi=family%20 income%20family%20type

Statistics Canada (c). *Persons in Low Income after Tax, by Number, 2000–2004* (last modified: 2006-03-28). http://www40.statcan.ca/l01/cst01/famil19b.htm

Statistics Canada (d). *Income in Canada – 2004.* Table 8-5 Cat. 75-201. http://www.statcan.ca/ english/freepub/75-202-XIE/2004000/tablesectionlist.htm

Statistics Canada. Jan 5, 2007. *Latest Release from the Labour Force Survey.* http://www.statcan.ca/ english/Subjects/Labour/LFS/lfs-en.htm

Statistics Canada. *Full-time and Part-time Employment by Sex and Age Group.* CANSIM, Table (last modified 2007-01-04). http://www40.statcan.ca/l01/cst01/labor12.htm

*Toronto Star.* Feb. 22, 2007. *Federal Surplus for Nine Months Hit $7.3 Billion.*

*Toronto Star.* Feb. 25, 2007. *EI Cash Rich, Service Poor.* A14.

Turcotte, Martin. Feb. 2007. "Time Spent with Family During a Typical Workday, 1986–2005." *Canadian Social Trends.* http://www.statcan.ca/english/freepub/11-008-XIE/2006007/pdf/ 11-008-XIE20060079574.pdf

United Nations. 2003. *Human Development Report.* United Nations Development Programme.

United Nations. 2006. *Human Development Report.* United Nations Development Programme.

Walkom, Thomas. January 27, 2007. "If You Feel Poorer You Are Not Alone." *Toronto Star.* F4.

# CHAPTER 12

# The Nature of Oppression and Anti-oppressive Policy Development

*Tracy A. Swan*

*. . . there is a need to pronounce on the issues, to take stands, to make voices heard, and to let the community know that thinking, sensitive, decent human beings are committed to people who are vulnerable, isolated and marginalized. Most of us have social justice. It would be nice to share it with the rest of the world which does not.*

*Stephen Lewis, 2000:8*

## INTRODUCTION

Oppression is a complex phenomenon that is not readily captured in a single chapter, and I am aware that others have written far more comprehensive and thoughtful discussions (Bishop, 2002; Carniol, 2005; Freire, 2000; Mullaly, 2002). Consequently, as I took up the task of writing about the nature of oppression and its relevance to policy analysis and development, I feared that I would not adequately convey the complexity of oppression on the few pages allotted. More significantly, I worried that in writing about oppression on a conceptual level, I would fail to convey or capture the felt experience that so many of our citizens struggle with on a daily basis. When we write about oppression in the abstract, this is often one of the unintended consequences; peoples' experiences of oppression become essentialized and their individual voices are muted. For me this situation would be the greater injustice, because most of what I know about oppression I have learned from others who navigate their lives on the margins of society and they deserve to be heard. However, not to write about oppression and speak to its relevance to Canadian social welfare policy was also not an option. There is a need, as Stephen Lewis states, to pronounce on issues of injustice whenever possible. To not do so is to contribute to that injustice through silence.

The nature of oppression is such that most agree one single definitive understanding does not exist. However, there are a number of significant concepts that, taken together, help to explicate the dynamic nature of oppression. I will initially highlight what many authors consider some of the key concepts that contribute to our understanding of oppression, and in so doing endeavour to address what it is, how it operates, and why it persists. Using heterosexism and homophobia as examples of structural oppression, I hope to demonstrate how various concepts dynamically operate and contribute to the marginalization of "queer" people and others who do not "fit" dominant images and beliefs of mainstream North American society. The chapter will also address three additional questions: Why is an understanding of oppression relevant to policy formulation and analysis? What might anti-oppressive policy development entail? By what criteria can we ascertain whether a policy perpetuates oppression or contributes to social justice?

To create a context for this discussion, I will initially briefly highlight a number of concepts contained in other policy frameworks that, on a conceptual level, suggest a more anti-oppressive and inclusive potential—specifically, social inclusion/exclusion and social or participatory citizenship. The chapter will also speak to the relevance of critical self-awareness to critical policy analysis.

# WHAT IS OPPRESSION?

Oppression takes many forms and has a major impact on the lives and well-being of many Canadian citizens and a vast majority of the world's citizens. Young (1990) indicates oppression has five faces: exploitation, marginalization, powerlessness, cultural imperialism, and violence (The box titled Forms of Oppression provides a brief definition and examples of the different forms of oppression). The experience of any form of oppression can be devastating emotionally, socially, and psychologically. However, the various faces are often interwoven, and people frequently experience multiple forms of oppression in their lives. While many who experience such oppression actively engage in daily acts of resistance (hooks, 1993; Foucault, 1980, 1990; Freire, 2000), for the vast many more, oppression can contribute to the death of all hope. Why then does oppression persist? This is a question that many well-meaning social workers and social work students often ask upon learning about the nature of oppression.

## Forms of Oppression

**Exploitation** refers to social processes whereby the dominant group is able to accrue and maintain status, power, and assets. In the current neo-conservative political environment that allows for significant corporate tax cuts, the gap between the poor and wealthy is increasing and there is a growing underclass in Canada.

**Marginalization** excludes whole groups of people from meaningful participation in society. It affects primarily people of colour, old and young people, many lone mothers and their children, Aboriginal peoples, and mentally and physically challenged people. For example, the voices of individuals who are marginalized have little or no influence on the nature of social policies that affect their lives.

**Powerlessness** affects the development of an individual's capacity and sense of efficacy. For the powerless, decision-making control is severely limited and the individual is exposed to disrespectful treatment and stigma because of her/his status. Many lone mothers on social assistance, for example, experience considerable public scrutiny by the welfare and/or child welfare systems. They also struggle with stigma associated with stereotypes of "welfare bum" and/or "bad mother."

**Cultural imperialism** occurs when the dominant group imposes its way of life, beliefs, values, and experiences on "others" and measures them by dominant norms. When people fail to meet the "norm," they are constructed as deviant by the dominant group and their own experiences/way of life become invisible. The most blatant example of cultural imperialism is reflected in the historical and current treatment of Aboriginal peoples in Canada.

**Violence** includes direct physical attack, harassment, intimidation, and ridicule. All forms of violence serve to stigmatize the person, group, and community. Fear of such violence also contributes to oppression. For example, many lesbian, gay, bisexual, transgendered, and transsexual individuals fear being "outed" because it will potentially expose her/him to other forms of violence and oppression (Adapted from Mullaly, 2002).

Part of the answer lies in the complex nature of oppression and part lies in our individual and collective responses to the challenges it presents to those of us who have more privilege. Mullaly (2007) posits that although oppression has different forms and levels of severity that may be experienced differently by individuals, it is characterized by "a common set of dynamics" between the dominant and subordinate groups (285). Oppression, therefore, is experienced by some and not others, because of their group affiliation.

## HOW AND WHY IS OPPRESSION MAINTAINED?

Oppression originates and operates through social structures and institutions. Carniol (1992) differentiates between primary structures and secondary structures. Primary structures are invisible and include classism, patriarchy and, associated with it, sexism and heterosexism, racism, ageism, ableism, imperialism/colonialism, and now globalization.[1] Secondary structures are concrete and refer to social institutions and systems such as the family, communities, educational and religious institutions, social services, and the media. All these systems perpetuate the world view of dominant society that is used as the benchmark by which "others" are measured and found wanting. Both primary structures and secondary structures reproduce all forms of oppression whereby different groups of people, often as a mere consequence of their birth, are marginalized in society. These include people who are poor, of colour, with (dis)abilities, women, children, older people, sexually oriented people other than heterosexuals, and immigrants. Other people, also often through an accident of birth, who are upper or middle class, white, able-bodied, male, between 19 and 60 or 65 years of age, heterosexual, and of European or North American descent, have privilege and power. In Figure 12.1, Dumbrill (2003) provides the following Spatial Analysis of Domination and Oppression. On the left, he highlights issues of class and on the right, he identifies other forms of oppression and those who are affected. In the middle is the dominant group, the mainstream who have more power and privilege.

Privilege provides access to power and power provides access to even more privilege. Those from the mainstream use their power to maintain their position and, in doing so, contribute to the oppression of others. However, those of us from the mainstream do not often recognize either our own privilege or how we contribute to the oppression of others. A number of factors protects us from this realization. Firstly, there is a dominant belief that Western societies and democracies are just and equitable. Secondly, oppression on a structural level is often quite covert or subtle and, therefore, more readily denied (Mullaly, 2007). And thirdly, most well-intended people from mainstream society find it very difficult to accept that they are oppressors (McIntosh, 1989; Narayan, 1994; Swan, 2002).

---

1   Globalization refers to the expansion of capitalism globally. It promotes free trade of goods and services between countries and has been a major force in the neo-conservative economic policies of major Western countries. Globalization also concentrates economic power in the hands of multinational/transnational corporations. International bodies such as the World Trade Organization, the World Bank, and the International Monetary Fund, which have a much greater influence over economic policies and practices than national governments, protect the rights of multinational corporations and, as a consequence, they continue to increase in scope and power (Hick, 2004; Mullaly, 2007).

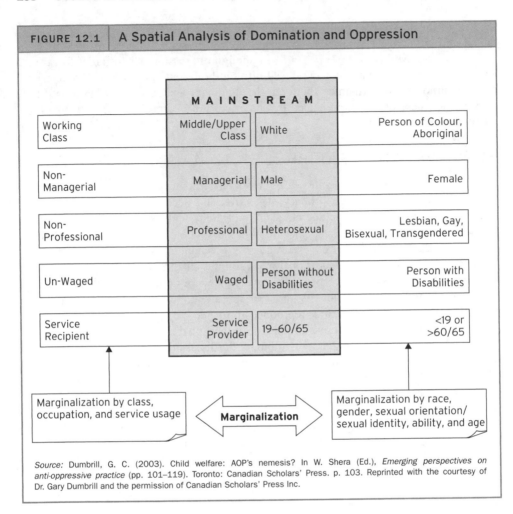

**FIGURE 12.1    A Spatial Analysis of Domination and Oppression**

*Source:* Dumbrill, G. C. (2003). Child welfare: AOP's nemesis? In W. Shera (Ed.), *Emerging perspectives on anti-oppressive practice* (pp. 101–119). Toronto: Canadian Scholars' Press. p. 103. Reprinted with the courtesy of Dr. Gary Dumbrill and the permission of Canadian Scholars' Press Inc.

# MULTIPLE LOCATIONS AND INTERLOCKING OPPRESSION

All the above might suggest that there are two mutually exclusive groups, the oppressed and those who oppress. However, people rarely possess only one social identity or occupy one social location. A person can occupy social locations whereby she/he experiences multiple forms of oppression, as well as occupy different locations of privilege. In other words, we can occupy quite different social locations simultaneously and be oppressed in some aspects of our lives and be the oppressor in others (Carniol, 2005; Mullaly, 2002). Having multiple locations, some of privilege and others where we are oppressed, creates conflict and competition within and across marginalized groups (Bishop, 2002). We may strive to eliminate oppression in those areas of our lives where we are oppressed and at the same time remain "blind" to the implications of our privilege for others who have different social identities. For an example of the nature of interlocking identities, please see the box titled Interlocking Social Identities.

## Interlocking Social Identities

To use a personal example, I am white, of British heritage, and was brought up in a middle class, traditional, nuclear family that attended a church of one of the dominant Christian denominations. With the exception of the need to wear glasses, I am able bodied. All of these factors indicate I am part of dominant society and have benefited from considerable privilege. However, I am a woman and a lesbian. This suggests that I have experienced sexism and gender oppression, as well as homophobia and oppression that springs from heterosexism. I have also seen my 60th birthday, and as such am beginning to experience ageism. As I grow older, I am aware that ableism will become a factor in my life. Given these different social identities (locations), it is evident that I am oppressed in some aspects of my life and am clearly privileged and an oppressor in others (Bishop, 2002). I may, therefore, be highly conscious of oppression that I experience on a daily basis, but remain unaware of the oppression that I perpetrate in other areas where I have privilege. For example, I have often taken my white privilege for granted, adamantly denying that I am a racist, while enjoying the benefits of that privilege at the expense of people of colour.

## CULTURE AND IDEOLOGY

Oppression operates on three levels: structurally, culturally, and individually (Dominelli, 1997; Mullaly, 2002; Thompson, 1997). Mullaly (2007) indicates that each level is "interdependent, interactive, and mutually reinforcing" and that:

> Oppression on a cultural level consists of those values, norms, and shared patterns of thinking and acting, along with an assumed consensus about what is right and normal, that taken together, endorse the belief in a superior culture. It acts as a vehicle for transmitting and presenting the dominant culture . . . as the norm (262).

Bishop (2002) suggests that structural oppression is based on three primary assumptions that are part of the fabric of our beliefs in society; separation, hierarchy, and competition. Similarly, Mullaly (2007) identifies other myths that we are all brought up to believe contribute to oppression. These include, among others, myths about scarcity of resources, myths about competition and hierarchy, myths about class, and myths about supremacy, which he indicates relates to beliefs in the supremacy of white, Western male culture. Additionally, there are myths about normalcy, which reflect mainstream norms and standards against which people are measured (i.e., there is a "normal family" and "normal behaviour"). There is a myth about individuality and, related to this, beliefs about fairness and how one can be successful in society. There are also specific myths that contribute to stereotypes, as well as particular myths that impact specific groups of marginalized people, for example, "myths about motherhood" that affect all women and contribute to gender oppression (Baines, Evans & Neysmith, 1998).

All these myths and beliefs as a whole, communicated through culture and secondary structures, constitute the dominant ideology that maintains structural inequity. Through both the written and spoken word, these myths persist and make up the dominant discourse that is generally understood and accepted unquestioningly. Because words have the power to construct, dominant discourse not only conveys taken-for-granted beliefs, but also reinforces ideas about the nature of those who are "different" from the mainstream (Foucault, 1980, 1972). More specifically, those who are different are oppressed through discourses that perpetuate stereotypical and pejorative images. For example, even though members of the GLBTQ[2] community have made some significant gains in respect to equal rights in Canada, oppression, in all its various forms, still persists (O'Neill, 2003). Through heterosexism and homophobia, the "dominant culture sustains an ideological environment that *justifies* (emphasis added) a range of institutional practices that exclude, stigmatize and dismiss lesbians" (Aronson, 1995, 10) and gay men. The box below provides a description of how heterosexist privilege is maintained *structurally* and *culturally* and demonstrates how heterosexism and homophobia combine to create various forms of oppression. It also describes how oppression can be experienced by many, but not all, queer youth on an individual level.

In a similar fashion, other myths and stereotypical images are perpetuated through dominant discourse: myths of individualism contribute to the construction of the "welfare bum," myths about the supremacy of white Western thought and culture combine with stereotypes of the "drunk Indian" and/or the construction of the "noble savage" and perpetuate oppression of Aboriginal peoples (King, 2003; Hart, 2002), and so on. What then, given the pervasive nature and power of these beliefs that constrain the lives of people on the margins, can be done to challenge them? With this question, we turn our attention to ideas about resistance.

## Homophobia and Heterosexism

We are all brought up, allowing for a few exceptions, to believe that all people are heterosexual and all families are composed of a man and a woman who come together to give birth to children. This belief and the assumptions we make that relate to it have major implications not only for other sexually oriented people, but also for all those who form families that do not coincide with this dominant image. Heterosexism not only marginalizes those who are not heterosexual, but also simultaneously protects and maintains the privilege for those who are. Heterosexist notions are perpetuated in the culture through dogma, stereotypes, and as noted, assumptions and myths. By assuming that all people are heterosexual, those who are straight do not have to entertain the notion of gay marriage or lesbian parents. Even though "they" may have the right to do both, gay men or lesbians who choose to marry and/or become parents do not have to be acknowledged in the same way as heterosexual marriages are honoured;

*(Continued)*

---

2  GLBTQ is an acronym for gay men, lesbians, bisexual and transgendered people and all others who self-identify as "queer."

*(Continued)*

and if I do not have to consider these rights, then laws that privilege heterosexual unions do not have to be extended to these "others" and in all these ways my privilege and way of life is protected. Heterosexist assumptions also mean that I do not see more subtle forms of oppression that make it, for example, almost impossible for those gay or lesbian couples wishing to celebrate their relationship to find anniversary cards that reflect the nature of that relationship, and so on. Additionally, when my heterosexist assumptions are challenged in some way, as was the recent case with gay marriage in Canada, discourse will reinforce and give "voice" to my dominant beliefs about family and what is "normal" through various social institutions and the media. I can also be sure that when my privilege is threatened that negative stereotypes and myths can be employed that will contribute to my heterosexist privilege. For example, the flighty, effeminate, and promiscuous gay men like the TV character Jack in *Will and Grace*, or the myth that gay men are pedophiles, can be evoked to protect the sanctity of the "heterosexual family unit" and contribute further to the stigma and oppression of all "queer" people. The media that contributes to these myths will assist in this enterprise, by predominantly depicting the family as heterosexual (also predominantly middle class, and, for the most part, white). In all these ways and more, heterosexism and homophobia combine to maintain heterosexual privilege and serve to silence and marginalize those who are other sexually oriented.

How this oppression is experienced on an individual level will vary depending on an array of other variables: other areas of oppression or privilege, personal history, emotional and psychological well-being, access to gay positive environment and supports, to name a few. However, to demonstrate the potential impact, consider the experience of many queer youth. For a gay or lesbian youth who is struggling with his/her sexual orientation, this means she/he is more likely to see such stereotypes in the media, and far less likely to find positive roles with whom to identify. Faced with pejorative images and homophobic dogma that tells him/her that s/he is "less than," the young person is more likely to struggle with internalized homophobia and to remain isolated and alienated from peers. He/she is more likely to live in fear of being "outed" and exposed to ridicule and stigma. Should s/he choose to come out, the young person is at greater risk of being rejected by family members, and is at greater risk of living on the street and encountering overt violence that is part of street life. Once on the street, he/she is likely to engage in street crime and prostitution to survive. It is also more probable that the young person will try to cope with the pain associated with oppression and self-alienation through drug use and other self-destructive behaviour. S/he is also at greater risk than his/her straight peers of attempting or committing suicide (Mallon, 1999; Morrow, 2006; Savin-Williams, 2005).

# THE NATURE OF RESISTANCE

An understanding of oppression is incomplete without also understanding the relevance of resistance and the many forms it can take. Resistance, like power, is a part of all relationships, because as Foucault (1990) posits, power and resistance exist only in relationship. Resistance can, therefore, be understood as an exercise of power and an expression of autonomy by those who are oppressed. Resistance takes many forms across a spectrum of activity from individual expression to global social movements. It can also occur in a multiplicity of positions and sites, on the personal, community, national, and global level. Regardless of the form it takes, however, resistance constitutes a refusal to accept the constraints imposed by dominant discourses and power relationships (Fook, 2002; Mullaly, 2002; Saulnier, 1996).

An individual expression of resistance that many social workers and social work students will recognize is the late, absent, angry, or otherwise disruptive client; the person who social work practitioners have traditionally labelled as "resistant," "unreliable," or "irresponsible." We may often fail to see the "annoying behaviour" as an exercise of autonomy and an expression of resistance to the power, authority, and control of either the professional or the agency (Mullaly, 2002). Another individual expression of resistance occurs when a person challenges stereotypes by claiming language generally used pejoratively by others to construct his/her identity. Many in the gay and/or lesbian community, for example, now self-identify as queer, and in so doing resist the dominant construction of who they are. In a similar vein, Mullaly (2002) suggests that negative stereotypes can be confronted by a reversing technique whereby the qualities or characteristics of the stereotype are applied to the dominant group. An example of this technique is demonstrated by the Heterosexual Questionnaire,[3] where homosexual stereotypes and dominant discourse is challenged by asking heterosexual people to respond to questions often asked of GLBTQ people. The following is a sample of the kinds of question contained in the questionnaire: "What do you think caused your heterosexuality? Is it possible that your heterosexuality is just a phase you may grow out of? Why are heterosexuals so promiscuous?"

Another form of resistance entails critiquing dominant discourses and contributing to the creation of alternative forms of discourse (Fook, 2002; Mullaly, 2002). Individually and collectively, women involved in the second wave of feminism developed a counter discourse such that today all forms of feminism present an alternative discourse that challenges male domination (Saulnier, 1996). Different forms of feminism also provide alternative discourses that challenge other forms of oppression. For example, Black womanism contributes to anti-racist discourse and global feminism contributes to the discourse that challenges globalization and capitalism by addressing the economic exploitation of women around the world (Saulnier, 1996).

Many individuals, groups, and communities also resist the dominant culture and reclaim lost traditions and/or create alternative cultures. Perhaps the most familiar example of this form of resistance is the efforts of Aboriginal peoples across Canada who have

---

3   The Heterosexual Questionnaire was originally developed by Martin Rochlin, Ph.D. (January 1977). The questions cited here are from the Advocates for Youth website (www.advocatesforyouth.org/lessonplans/heterosexual2.htm). In addition to working on the behalf of youth generally, they advocate for GLBTQ youth and have developed resource materials that can be used to promote a safe space for queer youth.

not only reclaimed their languages and traditions, but have also challenged stereotypes and critiqued the dominant white culture and its version of history (King, 2003; Hart, 2002). Finally, as noted above, national and global social movements[4] constitute another form of resistance. For example, when it was suggested that the recently won right of gays and lesbians to marry should be reopened for debate in the House of Commons, Egale[5] mounted a national Internet campaign encouraging citizens to contact their members of Parliament to encourage them to vote against the motion. On both a national and global level, the Council of Canadians, led by Maude Barlow, has actively critiqued Canada's economic, health, and environmental policy and programs, and addressed human rights issues nationally and internationally. The organization has also actively participated in global social movements such as the World Social Forum in Nairobi, Kenya, in January 2007, where representatives spoke to the impact of multinational corporations (Canadian Council of Canadians, Spring 2007).

## POLICY AND OPPRESSION

How then do these ideas about oppression and resistance relate to policy development and analysis? What might anti-oppressive policy formulation entail? And what challenges does this pose for individual social work students and social workers? I will conclude the chapter with some ideas that will hopefully assist social work students and practitioners in their efforts to contribute to the development of anti-oppressive and inclusive policy. Before these ideas are presented, however, it is important to first highlight a number of points about the nature of social and economic policy in Canada. It is clearly beyond the scope of this chapter to delineate the many variables and frameworks that inform policy development, but most critical policy analysts concur that many of the myths identified above sustain capitalism and globalization, and are embedded in policy frameworks employed to a greater or lesser degree by all political parties in Canada (Caragata, 2003; Hick, 2004; Graham, Swift, & Delaney, 2003; Mullaly, 2007; Mishra, 2005). As a consequence, economic and social welfare policies and the language they contain often reinforce the same beliefs and are another means by which the privilege of dominant society is maintained at the expense of those defined as "other." Additionally, it is recognized that for the better part of a decade and a half, all levels of government have engaged in a major retrenchment of social welfare policies, regardless of which political party is in power. This retrenchment is attributed to the globalization and influence of multinational corporations and the economic policies that they promote (Graham, Swift, & Delaney, 2003; Mishra, 2005).

---

4  Interested students and workers who wish to contribute to anti-oppressive policy on a national or international level can contribute to the work of social movements that focus on issues of oppression. Both the Council of Canadians (www.canadians.org), and the International Forum on Globalization (www.ifg.org/) address issues that pertain to globalization, while nationally, the Make Poverty History campaign (www.makepovertyhistory.ca) works to eliminate poverty in Canada. Recently they joined with international partner groups in the global call to action against poverty in a day of action to demand gender equality to end poverty.

5  Egale Canada is a national organization that advances equality for GLBTQ people and their families. In addition to carrying on a national campaign to defeat the motion to reopen debate of gay marriage, the organization is currently undertaking a countrywide campaign to make schools safer places for GLBTQ youth (www.egale.ca).

Given these realities, then, as the discussion of resistance might suggest, those who wish to address the oppressive nature of policies need to initially develop a capacity to critically analyze and deconstruct dominant discourse in order to challenge oppressive beliefs that are embedded in various policies that underpin practice and service delivery. Our individual capacity to do this begins with a focus on the "self" and entails the hard work of developing our capacity to deconstruct the many taken-for-granted assumptions and beliefs that constitute our own world view[6] (Kondrat, 1999; Swan, 2002). Critical reflection and self-examination is often the beginning step for many social work students who come to recognize, through this process, the pervasive nature of the dominant ideology (Swan, Ferriera, Cosby, Young, Cho, Sammon, Dumbrill, Lee, Palmer, & Westwood, 2005). Building on this understanding, they are better equipped to turn their gaze outward to identify the many overt and subtle ways in which dominant discourse perpetuates oppression. This entails recognizing how different discourses are embedded in policies that inform the services social work students come to provide.

In addition to deconstructing oppressive aspects of policy, we can contribute to the development of more inclusive and emancipatory policy by increasing our knowledge of a variety of other discourses that are relevant to the people for whom we provide service (Fook, 2002; Mullaly, 2002). In a child welfare context, for example, this could include, among others, feminist discourse on the construction of mothering or gendered roles, alternative discourse on the nature of family that recognizes the viability of different family forms, anti-racist and/or Aboriginal discourse, and discourse on identity formation of young people that challenges heterosexual assumptions. Equipped with these different perspectives, not only can we identify the oppressive nature of the assumptions that underpin policies, we can contribute to the development of more inclusive, anti-oppressive policy by drawing on concepts and language from alternative discourses (Swan & Sinnott, 2007).

In a similar vein, it is also important to learn about policy frameworks that offer the promise of *meaningful* inclusion and participation of those who experience oppression. Mullaly (2007) maintains that definitions of social justice and equality must include social rights, which he notes refers to the "full participation of everyone in society's major institutions and to the socially supported opportunities for all to develop and exercise their inherent capacities" (283). Social inclusion[7] and social or citizen participation are concepts that emphasize the relevance of meaningful and active participation of individuals whose lives are significantly constrained by oppression (Caragata, 2003; Lister, 1999; Wharf-Higgins, Cossom, & Wharf, 2003). While the concept of social inclusion/exclusion also

---

6   Grappling with the complexity of unmasking and naming oppression always entails coming to understand how we contribute to the very oppression we are trying to eradicate. For those of us whose identity is invested in seeing ourselves as good, caring, well-intentioned people, this can be a particularly difficult task. The feelings that are evoked by this realization, for example, guilt, sadness, and denial, can constitute a major hurdle to working alongside those who are marginalized. Yet it is a task that we all must take on daily, if we hope to work anti-oppressively.

7   Social inclusion/exclusion evolved in Europe during the 1980s to address growing social divisions. Although not a fully evolved framework, it is a major topic in policy discussions in Canada. The concept shifts the focus to non-economic aspects of society that contribute to social exclusion, such as access to education and health care, social cohesion, and community and political participation (Hick, 2004). With a focus on inclusion, citizen participation or social citizenship, based on the work of T. H. Marshall, has regained appeal (Wharf-Higgins, Cossom, & Wharf, 2003).

has limitations,[8] Graham, Swift, and Delaney (2003) indicate that the language of social inclusion

- factors in power relations in the analysis;
- includes many levels of experience, such as health, rights, quality of life and well-being;
- automatically involves the "social";
- focuses on barriers to inclusion; and
- stresses process rather than outcomes (i.e., the concepts contribute to discussions of citizenship and, by extension, to discussions that speak to what constitutes meaningful participation for those on the margins).

In many ways, social inclusion/exclusion provides an alternative discourse and the emphasis on social justice provides a different focus for policy and program evaluation. Further, the authors also suggest that social inclusion contributes to discussions of citizenship and, by extension, to discussions of citizen participation. What then constitutes meaningful participation of people who are oppressed?

## MEANINGFUL PARTICIPATION OF MARGINALIZED PEOPLE

For policy to be meaningful to citizens generally, they must see themselves reflected in it. Although they are intimately familiar with how the policies contribute to their oppression on a day-to-day basis, the majority of people who struggle with various forms of structural oppression have few meaningful opportunities either to participate in policy development or to critique existing policy and programs. Wharf-Higgins, Cossom, and Wharf (2003) suggest that their failure to participate in policy formulation has more to do with the nature of the participatory structures employed—committee meetings and public forums—than with a lack of desire to have a voice. Citizens who do participate tend to be educated, middle class individuals who are familiar with these structures and have the means to access them. Those who struggle with different forms of disadvantage may find the structures either intimidating and/or inaccessible for economic reasons because they work long hours, because of linguistic or cultural differences, and/or because their lives are such that they cannot make a sustained commitment to participate. Other barriers relate to how dominant discourses impact the relationship between the service user and agency. Various groups often experience humiliation and further oppression at the very hands of those who provide services on which they depend. Lone mothers, for example, whose lives are often scrutinized by both the welfare system and the child welfare system, live in fear of losing

---

8  Various authors note that the language of the social inclusion/exclusion concepts can be employed to support any political position, and that several parties in Canada have used the discourse to promote neo-conservative and neo-liberal agendas (Graham, Swift, & Delaney, 2003; Mullaly, 2007). Others highlight that, if not used with care, policy built on the concepts of social inclusion could reinforce conformity or homogeneity, rather than enhance diversity. Sin and Yan (2003), who focus on a position paper developed by the Laidlaw Foundation, speak to a number of problematic aspects of the proposal, one of which is the failure to recognize racial diversity. They, like Mullaly (2007), also argue that the social inclusion/exclusion ideology fails to address structural roots of oppression.

## An Anti-oppressive Policy Screen

Anti-oppressive policy and policy development

- Contributes to the "unmasking" of power relations
- Addresses the ingrained impact of oppression and social exclusion
- Recognizes differences and diversity within and across groups and in social arrangements
- Breaks down system barriers that hamper full participation

- Enhances meaningful participation of all citizens in the development, implementation, and evaluation of policies and programs that impact their lives
- Promotes social justice and the use of social justice as a screen for evaluation
- Facilitates the links between local, national, and international issues
- Facilitates the links between local, national, and international coalitions and movements

not only their primary source of income, but also their children. Understandably, they do not feel like full citizens with rights. Many lone mothers are also reluctant to participate because of a potential backlash that could have both psychological and severe economic consequences (Lessa, 2003; Wharf-Higgins, Cossom, & Wharf, 2003).

It follows that in order for those on the margins of society to meaningfully participate, social workers and those who wish to develop anti-oppressive policy must work to reduce the potential risks of taking part and find creative ways to facilitate inclusion. Wharf-Higgins, Cossom, & Wharf (2003) cite a number of methods such as citizen panels, visual and practical planning experiences in malls, in neighbourhoods, or culturally specific associations, and/or in churches as being successful in bringing together members of diverse communities. Beyond this, Leonard (1997) encourages us to counter the homogenizing tendency of welfare policy by encouraging co-authorship of joint narratives that give priority to a diversity of subjects. Social workers who engage in critical self-reflection and develop their capacity for critical empathy (Clark, 2003; Swan, 2002) are well situated to work collaboratively to develop joint narratives with diverse individuals and to contribute to policies that reflect their voices and experiences, in other words, policies to which they can relate.

Taken together, the discussions of resistance, policy, and oppression contain a number of suggestions that can assist both social work students and practitioners to deconstruct and critically analyze provincial and federal policies that inform their practice. To further assist with this analysis, dimensions/characteristics of anti-oppressive policy are presented in the box titled An Anti-oppressive Policy Screen, and a series of critical questions for policy analysis are outlined in the box titled Critical Questions for Policy Analysis.

The policy screen and the critical questions incorporate suggestions that flow from the discussion of social inclusion and citizen participation. Both may be used to evaluate the degree to which policies either perpetuate oppression, or promote the inclusion and meaningful participation of people who have had few opportunities to contribute to policies that impact their lives.

## Critical Questions for Policy Analysis

**Language & Discourse**

Does the policy perpetuate dominant myths and binaries such as independence and dependence and other discourses and/or stereotypes?

- Is the policy inclusive or does it perpetuate marginalization by failing to recognize differences or by being silent on issues?

- Does the policy reflect multiple voices and diversity of subjects and positions?

- Does the research on which the policy is based reflect joint authorship of narratives about problems, needs, and claims (Leonard, 1997)?

- Does the language of the policy reflect alternative discourses that are emancipatory and inclusive?

- How does the language and nature of the policy contribute to the construction of the service user/social worker relationship?

**Felt Experience**

When implemented, does the policy constrain the service user or contribute to her/his humiliation?

- If I was (name of client with whom you are very familiar), how would the language of the policy impact me?

- If I was (name of a client with whom you are very familiar), how would I experience the service that is guided by the policy?

- Do the policies or the procedures that guide your practice constrain you, the worker, in your efforts to work anti-oppressively?

# CONCLUSION

This chapter has presented a number of significant concepts that define the nature of oppression and also help to explain why oppression persists. The chapter has also endeavoured to address the relationship between oppression and social welfare policy. In speaking to this relationship the goal was also to provide students and social workers with a variety of ways in which they too can take up the challenge of contributing to the development of anti-oppressive policy. I have written this chapter with full awareness that taking on this challenge can be demanding and not without risks. I am also aware that for many, if not all, the demands of social work practice, on any given day, can be quite demanding, if not overwhelming. And yet, I contend we all need to look for and to create opportunities to address oppression. Although we are all inculcated with beliefs and values that make up dominant ideology and we tend, for the most part, to accept it unquestioningly, we too can engage in resistance and contribute to the creation of a counter discourse. We can, as Stephen Lewis encourages us to do, exercise the power we have, join with those who are more intimately acquainted with the nature of oppression, and work to create a world that is anti-oppressive and characterized by social justice. All social workers, regardless of their place of employment or the nature or method of practice, have a particular responsibility to take up Lewis's challenge. Our code of ethics is clear in this regard (Canadian Association of Social Workers, 2005).

# References

Aronson, J. (1995). Lesbians in social work education: Process and puzzles in claiming visibility. *Journal of Professional Human Services, 6 (1),* 5–26.

Baines, C., Evans, P., Neysmith, S. (1998). Women's caring: Work expanding, state contracting. In C. Baines, P. Evans, S. Neysmith (Eds.), *Women's caring: Feminist perspectives on social welfare* (pp. 3–22). Toronto: Oxford University Press.

Bishop, A. (2005). *Beyond token change: Breaking the cycle of oppression in institutions.* Halifax, Nova Scotia: Fernwood Publishing.

Bishop, A. (2002). *Becoming an ally: Breaking the cycle of oppression in people.* Halifax, Nova Scotia: Fernwood Publishing.

Canadian Association of Social Workers. (2005). *Code of Ethics.* http://www.casw-acts.ca.

Canadian Council of Canadians. (Spring 2007). *Canadian perspectives.* http://www.canadians.org.

Caragata, L. (2003). Neoconservative realities: The social and economic marginalization of Canadian women. *International Sociology, 18 (3),* 559–580.

Carniol, B. (2005). *Case critical: Social services and social justice in Canada.* 5th ed. Toronto: Between the Lines.

Carniol, B. (1992). Structural social work: Maurice Moreau's challenge to social work practice. *Journal of Progressive Human Service, 3 (1),* 1–20.

Clark, J. (2003). Reconceptualizing empathy for anti-oppressive, culturally competent practice. In W. Shera (Ed.), *Emerging perspectives on anti-oppressive practice* (pp. 247–263). Toronto: Canadian Scholars' Press.

Dominelli, L. (1997). *Anti-racist social work.* 2nd ed. London: Macmillan.

Dumbrill, G. (2003). Child welfare: AOP's nemesis? In W. Shera (Ed.), *Emerging perspectives on anti-oppressive practice* (pp. 101–119). Toronto: Canadian Scholars' Press.

Fook, J. (2002). *Social work: Critical theory and practice.* London: Sage.

Foucault, M. (1990). *Introduction, Volume 1: The history of sexuality (1978).* Reprint, New York: Random House.

Foucault, M. (1980). *Power/knowledge: Selected interviews and other writings 1972–77.* C. Gordon (Ed.). Brighton: Harvester Press.

Foucault, M. (1972). *The archaeology of knowledge and the discourse of language.* New York: Pantheon.

Freire, P. (2000). *Pedagogy of the oppressed, 30th anniversary editions.* New York: Continuum.

Graham, J. R., Swift, K. J., Delaney, R. (2003). *Canadian social policy: An introduction.* 2nd ed. Toronto: Prentice Hall.

Hart, M. A. (2002). *Seeking mino-pimatisiwin: An Aboriginal approach to helping.* Halifax, Nova Scotia: Fernwood Publishing.

Hick, S. (2004). *Social welfare in Canada: Understanding income security.* Toronto: Thompson Educational Publishing.

hooks, b. (1993). *Sisters of the yam: Black women and self-recovery.* Boston, MA: South End Press.

Kondrat, M. E. (1999). Who is the "self" in self-awareness: Professional self-awareness from a critical perspective. *Social service review, Dec*, 451–477.

King, T. (2003). *The truth about stories: A native narrative.* Toronto: The House of Anansi Press Inc.

Leonard, P. (1997). *Postmodern welfare: Reconstructing an emancipatory project.* London: Sage.

Lessa, I. (2003). Single motherhood in the Canadian landscape: Postcard from a subject. In A. Westhues (Ed.), *Canadian social policy: Issues and perspectives* (pp. 90–103). Waterloo: Wilfrid Laurier Press.

Lewis, Stephen. (2000). Keynote address. The joint conference of the International Federation of Social Workers & the International Association of the Schools of Social Work. Montreal, Canada.

Lister, R. (1999). Tracing the contours of women's citizenship. *Policy and Politics, 21 (1),* 3–16.

Mallon, G. (1999). *Let's get this straight: A gay- and lesbian-affirming approach to child welfare.* New York: Columbia University Press.

McIntosh, P. (1989). White privilege: Unpacking the invisible knapsack. *Peace & Freedom,* (July/August), 10–12.

Mishra, R. (2005). The political bases of Canadian social welfare. In J. Turner & F. Turner (Eds.), *Canadian social welfare,* 5th ed. (pp. 46–59). Toronto: Pearson Education Canada.

Morrow, D. F. (2006). Gay, lesbian, bisexual, and transgendered adolescents. In D. F. Morrow & L. Messinger (Eds.), *Sexual orientation & gender expression in social work practice. Working with gay, lesbian, bisexual & transgendered people* (pp. 177–195). New York: Columbia University Press.

Mullaly, Bob. (2007). *The new structural social work,* 3rd ed. Don Mills, ON: Oxford University Press.

Mullaly, Bob. (2002). *Challenging oppression: A critical social work approach.* Don Mills, ON: Oxford University Press, pp. 42–48.

Narayan, U. (1994). Working together across differences. In B. R. Compton & B. Galaway (Eds.), *Social Work Processes* (pp. 177–188). Belmont, California: Wadsworth Press.

O'Neill, B. (2003). Toward inclusion of gay and lesbian people: Social policy changes in relation to sexual orientation. In A. Westhues (Ed.), *Canadian social policy: Issues and perspectives,* 3rd ed. (pp. 331–348). Waterloo, Ontario: Wilfrid Laurier Press.

Saulnier, C. F. (1996). *Feminist theories and social work: Approaches and applications.* New York: The Haworth Press.

Savin-Williams, R. C. (2005). *The new gay teenager.* Cambridge, MA: Harvard University Press.

Sin, Rick & Yan, Miu Chung (2003). Margins as centres: A theory of social inclusion in anti-oppressive social work. In W. Shera (Ed.), *Emerging perspectives in anti-oppressive practice* (pp. 25–41). Toronto: Canadian Scholars' Press.

Swan, T. (2002). Anti-oppressive social work: Self-awareness and the relevance of social location. In B. Lee & M. Wolfson (Eds.), *Introductory readings in structural social work* (pp. 38–45). Monograph, McMaster University, Hamilton, Ontario.

Swan, T. & Sinott, R. (Winter, 2007). *The relevance of anti-oppressive practice & critical reflection in diverse fields of social work.* Presented at the Eastern Regional Integrated Health Authority social work week speaker series, March 23, 2007. St. John's, Newfoundland.

Swan, T., Ferriera, C., Cosby, R., Young, M., Cho, M., Sammon, S., Dumbrill, G., Lee, B., Palmer, S. & Westwood, A. (2005). *Looking at oneself: Struggling with critical empathy and critical reflectivity within AOP education.* Presented at Re-imaging social work: Seeing the forest and the trees. The Canadian Association of Social Work Conference, Congress of the Social Sciences & Humanities, May 29-June 1, 2005.

Thompson, N. (1997). *Anti-discriminatory practice.* London: Macmillan.

Wharf-Higgins, J., Cossom, J., & Wharf, B. (2003). Citizen participation in social policy. In A. West-hues (Ed.), *Canadian social policy: Issues and perspectives,* 3rd ed. (pp. 301–318). Waterloo: Wilfrid Laurier Press.

Young, I. M. (1990). *Justice and the politics of difference.* Princeton, NJ: Princeton University Press.

# CHAPTER 13

# Canada's Unique Psychosocial Realities

*G. Brent Angell and Katka Hrncic-Lipovic*

## CANADA'S UNIQUE PSYCHOSOCIAL REALITIES

What does being a Canadian mean and how is this identification distinct from life in other nations in the world? This seemingly simple question is likely difficult to answer for many people, regardless of whether they were born in or immigrated to the country. Indeed, the ethos of Canada stems from the diversity of its people's cultures, histories, and experiences, which are intimately entwined with the land itself. It is a nation marked by regional variation, which is conspicuously psychosocial and geophysical. Considered a land of migrants, the nation is often times described as a multicultural mosaic founded on tolerance and reinforced by legislation (Canadian Heritage, 1988). However, in addition to being multicultural, the mosaic is also vertical.

As Porter (1965) explains, immigrants to Canada have been selectively chosen over the years to meet certain predetermined needs, which often ascribe them to subordinate social niches. For example, the mass migrational push of people from Great Britain during the 1880s was largely comprised of individuals and families selected from the bottom echelon of British society. Migrating under the pretense of ensuring that Canada remained British, and escaping the harsh realities of impoverishment and classism, the newcomers were set the task of populating and developing the land with little in the way of preparation, personal resources, or government support. Porter further points out: "These indigents were shipped out by a variety of 'charitable' schemes, often said only to be devices to relieve the burden of poverty on English parishes" (p. 62).

As discussed in Chapter 10, the factors that push or pull people to immigrate are similar to those that affect intra and inter-provincial migrants within the country. Canadians have always been a people on the move to, within, and beyond the nation in search of safety, employment, and advancement (Amnesty International, 2007; Angell, 1992; Statistics Canada, 2004, 2007). In fact, the largest demographic changes within the provinces are a result of interregional migration and not due to international immigration (Statistics Canada, 2003a). This steady ebb and flow of people entering and traversing the country has contributed a great deal to the transformation of the nation, but relocation has also inimitably moulded the people. Carrying with them their psychosocial constructions of perceived and interpreted life experiences, these newcomers are continuously being engaged in transactional processes which pit and juxtapose their notions of who they are against who they are becoming. In short, they shape and are shaped by the environment.

Canada can be considered a diasporic nation of peoples who have been compelled or encouraged to leave their customary homelands or ways of life to start anew, while actively retaining their ethnic and cultural distinctiveness. It is a country characterized by "hyphenated" ethno-cultural people. Whether the founding Aboriginal, French, or Anglo peoples, or sundry other newcomers, being Canadian means something in addition to, rather than instead of. This then is the essence of the national psychosocial reality; a reality that envelops and contributes to the development of the peoples' individual and collective personae.

The importance of Canada's unique psychosocial reality for social work is founded in the very roots of the profession. As noted in Chapter 6 with the work of Blessed Marguerite Bourgeoys in 1653, Canada's first "social worker," the profession has been involved in providing assistance to and advocating for newcomers (Bellamy and Irving, 1986). As such, social workers are obliged to be aware of the multifaceted mosaic of differences that exist between and among the country's peoples and regions. The profession's practice perspective reminds practitioners to start their approach with the clients and their client systems. In so doing, social workers can bridge multicultural knowledge bases and build co-operative strengths-based partnerships. Of course, it would be naïve to expect that any one social worker could become ethno-culturally aware and competent across the spectrum of Canadian human diversity. However, it is reasonable to expect that a template for understanding can be achieved. With this in mind, the following discussion will focus on the diversity of Canada.

## OFFICIAL LANGUAGES IN CANADA

Canada is a multicultural and bilingual country with both English and French being its official languages (Office of the Commissioner of Official Languages, 2007). The official history of bilingualism dates back to 1867 with the passing of the *British North America Act*, which, under section 133, permitted the use of both languages in parliamentary debates and federal court proceedings (Canadian Heritage, 2007). Just over 100 years later, in 1969, Canada's first *Official Languages Act* was adopted by Parliament, which guaranteed equity to both English and French Canadians in parliamentary proceedings and dealings with federal government agencies. One of the objectives of the act was to preserve and further develop official language communities in Canada (Canadian Heritage, 2007). In the same year, New Brunswick became the first official bilingual province in Canada with the enactment of its first *Official Languages Act*.

Despite English and French being the official languages of Canada, the citizenry report more than 100 other languages as their mother tongues. In keeping with this, approximately one in six people report neither English nor French as their first language (Statistics Canada, 2002). Demographically, anglophones represent the majority of Canadians (59.1 percent), while francophones represent 22.9 percent, and allophones, or non-English or non-French speakers, comprise 18.0 percent of the population. Of note, Chinese is the third most common mother tongue (Statistics Canada, 2002). With respect to Aboriginal languages, Cree was the most common (80 000), followed by Inuktitut (29 700) and Ojibway (23 500). In terms of bilingualism, the 2001 Census data indicate that 17 percent of the Canadian population is bilingual in French and English (Statistics Canada, 2002).

Support for bilingualism in Canada remained stable between 1963 and 2002 (Parkin & Turcotte, 2004). Analyzing Canadians' attitudes toward language and bilingualism, Parkin and Turcotte (2004) have found that 77 percent of Canadians agree that the federal government should provide services in both English and French. The authors also find that the francophone majority in Quebec is far more likely to support the official languages policy and to be interested in learning a second language than are members of the anglophone minority in the province. Conversely, the anglophone majority across Canada is less likely to support putting more government resources into the promotion of bilingualism than is the francophone minority. Parkin and Turcotte (2004) maintain that the anglophone resistance towards putting more resources into promoting bilingualism may stem from the perception that bilingualism affects the lives of English-speaking Canadians by limiting employment opportunities for those who do not speak French. English speakers also feel that there are higher priority issues on which to spend tax dollars than bilingualism. Indeed, one in two Canadians believes that "English is the only language needed to succeed in Canada" (Parkin and Turcotte, 2004, p. 25).

Even though the majority of Canadians support bilingualism, a concern has been expressed that individuals belonging to visible minority groups encounter specific language barriers for career advancement in the federal public service sector (Public Service Human Resources Management Agency of Canada, 2005). This perception was investigated in a qualitative study (focus groups and in-depth interviews) by the Public Service Human Resources Management Agency of Canada, which sought to determine whether official language policies presented an employment barrier for visible minorities in the federal public service. The study found that official language barriers posed a significant employment barrier for individuals who were recent immigrants and whose first language was neither English nor French. However, while the study found that visible minorities did indeed have an increased degree of barriers to career mobility, these barriers were more likely to be the result of the organizational culture and attitudes from co-workers than the result of specific language-related policies. Furthermore, the conclusion was reached that the barriers that the visible minorities encountered were "no different, and no less reasonable or unfair for them than they are for everyone else" (Public Service Human Resources Management Agency of Canada, 2005, p. 10). However, given that in 2001, 33 percent of francophone, 26 percent of allophone, and only 4 percent of anglophone workers used more than one language at work (Statistics Canada, 2003b), the debate surrounding the official language requirements for the federal public service employees is likely to continue.

## DIVERSITY OF CANADA

According to Canadian Heritage (2004a), Canada was the first country in the world to adopt an official Multicultural Policy in 1971. This policy was instrumental in strengthening Canada's commitment to and support of "linguistic, ethno-cultural, and ethno-racial pluralism" (Canadian Heritage, 2004b, paragraph 2). This commitment was further demonstrated by the adoption of the Canadian Charter of Rights and Freedoms in 1982 and the passage of the *Canadian Multiculturalism Act* in 1988 (Canadian Heritage, 2004a, 2004b). The *Multiculturalism Act* "seeks to assist in preserving culture, reducing discrimination, enhancing cultural awareness and understanding, and promoting culturally sensitive institutional change at the federal level" (Canadian Heritage, 2004b, paragraph 6).

According to the 2001 Census, Canada's population originates from more than 200 different ethnic groups including North American First Nations, Métis, Inuit, French, British, Scottish, Irish, and many others (Statistics Canada, 2003a). On average, Canada welcomes 200 000 immigrants annually to the country from all over the world (Canadian Heritage, 2004a) and this action is reflected in the fact that 18.4 percent of the total population is foreign-born (Statistics Canada, 2003a). Only Australia has a higher percentage of residents born outside the country with 22 percent (Statistics Canada, 2003a).

Scholars like Howard-Hassmann (1999) argue that Canada's emphasis on diversity and multiculturalism may weaken the national sense of identity. She maintains that in addition to promoting differences, public policy should also stress the importance of "sameness and similarity" of Canadians as well (p. 535). However, there are some indications that this identification as Canadian may be already happening. According to the 2001 Census, the proportion of people identifying themselves as Canadian has increased from 31 percent in 1996 to 39 percent in 2001 (Statistics Canada, 2003a).

## CANADA'S CONSTITUTION AND THE CANADA–QUEBEC RELATIONS

Originally known as the *British North American Act* (1867), Canada's first *Constitution Act* was also passed in 1867 (Department of Justice Canada, 2007). It specified that Canada consisted of four provinces: Ontario, Quebec, Nova Scotia, and New Brunswick. The act "recognized Quebec's distinctiveness . . . including the official status of French in Quebec, and the protection of the province's civil law" (Government of Canada Privy Council Office, 2001, paragraph 19). Many years later, in 1968, the prime minister and the provincial premiers agreed to launch a constitutional renewal process, which would focus on redistributing federal and provincial powers and service provision roles. However, this initiative never materialized and the Canadian Constitution remained under British control.

In 1976, the people of Quebec elected the Parti Québécois, which called for a "dramatic distancing of Quebec from the rest of the Canadian federation." This influenced the federal government to renew the *Constitution Act* debate. Subsequently, a 12-item agenda for constitutional change was drafted and presented at the Conference of First Ministers in 1979. Unfortunately, the provincial premiers could not agree on any agenda items. Later that year, the Parti Québécois called for the creation of a "sovereignty-association" partnership between Canada and Quebec, which was relayed in a position paper reconsidering Canadian federalism (paragraph 48). In a referendum on May 20, 1980, and following a pledge from the prime minister that the government would immediately take action to renew the Constitution if Quebeckers voted no, the people of Quebec voted no to the creation of "sovereignty-association."

All provinces, with the exception of Quebec, accepted a new package of constitutional reforms, which included the revolutionary Canadian Charter of Rights and Freedoms. The Charter affirmed the federal government's commitment to social justice and equality for all people in Canada, including a reaffirmation of the "existing rights of Canada's Aboriginal peoples" (Government of Canada Privy Council Office, 2001, paragraph 57). Explicit in the Charter was the guarantee of full democratic, legal, and fundamental rights for all Canadians (Department of Justice Canada, 2007). The Quebec government argued that "Quebec's claims had been ignored [and] that a deal had been reached without Quebec's knowledge" and they rejected the partition package (Government of Canada Privy Council Office, 2001, paragraph 59). On November 5, 1981, the National Assembly of Quebec and the Quebec government refused to recognize the political legitimacy of the new proposed *Constitution Act* and began to amend their legislation. After the new *Constitution Act* was proclaimed on April 17, 1982, the Supreme Court of Canada ruled that Quebec had to respect the legality of the *Constitution Act* as it had "no veto in law or practice over partition of the Constitution" (paragraph 60). Another attempt by the Quebec government to seek special constitutional recognition was made during the Meech Lake Accord meeting of 1987, where Quebec sought status as a distinct society within Canada. Fortunately, for federalists, but unhappily for Quebec sovereignists, unanimous legislative agreement within the required three-year period did not occur and the Meech Lake Accord was never ratified (Government of Canada Privy Council Office, 2001).

In 1992, at Charlottetown, Prince Edward Island, a unanimous agreement, known as the Charlottetown Accord, was reached between the Government of Canada, the provincial governments (including Quebec), the territorial governments, and the representatives from Aboriginal First Nations, to recognize, among others, the right of Aboriginal peoples to self-government, the province of Quebec as a distinct society, and the power of "veto for all provinces over subsequent institutional reform" (paragraph 72).

Quebec's second referendum for sovereignty was held on October 30, 1995, when 49.4 percent of Quebeckers voted in favour of sovereignty. In December of that same year, the House of Commons and the Senate fully recognized Quebec as a distinct society. In 1996, Quebec along with Ontario, British Columbia, the Prairies, and the Atlantic region were given a regional veto that specified that changes and amendments to the Canadian Constitution could not be proposed by the Government of Canada without the consent of these regions.

Another important agreement between the Government of Canada and the province of Quebec was the Canada–Quebec Accord, which was signed in 1991 (Citizenship and Immigration Canada, 2002). Under this agreement, Quebec was granted the sole right to select its own independent immigrants and refugees for settlement in its province. The federal government's responsibility continues to be the definition of immigrant classes and the establishment of the level of immigrants allowed into Canada (Citizenship and Immigration Canada, 2002).

## FIRST NATIONS PEOPLE IN CANADA

As noted in Chapter 7, the First Nations inherent right to self-government was officially recognized by the Government of Canada in the *Constitution Act*, 1982, section 35(1) (Hawkes, 2001). Even though the Government of Canada recognizes the historical wrong-doings towards the First Nations people and promises to work towards renewing its relationship with them (Indian and Northern Affairs Canada, 2004), the implementation of these promises has been slow. Hawkes (2001) maintains that the Aboriginal peoples can achieve self-determination if they have greater autonomy exercised through self-government and if they demand and accomplish greater participation in the decision-making institutions of the state.

## THE RESIDENTIAL SCHOOL SYSTEM

Under the *Constitution Act* of 1867, the Government of Canada was granted full authority over the matters and lands of First Nations people in Canada (Hurley, 1999). The *Indian Act* of 1867 defined who was an Indian and gave authority to the Canadian government to exercise control over the legal rights of all registered Indians. To meet its obligation of providing education to the Aboriginal people as specified in the *Indian Act*, the federal government implemented a residential school system in 1874, which was operated in partnership with various religious and missionary organizations until 1969 when the government assumed sole responsibility for the schools (Indian and Northern Affairs Canada, 2004). The children were forcibly separated from their families and communities and put in residential schools where they were forbidden to speak their native language or engage in cultural and traditional practices.

It is estimated that approximately 100 000 children went through the residential school system (Indian and Northern Affairs Canada, 2004). The last federally owned residential school in Saskatchewan closed in 1996 (Indian and Northern Affairs Canada, 2004). Many years after the residential school system, Aboriginal people made public their experiences of abuse, neglect, harsh discipline, and punishment that occurred regularly in the schools.

In 1996, the Royal Commission on Aboriginal Peoples called for a public inquiry that would investigate and document the abuses that took place in the residential schools (Indian and Northern Affairs Canada, 1996).

The negative effects of the residential school system are long-lasting. Survivors of the residential school system have difficulty in terms of language proficiency, knowledge of traditional customs and norms, interpersonal trust, and community affiliation. Additionally, many Aboriginal people affected by the residential school system were harmed spiritually, physically, emotionally, and intellectually (Public Health Agency of Canada, 2006). As part of the healing for First Nations members directly or vicariously affected by the residential school system, a court settlement was reached on March 22, 2007 (Government of Canada, 2007). As part of this settlement, a Truth and Reconciliation Commission was established to provide a venue for those affected to share their stories and create an archive on this abysmal chapter in Canada's history. Nevertheless, this exercise of government power over the education of Aboriginal peoples can only be interpreted as an attempt to erode or destroy Aboriginal sovereignty, culture, tradition, value, and language with the alleged endgame being to forcibly assimilate Aboriginal people into mainstream Canada. This conclusion is supported by the findings of the Royal Commission on Aboriginal Peoples (Indian and Northern Affairs Canada, 1996). In a recent public opinion survey of Aboriginal and Northern affairs, Canadians identified health care (43%), education (18%), and governmental politics (15%) as government's top priorities while only one percent identified Aboriginal issues as a top priority (Indian and Northern Affairs Canada, 2005).

## IMPLICATIONS FOR SOCIAL WORK

Canada's changing demographics require social workers to be proficient in their understanding of and approach to those who are ethnically and culturally different from themselves. Social workers who have been educated in Canada should recognize that they operate from a Canadian set of social work values which have been and continue to be reinforced by the dominant culture. While it is not possible for social workers to completely separate themselves from the cultural influences of the dominant society, they must be conscious of their own limitations. Instead of resisting "otherness" or trying to fit it into something that already exists, "otherness" should be embraced and welcomed because it brings richness and completeness to our profession. The social work profession should remain flexible and inclusive. The multicultural mosaic that is Canadian, its rich history, and the ever-changing experiences of its people need to continue to inform the practice of social work and build on what we already know. Social workers not only should be knowledgeable about their client's current situation or recent life history, but also need to be aware of the chronology of push and pull factors that may have contributed to their client's current position and vulnerability. This awareness of historical and present influences will allow social workers to be more effective as practitioners and minimize the possibility of inadvertent or unconscious perpetuation of oppression and dominance.

## CONCLUSION

Canada's demography and topography shape the psychosocial realities of the nation. The diverse cultures and ethnicities that make up the country present abundant opportunities and challenges for a nation undergoing dramatic change as it adapts to the flood of new world views, beliefs, and customs. In the face of change, it will be important for the nation and its people to learn from the past. Instances of intolerance and injustice, such as the residential school system that victimized First Nations children, violated their culture, and threatened their very survival, must serve as a lesson to us all about the destructive power that can arise out of ignorance, indifference, and fear. Other historical influences, such as the tension surrounding Quebec–Canada relations and the passing of the first *Official Languages Act,* also speak to the strife that has helped influence the nation. Fortunately, we are a country that tries to learn from its mistakes. Canada is moving forward in a bid to create a just society characterized by acceptance of human difference and inclusion of all of our brothers and sisters who are determined to make the country strong and free. Social workers play an integral role in making this dream a reality by exposing and helping to correct historical and current injustices for all those who call this land home, and for all those who have yet to make Canada their home.

# References

Amnesty International. (2007). *Refugee protection in Canada.* Retrieved August, 23, 2007, from http://www.amnesty.ca/Refugee/Canada.php

Angell, G. B. (1992). *Interregional migration: Newfoundland women living in the city — an ethnography of push-pull and adjustment factors.* Unpublished Doctoral Dissertation.

Bellamy, D. & Irving, A. (1986). Pioneers. In J. C. Turner & F. J. U. Turner (Eds.), *Canadian social welfare* (2nd Ed.) (pp. 29–49). Toronto: Collier Macmillian Canada, Inc.

Canadian Heritage. (1988). *An act for the preservation and enhancement of multiculturalism in Canada.* Retrieved August 22, 2007, from http://www.canadianheritage.gc.ca/progs/multi/policy/act_e.cfm

Canadian Heritage. (2004a). *Canadian diversity: Respecting our differences.* Retrieved May 24, 2007, from http://www.canadianheritage.gc.ca/progs/multi/respect_e.cfm#ahead

Canadian Heritage. (2004b). *The Canadian Multiculturalism Act: 15 years later.* Retrieved May 24, 2007, from http://www.pch.gc.ca/progs/multi/reports/ann2002-2003/01_e.cfm

Canadian Heritage. (2007). *History of bilingualism in Canada.* Retrieved May 15, 2007, from http://www.pch.gc.ca/progs/lo-ol/biling/hist_e.cfm

Citizenship and Immigration Canada. (2002). *The Canada-Quebec Accord made easy.* Retrieved May 24, 2007, from http://www.cic.gc.ca/english/about/laws-policy/agreements/quebec/can-que-guide.asp

Department of Justice Canada. (2007). *Constitution Acts 1867 to 1982.* Retrieved May 24, 2007, from http://laws.justice.gc.ca/en/const/index.html

Government of Canada Privy Council Office. (2001). *The history of Canada's constitutional development.*

Government of Canada. (2007). *Indian residential schools settlement: Official court website.* Retrieved August 23, 2007, from http://www.residentialschoolsettlement.ca/English.html

Hawkes, D. C. (2001). Indigenous peoples: Self-government and intergovernmental relations. *International Social Science Journal, 53(167),* 153–161.

Howard-Hassmann, R. E. (1999). "Canadian" as an ethnic category: Implications for multiculturalism and national unity. *Canadian Public Policy, 25(4),* 523–537.

Hurley, M. C. (1999). *The Indian Act.* Government of Canada: Parliamentary Research Board.

Indian and Northern Affairs Canada. (1996). *Report of the Royal Commission on Aboriginal Peoples.* Retrieved May 25, 2007, from http://www.ainc-inac.gc.ca/ch/rcap/sg/cg_e.html

Indian and Northern Affairs Canada. (2004). *Backgrounder: The residential school system.* Retrieved May 26, 2007, from http://www.ainc-inac.gc.ca/gs/schl_e.html

Indian and Northern Affairs Canada. (2005). *The landscape: Public opinion on Aboriginal and Northern issues.* Cat. No. R1-23/2005E. Ottawa, ON: Minister of Indian and Northern Development.

Office of the Commissioner of Official Languages. (2007). *Federal legislation on official languages.*

Parkin, A. & Turcotte, A. (2004). Bilingualism: Part of our past or part of our future? *The CRIC Papers,13,* Centre for Research and Information on Canada.

Parliament of Canada. (2004). *Immigration: The Canada-Quebec Accord.* Retrieved May 24, 2007, from http://www.parl.gc.ca/information/library/PRBpubs/bp252-e.htm

Porter, J. (1965). *The vertical mosaic: An analysis of social class and power in Canada.* Toronto: University of Toronto Press.

Public Health Agency of Canada. (2006). *What were residential schools? What was their effect then and how do they affect families today?*

Public Service Human Resources Management Agency of Canada. (2005). *Official languages and visible minorities in the public service of Canada: A qualitative investigation of barriers to career advancement.* Retrieved May 15, 2007, from http://www.hrma-agrh.gc.ca/ollo/or-ar/ study-etude/Patterson/olvm-lomv-1_e.asp

Statistics Canada. (2002). *Profile of languages in Canada: English, French and many others.* 2001 Census Analysis Series Cat. No. 96F0030XIE2001005. Ottawa, ON: Minister of Industry.

Statistics Canada. (2003a). *Canada's ethno-cultural portrait: The changing mosaic.* 2001 Census Analysis Series Cat. No. 96F0030XIE2001008. Ottawa, ON: Minister of Industry.

Statistics Canada. (2003b). *Use of English and French at work.* 2001 Census Analysis Series Cat. No. 96F0030XIE2001011. Ottawa, ON: Minister of Industry.

Statistics Canada. (2004). *2001 Census: Multimedia.* 2001 Census Analysis Series Cat. No. 96F0030XIE2001006. Ottawa, ON: Minister of Industry.

Statistics Canada. (2007). *Mobility and migration.* 2006 Census Analysis Series Cat. No. 97-556-XWE2006012. Ottawa, ON: Minister of Industry.

# CHAPTER 14

# Agencies in General

*Barbara Decker Pierce*

## INTRODUCTION

Social agencies and human service organizations exist so that the services and resources of our social welfare system can be delivered to people in need. They are the contact points between government social policy and targeted populations, between a community's charitable aims and its members in need. Social service agencies and organizations must, therefore, have a physical presence, clearly defined purposes, and a set of characteristics that make up their unique identities.

In this chapter we will be discussing some aspects of social agencies and human service organizations, acknowledging that while they all have some common elements they are also quite diverse. They differ in regard to their histories, the needs they address, the clients they serve, the programs they deliver, the communities in which they are located, the philosophies of helping that their professionals and volunteers have adopted, and the availability of their funds.

As a result, all social agencies and human service organizations share a common core of features; each also has a unique set of traits that sets it apart from the others, even those in the same field of service.

## DEFINITIONS

A *social agency* is a formally structured unit, sanctioned by society, whose goals and activities focus on meeting human needs. Agencies vary in size from one-employee operations to those with hundreds of workers. The majority are considered *primary* social work settings with staffs consisting mainly of professional social workers. Agencies have locations, purposes set out in the form of mission and policy statements and programs designed to provide services to defined groups of clients.

Alternatively, *human service organizations* are likely to be *secondary* settings for social work practice; social work is only one of several professions that provide services in these multidisciplinary organizations. Hospitals, schools, government departments, or social planning bodies that "have as their stated purpose enhancement of the social, emotional, physical and/or intellectual well-being of some component of the population"[1] are common examples of human service organizations that employ social workers.

## THREE TYPES OF SPONSORSHIP AND FUNDING

The mandate to create social agencies and human service organizations rests with three major sectors of Canadian society—*government*, *voluntary*, and *commercial*—in what has been termed "a mixed economy of welfare."[2]

---

1  Brager, G., & Holloway, S. (1978), *Changing human service organizations: Politics and practice.* New York: Collier Macmillan, p. 2.

2  Lightman, E. (2003), *Social policy in Canada.* Don Mills, ON: Oxford University Press, p. 86.

The reasons for this mix of service providers in the history of social welfare development in Canada are many. From the nation's beginning, all levels of government have attempted to meet the social and health care needs of both citizens and immigrants. Initially, governments were strongly supported in this work by religious groups. Eventually other voluntary bodies, concerned about particular groups or social problems, emerged to take their place in the network of service providers. Despite an increasing role for government funding in meeting basic human need, volunteers and church groups still maintain a presence in the social service field, often entering into financial partnerships with some levels of government to establish needed services. The commercial sector is a relative newcomer to the field, filling gaps left by the government and the voluntary social service network with profit-making organizations.[3]

The pattern of social service delivery in Canada offers many examples of funding partnerships among the three sectors. Agencies obtain funds from one or several sources: through charitable donations, government grants, or fees for service. This section will examine the major characteristics of the government, voluntary, and commercial sectors and discuss the types of agencies each sponsors.

## Government Sector

Because the constitutional obligation to provide social welfare and health care services is divided between the federal and provincial governments—which in turn assign some of their responsibilities to municipal and local bodies—all three levels of government fund and support agencies or organizations through which these services are delivered. Many social services are seen as rights that accompany citizenship and are provided by legislation and funded by means of taxation.

Government agencies traditionally have had a larger presence than those in the other two sectors; this may be changing in the current debate in governments at all levels between those who support neo-conservative approaches, with a focus on curbing government expenditures on health and social welfare, and those who advocate strong government roles in social policy-setting and providing services.[4]

The final shape the government sector will take can be known only with the passage of time. What is clear now is that in the past 20 years, billions of dollars have been drained from the social security system, ending programs, closing agencies, curtailing services, and losing jobs.[5] While the federal and some provincial governments have recently experienced fiscal surpluses, much of this has been directed toward tax relief, debt repayment, and high priority program areas such as health care and the environment. For the most part social service agencies have not received an equitable share of government surplus funds. This shift in governments' funding priorities demands that the voluntary sector play a new role, one that Browne predicts will reflect the fact that the "non-profit organizations, especially those

---

3   Armitage, A. (1996), *Social welfare in Canada revisited: Facing up to the future* (3rd ed.). Don Mills: Oxford University Press, pp. 118–119.

4   Browne, P. (1996), *Love in a cold world: The voluntary sector in an age of cuts.* Ottawa: Canadian Centre for Policy Alternatives.

5   Graham, J. R., Swift, K. J., & Delaney, R. (2003), *Canadian social policy: An introduction.* Toronto: Prentice Hall, pp. 40–41.

that mobilize volunteers, are being touted either as substitutes for the welfare state or as agents for a new, leaner government."[6]

**Areas of Government Responsibility**  The Constitution has allocated the following welfare measures to either the federal or provincial jurisdiction: income support, health care, child welfare, employment insurance, vocational rehabilitation, housing, corrections, and services to veterans and First Nations citizens. Clearly, our society requires many types of agencies and organizations to deliver such a wide variety of services. These range from the computerized, information-processing environment of the federal department of Human Resources and Social Development Canada to the more informal setting of a municipal social service office where people apply in person for welfare benefits.

While federal departments with health and welfare responsibilities base their central offices in Ottawa, they also run a network of provincial, regional, and local agencies to ensure that people have relatively easy access to their services. For example, because Employment Insurance (EI) legislation demands their staff make direct contact with recipients to confirm that they meet eligibility and job-search requirements, a network of Human Resources Centres has been created across the country.

The Constitution also assigns the provincial governments and territories responsibility for health and welfare services that affect many Canadians' lives. These include physical and mental health care, institutions for the aged and those with disabilities, child welfare, aspects of corrections, and short-term and emergency income support. Each of these governments locates its central health and social welfare offices in its capital city, which is connected to a system of regional and branch offices. Each also funds human service organizations such as hospitals and residential treatment centres.

The provincial governments often delegate some of their responsibilities to municipal and local governments on the grounds that they are more in touch with community needs and better able to respond quickly and effectively. Typical of these kinds of responsibilities are emergency income support, homes for the aged, daycare, homemakers, home nursing, public health, and accommodation and food for transients and the homeless.

While the federal government covers the entire cost of its services and agencies from the country's tax base, it also shares the cost of selected provincial social services by transferring funds to the provincial governments. Provincial governments must raise the balance of the funds they need through their own means of taxation. In turn, municipal services and agencies receive a large portion of their funding from their province—occasionally with some added federal money—but they must supplement this money with local property taxes and other measures of revenue generation.

Through these complicated cost-sharing arrangements, social agencies often receive revenue from more than one level of government. In addition, most supplement their government funding with charitable donations and some have even added commercial endeavours to generate additional revenue. To add to the complexity of the Canadian system, each province presents a slightly different picture of the ways it mixes the public, voluntary, and commercial sponsorship of its social agencies and organizations. Studying the ways social services are delivered in Canada involves an understanding of the national picture as well as some knowledge of the pattern a specific province or region has adopted.

---

**6**  Armitage, A. (1996), *Social welfare in Canada revisited.* p. 81.

| TABLE 14.1 | Voluntary Sector and Charitable Donations |
|---|---|
| Number of Volunteer Organizations | 161 000 |
| Sector (excluding hospitals, universities, colleges) | |
| . Revenue | $75 billion |
| . Employees | 1.3 million |
| . Volunteers | 19 million |
| Charitable Donations (2004) | $8.9 billion |
| Charitable Donations to Social Service Agencies | $809 million |

*Source:* Imagine Canada. (2006). *The non-profit and voluntary sector in Canada.* Retrieved April 25, 2007, from www.imaginecanada.ca/Files/NSNVO/Sector_in_Canada_Factsheet.pdf
Canadian Centre for Philanthropy. (2004). *Charitable giving in Canada.* Retrieved April 25, 2007 from www.givingandvolunteering.ca/factsheets.asp.

## Voluntary Sector

Thousands of private agencies and organizations exist in Canada, sponsored by an array of charitable, philanthropic, or religious bodies; national organizations; special interest groups; and individual citizens. Some statistics illustrate the size of the voluntary sector (see Table 14.1).

Organizations in the voluntary sector provide both direct and indirect social services. One example of a *direct* service provider is Big Brothers. Its services include matching children who lack adult role models with volunteers who offer friendship, social support, and recreation through character-building activities. *Indirect* service organizations provide services that do not require face-to-face interaction with clients. These organizations, of which the Canadian Council on Social Development or the Kidney Foundation of Canada are examples, carry out a variety of activities. They raise funds, research, advocate for certain causes, and sponsor education or training endeavours, all to create a supportive environment for people suffering from health or psychosocial problems and to prevent the growth of the problems they target.

**Describing the Voluntary Agency** Every voluntary agency begins as a response to an unmet human need. When others in a community recognize a human need, their natural response is often to help. Their efforts become a collective effort to lessen the damaging effect of that specific deprivation on people. Helping consists of providing resources to those in need and developing strategies to prevent others from experiencing similar needs.

Efforts to help often begin with a needs assessment. This is a structured process that helps determine the severity and extent of an unmet need. Research is carried out to identify the incidence of a problem and its impact on people, what service responses are already available, and the cost of setting up effective programs to deal with it.[7] The

---

7   Reviere, R., Berkowitz, S., Carter, C. C., & Ferguson, C. G. (1996), *Needs assessment: A creative and practical guide for social scientists.* Washington: Taylor & Francis.

assessment determines the capacity of a community to meet its own needs, emphasizing people's abilities to solve their own problems within that community.

The voluntary sector is characterized by a flexible response to emerging social needs and problems. Chiefly it does not work through a cumbersome legislative process to develop a service or change a policy. In large measure the efforts of voluntary social service organizations have traditionally supplemented the more substantial and basic provisions governments have made. However, they also offer a sort of experimental social laboratory in which various approaches to meeting human needs can be tried and tested before society decides whether they should be incorporated into legislated services and government agencies.

Voluntary agencies and organizations vary according to such factors as the degree of public support for them, sources of funding, and the involvement of the target population in designing the program and running the agency. Agencies in the private sector offer services that respond to a broad range of human needs. These may include counselling for individuals, families, and couples; children's mental health facilities; psychological and social supports for clients suffering mental and physical health problems; social services designed for the special needs of women, children, the aged, those with disabilities, the bereaved, the poor, young offenders, and immigrants; recreational and socialization facilities for certain groups, such as children from impoverished families, the aged, and persons with disabilities; crisis intervention services in cases of family violence, child abuse, suicide, sexual assault, and incest; community information; debt counselling; job readiness; social planning; and fundraising.

Various levels of government and the voluntary sector form funding and policy-setting partnerships. These enable governments to deliver services sensitive to local values and standards and to foster the mutual care ethic the voluntary presence provides. Nonetheless, many voluntary organizations do not seek government sanction, particularly those based on the self-help model or whose purpose is to advocate for a special cause or group that may lead to a conflict of interest with the government.

**Creating a New Social Agency** In creating a new agency today, the first requirement remains the same: a group of people must share a common concern about some unmet human need. Group awareness does not have to arise spontaneously; it may need to be encouraged through education and leadership or the sharing of an ideology whose expression demands action. For example, the increase in services to abused women and their children grew out of the demands for justice that feminist groups made, yet many citizens have supported it who would not describe themselves as feminists—including the governments that now fund women's shelters and counselling services. Groups with differing philosophies develop a collaborative approach out of the greater public awareness of the frequency of spousal abuse and its devastating consequences on the abused women and children.

Whatever the origins of their concern, the founders of a voluntary social agency must all carry out a set of tasks that include the following, although not necessarily in this order: assembling a board of directors to represent the community; establishing a mission, goals, and objectives for the agency; seeking a reliable source of funding; possibly searching for a suitable partner in government or the voluntary sector; observing relevant government regulations; developing a constitution, bylaws, and policies; designing programs; setting a budget; finding quarters for the agency; hiring an executive director who must then employ staff; and publicizing the service. This process can take many months or years (more often the latter), but most of the voluntary social service agencies and organizations in Canada today have had to follow similar steps in creating themselves, whether sponsored by small local groups or by more powerful national bodies.

One common feature of the voluntary agency is its board of directors. To assure public accountability and the agency's close connection to the community, citizens are elected or appointed to a board. The board generally oversees the agency's operations, assuring the community that it is achieving its stated goals, that its programs are relevant and effective, and that it is spending funds responsibly. The board of directors legitimizes the agency's activities in the eyes of the community. In the same way, politicians and public servants legitimize the work of government agencies through accountability to the public. Board members may serve in advisory capacities only or they may form working committees that design policies, evaluate programs, or work more directly with clients.

**Funding Challenges** Funding is a constant concern to voluntary agencies. Although these organizations receive government funds for specific programs, much of the money that supports their services comes from a very uncertain source—charitable donations. Charitable dollars express the donors' concern for the well-being of strangers, and the collection of money is often based on cleverly orchestrated appeals to both the heart and the head, to the emotions of both pity and fear. People may pity those in need and have great sympathy for them or they may fear that adversity will befall them or those they love. A mixture of motives, including the "good citizen" approach, which corporate donors employ, produces donations of substantial sums to voluntary agencies each year. Charitable foundations are beginning to play an important role in supporting agency-based programs and initiatives. These may be community foundations, endowments sponsored by specific families, or money collected as an expression of concern about a particular social problem or illness. While charitable donations play an important role in the funding of organizations, this dependence on charitable revenue has sometimes led to fierce competition among charitable groups and to donation fatigue among potential donors.

In addition, charitable campaigns are extremely vulnerable to any public perception that funds being collected are not being used wisely or are being applied to a controversial service. Voluntary agencies will often avoid taking a stand on contentious issues or offering services that might attract public criticism. This does not mean that the voluntary sector never addresses "unpopular causes." However, these causes must be presented to the public in such a way as to elicit the maximum amount of understanding, empathy, and acceptance for the client group affected in order to attract those charitable dollars.

## Commercial Sector

A lack of services in some areas of human need has encouraged entrepreneurs to move into the area of social service in the hope of realizing profits—an objective that they may well combine with more altruistic motives. The commercial or profit-making sector is a small and gradually increasing part of the social welfare system. It provides services in areas where neither the government nor voluntary groups wish to assume responsibility, usually because the cost of fully meeting the particular need over time would be substantial.

The recent policy objectives of fiscal restraint and privatization have made the purchase of services from commercial providers attractive to governments. There are other reasons for their support of for-profit operations as well. Private service delivery includes such advantages of increased efficiency through competition, more clearly defined and flexible services, fewer fixed costs than established government services would incur, and the possibility of changing providers if one provider's service proves unsatisfactory. Disadvantages consist of uncertainties related to program design and objectives, quality control, and potential disruption for clients if contracts are terminated.[8]

**Concerns about Commercial Social Services** There are additional objections to for-profit providers involved in social welfare.

Philosophically, the money-making objectives of the commercial sector conflict with the mutual support ethic of social welfare and social work.[9] Some cite realistic fears that if the commercial sector becomes too large a part of social welfare or obtains a monopoly in any one field of service, the poor may not be served at all because they will not be able to afford the fees. Quality control is difficult for governments to exert at a distance, and in some areas there are minimal regulations to establish standards of care and protect clients.

Commercial providers are always caught between their contract to provide service and their need to show a profit. There may be times when these agencies redesign or reduce services in the interest of financial gain, resulting in inadequate service to clients. On the other hand, some critics take the position that government should get out of the business of providing social services directly in favour of contracting out to the voluntary and commercial sectors while retaining the right to set policies, budgets, and standards. Issues related to ideology, efficiency, quality of service, cost, and accountability continue to be hotly debated while the commercial sector grows and thrives.[10]

**Developments in the Commercial Sector** Many forces encourage this sector's growth. They include both the current economic policies of all levels of government and the increasing demand for service in certain areas. Commercial agencies and organizations seem to respond faster than the government or voluntary sectors in such areas as residential care for emotionally disturbed children; group homes for discharged psychiatric patients; facilities for youths in conflict with the law; chronic care, nursing homes, and residential care for the aged; and operating support services such as home nursing and homemaking.

Employee Assistance Programs (EAPs) are one example of a growth area in the commercial field. Employers establish EAPs by purchasing a block of counselling time from

---

**8** Armitage, A. (1988), *Social welfare in Canada: Ideals, realities and future paths* (2nd ed.). Toronto: McClelland & Stewart, p. 226.

**9** Wilensky, H., & Lebeaux, C. (1965), Conceptions of social welfare. In H. Wilensky and C. Lebeaux (Eds.), *Industrial society and social welfare.* New York: Free Press.

**10** Lightman, E. (2003), *Social policy in Canada*, pp. 93–99.

an organization, which employees can use anonymously and without charge. EAP services address such problems as family conflict, addictions, child management, and bereavement. Employers provide these services as an employee benefit to maintain their employees' work performance at acceptable levels, despite the disturbing situations the employees may be facing in their home lives.[11]

On balance, this mix of agency sponsorship, which has been referred to as a "blurring of the sector boundaries,"[12] appears to work fairly well, although inadequacies can be found in the social services that all three sectors provide.[13] Answers to the question of what an ideal service delivery model should be are elusive. One aspect of the issue with particular significance for Canada is the challenge of providing services in isolated and sparsely populated areas, such as rural and northern communities. Government intervention in this situation is clearly necessary as neither the voluntary nor the commercial sector is able or willing to offer adequate social services to these small, scattered populations.

# INTERNAL MANAGEMENT AND THE BUREAUCRATIC STRUCTURE

Each social service agency is guided by mission and policy statements that outline the agency's goals and objectives. From these the agency develops a strategic plan that identifies the tasks necessary to carry out its mission. This plan then becomes the blueprint for structuring the agency into specialized work units or departments.

As is the case in most modern institutions, the social welfare system operates through a bureaucratic structure and processes. This framework enables its agencies to carry out their complex tasks. Bureaucratic rules and regulations allow an even-handed distribution of social welfare goods and services to clients according to agency policy. Benefits do not depend on the workers' personal preferences, except when the regulations state that the provider can exercise its own judgment in providing or withholding a benefit in individual cases.

Nevertheless, the bureaucratic model and the objectives of social welfare and social work fit together only imperfectly. The very formality and regulation that organizations need to run efficiently also make for a rigidity that hinders their adapting easily to the unique nature of the human beings who come to them with their different needs.

## Issues Affecting Bureaucratic Organizations

Bureaucracies present problems for both workers and clients. Clients may find the intricate nature of the bureaucracy hard to deal with because they do not fully understand the rules or how best to interpret regulations in order to qualify for service. Applying for a benefit demands that clients put forward the most convincing case possible on their own behalf and that they advocate for themselves with some skill. Unfortunately, they often run into

---

11 Brothers, C., & Brothers, J. (2001), Industries and the provision of social services. In J. C. Turner and F. J. Turner (Eds.), *Canadian social welfare* (4th ed.). Toronto: Pearson Education.

12 Chappell, R. (2001), *Social welfare in Canadian society.* Scarborough, ON: Nelson Thomson Learning, p. 119.

13 Davies, L., & Schragge, E. (1990), *Bureaucracy and community.* Montreal: Black Rose Books.

this expectation when they are under the most stress. They may find going through the necessary steps to obtain this help from a social agency discouraging or even intimidating; the agency may request that they share personal information with strangers or fill out extensive application forms. These expectations combined with the possibility of rejection and the reality of waiting lists or possible referrals to other service providers cause stress for prospective clients.

The sponsorship and size of the agency usually determine the extent to which an agency follows the bureaucratic model. Large government organizations normally rank highest on the bureaucracy scale with small voluntary agencies ranking lower, but despite differences in degree, bureaucratic features are found in almost all human service agencies and organizations.

## Managing the Agency

Bureaucratic structure makes the agency's management possible. Qualified staff can be assigned to specialized departments and their activities co-ordinated efficiently. Arranging positions in a hierarchy and allocating work to assigned units eliminates confusion about who should be doing which tasks and in what sequence.

Managers frequently supervise performance. They monitor and co-ordinate the work of the staff. It is their responsibility to see that standards of performance are adequate and that the overall organizational plan is being implemented. Recent cutbacks in social services and health care funding have resulted in fewer managers and supervisors of social work in practice settings. A whole layer of middle management seems to have been stripped out of the agency structures in many fields. Consequently, social workers are expected to practise far more independently and they have fewer opportunities in terms of support, consultation, and guidance from colleagues than was the case in earlier decades.

The number of levels into which staff is organized varies from agency to agency. Small agencies may have only two levels: front-line workers who serve clients face to face and a director who oversees the operation. Larger agencies need internal structures to manage their staff: front-line workers, department heads, middle management, co-ordinators, consultants, and an executive director. Organizational charts for complex agencies can be drawn to indicate reporting responsibilities and to specify the correct channels through which to send information.

## Social Work within a Bureaucracy

The bureaucratic structure causes much tension for social workers, especially when "individualization is sacrificed to proceduralism; when efficiency becomes more important than quality of service; and when administrative accountability serves to stifle practitioner creativity and constrain the exercise of professional judgment."[14]

However, Resnick and Patti suggest features such as participatory decision-making, maximum professional autonomy, non-hierarchical communication patterns, and consultative

---

[14] Patti, R. J. (1980), Internal advocacy and human service practitioners: An exploratory study. In H. Resnick and R.J. Patti (Eds.), *Change from within: Humanizing social welfare organizations*. Philadelphia: Temple University Press, p. 287.

leadership as approaches that can be taken by an organization to modify the negative impact of rigid bureaucracy on both social workers and service to clients.[15]

Besides the formal structure of an agency there exists a hidden, powerful substructure that cannot be drawn on a flow chart. Nonetheless, it contributes greatly to high or low morale among staff members. This is the network of peers who develop their own relationships through their daily interaction and shared perspectives. The informal network can strengthen or weaken the agency, depending on whether or not the members agree with the direction the agency is taking and the administration's methods for settling differences and allocating resources.[16] The informal network functions in many ways: it gives emotional support to its members, allows them to complain without confronting the administration, controls aspects related to the quality and amount of work expected of workers, and corrects errors administration makes through the many decisions and adjustments that frontline workers can make.

## Power within the Bureaucracy

Power influences much of what occurs in an organization. Those possessing the power can carry out their wishes despite opposition and exercise command over resources. Power attaches to position.

Those at the top of an organization have more and those at the bottom less, at least theoretically. A major factor determining the amount of power a person actually has in the workplace is his or her personal power—the individual's natural ability to influence and lead others. It sometimes happens, because of a lack of personal power, that those highly placed in a hierarchy are unable to exercise the full measure of their authority while workers lower in the hierarchy, those with a good measure of personal power, exercise more influence than their jobs warrant. Ideally, the workers in a social agency should command enough power to carry out their own duties, but not enough to allow them to interfere in other workers' appropriate use of their own power.

Staff members need to believe that the people who control the organization—the administrators, board members, civil servants, or commercial operators—are exercising their power legitimately, with the ultimate well-being of clients, staff, and organization more important than their own personal benefit. Without this belief it is difficult for workers to remain committed to the organization, to adhere to regulations, and to work under constraints. Most social agencies make provisions for workers to share a part of organizational power through their participation in decision making. Membership on planning committees, representation on the board of directors, and a consultative approach to developing internal policies are some of the ways staff may share power. Unionization has given some social service workers an additional power base from which to exert influence on their agencies and control some of the conditions of their work.[17]

---

**15** Resnick, H., & Patti, R. J. (Eds.). (1980), *Change from within: Humanizing social welfare organizations*. Philadelphia: Temple University Press, pp. 6–7.

**16** Gibelman, M. (2003), *Navigating human service organizations*. Chicago: Lyceum Books, p. 115.

**17** Foley, J. (1999), Professional associations in Canada. In F. J. Turner (Ed.), *Social work practice: A Canadian perspective*. Scarborough: Prentice-Hall.

# Changing the Agency from Within

At times, the professionals involved in the provision of social services may wish their agencies or organizations would change in some way. Often they are frustrated by the unresponsive nature of their own bureaucracies. Social workers promise in their code of ethics to seek change when they believe that their clients' well-being is in jeopardy because of circumstances in their organizations' workplaces.[18]

What circumstances could motivate social workers to confront management and possibly risk losing their jobs to protect clients? Mullaly identifies these conditions within social agencies. Policies and programs that force clients to accept roles or engage in behaviours that sustain and sanction oppressive relationships are clear targets for front-line action. As well, overbearing supervision, reward systems that favour administrative convenience over client service, and caseloads far too large for individual workers to manage can lead social workers to demand change.[19]

Social workers can adopt one of three positions in their efforts to bring about agency change. The first calls for the social worker to exercise some skill within agency regulations. Here the professionals act as advocates on their clients' behalf while fulfilling the role of "good bureaucrats," those who can function effectively within their organizations without compromising larger social work values.

As organizational change takes time, Pruger counsels workers to develop a philosophical approach and set of skills that will make them competent, active participants in shaping the life of the organization as it develops. A social worker with patience, high energy, and the ability to think independently can enlarge his areas of discretionary judgment, and so earn the power to interpret rules and regulations as liberally as possible, in his clients' interests.[20] This is an appropriate use of personal power and influence.

Working within the system can be an effective process, but circumstances may persuade the professionals involved that they must act directly and openly to bring about some kind of change in their organizations. In this second approach, several strategies are available. Resnick and Patti outline both collaborative and adversarial methods for altering agency patterns and policies.[21] Change is as difficult for social agencies as it is for human beings, and in attempting to initiate change the authors counsel workers to try collaborative methods first. Adversarial approaches often polarize an issue and harden the agencies' resistance to change. When social workers elect to collaborate in order to change some aspect of their agencies' operations, they are applying a problem-solving model to their agencies' processes. Workers interested in creating organizational change can provide information, present alternative approaches, ask permission to try innovative or experimental practices, produce statistical data to support the need for change, and point out the negative impact that current rules may have on clients.

If agencies resist this slow-moving, incremental process or it is otherwise ineffective, the final method available to workers is confrontation. Being adversarial in seeking agency

---

**18** Canadian Association of Social Workers. (2005), *Code of ethics*. Ottawa.

**19** Mullaly, B. (1997), *Structural social work: Ideology, theory and practice* (2nd ed.). Don Mills, ON: Oxford University Press, p. 181.

**20** Pruger, R. (1973), The good bureaucrat. *Social Work, 18*, 26–32.

**21** Resnick, H., & Patti, R. J. (1980), *Change from within*.

change is stressful and can be hazardous for workers; those who actively oppose their employer's methods of operating inevitably provoke anger and conflict. Nevertheless, putting the well-being of clients first may make this a necessary choice. Adversarial tactics on an ascending scale of intensity include submitting petitions, encouraging staff not to comply with a disputed regulation, initiating conflicts at meetings, using the media to publicize the problem (with all the attendant threats of loss of public support and funding), instituting work stoppages or strikes, and litigating (as a last resort). Social workers participate actively in shaping their agencies' responses to meeting clients' needs. They need to be skilled, knowledgeable, and courageous in playing their parts well.

## Management Practices and Agency Costs

In an attempt to answer the question of how best to manage the inner workings of the social agency so that staff members perform well and deliver the most cost-effective services to clients, a large body of literature[22] and an active consultation business for management experts have developed. Both structure and flexibility seem to be fundamental. Social workers are more likely to work effectively when they accept organized work patterns and can see that the values of the profession are being observed.

As social agencies deal with human problems on a case-by-case basis, every person who requests service must be assessed for eligibility, her situation documented and recorded, and outcomes of the intervention evaluated before closing her case. Dealing with requests for service is termed "intake" and the responsibility is often assigned to specialists who assess whether the client's need falls within the agency's mandate and resources. These specialists then recommend acceptance of the client or her referral to another source of help.

In providing social work services to clients, workers are guided by agency policy and written procedures or protocols. The latter are detailed lists of steps for staff to take in specific types of cases. For example, in a child welfare agency, workers always follow certain procedures in investigating and dealing with a complaint of child abuse. Although the use of protocols tends to standardize procedures in a somewhat rigid way, it also ensures a uniform quality of service delivery in that the workers carry out all the essential steps and minimizes their possible oversight or incompetence.

All agencies maintain client records that usually contain short case histories and periodic notes about a client's progress, as well as a closing summary of all that occurred during the agency's contact with him. More comprehensive recordings are of particular importance in cases involving child abuse or custody disputes when there may be legal proceedings, and they are invaluable should a social worker be accused of malpractice. Contents of the record are confidential and cannot be used outside the agency without the client's permission or a court order.

Most workers also develop their own systems of personal information that allow them to keep track of their work commitments with appointment books, day sheets, and working notes. Workers need to keep careful records of their daily activities because they must periodically provide their agencies with statistical breakdowns of how they spend their time. Computers are an increasingly important feature for managing case records, performing statistical analysis, and communicating among workers and other agencies.[23]

---

**22** Lewis, J.A., Lewis, M.D., Packard, T., & Souflee, F. (2001), *Management of human service programs* (3rd Ed.). Belmont, CA: Wadsworth.

**23** Perlmutter, F. D., Bailey, D., & Netting, F. E. (2001), *Managing human resources in the human services: Supervisory challenges.* New York: Oxford University Press, ch. 4.

Workers often see reporting on their statistics as tedious, but the statistical analysis of agency data is an important management tool. Statistical data yield information about the characteristics of the people the agency serves, changing needs in the community, referral sources to the agency, outcomes of interventions used, case conferences held, and education or training sessions attended. The administration uses this information to demonstrate accountability for agency costs to its board of directors, funders, government regulators, and the larger community. Administrators can also discern trends in requests for service, as the profile of human need changes over time, with some needs increasing as others diminish in importance. As well, administrators and managers can compare workers' productivity, which is information that can lead to performance improvement, better allocations of talents, or additional training.

## PROGRAM EVALUATION

At all times, but perhaps especially in times of fiscal restraint, agencies must justify their expenditures. They do this in part by measuring the impact their programs have in helping their clients deal with their problems or in alleviating the social problems the agencies target. For example, if an agency offers education and training to youths who have dropped out of school, they could measure their program's effectiveness by keeping track of the percentage of clients who find employment or who go on to higher education following their agency's intervention, compared with the employment of a similar group the agency does not serve. It is reasonable to expect that if the program demonstrates effectiveness over time, a network of such services would lower the number of youths who are unemployed, which in turn would affect local unemployment rates.

Deciding what to choose as valid indicators of successful outcomes is a problem for those who evaluate the success or failure of social programs. Numbers alone are not enough, nor is an emphasis on how many dollars have been saved. Somehow an agency evaluating its own performance over time must identify variables that measure the impact of a service in terms of personal growth, family harmony, community strength, or other specific goals that the agency has expressed.

## NEW AND EMERGING NEEDS

We live in an age of rapid social change and rising expectations for personal happiness. These forces converge to make our society more aware of the variety and extent of human need than ever before possible. Not only do we recognize new needs, but we have the capability and often the will to try and relieve them by taking action. Hence, we continually create new agencies and organizations with special programs designed to correct contemporary problems in living.

We speak of "new" needs, but the term actually has two meanings: some needs that have always existed but are newly uncovered because they can now be discussed and dealt with openly, or alternatively, some needs we have never before experienced that have arisen as a result of some change in society or the environment.

For example, violence in the family, especially against women, is not new. What is new is society's powerful response against it. In collaboration with strong legislation, a variety of services for abused women and their children have been developed—legal advice clinics, shelters, and transition houses.

With the advent of HIV and AIDS in the early 1980s, an entirely new and unanticipated area of human need appeared. Agencies and services of many types, such as hostels, hospices, and counselling programs, are being established to respond to the needs of these patients and those related to them. Here we have an opportunity to study the many human reactions to a tragic social problem. Many segments of the voluntary community have reacted with generous support while governments have often operated at arm's length, perhaps because of the perceived political risks they would run in seeming to endorse people with stigmatized illnesses.

New agencies sometimes appear as our society finds innovative ways to cope with "old" needs. Bereavement services are one such instance. People have always had to deal with death, and recent advances in therapeutic counselling and the use of mutual support groups offer the possibility of relieving human suffering and preventing family breakdowns after the deaths of loved ones.

Self-help/mutual support are long-established methods of helping others. The strengths to be found through mutual aid are being applied to current problems caused by changing social forces. For example, mutual support groups are being developed to assist farmers whose livelihoods are threatened by poor economic times, to help the victims of incest and rape, to encourage widowed people to live more fully, and to allow the adult children of alcoholic parents to overcome negative influences from their past. Self-help and professionally directed services developed for First Nations clients both on and off the reserves help them deal with problems of cultural adjustment, work readiness, addictions, and personal development. The government and the private sectors unite to help the elderly through a variety of community-based agencies that offer recreation, retirement counselling, home support, and nursing services. As a country that encourages the immigration of people from many other cultures, Canada supports a network of services to assist the newcomers in their adjustment or "settlement" in their new country. Professionals in health and social welfare today see using cultural interpreters as necessary so that they can provide their services in a culturally and linguistically sensitive manner.

In this era of information overload, many clients discover that finding out the correct facts regarding an appropriate service is difficult. One type of agency has been created to guide clients through the maze of resources available. Information centres collect and categorize vast amounts of data on legislation; social, health, and community agencies; and human rights. As well as giving clients clear facts relevant to their situations, information centres also refer them directly to specific services.

The creation of the multi-service centre represents another step toward simplifying help-seeking. Several agencies staff this organization, from both the government and the voluntary sectors, so that clients with complex problems can find the many resources they need there. Rural settings are finding the multi-service concept particularly useful.

## CONCLUSION

From the information contained in this chapter it is apparent that the safety net that covers Canada in support of the needy and the vulnerable among us is woven of strong fibres. Social agencies, human service organizations, social workers, health care professionals, volunteers, social policies, and funding sources constitute the strands.

Like all human institutions, agencies and organizations have problems. Yet, flawed as these organizations might be, their mere existence offers concrete evidence of that aspect of the human spirit that moves us to care for strangers' well-being. It would be difficult to visualize Canadian society without them.

# CHAPTER 15

# Industries and the Provision of Social Services

*Catherine Brothers and John Brothers*

## INTRODUCTION

Until the 1980s, Canadian social workers might have expected to spend their entire careers employed within not-for-profit agencies funded through government and charitable sources. Until that point, many Canadians viewed fully funded social work services as the responsibility of the state, religious groups, and philanthropic individuals and organizations.

"User fees" have existed for 75 years in non-government social agencies, particularly the family service agencies, out of a belief that those who were able to afford services ought to contribute their fair share towards the cost, thus making available resources go further for those who are unable to pay. Over the past 50 years, another "payer"—funding source—and a new area of social work practice has emerged across Canada—namely, social work within industry. Increasingly, employers are viewing social work as a positive, relevant, and meaningful resource in the workplace. Social workers, in both not-for-profit and for-profit organizations, are aggressively marketing their services to workplaces.

This chapter explores issues related to the current practice of social work in workplaces. The goals of social work practice are to help individuals reach their maximum potential and to work with community members to ensure that all have equal opportunity to reach that maximum potential. This distinct and unique orientation within the social work profession towards building both strong individuals and healthy communities inspires the practice of social work in workplaces. The social worker's knowledge and skills in the areas of both clinical practice and community development provide the framework for delivering social work services within industry. The social worker's values and training are most relevant to understanding the perspectives of both the employee and the employer and to facilitating mutually beneficial interactions.

## HISTORICAL CONTEXT

A brief overview of history puts into context that, from the earliest days of professional social work, workplace issues have been considered fundamental components of individual well-being. Although the practice of social work within industry tends to be viewed as a recent development, industrial social work was, in fact, one of the first areas of social work activity.

In the late 1800s, the social worker, initially known as a "welfare secretary," played a key role in American industry's social welfare movement.[1] The welfare secretary was the initiative of beneficent owners and management, and that person's role was to improve the social well-being and morale of employees, especially those of female employees and minority groups. The welfare secretary organized recreational activities and supported means of meeting employees' basic living needs, such as housing. Most historians view the welfare secretary's form of social work as the origin of the human resources

---

1 Significantly, the New York School of Social Work and the Bryn Mawr School of Social Work offered specialized courses in industrial social work in the first quarter of the twentieth century.

profession. Originally a popular position, the welfare secretary came to be viewed with mistrust and eventually fell from grace as the union movement emerged, which perceived this position as employers' paternalism and manipulation.

The present practice of social work within industry began with concerns about the impact of alcohol abuse within the workplace. High absenteeism rates and accidents on the job, both personal and in the manufacturing process, were adding to labour and production costs.

Over the past 150 years, with the exception of the Prohibition years, the use of alcohol was freely condoned, and even encouraged, in many workplaces. Until the 1970s, it was not unusual for employees of Canadian breweries and distilleries to be rewarded with servings of alcohol during their working hours. Everywhere, however, a person endured a great stigma as a "drunk" or an "alcoholic." Until the introduction of Alcoholics Anonymous in 1935, alcohol abuse was considered a symptom of moral degeneration and personal failure. Counselling services for substance abusers, rather than discipline, were assumed to lessen such costs and to improve employee morale and performance.

In 1992, the Conference Board of Canada published a report by Shahid Alvi, *Corporate Responses to Substance Abuse in the Workplace*. Alvi reported that the founding of Alcoholics Anonymous in 1935 led to employer-sponsored rehabilitation programs in organizations like DuPont and Eastman Kodak in the United States. He also identified Canada's first occupational alcohol abuse program, created at Bell Canada in 1947. Throughout Canada and the United States, from the 1940s to the 1970s, recovered alcohol abusers, who had positive affiliations as peers within the workplace and strong ties with Alcoholics Anonymous, tended to provide workplace counselling programs.

In Ontario, over the past 50 years, the Addiction Research Foundation (ARF)—now the Centre for Addiction and Mental Health—an agent of the province, played a major role in helping workplaces to care for the social, emotional, and psychological well-being of their employees. The Addiction Research Foundation strongly promoted policies and workplace interventions related to alcohol and drug abuse. The foundation advocated strongly for rehabilitation rather than discipline and dismissal. During the 1970s, the ARF placed more than 50 consultants throughout Ontario, helping hundreds of corporations to recognize and deal with employees with problems related to substance abuse. The ARF emphasized helping workplaces to identify problem employees and then constructively manipulating them into treatment. Since the mid-1970s, the foundation shifted from a narrow focus on substance abuse to organizational interventions, encouraging workplaces to adopt more holistic and "broad-brush" approaches.

In 1998, the ARF merged with three other major providers of addiction and mental health services in Ontario to form the Centre for Addiction and Mental Health. As in the general practice of social work in industry, this merger acknowledges the complexity of psychosocial issues and the need for collaborative relationships in finding solutions.

Using the language of the marketplace, social work practice in industry is often referred to as Employee Assistance Programs (EAPs) or Employee and Family Assistance Programs (EFAPs). Generally, EAPs aim to help employees find solutions to a broad range of personal and family problems. Prevention, promotion of wellness, and reduction of workplace problems remain constant goals of these programs.

Many non-profit and family service agencies began providing EAPs in the late 1970s and early 1980s. At that time, family service agencies provided most of the social work services within workplaces, and they were optimistic that these services, paid for by the employers, would provide margins of profit sufficient to enable the non-profit agencies to enhance their services to poor and marginalized persons. As more private practitioners and national and international for-profit EAP providers entered the field, however, the profit margins shrank and competition intensified. It is impossible to determine how many workplaces in Canada use social work services today, but the number is growing weekly. Most medium- and large-sized industries offer some form of professional counselling services to their employees.

The organizational trend, throughout the 1990s, among both local social work providers and large national and international providers, was to develop networks of social work affiliates who can provide services to work sites throughout North America.

During the 1990s, the trend in social work services to industry expanded from a focus on reducing workplace problems to a wider perspective that included prevention and promotion of health and wellness. There was gradually less emphasis on the identification of workplace problems by supervisors, and an increasing emphasis on the importance of employee-initiated self-referrals. The present EAP strategy offers a range of social work services from which the employee may choose, rather than the mandated or involuntary referrals of the past.

In the first decade of the 21st century, dominant issues for social work in workplaces have become diversity, violence in the workplace, overwork, presenteeism, an aging workforce, outsourcing, skilled labour shortages, and the impact of globalization. Throughout the country there has been a shift from industrial to knowledge- and service-based workplaces. The pace of work, fuelled by the proliferation of technological advances, is a major issue as more and more employees are connected to the Internet and their workplaces 24-7 through computers, cell phones, and wireless devices. The workforce has become more ethnically diverse as more immigrants fill gaps in the labour force and allow for economic growth. Greater numbers of newcomers to Canada come from Asia than from Europe, as was the traditional immigration pattern.

The increasing trend to offer EAP services by phone and Internet remains controversial. It is argued that the Internet fits the culture and lifestyle of younger employees, provides convenience, and improves both access to service and confidentiality. On the other hand, there are concerns about misdiagnosing clients without face-to-face interactions as well as concerns about safety and mandatory reporting requirements related to family violence and child abuse. There can be no doubt that Internet and tele-therapy are becoming more prominent—sometimes driven by the EAP providers' need to be cost-conscious in delivering service. Much work remains to be done in the area of regulating providers of such technology-based therapy and evaluating its effectiveness. A good argument can be made for a combination of Internet-based EAP services with face-to-face counselling.

## TARGET POPULATION OF SOCIAL WORKERS IN INDUSTRY

There are a variety of workplaces that employ social workers: hospitals, universities, schools, government offices, firms of professional engineers and architects, factories, financial institutions such as banks and credit unions, chartered accountancy firms, bus and aviation companies, police and fire departments, and gas bars and convenience stores. It is hard to imagine a workplace that would not benefit from access to these services. While large workplaces remain a target for marketing social work services to employees, since 2000 there has been an increasing emphasis on making social work services available to small and medium-sized local businesses.

Social workers help both the employee and his or her family members, either individually or together, to find solutions for the stressors in their daily lives. For social workers in industry, the target population encompasses all levels of employees, including members of boards of directors, owners, senior management, supervisors, and front-line workers.

With growing awareness of the many challenges that small and medium-sized businesses face in remaining efficient and competitive in the global economy, there is a new role emerging for social workers. Many small and medium-sized businesses do not have skilled human resource departments or professionals. The efficiency and productivity of small and medium-sized businesses depend upon their human capital. Workplaces are impacted by the personal, relationship, psychological, and social problems of their employees. In 2007, the Government of Canada funded a three-year, 1.7 million dollar pilot project for the Catholic Family Counselling Centre in Kitchener-Waterloo, Ontario, to collaborate with twenty small and medium-sized business partners in developing an innovative model for helping business owners to address the psychosocial challenges of their employees. Using up-to-the-minute technology, this project will assess the impact of developing an interactive Web-portal and in-the-moment coaching for owners and supervisors. While the goal is to improve the capacity of workplaces to promote well-being in their employees, clearly the measurement of success will be improvements in the productivity and achievements of workplaces.

## Types of Problems and Issues

In 1991, the Alberta Alcohol and Drug Abuse Commission reaffirmed that substance use in Canadian workplaces remains a significant concern. Although excessive use of alcohol and drugs seems to be declining in Canadian society, we cannot overstate the enormous threat that these forms of substance use pose to the workplace. We have worked in several industries devastated by the deaths of many employees in alcohol-related workplace accidents.

Depression is a primary reason for employees seeking EAP counselling. Statistics Canada estimates that nearly one in five Canadian workers suffers from stress owing to home or work issues. Much has been said about the challenges of balancing work and family expectations. Depression is responsible for the greatest percentage of lost productive work time, and about one-third of all disability claims are related to depression and stress. The World Health Organization (2001) has estimated that depression will be the second-leading cause of disability worldwide by the year 2020.

One of the largest problems facing employers in the next ten to fifteen years will be handling the challenges faced by the aging "baby boomer" population. EAP services need to better address the needs of older workers. While there has been a trend towards earlier retirement over the past twenty years, there are also new dynamics created by the removal of mandatory retirement ages.

Industries grappling with high rates of absenteeism and presenteeism look to social work to play a role in solving these problems. Historically, missing work was considered a major problem in workplaces. Recently, there has been a growing recognition that greater problems are associated with presenteeism, wherein employees preoccupied with a range of problems show up for work, but with a negative attitude and limited capacity that interfere with many aspects of workplace relationships and outputs. Presenteeism can also refer to the problems associated with overwork, when an employee has lost the balance between work and fun or family life.

In working with individual employees, the social worker understands that conflicting stresses related to work and family responsibilities may lead to either absenteeism or presenteeism. Appreciating the stresses that families face, many social workers have advocated flexible hours in industry. They will often advocate for employees regarding essential child care and elder care resources.

Social workers have successfully helped industries improve their policies regarding time off for family responsibilities. One human resources manager with no children of his own reminded a concerned social worker quite firmly that "either these people want to work, or they don't. A job is a job!" Three years later, the same manager, with a working wife and two young children of his own, introduced a policy into his own workplace that permitted employees to use their "sick days" to fulfill family responsibilities, such as caring for a child too ill to be brought to the child care provider.

Most frequently, social workers are treating a broad range of marital and family problems in industry. Many employees have stress-related problems that are often related to the conflicting demands of work and family life. Conflicts among employees and difficult people in the workplace are common concerns. Other problems include sexual harassment, workplace violence, living with shift work, feelings of being wronged in the workplace, financial worries, gambling problems, illness, and long-term disabilities. Employees seek out social workers' help in coping with the pressures of mergers, downsizing, early retirement, and employers' expectations that they accomplish more and more work with less job security and fewer resources. Employees often feel they have very little control over the major decisions that affect their whole lives. Working within boards of education, for example, social workers help teachers and principals cope after they have been transferred or reassigned with little or no consultation. Social workers in industry also address tensions in the workplace related to ethnicity, culture, or sexual orientation.

During the 1990s, social workers across Canada became increasingly involved in interventions related to sudden critical incidents and traumatic accidents. These could be workplace violence; industrial accidents; suicide; murder; robberies; rescue attempts; car, bus, and plane accidents; and fires. When such tragic events happen, social workers can respond immediately with well-defined strategies of stress management, debriefing, defusing, and damage control.

## "Where the Client Is At"

The presence of social work within industry reflects major changes within the Canadian family. During the 1994 International Year of the Family, the Vanier Institute of the Family in Ottawa published an excellent document in partnership with the Conference Board of Canada, *The Work and Family Challenge: Issues and Options* (Alvi 1992). According to Alvi, its author, almost 60 percent of Canadian women are in the labour force and they account for more than 40 percent of the whole labour force. Further, in the last 30 years, the dual-income family has replaced the "traditional" family unit of a mother at home, a working father, and two children. More than half of our society's women with children younger than six years of age are in the labour force. The Vanier document goes on to describe the high stress levels plaguing so many men and women under constant pressure to juggle their work and family priorities. Given the challenges today's families face, it makes good sense that social workers be "where the client is at"—that is, in the workplace.

Workplace clients may ask for specific help that social workers do not consider appropriate. Such might be the case in matters of family violence, for example, where an abusive spouse requests couple counselling with their battered partner. Similarly, a separated employee may demand that the social worker prepare a report for the court in support of his desire for child custody or access. As in other social work settings, the professional social worker may have to confront a client regarding the consequences of her own behaviour. This is a sensitive challenge within industry, where the employer expects to be pleased with the social worker's efforts and, at the same time, the social worker must act according to professional knowledge and within legal child protection reporting requirements. To begin "where the client is at," the social worker in industry must also sort out when social work treatment is appropriate and when a client simply needs information and access to other resources. Negotiating these differences with clients can be difficult. Another ethical and practical dilemma frequently faced by social workers whose service is purchased by employers is working within caps on the number of counselling services, or limitations in the scope of services that the employer has agreed to pay for.

## ATTITUDES TOWARDS SOCIAL WORK SERVICES IN INDUSTRY

Not very long ago, considerable stigma was attached to a person's receiving professional social work services, many of which were involuntary. The decision to seek social work services was a personal and private matter, and gender roles meant that women were the majority of social work clients. Today, access to social work services is viewed as a standard workplace benefit. Male and female employees are looking to their workplaces for benefits packages that include access to counselling from professional social workers. Rather than the old stigma attached to seeking professional mental health services, employees now expect that employers will provide counselling benefits and that co-workers with problems will "get some help and deal with it." Industry leaders consider it "good business" to form partnerships with social workers in promoting individual and family well-being.

Larger social factors in Canada have also contributed to the growing role of social work in industry: the rise of social movements, such as consumerism, environmental protection, and the rights of the individual as reaffirmed in the repatriation of the Constitution of Canada. We hear more people in industry discussing the importance of both "high tech" and "high touch." Twenty years ago, open dialogues on compassion and spirituality in the workplace would have been highly unusual. Today such conversations are held more and more frequently in many workplaces.

Employers appreciate the value of loyal and healthy employees and of a positive public perception that they care about their employees and are building a better community. Society increasingly recognizes the importance of the relationship between a healthy economy and healthy individuals and families. For example, in 1999, it was remarkable to witness the Vancouver Board of Trade presenting a solid business plan to the federal minister of finance as to why early childhood supports and interventions are the core of a strong economy.

In the workplace, social workers are recognized for their profound belief in the worth and dignity of each person and in the community's role in sustaining and enhancing this approach. These beliefs make an excellent starting point for helping both the employee and the employer pursue mutually beneficial goals.

A business that makes a real and visible commitment to supporting social work practice within its enterprise is generally a business that thrives. It enjoys positive workplace morale and is valued as a "good" employer in the community. An industry demonstrates a commitment to its employee assistance program through lots of communications with its employees about readily available social work services, frequent and regularly scheduled training and orientation sessions conducted by social workers, and articles in business newsletters and on the company's Web site or intranet about the value of social work services in the workplace.

Companies with low morale and/or lots of mistrust often impose extra barriers on their employees to accessing social work services, such as imposing user fees or requiring that any employee's access to the service be approved internally. Top management in such companies does little to convey its belief in the importance of the social work program. It restricts distribution of education and promotion materials. Either the owners or the union members may have pressured top management into providing the social work services, while management's attitude toward social work value is skeptical. "Buy-in" at the top is essential!

## THE ROLE OF LABOUR UNIONS

Union counsellors and union peers play very significant roles in encouraging employees to use social work services. The social worker in industry appreciates the importance of understanding the corporate culture and recognizing the people who employees normally seek out for their information, support, and referral. The social worker will build links with existing support networks within the industry, especially with labour leaders and union counsellors.

Unions have been both supportive and proactive in promoting these social work services. Union leaders, however, remain vigilant about warnings against placing too much emphasis on services to individuals in distress; this focus may perpetuate the notion that the employees' "personal" problems lie at the bottom of their work-related stress. As much as they support EAPs, unions are concerned about letting employers off the hook in addressing organizational issues that affect the health and well-being of their employees. Some union leaders see social work in industry as a Band-Aid approach to problem solving that detracts from the employers' responsibility to establish positive environments and proper working conditions.

Labour unions have led the way in sponsoring many EAPs across Canada. In reporting on the state of these in Canada in 1991, the Alberta Alcohol and Drug Abuse Commission (Wnek, 1991) discovered that most unionized companies in Canada provide these programs under the joint sponsorship of labour and management. In both Ontario and Saskatchewan, almost two-thirds of those organizations with unions have both union and management representation, as do more than half of the federally regulated transportation companies (Macdonald et al., 2006).

The Canadian Labour Congress has developed union counselling programs across Canada to train union counsellors within industry. Social workers participate in delivering these programs, which focus on training union counsellors to help their peers access the supports and services they need.

# CONFIDENTIALITY

Confidentiality, integrity, and honesty are cornerstones of the social work profession. Employers and employees quickly size up social workers and decide whether they can trust them. While the social workers might be helping both management and line employees, it must be absolutely clear to everyone that they will not convey any information about clients to anyone else in the workplace. All social work reports that are sent to the workplace contain only non-identifying information—number of clients, number of units of service, lists of presenting problems, and clinical outcomes—none of which jeopardizes the identity of any individual employee.

For social workers employed in industry, it is critical to sort out with the industry or the "payer" the question of who "owns" the social work records. When industry contracts with off-site social work providers, the provider will find it easier to establish ownership and confidentiality of client records. The matter becomes more complex when the social worker is an actual employee of the workplace, working within the industry. The social worker with an off-site provider must anticipate that the funding organization will want to verify that the services it is paying for have, in fact, been provided. Such verification may include an audit of client records. The social worker needs to plan for this eventuality with the employer in advance, agreeing on procedures that do not disclose to the employer any names or identifying information about the employees. Privacy legislation introduced in 2004 across Canada further protects the employee confidentiality.

Social workers will want to clarify with the workplace beforehand how they are going to deal with requests for service from the children of employees and how they will deal with employees or family members who threaten to harm themselves or others.

# PROMOTION OF SOCIAL WORK SERVICES WITHIN INDUSTRY

New technology, especially the Internet, has led to a profound change in the way employees learn about social work services and their employee assistance programs. Before 2000, most of the education about social work services was done through printed materials and face-to-face meetings and workshops. Today, the Internet is the major vehicle for educating employees about available employee assistance programs. This shift has challenged many providers of social work services to become much more technologically relevant and competitive.

Reputation and credibility are paramount in establishing and maintaining employee assistance programs. Employees who have been helped will readily advise their friends and colleagues of the service. Equally important, if employees have any suspicion whatever that they cannot trust the social worker, word of that will also spread quickly. The emphasis for the social worker in industry is on delivering excellent customer service. Once an employee assistance program has been established, it takes constant attention to good customer care to maintain that contract. Most EAP contracts are for a fixed period of time and then the company will go out to the marketplace again for competitive quotes.

# TIME

There are very specific time requirements related to providing social work in industry. When social work services are attached to benefits in the workplace, employees will expect immediate access to those services. Consequently, social workers are keeping pace with the most up-to-date developments in technology and communication devices. Most contracts between the social worker and the workplace establish that the employee will have access to a social work session within 24 to 48 hours from the time of referral and that critical incidents and emergencies will be treated immediately.

The emphasis on accessible social work services within industry has introduced a whole new dimension to the concept of "time." Employee assistance providers compete with one another, and this has raised the standards regarding time expectations. Twenty-four-hour accessibility, wide-area dialling, evening hours, weekend appointments, telephone counselling services, and interactive Internet communications have all become common tools of social work practice.

Time presents another major challenge. Contracts between the social worker and the industry must define the number of social work sessions to which an employee and family members are entitled, generally on an annual basis. Many contracts in Canada limit the employee to an average of six sessions per year, to be paid for by the employer. Sometimes the employer will "cap" the amount to be paid to the social worker rather than "cap" the number of sessions. For example, both parties will negotiate the maximum payment to the social worker in one year, and the social worker will agree to provide the service to all employees within that fixed amount.

When an employer agrees in the contract to pay for only one to three sessions, the social worker faces an ethical dilemma. The American practice of "managed care" has influenced benefits in the Canadian workplace. Typically, the "managed care" model emphasizes the information and referral role of the social worker and restricts the number of eligible sessions. Some social workers have declined requests to provide services that are capped at one to three sessions on the basis that agreeing to enter into such a limited treatment relationship is impractical, imprudent, and unethical. Others take the position that some social work intervention is better than none, and they focus on helping their employee clients sort out what they can within the limited time frame.

## STRATEGIC ALLIANCES IN PROVIDING SOCIAL WORK SERVICES TO INDUSTRY

Today's global economy means that many industries, large and small, operate from multiple sites. A company often does business in different cities and provinces across Canada, across North America, and internationally. Head office generally expects that the employees at all work sites will have equitable access to benefits.

The social worker negotiating the provision of social work services with head office needs to have a plan to provide those services for all of the company's employees throughout Canada and the United States. Accordingly, social worker organizations have developed strategic alliances and joint ventures similar to those that businesses enter throughout the world.

Since the late 1970s, family service agencies have allied themselves as member agencies of Family Service Canada to organize access to FSEAPs (Family Service EAPs) across the country. Typically, one family service agency will hold the "master contract" for the social work in a particular workplace, and employees across Canada may access this help through their local family service agency. These agencies also belong to national and international associations of employee assistance providers that offer networks of experienced and qualified social workers who deliver such services throughout North America.

On a typical workday, a family service agency in Kitchener, Ontario, arranged for social work services for the employees of a Canadian-owned company at work sites in Phoenix and Chicago and received calls from Detroit and Houston, requesting the same services for the local employees of the client's American-owned companies. Services provided at this Kitchener agency within a short time frame included critical incident debriefing services, wherein social workers treated local bus drivers who suffered the emotional impact of a fatal bus accident across the American border. Crisis intervention services with employees on a construction site who had just witnessed the electrocution of a co-worker were deemed essential in coping with this tragedy. The agency conducted another debriefing for the executives of a local company who had been traumatized by a frightening non-fatal crash of their small plane on a business trip to the United States. The agency also arranged services in Minnesota for a Kitchener truck driver after he was victimized in an armed robbery.

Strategic alliances are evident in the collaborative networks social workers are building to ensure workplaces can access a range of social work and health promotion activities. More individual social workers are providing services that emphasize wellness and holistic health. While expectations of the eclectic social worker remain high related to providing individual, couples', family, and group counselling, there is an increasing trend for collaborative work within all disciplines. Employee assistance programs often combine the expertise of social workers with other professionals in areas such as psychology, spiritual care, occupational therapy, career counselling, credit counselling, and nutrition counselling.

## IMPACT ON THE SOCIAL WORKER'S OWN WORKPLACE

One would not expect someone who does not own life insurance herself to be able to sell life insurance to others. Similarly, to provide congruent social work services in industry, practices within the social workers' own workplaces become more significant.

As social workers become more involved in industry, they pay more attention within their own workplaces to the importance of continuous quality improvement, staff training and development, positive working environments, strong employee morale, access to their own EAP benefits—for themselves—employee rewards, and employee incentives. To promote family-friendly practices within industry, social workers have renewed their emphasis on family-friendly policies within their own workplaces. As they support other employees during times of rapid technological growth, so they too need the same support within their own workplaces. As social workers support those in industry who pursue the clarification of values and spirituality, so social workers now express interest in the same matters in their own places of employment. As they encourage other workplaces to make sure that working parents can receive the reassuring "I'm home! What's to eat?" phone call or email at work every afternoon, so the values of such family practices and accessibility have become topics of more open dialogue in the social workers' workplaces, too.

## INTERNAL VERSUS EXTERNAL SOCIAL WORK SERVICES WITHIN INDUSTRY

There has been long-standing debate related to the pros and cons of internal versus external models of providing social work within the workplace. In the internal EAP, the social worker is visible and present within the workplace. Some industries, typically large organizations with considerable resources, employ their own social workers with offices within the workplace. These workers may offer a range of education, wellness, and recreational activities for staff and serve as information and referral resources to a wide array of community, legal, child care, and elder care resources. Other companies employ their own internal social workers, and, to maintain privacy and confidentiality, the social workers are located off-site and tend to specialize in more in-depth social work treatment services.

Social workers within internal EAPs have the opportunity to interact with employees and management on a regular basis. They may provide a more personal approach towards helping. They are able to build trust and healthy working relationships on a continuous basis and have the advantage of day-to-day informal interactions within the workplace. A good social worker in industry earns credibility as someone who can contribute to the organization. In sudden crises, the internal social worker responds quickly and has enough background information to plan an immediate and relevant response. On the negative side, the same social worker may easily be viewed as connected to top management and may have trouble earning employees' trust. While the value of relationships between the internal social worker and the industry is obvious, social workers deal with very significant challenges in maintaining professional social work relationships with clients who are also colleagues.

When a company or an industry enters into a contract with an external social work provider, the provider may supply the services on-site, but the vast majority of these are offered off-site. One food manufacturing company, with primarily female workers and a number of problems related to absenteeism, wanted on-site services both to control costs and to ensure employees' accessibility to information about child care resources. The social worker from the family service agency began with an office beside the human resources department—not the ideal position in terms of privacy or confidentiality. But it was a start and it did raise company awareness about the availability of social work help. Before long, employees were calling the family service agency and asking the social worker if they could meet off-site, to deal with private family matters.

By starting where the customer was "at," this particular social worker successfully established trust and credibility with the human resources manager, and that EAP has now moved to an off-site service location. One of the ways the social worker built the positive relationship with the human resources manager was by participating in a golf game! Social workers are finding that this kind of marketing technique, long familiar in business, has become applicable to their building their own relationships at all levels within industry.

Most employers prefer to sign contracts with external social work providers who can provide access to a diverse range of experienced social workers. Once these contracts are established, the industry has little bureaucracy to manage. Employees have access to social work services with minimal involvement on the part of the employer. Through strategic alliances and partnerships, the social worker takes on the responsibility of ensuring that all the industry's employees have access to service, regardless of the work-site location. To many, the services of an external social worker seem more objective. The external social worker can tailor a specific approach to service provision to suit the specific issues of individual workplaces.

## OUTCOME MEASUREMENT

To be taken seriously within industry, social workers must demonstrate their accountability and their commitment to continuous quality improvement. Until recently, they measured the impact of their services by reporting on utilization rates, changes in absenteeism, accident rates, and, most frequently, employee or client satisfaction. Attempts to describe the changes taking place in the lives of those who have used social work services were limited to inferences drawn from rates of utilization, lists of presenting problems, and client satisfaction surveys.

Social workers are now using tools that measure in concrete, observable terms the major personal and family changes in the persons who use social work services. Specific measurements are used to demonstrate to the employer behaviour and mental health changes that impact the employee's functioning in the workplace.

The literature on healthy workplace outcomes and organizational health focuses on addressing the relationship between employee health and workplace outcomes. As a framework for healthy workplaces, the National Quality Institute has developed a resource for Canadian businesses called the Canadian Healthy Workplace Criteria. The literature, as reported by Health Canada (2004), outlines a healthy workplace in terms of "holistic workplace health," which includes physical, social, personal, and developmental support "to improve overall employee quality of life both within and outside of the workplace."

Prudent social workers will involve workplaces in determining the outcomes to be measured. The workers who present evaluation reports that do not measure changes valued by the workplace will be defeating themselves. Most frequently, clients, workplaces, and social workers all agree on the areas where change is most valuable, but the quality of the communication that goes into determining the areas of shared belief is critical.

Increasingly, industries will expect social workers to produce solid evaluation methods by which to analyze both client outcomes and program benefits. Social workers recognize the common sense behind the paying customers' expectations of specific services with demonstrated outcomes.

## CONCLUSION

In the late 1800s, social workers began working in industry as "welfare secretaries." In the twenty-first century, a different and strong role has evolved for social work practice in the workplace. While no statistics are available to confirm the extent of the practice within industry, it is increasingly apparent that employees in most large workforces in Canada have access to social work services, and the profession is making constant progress in reaching small and medium-sized businesses. The profession of social work is recognized as an integral partner in supporting employees and employers in Canadian workplaces.

# References

Alvi, S. (1992). *Corporate responses to substance abuse in the workplace.* Ottawa: Conference Board of Canada.

Alvi, S. (1994). *The work and family challenge: Issues and options.* Canada Committee for the International Year of the Family 1994. Ottawa: Conference Board of Canada.

Annett-Lawrence, N. & Oattes, A. (2006). *Catholic Family Counselling Centre: Meeting the needs of EAP clients.* Unpublished research paper by MSc(OT) Candidates, McMaster University Health Sciences.

Bilsker, D., et al. (2004). *Depression & work function: Bridging the gap between mental health care and the workplace.* Retrieved from www.mheccu.ubc.ca/publications.

Cooper, C. & Highley-Marchington, C. (1997). *Employee assistance programmes and workplace counselling.* Toronto: John Wiley & Sons.

Csiernik, R. (2004). What to look for in an external EAP service. *Canadian HR Reporter, 18,* 7.

Csiernik, R. (2005). *Wellness and work: Employee assistance programming in Canada.* Toronto: Canadian Scholars' Press.

Fleming, C. W. (1979). Does social work have a future in industry? *Social Work, 24.5,* 183–85.

Foster, Z., Hirsch, S., & Zaske, K. (1991). Social work role in developing and managing employee assistance programs in health care settings. *Social Work in Health Care, 16.2,* 81–95.

Hartwell, T. D., Steele, P., et al. (1996). Aiding troubled employees: The prevalence, cost, and characteristics of employee assistance programs in the United States. *American Journal of Public Health, 86.6,* 804–08.

Health Canada. (1999). Influencing employee health. *Canadian Fitness and Lifestyle Research Institute, 1,* 2–9.

Health Canada. (2004). About Healthy Workplace. Retrieved January 28, 2006, from 222.nqi.ca/healthyworkplace.

Hockley, D. (1992). Assisting employees at B.C. Tel. *Canadian Business Review.* Ottawa: The Conference Board of Canada.

Kelloway, E. K. & Day, A. L. (2005). Building healthy workplaces: What we know so far. *Canadian Journal of Behavioural Science, 37,* 223–35.

Lowe, G. (2002). Here in body, absent in productivity: Presenteeism hurts output, quality of work-life and employee health. *Canadian HR Reporter, 15,* 5–8.

Macdonald, S., Csiernik, R., Durand, P., Rylett, M. & Wild, T. C. (2006). The prevalence and factors related to Canadian workplace health programs. *Canadian Journal of Public Health, 97(2),* 121–25.

McKibbon, D. (1993). EAPs in Canada: A panacea without definition. *Employee Assistance Quarterly, 8.3,* 11–29.

Massey, M. & Csiernik, R. (1997). Community development in EAP: The employee assistance program council of Hamilton-Wentworth. *Employee Assistance Quarterly, 12.3,* 35–46.

National Quality Institute. (2006). *About NQI.* Retrieved from www.nqi.ca/about.

Ozawa, M. N. (1980). Development of social services in industry: Why and how? *Social Work, 25.9,* 464–70.

Popple, P. R. (June 1981). Social work practice in business and industry, 1875–1930. *Social Service Review,* 257–69.

Rafter, M. V. (2004). EAPs tout the benefits of dial-up counselling in place of face-to-face. *Workforce Management, 83,* 75–77.

Ramanathan, C. S. (1992). EAPs response to personal stress and productivity: Implications for occupational social work. *Social Work, 37.3,* 234–39.

Reina, Dennis S., & Reina, Michelle Reina. (March/April 2004). Rebuilding employee trust during change. *Behavioural Health Management, 24.2.*

Ruiz, G. (2006). Expanded EAPs lend a hand to employers' bottom lines. *Workforce Management, 85,* 46–47.

Simson, S. (2004). Measuring the quality of an EAP. *Canadian HR Reporter, 18,* 8.

Solomon, R. M. & Usprich, S. (1993). *Consent, negligence and confidentiality: A legal primer for Canadian employee assistance programs.* Ottawa: Canadian Centre on Substance Abuse.

Stimson, J. (1990). *Employee and family assistance program and the assessment and referral service: "A successful model."* Canada: MacMillan Bloedel.

Vu, U. (2004). Solving the EAP puzzle. *Canadian HR Reporter, 18,* 5.

Wang, J. & Patten, S. B. (2001). Perceived work stress and major depression in the Canadian employed population, 20–49 years old. *Journal of Occupational Health Psychology, 6,* 283–289.

Warley, Raquel. (1st Quarter, 2004). Assessment in an EAP setting. *Journal of Employee Assistance, 34.1* (Arlington, VA).

Wirt, G. L. (1998). The ABCs of EAPs. *HR Focus, 75,* S12.

Wnek, I. (1991). *Employee assistance programs in Canada.* Alberta: Alberta Alcohol and Drug Abuse Commission.

# CHAPTER 16

# Canadian Approaches to Income Security

*John R. Graham*

## INTRODUCTION

Many people reading this textbook are considering careers in the helping professions. Of these, a substantial proportion probably hopes to provide direct services to clients. This chapter will be especially relevant to these readers, as well as to students interested in social policy analysis.

Economic need is one of the most pervasive issues to arise out of any helping encounter between a social worker and client. As Chapter 6 elaborates, before the development of a comprehensive welfare state in the 1940s and 1950s, Canadians who lived in poverty had few places to turn for help. They were expected to be self-reliant. If, however, they had to seek help from others, ordinarily they would go first to family, then to friends, and then to community institutions such as the church or a charity (Graham, 1992; Splane, 1965). When these resources were exhausted, the poor accessed "unemployment relief"—the precursor to contemporary social assistance (Graham, 1996; Struthers, 1983).

In today's world, a far more elaborate system of income security exists, encompassing all three levels of government in Canada—and hence different offices with which a social worker might be in contact—and applying to a wide spectrum of categories. Different income security programs have been designed for

- single-parent families (income support programs—the exact name varies by province);
- families with children (Canada Child Tax Benefit);
- individuals who have been unemployed for a long time (income support programs— the exact name varies by province);
- individuals who have recently lost their jobs (Employment Insurance);
- youths who do not live with parents or guardians (income support programs—the exact name varies by province);
- individuals who are injured in the workplace (Workers' Compensation);
- people with disabilities (income and health benefit programs—the exact name varies by province);
- the elderly (Canada Pension Plan, International Benefits, and Old Age Security—which includes the Guaranteed Income Supplement and Spousal Allowance programs; some provinces have top-up programs for the elderly poor);
- government-assisted refugees new to Canada (Resettlement Assistance Program);
- veterans of wars (War Veterans' Allowance); and
- other categories.

Social workers need comprehensive familiarity with this system in order to help their clients identify particular program(s) for which they are eligible and ensure their prompt and full access to these programs. Social workers' success in this task may prove crucially important to a client. It may make the difference, for example, between clients' going hungry or having food, being homeless or being able to find accommodation, feeling desperate or feeling hopeful, being trapped in poverty or having the means to improve their standard of living.

## POVERTY IN CANADA

Poverty is defined as having insufficient means of subsistence. There are two ways of thinking about poverty: in absolute and relative terms. *Absolute poverty* denotes a standard of living so low that a person cannot obtain adequate nutrition or shelter. Many homeless people in Canada may be described as living this way. One lives in *relative poverty*, in contrast, if one has insufficient means in relation to prevailing community standards. So, for example, individuals who have food to eat and a roof over their heads may still be defined as poor in relative terms (Graham, Swift, & Delaney, 2008). Notions of poverty in that sense necessarily vary from place to place and over time. In Northern Canada, as an example, possessing a warm winter coat is essential to survival and the lack of it aptly indicates poverty, whereas in a tropical climate a warm winter coat is not essential.

### Measures of Poverty

The measure of poverty is a systematic tool that enables determination of the level of income below which an individual or family is said to be living in poverty. One of the most frequently cited measures of poverty derives from the federal government's Statistics Canada: the "low income cut-off," or LICO.

The LICO is based on the share of income an average Canadian family devotes to food, clothing, and shelter—and hence assesses relative poverty by applying community standards to the prevailing benchmark—and then adds 20 percent to this amount. Any family that must spend more than this share of its income on such basic necessities is described as living in poverty (Ross, Scott, & Smith, 2000). Another measure of poverty is the "low income measure," or LIM. The LIM is equivalent to 50 percent of the median family income. Variations in the LIM are based on the quantity and age of members in a family (Statistics Canada Income Statistics Division, 2006). Other organizations have come up with measures of poverty that differ from the LICO and the LIM—either higher or lower; a number of reference sources delve into poverty-line distinctions in greater detail (National Council of Welfare, 1999; Ross, Shillington, & Lochhead, 1994).

A recent measure that is gaining prominence in poverty-related discussions is the Market Basket Measure (MBM). This measure differs from the LICO because it is based on the actual market costs of shelter, food, clothing and footwear, transportation, and other goods and services—such as hygiene products or furniture (Human Resources and Social Development Canada, 2006). It is an important measure within the discussion because it is calculable to a specific community, rather than being applicable to all Canadians. It also includes a wider scope of goods that have been deemed necessary for life; unlike for the LICO, transportation, furniture, and various other products are included when calculating the threshold between low income and income that is sufficient to meet one's individual and/or familial needs. All discussion in this chapter, however, will refer to the LICO, unless otherwise stated.

Four points are essential in any discussion of measures of poverty:

1. All measures of poverty are relative.

2. All measures of poverty are arbitrary.

3. Measures of poverty measure the incomes of *groups* of people and not individual need.

4. Any poverty line may be called into question because of points 1 to 3 above (National Council of Welfare, 1999).

## Who Is Poor?

Social programs in the post-World War II period gradually began to make progress against poverty, but over the past 30 years few new inroads have been made. Indeed, in 2004—the most recent year for which statistics are available (Figure 16.1)—11.7 percent of Canadians fell into a low-income category (Statistics Canada, 2007a)—compared to 15.7 percent in 1996 (Statistics Canada, 2006).

What factors contribute to poverty in Canada? One is the growing inability of provincial minimum wage levels to keep pace with inflation (Battle, 2003). As other chapters in this book point out, other issues associated with poverty are ideology, patriarchy, racism, and other structural matters. Overall, the rate of household poverty rose in the 1990s from levels in the 1980s and 1970s.

But one point cannot be overstated: different age cohorts are affected quite differently. Seventeen percent of seniors are thought to be poor today as opposed to rates of 30 percent in the 1980s (Hick, 2004). An appalling fact: many young Canadian families are likely to be poor. According to the 2001 Census, the poverty rate of lone-parent families with children passed the 50 percent mark for the first time in at least 20 years—a rate that most readers will agree is deeply troubling (Hick, 2004).

Child poverty rates continue to be a great concern; in 2004, the most recent date for which there are data, 865 000 children under the age of 18 were living in poverty (National Council of Welfare, 2006). This represents 12.8 percent of all Canadian children, a figure that still falls short of many advocates' demands for a total end to childhood poverty. Lone-parent families, particularly female-headed families, continue to be most vulnerable to poverty; in 2004, of the 550 000 lone-parent families headed by women in Canada, statistics showed a shocking 36 percent with low income.

Aboriginal peoples, minority peoples, and peoples with disabilities are also vulnerable to poverty, historically and presently (Ross, Scott, & Smith, 2000; Statistics Canada, 2002). Data collected during the 2001 Census illustrate that, based on the LICO measure, 38.0 percent of Aboriginal peoples and 38.0 percent of visible minorities, and based on the MBM, 35.8 percent of persons with disabilities were poor in 2000 (Human

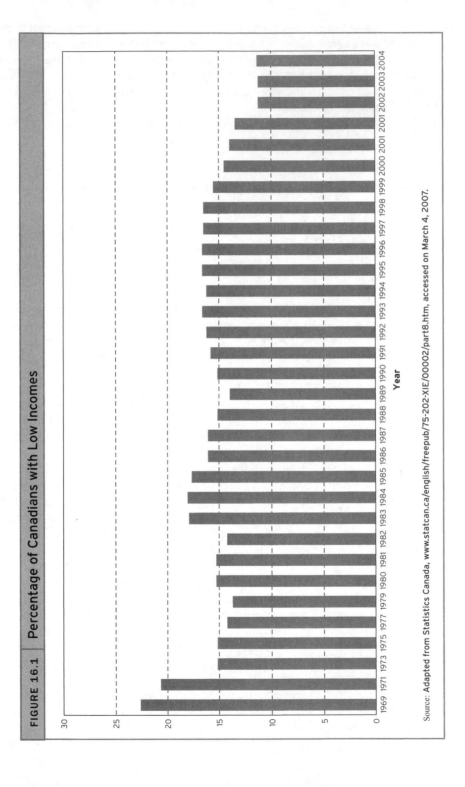

**FIGURE 16.1**   Percentage of Canadians with Low Incomes

Source: Adapted from Statistics Canada, www.statcan.ca/english/freepub/75-202-XIE/00002/part8.htm, accessed on March 4, 2007.

Resources and Social Development Canada, 2006; Statistics Canada, 2003). These rates are significantly higher than the 2002 national average, based on the Statistics Canada post-income tax LICO measure, of 11.6 percent (Human Resources and Social Development Canada, 2006). They are also high when compared to the national incidence of poverty, 13.7 percent, expressed by the 2002 MBM (Human Resources and Social Development Canada, 2006).

People's abilities to climb out of poorly paying jobs are limited; fewer than half of those Canadians with low-paying jobs in 1996 had jobs that were not low-paying five years later (Janz, 2004). At the same time, income inequality has increased in Canada, as it has in many other advanced industrialized countries (Morissette, Zhang, & Drolet, 2002). According to one report, the wealthiest 10 percent of Canadian families held 58 percent of the country's wealth in 2005, while the poorest 10 percent had average wealth in negative figures, or more debts than assets (Morissette & Zhang, 2006).

Chronological age (how old one is) and age cohort status (in what year/decade one was born) are among the myriad factors influencing wealth and poverty. Take the concept of median wealth, the midpoint of the income spectrum, the value compared to which half of the units in the population has lower incomes and half has higher incomes. Between 1984 and 2005, among families whose major income recipient was 25 to 34 years old, median wealth fell by 50 percent; in contrast, among those families whose major income recipient was at least 65 years old, median wealth increased 59 percent (Morissette & Zhang, 2006). The proportion of those with no financial wealth continues to increase in Canada. For all families, 24 percent have no financial wealth (such as a house as equity), an increase of 4.3 percent since 1999. A most appalling statistic is as follows: Canadian families headed by female lone parents have the least financial wealth as a population subgroup. Of all single parent families, both male and female headed, 40 percent are living in poverty (Morissette & Zhang, 2006). Home equity accounts for the largest determinant of financial wealth for families in Canada. With changes and restrictions to publicly based retirement income security programs such as the OAS, the federal government is encouraging people to deposit greater amounts of money into private Retirement Savings Plans. Research identifies that many of those families that do not have assets in retirement savings plans also do not own their own homes (Statistics Canada Pensions and Wealth Surveys Section, 2005).

Poverty was especially acute among families whose main income recipient was aged between 25 and 34 and had no university education, families whose major income recipient had a limitation of some kind regarding work, unattached individuals less than 65 years of age, and immigrant families who had been living in Canada for less than 10 years (Morissette, 2002).

## UNEMPLOYMENT IN CANADA

Unemployment remains a key cause of poverty in Canada, and the threat of unemployment is one of the continuing major risks of modern life. Many couples have both spouses in the workforce, while many other families are only a job loss away from poverty.

National jobless rates have increased gradually from 3.1 percent in the 1940s, to 5 percent in the 1960s, 6.7 percent in the 1970s, 9.3 percent in the 1980s, and an average of

9.8 percent in the 1990s. Average levels in the 1990s were the highest they had been since the Great Depression of the 1930s, when unemployment averaged 13 percent throughout that decade, peaking at 25 percent in 1933 (Graham, 1995; Torjman, 1998a; Torjman & Battle, 1999). Rates appear to have fallen modestly since then—from 11.3 percent in 1992 to 6.7 percent in January 2007 (Statistics Canada, 2007b). But these vary significantly by region, level of education, and other parameters.

Yet we cannot take these numbers at face value, for official unemployment rates do not include those unemployed Canadians so discouraged that they have given up searching for jobs. Nor do official numbers count the underemployed. Those who would like to work longer hours and can find only part-time employment, known as "involuntary part-timers," account for 25.8 percent of all part-time workers in Canada, a figure that is the third highest when compared to 17 other developed countries (Canadian Policy Research Network, 2006). Applying this figure to current labour market characteristics, relating to full- and part-time work, provides an estimate of 4.5 percent of all employment accounting for involuntary part-time work (Statistics Canada, 2007c). The prevalence of involuntary or voluntary part-time work in Canada highlights the reality that securing employment is no guarantee people will be able to financially support and provide for themselves and/or their families and essentially avoid poverty. Indeed, the number of working-poor households, those in which one or more income earners were employed for at least 40 weeks of a year, or 1500 hours of earnings, has been increasing since 1981 (see Ross, Scott, & Smith, 2000; Fleury & Fortin, 2006). The proportion of part-time workers in the labour force (voluntary and involuntary) has also been increasing, so that it now constitutes nearly 20 percent of today's workforce (Statistics Canada, 2007c). The number of people holding multiple jobs has also risen significantly; nine percent of Canadians can be so categorized (Shields & Wilkins, 2006).

Unemployment varies significantly by region. Levels are much higher in the Atlantic provinces and Quebec. In January 2007, as one example, unemployment in Newfoundland stood at 18.1 percent, in Prince Edward Island at 13.9 percent, in New Brunswick at 8.8 percent, in Nova Scotia at 8.9 percent, and in Quebec at 8.8 percent; Ontario, on the other hand, had levels of 6.6 percent, British Columbia had 4.8 percent, Manitoba had 5.1 percent, Alberta had 3.7 percent, and Saskatchewan had 4.6 percent (Statistics Canada, 2007b).

This chapter discusses income security programs, which are defined as social programs that provide cash payments to recipients. Income security programs provide individuals, or families, with money in a variety of circumstances. Some programs cover various social risks that preclude or limit employment, such as disability, poverty, sickness, or unemployment. Other programs provide money to individuals in various stages of life: for example, to the elderly, or to sole parents whose child-rearing responsibilities preclude their full employment.

## Selective Programs

There are two major forms of income security programs: *selective* and *universal*. Each carries its own assumptions. Selective programs have a long history, stretching back to Elizabethan poor relief in England, and were brought to Canada with European colonizers.

"Unemployment relief" was a selective program, as is its contemporary successor, general welfare assistance, also called "social assistance" or "a social allowance." A selective payment usually involves a transfer of money from a level of government to an individual.

Eligibility for selective programs is based on a means test. Social workers carry out means tests to evaluate, first, a person's financial resources—income, assets, debts, and other obligations—and, second, other criteria such as the applicant's number of dependants or level of health.

Selective programs are subject to several criticisms. They may personalize problems of poverty rather than focus attention on broader societal structures beyond an individual's control that may create the conditions for poverty. One such economic change would be the closing of a pulp-and-paper mill in a one-industry town, leading to loss of employment for the man applying to a selective program. Selective programs, likewise, may stigmatize people who, through factors outside their own immediate control, face a temporary or permanent loss of income.

These programs devote considerable administrative resources to monitoring the lives of individual clients rather than focusing on broader community and societal changes that might improve the clients' opportunities in life. Proponents, on the other hand, believe that selective programs are the most efficient means of targeting money to those in need. As well, means tests, some believe, may motivate—to others, coerce—recipients to return to the workforce.

## Universal Programs

Universal programs provide cash benefits to *all* the individuals in a society who fall into a certain category. They differ from selective programs in that eligibility to them is a right of citizenship, rather than a requirement that one prove personal eligibility through a means test.

The implications are many. A recipient's level of specific needs, or economic status, is not taken into account when determining eligibility. Where selective programs focus on an individual claimant's worthiness to receive benefits, universal programs operate under manifestly different assumptions. The state expresses a responsibility to provide income security for all citizens, and society implicitly recognizes the existence of conditions beyond an individual's control and that might impede one's economic well-being. Stigma has little place in a universal program, since all people, regardless of their levels of need, may have access to benefits as long as they fulfill eligibility conditions—such as being the required age in the case of Old Age Security.

While universal programs may target a greater amount of money to a greater number of people, including the well-to-do, many argue that the income tax system should counterbalance payments to the rich—and not the social program itself. In a progressive income tax system, the proportion of taxes one pays increases with earnings; those with a greater ability to pay more do so. In a regressive tax system, in contrast, taxes are not collected on an ability-to-pay basis.

Regressive and progressive are relative terms, and the most extreme instance of a regressive tax—such as a sales tax—is one levied equally on all.

How so? Whether a person paying a sales tax is below the poverty line or is the president of a major bank, the sales tax charged remains the same percentage for each. Canada's tax system is somewhat—although far from completely—progressive. Thus, higher income earners pay a greater proportion of their money as income tax than do those in the lower income categories. The argument may be made that universal programs do not wrongfully direct monies to the better-off, given the existence (or potential existence) of a progressive income tax system (Muszynski, 1987). What is more, with everyone receiving benefits from a universal program, some argue that the middle and upper classes are politically co-opted into supporting the program, and so the benefits are less likely to be reduced in scope or eligibility than they would be in a selective program geared only towards the less politically powerful poor (Titmuss, 1958, 1987).

Universal programs came to the fore during World War II. But their presence has been systematically eroded over the past 35 years as selective programs have found new favour. The reasons for this erosion are complex, and at least part of the explanation rests with the emergence of neo-conservative ideology.

## Demogrant, Social Assistance, Social Insurance

Several other terms are used to describe income security programs, so knowledge of them and their effective use is essential to social work practice.

A *demogrant* is a cash payment to an individual or family based on a demographic characteristic (usually age) as opposed to need; one example is Old Age Security.

*Social assistance* refers to selective income-security programs that apply a means or needs test to determine eligibility; these are often administered at the provincial or local government level, depending on the province.

*Social insurance* refers to income security programs in which eligibility for benefits is determined by a person's previous record of contribution and in the event of a particular contingency, such as unemployment, retirement, injury, or widowhood. Examples of these include the Canada Pension Plan and Employment Insurance (Armitage, 1996).

## Government Jurisdiction

Sections 91 and 92 of the Canadian Constitution, which define federal and provincial government jurisdictions, allocate responsibility for social welfare to the provinces. Hence, many income security programs are administered at this level of government. But federal government participation has been equally important, since this jurisdiction has the greatest capacity to generate revenue, through income tax, tariffs, and corporate taxes.

Ottawa provides funding for the cost-sharing of major social programs, which the provinces deliver under the Canada Assistance Plan (1966–1996) and its successors, the Canadian Health and Social Transfer (1996–2004), which has been split into the Canada Health Transfer (CHT, 2004) and the Canada Social Transfer (CST, 2004). Other social programs, as will be elaborated, have also emerged at the federal government level, and some, such as Employment Insurance, through constitutional changes.

Municipal governments, considered "creatures of the provinces," have limited constitutional jurisdiction and can be created or disbanded at the will of a provincial government. For centuries, social welfare in England, and then in Canada, came under the jurisdiction of local government. This explains why, in some provinces, programs such as general welfare assistance (a specific example of social assistance) have continued to be partially funded and entirely administered by local governments.

**The Canada Health and Social Transfers (CHT and CST, 2004)** Perhaps the apex of the creation of a universal welfare state in Canada was the Canada Assistance Plan introduced in 1966 (CAP, 1966–1996). The CAP was a funding agreement that enabled the federal government to cost-share with the provinces those constitutionally prescribed provincial responsibilities for the delivery of education, health, and social service commitments. The CAP was a landmark social policy, allowing the federal government to ensure minimum standards of service delivery, relatively equal standards of services across the provinces, and a reliable funding base to achieve these ends.

The CAP started to unravel in the mid-1970s as changes in cost-sharing arrangements eroded the amount of money transferred to provinces. By 1992–1993, the federal share of CAP transfers to the country's three wealthiest provinces was down to 28 percent in Ontario and 36 percent in British Columbia and Alberta (National Council of Welfare, 1995). The CAP had ceased to be a 50-50 cost-shared relationship. Many provinces, in turn, downloaded significant financial responsibilities of their own onto local governments for funding and delivering social service programs such as social assistance, supported housing, home care, daycare, and other services.

Those who know this history appreciate that local governments were responsible for funding and delivering most Canadian social programs until the end of the 1930s. During the Great Depression of that decade, many local governments went bankrupt and most could no longer afford the costs of delivering the programs, a significant precedent set in the wartime creation of a comprehensive welfare state.

Ironically, few proponents of municipal downloading appreciate why service funding and delivery were uploaded to higher levels of government some 75 years ago. As part of this downloading process, none consider expanding municipal fiscal capacity, which is based entirely on the property tax and hence is very limited and restrictive (Graham, 1995).

The CHST, which replaced the CAP in 1996, resulted in a 15 percent decrease in federal transfers to provinces intended for health, post-secondary education, and social services over the previous two years (Scott, 1998). The provinces, for their part, reduced benefit rates for social assistance and other programs. The CHST has also removed enforceable federal government standards, so the provinces are now free to allocate the money they receive in whatever ways they wish—even if this means substantially reducing program entitlements and restricting eligibility and access.

One of the country's foremost social policy think-tanks, the Caledon Institute of Social Policy (CISP), contends that this change in enforceability "constitutes one of the worst mistakes in the history of our social security system." It turns back "the social policy clock" to a period of minimal standards and far greater risks for society's most vulnerable (Torjman & Battle, 1995a, p. 5). "There will be no guarantee of a safety net in the country," a second CISP document points out (Torjman & Battle, 1995b, p. 2). This one piece of legislation—that passed in the federal House of Commons in 1995 and that created the CHST—highlights the profound significance of social policy in directing social work practice and affecting the lives of many social work clients.

The 2004 split of the CHST created two new entities: the Canada Health Transfer (CHT) and the Canada Social Transfer (CST). The CST is a federal block transfer to the provinces and territories in support of post-secondary education, social assistance, and social services, including early childhood development and early learning and child care. The CHT is the primary federal transfer to the provinces and territories in support of health care.

Progressive social-policy research organizations such as the Canadian Council on Social Development (CCSD) are concerned that the CST will perpetuate the under-funding of social and education programs in Canada. It proposes improved federal government funding, mechanisms to evaluate outcomes, and, to that end, the further splitting of the CST into programs for social welfare and post-secondary education, respectively (CCSD, 2004). Furthermore, the CCSD has also identified the need to generate an improved sense of accountability within the federal government for the promotion and implementation of social programs in Canada. This would include the creation of a national agenda and the use of specific measures to evaluate program outcomes (CCSD, 2005)—all of which act as critical components that have long since been lost with the initial demise of the Canada Assistance Plan.

## MAJOR INCOME SECURITY PROGRAMS IN CANADA

Several levels of government deliver income security programs. They constitute part, but not the whole, of transfers to persons and transfers to the governments, as shown in Table 16.1. The following program descriptions are deliberately succinct and simplified, covering major aspects of eligibility and benefits while omitting minor details that are too numerous to discuss here. More comprehensive analyses can be found in other sources (see Durst, 1999; Guest, 1997; McGilly, 1998).

### Federal Government Programs

**Employment Insurance (EI, 1996–)** This was previously known as Unemployment Insurance (1940–1996). There are three ways to obtain EI: loss of job through termination, temporary disruption of work because of illness, and application for maternity/parental benefits. EI is based now on the number of hours, rather than weeks, worked—which is a fairer practice for part-time workers and those holding several jobs.

| TABLE 16.1 | Federal Government Select Expenditures, 2005–2007 | | |
|---|---|---|---|
| Expenditures | Actual | Estimate | Projections |
| ($Billions) | 2004–2005 | 2005–2006 | 2006–2007 |
| Transfers to persons | 51.3 | 53.2 | 56.3 |
| Transfers to governments | 42.0 | 40.9 | 40.1 |
| Direct program spending | 83.1 | 85.2 | 92.4 |
| Total program expenses | 176.3 | 179.2 | 188.8 |

Source: Department of Finance, *The Budget Plan 2006: How the budget breaks down government expenses,* http://www.oag-bvg.gc.ca/domino/reports.nsf/html/20061100xe04.html

The entrance requirements have become more stringent over the past 15 years but continue to vary depending on the job type and the rate of unemployment in the region where the claimant lives. For example, in areas with high unemployment (above 13 percent), a claimant must prove work for a minimum of 420 hours, whereas in places of low unemployment (less than 6 percent), he or she must prove 700 hours of work to be eligible to apply (Human Resources and Social Development Canada, 2007). In some further cases an individual may have to acquire a total of 910 hours if that individual was in the workforce for the first time or returning after a two-year absence (Service Canada, 2007).

A May 2004 report indicates that only 42 percent of Canada's jobless received benefits the previous year, owing to increasingly severe restrictions on eligibility (Human Resources and Skills Development Canada, 2004). Many people fall through the cracks because, for example, they were not in the workforce long enough to be eligible for the program, did not work enough hours, or their EI benefits ran out (Human Resources and Skills Development Canada, 2002). Most recipients receive up to 55 percent of their average weekly-insured earnings, the result of incremental drops in entitlement from as high as 64 percent of working wages in the 1970s (Battle, 2002).

As of January 2007, the maximum benefits payment is $423 per week. The program used to be funded by the federal government, the employer, and the employee; now it is funded only by employer and employee contributions. Further, restrictions—with regard to the length of time during which an individual can receive benefits—exist that are geographically specific. The length of time a claimant can receive employment insurance ranges from 36 to 45 weeks. Also, those claimants that can be covered for 45 weeks live in economic regions where the minimum requirements for accrued hours of work is less than those claimants covered for the mere 36-week period (Human Resources and Social Development Canada, 2007).

**Canada Pension Plan/Quebec Pension Plan (CPP/QPP, 1966–)** The Canada Pension Plan and the Quebec Pension Plan are insurance plans to which people must contribute during their working years. Both were created the same year and are similar in design; the QPP is administered by the Quebec provincial government and is solely for those working in that province, and the CPP is administered by the federal government and is for those in all provinces other than Quebec. CPP and QPP also comprise survivors' pensions for the spouses of deceased pensioners, disability pensions, and children's and death benefits. Eligibility is based on past contributions to the plan.

In instances of retirement (as distinct from disability or a spouse's death), it is paid to contributing claimants older than age 60 and is intended to replace about 25 percent of the income the claimant paid into the plans. As of January 2007, maximum benefits are $863.75 per month for retirement payment, $1053.77 for disability payments, $518.25 for spousal survivor payments (ages 65 or older), and $204.68 for children's survivor payments.

Employer and employee contributions fund the programs. These contribution rates were low and level from 1966 to 1986, and have risen gradually since that time. Over the next two decades, they are expected to nearly double (Battle, 1997). The plans are considered social insurance.

**Old Age Security (OAS, 1952–)** The Old Age Security pension is a monthly benefit for people 65 years of age or older. It originated in 1927 as a selective, means-tested program and was transformed into a universal program in 1952. As a universal program, employment history does not play a part in eligibility, and a claimant need not be retired to be eligible.

Those on OAS pensions are subject to federal and provincial income tax on their incomes. Those with higher incomes also repay part or all of their benefits through the tax system (Government of Canada, 1999).

Some argue that OAS ceases to be a universal program owing to this so-called claw-back of the benefits of higher-income-earning Canadians through the income tax system. It precludes many people from full entitlement and a substantial number from ever receiving any compensation. Moreover, clawback amounts have systematically increased since the late 1980s.

As of January 2007, the maximum benefits are $491.93 per month. The program is financed from federal government general tax revenues and is considered a demogrant.

**Guaranteed Income Supplement (GIS, 1967–)** The GIS was established to supplement the earnings of low-income OAS recipients. It is administered under the OAS program. Eligibility is determined by need and may increase or decrease according to the claimant's overall yearly income.

As of January 2007, maximum benefits are $620.91 per month for a single applicant, and $410.04 for the spouse of an applicant. The federal government's general tax revenues fund the program and it is considered social insurance.

**Spouse's Allowance (SPA, 1976–)** The Spouse's Allowance was established to provide income to the spouse of an OAS pensioner, either a widow or a widower. Like the GIS, eligibility is based on need, and the allowance is provided only to those within certain income limits. The SPA stops when the recipient turns 65 and becomes eligible for the OAS, or when the recipient moves out of the country or dies.

Maximum benefits as of January 2007 are $901.97 per month for a beneficiary married to an OAS pensioner, and $999.81 for those widowed from a former OAS pensioner. The federal government's general tax revenues fund the program and it is considered social insurance.

**Veterans' Pensions (VP, 1919–)** Those members of the armed forces who incur disabilities during wartime (Active Force), peacetime (Special Duty Area), or other service are eligible for the VP. The amount of pension is determined by degree of disability, and varies accordingly; maximum rates as of January 2007 are $2221.08 for the pensioner and $555.27 for spousal recipients per month. The program is funded from federal government general tax revenues and is considered a demogrant.

**War Veterans' Allowances (WVA, 1930–, with origins in World War I)** This income-related program ensures a minimum annual income for wartime service veterans who served in World War I, World War II, or the Korean War. Eligibility is based on financial and service eligibility and age, with a minimum qualifying age of 60 for a man and 55 for a woman. Survivors' allowances are also available.

As of June 2006, maximum benefits are $1176.50 per month for single claimants, and $1787.95 for those living with a spouse and/or with one child. This program is funded from federal government general tax revenues and is considered a form of social assistance.

**Resettlement Assistance Program (RAP, 1998–)** Administered by the Ministry of Citizenship and Immigration (MCI), the Resettlement Assistance Program (RAP) provides various supportive services, as well as financial assistance for up to one year after the recipient's arrival, to government-assisted refugees arriving in Canada. In many instances, funding may also be provided via cost-sharing sponsorship agreements between MCI and sponsorship agreement holders at the local, regional, and national levels.

As Chapter 10 explains, almost all newcomers to Canada are independent-class immigrants or sponsored by others, such as Canadian family members. A small proportion are Convention refugees, defined as having "a well-founded fear of persecution in his or her country of origin because of race, religion, nationality, membership in a social group, or political opinion" (Government of Canada, 2007). The RAP is only for refugee-class immigrants.

Benefit levels are usually identical to provincial social-assistance rates and are intended to provide necessary resources for food, shelter, and clothing, and to provide an opportunity for the immigrant to enrol in language classes and obtain a job.

The RAP emerged out of what used to be called the Adjustment Assistance Program, which originated during World War II. It parallels the Immigrant Loans Program, also intended to assist recipients in their resettlement process. Local, regional, and national immigration-service organizations provide hands-on transition assistance in a refugee's attainment of housing, education, employment, and other services; the RAP is delivered in collaboration with these organizations. The program is funded from federal government general tax revenues and is considered a form of social assistance.

**Canada Child Tax Benefit, (1998–)** This tax benefit is made up of three parts: (1) the Canada Child Tax Benefit (CCTB), a tax-free monthly payment made to eligible families to assist with the cost of rearing children under the age of 18; (2) the National Child Benefit Supplement (NCBS), a monthly benefit for low-income families with children created through the National Child Benefit (NCB), the joint federal-provincial initiative; and (3) the Child Disability Benefit, a tax-free benefit for families caring for a child under 18 with a severe or prolonged mental or physical disability (Canada Revenue Agency, 2007). The benefits are usually paid to the mother of the child if the child lives with her.

The amount differs according to family income, number of children, and their ages. The CCTB is tax-free, and in all provinces except for Alberta may be as much as $3199.92 per child per year (in Alberta, payments are less when the children are younger and more when they are older, but are intended to average out over 18 years to be equivalent to payments in other provinces). As of January 2007, the supplement annually provides $162.08 monthly for the first child and $143.33 for the second in families whose yearly income is less than $20 435.

The CCTB and its predecessor, the Child Benefit, replaced the following three things: the Family Allowance (1944–1992)—a universal demogrant form of income security provided to all mothers of children under the age of 18—and refundable and non-refundable tax credits. The CCTB is considered a form of social assistance. It is an excellent example of a formerly universal program (the Family Allowance) that has been replaced by a selective/income-tested program (the CCTB). Many commentators criticize the program for providing inadequate benefits in light of pervasive child poverty (Freiler & Cerny, 1998).

## Provincial Government Programs

**Workers' Compensation (WC, 1914–)** Workers' Compensation is designed to make payments and cover rehabilitation and medical costs for those workers who have been injured on the job. In the case of workplace death, it also provides payments to an employee's survivors.

It was first introduced in Ontario and subsequently spread to other provinces. Assistance levels vary from province to province. Eligibility criteria are stricter now than in the past, and benefits have been reduced in scope.

In Alberta, benefits as of 2005 are 90 percent of net income up to $62 600 (Government of Alberta, 2007), and in Ontario, 85 percent of net income up to $71 800 (Government of Ontario, 2007). In other provinces, benefits may be as low as 75 percent, but the maximum net may be larger than the case of, say, Ontario's (McGilly, 1998). The program is funded by worker and employee contributions and is considered a form of social insurance.

**Social Assistance (SA, Various Years)** Social assistance, often called welfare or public assistance, helps people in need who are not eligible for other benefits, and is one of the most important income security programs with which a social worker should be familiar. It is typically delivered to three broad categories of people: (1) families with dependent children in need (often long-term need); (2) individuals with disabilities (often long-term need); and (3) individuals or families in short-term need. These three programs may have different names and may be administered out of different offices. The last category mentioned—intended for short-term assistance—is seen as an income program of last resort. Benefit payments help pay for food, shelter, fuel, clothing, prescription drugs, and other health services.

Eligibility rules and the amounts of payment differ from province to province; for example, in some provinces, the municipalities continue to administer and/or partially fund programs. Especially in short-term need assistance, means tests tend to prevail. Applicants must be of a certain age, usually between 18 and 65, but some provinces have provisions for minors under the age of 18 not living with a legal parent or guardian. Full-time students of post-secondary education, under certain circumstances, may be eligible for assistance in some provinces but not in others. Single parents must try to secure court-ordered maintenance support to which they are entitled. Those on strike are usually not eligible for assistance, nor are sponsored refugees or sponsored family-class immigrants during their period of sponsorship.

In general, social assistance is granted if a household's net assets are less than the cost of regularly recurring basic needs for food, shelter, and other necessities. Fixed and liquid assets are usually examined, and most provinces exempt the value of a car, a principal residence, furniture, and clothing. In most provinces, other assets—cash, bonds, securities that are readily convertible to cash, the value of life insurance—are limited by household size and employability. Applicants are usually required to convert non-exempt fixed assets into liquid assets and deplete those assets before qualifying for welfare (National Council of Welfare, 1997–1998).

Benefit rates fall well below LICO measures of poverty, as indicated in Table 16.2. Definitions of eligibility, and benefit rates, have also tightened in recent years (National Council of Welfare, 2004). During its first term in administration, for example, Ontario's Progressive Conservative government in 1995 slashed social assistance by a remarkable 21

| TABLE 16.2 | Social Assistance Benefits for Select Provinces, 2005 | | | |
|---|---|---|---|---|
| Family Type | Total Welfare Income | Poverty Line | Poverty Gap | Total as % of Poverty Line |
| **Newfoundland & Labrador** | | | | |
| Single Employable | $8198 | $17 895 | $-9697 | 46% |
| Person with a Disability | $9728 | $17 895 | $-8167 | 54% |
| Single Parent, One Child | $16 181 | $22 276 | $-6095 | 73% |
| Couple, Two Children | $19 578 | $33 251 | $-13 673 | 59% |
| **Quebec** | | | | |
| Single Employable | $6947 | $20 778 | $-13 831 | 33% |
| Person with a Disability | $10 063 | $20 778 | $-10 715 | 48% |
| Single Parent, One Child | $15 395 | $25 867 | $-10 472 | 60% |
| Couple, Two Children | $20 704 | $39 610 | $-17 906 | 54% |
| **Ontario** | | | | |
| Single Employable | $7007 | $20 778 | $-13 771 | 34% |
| Person with a Disability | $12 057 | $20 778 | $-8721 | 58% |
| Single Parent, One Child | $14 451 | $25 867 | $-11 416 | 56% |
| Couple, Iwo Children | $19 302 | $38 610 | $-19 308 | 50% |
| **Alberta** | | | | |
| Single Employable | $5050 | $20 778 | $-15 728 | 24% |
| Person with a Disability | $7851 | $20 778 | $-12 927 | 38% |
| Single Parent, One Child | $12 326 | $25 867 | $-13 541 | 48% |
| Couple, Two Children | $19 497 | $38 610 | $-19 113 | 50% |
| **British Columbia** | | | | |
| Single Employable | $6456 | $20 778 | $-14 322 | 31% |
| Person with a Disability | $10 656 | $20 778 | $-10 122 | 51% |
| Single Parent, One Child | $13 948 | $25 867 | $-11 919 | 54% |
| Couple, Two Children | $18 466 | $38 610 | $-20 144 | 48% |

Source: Adapted from National Council of Welfare, *Welfare Incomes 2005*. www.ncwcnbes.net/documents/researchpublications/ResearchProjects/WelfareIncomes/2005Report_Summer2006/ReportENG.pdf

percent. Workfare has also been introduced in some instances—where recipients are expected to undergo training programs and/or other forms of work-related activities in return for benefits, and some provinces are exploring the introduction of a lifetime maximum for which people may receive some forms of social assistance.

The program is funded by federal and provincial monies under the CST, and in some instances partially by municipal governments. It should also be noted that funding arrangements with the federal Department of Indian and Northern Affairs pay for the delivery of social assistance programs in Aboriginal reserves; benefit rates and eligibility criteria are almost always identical to the prevailing provincial rates and criteria.

As the Caledon Institute of Social Policy points out, it may be wiser to approach social assistance as a human resource strategy issue rather than as workfare (Torjman,

1996a). Workfare implies compulsory labour and mandatory participation in designated activities. A human resource strategy, in contrast to workfare, is voluntary. Ideally, numerous stakeholders can collaborate in both—industries, educators, social welfare, and justice. Both also are supposed to provide a range of options including job search, academic upgrading, skills training, and employment creation, but some argue that workfare emphasizes these less. A human resource strategy "also ensures" more explicitly "that appropriate supports are in place—notably, high-quality, affordable child care and transportation subsidies—so that recipients can move off welfare" (Torjman, 1996a, p. 1). Finally, and perhaps most importantly, a human resource strategy promotes, rather than destroys, human dignity and well-being.

Some provincial governments have sought to revise their social assistance programs previously targeted for children and families and align these with the federal CCTB. British Columbia was the first to consider a federally–provincially integrated child benefits system payable to low-income families with children, and other provinces such as Saskatchewan, Quebec, and New Brunswick are doing the same (Battle & Mendelson, 1997). Earnings supplement programs for working-poor families are also available in several provinces.

**Provincial Top-Ups for the Elderly (Various Years)** The combined OAS and GIS supplements are low enough to qualify most elderly couples in most provinces for social assistance. To avoid having elderly SA recipients, some provincially administered income-supplement programs have been introduced.

Benefit rates vary from province to province, and are intended to raise incomes of recipients to roughly the income levels of public assistance recipients. For example, the Saskatchewan Income Plan provides a maximum of $90 per month to a single claimant and $72.50 to one who is married (Government of Saskatchewan, 2007). The Ontario Guaranteed Annual Income System (GAINS) provides a maximum of $83 per month (Government of Ontario, 2007). Some other provinces have no such equivalent programs. Provincial top-ups for the elderly are selective social assistance programs, funded jointly by federal and provincial monies under the CST.

## CONCLUSION: DIRECTIONS FOR TOMORROW

Income security policies work best when they are applied collaboratively with other social and economic policies, and when they are successful at addressing categories of people who are most in need.

The disgraceful incidences of poverty among Aboriginal peoples, children, persons with disabilities, and women, among other social groups, ought to compel more comprehensive and successful policy responses. Disability pensions within the CPP, for example, have been criticized for not allowing beneficiaries who can work irregularly or part-time to do so—unless they are willing to forfeit all their benefits (Torjman, 1997). Some likewise argue that social assistance programs should be designed to provide income top-ups to low-income labourers, and that social programs should provide special transportation, child care, and other supports necessary to full and vital functioning in and beyond the workplace (Torjman, 1996a, 1996b, 1997, 1998a, 1998b, 1999).

So too might policies be delivered in ways that more sensitively appreciate people's diverse positions in terms of the basis of age, ethnicity, gender, geography, race, religion, and range of ability, among other parameters. In 2002, low-income rates of immigrants during their first full year in Canada were 3.5 times that of the Canadian-born, and were 3.2 times greater in 2004. A similar, disturbing trend of higher rates of poverty compared with national averages is observed among all immigrants in Canada who have been in the country for ten years or less (Picot, Hou, & Coulombe, 2007). The implications are considerable. People new to Canada may have little appreciation of, or experience with, a welfare state and may require especially skilful and competent social work assistance to help them gain access to its income security programs. As well, there are some profound and troubling questions regarding immigrant peoples' full access to labour markets (Galabuzi, 2006).

More generally, income security policies are thought to reflect the national will. On the surface, this appears to be self-evident, and certainly plausible, yet as a growing body of policy literature points out, the forces of globalization are calling into question the limits of the state (Graham, Swift, & Delaney, 2008). As companies compete in an increasingly international marketplace, the demands on national governments to restrict their welfare states may grow. Some corporate leaders seek minimalist tax structures and minimal corporate contributions to income security, health insurance, and other forms of publicly administered programs. We in Canada are also prone to the assumption of American values in virtually all we think and do (Grant, 1965, 1969). Given the growing presence of American political culture in Canada, in part reinforced by the North American Free Trade Agreement, Canadian politicians have looked south of the forty-ninth parallel for political precedents. Many analysts are struck by the strongly American influences in contemporary Canadian social welfare retrenchment and workfare (Torjman, 1997, 1998b).

By virtue of its geography, Canadians have always appreciated the necessities of survival and of caring for one another to that end. The state has been an important instrument in Canadian history, expressed in the pragmatic conservativism of Sir John A. Macdonald's nineteenth-century national policy of tariffs and westward settlement, in the Tory and social democratic ideologies that have distinguished our political life from that of the United States, and in the welfare state of the twentieth century. The choices we make in the twenty-first century cannot help but refer to what has come before. These choices could also reflect what we agree as a society should be our destiny. But will they?

# References

Battle, K. (1997). *Targeted tax relief.* Ottawa: Caledon Institute of Social Policy.

Battle, K. (2002). *Social policy that works: An agenda.* Ottawa: Caledon Institute of Social Policy.

Battle, K. (2003). *Minimum wages in Canada: A statistical portrait with policy implications.* Ottawa: Caledon Institute of Social Policy.

Battle, K., & Mendelson, M. (1997). *Child benefit reform in Canada: An evaluative framework and future directions.* Ottawa: Caledon Institute of Social Policy.

Caledon Institute of Social Policy. (1996). *Roundtable on Canada's aging society and retirement income system.* Ottawa: Caledon Institute of Social Policy.

Canadian Council on Social Development. (2001). *Canadian welfare incomes as a percentage of the poverty line by family type and province, 2001.* Accessed at www.ccsd.ca/factsheets/fs_newpl01.htm

Canadian Council on Social Development. (2004). *What kind of Canada? A call for a national debate on the Canada Social Transfer.* Ottawa: CCSD.

Canadian Council on Social Development. (2005). *Canada failing to stop child poverty.* Ottawa: CCSD Media. Retrieved March 7, 2007, from: www.ccsd.ca/media/2005/cpprairies.htm

Canadian Policy Research Network. (2006). International comparisons of job quality: Incidence of involuntary part-time employment. Online Publication: Work Network of Canadian Policy Research Network. Retrieved March 30, 2007, from: http://www.jobquality.ca/indicator_e/security001.stm

Canada Revenue Agency (2007). *Canada Child Tax Benefit.* Ottawa: Author. Retrieved May 15, 2007, from: www.cra-arc.gc.ca/benefits/cctb/menu-e.html

Department of Finance. (2006). *The Budget Plan 2006: How the budget breaks down government expenses.* Accessed at www.oag-bvg.gc.ca/domino/reports.nsf/html/20061100xe04.html

Durst, D. (Ed.). (1999). *Canada's national child benefit: Phoenix or fizzle?* Halifax: Fernwood.

Fleury, D., & Fortin, M. (2006). *When working is not enough to escape poverty: An analysis of Canada's working poor.* Ottawa: Human Resources and Social Development Canada.

Freiler, C., & Cerny, J. (1998). *Benefiting Canada's children: Perspectives on gender and social responsibility.* Ottawa: Status of Women Canada.

Galabuzi, G. E. (2006). *Canada's economic apartheid: The social exclusion of racialized groups in the new century.* Toronto: Canadian Scholars' Press.

Government of Alberta. (2007). *Alberta Workers' Compensation Board.* Accessed at www.wcb.ab.ca/pdfs/wage_loss.pdf.

Government of Canada. (1999). Human Resources and Development Canada Web site. Accessed at www.hrdc-drhc.gc.ca

Government of Canada. (2007). Citizenship and Immigration Canada Web site. Accessed at www.cic.gc.ca/english/refugees/asylum-1.html#convention

Government of Ontario. (2007). *Ontario workplace safety and insurance board.* Accessed at www.wsib.on.ca/wsib/wsibsite.nsf/public/BenefitsLOE

Government of Ontario. (2007). *Ontario guaranteed annual income system (GAINS).* Accessed at www.trd.fin.gov.on.ca/English/tax/credit/gains

Government of Saskatchewan. (2007). *Saskatchewan income plan.* Accessed at www.dcre.gov.sk.ca/financial/SIPoverview.html

Graham, J. R. (1992). The Haven, 1878–1930: A Toronto charity's transition from a religious to a professional ethos. *Histoire Sociale/Social History, 25.50,* 283–306.

Graham, J. R. (1995). Lessons for today: Canadian municipalities and unemployment relief during the 1930s Great Depression. *Canadian Review of Social Policy, 35,* 1–18.

Graham, J. R. (1996). An analysis of Canadian social welfare historical writing. *Social Service Review, 70.1.,* 140–158.

Graham, J. R., Swift, K., & Delaney, R. (2008). *Canadian social policy: An introduction* (3rd ed.). Toronto: Allyn and Bacon.

Grant, G. (1965). *Lament for a nation: The defeat of Canadian nationalism.* Toronto: Anansi.

Grant, G. (1969). *Technology and empire: Perspectives on North America.* Toronto: Anansi.

Guest, D. (1997). *The emergence of social security in Canada* (3rd ed.). Vancouver: University of British Columbia Press.

Hick, S. (2004). *Social welfare in Canada: Understanding income security.* Toronto: Thompson Educational Publishing.

Human Resources and Skills Development Canada. (2002). *The employment insurance coverage survey.* Ottawa: Human Resources Development Canada.

Human Resources and Skills Development Canada. (2004). *Employment insurance and regular benefits.* Accessed at www.hrsdc.gc

Human Resources and Social Development Canada. (2007). Employment Insurance Program Characteristics. Ottawa: Author. Retrieved March 29, 2007, from: http://srv200.services.gc.ca/iiws/eiregions/geocont.aspx

Human Resources and Social Development Canada. (2006). *Low income in Canada: 2000–2002 Using the Market Basket Measure.* Ottawa: Author. Retrieved March 7, 2007, from: www.hrsdc.gc.ca/en/cs/sp/sdc/pkrf/publications/research/2002-000662/SP-628-05-06e.pdf

Janz, T. (2004). *Low-paid employment and moving up.* Ottawa: Statistics Canada.

McGilly, F. (1998). *An introduction to Canada's public social services.* Don Mills, ON: Oxford University Press.

Morissette, R. (2002). On the edge: Financially vulnerable families. *Canadian Social Trends, 67,* 13–17.

Morissette, R., & Zhang, X. (2006). Revisiting wealth inequality. *Perspectives on Labour and Income,* vol. 7, no 12, December. Statistics Canada Catalogue no. 75-001-XIE.

Morissette, R., Zhang, X., & Drolet, M. (2002). Wealth inequality. *Perspectives on Labour and Income,* vol. 3, no. 2, February. Statistics Canada Catalogue no. 75-001-XIE.

Muszynski, L. (1987). *Is it fair? What tax reform will do to you.* Ottawa: Canadian Centre for Policy Alternatives.

National Council of Welfare. (1995). *The 1995 budget and block funding.* Ottawa: National Council of Welfare.

National Council of Welfare. (1997–1998). *Welfare incomes 1996.* Ottawa: National Council of Welfare.

National Council of Welfare. (1999). *A new poverty line: Yes, no, or maybe?* Ottawa: National Council of Welfare.

National Council of Welfare. (2006). *Welfare incomes 2005.* Vol 119. Ottawa: National Council of Welfare. Accessed at www.ncwcnbes.net/htmdocument/reportWelfareIncomes2005/WI2005EN Grevised.pdf

National Council of Welfare. (2004). *Income for living?* Vol. 120. Ottawa: National Council of Welfare.

Picot, G., Hou, F., & Coulombe, S. (2007) *Chronic low income and low-income dynamics among recent immigrants.* Catalogue no. 11F0019MIE — No. 294. Ottawa: Statistics Canada.

Ross, D. P., & Lochhead, C. (1998). Poverty. In *1998 Canadian Encyclopedia CD ROM.* Toronto: McClelland & Stewart.

Ross, D. P., Scott, K. J., & Smith, P. J. (2000). *Canadian Fact Book on Poverty – 2000.* Ottawa: Canadian Council on Social Development.

Scott, K. (1998). *Women and the CHST: A profile of women receiving social assistance in 1994.* Ottawa: Status of Women, Canada.

Service Canada. (2007). *Employment insurance and regular benefits.* Ottawa: Author. Retrieved March 7, 2007, from: www1.servicecanada.gc.ca/en/ei/types/regular.shtml#Qualifying

Shields, M., & Wilkins, K. (2006). *Findings from the 2005 National Survey of the Work and Health of Nurses.* Ottawa: Statistics Canada, Health Canada, and the Canadian Institute of Health Research.

Splane, R. B. (1965). *Social welfare in Ontario, 1791–1893: A study of public welfare administra-tion.* Toronto: University of Toronto Press.

Statistics Canada. (2002). *Analysis of income in Canada.* Ottawa: Statistics Canada. Accessed at www.statcan.ca/english/freepub/75-203-XIE/00002/part8.htm

Statistics Canada. (December 16, 2003). Total Income Groups in Constant (2000) Dollars, file no. 97F0020XCB2001073. Ottawa: Author. Retrieved March 29, 2007 from: www12.statcan. ca/english/census01/products/standard/themes/RetrieveProductTable.cfm?Temporal=2001&PID =60960&APATH=3&GID=355313&METH=1&PTYPE=55496&THEME=54&FOCUS=0&A ID=0&PLACENAME=0&PROVINCE=0&SEARCH=0&GC=99&GK=NA&VID=0&VNAM EE=&VNAMEF=&FL=0&RL=0&FREE=0

Statistics Canada. (2004). *CANSIM Table 202-0102—Average earnings by sex and work pattern.* Ottawa: Statistics Canada.

Statistics Canada Pensions and Wealth Surveys Section. (2005). *The wealth of Canadians: An overview of the results of the survey of financial wealth.* Ottawa: Author. Catalogue No. 13F0026MIE.

Statistics Canada, Income Statistics Division. (2006). *Low Income Cut-offs for 2005 and Low Income Measures for 2004.* Catalogue no. 75F0003MIE. Ottawa: Statistics Canada.

Statistics Canada. (2006). *Low wage and low income.* Catalogue no. 75F0002MIE. Ottawa: Statistics Canada.

Statistics Canada. (2007a). *Income in Canada.* Accessed at http://dsp-psd.tpsgc.gc.ca/Collection/ Statcan/75-202-XIE/75-202-XIE2004000.pdf

Statistics Canada. (2007b). *Labour force information.* Statistics Canada, CANSIM, Table 282-0001 and Catalogue no. 71-001-XIE.

Statistics Canada. (2007c). *Labour force survey release.* Ottawa: Author. Retrieved March 30, 2007, from: www.statcan.ca/english/Subjects/Labour/LFS/lfs-en.htm

Struthers, J. (1983). *No fault of their own: Unemployment and the Canadian welfare state, 1914–1941.* Toronto: University of Toronto Press.

Titmuss, R. M. (1958). *Essays on the welfare state.* London: George Allen and Unwin.

Titmuss, R M. (1987). *Selected writings of Richard M. Titmuss: The philosophy of welfare.* London: Allen and Unwin.

Torjman, S. (1996a). *Workfare: A poor law.* Ottawa: Caledon Institute of Social Policy.

Torjman, S. (1996b). *History/hysteria.* Ottawa: Caledon Institute of Social Policy.

Torjman, S. (1997). *Welfare warfare.* Ottawa: Caledon Institute of Social Policy.

Torjman, S. (1998a). *Community-based poverty reduction.* Ottawa: Caledon Institute of Social Policy.

Torjman, S. (1998b). *Welfare reform through tailor-made training.* Ottawa: Caledon Institute of Social Policy.

Torjman, S. (1999). *Dumb and dumber governments.* Ottawa: Caledon Institute of Social Policy.

Torjman, S., & Battle, K. (1995a). *Can we have national standards?* Ottawa: Caledon Institute of Social Policy.

Torjman, S., & Battle, K. (1995b). *The dangers of block funding.* Ottawa: Caledon Institute of Social Policy.

# CHAPTER 17

# Our System of Health Care

*Ted McNeill and David Nicholas*

Canada's system of health care is important to Canadians; each of us values our health and that of our loved ones in particular. Other priorities pale if we are faced with threats to our health and survival. Consequently, the organization and administration of our health care system is of interest to Canadians. Indicative of the importance of health care to Canadians, a recent survey to identify the greatest Canadian of all time resulted in the selection of Tommy Douglas, the founder of Medicare as we know it today.

This chapter explores various dimensions of Canada's health care system, including its organization and policy framework, challenges facing the system, and a discussion about the implications for social work.

## CANADA'S SYSTEM OF HEALTH CARE

Universal health care in Canada is a hallmark of contemporary Canadian society. Enshrined in the *Canada Health Act*, health care incorporates five overarching principles:

1. **Universality**—public health care insurance must be provided to all Canadians.

2. **Comprehensiveness**—medically necessary hospital and physician services are covered by public health care insurance.

3. **Accessibility**—financial or other barriers to the provision of publicly funded health services are discouraged, so that health services are available to all Canadians when they need them.

4. **Portability**—all Canadians are covered under public health care insurance, even when they travel within Canada and internationally, or move from one province to another.

5. **Public administration**—provincial and territorial health care insurance plans are to be managed by a public agency on a not-for-profit basis. (This principle says nothing about the ownership structure of a health service *delivery* institution.)

Despite these guiding principles, challenges associated with our current health system and the vast geographic landscape of Canada do not permit easy or complete implementation of all these guiding principles.

Health care in Canada is complex in that it is federally mandated, but provincially administered. In 1996, the Canada Health and Social Transfer replaced the Canada Assistance Plan. This change had substantial impact on the nature of the social safety net in Canada, and limited the availability of some services.

Health care services are organized primarily around the treatment of diseases and chronic health conditions. Currently, a system of health care service delivery is available in each province and territory, and includes institutional care such as acute care hospitals, community hospitals, rehabilitation hospitals, chronic care facilities, and community-based care in agencies, doctors' private offices, and in the homes of Canadians through services such as public health and homecare. Traditionally, the emphasis has been on providing medical care to those who are sick, delivered primarily by physicians and nurses. This is a cornerstone of Canada's health care system and remains an essential component. But, increasingly, care is understood as complex and is provided by health care teams, consisting of various additional disciplines which contribute specialized knowledge such as physiotherapists, pharmacists, dieticians, speech language pathologists, and social workers. These services are primarily publicly funded, reflecting various jurisdictions and partnership arrangements among federal, provincial, and municipal levels of government.

Drastic changes in Canada's health care system are reported to have occurred over recent decades (*Health Care in Canada*, 2000). Changes include decreased hospital beds, admission rates, and length of hospital stay. Notwithstanding these shifts, key principles remain, most notably, the fact that access to universal health services is highly valued in Canada. Currently, this includes public coverage for physician fees, hospitalization costs, medications for in-patients, medical tests, and extended health services, including outpatient health programs and homecare.

Public opinion polls indicate a decrease in satisfaction among Canadians; however, health status, as indicated by life expectancy, has reportedly improved in Canada over the last decade. After numerous task forces and royal commissions to examine ways to foster greater effectiveness and efficiency, multiple options have been recommended. A central tenet of these options has been the regionalization of the health system whereby regional bodies would assume responsibility for coordinating the local health system. This model was first implemented in Saskatchewan and since has been integrated across Canada. However, obstacles related to this regionalized co-ordination of services have been reported, including decreased efficiencies related to a smaller economy of scale, vast amounts of information and communication coordination needed, and possibly increased costs (Church & Barker, 1998). What is less clear is the impact of regionalization of health services on consumers, and the toll of reduced services on family members who have often been called on to provide significant caregiving for their ill family member due to decreased health services.

In 2001–02, the Romanow Commission, headed by the former provincial premier of Saskatchewan, Roy Romanow, was appointed to advise the federal government on how to ensure access to sustainable, timely, affordable, and quality health care services for all Canadians. On November 28, 2002, Romanow released his final report, *Building on Values: The Future of Health Care in Canada* (Romanow, 2002). The report upheld Canadian values favouring a universal health care system that protects against catastrophic illness; however, there was also recognition in this report for limits to spending for health care. Specific concerns noted about the current health system included lengthy waiting times for services; unavailable services; demands that periodically exceed supply; inaccessible or inconvenient locations of service; some services not covered financially; and cultural, linguistic, and class barriers to receiving service. In a follow-up meeting of First Ministers in 2004, recommendations for health care reform addressed key priorities, including financial support for reduced waiting times for procedures, a strategic health human resource plan to attract key health care providers, increased homecare services, primary care reform, access to health care in northern Canada, a national pharmaceutical strategy, prevention and public health, health innovation, and greater accountability to the public.

## INTERNATIONAL PERSPECTIVES

Despite its challenges, most Canadians are proud of the health care system; however, they may be surprised to learn that key indicators suggest Canada lags behind many other industrialized nations. Although Canada's system performs better than that of our closest neighbour, the United States, it is a dubious distinction since the US routinely scores at or near the bottom on population health indicators such as infant mortality and longevity of life.

These findings are surprising and troubling given the wealth and resources available in a country such as the United States, but they point to organizational and contextual considerations beyond pure funding availability for understanding the health status of national populations and the system of health services delivery.

## HEALTH CARE IN CONTEXT

As we consider Canada's health care system, how we understand "health" merits some exploration. Because health care services are delivered to individuals at the micro level, the larger social, political, and economic context in which health is embedded can be obscured. Moreover, health is more than merely the absence of ill health. Rather, health is conceptualized by the World Health Organization (WHO) as ". . . a state of complete physical, mental, and social well-being. . . ." Although this definition was developed in 1946, it remains relevant today in the way that it formulates health to include mental and social well-being in addition to physical health. In this way, it serves as a catalyst to understand health, and the provision of health care, in broader rather than narrower terms.

Research has been developing over many years that points to the importance of contextual factors in the etiology of illness and disease. This research identifies broad social factors as powerful predictors of health. In a recent publication of the WHO, reporting an analysis of research conducted across many countries and health care systems, it was concluded that there is a ". . . remarkable sensitivity of health to the social environment and to what have become known as the social determinants of health" (Wilkinson & Marmot, 2003, p. 7).

At a recent WHO assembly, the social determinants of health were described as ". . . the social conditions in which people live and work. Good medical care is vital, but unless the root social causes that undermine people's health are addressed, the opportunity for well-being will not be achieved" (Garrido, 2006).

In Canada, a national consensus conference at York University in Toronto identified the broad determinants of health in the Canadian context (*The Social Determinants of Health: An Overview of the Implications for Policy and the Role of the Health Sector, 2002*). The following factors were identified as key influences shaping health:

- Early life experiences (i.e., ensuring conditions for all families that facilitate a healthy and secure attachment between parent(s) and their child(ren) and the availability of high-quality daycare)
- Education (i.e., availability of high-quality public schooling to prepare children for productive lives, including lifelong learning and job training opportunities)
- Food security (i.e., availability of nutritious, healthy, and affordable foods)
- Housing (i.e., availability of quality, affordable housing)

- Health care services (i.e., availability of accessible health services)
- Social safety net (i.e., availability of programs and services to support individuals and families)
- Social exclusion (i.e., toxic effects of discrimination and exclusion due to race, sexual preference, disability, gender, etc.)
- Income and its distribution (i.e., growing gap between high- and low-income families, including the impact of poverty)
- Employment and working conditions (i.e., safe working conditions with adequate pay and benefits)
- Unemployment and employment security (i.e., availability of secure full-time jobs with access to employment training and benefits for those who are out of work)

Historically, the connection between health and the social environment has received much speculation and theoretical exploration. In the 1970s, under Canada's Minister of Health at the time, Marc Lalonde, Canada took a leadership role in the world by advancing a vision for health care that included the integration of many influences that affect health, including factors found in both the social and physical environments that form the context in which individual health is immersed. Subsequently, countries such as Sweden and other northern European countries have assumed a leadership role in unravelling the ways in which the social environment in particular affects individual health.

The evolution of Canada's health care system has been shaped in part by a worldwide move to neo-conservative/neo-liberal governments and political philosophies which extol the virtues of small governments, low taxes, and, consequently, fewer programs and services for individuals and families. The trend to globalization and the increasing power of multinational corporations, and, with it, the desire of national governments to provide attractive investment conditions for businesses, create a challenging environment in which to provide adequate services for children and families. The governments of Ronald Reagan and George Bush Sr. in the United States and Margaret Thatcher and John Major in Britain were key forces on the world stage. In Canada, both Liberal and Conservative federal governments embraced a conservative fiscal agenda. The drive to reduce taxes and eliminate government debt resulted in substantial cuts to programs and services. Due in part to these government cutbacks, health was more likely to be understood in narrow rather than broader ways, and health care services emphasized medical care.

Consistent with this broad trend, medical researchers worldwide made great strides to understand the biology and genetic foundations of diseases and to advance this essential paradigm for understanding health. However, epidemiologists and social scientists continue to examine the social and environmental factors and have begun to uncover important connections to health.

## CONCEPTUAL FRAMEWORKS FOR UNDERSTANDING HEALTH

Increasingly, health has come to be understood in dynamic terms, requiring a multi-factorial approach. The following models have emerged (Raphael, 2004). They are not mutually exclusive, rather complementary in the sense that each contributes to an integrated understanding of health (or ill health).

1. Genetic and biological factors: This model recognizes the interplay of genetic and bio-logical factors in determining the health of individuals. This is the model most famil-iar to health care professionals.

2. Behavioural and lifestyle factors: There is a growing understanding that the life choices people make affect their health positively and/or negatively (e.g., nutritional intake, exer-cise, smoking, use of drugs, alcohol, etc.).

3. Social determinants of health: These are presently the least understood but may have the most profound impact on the health of individuals and populations. These include the impact of poverty, social exclusion, housing conditions, access to nutritious food, etc.

In addition to these Western models for understanding health, the influx of new Canadians from countries around the world has brought other traditions for understand-ing health, some stretching back thousands of years. These models enrich our under-standing of health and provide complementary and alternative therapies such as acupuncture, massage, therapeutic touch, and traditional Chinese medicines that provide a choice to consumers.

## IMPLICATIONS FOR HEALTH OF CANADIANS

It is evident that health has emerged as a complex phenomenon that requires multiple perspectives for a comprehensive understanding of both its etiology and treatment options for optimal care. Consideration of the social determinants of health and the way that society is organized helps to explain differential health outcomes for some Canadians. For example, data from Health Canada indicates that Aboriginal Canadians experience higher rates of chronic diseases and infectious diseases (e.g., First Nations/Inuit tuberculosis rates are 6–11 times higher than rates for other Canadians). In addition, a gap in life expectancy of Aboriginal men and women compared to the non-Aboriginal population exists. On average, First Nations men live 8.1 years less than other Canadian men, and First Nations women, 5.5 years less than other Canadian women (*First Nations Comparable Health Indicators, 2005*). The suicide rate among First Nations youth is 5–6 times higher than the national average, and for Inuit youth it is 11 times higher. Suicide is the single greatest cause of injury-related deaths among Aboriginal peoples.

Other minority groups experience similar patterns of poorer health outcomes. When socio-economic status is considered, a disturbing picture emerges. A significant burden exists for the approximately 15% of Canadian children living in poverty. For example, Canadian children living in low-income families are more likely to experience

- greater incidence of a variety of illnesses
- hospital stays
- accidental injuries
- mental health problems
- lower school achievement and early dropout
- family violence and child abuse

In fact, children from low-income families show higher incidences of any health-, social-, or education-related problems, however defined (*The Health of Canada's Children, 2000*).

These patterns of health outcomes are most evident when examined from a population health perspective. Approaches to understanding health that emphasize only individual perspectives are likely to obscure the broader social conditions that individuals do not control and yet impact their health. These narrow perspectives can also lead to the stigmatization of individuals by "blaming" them for their ill health, which compounds the injustice. In fact, individual behavioural and/or lifestyle approaches are weak predictors of health compared to socio-economic and demographic factors. For example, most relevant scholarship places living conditions as four to five times as important as health care in predicting health outcomes (Raphael, 2004).

## ACCESS TO HEALTH SERVICES

These health outcome patterns are evident across Canada, and awareness is growing about the importance of examining these factors within the context of a population health perspective. Issues related to access to care continue to be a concern despite being a core principle of Canada's system of health care. For example, the Ontario Quality Health Council, a provincially funded agency that operates at arm's length from the government, recently concluded in their first annual report that ". . . some groups, in particular the poor, immigrants, rural residents, and Aboriginals, face greater difficulties in getting care" (*Annual Report: Ontario Quality Health Council,* 2006).

This finding may help explain Canada-wide survey data which found that a total of 15% of Canadians had difficulty accessing routine medical care, and 23% reported difficulty accessing care for minor health problems (*Canadian Community Health Survey,* 2003; *Health Services Access Survey,* 2003). Persons who lacked a regular family physician were at greater risk as this group was twice as likely to have problems obtaining health care services as opposed to those with a regular family physician. Younger persons more often reported difficulty accessing health care services, as did those with less than high school education. Of note, Canadians who had difficulty accessing medical care reported poorer health.

Given the diverse cultural makeup of Canada, it is important to note that recent immigrants (those living in Canada for less than five years) are almost two and a half times more likely to report difficulties acquiring care for minor health problems. Over time, however, this disparity appears to ease as immigrants living in Canada for more than five years report experiencing difficulty accessing health care less frequently.

## IMPLICATIONS FOR GOVERNMENT PLANNING AND HEALTH CARE INSTITUTIONS

As indicated above, it is increasingly evident that our understanding of health must be informed by multiple perspectives, and by extension that Canada's health care system must reflect this. With the explosion of knowledge that is occurring, advocates of evidence-based decision making are hard pressed to make sense of the competing considerations for health care spending. Many compelling issues such as long surgical wait times, availability of prescription medications to all who need them, maintenance of the public system of health care services, and an impending crisis due to the lack of health professionals because of the needs of the surging aging population all demand government attention. Most of these issues require government funding at least as part of the solution.

Historically, as Canadians' values regarding the importance of health care evolved, so did government expenditures. For example, in Ontario, the top government expenditure in the 1940s was for transportation and infrastructure. In the 1950s and early '60s, spending on education became the top priority. However, by the late 1960s, health emerged as the highest priority, capturing the largest proportion of total government spending. Accounting for population growth and inflation, health care spending has risen steadily since the 1970s, and, by 1997, it accounted for 8.9% of Canada's economic output. At the provincial level, in a recent presentation, former Premier of Ontario Bob Rae lamented that overall health expenditures totalled approximately 34% of the provincial budget in the early 1990s, but had increased to approximately 45% in the span of 10 years. Such dramatic spending increases are unsustainable. Moreover, this change occurred during a time of unprecedented government cutbacks to balance budgets. Although hospitals experienced budget reductions, the proportion of reductions in other ministries was much higher—to the point that the government all but abandoned social housing programs and reduced welfare rates to punishing levels.

An unmistakable conclusion is that the continuing rise of government expenditures for health is unsustainable. The potential opportunity costs and broader implications are compelling reasons to re-examine the current approach of governments to health care. A reconciliation regarding the finite resources of governments is needed and will result in tough decisions about where resources should be allocated. In the case of health care, there is public demand for high-tech care, access to costly designer drugs, organ transplantation, and joint replacements for all who need them. These command huge expenditures and lead some to advocate for private health care options while others express concern about potential harms associated with two-tiered health care. They worry that the number of publicly funded procedures will shrink dramatically as those with the financial means access for-profit care with the consequence that demand on governments to provide public funding will diminish, leading to two-tier health care. As an example of these varied positions, recent legislation in Alberta substantially expanded the range of treatments and procedures that can be provided outside a publicly administered hospital (*Bill 11: An Act Respecting the Delivery of Health and Community Services and the Establishment of Regional Health Authorities*, 2006). Amidst massive opposition to this bill on the grounds that private health care threatens the central tenets of universal and equitable health care, the role of private, for-profit clinics nonetheless appears to be in place. Whatever the outcome of these debates across the rest of the country, they are unlikely to end soon given the rise in health care costs and the range of strongly held views about the importance of health care services.

As these debates occur, the pressure for enhanced funding for medical and surgical procedures continues. Issues of access to health care services and racial inequities in health outcomes are also compelling issues for governments to address. A primary means for governments to address these and other important issues is through the health and social policy arenas. However, a distinction must be made between policies that attempt to address the way the current system operates in order to ensure greater fairness and consistency of services and health outcomes and those that seek to alter the conditions in which people live that produce the adverse health impacts in the first place (Raphael, in press). The first relates to social welfare programs and other forms of assistance to assist those in poverty and other vulnerable populations, while the latter addresses the structural organization of society such as tax, trade, and business regulation that creates the unequal distribution of resources in the first place.

Such a structural approach is truly preventive in the sense that it addresses the underlying causes of inequities that lead to adverse health outcomes as opposed to addressing the fallout or implications of the current system. As research continues to demonstrate the strong connection between health and the social world, spending on programs that focus on the structural issues that produce and maintain poverty and other adverse living conditions will continue to resonate.

These are challenging issues for any government because addressing the "causes of the causes" of ill health may not produce immediate benefits, at least not benefits that are immediately apparent. As we embark on planning for the future of health care in Canada, the tasks and controversies will be accompanied by challenging considerations on all sides of these key debates. In these deliberations, it is likely that decisions will reflect, in part at least, the political ideology of the governments in power at the time. In a recent Canadian study entitled *Politics and Health Outcomes*, an empirical link has been demonstrated between a government's political ideology and the health of its citizens. There has been much debate in the past about whether such a relationship exists. Many have assumed such a correlation, but there has never been any scientific evidence. According to this study, it was found that governments that provide services to correct for social inequalities tend to improve the health of the whole population (Navarro et al., 2006).

This finding has important implications for government planning; however, it would be short-sighted to assume that governments have sole responsibility for decisions about the allocation of health care resources. While governments carry the largest responsibility, health care institutions, agencies, and even individual practitioners also have important roles to play. Decisions about how resources are allocated within institutions and agencies are made with some degree of autonomy and reflect the priorities of the individual institution or agency. This becomes a political issue within institutions as they allocate finite resources to the range of programs and services necessary to provide health care. The beliefs, values, characteristics, and professional backgrounds of the decision-makers become relevant in this process. Agencies and institutions face incredible challenges to keep informed about new knowledge that is exploding in the health care field, and thus the decision-making process must be informed by individuals with complementary educational backgrounds and experience for effective institutional planning. There can be little debate that a biopsychosocial approach is needed for promoting well-being, responding to quality of life considerations, and treating those suffering from ill health.

## SOCIAL WORKERS IN HEALTH

Social work in health care has emerged over a long history of increased recognition of the complexities associated with caring for those with an illness or chronic health condition. It has followed a historical shift whereby ill persons were, in an earlier era, largely cared for at home. American history records the development, in the 1700s, of buildings constructed to house those affected by pandemic conditions. Later, almshouses were constructed for care of those who were aged, orphaned, vagrant, or physically or mentally ill (Gehlert & Browne, 2006). By the mid-1700s, the ill were separated from the poor and vagrant in wards or buildings that eventually came to be known as hospitals. The collaboration of social work and medicine stemmed from early partnerships between hospitals and charity societies. An early and close partnership between the Johns Hopkins Hospital and the Charity Organization Society in Baltimore fostered ideas for collaboration between social work and medicine (Gehlert & Browne, 2006). In England, similar processes were underway at the Royal Free Hospital in London where the hospital began screening patients for poverty as early as 1874, and, by 1895, a hospital almoner was hired.

The first noted social work department in a Canadian hospital was at the Montreal General Hospital, established in 1911. As health expenditures expanded rapidly in the 1960s and '70s, social work departments became established services in hospitals. More recent developments have included many changes in how health care is organized and managed. For instance, approaches to organizational management have dramatically shifted, creating both pressures and opportunities for social workers. In health care, administrative governance, such as program management and matrix management, have impacted the delivery of social work services, sometimes resulting in the erosion or even elimination of social work department structures. The era of the 1990s witnessed a reduction of social work departments in health care facilities across Canada although individual social workers continued to be employed within these settings.

These changes precipitated a crisis within social work and other professional disciplines within hospitals which, in turn, created both challenges and opportunities to recreate the field in proactive ways. Social workers, as experts in managing change (Globerman, 1999), found themselves, and continue to find themselves, in a position of needing to demonstrate leadership in responding to the demands of a resource-limited health care environment. For instance, social workers must work creatively in redesigning their practice to ensure a relevant and vibrant role in the context of the interprofessional delivery of health care.

Given the complexity associated with providing specialized health care services and the growing recognition that the knowledge and skills of various disciplines are needed to address the range of health care needs of patients and their families, it is essential for social workers to develop evidence-based models of practices and to understand the context of their own and others' roles in the delivery of patient care. Multidisciplinary care has given way to interprofessional care, which emphasizes collaboration across disciplines and includes attunement to scopes of practice, communication, mutual decision-making, and team functioning.

The foregoing has implications for how social workers practice regardless of the particular field in which they work. In the health care field, social workers are primarily employed in hospitals and other institutional settings. They usually work as members of an interprofessional health care team where they contribute collaboratively with professionals from other health disciplines to provide care to patients and their families. The social work role is dynamic and multifaceted. A key function is to provide psychosocial assessments that consider the patient's and family's strengths, attitudes, feelings, cognitions, meaning of the illness, interactions, social supports, and problem-solving abilities within their cultural and spiritual context. Social workers develop and implement a plan of care which addresses mental health issues, adaptation, adherence to treatment, and quality of life as appropriate to the patient's situation. In addressing chronic and/or life threatening conditions, the social worker may be involved with issues of loss, palliation, and bereavement. Drawing on a variety of possible interventions and working in collaboration with the patient and family, the social worker employs such strategies as crisis intervention, individual and family counselling, group work, consultation, case management, community outreach, and advocacy. Social workers often serve as a bridge to the community to access community-based resources that may be beneficial to the patient and family. In many hospitals, social workers provide an important discharge planning role to assist patients to transition to other institutions that can provide the level and type of care that is needed. Concern about individuals in need of protection due to child neglect or abuse, elder abuse, or domestic violence is a regular reason for referral to a social worker. It is evident that social workers bring relevant knowledge, skills, and judgment necessary to address a broad variety of health-related issues and are a valuable resource on health care teams.

A capacity to bring a variety of "lenses" to understanding clients is needed. In addition to the capacity to empathically understand the experience of individuals in terms of their emotional and psychological functioning, approaches informed by the interpretive paradigm such as narrative therapy and some depth psychology models that emphasize the relevance of individual meanings in the interpretation of experiences and events are beneficial. A capacity to understand behaviours and symptoms within their context, beginning with the important context of the family and the relationships in which the individual is embedded is essential. Family systems theory and the social ecological model are effective in drawing our attention to important factors beyond the individual. In addition, structural elements of society and the existence of broad social forces such as poverty, racism, and stigma are important perspectives that situate and contextualize persons relative to their health and well-being. An orientation to anti-oppressive practices provides an essential dimension of understanding when the goal is to advance social justice by intervening in the environment in which the individual is immersed. Drawing on various lenses such as those described above to understand individual and family is likely to identify distinct targets for intervention. Clinical judgment and an understanding of client preferences are needed to decide which approach should be emphasized.

While competing demands, such as fiscal pressures, impinge on the breadth and depth of services delivered by social workers, the theoretical underpinnings and values of the profession ground the role and contribution that social workers bring to health care teams and ultimately to the lives of patients and families. Considering the varied theoretical approaches available to social work, a shift to evidence-based practice is challenging but necessary. Social work's respect for the plight of marginalized persons, its nuanced understanding of health care processes and its attunement to change strategies cumulatively point to the potential leadership of social work in health care planning.

Social work is well positioned to thrive in an environment of understanding health in broad terms with attention to the context in which patients live. In fact, social workers are likely to be more aware of the influence of the social determinants of health discussed earlier and have an important educational and advocacy role to expand awareness of the interplay of multiple factors in shaping health. Social workers must understand the literature, both theoretical and empirical, that demonstrates the remarkable sensitivity that humans have to the social environment. Equally important is the knowledge that health inequities exist and that some individuals and groups are more likely to experience poorer health outcomes as a direct result of the influence of these determinants of health.

Informed with this knowledge, social workers have a key role to address issues on various levels as they impact on their client population. They may serve as a catalyst within their organization to provide interventions to target those at greater risk of experiencing poorer health outcomes. In hospitals, solutions rest on getting "buy in" at the team level, as well as within the executive and board. While a social justice framework is an essential perspective, it is often a hard sell in institutions that may not fully appreciate these realities and are usually grappling with competing values and priorities. Consequently, promoting an approach that advocates special accommodation only of those who are marginalized or oppressed can lead to resentment that may not result in success. Finding benefits for the organization are also needed, which may include pride of leadership, higher levels of positive patient outcomes, a more satisfied workforce that feels positive about their work, or being an exemplar of best practices.

## ROADMAP FOR THE FUTURE

As in previous eras, the health care field will continue to evolve in both predictable and unpredictable ways. An interesting trend is the blurring of boundaries between health and social programs due to the recognition of the intimate role that the social environment plays in contributing to the health (or ill health) of Canadians. It is increasingly evident, supported by research, that there is a dynamic and complementary relationship between these fields and there is a need to further their development and integration. In turn, this will have implications for social work practice and represents an opportunity for social workers to contribute to a more comprehensive understanding of health, as well as the implications of social conditions on the lives of Canadians. Attention to the social determinants of health, while cognizant of other important considerations, offers an inherently preventive approach to optimizing the health of Canadians and, in this way, provides an alternative to an emphasis on sickness and ill health alone. Given social work's expertise in understanding contextual factors that influence health, a natural fit exists to create partnerships to advance this understanding. At the systems level, social work and public health share an interest in the social determinants of health and efforts to mitigate adverse effects of risk factors associated with them.

Whether the complementarity between health and social programs will lead to greater integration within government planning and funding is yet to be seen. There will continue to be tension related to decisions about priorities within the health care system and the allocation of resources to advance those priorities. Finite resources and seemingly infinite needs will continue to pressure governments and institutions to look for better ways to adjudicate resource distribution. An emphasis on evidence-based decision-making and a growing concern about moral and ethical issues related to social justice are imperative in advancing this complex process.

Because the health care system is shaped by policies, social work has an important role to expand the debate. To this policy development process, social workers bring key knowledge, skills, and values that can help to inform health care planning. Decisions about health care priorities and the allocation of resources are shaped by multiple factors, including values, and research on population health needs. Developing social work leaders to contribute to this process is critical. To optimize this role, leadership is needed within the discipline to prepare future leaders who can contribute to the policy planning process and to health care administration.

At the micro level of delivering services to patients and their families, social workers will practice in a system that seeks to balance and integrate current trends, including an emphasis on patient safety, increasing use of technology, availability of newer and increasingly costlier drugs, consideration of quality of life, evidence-based practice, patient and family-centred care, interprofessional practice, a growing awareness of health inequalities, and the need for greater social justice. Social workers are well positioned to contribute constructively to the evolution of Canada's health care system both clinically and by creating new knowledge through research to inform practice. Toward this aim, social workers will be called to new levels of reflection and leadership to shape Canada's health care system of the future. The years ahead will surely present challenges, yet simultaneously offer opportunity and excitement for social work in Canada.

# References

*Annual Report: Ontario Quality Health Council.* (2006). Government of Ontario.

*Bill 11: An Act Respecting the Delivery of Health and Community Services and the Establishment of Regional Health Authorities.* (2006) Government of Alberta.

*Canadian Community Health Survey.* (2003). Stats Canada.

Church, J., & Barker, P. (1998). Regionalization of health services in Canada: A critical perspective. *International Journal of Health Services*, 28(3), 467–486.

First Nations Comparable Health Indicators. (2005). Government of Canada.

Garrido, P. I. (2006, May 22). *Presidential Address.* Paper presented at the 59th World Health Assembly, World Health Organization, Geneva.

Gehlert. S. (2006). The conceptual underpinnings of social work in health care. In *Handbook of Health Social Work* (S. Gehlert and T.A. Browne, eds.). Hoboken, NJ: John Wiley and Sons, Inc.

Globerman, J. (1999). Hospital restructuring: Positioning social work to manage change. *Social Work in Health Care*, 28(4), 13–30.

*Health Care in Canada.* (2000). Government of Canada.

*The Health of Canada's Children.* (2000). Canadian Institute of Child Health.

*Health Services Access Survey.* (2003). Stats Canada.

Navarro, V., Muntaner, C., Borrell, C., Benach, J., Quiroga, A., Rodriguez-Sanz, M., et al. (2006). Politics and health outcomes. *Lancet,* 368(9540), 1033–1037.

Raphael, D. (Ed.). (2004). *Social Determinants of Health: Canadian Perspective.* Toronto: Canadian Scholars' Press.

Romanow, R. (2002). *Building on Values: The Future of Health Care in Canada.* Government of Canada.

*The Social Determinants of Health: An Overview of the Implications for Policy and the Role of the Health Sector.* (2002). Public Health Agency of Canada.

Wilkinson, R., & Marmot, M. (Eds.). (2003). *The Social Determinants of Health: The Solid Facts* (2nd ed.). Copenhagen: World Health Organization.

# CHAPTER 18

# Community Capacity Building: A Re-conceptualization of Services for the Protection of Children

*Ken Barter*

## INTRODUCTION

There is a plethora of child welfare research and information from parents, social workers, and Aboriginal communities that Canada's child protection systems are significantly challenged. They are systems well recognized to be reactive in approach and crisis-driven (Swift & Callahan, 2006; Cameron & Freymond, 2006; Bennett & Blackstock, 2006; CASW, 2005, 2003; Barter, 2005, 2004; Kufeldt & McKenzie, 2003; Wharf, 2003; Prilleltensky, Nelson, & Peirson, 2001). A consensus is emerging that it is no longer acceptable to engage with children and families who require protective intervention services in a reactive manner that stems from moral panic on the part of the public in reaction to a crisis such as a death or injury of a child known to or in the care of child protection authorities. Research is clear in suggesting it is not possible nor responsible to assume that one intervention strategy can appropriately respond to the complex and chronic needs of children and families. Engaging in the ongoing pendulum swing from rescuing children on the one end and preserving families on the other is simply not sufficient (Lindsay, 2004; Lindsay & Henly, 1997). Both paradigms are not producing desirable outcomes nor making a significant difference in the lives of vulnerable children and families (Trocmé, 1999).

The absence of positive outcomes is well-documented. The extent of social injustices can be seen with the continuing critical problem of child and family poverty; the pervasiveness of child maltreatment; the increasing numbers of children, particularly Aboriginal children, in the care of the state; the continuing crises in foster care; the increase in the use of food banks by families with children; the continuing absence of investments in prevention and early intervention strategies; the increase in violence within families, schools, and communities; and the ever-continuing negative public attitudes towards poor and disadvantaged citizens (Campaign 2000, 2006; Trocmé et al., 2005; Lundy, 2004; Kufeldt & McKenzie, 2003; Willms, 2002; Barter, 2002, 2003; Trocmé et al., 2001; Conway, 2001; Prilleltensky et al., 2001).

These undesirable outcomes continue despite comprehensive changes that have taken place in many child welfare jurisdictions. These changes tend to be organizational in nature with increased emphasis on accountability, risk assessment instruments, integration of services, the shift from government to community-based delivery of child welfare services, efficiency standards, working protocols, and legislative policy changes. The current emphases on risk assessment and risk management are attempts to try and make the future calculable in terms of abuse and neglect. It is all about trying to bring about consistency in investigations and decision making so interventions with children and families are defensible (Wharf, 2002; Barter, 2002). This consistency and defensiveness have created organizational climates that are more rules- and procedures-driven, as opposed to being professionally and clinically driven based on relationship building. What is really taking place in the lives of the majority of families who come to the attention of child protection systems, such as injustices associated with poverty, violence, isolation, discrimination, homelessness, and loss of hope and opportunities, is skirted.

This chapter sounds the call to say enough is enough. It challenges what has been happening in child protection systems based on evidence that suggests the ultimate goals of improving situations for children and families in need of assistance and support, as well as improving working conditions for workers, are far from being realized (CASSW, 2005). Based on this evidence, the chapter puts forth community capacity building as a comprehensive approach and a re-conceptualization of services for the protection of children. Implications for social work practice in child protection and social work education are also explored.

## ENOUGH IS ENOUGH

Enough is enough for several reasons. First, the complexity, unpredictability, and uncertainty that permeate much of the terrain of child protection work demand a different approach. The current emphasis on evidence-based and competency-based approaches to practice, for example, are not necessarily conducive to engaging and creating opportunities for change, particularly with citizens who are marginalized and excluded. Although the emphasis on evidence-based practice may have obvious attractions in terms of improving accountability and effectiveness of services, as well as having potential for cost efficiency, its contribution to tackling poverty and oppression and other social injustices is less clear (Stepney, 2000). Evidence is not new to child protection work. Yet, despite efforts to address this evidence—for example, child deaths and increases in child maltreatment—situations for children and families and for workers in child protection systems have not dramatically changed. What has changed, however, is the emphasis on rules, tools, techniques, and conformity to procedures and mechanisms for obtaining and measuring competencies. This emphasis reduces the complex personal, professional, and social issues associated with child protection work to problems of bureaucratic administration.

Competency-based practice is an example of a bureaucratic approach. Yet this practice has many shortcomings (Adams, 2002; Stepney, 2002; Rossiter, 2002). Adams (2002) identifies six main criticisms of competency-based approaches: (1) they tend to focus on expertise that is more suitable to bureaucratic work settings; (2) they fragment practice into artificially discrete elements; (3) they bring about a narrowing of ideas that are consistent with outcome-based activity rather than divergent thinking and an emphasis on the value of process; (4) they concentrate on measurable aspects of people's performance; (5) they overemphasize techniques and skills at the expense of values and critical reflection; and (6) they emphasize acquiring specified techniques rather than developing approaches based on critically reflective practice. As pointed out by Dominelli (1996), many of the realities associated with child welfare are structural problems. These problems cannot be dealt with by a competency-based approach which presupposes that what needs to be done for children and families is known and infallible, that resources are adequate to deal with situations facing families, and that social work relationships operate in a vacuum.

Second, child welfare authorities and social workers alike have acknowledged the errors associated with the policies of assimilation and integration that have had a devastating impact on Aboriginal children, their families, and their communities. These policies were a blatant imposition of power and authority by the dominant white culture oppressing Aboriginal values, lifestyles, and social and political structures. Child welfare practices have been a major factor in this oppression and the deterioration of Aboriginal cultures in Canada (Sinclair et al., 1991). Yet, despite this history, there are more Aboriginal children in the care of the child welfare and justice systems today than there were at the height of the residential schools era (Blackstock, 2003). Is colonization still very much alive? Are oppressive policies and practices within child welfare organizations being sustained? There is an urgent requirement for dialogue and change in order to facilitate First Nations and Aboriginal control and leadership in child welfare so interventions are in accordance with their culture, beliefs, and values (Brubacher, 2006; Mandell et al., 2006; Bennett & Blackstock, 2006; MacKenzie & Flette, 2003).

Third, risk assessment and risk management paradigms currently dominate child protection work. Child abuse and neglect investigations, which is essentially crisis work, take precedence. These emphases have created within the general public and with child-serving professionals the idea that child protection consists of reporting and investigating, being "forensic" units with a blaming dimension attached, and establishing who is accountable (Lindsey, 2004; Melton, 2003; Wharf, 2003; Roberts, 1991). As a result, child welfare agencies are coerced into devoting the majority of resources to these activities. Evidence gathering and preparation of actual or potential court action have shifted human and fiscal resources from prevention, early intervention, and family support to activities that usually result in significant disruption of family life with little by way of positive outcomes. Investigative work tends to place workers in positions of doing more judging than helping, more investigation than relationship building, more following rules and protocols than creative intervention and risk taking, more relying on tools and instruments than professional integrity and assessments, more attending to the needs of the organization to avoid scandal than to the needs of families and children, and more reacting after family breakdowns than interventions to prevent breakdowns. Investigative work has distracted child protection agencies from ways in which the law and policy can be used to help families and communities become safer for children. These realities in children's protection organizations make it practically impossible to carry out the necessary interventions to realize desirable outcomes for children and families (Lindsey, 2004; Wharf, 2003; Turnell & Edwards, 1999; Berg & Kelly, 2000; Prilleltensky et al., 2001).

Fourth, work in statutory settings has always caused considerable difficulties for social workers in terms of practice and relationship building. Values of social justice, self-determination, and empowerment place social workers in positions where they have to carefully negotiate through a minefield of moral and ethical dilemmas (Dominelli, 1999). Social work values often challenge the rigidity attached to bureaucracies with their focus on efficiency, consistency, accountability through extensive paperwork, and surveillance/supervision tasks associated with risk assessment and risk management. These emphases tend not to be balanced with professional social work principles and expectations. Hence, there are many tensions in practice. Lafrance (2003) captures these tensions under three categories. The first is what he refers to as a *process versus task* tension. Even though relationship building is one of the best attributes for good child protection work, the overemphasis on rules and procedures interfere with this being done and de-humanizes the interaction between workers and clients. The second is that of *creativity versus prescription*, meaning that the application of prescribed rigid procedures stifles worker discretion, creativity, flexibility, and professional practice. The final tension, *community partnership versus isolation*, indicates failure on the part of child welfare organizations to support advocacy, educate the public, and be involved in building community capacities in terms of informal support networks for children and families. As stated by Lafrance: "The overall paradigm in child protection agencies seems to be moving toward increasing power and control over clients and away from interpersonal elements necessary for the achievement of child welfare activities which are central to agency goals" (p. 151). MacAulay (2003, 2002) identifies these tensions between community and family resource centres throughout Canada and child protection authorities. The characteristics of these centres in terms of flexibility, comprehensiveness, responsiveness, community rooted-ness, being parent driven and respectful of process and relationship building are not necessarily congruent with child protection practices. She suggests the critical need to find a common ground.

Tensions such as these have created working conditions where creativity is replaced with conformity, idealism with cynicism, collective sharing with turf protection, and where critical questions, challenges, and new ideas are oftentimes feared and avoided. They are also working conditions where professional social work practice, as the primary practice profession in child protection, is not embraced for its values, ethics, and principles. These working environments contribute to the ever-increasing emphasis on control, efficiency, accountability, technical proficiency, and endeavouring to find clinical solutions to structural problems.

Finally, enough is enough when you consider the evidence brought forward through the report entitled *Child Welfare Project: Creating Conditions for Good Practice,* produced by the Canadian Association of Social Workers (CASW, 2003). Data collected across Canada from over one thousand social workers involved in child protection identified issues of low worker morale, fears of liability and prosecution, lack of experienced and trained social workers, inadequate financial and human resources to respond to demand, the adversarial process of investigation, and the overall residual approach to child protection work. According to the report, "the most powerful messages from all the data are that the demands of the work environment overwhelmingly impede the use of relationship as a catalyst for change, and that social workers feel keenly the lack of visible and public support for good practice" (CASW, 2003, p. 21). Of equal significance in the report is the statement suggesting "there is a sense that many of these practitioners feel lonely and isolated, and that there is a pervasive sense of powerlessness and fear" (p. 21). The irony is that the senses of powerlessness, fear, and frustration being felt by social workers are the same feelings been experienced by the parents and families who require protective intervention services. How can those who feel unsupported, powerless, and hopeless engage in building helping relationships with others who need support, encouragement, and hope in order to appreciate their strengths and discover their personal power to address and problem-solve issues related to their oppression and poverty?

That enough is enough is obvious. Barter (2005) captures the essence of this when he suggests that: "If we in Canada were assigned the task to deliberately design systems that would frustrate the professionals/para-professionals who staff it, anger the public who finance it, alienate those who require its services and programs, invest in reactive responses to cope with symptoms of problems as opposed to being proactive, systems whose mandate is not shared and embraced by other public child serving organizations, and systems that would serve to be the scapegoat and bear the brunt of public criticisms should a child be harmed in any way, we could not do a better job than our present children's protection systems" (p. 317).

It is time for re-conceptualization and more comprehensive and responsive ideas. Community capacity building represents such a re-conceptualization and idea.

## COMMUNITY CAPACITY BUILDING—THE CONCEPT

Community capacity building challenges the premise that child abuse and neglect are individual/family problems amenable to clinical solutions (Dominelli, 1999). Rather, it is about being responsive and comprehensive not only with respect to protective interventions with children and families but also with the many complex issues associated with child protection. It is about extending interventions beyond the four walls of parenting. It is an approach that is just as concerned about the abuse and neglect of children by society as it is with the abuse and neglect by parents. This takes the intervention into the social and political arena where poverty, poor neighbourhoods, violence, and discrimination are seen as critical dimensions to be addressed.

Community capacity building is about bringing services to children and families out of the professional/bureaucratic paradigm and into the citizen/family/community paradigm. Experiences in child protection suggest that the professional/bureaucratic environment is not necessarily the right environment for creating opportunities where caring, investment, and compassion take place. Instead, it is an environment that is governed by rigid policies and procedures, where the power remains with high-level bureaucrats who are isolated from the grass roots, where the thinking is compartmentalized and often reactive in attempts to fix things, where there is unwarranted political involvement, where the system is closed and not necessarily user or family friendly, where professional autonomy is stifled, and where those who seek services or provide services are not seen as equal partners in the decisions. In these environments, the traditional top-down programmatic fix-it approach, also referred to as a "knowing-in-action approach," dominates (Fabricant & Burghardt, 1992). This approach fails to acknowledge that many of the issues facing children and their families, as well as their communities, elude hierarchical and bureaucratic approaches. It is no longer appropriate to just throw money at problems that are only growing worse (Schorr, 1988). Also not helping is blaming citizens who require assistance for iatrogenic practices of human service professionals and their organizations.

The citizen/family/community paradigm suggests that public services and programs be more community-based, with communities assuming responsibility for governance based on the goals and priorities they see as important for the well-being of citizens. Expectations associated with community capacity building include partnership, inter-professional team work, client participation and involvement, staff empowerment, user-friendly services, primary prevention and promotion, community development, seamless systems of delivery, integrated programs and services, and community decision making and governance. Community capacity building is about caring, respect, acceptance, and personal and social power. Instead of a knowing-in-action approach, community capacity building is a "reflection-in-action approach" (Fabricant & Burghardt, 1992). Reflection is a process of dialogue, analysis, and consciousness raising. This process creates opportunities to challenge thinking, revisit assumptions and beliefs, consider new approaches to service delivery, and connect and build relationships with people.

Community capacity building is about collaboration, innovation, and a willingness to relinquish power and control. To do this appropriately means operating on the understanding that individuals, families, and communities understand their own needs. Extending them the trust, respect, autonomy, and opportunity to develop this understanding is essential. Parents and citizens are critical resources and partners in community capacity building. Seeing them as such means creating opportunities for their involvement in child protection service delivery in a way that not only focuses on their problems or issues but taps into their creative talents and strengths. For example, in current child protection systems, are parents who require protective interventions invited to participate in policy and management decisions? Are they invited to act in an advisory or evaluative capacity in terms of service delivery? Are interested citizens and volunteers asked to participate? Are child protection workers and agencies creating opportunities for such participation? Creating these opportunities for active participation involves a willingness to renegotiate and build relationships in order to begin crossing traditional professional and bureaucratic boundaries. Flexibility must exist whereby professionals, systems, and the people they serve can work collaboratively on common issues of concern. This willingness means challenging traditional practices and assuming new roles and expectations in newfound relationships. It means venturing away from familiar practices and moving toward non-traditional settings and hours of work.

Community capacity building is about connecting personal difficulties and public issues. This connection suggests a personal-trouble response of support, counselling, and membership and a public-issue response that will build community capacity. Integrating these two concepts suggests the importance of social work, as the predominant profession involved, to be concerned about a general rather than specialized approach to practice (Ife, 1997). Such an approach requires grasping a broader domain in which social problems and solutions necessitate the investment of many institutions and professions, only a small portion of which will be social workers involved in child protection. Grasping a broader domain supports the importance of embracing an emancipatory approach (Dominelli, 2002) to working with people and moving beyond the traditional therapeutic and maintenance approaches. Whereas therapeutic approaches focus on individuals and their psychological functioning, the maintenance approach is basically one of helping people cope through the dissemination of information about resources and sharing practice wisdom of what seems to work for people. The maintenance approach relies on the social worker as expert, and on their authority under public legislation such as is found in child welfare. An emancipatory approach recognizes the critical reality that the protection of children touches on issues related to poverty, violence, diversity, health, justice, gender, and the community.

An emancipatory or anti-oppressive approach challenges what has taken place within child protection organizations—the transformation of social work practitioners into managers of scarce resources, co-ordinators of services, and assessors of risks. With this transformation comes the loss of professional discretion, erosion of professional identity, and a move away from professional practices based on relationship building and creating opportunities for justice and equality. Community capacity building challenges this transformation and suggests moving social workers away from being office-bound, rules-driven, and arm's length from parents, families, and communities (Wharf, 2002; Jordan, 2000).

Community capacity building is sensitive to the reality that the authority of child protection workers is often resisted by people with whom they work, particularly since many people come into contact with their systems through third party referrals (for example, by the police, schools, mental health) rather than through self-referral. In many instances, social work is viewed with low regard and suspicion. People often think the services of social workers are to be avoided wherever possible given there is an association of these services with failure and stigma (Jones, 2002). Added to this has been the growing public criticism for the profession's failure to manage high-risk populations, especially in the areas of child protection and mental health. Social workers are seen as problematic, they are labelled "do-gooders," and there is a dimension of blame that they have done little by way of offering solutions to eradicate poverty, violence, oppression, and other social problems (Allen-Meares & DeRoos, 1997). These public perceptions are critical features in influencing policy, management, political, and organizational decisions. They go an equally long way in swaying what people think of the profession. Community capacity building is an opportunity to educate, participate, and transform the current image of social workers involved in child protection.

Community capacity building embraces the definition of child welfare put forth by Barter (2005a) which suggests that "child welfare is a collaborative process between community, families, and child serving organizations and professionals. That process aims to reclaim these parties' strengths and capacities to develop the necessary preventative, supportive, supplementary, substitute, and advocacy services that respect children's rights to health and well-being and to actively seek to influence and change the social, economic, and political policies that affect children and their families" (p. 321). This definition moves away from defining child welfare too narrowly. Instead, it proposes a new vision for child protection services that reflects the importance of family-centred practice and building community capacities. Family-centred interventions recognize parents as collaborative partners where they are seen as having strengths and capabilities within the context of their families, neighbourhoods, and communities. As such, there is sensitivity to culture, coping mechanisms, the importance of parent-to-parent support, and the involvement of parents in processes that impact upon them. A family-centred approach supports child-centred interventions. Hooper-Briar and Lawson (1994) suggest that family-centred interventions connect children, parents, families, neighbours, and communities. They put forth the premise that if interventions try to do things to, and for, children and youth, things which parents could do themselves if they had the necessary supports and resources, then interventions are child-centred. By comparison, the family-centred approach offers a framework that assumes a more ecological and social justice perspective in working with children, families, and communities. Where the ecological perspective is based on principles of holism, sustainability, diversity, and equilibrium, the social justice perspective recognizes structural disadvantage, empowerment, needs, rights, and participation (Ife, 1995). These principles connect personal difficulties and public issues, hence assuming a dual response to working with children, parents, and citizens.

Building community capacity to protect children is a people-centred approach with emphasis on building capacity "of" people, "by" people, and "for" people (Barter, 2001). "Of people" suggests enhancing, strengthening, and renewing people's capabilities, personal skills, self-knowledge, and self-awareness. This heightens the capacity for self-determination in identifying needs and interests that are important for them based on their experiences. "By people" suggests commitment, engagement, application of enhanced capabilities, skills and knowledge, participation, collaboration, self-governance, and ownership. "For people" implies mobilization of capacities to take action and work toward change, equal opportunities, and access to resources that are sustained in order to promote collective good. Building capacities of people, by people, and for people essentially means mutual investment and commitment on the part of all stakeholders to collaboratively partner and work together. This partnership is paramount.

## COMMUNITY CAPACITY BUILDING—THE EVIDENCE

There is a consensus for change. Evidence suggests that public child protection agencies can no longer carry out a protection mandate and services without an investment in prevention and early intervention, they can no longer assume responsibility for the care and custody of children in a foster care system where resources are limited or not available, they can no longer provide counselling and supportive services in a framework of poverty, and they can no longer present an image to the community and the children and families they serve that they are in a position of power and influence to adequately fulfill a protection mandate alone. These agencies are in a difficult bind. The expectations from the public with regard to children and families are high. The statutory duties to prevent and detect child abuse, to investigate allegations of abuse and neglect, to work in assisting and supporting families in order to prevent further abuse and neglect, and to assume responsibility for parenting children who have been apprehended from their families due to the severity of abuse and neglect take place whereby any one of these duties is being carried out at the expense of the others. This leaves the agencies and the workers vulnerable. It is with this situation that they are criticized for either intervening too soon, or, in the event of a child's being hurt, not intervening soon enough.

Community capacity building represents an alternative approach to the current dominant risk paradigm. There is evidence to suggest that community capacity building does realize positive outcomes for children, families, and communities. This evidence can be seen, for example, in adherence to the philosophy and principles underpinning the Canadian Association of Family Resource Programs. Throughout family and community resource centres across Canada, interventions are taking place that recognize the significance of relationships. Relationships within these centres are built on the principles of inclusion, power sharing, respect for diversity, parent leadership, and partnership. Resource programs and centres are community-based and responsive to family and community needs. They offer support and advocate for parents, and they take a community capacity building approach (MacAulay, 2003). The emphasis on promotion of wellness and prevention are strong program principles that are followed. As stated previously, there are tensions between family resource programs and child protection. The challenge is to begin a partnership to seek out a common ground for both to work in the best interests of children and families (Barter, 2004; MacAulay, 2003, 2002). This will mean a shift in approach on the part of child protection systems to move from the risk assessment and management paradigm to a community capacity building paradigm (Wharf, 2002).

Other examples of desirable outcomes being realized through community social work, community organizing, and community control are identified in Wharf's (2002) *Community Work Approaches to Child Welfare* text. The Neighbourhood House Project in Victoria and the Hazelton Office of the Ministry for Children and Families (Wharf, 2002) have demonstrated that partnership and involvement of parents and families in a respectful fashion does realize desirable outcomes in assisting families to overcome difficulties. McKenzie (2002) and McKenzie and Flette (2003) explore the significance of community capacity building to nine First Nations communities by the West Region Child and Family Services in Western Manitoba. These authors, similar to Connors and Maidman (2001) and Blackstock (2003), suggest that a capacity building approach in Aboriginal and First Nations communities is the essence of self-government and control over child welfare service delivery. Within the more than one hundred First Nations Child and Family Service Agencies across Canada (Blackstock, 2003), initiatives and developments are underway using the attributes and principles not only of successful programs from a research perspective but, more importantly, from First Nations values and beliefs associated with respect, sharing, co-operation, and holism (Connors & Maidman, 2001). In the book *Breaking The Rules: Transforming Governance in Social Services* (Bellefeuille et al., 1997), it is suggested there is a better way to approach social services in Aboriginal communities. This better way is premised on such factors as respect for differences, relationships, best interests of people, believing in people's capacity, and acknowledging that quick fixes do not work. These are critical dimensions to embrace in meeting the challenge of shifting from the risk paradigm to the community capacity building paradigm. It has been demonstrated that interventions within Aboriginal communities such as Aboriginal Head Start; Children's Circle Program; sexual abuse treatment programs; healing practices for adult family members using professional, lay, and traditional interventions; home visitations; family healing lodges; and Community Holistic Circle Healing are realizing desirable outcomes (Brubacher, 2006; Connors & Maidman, 2001).

Lee and Richards (2002) in writing about the Community Development and Prevention Program of the Children's Aid Society of Toronto (CAST) describe another example of a community building approach. The benefits realized through CAST include citizen participation, organizational involvement, a sense of community, social learning, and resource development in terms of programs and services at the community level. The Highfield Community Enrichment Project in the northwest area of Toronto suggests that with a community development approach, desirable outcomes can be realized in terms of reducing child maltreatment and enhancing family functioning. The Ontario Better Beginnings, Better Futures initiative, the funding source for the Highfield Project, is distinguished by its strong commitment to community development and citizen participation.

A three-year community capacity building project in St. John's, Newfoundland and Labrador, entitled the Chalker Place Project[1] is yet another example of bringing about

---

1    The Chalker Place Project was funded by the National Crime Prevention Strategy's Crime Prevention Partnership program, a division of Public Safety and Emergency Preparedness Canada. The project ran for three years (2003–2006) and was entitled Building Community Capacity for the Health and Well-Being of Children: A Framework for Action. The author was the principal investigator. The project had three main goals: (1) To increase focus on community capacity building in services and programs geared towards the protection of children, healthy child development, family violence, and family support; (2) To increase focus on early intervention with children and families in an identified neighbourhood; (3) To develop and increase understanding of a framework for building community capacity in order to create a supportive and safe community for children and parents. The evaluation conducted throughout the three years gave a resounding yes that community capacity building does make a difference in the lives of children and parents and it is a reasonable process to use in working with families for the health, well-being, and protection of children.

positive outcomes for families and their neighbourhoods. Of significance in this project is the emphasis placed on the determinants of health from the point of view of hope and opportunity, relationships, and community. The formal child protection system invests primarily in the protection determinant with little investment in the other three. The Chalker Place experience has demonstrated the importance of all determinants and the benefits that are realized when there is a process to connect with parents that does not involve the authority role that comes with protection. Parents thrive on social connections in terms of parenting programs, programs for children, being involved in leadership roles within their community, working with other parents on joint community projects, being consulted for advice, having opportunities for training, and being involved as volunteers. It is these connections and relationships that bring about hope, create opportunities, and that in turn provide a sense of belonging and community. Building on these determinants not only increases protective factors and reduces risk factors for children, but also invests in a real way in early intervention and prevention. Community capacity building is an approach to protect children but it does so through a process of caring, respect, acceptance, relationship building, and involvement as opposed to investigation.

The Chalker Place experience reinforced what is stated in the literature about how the risk assessment and risk management approach to child protection leave in the background issues of poverty, oppression, social injustices, and power imbalances. Yet these are the very reasons why many parents and families require assistance or protective intervention services. Connecting with the parents and the Chalker Place community brought these issues front and centre. Through their community resource centre, parents worked in partnership with others to take steps to deal with some of these pervasive issues, for example, establishing a community food bank, developing cost-free programs for children, running clothing exchanges, and other developments. Community capacity building creates these opportunities to advocate for and take action to deal with fundamental issues facing parents and families on a day-to-day basis. It is truly an "of" people, "for" people, and "by" people process.

The Chalker Place experience is not about change but innovation, not about welfare but justice, not about wielding power but discovering it, not about programmatic "fix it" approaches but about distributive collaborative approaches, not about programs and services that are rule- and procedures-driven but about programs and services that are vision- and value-driven. It is about creating opportunities and interventions that are heavily invested in prevention and early involvement as well as treatment.

## IMPLICATIONS FOR SOCIAL WORK PRACTICE AND EDUCATION

Community capacity building is about connecting with parents and their neighbourhoods through appreciation for process and relationship building. To embrace community capacity building in practice means that current relationships that exist between child protection systems and parents and families, as well as with other key community and professional stakeholders, must be renegotiated. Central to this renegotiating process is an acknowledgment that current child protection policies and practices are not realizing desirable outcomes (Barter, 2005b). There is a consensus in child welfare literature and research that the status quo is unacceptable and that more comprehensive approaches, such as community capacity building, are deemed necessary. Juxtaposed to this is an understanding of the following in terms of practice and relationship building/renegotiation (Barter, 2002):

1. It is important to alter the existing power relationships between parents requiring protective intervention services and social workers involved in child protection. The voice of the professional cannot substitute for the voice of parents.

2. It is important to acknowledge that child protection requires collaborative partnerships between families and youth, professionals and their organizations, and citizens and their communities.

3. It is important to shift from the idea that professionals and their organizations are the sole experts. Acknowledging parents and communities as critical resources and partners with varying degrees of expertise is essential.

4. It is important to understand that protecting children is a community responsibility requiring the collaboration of all stakeholders. Collaboration is more than either co-ordination or co-operation. It is the willingness to mutually invest in a common vision and goal and to do things differently.

5. It is important to be innovative whereby opportunities are stressed rather than problems, where collective intelligence, strengths, and diversity are appreciated and where individual and community empowerment is facilitated. This is critical in partnering with Aboriginal peoples and their communities.

Equally important in practice within a community capacity building framework are the principles put forth by Seita (2000). His suggestion is that a major shift in child welfare practices would occur with the adoption of four key principles: (1) connectedness (promoting close, positive relationships); (2) dignity (courtesy, respect, and safety); (3) continuity (continuous belonging to a group, family, community); and (4) opportunity (capitalizing on one's strengths, and forming a personal vision). Embracing concepts and principles such as these places child protection work within the realm of being more holistic and wellness oriented. It is for this reason that community capacity emphasizes the significance of the four key determinants of health—protection, relationships, hope and opportunity, and community (Guy, 1997). When working with children and families, all four determinants require investments in planning. Currently, it is protection that is emphasized with little or no emphasis on the other three. Embracing all four determinants suggests extending questions beyond just the protective plan to include plans for hope and opportunity for the children and parents, plans for ongoing and sustaining relationships, and plans for a sense of community and belonging. All four determinants require as much in terms of assessments as does the assessment of risks, whether the intervention plan is either the removal of risks or the removal of children. Current risk assessment procedures and tools tend not to emphasize environmental influences and the critical dimensions associated with the four key determinants of health (Wharf, 2003; Callahan, 2001). These dimensions include income and social status, social support networks, education, employment/working conditions, social environments, physical environments, personal health practices and coping skills, health services, gender, and culture.

Of equal significance for practice in community capacity building is the emphasis on extending interventions beyond the family to include interventions with public child welfare organizations and their professionals, as well as with citizens and their communities. Each are communities of individuals connected by relationships, difficulties, common challenges and vulnerabilities, and interdependence. A commitment to community capacity building requires a rethinking of current practices and an appreciation of the importance of integrating individual and community practices—in other words, connecting personal difficulties to public issues. Making this personal-political connection conveys a message that community has a role in protecting the health and well-being of children. The current emphasis on interventions being primarily with children and families, independent of other professionals, child-serving organizations and the community, continues to frame child protection in a narrow way and fails to bring issues impacting on children and families into the broader social and political realm.

Community capacity building also challenges language used in child protection work. Child protection families are most commonly referred to as "cases." "Treating people as cases dehumanizes them" (Wharf, 2000, p. 132). The term represents classification and categorization for purposes of management control and administration. It does little to recognize children, parents, and families as citizens who have rights to services and basic needs. Categorizing children and parents as "cases" presents the same disrespect as the term "client." "Client," similar to words like "patient" or "customer," implies that a person has less knowledge, information, expertise, or resources than the professional. Rather than being seen as an equal person, "client" denotes someone of concern and requiring professional attention rather than someone who can make a contribution. Social work education tends to promote "clientism" (Parsloe, 1990) or the effort to "clientize" people (Smale, 1995). Doing so shares with racism, sexism, and ageism in that it devalues a particular group of people by those with power. Community capacity building recognizes people requiring services, as well as people providing services, as citizens, each with their own skills, resources, strengths, and vulnerabilities. The term "citizen" supports emancipatory practice. The person is seen in the context of the broader domain and individual and public issues are to be understood and connected, each having roles and responsibilities in bringing about innovation. Many initiatives associated with the Community Action Program for Children (CAPC) use the term "participant" as opposed to "client." The term denotes equality among all those involved, both professionals and those being served.

Another language issue is the term "at risk." Swadener and Lubeck (1995) promote the term "at promise." The notion of children and families being "at risk" promotes deficit model assumptions and discourse which tend to locate problems or pathologies in individuals and families rather than in institutional structures that create and maintain inequality. "At promise" conveys the importance of locating many problems faced by parents and children outside the family. It focuses attention on the larger contexts within which families struggle and where change is required both individually and structurally. Viewing children and families as "at promise" enhances the possibilities of constructing authentic relations where active listening and learning from one another take place (Muluccio & Anderson, 2000; Waldfogel, 1998). Abandoning "clinical" labels is equally important. Terms such as "behaviour disorder," "dysfunctional," "disruptive," and "disturbed" remain a part of practice language. According to Seita (2000), "these terms border on the derisive, are disrespectful of our children, focus on so-called weaknesses, fail to recognize the social context, and may contribute to negative, judgmental, and punitive practices by those in the child welfare field and by society in general" (p. 80). Even the word "protection" presupposes that children need to be protected from their parents. "The concept of child protection automatically pits the child against the parent, since a child cannot exist without a parent, and one ceases to be a parent without a child" (Turnell & Edwards, 1999, p. ix). Community capacity building avoids language where parents feel devalued and judged.

In terms of social work education and preparation for child welfare practice, it is important to have a consensus on curriculum content. Close collaboration is required between schools of social work and child welfare organizations whereby discourse can occur around the impact of managerialism, the contract culture that is emerging in health and social services, and the imposition on social work education and training of a competency-based approach to practice. All are changing the nature of practice. Theory-based and value-driven aspects associated with professionalism, ethics, social justice, critical thinking, and reflective practice are antithetical to this change. The challenge is finding a balance that not only upholds the "art" and "science" of social work, but also prepares students for the reality of the working environment. This reality comes in several forms. For example, social work education cannot take place without acknowledgment that most social workers will work in hierarchical organizations with much of their work being controlled by bureaucratic rules and procedures. Bureaucracies tend not to be environments that embrace the "art" of social work where social workers are expected to exercise autonomy, creativity, critical thinking, and re-conceptualization abilities. Social workers need to understand the challenges associated with being a professional, although not necessarily hired to be so in a true sense. Instead they become "bureau professionals" who must strive for a balance of being loyal to the profession and the bureaucracy. Social work education cannot ignore this reality. Students must know about being the bureau professional and know how bureaucracies operate.

Also of significance in social work practice and education in child welfare is technology. The current emphasis in social work education on "hi-touch" (feelings, impressions, intuition) must be extended to integrate "hi-tech" (hypertechnology). Computer technology poses many critical challenges. As computers enter more and more into the day-to-day practices of social workers, there has to be a balance between computers meeting a financial efficiency and organizational agenda as well as fulfilling social work practice expectations in terms of relationship building and face-to-face dialogue. It is important that computer technology does not become dehumanizing and instead operates to facilitate professional practice, as opposed to creating barriers to working with vulnerable populations.

Of equal significance is embracing diversity. The knowledge base of social work needs to expand to include a broader spectrum of populations. Social workers need to be prepared to work within a multicultural society and understand the impact of migration, oppression, colonization, and marginalization. As pointed out by Lacroix (2003), it is important for teaching and learning in social work to move from ethnocentricity to ethnorelativism. Where ethnocentricity refers to being centred in one's own world, ethnorelativism is the ability to not only accept and respect cultural differences, but also the empathic ability to shift to another cultural world view. Creating opportunities within social work education for students to understand and appreciate different cultures will mean engaging individuals from diverse cultures and backgrounds within the classroom as well as with field placement opportunities within different cultures. Past experiences of Aboriginal peoples with social workers would suggest the critical importance of embracing diversity.

The theory of instruction is also an important consideration in educating social workers and preparing them for practice in child welfare. It is suggested that rather than relying on the art and science of teaching children ("pedagogy," which translates into providing practical experience and related opportunities), there is a need to adopt "andragogy," the art and science of helping adults learn to become social workers. Becoming a social worker is about self-awareness and shaping attitudes and values. This is done more through experience and example than by didactic teaching. Students must be treated as adults and be active participants with others in their learning. It is important for social work schools to create this type of learning environment, an environment that appreciates collaborative partnerships between faculties and students, that supports sharing power, that learns by doing and seeing, and where social work values and principles are more than just words but are seen in action. There is a requirement for just as much emphasis on learning as well as teaching.

## SUMMARY

Community capacity building represents a fundamental shift in thinking from the traditional approach in protecting children. As put forth in this chapter, the protection of children is a community responsibility involving parents, law enforcement officials, courts, mental health workers, teachers, and other citizens. All have an important role to play. When these roles come together in the best interests of children, families, and communities, as evidenced from community capacity building initiatives, positive outcomes are realized. Within these various roles, the social work profession is critical. Not only is child welfare recognized and sanctioned as the domain of social work (Callahan, 1993), it is a field of practice requiring what social work stands for in terms of its ethics, values, and principles. Being the predominant profession in child welfare, social work is well placed to be influential in advocating and facilitating innovation, collaboration, and the research/policy connection to practice and in assuming a leadership role to build community capacities for the protection of children.

## References

Adams, R. (2002). Social work processes. In R. Adams, L. Dominelli, & M. Payne (Eds.). *Social work: Themes, issues and critical debates* (2nd ed., pp. 249–266). New York, NY: Palgrave.

Allen-Meares, P. & DeRoos, Y. (1997). The future of the social work profession. In M. Reisch & E. Gambrill (Eds.). *Social work in the 21st century* (pp. 376–386). London: Pine Forge Press.

Barter, K.A. (1996). Collaboration: A framework for northern social work practice. In R. Delaney, K. Brownlee, & K. Zapf (Eds.). *Issues in northern social work practice* (pp. 70–94). Thunder Bay: Centre for Northern Studies, Lakehead University.

Barter, K. (1997). Rethinking values and beliefs in child protection: A challenge for social work. *Child & Family: A Journal of the Notre Dame and Family Institute*, 1(2), 6–15.

Barter, K. (2000, Summer). Renegotiating relationships in child protection. *Canada's Children*. Ottawa: Child Welfare League of Canada, 35–38.

Barter, K. (2001). *Capacity building as a core element of evaluation: A literature review.* Paper prepared for Population and Public Health, Atlantic Regional Office, Health Canada.

Barter, K. (2002, Spring). Enough is enough: Renegotiating relationships to create a conceptual revolution in community and children's protection. *Canada's Children*. Ottawa: Child Welfare League of Canada, 28–29.

Barter, K. (2003, Spring). Strengthening community capacity: Expanding the vision. *Relational Child and Youth Care Journal*, 16(2), 24–32.

Barter, K. (2004). A community approach to child protection. *Perspectives*, 1(1), 27–32.

Barter, K. (2005a). Re-conceptualizing services for the protection of children. In J. Turner & F. Turner (Eds.). *Canadian social welfare* (5th ed., pp. 316–332). Toronto: Pearson Education Canada, Inc.

Barter, K. (2005b). Alternative approaches to promoting the health and well-being of children: Accessing community resources to support resilience. In M. Ungar (Ed.). *Handbook for working with children and youth: Pathways to resilience across cultures and contexts* (pp. 343–356). Sage Publications Inc.

Bellefeuille G., Garrioch, S. & Ricks, F. (1997). *Breaking the rules: Transforming governance in social services*. Thompson, Manitoba: Awasis Agency of Northern Manitoba.

Bennett, M. & Blackstock, C. (2006). First Nations child and family services and Indigenous knowledge as a framework for research, policy and practice. In N. Freymond & G. Cameron (Eds.). *Towards positive systems of child and family welfare: International comparisons of child protection, family service, and community caring systems* (pp. 269–288). Toronto: University of Toronto Press.

Berg, I. K. & Kelly, S. (2000). *Building solutions in child protective services*. New York: W. W. Norton & Company.

Blackstock, C. (2003). First Nations child and family services: Restoring peace and harmony in First Nations communities. In K. Kufeldt & B. McKenzie (Eds.). *Child welfare: Connecting research, policy, and practice* (pp. 331–342). Waterloo, Ontario: Wilfrid Laurier University Press.

Brubacher, M. (2006). *Coming home: A story of Tikinagan child and family services*. Tikinagan Child and Family Services: Sioux Lookout, Ontario.

Callahan, M. (1993). Feminist approaches: Women recreate child welfare. In B. Wharf (Ed.). *Rethinking child welfare in Canada* (pp. 172–209). Toronto: McClelland & Stewart.

Callahan, M. (2001) Risk assessment in child protection services: No: 'These tools... do not reduce risk for children.' *Canadian Social Work Review,* 18(1), 157–162.

Callahan, M. & Wharf, B. (1993). The case for removing child abuse and neglect investigations from the mandate of child welfare. In *Rethinking social welfare: People, policy, and practice* (pp. 87–108). Sixth Biennial Social Welfare Policy Conference, St. John's, NL.

Cameron, G. & Freymond, N. (2006). Understanding international comparisons of child protection, family services, and community caring systems of child and family welfare. In N. Freymond & G. Cameron (Eds.). *Towards positive systems of child and family welfare: International comparisons of child protection, family service, and community caring systems* (pp. 3–26). Toronto: University of Toronto Press.

Campaign 2000. (2006). *Child poverty in Canada: Report card 2005*. Toronto: Child Poverty Action Group.

Canadian Association of Social Workers. (2003). *Child Welfare Project: Creating Conditions for Good Practice*. Ottawa: Canadian Association of Social Workers.

Canadian Association of Social Workers. (2005). *Working conditions for social workers and linkages to client outcomes in child welfare: A literature review 2005*. Ottawa: Canadian Association of Social Workers.

Carniol, B. (1995). *Case critical: Challenging social services in Canada*. Toronto: Between The Lines.

Connors, E. & Maidman, F. (2001). A circle of healing: Family wellness in Aboriginal communities. In I. Prilleltensky, G. Nelson, & L. Peirson (Eds.). *Promoting family wellness and preventing child maltreatment: Fundamentals for thinking and action* (pp. 349–418). Toronto: University of Toronto Press.

Conway, J. F. (2001). *The Canadian family in crisis* (4th ed.). Toronto: James Lorimer & Company Ltd., Publishers.

Dominelli, L. (1996). De-professionalizing social work: Anti-oppressive practice, competencies and postmodernism. *British Journal of Social Work,* 26, 153–175.

Dominelli, L. (1999). *Community approaches to child welfare*. Burlington, VT: Ashgate Publishing Company.

Dominelli, L. (2002). Anti-oppressive practice in context. In R. Adams, L. Dominelli & M. Payne, (Eds.). *Social work: Themes, issues and critical debates* (2nd ed., pp. 3–19). New York, NY: Palgrave.

Fabricant, M. B. & Burghardt, S. (1992). *The welfare state crisis and the transformation of social service work*. New York: M. E. Sharpe, Inc.

Graham, J. & Barter, K. (1999). Collaboration: A social work practice method. *Families in Society: The Journal of Contemporary Human Services*, 80(1), 6–13.

Guy, K. A. (Ed.). (1997). *Our promise to our children*. Ottawa: Canadian Institute of Child Health.

Hooper-Briar, K. (1996). Building new capacities for work with vulnerable children, youth, and families. In K. Hooper-Briar & H.A. Lawson (Eds.). *Expanding partnerships for vulnerable children, youth, and families* (pp. 352–361). Alexandria, Virginia: Council on Social Work Education.

Hooper-Briar, K. & Lawson, H. A. (1994). *Serving children, youth and families through interprofessional collaboration and service integration: A framework for action*. Oxford, OH: The Danforth Foundation and the Institute for Educational Renewal at Miami University.

Ife, J. (1995). *Community development: Creating community alternatives—vision, analysis and practice*. Melbourne, Australia: Longman.

Ife, J. (1997). *Rethinking social work practice: Towards critical practice*. Melbourne, Australia: Longman.

Jones, C. (2002). Social work and society. In R. Adams, L. Dominelli & M. Payne, (Eds.). *Social work: Themes, issues and critical debates* (2nd ed., pp. 41–49). New York, NY: Palgrave.

Jordan, B. (2000). Conclusion: Tough love: Social work practice in UK society. In P. Stepney & D. Ford (Eds.), *Social work models, methods and theories* (pp. 139–146). Dorset: Russell House Publishing.

Kufeldt, K. & McKenzie, B. (Eds.). (2003). *Child welfare: Connecting research, policy, and practice* (pp. 79–99). Waterloo, Ontario: Wilfrid Laurier University Press.

Lacroix, M. (2003). Culturally appropriate knowledge and skills required for effective multicultural practice with individuals, families, and small groups. In A. Al-Krenawi & J. Graham (Eds.), *Multicultural social work in Canada* (pp. 23–46). New York: Oxford University Press.

Lafrance, J. (2003). *Social work practice and child welfare—paradox and possibility*. Paper presented at the Canadian Symposium of Child and Family Services Outcomes (pp 145–153). Calgary, Alberta: Canadian Outcomes Institute.

Lee, B. & Richards, S. (2002). Child protection through strengthening communities: The Toronto Children's Aid Society. In B. Wharf (Ed.). *Community work approaches to child welfare* (pp. 93–115). Peterborough, ON: Broadview Press.

Lindsey, D. (2004). *The welfare of children*. New York: Oxford University Press.

Lindsey, D. & Henly, J. R. (1997). The future of child welfare. In M. Reisch & E. Gambrill (Eds.), *Social work in the 21st century* (pp. 100–119). London: Pine Forge Press.

Lundy, C. (2004). *Social work and social justice: A structural approach to practice*. Peterborough, ON: Broadview Press.

MacAulay, J. (2002). *Tensions and possibilities: Forging better links between family resource programs and child welfare*. Ottawa: Family Resource Programs Canada.

MacAulay, J. (2003). Searching for common ground: Family resource programs and child welfare. In B. Wharf (Ed.). *Community work approaches to child welfare* (pp. 163–180). Peterborough, ON: Broadview Press.

Mandell, D., Blackstock, C., Carlson, J. C. & Fine, M. (2006). From child welfare to child, family, and community welfare: The agenda of Canada's Aboriginal Peoples. In N. Freymond & G. Cameron (Eds.). *Towards positive systems of child and family welfare: International comparisons of child protection, family service, and community caring systems* (pp. 211–236). Toronto: University of Toronto Press.

McKenzie, B. (2002). Building community in West Region Child and Family Services. In B. Wharf (Ed.). *Community work approaches to child welfare* (pp. 1152–1162). Peterborough, ON: Broadview Press.

McKenzie, B. & Flette, E. (2003). Community building through block funding in Aboriginal child and family services. In K. Kufeldt & B. McKenzie (Eds.). *Child welfare: Connecting research, policy, and practice* (pp. 343–354). Waterloo, ON: Wilfrid Laurier University Press.

Melton, G. B. (2003). *Mandatory Reporting: A Policy without Reason*. Commentary prepared for virtual discussion sponsored by the International Society for Prevention of Child Abuse and Neglect.

Muluccio, A. N. & Anderson, G. R. (Eds.). (2000, January/February). Future challenges and opportunities in child welfare. *Child Welfare*, LXXIX(1).

Parsloe, P. (1990). Social work education in the year 2000. *International Social Work*, 33, 13–25.

Prilleltensky I., Nelson G. & Peirson L. (2001). *Promoting family wellness and preventing child maltreatment: Fundamentals for thinking and action*. Toronto: University of Toronto Press.

Roberts, D. (1991). Child protection in the 21st century. *Child Abuse & Neglect*, 15(1), 25–30.

Rossiter, A. (2002). The social work sector study: A response. *Canadian Social Work Review*, 19(2), 341–348.

Saleebey, D. (1994, July). Culture, theory, and narrative: The intersection of meaning in practice. *Social Work*, 39(4), 351–359.

Schorr, L. B. (1988). *Within our reach: Breaking the cycle of disadvantage*. Toronto: Doubleday.

Schorr, L. B. (1998). *Common purpose: Strengthening families and neighborhoods to rebuild America*. New York: Anchor Books.

Seita, J. R. (2000). In our best interest: Three necessary shifts for child welfare workers and children. *Child Welfare*, LXXIX(1), 77–92.

Sinclair, M., Phillips, D. & Bala, N. (1991). Aboriginal child welfare in Canada. In N. Bala, J. P. Hornick & R. Vogl (Eds.). *Canadian child welfare law* (pp. 171–194). Toronto: Thompson Educational Publishing.

Smale, G. G. (1995). Integrating community and individual practice: A new paradigm for practice. In P. Adams & K. Nelson (Eds.). *Reinventing human services: Community-and family-centred practice* (pp. 59–80). New York: Aldine De Gruyter.

Smale, G. G. (1998). *Managing change through innovation*. London: National Institute for Social Work.

Stepney, P. (2000). Implications for social work in the new millennium. In P. Stepney & D. Ford (Eds.). *Social work models, methods and theories* (pp. 9–19). Dorset: Russell House Publishing.

Swadener, B. B. & Lubeck, S. (1995). *Children and families "at promise."* Albany: State University of New York Press.

Swift, K. & Callahan, M. (2006). Problems and potential of Canadian child welfare. In N. Freymond & G. Cameron (Eds.). *Towards positive systems of child and family welfare: International comparisons of child protection, family service, and community caring systems* (pp. 118–150). Toronto: University of Toronto Press.

Trocmé, N. (1999). Canadian child welfare multi-dimensional outcomes framework and incremental measurement development strategy. In J. Thompson & B. Fallon (Eds.). *The first Canadian roundtable on child welfare outcomes: Roundtable proceedings* (pp. 30–54). Toronto: University of Toronto Press.

Trocmé, N., Fallon, B., MacLaurin, B., Daciuk, J., Felstiner, C., et al. (2005). *Canadian incidence study of reported child abuse and neglect—2003*. Ottawa: Minister of Public Works and Government Services Canada.

Trocmé, N., MacLaurin, B., Fallon, B., Daciuk, J., Billingsley, D., Tourigny, M., et al. (2001). *Canadian incidence study of reported child abuse and neglect*. Ottawa: Health Canada, Government of Canada.

Turnell, A. & Edwards, S. (1999). *Signs of safety: A solution and safety oriented approach to child protection casework*. New York: W.W. Norton and Company.

Waldfogel, J. (1998). *The future of child protection: How to break the cycle of abuse and neglect*. Cambridge, MA: Harvard University Press.

Wharf, B. (1993). Rethinking child welfare. In B. Wharf (Ed.). *Rethinking child welfare in Canada* (pp. 210–230). Toronto: McClelland & Stewart.

Wharf, B. (2000). Cases or citizens? Viewing child welfare through a different lens. *Canadian Social Work*, 2(2), 132–139.

Wharf, B. (Ed.). (2002). *Community work approaches to child welfare*. Peterborough, ON: Broadview Press.

Wharf, B. (2003). Addressing public issues in child welfare. In K. Kufeldt & B. McKenzie (Eds.). *Child welfare: Connecting research, policy, and practice* (pp. 421–428). Waterloo.

Willms, J. D. (Ed.). (2002). *Vulnerable children: Findings from Canada's national longitudinal survey of children and youth*. Edmonton, Alberta: University of Alberta Press.

# CHAPTER 19

# Youth and Youth Services

*Teri Kay and Melanie Cohen*

## INTRODUCTION

Adolescence is one of the most chaotic stages of life. It is marked by rapid body changes both anatomically and physiologically (Borhek, 1988). According to Erik Erikson (1963), identity formation is the most important developmental task of adolescence.

Included in the general framework of adolescence is the development of complex problem-solving skills and values that are learned in part through peer group interaction (Hartup, 1983). More and more youth rely on their peers for support that the family previously provided (Douvan and Adelson, 1966). It is a time of exploration for friends who will be trustworthy and loyal. It is also a time of conformity as young people search for acceptance as members of the group. Interests, use of language, hairstyle, and dress are among the characteristics teens share and learn from one other. Peer groups also provide the opportunity to experiment with new behaviours and assume adult roles in a context that facilitates their individual development of self-identities and sense of self-worth (Erikson, 1963).

Peer relationships and the support they provide can enhance self-esteem and well-being. Conversely, rejection by friends can create adjustment problems, anxiety, or involvement in socially inappropriate or deviant activities. Although inconclusive, studies show that teens who smoke cigarettes or use alcohol and other drugs usually have friends who engage in the same activities (Dingis and Oetting, 1993).

Families, too, play a major role in influencing teenagers' behaviour both positively and negatively. We see many "troubling trends" in our society regarding marriage and family life. In general, the number of divorces, remarriages, single-parent families, teenage pregnancies, poor families, families affected in some way by AIDS (Acquired Immune Deficiency Syndrome), and families reporting family violence have all increased. These statistics indicate a decline in the quality of family life, affecting our children and youths most profoundly.

Complex family structures are emerging that challenge our traditional definition of family and test our ability to search for the strengths, the necessary supports, and the areas of prevention to enable us to treat some of these problematic issues. What are some of the issues facing youths today?

## THE CHANGING FAMILY

Each year a growing number of parents face what may be the greatest test of their parenthood—helping their children deal with the breakup of the family unit. The parents of teens know the unique challenge of parenting this age group, and breakup can have a powerful impact on teenage children. The effects can include periods of mourning and sadness, tiredness, lack of concentration and poor school performance, angry outbursts, and challenges to parental authority.

As with a child of any age, it is important not to involve the teenager in the parental dispute. To do so invites the teenager's resentment and bitterness toward both parents. What is clear from the research (Wallerstein and Blakeslee, 1989) is that the post-divorce relationship between the parents becomes the most important feature in shaping the emerging identity of the adolescent. Children of all ages fare much better when their parents can set aside their spousal differences and co-operate around the children. Allowing teens to make choices about visitation, holidays, primary residences, and meeting new mates improves the chances of building a new and viable family structure.

In most communities across Canada, family service agencies offer programs for the changing family. They range from education and information about the process, alternative-dispute resolution, and the impacts on children and youths, to counselling programs for parents and children, grandparents, and step-parents. What to Tell the Kids, Successful Step-Parenting, Shared Parenting, Adolescence: A Trying Time for Teens, The Importance of Grandparents, and Single Again are examples of the programs these agencies offer. Family Service Canada generally accredits service agencies and they provide their services on a sliding-fee scale.

Inquiries about discussion groups with other teens should also be made at schools, religious institutions, and community associations. If they do not exist, parents could request that they be created.

## LIFESTYLE CHOICES

During this time of rapid change and growth, teens are also balancing a number of their own lifestyle choices. These choices can have a direct impact on their futures and on their present lives.

For many teens, adolescence is a time of exploration and a healthy search for identity and future career path. But those living in marginalized environments often find it a time marked by vulnerability and destructive behaviour. Too many teenagers live in environments characterized by poverty, abuse, and family breakdown. Any one of these factors can lure teens to abuse drugs and/or alcohol. Substance abuse is a problem not only for marginalized youths, but also for youths in general. According to U.N. Chronicle (1998), which refers to the *Report of the International Narcotics Control Board* for 1997, "Drug abuse . . . is now also emerging as a part of a youth subculture that is quickly spreading around the globe a benign image of drugs. . . . Drugs such as methamphetamine, 'ecstasy' and other amphetamine-type stimulants—drugs closely associated with the 'rave' or dance scene—are growing in popularity. . . ."

The false comfort of drugs can have disastrous results not only psychologically and physically, but also through the users' increased exposure to major health risks such as AIDS.

In April 1998, the United Nations International Drug Control Program (UNIDCP) sponsored a five-day get-together for youths in Banff, Alberta. More than 150 young people from 33 countries met and discussed their experiences and shared their ideas about drug prevention. While some focused on the problem of marginalized youths, others saw drugs as part of current youth culture, an image aided by music, television, and movies.

One of the major outcomes of this conference is a developing global network made possible through the proliferation of computers and the worldwide Internet. Equally important is the notion that youths need to be heard and empowered to become part of the solution rather than simply the problem.

Schools are the obvious venue for drug and alcohol prevention programs. While many schools across the country have such programs, others need to be supported and encouraged. Family Life Education programming is perceived as one of the most effective means of prevention. While some schools offer such courses, parents and youths are encouraged to advocate for changes to the curriculum that would also include mandatory drug and alcohol prevention programs.

Excellent films have been created. One of these is an animated cartoon, *Goldtooth*, produced by the Canadian non-governmental organization Street Kids International (SKI). It is an action-adventure film about substance abuse. *The Karate Kid*, another SKI film, deals with health issues such as HIV/AIDS. These two cartoons help both youth workers and teens work together.

In a similar vein, increasing numbers of youths are involved in gambling. Based on the South Oaks Gambling Screen (SOGS), 4 percent of adolescents between the ages of 12 and 19 in Ontario are probable pathological gamblers and another 33 percent have some gambling problems. In a study of 702 adolescents between the ages of 15 and 18 years, correlates of problem gambling include school difficulties, regular drug use, delinquency, parental gambling, and being male (Insight Canada Research Survey, 1993). Casino gambling is restricted to people over the age of 18 years, making it an adult activity; however, this fact has not deterred or prevented teens from gaining access to gambling establishments. Many young people report they can enter casinos with relative ease, and 79 percent reported that their parents knew about their gambling (Acuri et al., 1985). Adults in general do not consider gambling a dangerous activity for adolescents, and the very fact that our society views gambling as a pleasurable adult activity adds to its attraction for many young people. Some gambling activities such as sports pools and raffles do not even attempt to restrict young people.

The level of involvement of adolescents in gambling, the growth of gambling activities in Canada, and the lessons learned from the literature all support the need for education and prevention programs in schools. Adults who work with young people are aware that gambling does not have the recognition that alcohol or drug abuse does, yet the incidence of cross-addiction has been documented as high; substance abusers are about six times as likely to be addicted to gambling as the general population (Gambino, Fitzgerald, Shaffer, and Renner, 1993).

Addressing substance abuse and gambling problems in adolescence requires partnerships. Schools have neither the time nor the skill to develop effective experiential programs. By virtue of their training, social service providers can bring such an approach into classroom learning and could usefully bridge the two systems. The Toronto District School Board (TDSB) and the Jewish Family and Child Service (JF and CS) have formed such a partnership. Classroom presentations are jointly created from input from the teachers and the students and facilitated by an outreach social worker from the TDSB or JF and CS.

Schools throughout the country have developed peer-mentoring programs with social service agencies. These programs recognize the importance of teens talking with teens and they help identify young people at risk. Programs such as conflict resolution are gaining momentum, too, as schools struggle to curb violence on school grounds and in the classrooms. Youth involvement is essential to the success of these programs.

Most communities offer community information services. The Kids Help Phone, for example, can be reached through 1-800-668-6868 or http://kidshelp.sympatico.ca/ and is available across Canada.

Most communities also offer 12-step programs for teens and parents through Alcoholics Anonymous and Gamblers Anonymous.

## LEAVING HOME

Leaving home is often associated with obtaining higher education, training, or job enhancement; however, some young people leave home because their parents can no longer care for them or because their family situations are intolerable. Many teens cannot live independently, and the need for substitute care is obvious. Their issues require a variety of support systems, including specialized foster homes, group homes, children's mental health centres, hostels, and maternity homes.

Most communities have some of these services, and some communities have set up a point of centralized access to these resources through children's mental health centres. Other services can be accessed through the Children's Aid Society and family service organizations. Unfortunately, more and more youths are finding their way to the streets and becoming part of Canada's growing number of homeless. These adolescents are without the benefit of adult guidance and must make decisions on their own at a time when they are ill-equipped to do so. These young people face severe challenges, including exploitation and abuse. While overall statistics are scant, it is believed that a disproportionate number of gay and lesbian youths are part of the army of street youths. These teens are homeless because they are no longer welcome at home, not by choice.

Street youths usually rely on the public for their day-to-day subsistence. They beg, scrounge, wash car windows, and perform other "services" that consumers generally do not appreciate. Street youths run the risk of being abused, developing health problems, using drugs, and becoming involved in criminal activities.

Services for street youths are mainly non-traditional. Youth organizations often reach out to this population by placing youth workers on the streets. As street youths are primarily a problem of urban centres, cities such as Toronto, Calgary, Edmonton, and Vancouver have specialized programs that work in conjunction with hostels and police.

The *Protection of Children Involved in Prostitution Act*, introduced in Alberta on February 1, 1999, is the first attempt to allow police and social workers to remove girls younger than age 18 from the streets for 72 hours with or without their consent. In addition, the law allows for fines of up to $25 000 and jail terms of two years less a day for pimps caught with juvenile prostitutes.

In the first 10 weeks of the law's enforcement, the number of juvenile prostitutes on the streets of Calgary dropped dramatically. Other provinces are watching the results very closely, and similar laws may be enacted in Ontario and British Columbia (*Toronto Star*, 1999).

Teens involved in criminal behaviour are dealt with under the *Young Offenders Act*, 1985. The act covers children from ages 12 to 17 who commit offences and allows for youths to be treated and rehabilitated in specialized institutions called training schools. Specialized juvenile courts hear the offences and determine their outcomes. Unlike adult courts, juvenile courts emphasize rehabilitation. The act is a federal statute but the provincial governments administer and operate the facilities required to assist in the process. Although programs may vary, all are designed to meet the education, recreation, and counselling needs of youths.

## NEWCOMERS

In 1998, the Department of Citizenship and Immigration Canada, Settlement Directorate, Ontario Region, conducted a province-wide consultation on the needs of newcomers to the country. The consultation concluded that families and children need greater access to settlement services. The consultation has since resulted in a pilot project in Toronto, which began in mid-1999 and concluded in mid-2000, a partnership between the Toronto District School Board and the community settlement agencies, which are funded by the federal government.

The project intended to expand access to traditional settlement services by moving them into the elementary and secondary schools, which acknowledge that newcomer families require outreach services. Many of these families do not access traditional agencies.

Most communities in Canada today have a definite multicultural representation. One principal in Toronto recently remarked that 77 different languages are spoken in his school. The related challenge for families, schools, and social workers is enormous, particularly when prevention programs are being eliminated.

In addition to issues of normal adolescent development, students from other countries face language and cultural differences, and perhaps unfamiliar vocation and education choices. Some may have learning difficulties; others may be traumatized by coming from countries where they or their families endured discrimination and/or terror.

In addition to learning new language skills and finding employment, families often find their children adjust more quickly and easily to Canadian daily life than the adults do. Family conflicts can arise as the adolescent opts for the norms and values of the prevailing youth culture rather than those of the family's traditions. Teens' language skills often develop beyond those of their parents and can complicate family matters even further. Frequently, the teens are asked to take on the role of translator to help the family acquire needed services. Neither their parents nor the teens themselves always welcome this role reversal. Teachers struggle to understand issues affecting these students, but the influx of so many different cultures makes their job overwhelming.

The initiative of the Ministry of Culture and Immigration, therefore, holds great promise. It is a model that can be repeated in other communities. It also recognizes that reaching out to families and teens in schools is a more accessible and more comfortable route for parents to accept.

## EATING DISORDERS

In Western society, chronic dieting has become very common. Not only is dieting, as Rodin et al. (1985) suggest, a way of life for many, but it often starts in early adolescence. Rodin et al. (1986), using a random sample of male and female undergraduates, discovered that weight and body shape were the central determinants of a female's self-perception of her attractiveness much more than they were for the males.

Dieting often precipitates eating disorders. *Woman's Health Weekly* (1995) reported the following definitions by Dr. Donald Durham, a leading authority on eating disorders and the keynote speaker at a symposium at Texas Christian University:

- Anorexia nervosa is characterized by a body weight of 15 percent or more below normal, refusal to gain or maintain normal weight, and a phobic fear of weight gain that takes on irrational proportions.
- Bulimia nervosa, characterized by episodes of binge eating and purging, is more prevalent than anorexia. Secret binges, in which the patient might consume 20 000 calories at once, are followed by self-induced vomiting, use of laxatives and diuretics, fasting, and compulsive exercise.

- Compulsive overeating, also known as binge-eating disorder, is characterized by binge eating without extreme weight-control measures.

Eating disorders are about more than an obsession with food; they are a reflection of a person's body image, self-esteem, sense of belonging, and societal and peer pressure. Eating disorders kill if left untreated. Treatment often involves hospitalization, antidepressants, nutritional planning, counselling, 12-step programs, support groups, and family therapy.

While eating disorders are considered a major problem among adolescents, the problem continues to be surrounded by a strange silence/secrecy. As a society, our focus continues to be on appearance and the notion that "thin is in."

In school, girls often form cliques and, within these groups, members struggle to be cool or to be perceived as leaders. A girl may have more status if she diets, takes appetite suppressants, and exercises feverishly. Some girls watch each other at lunchtime and focus more on what is on their plates than what is in their books. How many brilliant minds are we losing to these diseases?

Parents and youths are encouraged to become informed about eating disorders and their devastating effects. Only one-half of all persons diagnosed with anorexia recover fully, and one out of every 30 dies as a result (Patton, 1989).

Here are some recommended self-help books:

Bruch, H. 1998. *The gold cage: The enigma of anorexia nervosa*. Cambridge, MA: Harvard University Press.

Cash, T. 1995. *What do you see when you look in the mirror? Helping yourself to a positive body image*. New York: Bantam Books.

Cooper, P. 1995. *Bulimia nervosa and binge eating: A guide to recovery*. New York: University Press.

## DATING VIOLENCE

### Definitions and Facts about Dating Violence from the National Clearing House on Family Violence—Canada (1995)

Dating violence is defined as any intentional sexual, physical, or psychological attack on one partner by the other in a dating relationship. The definition takes all abuse seriously. It acknowledges that although both women and men may act abusively, the abuse of women by men is more pervasive and usually more severe.

Dating violence is a serious problem in Canada, but there are still only limited statistics to assess its extent. However, between 16 percent and 30 percent of women surveyed say they have experienced at least one physical assault by a male dating partner. Studies on sexual violence are less clear-cut because of the low reporting rate. Surveys suggest that 45 percent of the women surveyed state that they have been victimized since leaving high school.

Canadian, British, and US studies indicate that women are at far greater risk of being assaulted by men they know.

In order to work with youths involved in violent dating relationships it is important to understand their social context. Developmentally, adolescence is a time of confusion and vulnerability. This is especially true for a young woman in love. Young women may absorb the romantic fantasies featured in movies, on television, and in magazines in addition to the covert pressure of family and friends asking "Do you have a boyfriend?" Having a boyfriend certainly may increase one's status among peers. Having a boyfriend may also increase one's value in a couple-oriented society. These pressures, and the other challenges of adolescence, can create a needy young woman searching for acceptance. In her interviews with 11 dating-violence survivors, Rosen (1994) found that the interviewees were all experiencing difficult times when they met their boyfriends. They saw their boyfriends unrealistically and allowed themselves to be swept away by men who they thought would make their lives easier.

Not only is there pressure to be in a relationship, but there is pressure to stay in the relationship as well. Many young women believe that staying in a relationship is so important that a violent relationship is better than no relationship at all.

Work on this issue is necessary on both a formal level and an informal one. The formal level refers to sending public messages about non-violence through institutions such as schools and universities. Informal work involves the work of individual social workers who meet with adolescents and the parents of adolescent children.

The most obvious place to begin working on preventing dating violence is in the schools. Educational institutions have a tremendous responsibility to address violence and take an active stand against it. Again, policies need to be backed up with education. Hird (1995) reported that most Canadian provinces have produced at least one course for students that includes information on family violence. The next step is to expand the definition of family violence to include dating violence, and then to make such courses mandatory.

Parents, teachers, school nurses, principals, and janitors—everyone in the school community who may recognize the signs—need to be educated about dating violence. At the university level this training includes security personnel, residence staff, and health services. Also, students must be educated to identify the signs of dating violence in friends. It is critical that all youths be informed.

It is especially important at the university level for three reasons. First, Carlson (1987) points out that men who attend higher education are more receptive to "talking" interventions. Second, it is at university age that many people enter their first serious relationship. Last, many students are away from home for the first time and may be more anxious to be in relationships.

Part of the work that can be done on a more informal level is for parents, teachers, and social workers to be more open when discussing sex and relationships. Developmentally, youths not only tend to disengage from their parents at this age but also view adult help as a complicating factor (Mercer, 1998). Parents and teachers can play a part in making themselves more accessible to adolescents. Through better communication a youth may feel more comfortable approaching an adult. As well, with more information about safe, consensual sex and reciprocal relationships, young people may recognize violence in their relationships faster. Litch Mercer (1988) supports open discussions, especially given that sexuality is transmitted through society as pornography, rape, seduction, and romanticism. When we do not engage in discussions about sexuality and relationships with teens, the young people have no evidence or information to counter those particular images.

Routinely, parents need to ask their daughters (and sons) about their dating relationships. Sometimes simply asking shows youths that their parents care. Parents need to learn how to recognize the signs associated with abusive relationships. Also, they need to know the steps to take if they suspect violence. Rosen (1994) describes interviews conducted with young women in which their parents reportedly saw the violence without really perceiving it. Ignoring such signs not only puts a daughter at risk but also sends her a message that the violence is acceptable.

Social workers as well can play an important part in protecting youths from violent dating relationships. Like parents, we can be more open to discussing sexuality and relationships. Obviously, we must do this when we work directly with survivors of dating violence. In fact, questions about violence need to be a part of the assessment interviews in all contexts (Bergman, 1992). School social workers must try to monitor sudden changes in student behaviour and attitude. Exploring the changes and asking questions may bring a problem to the worker's attention. Often this is a key step that health professionals and social workers overlook when they work with abused women. For example, an emergency room physician may treat a young woman's broken arm, but does not treat her by pressing for details of how the injury happened.

When working with youths who are involved in violent dating relationships, it is very important that the social worker send a strong message against violence. At all stages of a relationship, women need information about violence that dispels myths, explores sex-role socialization, and helps them identify dangerous situations (Mills and Granoff, 1992).

In her article, Rosen (1994) discusses the treatment goals when working with survivors of violence. Assuring the safety of the client is paramount. This requires creating a safety plan, informing the woman about available resources, and possibly informing her guardians and the police about the situation. The therapist must refuse to minimize the violence and emphasize that violence is a crime. The second step is to help the client expand her perspective by reading literature on the cycle of violence and the common characteristics of abused women. This will help her see the abuse from a more detached point of view and help her realize she is not alone. The last step is to empower her to establish more appropriate boundaries between herself and her partner, and to strengthen her connections to friends and family.

Male youths need resources on the issue as well. Research has suggested that young men often turn to other male friends for support (DeKeseredy and Hinch, 1991). With the help of these friends, a young man may minimize and accept the violence. Offering alternatives for men therefore is essential. This can be accomplished through peer counselling, university-run groups, and late-night hotlines.

## IMPACT OF THE INTERNET ON YOUTHS

The Internet is often referred to as "the information highway." It serves people's business, shopping, and banking needs, is used for research purposes, and much more. In today's society, one has to ponder the question: "Is the Internet a friend or foe to the youths of today?" Youth Culture, Inc., a publisher and market research company that targets teens, conducted the Canadian Teen Landmark Study on the Internet, which is supported by a survey done by Northern Research Partners. The survey questioned 1000 young Net surfers between the ages of 12 to 17 and 450 parents. It estimated that 85 percent of Canada's 2.4 million teens use the Internet, connecting for an average of 9.3 hours per week (Newsbytes, 2000).

Since such a large number of teens use the Internet, the next question is "How useful is the time spent while surfing the information highway?" The Young Canadians in a Wired

World survey canvassed 5682 students between the ages of 9 and 17 in schools across Canada. According to this survey, 57 percent spend their time downloading and playing music, 56 percent send and receive email, 50 percent surf for fun, 48 percent play and download games, 40 percent send instant messages, 39 percent use chat rooms, and only 38 percent spend their time doing homework (Media Awareness Network, 2001).

An alarming finding from the Young Canadians in a Wired World survey is that more and more youths are entering private and adults-only chat rooms. Children lack supervision and rules regarding Internet use at home. Youths most commonly enter these chat room sites when they are alone, whether that is at home, in Internet cafes, or elsewhere. What is even more alarming is that not only do teens enter inappropriate chat rooms, they often also meet in person with the people they have previously spoken with only on the Internet. According to the survey, 73 percent of males and 27 percent of females were likely to put themselves at risk in this way (*Young Canadians in a Wired World: The Student's View*, 2004)

## GAY AND LESBIAN YOUTH

Growing up can be an extremely trying and complex time for adolescents. A large part of growing up revolves around the formation of one's sexual identity. It is quite normal and healthy for children and teenagers to explore and experiment with their sexuality. They may do this with same-sex partners or with partners of the opposite sex. For those who have thought about and/or actively experimented with same-sex partners, anxiety may persist. "Homosexuality" is "the persistent sexual and emotional attraction to someone of the same sex" (American Academy of Child and Adolescent Psychiatry [AACAP], 2002).

Misperceptions, myths, and stigmas regarding sexual orientation can complicate the social, emotional, and physical processes of teenage development (Vare and Norton, 1998). A previously misconceived notion is that homosexuality is a mental illness or disorder. Parents and loved ones should understand that homosexuality is not a mental illness and that the causes of homosexuality are not fully understood. Sexual orientation is not a matter of choice.

Another misconception according to Remafedi and Blum (1986) is that only those with homosexual identities engage in sexual activity with people of the same sex. In reality, adolescence can be a time of experimentation with partners of both sexes. Sexual activity alone does not necessarily indicate sexual orientation.

The stigma surrounding homosexual behaviour hinders the ability of gay and lesbian youths to confront the confusion they may be experiencing regarding their emerging identities. Because of this, many teens may opt to engage in avoidance strategies, such as denial of their homosexuality. These avoidance strategies can be manifested as specific behaviours, such as limited interaction with the same sex to prevent being "found out" and the refusal to explore the subject of homosexuality.

Health and psychosocial difficulties often surface with youths who identify themselves as homosexual. Some of these difficulties include deteriorating school performance, truancy, running away from home, substance abuse, the need to consult mental health professionals, juvenile prostitution, and psychiatric hospitalization (Vare and Norton, 1998).

In spite of the fact that as a society our knowledge about being gay and lesbian has increased, our youths still worry about various related concerns. These range from feeling different from their peers, feelings of guilt or anxiety provoked by loved ones' reactions, and fears about being teased and ridiculed, sexually transmitted diseases, discrimination, rejection, and exposure to harassment by others around them.

Social isolation and low self-esteem are common in gay and lesbian teens. Depression is also common among gay and lesbian youths, and it frequently is a factor leading to suicide. According to the AACAP, recent studies have shown that gay and lesbian youths account for a significant number of deaths by suicide (2002). In conjunction with this, there is a blatant lack of emotional support for gay and lesbian youths. Rejection can originate from parents, family members, educators, and peers. It is vital that we help youths, whether heterosexual or homosexual, to feel wanted, worthy, and able to express their identities. Acceptance must be our future.

Parents may have difficulty accepting their teens' homosexuality; therefore, they may find organizations such as Parents, Families and Friends of Lesbians and Gays (PFLAG) useful. Parents may turn to counselling for gay and lesbian youths; however, no one should expect counselling to change people's homosexual orientation. Doing this can confuse teens and only perpetuate their anxiety by reinforcing negative thoughts and emotions that they have already been dealing with (AACAP, 2002). The purpose of counselling should be to help youths feel free and able to address their feelings openly and in an environment in which they feel safe.

## YOUTH SUICIDE

Rates of depression are below 1 percent before puberty, but shoot up to 8 percent to 10 percent following puberty (Cooper, 2004). A large percentage of Canadian teens suffer from depression, which is one of the main causes of suicide among youths. Suicidal teens often have feelings of overwhelming hopelessness, which stem in turn from feeling unloved, unworthy, and not good enough (Cooper, 2004). Teen suicide is the second leading cause of death among youths, after motor vehicle accidents, according to Health Canada sources (UBC Public Affairs, 2001, and the Canadian Psychiatric Association, 1995). According to the Psychology Association's Professor Paul Hewitt, about 700 children and teens die every year in Canada by suicide (UBC Public Affairs, 2001).

Why do young people commit suicide? There is a general agreement that young people kill themselves when they feel hopeless about a situation and believe that it will never change. Suicide appears to be a response to "intolerable pain."

Several other factors can also contribute to teen suicide; biological factors are among them. A person may succumb to clinical depression owing to a chemical imbalance, a physical disability, a learning disability, the chemical changes of puberty, or a physical dependency on drugs or alcohol. Emotional issues can also lead to suicide among youths— sadness, stress, impulsive behaviour, feelings of powerlessness, loss, grief, low self-esteem, anger or rage, guilt, hopelessness, feeling overwhelmed, anxious, confused about sexual identity/orientation, and an emotional dependency on chemical substances.

Intellectually, youths may find it difficult to communicate their feelings. They may feel pressure to achieve or perform, criticize themselves very harshly, view death unrealistically, want to exact revenge, and may exaggerate their own faults, any or all of which may also contribute to suicide.

Finally, there are also social reasons behind young people's committing suicide. They may suffer isolation, withdrawal, friendlessness, and a lack of social skills; they may be unpopular, feel they do not belong, feel embarrassed before their peers, or be labelled "crazy," "stupid," or just "different." They may have troubles at home, at school, or with the law and may be runaways (The Acadia Hospital, 2003a).

Knowing the suicide warning signs is the first step in helping a child or teen in need. It is important to remember that no single sign can be taken as a concrete indicator of suicide. Look for a pattern. Look for direct statements: for example, "I want to die" or "Life sucks and I want to get out." Observe behaviour, such as a lack of energy, boredom or disinterest, teariness and sadness, and anger or destructive behaviour. For environmental warning signs, look for previous suicide attempts by a family member or friend, problems at school, family violence, sexual abuse, and major family change (The Acadia Hospital, 2003b).

There are many ways to help when a person admits to having suicidal feelings. It is very important to listen to young people, to talk openly with them about suicide, remain calm, be positive, realize your own limits, emphasize alternatives, and know what resources are available to help. It is crucial to find professional help following your initial interaction with the youth in question. Notify the primary-care physician, local hospital, mental health agency, school guidance counsellor, or another trusted professional in your community. Two specific organizations that may be useful are the Acadia Hospital-Access Centre and the Youth Crisis Stabilization Program, a program run by Community Health and Counselling Services.

In cities across Canada, there are emergency mental health–assessment and crisis counselling teams. In Halifax, Nova Scotia, the IWK Children's Health Centre's Intervention Facility is open 24 hours a day, seven days a week. Some other helpful resources are the Suicide Information and Education Centre—www.suicideinfo.ca; The Kids' Help Phone—www.kidshelp.sympatico.ca/en; and the Canadian Mental Health Association for Suicide Prevention—www.suicideprevention.ca.

## CONCLUSION

Working with adolescents is complex and it requires the expertise of a variety of professionals, including social workers, teachers, physicians, police officers, parents, and teens themselves. Social workers bring to the mix an ability to work with a variety of systems and organizations to encourage partnerships and inclusivity. Social work methods range from prevention and education to group and classroom participation, from advocacy and outreach to individual group and family counselling.

Youth issues present social workers with a formidable set of challenges and tasks. Social workers, however, must remember what it was like to be a young adult. This means keeping in mind the importance of "fitting in," the profound influence of the media on values and styles, and simply how scary it can be to grow up.

# References

The Acadia Hospital. (2003a). *Why do youth commit suicide?* Retrieved Sept. 16, 2004, from http://acadiahospital.org/Youth+Suicide+Prevention/Why+Do+Youth+Commit Suicide%3f.htm

The Acadia Hospital. (2003b). *Warning signs.* Retrieved Sept. 16, 2004, from http://acadiahospital.org/Youth+Suicide+Prevention/Warning+Signs.htm

Acuri, A. F., Lester, D., and Smith, R. D. (1985). Shaping adolescent behaviour. *Adolescence, 20.* 935–938.

Addiction Research Foundation. (1995). *Insight Canada research survey 1993.*

American Academy of Child and Adolescent Psychiatry (AACAP). (2002). *Gay and lesbian adolescents.* Retrieved Sept. 16, 2004, from www.aacap.org/publications/factsfam/63.htm

Bergman, Libby. (1992). Dating violence among high school students. *Social Work, 37.1.* 21–27.

Borhek, M. (1988). Helping gay and lesbian adolescents and their families. *Journal of Adolescent Health Care, 9.* 123–128.

Canadian Psychiatric Association. (1995). *Youth and mental illness.* Retrieved Sept. 16, 2004, from www.mentalhealth.com/book/p43-yout.html

Carlson, Bonnie E. (January 1987). Dating violence: A research review and comparison with spouse abuse. *Social Casework: The Journal of Contemporary Social Work.* 16–23.

Cooper, Jen. (2004). *Teen Suicide: What causes it, and how do we prevent it?* Retrieved Sept. 16, 2004, from www.mindful-things.com/Features/features_TeenSuicide.html

DeKeseredey, Walter, and Hinch, R. (1991). Premarital woman abuse. In *Woman abuse: Sociological perspectives.* Toronto: Thompson Educational Publishing.

Dingis, M. M., and Oetting, E. R. (1993). Similarity in drug use patterns between adolescents and their peers. *Adolescence, 28.110.* 253–266.

Douvan, E., and Adelson, J. (1966). *The adolescent experience.* New York: Wiley.

Erikson, E. 1963. *Childhood and society* (2nd ed.). New York: W. W. Norton.

Gambino, B., Fitzgerald, R., Shaffer, H. J., and Renner, J. (1993) Perceived family history of problem gambling and scores on SOGS. *Journal of Gambling Studies, 9.2.* 169–184.

Hartup, W. W. (1983). Peer relations. In E. M. Hetherington (Ed.), *Handbook of child psychology; Socialization, personality and social development* (Vol. 4). New York: Wiley.

Hird, Myra Jean. (1995). Adolescent dating violence: An empirical study. *Intervention, 100.* 60–69.

Litch Mercer, Shirley. (1988). Not a pretty picture: An exploratory study of violence in high school dating relationships. *New Feminist Research, 17.2.* 15–23.

Media Awareness Network. (2001). Retrieved Sept. 16, 2004, from www.media-awareness.ca/english/index.cfm

Mills, C. S., and Granoff, B. J. (November 1992). Date and acquaintance rape among a sample of college students. *Social Work, 37.6.* 504–509.

Newsbytes. (2000). *Teens cut back on TV to surf the Net.* Retrieved Sept. 16, 2004, from http://jimbo.canadacomputes.com/story_3365_24

*Newsweek.* (1993). Boy meets girl, boy beats girl. December 13.

Patton, G. (1989). The course of anorexia nervosa. *British Medical Journal, 299.* 39–140.

Rodin, J., Silberstein, L. R., and Striegel-Moore, R. H. (1985). Women and weight: A normative discontent. In E. M. Hetherington (Ed.), *Nebraska Symposium on Motivation, 32.* Psychology and gender. 267–307.

Rodin, J., Silberstein, L. R., and Striegel-Moore, R. H. (1986). Toward an understanding of risk factors for bulimia. *American Psychologist, 41.* 246–263.

Rosen, Karen H. (August 1994). Empowering young women in violent date relationships. *Family Therapy News.*

Silverstein, Shel. (1981). *A Light in the Attic.* New York: Harper and Row.

*Toronto Star.* (1992). New law allows police and youth workers the authority to get juvenile prostitutes off the street for 72 hours. April 18.

UBC Public Affairs. (2001). *UBC researcher probes perfectionism as suicide predictor in youth.* Retrieved Sept. 16, 2004, from www.publicaffairs.ubc.ca/media/releases/2001/mr-01-47.html

UN Chronicle. (1998). Turning to kids . . . before they turn to drugs. *U.N. Chronicle, 35.2.* 14.

Wallerstein, Judith S., and Blakeslee, Sandra. (1989). *Second chances.* New York: Ticknor and Fields.

*Women's Health Weekly.* (1995). Eating disorders. December 4.

*Young Canadians in a Wired World: The Student's View.* (2004). Retrieved Sept. 16, 2004, from www.mediaawareness.ca/english/special_initiatives/surveys/phase_one/students_survey.cfm

# CHAPTER 20

# Services for Families

*Margaret Fietz*

## INTRODUCTION

The family is the cornerstone of well-being in Canadian society. For the purposes of this discussion, the family is defined in its most inclusive and broadest sense. In the current social context in Canada, family structures are very diverse and complex. While raising children continues to be one of the most prevalent and important responsibilities of family, the additional roles of maintaining stable nurturing relationships for adult couples and family care of seniors are emerging as essential for societal well-being.

At all levels of government, social policy to support families has not developed sufficiently in Canada to provide consistent focus, services, and supports. Philosophically, families in Canada are perceived as being private and responsible for their own well-being. Debate continues on how involved others should be in family affairs, whether that be how to raise children, who is responsible for care of the elderly, or how much external protection is given in situations of spousal abuse, etc. Debate continues on the private rights of parents over children vs. societal norms and Canada's signed international agreements such as the United Nations Convention on the Rights of the Child and its contribution to *A World Fit for Children* (2002).[1]

Federal and provincial government policies do not consistently provide for standards that would support the essential roles that family members need to fulfill. In addition, contrary to the rhetoric that may imply something else, the primary focus of governments in Canada today appears to be one of getting re-elected. Therefore, any change in government can result in a rearranging or dissolution of previous policies, be they helpful to families or not.

In spite of this, there is historically a well-developed system of services, some government initiated and some voluntary, to assist families to develop, grow, benefit from their relationships, and fulfill their responsibilities.

This chapter intends to stimulate the discussion of how families could be more systematically supported in Canada through a) social policy development and b) balanced responsibility of governments, communities, and families. The discussion will focus on the promotion of common values, existing family strengths, and Canada's societal strengths and potential.

## FAMILY IN CANADA TODAY

Every individual is born into a "family" and maintains certain family ties throughout a lifespan. Whether a child grows up with its biological parents, adoptive parents, stepparent, or other caregivers, the child maintains ties to family members and by the nature of human social relationships benefits from and has obligations to these people throughout life.

One of the major challenges is finding an agreed-upon definition of "family." For the purposes of this chapter, family is defined as consisting of two or more people, whether living together or apart,

---

1   Government of Canada. 2002. *A World Fit for Children*. GoC Catalogue Number H39-633/2002-MRC.

related by blood, marriage, adoption, or a commitment to care for one another (Family Service Association of Toronto). Family is not defined by age, offspring, or sexual orientation.

While the definition of family may not seem noteworthy, it determines how policies and practices affecting families are developed. For example, as more couples grow into old age together, their need to have access to shared housing in nursing facilities must be acknowledged and accommodated. The couple is "a family." "The nature of a family is its essential characteristics and qualities…it is characterized by its unconditional concerns or commitment for the total well-being of its members and itself" (Yuen and Skibinski, 2003, p. 204).[2]

The majority of research in Canada has been conducted on families with children under the age of 18. Canadian Council on Social Development's *Stats and Facts: Families: A Canadian Profile* provides a useful analysis of the characteristics of families with children.[3]

In 2001, there were 8.4 million families in Canada: 70.4% were married couples, 13.8% were common-law relationships, and 15.6% were lone-parent families. Average family size was 3.0 persons. Between 2002 and 2003, the divorce rate increased by only 0.7%. In 2003, 63.4% of women with children under 3 were employed, while 76.5% of women with children aged 6-15 were employed. In 2003/04, only 15.5% of children aged 0–12 could be accommodated in regulated child care spaces.

## FACTORS INFLUENCING FAMILY WELL-BEING IN CANADA

Most families in Canada are doing very well. Canadian Council on Social Development's *Progress of Canada's Children and Youth,* 2006,[4] reported on the achievements for children in health, education, recreation, and social development. The report also documents the situation for families who are not doing as well.

Many families in Canada are exhibiting strengths, creativity, and resiliency; they're doing their best. With an ever-increasing participation of women in the workforce and more part-time and self-employed employment, family life patterns are changing. Families are relocating, mostly to Alberta, for better-paid employment, leaving behind their extended family support networks. As Canada engages in more military combat, military families are dealing with increased anxiety about their spouse's or adult children's safety and with their own grief. Canada's major cities have social problems that are not easily rectified. Canada is experiencing lower birth rates and changing demographic patterns. Advances in technology and new medical procedures have resulted in more frail, ill, and disabled people being cared for at home.

As more and more couples delay having children until their late 30s or 40s,[5] more adults find themselves simultaneously trying to fulfill three major roles: that of parent,

---

2   Yuen, F., Editor. 2005. *Social Work Practice with Children and Families: A Family Health Approach.* New York: The Hayward Press Inc.

3   Scott, K. 2005. *Stats and Facts.* Canadian Council on Social Development.

4   Canadian Council on Social Development. 2006. *The Progress of Canada's Children and Youth.*

5   Beaujot, R. 2004. Delayed Life Transitions: Trends and Implications. *Contemporary Family Trends.* Ottawa: Vanier Institute of the Family.

care manager of an aging parent, and supportive adult partner. When planners, researchers, and social policy developers see these roles as separate, services are not developed to meet the family's needs.

In addition, the current conservative political climate that is based on beliefs that "less government support of social infrastructure is best" and "let families create their own solutions," combined with the popularity of tax reduction, has resulted in less funding being available for community-based facilities that previously supported families, such as neighbourhood schools, community homes for the aged, and hospitals. While these societal changes have had a profound impact on family life, social policy has not developed to provide supportive services to mitigate the negative effects of these changes.

The impact of unemployment, poor health, lack of formal education, and financial poverty on child development and adult and family functioning is well-documented and substantially addressed in other chapters. However, it is important to note that disparities in access to health care, housing, educational achievement, and future economic security exist for Aboriginals, recent immigrant groups, persons with disabilities, single persons, the near-elderly, and families on social assistance across Canada.[6] These groups are growing poorer while there is an increasing concentration of wealth among Canada's richest families.[7] This imbalance of power is both real and perceived and has impacted on the development, or lack thereof, of family policy in Canada and on the development of family-supportive services. The political swing to "every family being responsible for its own well-being" has only increased the challenges of being financially poor.

## FAMILY POLICY AND THE SOCIAL SERVICE DELIVERY SYSTEM

Services in Canada for families have developed through two major venues: the voluntary sector and government. Historically, Canadians have been known for their caring and sharing approach to others. Individuals, families, and communities have helped others who are vulnerable or less fortunate and developed services to meet community needs. When some services became government responsibilities, voluntary community groups changed their mandates from ones of meeting basic human needs (food, shelter, clothing) to more supportive and preventive types of services. Voluntary organizations such as Family Service agencies in Vancouver, Edmonton, Toronto, Ottawa, and Montreal began in the early 1900s as providers of food and shelter for the homeless and for widows with children after World War I, and then changed their mandates to become counselling and community family support programs. Along with the advent of income tax in Canada (1917), family allowances, and government-funded medicare in the 1950s, other "social safety net" services gradually became available to Canadians.

Services for families can be viewed through two lenses: strengths and deficits. The service delivery system in Canada has developed in both ways, with, unfortunately, the deficit approach predominating. The deficit approach led to the development of one-dimensional

---

6  Scott, K. 2005. *The World We Have: Towards a New Social Architecture*. Canadian Council on Social Development.

7  Saez, E., Veali, M. 2003. *The Evolution of High Incomes in Canada, 1920–2000*. National Bureau of Economic Research Working Papers.

services—services based on a problem or disease entity (such as drug addiction, spousal abuse, or Alzheimer's), requiring eligibility to be determined prior to service and limiting service to the identified person, not the family unit. The deficit approach implied that the problem was the person or family's "fault" and that the person could be "fixed." It tended to ignore other social factors that were contributing to the problem, as well as ignoring the strengths that a person might have to apply to improving life. In recent years, the strengths-based approach and "family health" approach have provided useful analyses to underscore the complexity of families fulfilling their multi-responsibilities and their need for support-ive social policies and programs to do so.

Some families are able to deal with adversity and hardship and continue to provide nurturing environments for their members, while others cannot. The *strengths and assets-based perspective*[8] is based on the premise that people want to do what is best for themselves and others and that each person has some skills and strengths to con-tribute. Because preventive services are under-funded in Canada, programs focusing on strengths development and protective factors to increase resiliency in individuals and families are always at risk within the current social and political context. Thrive Canada, Family Service Canada's *Families and Schools Together Canada©* programs, as well as many other voluntary service organizations are promoting this approach and are demonstrating through applied research the effectiveness of assets-based individual, family, and community development. The reciprocity of social capital depends on adopting the strengths and assets-based perspective of valuing each individual's ability to contribute to family, community, and society so that those who presently cannot become those who can.

As Canadian society changed and communities' needs changed, communities used their strengths and caring approach to develop needed services. However, services have developed in an inconsistent way across Canada. Some geographic areas and cities devel-oped interconnected systems of services while others had very few resources. As this piecemeal approach grew and continues to grow, it means that rural and northern commu-nities in Canada continue to be under-serviced. This is in part due to the following factors: Canada's geography, concentrations of populations, weather, economy, and diverse popula-tion groups. These factors, in concert, present major challenges to having a well-developed, interconnected system of social and health services for families. This is further complicated by the lack of family policy and oppositional philosophic views on family matters. As a country, Canada has not decided whether or not and to what extent it will sup-port families.

## ROLE OF GOVERNMENTS

### Federal Government

While the federal government has legislation that supports families, it does not have an over-arching family policy to provide a framework and commitment to supporting fami-lies, through legislation, policies, resources, and services.

---

**8** Saleebey, D. 2002. *The Strengths Perspective in Social Work Practice.* U of Kansas. NY: Allyn & Bacon.

Some attempts at developing a formal policy position for children and families have been made. The National Children's Agenda, adopted in 2000, was intended to provide a comprehensive framework for integrated provincial/territorial and federal initiatives. Former Prime Minister Jean Chrétien did appoint Senator Landon Pearson as Canada's Children's emissary at the United Nations. Co-ordinated by the Ministries of Health and Social Development, Canada developed its position paper on A World Fit for Children (2005)[9]; however, no mechanisms exist in legislation to ensure that Canada fulfills its promises and targets neither in that commitment, nor in its commitments as a signatory to the UN's Declaration on the Rights of a Child.

The federal government does provide for economic support for families through tax and transfer programs, the Child Tax Benefit, Health and Social Transfer payments, and through Employment Insurance with extended parental leave provisions and some caregiver support recognition.[10] However, although it almost happened (2006), there is no systematic, regulated child care program in Canada and no systematic elder care support program. There is an increasing reliance on family and informal care giving of the elderly, the burden of care being assumed by women.[11] At the same time, grandparents and other older relatives are providing considerable and ongoing childcare services to young children. The disabled community in Canada has had to fight for support with successive governments.

Specific programs, such as the Early Childhood Development Initiative (ECDI), provided funding support for services through provincial governments until these programs ended in 2006. However, these kinds of programs varied greatly across Canada, and provinces and territories were not accountable for meeting targets. Other inequities continue to exist. For example, funding for protective child care services in Aboriginal communities (a federal responsibility) has been less on a per capita basis than for children in protective services under provincial and territorial jurisdictions.[12] Aboriginal children in need have been subject to extraordinary jurisdictional battles while waiting for services.[13]

No mechanism exists within the federal government to co-ordinate or integrate family-related policies among ministries. While the federal government has a ministry specifically to support business, including small businesses—Industry Canada—it has no equivalency for the family. Many of the voluntary organizations providing services to families had access to funding through various ministries' programs, research initiatives, and special projects. However, these programs are not part of a framework or plan.

In June 2000, through the efforts of an umbrella group of national voluntary organizations, the federal government funded the Voluntary Sector Initiative (VSI) as a method to

9    Torjman, S. 2005. *A World Fit for Children*. Caledon Institute of Social Policy.

10   Lefebvre, P., Merrigan, P. 2003. Assessing Family Policy in Canada: A New Deal for Families and Children. *Choices*. Institute for Research in Public Policy.

11   Canadian Policy Research Networks. 2005. *A Healthy Balance: Caregiving Policy in Canada: A Backgrounder*. Family Network. www.cprn.com.

12   Loxely, L., DeRiviere, L., Prakash, T., Blackstock C., Prokop, S. 2005. *The Journey Continues*. The National Policy Review on First Nations Child and Family Services Research Project. Phase Three. First Nations Child and Family Caring Society.

13   First Nations Child and Family Caring Society. 2005. *Joint Declaration of Support for Jordan's Principle to Resolving Jurisdictional Disputes Affecting Services to First Nations Children*. www.fncfcs.com

both organize and integrate the support being given to the voluntary sector across ministries and to acknowledge and support the voluntary sector as the third sector (government, corporate, and voluntary) essential to Canada's well-being. This five-year initiative provided infrastructure funding, an improved regulatory environment, and recognition of the importance of the voluntary sector to the economy and to individual, family, and community development. While progress was made throughout the years of the VSI, with a change in federal government in 2006, most gains and integrated funding support provided to the voluntary sector disappeared.

## Provincial/Territorial and Municipal Governments

To date, Quebec is the only province in Canada with a legislated family policy and a Minister of State for Family Policy. In the fifth edition of *Canadian Social Welfare*, Jack Spence provided a detailed description of the Quebec government's approach to family policy. While the existence of such a policy continues to be an important factor in supporting families, Quebeckers have had to fight to keep access to affordable, universal child care. As well, some of the services within the CLSC system (Centre Locale Service Communitaire) have now been designated as "targeted" for specific population groups rather than being available to all families, thus undermining the basic premise of Quebec's family policy: that all families need support and recognition for the important contribution they make to their members and, thus, to society.[14]

Federal/provincial jurisdictional issues continue to complicate the already complex funding situation. For example, provinces and territories argue that they are already providing huge support to families through education budgets. However, as school boards have less and less control over budget allocations in most provinces and territories, and as demographics change, many schools are being closed and children must travel by bus to schools outside their own neighbourhoods. This creates other challenges for families for transportation, child care, physical activity and recreation time, and for building a sense of community belonging. Schools, which used to be a place of support for parents, are no longer available for after-school or family and adult programs. Special needs programming has been severely cut back in most schools.

Another example of legislated policy detrimental to families is the one whereby provincial and territorial governments generate revenues from provincially regulated lotteries and gambling. The result is that gambling has become a family policy issue[15] that is critically incapacitating many families in Canada today.

In turn, municipalities struggle with both providing services within their current tax bases and the popular "no tax increases or reduced taxes" citizen mentality. The downloading of many services for families to municipalities by provincial/territorial governments (trickling down from the federal government) has made it difficult for municipalities to adopt policies that would support families to fulfill their functions.

---

14    Baril, R., Lefebvre, P., Merrigan, P. 2000. Quebec Family Policy: Impact & Options. *Choices*. Institute for Research in Public Policy.

15    Moscovitch, Arlene. 2006. *Gambling with Our (Kids') Futures: Gambling as a Family Policy Issue*. Vanier Institute of the Family.

# SERVICES AVAILABLE FOR FAMILIES

Canadians have demonstrated a concern for strengthening families in every community across Canada. "Non-profit and voluntary sector organizations are a vital part of every community. They provide a wide range of essential services and programs that touch virtually all aspects of our society. . . . These organizations help establish the connections among citizens, communities, and governments that build social capital and sustain democracy."[16] While service development is varied and thus not consistently available, services for families do exist and are demonstratively effective in improving individual functioning at home, work, and community and in strengthening family life.[17]

Some service networks are specifically focused on families, some on children, while others may have developed to address a specific topic, disease, or syndrome with adjunct programs for family members. Mandated child protection services are discussed in Chapter 18.

While some of these local services developed in the early 1900s, the rapid growth of voluntary service organizations occurred in the 1960s and 1970s. The 1980s saw the development of national organizations to integrate and support the work of local organizations. These national voluntary organizations, such as Family Service Canada, Canadian Child Care Federation, Boys and Girls Clubs of Canada, and Big Brothers & Big Sisters of Canada, have been instrumental in promoting the availability of services for families and in developing quality assurance programs, national accreditations, and outcome evaluation systems to provide systemized quality programming across Canada.[18]

Finding specific information about a needed service has been a constant challenge. In addition to many of the formal systems that make information available, such as Community Information Services, the Internet has significantly improved access to information. However, the co-ordination of care services, especially for the elderly, has increasingly become the responsibility of family members.

Some of the major family-serving networks are listed here.

**Family Service Agencies** There are approximately 120 Family Service agencies across Canada, all independent, registered charities providing services to support and strengthen individuals and families throughout the lifespan. These agencies provide professional services for serious relationship problems such as abuse and violence, separation, divorce, and mental health issues at no or low cost. In addition, family strengthening programs such as Families and Schools Together Canada, Roots and Wings, Family to Family Ties, You and Your Aging Parent, as well as family education workshops, group services for separated and divorced families and children, and other community development programs are provided. Over the years, these agencies have developed and changed their services to meet the particular needs of their communities. Family Service agencies have worked in partnership with immigrant and ethnic groups and, more recently, with Aboriginal groups to strengthen community services for these families.

---

16  Scott, K. 2005. *The World We Have: Towards a New Social Architecture.* Canadian Council on Social Development, p. 14.

17  Stephenson, Kathleen. 2005. *Family Service Canada's Outcomes Evaluation: Aggregate Report 2005.* Family Service Canada.

18  Family Service Canada. Family Service Ontario. 1984. Canadian Family Services Accreditation Program. Toronto.

Family Service Canada, whose vision is *Strong Families in a Caring Society*, provides leadership training and national program development. They also advocate on policies and legislation that advance family well-being to support the efforts of its community-based member agencies. In addition, it manages the Family Services Employee Assistance Program (FSEAP) as local Family Service agencies contract with employers to provide employer-paid EAP services.

**Family Resource Programs** There are approximately 700 Family Resource programs or centres across Canada. Partially funded by a federal government program, CAPC, these centres provide local neighbourhood facilities for parents to interact with other parents and to receive resources and parent education and support for maximizing and nurturing their children's development. Supported by the Canadian Association of Family Resource Programs (FRP), these agencies provide a friendly, important place to receive educational assistance, assess child development milestones, participate in community events, and develop a sense of belonging within a community. FRP Canada develops educational materials, facilitates workshops and regional educational opportunities, and conducts research on parenting matters.

**Military Family Resource Programs** There are 30 Military Family Resource programs in Canada and three Canadian programs internationally. These centres, located on Canadian forces bases, provide a variety of services for military families. In addition to the kinds of services provided by non-military family resource centres, these centres assist family members in preparing for the absence of a spouse, dealing with anxiety of a spouse being in dangerous combat situations, and working through loss and grief. With Canada's increased military involvement since 2004, Military Family Resource centres have become essential services to military families.

**Other Community Programs** Boys and Girls Clubs, Big Brothers and Big Sisters organizations, child care centres, and other similar child-centered organizations also provide supportive services to parents. At the service delivery level, there is recognition that for service outcomes for children to be effective and lasting, family members need to be part of the service plan. Supported by national organizations providing leadership training and quality assurance, these types of services are an integral part of Canadian community life.

**Home Support and Homecare Services** Services for families with family members who are acutely ill, chronically ill, or disabled and elderly are provided predominantly through homecare programs and by government-initiated financial support. Homecare insurance can be purchased through private health insurance plans. However, services available from provincially funded homecare programs are not consistent across Canada. Many families report difficulties with homecare services—lack of case management, inadequate hours of service, frequent changes of paid caregivers, and inadequate recognition of the needs of unpaid caregivers. "Simply put, unpaid caregivers in Canada are doing more than ever before: more hours of care and work, more juggling of multiple responsibilities, more managing of multiple services and providers, more negotiating and advocating for care, more complex care."[19]

---

**19** Canadian Policy Research Networks. 2005. *A Healthy Balance: Caregiving Policy in Canada: A Backgrounder*. Family Network. www.cprn.com, page 8.

Seniors centres, home support agencies, and case management services provided by the voluntary sector deliver many services for seniors and disabled adults such as Meals on Wheels, home maintenance services, respite services, friendly visiting, advocate services, and volunteer drivers to appointments—many of which are essential to the health and well-being of the service recipients. However, the majority of care at home continues to be provided by family members who are at risk from the stress of managing multiple roles.

This chapter cannot in any way itemize the numerous social and health services that provide support to families in Canada. The existence of these services is a demonstration of Canadians' concerns about and belief in the importance of family. The voluntary service sector is often misrepresented as not needing support because of a simplistic view that services are delivered by volunteers. While volunteers are an important part of voluntary service organizations, they must be supported by a paid, professional infrastructure. Non-profit and charitable organizations must abide by the same laws as any other employer in Canada: employment standards, accounting and fiscal reporting obligations, health and safety, security and privacy legislation, etc. They are expected to operate efficiently and effectively, supported by sound management and governance practices.

However, most of these organizations operate without any ongoing stable source of revenue. Managers of these organizations spend an inordinate amount of time searching for funding from multiple sources. Most funding is now short-term and project-based.[20] In addition, these agencies are expected to be accountable to all funding sources through different accountability formats. While funders and users of services need to know that funds are being spent responsibly and that services are meeting quality standards, the work required to produce accountability reports is far more than the funding warrants and is not paid for by the funders. Infrastructure funding for this sector does not exist.

Services for families do exist in Canada today. However, these services are not part of a comprehensive or supportive family framework. There is no "made in Canada" model applicable to all regions of Canada. The service delivery system is not supported by infrastructure funding that would ensure the existence of basic services and their subsequent augmentation and support by communities and families to meet a variety of cultural and ethnic needs. Vulnerable families are being left behind as government policies favour tax reduction and create other programs and tax incentives that are not available to poor families and recent immigrants.

## TOWARDS A NEW SOCIAL ARCHITECTURE FOR STRONG FAMILIES IN A CARING SOCIETY

"Bringing our policies for families up to date is essential. Failure to support families adequately imposes significant costs on the economy."[21] Policy-makers in this country are beginning to discuss developing a new "social architecture" for Canada. Basing this development on concepts of Canada needing to invest both in individual skill development for individual well-being and market economy production while investing simultaneously in

---

**20**   Scott, K. 2003. *Funding Matters: The Impact of Canada's New Funding Regime on Nonprofit and Voluntary Organizations.* Canadian Council on Social Development.

**21**   Hay, D. 2006. Strengthening Canadian Families. *Connecting People and Policy No. 1.* Canadian Policy Research Networks.

protective programs for vulnerable groups, emerging social policy indicates a "shared mix of contributions from the market, state, community, and family."[22] Furthermore, Jensen argues "a commitment to common and shared citizenship means that social risk should be pooled. Governments have a responsibility to use their taxing, spending, and regulatory powers to cover risks that are beyond the capacity of families to address alone. Any social architecture will, therefore, provide a mix of universal, progressive, and targeted programs.

Simply put, all families in Canada need support and recognition for the important contributions they make to Canadian society. Vulnerable families need additional assistance and resources, which are best developed as part of an overall framework that supports the multiple family roles of child development, sustaining adult relationships, and caregiving within regional, ethnic, and culturally appropriate environments.

Policy-makers and governments must find ways to develop policies and programs together—respecting the interdependent nature of government intervention with community and individual family intervention. All levels of government need to create strategies that share funding and delivery responsibilities, not download programs and services from one level to another. Recognition of the shared responsibility of governments and citizens for family well-being would result in base support for an infrastructure of services. Such a planned approach would be a partnership with voluntary sector fundraisers, such as the United Way and community foundations, as well as informed community groups.

Given the earlier discussion on the factors that have affected the development of services for families in Canada, new approaches are needed to address the inequities in the current system. Funding mechanisms are most often organized around a single, identified problem or for a specific ethnocultural group, making the service unavailable for other family members and creating gaps in service for those who don't quite "fit" a specific category. If families are to be truly supported, then, in addition to the identified service recipient, all family members must be eligible for services. The current system reserves service only for the identified client, thus negating the impact of a problem on the family unit and discounting the family's potential for assisting in the change or care process.

Organizing services based on what families need to fulfill their functions would change the service delivery paradigm. Such an approach would require the co-operation of employers, educators, housing developers, urban planners, etc., as well as the population groups in Canada that hold onto a "services only for my group" approach. Canada's multiculturalism and separation of Aboriginal affairs has contributed to both a lack of services and an impenetrable maze of service delivery mechanisms. For example, services for abused women are available in most parts of Canada. However, when a woman no longer meets the definition of "being abused," services are no longer available to her. Similarly, non-Aboriginal service organizations may not offer services to Aboriginal families, believing that they have access to such services on reserves or through off-reserve agencies. A new social architecture needs to rethink the traditional ways that services have been organized and delivered.

Valuing "family" and understanding its importance to a healthy, viable country is essential to a new social architecture. Basing policy development on a shared responsibility of

---

22   Jensen, J. 2004. *Canada's New Social Risks: Directions for a New Social Architecture.* Executive Summary (pp. viii–ix). Canadian Policy Research Networks.

governments, corporations, community, and family will ensure a measure of independence, inter-dependence, and will protect at-risk, vulnerable families. Having a well-articulated family policy and a subsequent infrastructure of policies, services, and programs supported by government funding and public/charitable funding would greatly improve family outcomes and support Canada's people and economy. Countries that clearly support family roles and functioning provide economic, workplace, educational, health, and social supports for family members.

## CONCLUSION

Well-functioning families are essential to Canada's well-being. In order for this to be realized in Canada, all families need a societal support system that values family roles and enables families to fulfill their multiple roles and obligations. The responsibility of government is to ensure that such a system exists and that the factors negatively affecting optimum family functioning are eliminated for all families including Canada's vulnerable family groups. Canada can legislate a comprehensive family policy. The off-loading or trickle-down effect of past political decisions can be reversed. Communities can best plan and make services available to families with the help of local voluntary sector service organizations that are supported through infrastructure funding and by national organizational structures.

Canada's vast geographical area, regional differences, and its culturally diverse, relatively small population mitigate against the development of one service delivery system that could be cost-efficient and effective in supporting family-functioning in every community in Canada. One model is unlikely to fit all.

However, Canada's history and its current voluntary sector demonstrate that with increased recognition of the contributions of family life and the creation of funded infrastructure support, communities can and will deliver unique service systems to support families across the country.

# References

Henderson, N., Benard, B., Sharp-Light, N., Eds. 2006. *Resiliency in Action*. 2nd Edition.

Phipps, Shelley. 2006. Working for working parents: the evolution of maternity and parental benefits in Canada. *Choices*. Institute for Research in Public Policy.

Roehlkpartain, Eugene C. et al. 2004. *Building Strong Families*. YMCA of USA.

Schlesinger, Ben. 1998. *Strengths in Families: Accentuating the Positive*. University of Toronto.

Search Institute. Developmental Assets[TM]. www.search-institute.org

Thrive! The Canadian Centre for Positive Youth Development. www.thrivecanada.ca

Voluntary Sector Initiative. 2000. www.vsi-isbc.ca

# CHAPTER 21

# Services for Older Adults

*Kerri-Ann Fitzgerald and James Gladstone*

## INTRODUCTION

Older adults represent a large proportion of the general population in Canada. It is estimated that by 2021, seniors will represent 18% of Canada's population, compared to 12.5% in 2000 (NACA, 2005). An increasing number of older persons will experience one or several of the major life events often associated with aging, namely, caregiving, widowhood, and relocation to a long-term care institution.[1] These major life events represent the focus for the rest of the chapter because of their significance for social work practice. Historically, social work has long been concerned with people in the context of their own environments, and each of these major life events (caregiving, widowhood, and relocation) represent change in people's environments, be it the physical, family, or work situation. These transitions frequently demand the attention of social work practitioners to reduce the stress often associated with these experiences.

Because these events are often perceived as stressful, they will be described and analyzed in terms of a stress model. Stress is mediated by coping behaviours, which in turn may involve the utilization of resources, including formal services (Pearlin et al., 1990). Before a person employs coping strategies, however, the stressor will be appraised, in the course of which the person affected attaches a subjective meaning or significance to the stressful event (Lazarus and Folkman, 1984).

This process also takes place within contexts of older adults' socio-demographic statuses. Older adults represent a heterogeneous group in Canada as they differ by age, marital status, health, ethnic, and historical backgrounds (NACA, 2005; Novak, 1997). These contextual factors are important since older persons may have different access to the resources they need to cope successfully (Pearlin et al., 1990). Examples of these factors will be provided throughout this chapter and highlighted in service discussions for social work practitioners.

## MAJOR LIFE EVENTS

### Caregiving

It is generally acknowledged that providing ongoing care for an older adult is perceived as stressful. The caregiving experience is primarily associated with stress, burden, and negative physical and mental health outcomes (Myers, 2003; Pinquart and Sorensen, 2005a). It has become known as a normative family stress that typically extends over numerous years (Myers, 2003).

Primary caregivers are most likely to be female (Guberman, Maheu, and Maille, 1992; Canadian Study on Health and Aging, 1994), and gender differences arise in relation to men and women's caregiving tasks. While men do perform caregiving duties, they usually provide types of care that differ

---

[1] The field of aging is very broad, and there are additional important life events related to aging, such as retirement, that are not included in this chapter. Social workers may provide professional services to assist older adults with the transition to retirement. For a summary of work on retirement and the above-mentioned stress model, refer to Turner and Turner, *Canadian Social Welfare,* 5th Edition (Toronto: Pearson Education Canada, Inc., 2005).

from that of women; the latter are more likely to provide personal assistance (Miller and Cafasso, 1992). In addition, significantly more husbands providing care for their spouses receive help with household chores from their spouses than do their female counterparts providing care for their husbands (Ingersoll-Dayton and Raschick, 2004). These findings fit with the Western societal view that family members in general, and women in particular, are expected to care for older relatives. The strength of these societal values has led some scholars (Aronson, 1990; Walker, 1991) to question whether the state is shifting the burden of caring for families onto women.

**Stress** There is consensus among research findings that caregivers are at risk of experiencing physical and mental health complications. With respect to mental health issues, caregivers have been found to experience high levels of distress, depression, demoralization, anxiety, and psychiatric symptomatology such as insomnia, headaches and excessive irritability (Myers, 2003).

Researchers have cited some contextual factors related to caregiving stress, including the caregiver's relationship to the person receiving care, his or her co-residency, type of illness, and ethnicity. Myers' (2003) literature review found that caregiving spouses had higher levels of depression, lower levels of life satisfaction, and lower participation levels in social activities compared to other family caregivers. Reasons for these outcomes may be that spouses tended to provide the most comprehensive care, provided caregiving duties for longer durations, and spent the most hours per week on caregiving tasks. However, Jutras and Veilleuz (1991) and Young and Kahana (1989), found that spouses experienced less stress than adult child caregivers.

According to Mittelman (2005), caring for a person with dementia involves different stressors than caring for a person without dementia. As more time to perform caregiving duties is required, there is a greater impact on employment, more caregiver strain, increased mental and physical health problems, as well as heightened family conflict. Other stressors involved in caring for a person with dementia have been cited as adapting to the novelty of the caregiving situation, its unpredictability, long duration, the management of behavioural and memory disturbances, financial expenditures, and the challenge of negotiating a degenerative illness of a loved one (Long et al., 2004).

Recognition of the role of ethnic, cultural, and geographic factors in caregiving stress is also important. For example, Latino caregivers have been found to show more depressive symptomology than Caucasian caregivers, and Latino caregivers tend to have higher levels of personal and role strain than African-American caregivers (Long et al., 2004). This might be related to the fact that African-American caregivers have had to deal with other major life stresses, namely oppression and discrimination, and that they place caregiving stress in a different perspective (Pinquart & Sorensen, 2005b).

Aside from the primary sources of stress embedded in caregiving, secondary sources of stress which stem from the primary stressors may also arise. The demands associated with working outside the home may become a secondary stressor. Caregivers who devote a lot of time and energy to a dependent older person may find it difficult to maintain outside employment, and this in turn can represent an additional stressor in their lives. Scharlach, Sobel, and Roberts (1991), however, suggest that the critical factors associated with occupational stress may not be working outside the home as such, but the degree of job flexibility inherent in their outside work, and the support provided by co-workers and supervisors regarding their caregiving.

A further point bears mentioning. While the amount of research related to caregiver stress has grown in the past number of years, very little is known about the perceptions or experiences of the older person receiving such care. In one of the few studies addressing this issue, Aronson (1991) found that older mothers felt ambivalent about receiving care from their daughters. The older women wanted to retain their independence, yet were concerned about their own deteriorating health and need for security.

**Appraisal** The meanings that caregivers attach to their caregiving experiences influence the coping strategies they employ to manage stress. Hasselkus (1998) found that caregivers may question their personal capabilities, feeling that someone else could perform the caregiving role better than themselves. Or they may take responsibility for somehow causing the situation, feeling that if they had recognized their older relative's symptoms earlier, the care recipient's health might not have deteriorated so far.

Farran et al. (1991) have pointed to the loss and powerlessness caregivers often feel. Some caregivers mourn the loss of their relationships with older impaired relatives. At the same time they may feel powerless in their choices to become caregivers and feel incapable of rebalancing their lives once they have done so.

Some studies, however, suggest that some caregivers may attach more positive interpretations to their caregiving experiences. For example, Gallagher-Thompson et al. (1998) found that caregiving has the potential to help care providers feel useful, and can increase feelings of self-worth, confidence, and companionship. Taking an existential approach, Farran (1997) refers to caregivers who feel fulfilled by their ability to "rise to the occasion" or who may feel "transformed" by their caregiving experience.

**Coping** In the stress model, effective coping is often associated with the use of social supports. According to Logsdon and Robinson (2000), social support is considered to be the "greatest moderator" of the effects of caregiving stress. Several studies have suggested that caregiving spouses are more likely than other caregivers to provide support alone (Tennstedt, McKinlay, and Sullivan, 1989), although this might not be true for all cultural groups (Miller and McFall, 1991). Myers (2003) found that spouses are a particularly vulnerable group, as they tend to participate less in social activities than do other family members providing the caregiving role, and may, therefore, have access to fewer social supports.

In examining coping strategies, it is important to recognize the influence of culture and ethnicity as well as the type of chronic illness experienced by the older adult. For example, the presentation of negative feelings is less acceptable (and avoidance is more adaptive) among Chinese caregivers compared to American caregivers (Long et al., 2004). With respect to types of chronic illnesses and caregivers' coping styles, it has been found that caregivers may be more reluctant to draw on social support when their relative is suffering a form of cognitive impairment (Montgomery and Borgatta, 1989). Caregivers may be self-conscious about their relative's public behaviour or may perceive a social stigma attached to that impairment. Additionally, as the type of illness progresses and the related characteristics and symptoms change, so might the coping strategies in order to manage the situation (Mittelman, 2005). This may involve a continuous appraisal of the caregiving circumstance, as well as adaptation to new coping strategies.

**Services** Numerous studies have shown that caregivers are reluctant to use formal services. A trend exists whereby caregivers seek services when they have reached a period of crisis

(Montgomery and Borgatta, 1989). This is especially true of those caregivers caring for persons with dementia (Canadian Study of Health and Aging, 1994). Spouses in particular are likely to try to provide care on their own (Tennstedt, McKinlay, and Sullivan, 1989), predominantly when their husbands or wives have dementia (Canadian Study of Health and Aging, 1994).

Sorenson, Pinquart, and Duberstein (2002) describe the following types of services and interventions that may be delivered to support caregivers: (1) psycho-educational interventions are structured programs that share information about the disease process and train the caregivers to respond to disease-related challenges; (2) supportive interventions refer to professionally led and peer-led unstructured groups that build relationships among participants, and address caregivers' feelings and coping strategies; (3) respite/adult day care involves assistance with care-receivers' personal care and activities of daily living to provide relief to the caregivers; and (4) psychotherapy involves a therapeutic relationship with a trained professional to teach coping strategies such as self-monitoring, time management, and emotional reactivity management.

Aneshensel et al. (1995) suggest that different types of services might be needed at different points of the "caregiving career." They posit that education is of greatest importance when caregivers first begin to assume their role. They need information about their relatives' diseases, the causes, what lies ahead, and what practical issues relate to the relatives' care. At later stages, the caregivers may benefit more from interventions directed at stress management. Mittelman (2005) advocates that interventions for caregivers be delivered over a long period of time as the nature of the chronic illness changes and, in turn, impacts the caregiver. Greater service options may also be available in the forms of telephone-based and Web-based counselling and support (Mittelman, 2005; Shultz et al., 2002). These technologies, for example, can increase service accessibility to caregivers who are homebound because of their own or the care recipient's health, or because of geography or difficulty with transportation (Smith and Toseland, 2006).

Sorenson, Pinquart, and Duberstein (2002) recommend that interventions encompass the spouses' affective aspects of caregiving, potential health risks, financial issues, and shrinking social networks. They suggest that dementia caregivers benefit less from the above interventions compared to non-dementia caregivers, and recommend that respite care be provided in conjunction with training. An important insight is that individual interventions may be more effective in enhancing caregiver well-being, while group interventions may be more effective at alleviating the symptoms of the person receiving care. Therefore, it is helpful for the service provider to collaborate with the caregiver and care-recipient in determining what type of support is most needed and to adapt the interventions accordingly. There may be differences in the extent to which caregivers access formal services, depending on race. Miller and Guo (2000), for example, found that Caucasian caregivers were more likely than African-Americans to use formal services because of structural barriers within society.

## Widowhood

The loss of a spouse is one of the most traumatic experiences associated with aging. It is described as a highly disruptive experience that is often followed by a time-limited period of acute grief (Shear and Shair, 2005). The grief associated with such a loss can manifest itself through physical or psychological symptoms and can affect every aspect of the survivor's life (Kastenbaum, 1986). Women tend to experience widowhood more than men owing to their longer life expectancy, and to the Western social norm for men to remarry in their later years because they have a greater choice of potential mates (Lopata, 1996).

**Stress** There is extensive research on the relationship between stress and widowhood. Gillies and Neimeyer (2006) list numerous stressors that widowed persons often experience, including longing and yearning for the deceased; intrusive thoughts about and images of the deceased; intense emotional episodes of sadness, social withdrawal and isolation; and feelings of meaninglessness and hopelessness. In describing the most stressful impact of bereavement, Kastenbaum (1986) states the most intense period of grief usually persists from one to six months and is characterized by numbness and despair, followed by symptoms of dizziness, headaches, body aches, loss of appetite, and sleep disturbances. As the physical reactions subside in intensity, the bereaved person may feel anger, confusion, and anxiety. According to Kastenbaum (1986), throughout the first year the survivor continues to move away from a complete focus on the loss, yet may continue the grieving process for a minimum of two years. Carnelley et al. (2006) examine the time course of grief, and note that most research studies concentrate on the first few years post-loss. Their study indicated that widowed persons continued to talk, think, and feel emotions about their lost spouses decades later.

Studies have shown that the most severe problem perceived by both widows and widowers is loneliness (Lopata, 1996). According to Beal (2006), older women report more loneliness than their male counterparts. Experiencing loneliness in widowhood appears to be a Western phenomenon since it is not as evident in non-Western communities where there is a high degree of interaction between extended families and neighbours (Lopata, 1996).

Additional factors that influence stress in widowhood are age, gender, and race. Support services differ depending on the age of the consumer and gender; men tend to be less accustomed than women to developing and accessing social support (Lopata 1996); and the experience of widowhood appears to be less difficult for African-American women than for Caucasian women, possibly because African-Americans have a more expanded social support network (Elwert and Christakis, 2006).

**Appraisal** Little has been written about the subjective meanings that are attached to grief or bereavement. In an earlier reference made on this subject, Martin Matthews (1980) referred to "anticipatory isolation" and stated that women were more likely than men to think about widowhood as a possible effect in their lives. While a person may engage in this thought pattern, other research (Hill, Thompson, and Gallagher, 1988) suggests that it does not necessarily reduce the intensity of the survivor's grief reaction after the spouse's death.

Lopata (1996) states that in appraising the experience of widowhood, one must construct a self-concept that distinguishes between past and present attachments and sentiments. Gillies and Neimeyer (2006) also examine the role of appraisal in bereavement. According to this research, three activities of meaning-making, or reconstruction, are involved in the grieving process. In the first stage, sense-making, the bereaved person poses questions to make sense of the loved one's death. The second stage, benefit-finding, involves identifying benefits related to the grieving experience in order to find new and positive meaning in life. In the third stage, identity change, the bereaved person may reconstruct himself or herself in response to the new reconstructed meaning. Gillies and Neimeyer (2006) and Lopata (1996) suggest that educational, maturational, personal, and social resources may influence the extent to which one engages in these activities of appraisal.

**Coping** To manage the stress of widowhood, the survivor may draw upon internal as well as external resources. In drawing upon an internal resource, one may develop feelings of competence by learning new skills and making decisions in new situations (Lopata, 1996). According to Lopata (1996), educated and middle-class women tend to have more personal resources to help them cope, including finances, health, knowledge, and self-confidence.

Several studies identify external resources used in coping with widowhood. Maintaining frequent contact with significant others is an example of an external resource, and is associated with a lower incidence of depression (Dimond, Lund, and Caserta, 1987). Widows may also draw upon external resources to combat loneliness by keeping busy, developing new roles and relations, and focusing on their social roles such as mother or friend (Lopata, 1996). Relationships with friends are subject to change following the death of a spouse, whereas relationships with family members are likely to remain stable (Connidis, 1989). However, Morgan (1989) has shown that widows do not always interpret gestures by friends and family as being supportive. Research highlights the importance of caregiving widows, receiving social support before relatives are deceased (Bass, Bowman, and Noelker, 1991). Sankar (1991) has found that the meaning that caregivers associate with the support they receive during the caregiving period has implications for their relationships with others following their relatives' deaths.

**Services** Western society has developed economic, emotional, and social support resources to respond to the stresses associated with widowhood (Lopata, 1996). Social security benefits and supplementary grants are available to widows aged 65 and older, who may need these monies to pay for basic necessities of life (Lopata, 1996). Community and religious programs also exist (Lopata, 1996). One of the more effective means of attaining social support is through self-help groups, which emphasize a process of mutual support (Lieberman and Videka-Sherman, 1986; Lopata, 1996; Silverman, 1986).

It is important for service providers to recognize that widows vary in the extent to which they access social support (Utz et al., 2002). Constraints affecting this access include lack of transportation, poor health, and language or literacy barriers. Furthermore, Lopata (1996) points out that the women least likely to access social support are socially isolated, are of working class backgrounds with limited education, are sporadically employed, and are not connected with a religious community. These barriers need to be taken into consideration when creating and delivering bereavement support services.

## Relocation to Long-Term Care Facilities

Long-term care is often portrayed as having two distinct parts, a formal and institutional side versus a more informal and social side (Gubrium, 1993). In this section, we consider the formal and informal aspects of relocation to a long-term care facility to overlap with each other.

A combination of various risk factors for older adults has been associated with the move to a long-term care facility. These factors include a person being over age 85, having unmarried status, living alone, having been recently admitted to a hospital, experiencing difficulty with activities of daily living, and having a form of cognitive impairment (Shapiro and Tate, 1988). Carriere and Pelletier (1995) found that the rate of institutionalization in Canada differs by region, the likelihood of living in facilities being greater in Quebec, Ontario, and the Prairies, and less so in British Columbia and the Maritimes. This is possibly due to differences in the way that provincial policies influence the distribution of services to older persons. Some American studies (for example, Mui and Burnette, 1994) have suggested that rates of relocation may also differ according to race and culture.

**Stress** The anticipation of moving away from home to a long-term care institution, as well as the move itself, can be a stressful experience for older people and their families (Davies and Nolan, 2004). Whether an older adult chooses to relocate to a long-term care facility or whether someone else makes that decision, such as a physician or a hospital discharge planner, the thought of moving to a long-term care facility can produce feelings of loss, depression, and a sense of helplessness in the older adult. As Solomon (1982) has pointed out, relocation represents a public acknowledgment of one's diminished capacity to care for oneself. Studies to date have focused exclusively on heterosexual elders. Research by Cosby (2005) and Cosby and van Berkel (2006) suggest that relocation can be especially stressful for lesbian and gay elders who may be discriminated against because of their sexuality.

Lee, Woo, and Mackenzie (2002) have pointed out that socio-cultural values play a role in elders' adjustment to life in long-term care facilities. For example, this study suggests that feelings of shame related to relocation are dominant in the Chinese community, not only for the resident, but also for the entire family system as the family is expected to care for aging parents. The National Advisory Council on Aging (2005) suggests that seniors of ethnic minorities may experience stress in adjusting to life in nursing homes because of a loss of family, loss of culture (including the ability to communicate in their own language), and a loss of community.

Family members may also find the anticipated move stressful. Even primary caregivers who have spent years attending to relatives, and who may be near the "breaking point," may feel guilty about "abandoning" their relatives (Rosenthal and Dawson, 1991). In Zarit and Whitlach's (1992) study, caregivers were especially concerned about the quality of the facilities, their relative's safety, and whether their relatives would be upset living in the facilities.

While family caregivers may experience reduced role overload following their relatives' moves (Aneshensel et al., 1995), the emotional strain of their caregiving often continues after the relocation. A study by Tornatore and Grant (2002), for example, suggests that ongoing caregiving is particularly difficult for those who are older, have spent a shorter period of time in the caregiver role before the relocation, and are currently more involved in providing hands-on care. Another study by Whitlach et al. (2001) finds an association between caregivers' depression and the extent to which they perceived that their relatives adjusted to their new living arrangements.

**Appraisal** The term "long-term care" in the context of older persons conveys an array of images and meanings. Rojiani (1994) conducted research that showed that an older woman living with long-term care needs viewed long-term care in a way that was vastly different from how it was thought of in the policy, practice, and research contexts around her. Rojiani demonstrated how professional conceptualizations of long-term care as a distinct service contradicted the care recipient's understanding of long-term care as a personal loss.

Bowers, Fibich, and Jacobson (2001) show how older adults have different interpretations of the quality of care they receive in long-term care facilities. In this study, satisfaction with care was found to be associated with the way that the residents viewed themselves in relation to the staff. Older persons appeared to rate their care differently, depending on whether they saw themselves as consumers of service or as friends with the staff.

Gladstone's (1995a, 1995b) study of older married couples revealed why some spouses felt positively about moving, or having their partners move to a long-term care facility. Some spouses felt that they would no longer be a burden on their husbands or wives who had cared for them when they were living in the community. Some felt overwhelmed by the amount of caregiving that they had to perform and looked forward to the assistance offered to them and their partners by the facilities. Others felt relief that they would no longer have to worry about their husbands' or wives' security and safety.

**Coping** Older adults manage the stress associated with relocation in various ways. Steele, Pinquart, and Sorensen (2003) identified four styles of coping that older people use when planning for future long-term care needs. These include avoiding, thinking, planning, and consenting. Older adults who were categorized as "thinkers," who thought about their future care needs but were unable to determine how these needs could be met, showed the highest levels of distress and reported the lowest levels of satisfaction in terms of preparing for long-term needs. On the other hand, seniors categorized as "planners," who made concrete plans, as well as "consenters" who accepted plans made by significant others, reported the highest levels of satisfaction in terms of preparation.

Nakashima et al. (2004) have also examined older adults' decision-making styles with regards to moving to long-term care settings. Older persons who used an autonomous approach made independent care decisions. Older persons who used a collaborative approach worked with their family members by sharing information and problem solving together. Older adults who used a delegated approach fit into three sub-types—total delegation, active delegation, and passive delegation—and involved the older person's leaving the decision making to a family member. Relocating to a long-term care environment is not always a negative experience. Seniors may experience a positive transition and take part in new activities and social relations (Gladstone, 1991).

Family members also manage the stress associated with relocation in different ways and may progress through various stages of coping. Accordingly, Strang et al. (2006) studied the ways that family members of seniors with dementia coped during the period of waiting and transition. The themes of crisis, synchronicity, control, and reciprocity appeared in the waiting period for placement to occur, while different themes including deeply bonded relationships, attempts at continuity, and managing the change occurred following the placement.

Family relationships, expressed in terms of regular visiting, and the provision of care continue once an older person has moved to a long-term care setting (Port et al., 2001; Yamamoto-Mitani, Aneshensel, and Levy-Stroms, 2002; Bowers, 1998; Ross, Rosenthal, and Dawson, 1997). Changes that occur in the provision of care are related more to a refocusing of care or to finding an alternate way of expressing care rather than to the termination of care (Gladstone, Dupuis, and Wexler, 2006). Family members may consolidate their position within the facilities by carefully negotiating their relationships with staff (Gladstone and Wexler, 2002a, 2002b). Visiting and continuing to provide assistance to their relatives after relocation represent ways that family members demonstrate commitment and a sense of closeness towards their relatives in long-term care facilities.

**Services** Social work practitioners have the opportunity to influence the way that relocation to a long-term care facility is perceived (Davies and Nolan, 2003). Practitioners can assist both older residents and their family members in adjusting to this life transition. Nakashima et al. (2004) suggested that older adults and their families participate in advanced care planning in order to reduce feelings of helplessness and frustration at the onset of a crisis that demands sudden relocation. They also recommend that social workers and their multidisciplinary colleagues use clear communication and avoid jargon when assisting with decision-making stages. Finally, social workers are encouraged to support client self-determination as much as possible in order to help the older adult experience greater satisfaction with the relocation experience. Kayser-Jones (2002) also points out the importance of attending to the psychosocial, spiritual, and cultural needs of older residents and families, especially at the end of the older adult's life. It is important to address the holistic nature of the older person and to place her or him in a social context when providing supportive services during relocation.

# CONCLUSION

While the focus of this chapter has been the stressful aspects of these life transitions, it should be remembered that older adults are a heterogeneous group, characterized by individual differences, as are members of every age cohort. Consequently, these transitions are not necessarily experienced as stressful by everyone. Horowitz (1985) and Cohen et al. (1994), for example, have stated that caregivers may derive a sense of satisfaction if they feel that they are successfully able to handle the situation, meet a perceived obligation, or act as role models for their own children. Lopata (1996) has distinguished between life circumstances when a person may or may not grieve the loss of their spouse, and illustrated how varying personal and environmental resources influence how widows cope with loss. Steele, Pinquart, and Sorensen (2003) highlighted that a variety of personality constructs and coping styles influence levels of satisfaction in moving to long-term care facilities.

Each of these major transitions is a process, rather than a discrete event that takes place at any one moment in time. Aneshensel et al. (1995), for example, have referred to the "careers of caregivers." Carnelley et al. (2006) refer to the "time course of grief," and show that bereavement can occur over decades. Strang et al. (2006) have identified various psychological stages that family members may experience over time as older relatives are relocated to long-term care facilities.

**Service Implications** This conclusion has implications for practice and policy. If each of these transitions unfolds as a process, then older adults and their families may have different types of needs at different stages that can be placed within the context of their age, marital status, health, ethnic, and historical backgrounds. In accounting for the above-mentioned research findings and older adults' unique qualities, social work practitioners have the opportunity to help reduce the stresses that are often associated with caregiving, widowhood, and relocation to long-term care facilities.

In order for services to be effective in addressing the aforementioned stresses, they need to be available, accessible, acceptable, and co-ordinated. Wallace (1990) refers to gaps in the continuum of services as "no-care zones" whereby the services provided are not appropriate to meet elders' needs. In order to avoid the "no-care zone" he stresses availability, accessibility, and acceptability in service delivery. Availability determines whether a service is provided on the basis of a particular need. Although demand for services to address particular needs may exist in rural parts of Canada, they may not be made available due to geographic-related barriers (Novak, 1997). Once a service is provided, however, it should be accessible to the population that needs it in terms of transportation, physical mobility, finances, and knowledge of its existence. Furthermore, it must be acceptable in the sense that clients who need the service are willing to access it. New immigrants and seniors from a wide variety of ethnic groups may be reluctant to utilize services if cultural differences (such as customary practices and dietary requirements) are not taken into consideration (NACA, 2005; Novak, 1997).

Lastly, it is essential that social services are co-ordinated. This is especially important when several Canadian social programs are currently undergoing restructuring, adjustment, and adaptation phases that may lead to fragmented and unco-ordinated services (Aronson, 1999). The National Advisory Council on Aging (1999) promotes co-ordination of services for older persons, and uses the term "systems harmonization" to encourage the integration of community care, long-term care, social services, and health services. It is important that service providers be cognizant of these service implications when working towards the establishment of services that reflect the diverse needs expressed by Canadian seniors.

# References

Aneshensel, C.S., Pearlin, L.I., Mullan, J.T., Zarit, S.H., & Whitlatch, C.J. 1995. *Profiles in caregiving: The unexpected career*. San Diego: Academic Press.

Aronson, J. 1990. Old women's experiences of needing care: Choice or compulsion? *Canadian Journal on Aging*. 9. 234–247.

Aronson, J. 1991. Dutiful daughters and undemanding mothers: Constraining images of giving and receiving care in middle and late life. In C. Baines, P. Evans, & S. Neysmith (Eds.), *Women's caring: Feminist perspectives on social welfare* (pp. 138–168). Toronto: McClelland & Stewart.

Aronson, J. 1999. Conflicting images of older people receiving care: Challenges for reflexive practice and research. In S. Neysmith (Ed.), *Critical issues for future social work practice and aging persons* (pp. 47–69). New York: Columbia University Press.

Aronson, J. 2002. Elderly people's accounts of home care rationing: Missing voices in long-term care policy debates. *Aging and Society*. 22. 399–418.

Bass, D.M., Bowman, K., & Noelker, L.S. 1991. The influence of caregiving and bereavement support on adjusting to an older relative's death. *The Gerontologist*. 31. 32–42.

Beal, C. 2006. Loneliness in older women: A review of the literature. *Issues in Mental Health Nursing*. 27. 795–813.

Bowers, B.J. 1998. Family perceptions of care in a nursing home. *The Gerontologist*. 28. 361–368.

Bowers, B.J., Fibich, B., & Jacobson, N. 2001. Care-as-service, care-as-relating, care-as-comfort: Understanding nursing home residents' definitions of quality. *The Gerontologist*. 28. 361–368.

Canadian Study on Health and Aging. 1994. Patterns of caring for people with dementia in Canada. *Canadian Journal on Aging*. 13. 470–487.

Carnelley, K.B., Wortman, C.B., Bolger, N., & Burke, C.T. 2006. The time course of grief reactions to spousal loss: evidence from a national probability sample. *Journal of Personality and Social Psychology*. 91. 476–492.

Carriere, Y., & Pelletier, L. 1995. Factors underlying the institutionalization of elderly persons in Canada. *Journal of Gerontology: Social Sciences, SOB*, S164–S172.

Cohen, C.A., Pushkar Gold, D., Shulman, K.I., & Zucchero, C.A. 1994. Positive aspects in caregiving: An overlooked variable in research. *Canadian Journal on Aging*. 17. 330–345.

Connidis, J.A. 1989. *Family ties and aging*. Toronto: Butterworths.

Cosby, R. October 2005. *Will they be safe?: A qualitative research study on staff attitudes toward same-sex couples living in long-term care*. A presentation at the Canadian Gerontology Association 2005. Annual Conference, "Navigating the Winds of Change. Halifax, Nova Scotia.

Cosby, R., and van Berkel, C. April 2006. *Homosexuality is wrong: Looking at staff attitudes in long-term care*. A presentation at the Ontario Gerontology Association. Annual Conference. Toronto, Ontario.

Davies, S., & Nolan, M. 2004. Making the move: Relatives' experiences of the transition to a care home. *Social Care in the Community*. 6. 517–526.

Dimund, M., Lund, D.A., & Caserta, M.S. 1987. The role of social support in the first two years of bereavement in an elderly sample. *The Gerontologist*. 27. 599–604.

Elwert, F., & Christakis, N.A. 2006. Widowhood and race. *American Sociological Review*. 71. 16–41.

Farran, C.J. 1997. Theoretical perspectives concerning positive aspects of caring for elderly persons with dementia: Stress/adaptation and existentialism. *The Gerontologist*. 37. 250–256.

Farran, C.J., Keane-Hagerty, E., Salloway, S., Kupferer, S., & Wilken, C.S. 1991. Finding meaning: An alternative paradigm for Alzheimer's disease family caregivers. *The Gerontologist*. 31. 483–489.

Gallagher-Thompson, D., Coon, D.W., Reivera, P., Powers, I., & Zeiss, A.M. 1998. Family caregiving: Stress, coping, and intervention. In M. Hersen & V.B. Van Hasselt (Eds.), *Handbook of Clinical Geropsychology* (pp. 469–493). New York: Plenum.

Gillies, J., & Neimeyer, R.A. 2006. Loss, grief, and the search for significance: Toward a model of meaning reconstruction in bereavement. *Journal of Constructive Psychology*. 19. 31–65.

Gladstone, J.W. 1991. *Elderly married persons relocating to institutions: Implications for mutual caregiving*. Paper presented at the International Conference on Care of the Elderly, Hong Kong.

Gladstone, J.W. 1995a. The marital perceptions of elderly persons living or having a spouse living in a long-term care institution in Canada. *The Gerontologist*. 35. 52–60.

Gladstone, J.W. 1995b. Elderly married persons living in long-term care institutions: A qualitative analysis of feelings. *Ageing and Society*. 15. 493–513.

Gladstone, J.W., Dupuis, S.L., & Wexler, E. 2006. Changes in family involvement following a relative's move to a long-term care facility. *Canadian Journal on Aging*. 25. 93–106.

Gladstone, J.W., & Wexler, E. January/February 2000. A family perspective of family-staff interaction in long term care facilities. *Geriatric Nursing*. 16–19.

Gladstone, J.W., & Wexler E. 2002a. Exploring the relationships between families and staff caring for residents in long-term care facilities: Family members' perspectives. *Canadian Journal on Aging*. 21. 39–46.

Gladstone, J.W., & Wexler, E. 2002b. The development of relationships between families and staff in long-term care facilities: Nurses' perspectives. *Canadian Journal on Aging*. 21. 217–228.

Guberman, N., Maheu, P., & Maille C. 1992. Women as family caregivers: Why do they care? *The Gerontologist*. 32. 607–617.

Gubrium, J. 1993. *Speaking of life: Horizons of meaning for nursing home residents*. New York: Walter de Gruyter, Inc.

Hasselkus, B.R. 1998. Meaning in family caregiving: Perspectives on caregiver/professional relationships. *The Gerontologist*. 38. 342–352.

Hill, C.D., Thompson L.W., & Gallagher, D. 1988. The role of anticipatory bereavement in older women's adjustment to widowhood. *The Gerontologist*. 28. 792–796.

Horowitz, A. 1985. Family caregiving to the frail elderly. In P. Lawton & G. Maddox (Eds.), *Annual Review of Gerontology and Geriatrics*, Vol. S (pp. 194–246). New York: Springer.

Ingersoll-Dayton, B., & Raschick, M. 2004. Relationship between care-recipient behaviours and spousal caregiving stress. *The Gerontologist*. 44. 318–327.

Javenic, M.R., & Connell, C.M. 2001. Racial, ethnic, and cultural differences in the dementia caregiving experience: Recent findings. *The Gerontologist*. 41. 334–347.

Jutras, J., & Veilleux, F. 1991. Informal caregiving: Correlates of perceived burden. *Canadian Journal on Aging*. 10. 40–55.

Kastenbaum, R.J. 1986. *Death, society and human experience*. Columbus, OH: Charles E. Merrill.

Kayser-Jones, J. 2002. The experience of dying: An ethnographic nursing home study. *The Gerontologist, Special Issue*. 3.42. 11–19.

Keating, N.C., Fast, J., Dosman, D., & Eales, J. 2001. Services provided by informal and formal caregivers to seniors in residential continuing care. *Canadian Journal on Aging*. 20. 23–45.

Keating, N., Fast, J.E., Connidis, I.A., Penning, M., & Keefe, J. 1997. Bridging policy and research in eldercare. *Canadian Journal on Aging, Special Issue Supplement*. 22–41.

Lazarus, R.S., & Folkman, S. 1984. *Stress, appraisal, and coping*. New York: Springer.

Lee, D.T.F., Woo, J., Mackenzie, A.E. 2002. The cultural context of adjusting to nursing home life: Chinese elders' perspectives. *The Gerontologist*. 42. 667–675.

Lieberman, M.A., & Videka-Sherman, L. 1986. The impact of self-help groups on the mental health of widows and widowers. *American Journal of Orthopsychiatry*. 56. 435–449.

Logsdon, M.C., & Robinson, K. 2000. Helping women caregivers obtain support. Barriers and recommendations. *Archives of Psychiatric Nursing*. 14. 244–248.

Long, C., Krisztal, E., Rabinowitz, Y., Gillispie, A., Oportot, M., Tse, C., Singer, L., Gallagher-Thompson, D. 2004. Caregiver stress and physical health: The case for stress management therapy. *Clinical Psychologist*. 8. 22–28.

Lopata, H.Z. 1996. *Current widowhood: Myths and realities*. Thousand Oaks, CA: Sage Publishers.

Martin Matthews, A. 1980. Women and widowhood. In B.W. Marshall (Ed.), *Aging in Canada* (pp. 145–153). Markham, ON: Fitzhenry and Whiteside.

McPherson, B.D. 1983. *Aging as a Social Process*. Toronto: Butterworth.

Miller, B., & Cafasso, L. 1992. Gender differences in caregiving: Fact or artifact? *The Gerontologist*. 32. 498–507.

Miller, B., & Guo, S. 2000. Social support for spouse caregivers of persons with dementia. *Journal of Gerontology: Social Sciences*. 55B. S163–S172.

Mittelman, M. 2005. Taking care of the caregivers. *Current Opinion in Psychiatry*. 18. 633–639.

Montgomery, R.J.V., & Borgatta, E.F. 1989. The effects of alternative support strategies on family caregiving. *The Gerontologist*. 29. 457–464.

Morgan, D. 1989. Adjusting to widowhood: Do social networks really make it easer? *The Gerontologist*. 29. 101–107.

Mui, A.C., & Burnette, D. 1994. Long-term care service use by frail elders: Is ethnicity a factor? *The Gerontologist*. 34. 190–198.

Myers, J. 2003. Coping with caregiving stress: A wellness-oriented, strengths-based approach for family counselors. *The Family Journal*. 11. 153–161.

Nakashima, M., Chapin, R., Macmillan, K., & Zimmerman, M. 2004. Decision making in long-term care: Approaches used by older adults and implications for social work practice. *Journal of Gerontological Social Work*. 43. 79–102.

National Advisory Council on Aging. 2002. 1999 and beyond: Challenges of an aging Canada.

National Advisory Council on Aging. 2005. Seniors from ethnocultural minorities: Seniors on the margins.

Novak, M. 1997. *Aging & Society: A Canadian Perspective*. Scarborough: International Thomson Publishing.

Pearlin, L.I., Mullan, J.T., Semple, S.J., & Skaff, M.M. 1990. Caregiving and the stress process: An overview of concepts and their measures. *The Gerontologist*. 30. 583–594.

Pinquart, M., & Sorenson, S. 2005a. *Caregiving Distress and Psychological Health of Caregivers*. New York: Nova Biomedical Books.

Pinquart, M., & Sorensen, S. 2005b. Ethnic differences in stressors, resources, and psychological outcomes of family caregiving: A meta-analysis. *The Gerontologist*. 45. 90–106.

Port, C.L., Gruber-Baldini, A.L., Burton, L., Baumgarten, M., Hebel, J.R., Zimmerman, S.L., & Magaziner, J. 2001. Resident contact with family and friends following nursing home admission. *The Gerontologist*. 41. 589–596.

Rojiani, R. 1994. Disparities in the social construction of long-term care. In C. Reissman (Ed.), *Qualitative Studies in Social Work Practice* (pp.139–154). USA: Sage Publications, Inc.

Rosenthal, C.J., & Dawson, P. 1991. Wives of institutionalized elderly men: The first stage of the transition to quasi-widowhood. *Journal of Aging and Health*. 3. 315–334.

Ross, M.M., Rosenthal, C.J., & Dawson, P.O. 1997. Spousal caregiving in the institutional setting: Task performance. *Canadian Journal on Aging*. 16. 51–69.

Sankar, A. 1991. Ritual and dying: A cultural analysis of social support for caregivers. *The Gerontologist*. 31. 43–50.

Scharlach, A.E., Sobel, E.L., & Roberts, R.E. 1991. Employment and caregiver strain: An integrative model. *The Gerontologist*. 31. 778–787.

Schultz, R., O'Brien, A., Czaja, S. Ory, M., Norris, R., Martire, L.M., Bele, S.H., Burgio, L., Gitlin, L., Doon, D., Burns, R., Gallagher-Thompson, D., & Stevens, A. 2002. Dementia caregiver intervention research: In search of clinical significance. *The Gerontologist*. 42. 589–602.

Shapiro, E., & Tate, R. 1988. Who is really at risk of institutionalization? *The Gerontologist*. 28. 237–245.

Shear, K., & Shair, H. 2005. Attachment, loss, and complicated grief. *Developmental Psychology*. 47. 253–267.

Silverman, P.R. 1986. *Widow to widow*. New York: Springer.

Smith, T.L., & Toseland, R.W. (2006). The effectiveness of a telephone support program for caregivers of frail older adults. *The Gerontologist*. 46. 620–629.

Solomon, R. 1982. Serving families of the institutionalized age: The four crises. *Journal of Gerontological Social Work*. 25. 83–96.

Sorenson, S., Pinquart, M., & Duberstein, P. 2002. How effective are interventions with caregivers? An updated meta-analysis. *The Gerontologist*. 42. 356–372.

Steele, M., Pinquart, M., & Sorensen, S. 2003. Preparation dimensions and styles in long-term care. *Clinical Gerontologist*. 26. 105–122.

Strang, V.R., Koop, P.M., Dupuis-blanchard, S., Nordstrom, M., & Thompson, B. 2006. Family caregivers and transition to long-term care. *Clinical Nursing Research*. 15. 27–45.

Stroebe, W., & Stroebe, M.S. 1993. Determinants of adjustment to bereavement in younger widows and widowers. In M.S. Stroebe, W. Stroebe, & R.O. Hanson (Eds.), *Handbook of bereavement: Theory, research and intervention* (pp. 208–226). New York: Cambridge University Press.

Tennstedt, S.L., McKinlay, J.B., & Sullivan, L.M. 1989. Informal care for frail elders: The role of secondary caregivers. *The Gerontologist*. 29. 677–683.

Tornatore, J.B., & Grant, L.A. 2002. Burden among family caregivers of persons with Alzheimer's disease in nursing homes. *The Gerontologist*. 42. 497–506.

Turner, J.C., and Turner, F.J. 2005. *Canadian Social Welfare* (5th Edition). Toronto: Pearson Education Canada, Inc.

Utz, R.L., Carr, D., Neese, R., & Woortman, C.B. 2002. The effect of widowhood on older adults' social participation: An evaluation of activity, disengagement, and continuity theories. *The Gerontologist*. 42. 522–533.

Wadley, V.G., & Haley, W.E. 2001. Diagnostic attributions versus labeling: Impact of Alzheimer's disease and major depression diagnoses on emotions, beliefs, and helping intentions of family members. *Journal of Gerontology: Psychological Sciences*. 56B. 244–252.

Walker, A. 1991. The relationship between the family and the state in the care of older people. *Canadian Journal on Aging*. 10. 94–112.

Wallace, S.P. 1990. The no-care zone: Availability, accessibility, and acceptability in community-based long-term care. *The Gerontologist*. 30. 254–261.

Whitlach, C.J., Schur, D., Noelker, L.S., Ejaz, F.K., & Looman, W.J. 2001. The stress process of family caregiving in institutional settings. *The Gerontologist*. 32. 665–672.

Yamamoto-Mitani, N., Aneshensel, C.S., & Levy-Stroms, L. 2002. Patterns of family visiting with institutionalized elders: The case of dementia. *Journal of Gerontology: Social Sciences*. 57B. S234–S246.

Young, R.F., & Kahana, E. 1989. Specifying caregiver outcomes: Gender and relationship aspects of caregiving strain. *The Gerontologist*. 20. 649–655.

Zarit, S.H., & Whitlatch, C.J. 1992. Institutional placement: phases of the transition. *The Gerontologist*. 32. 665–672.

# CHAPTER 22

# Persons with Disabilities: Barriers to Their Full Participation in Society

*Doreen M. Winkler*

## INTRODUCTION

### Who Are Persons with Disabilities?

Consider the impact of the following vignette in arriving at your answer.

A young, blind Crown attorney was cross-examining a defendant when suddenly there was a commotion in the court room, totally disrupting the proceedings. The Crown attorney, baffled by the noise, stopped in mid-sentence to ask the clerk standing next to him what was happening.

"Oh," said the clerk "the lights have all gone out."

"Your Honour!" cried the defence counsel, no longer able to read his notes in the darkened room, "I cannot continue . . . I assume that in all the confusion, you will want to adjourn this matter to another day."

"Your Honour," the blind Crown attorney declared, "I am fully prepared to continue. May we not proceed with the case?"[1]

Thus, in an instant, forty-nine people in the courtroom that day became disabled and the one who was disabled discovered that his disability had vanished.

This account of a simple incident startlingly reveals that, whether permanent or temporary, disability is not far from any one of us on this planet. Disabilities are everyone's concern.

As Carol Krause observes: "Disability is more normal than we often think. Almost all of us will experience some sort of disability at one point in our lives—maybe through age, maybe through broken limbs, or maybe through the onset of mental illness."[2] This theme is amplified by David Lepofsky who argues that most people really don't know about disabilities or simply would rather not have to think about them. Yet "disability eventually touches everyone's life. Everyone either now has a disability, or knows someone near and dear to them who has a disability, or will acquire a disability in the future. There are only two kinds of people in society: those who have a disability now, and people who have a disability in waiting—(i.e., those who will get one later)."[3]

Lepofsky reports that during the 1990s, 77% of Canadians surveyed knew someone with a disability with whom they were in close contact. According to the research Lepofsky cites, during the 1990s,

---

1  This story was told to the writer by Mr. Jim Sanders, President and Chief Executive Officer of the Canadian National Institute for the Blind, Toronto: February 6, 2007.

2  Carol Krause, ed., *Between Myself and Them: Stories of Disability and Difference*. (Toronto: Second Story Press, 2005), p. 1.

3  M. David Lepofsky, "The Long Arduous Road to a Barrier-Free Ontario for People with Disabilities, The History of the *Ontarians with Disabilities Act* —The First Chapter," in *National Journal of Constitutional Law,* 15:2, April 2004, p. 132.

17% of all Canadians had a disability. During the late 1990s, the Ontario government estimated that the number of persons with disabilities in that province alone rose from 1.5 million to 1.9 million. This is a clear indication that the number of people with disabilities is steadily growing.[4]

It is widely known that aging is the major cause of disability. In recent years Canada's aging population has greatly increased and is likely to continue to do so as the baby boomers (born 1946–1961) reach retirement and the years beyond. It is reasonable to assume that in the very near future more goods, services, and facilities designed to meet the needs of persons with disabilities will be required. Also, greater demands will be placed upon professionals and all providers of health care and social services to meet the specific needs of this population. What is of even greater urgency is that people in all sectors of society take immediate steps to remove, and cease to create new, barriers that persons with disabilities face in their efforts to achieve equality. Although the Charter of Rights and Freedoms as well as human rights codes are in place to protect persons with disabilities, barriers of many kinds still exist and are being created that prevent them from achieving their desired level of independence and from fully participating in all that our society has to offer.

This chapter examines aspects of disability in the context of some of the major barriers persons with disabilities face on a daily basis. Emphasis is placed on attitudinal barriers which are more elusive and, therefore, more difficult to eradicate, for reasons to be given. To conclude, suggested methods of changing attitudes and thus potentially tearing down attitudinal barriers will be offered.

## DEFINITIONS

A general definition of the term "disability" is any degree of physical, sensory, or mental impairment. However, a more comprehensive one is essential for a thorough understanding of the term. A detailed definition was offered to the United Nations General Assembly: "Article 1 . . . Persons with disabilities include those who have long-term physical, mental, intellectual, or sensory impairments which in interaction with various barriers may hinder their full and effective participation in society on an equal basis with others."[5]

Two additions to this definition might well be made. The first is that short-term disabilities can also create hardships and barriers for some people and they are often overlooked. In addition, emotional disabilities can be identified as disabilities, separate and apart from mental or intellectual ones. For example, when a person loses a child or a spouse and attempts to go through the various stages of the grieving process, that person can become immobilized in one of the many emotions that accompanies grieving. The person may get "stuck" and never accept the death or recover from the grief for their loss. Their disability is emotional in that they are unable to resolve the grief and complete the mourning process for their loved one who has died.

---

4   Lepofsky, pp. 132–3.

5   Final report of the Ad Hoc Committee on a Comprehensive and Integral International Convention on the Protection and Promotion of the Rights and Dignity of Persons with Disabilities, in a draft resolution of a Convention on the Rights of Persons with Disabilities, to be submitted to the General Assembly at its sixty-second session in March 2007, Article 2, p. 5.

Mel Basbaum refers to the World Health Organization's (WHO) distinction between *disability* and *handicap*: "A disability is any restriction or lack of ability to perform in a manner considered normal. Disabilities are the consequence of impairment representing a disturbance at the level of the individual . . . reduction of the individual's ability to perform certain physical functions. A handicap . . . is a disadvantage that prevents the individual from fulfilling a role or conforming to the expectations or norms of society."[6]

In common usage these terms are often used incorrectly as synonyms, although disabilities are intrinsic whereas handicaps are situational. A person with a visual disability who attends a symphony concert is in no way handicapped in listening to the music. The distinction between "disability" and "handicap" is useful in that many of the barriers that face disabled persons are handicaps to them and not the direct result of their disability. For example, a person who is mobility-challenged and uses a wheelchair competently is barred from entry to a building that has a set of stairs but no ramp. The lack of a ramp is a barrier that handicaps him from getting where he wants to go. It does not relate directly to his disability, to which he has made a good adjustment.

Finally, a "disability" as defined in the *Accessibility for Ontarians with Disabilities Act* (AODA) 2005 is

a.   "any degree of physical disability, infirmity, malformation, or disfigurement that is caused by bodily injury, birth defect, or illness and, without limiting the generality of the foregoing, includes diabetes mellitus, epilepsy, a brain injury, any degree of paralysis, amputation, lack of physical co-ordination, blindness or visual impediment, deafness or hearing impediment, muteness or speech impediment, or physical reliance on a guide dog or other animal or on a wheelchair or other remedial appliance or device;

b.   a condition of mental impairment or a developmental disability;

c.   a learning disability, or a dysfunction in one or more of the processes involved in understanding or using symbols or spoken language;

d.   a mental disorder; or

e.   an injury or disability for which benefits were claimed or received under the insurance plan established under the *Workplace Safety and Insurance Act, 1997*."[7]

For purposes of this chapter, the definition of "disability" will be the following:

A disability is a long-term or short-term physical, mental, intellectual, emotional, and/or sensory impairment that may, in interactions with certain barriers, prevent a person from fully participating in society.

A "barrier," in its simplest form, is a structure or object that impedes movement. It can be an obstacle or circumstance that separates things or keeps people apart from one another or from having access to something they need, or that prevents advancement to a position or goal.

A more precise and legal definition is given in the AODA, 2005, as: "a 'barrier' means anything that prevents a person with a disability from fully participating in all aspects of

---

6   Mel Basbaum, "Services for the Physically Disabled," in Joanne C. Turner and Francis J. Turner, eds., *Canadian Social Welfare* (Toronto: Pearson, 2005), p. 384.

7   *Accessibility for Ontarians with Disabilities Act* (AODA) 2005, S.O. chapter 11, part I, Definitions, 2005, c. 11, s. 2.

society because of his or her disability, including a physical barrier, an architectural barrier, an information or communications barrier, an attitudinal barrier, a technological barrier, a policy, or a practice."[8]

The types of barriers that confront persons with disabilities are many and varied. Some of them are concrete and physical, such as a set of stairs at an entrance to a building with no ramp for physically challenged persons who use a wheelchair, scooter, or walker. Others are latent and much more difficult to detect, such as psychological ones. For example, a disabled person may be in competition for a job promotion with one or more non-disabled persons. A non-disabled candidate may be chosen although the disabled one has equal or better qualifications, a demonstrated ability to do the work, and more time on the job. Although there could be many reasons for the rejection of the disabled applicant, reasons (lacking supporting evidence) may be given to camouflage the real one, namely, that the employer prefers to hire someone without a disability. Whether they are deliberate or inadvertent, covert barriers in the form of attitudinal barriers are the most difficult to identify and, therefore, to remove or prevent.

An "attitude" is a complex mental state involving beliefs and feelings, as well as values and dispositions to act in certain ways. An attitude may be expressed openly by an individual's words, facial expression, and body language. On the other hand, attitudes can be hidden or masked by overt behaviours and appearances in order to conceal conscious or unconscious feelings. For example, a non-disabled person may offer to help a blind or vision-impaired person to cross a busy intersection by approaching them with exaggerated concern for their safety in order to conceal an uncertainty about how to offer help or a fear of blindness. An attitude of prejudice against someone with a particular disability can result in discrimination, one of the most obvious and powerful attitudinal barriers faced by persons with disabilities in becoming equal participants in society. The U.N. proposed Convention on the Rights of Persons with Disabilities defines "discrimination" as follows:

> Discrimination on the basis of disability means any distinction, exclusion, or restriction on the basis of disability which has the purpose or effect of impairing or nullifying the recognition, enjoyment, or exercise, on an equal basis with others, of all human rights, and fundamental freedoms in the political, economic, social, cultural, civil, or any other field. It includes all forms of discrimination, including denial of reasonable accommodation.[9]

It is a logical deduction then that many attitudinal barriers emerge from prejudice and discrimination. Others arise from lack of knowledge, misinformation, failure to seek or accept new information, and rigid adherence to stereotypes and myths concerning disabilities.

## THE NATURE OF DISABILITIES

Disabilities encompass many different conditions with many differing characteristics. When most people think of disabilities they tend to think only of physical ones or at least of ones with visible manifestations. Examples are blindness or visual impairment, deafness or being hard-of-hearing; speech impediments, cerebral palsy, a wide range of mobility impairments, and various neurological diseases. However, it is important to emphasize that the list of disabilities reaches far beyond the physical. Some disabilities are visible while

---

**8** AODA 2005, c. 11, s. 2.

**9** In a draft resolution of a Convention on the Rights of Persons with Disabilities, submitted to the General Assembly at its sixty-second session in March 2007, Article 2, p. 5.

others are, or appear to be, invisible such as an acquired brain injury. Some individuals' disabilities may not be immediately apparent such as a developmental or intellectual disability, a learning disability, or a mental disorder. People can have congenital disabilities while others acquire them later in life.

Many people can and do have more than one disability and it may not be readily apparent which of their conditions is the most disabling for them or troublesome to those with whom they interact. For example, a blind or vision-impaired person who, having made a satisfactory adjustment to their vision loss, may be much more disabled by their acute or chronic depression than by their blindness. A person who is totally deaf may have learned to function well in most areas of life but suffer from severe, recurrent, and disabling episodes of schizophrenia or a bipolar disorder.

For this reason, disabilities cannot be fitted into compartments, nor completely grouped together as, for example, the physically challenged. Each disability is an entity with its own particular characteristics. Further, each person with a disability is a unique individual whose disability is but one characteristic that combines with the variety of other characteristics that makes each person a unique human being.

A further dimension is supplied by Basbaum who claims that "the issues facing someone with a disability do not result purely because of a physical or mental disability; rather, they concern the fit of such disabilities with the person's social, attitudinal, architectural, economic, and political environment. While there exists a wide variety of disabilities, each with its own features and needs, it should be obvious . . . that many of the problems confronting the disabled owe, at least as much, and probably more to issues of public will and attitudes as they do to an individual's or group's specific impairment and disability."[10]

This is inherent in Lepofsky's observation that "persons with disabilities tend to be among society's most disadvantaged. They are over-represented among Canada's poor. . . . They are over-represented among those who must depend on dwindling social assistance programs. . . . They are disproportionately vulnerable to the arbitrary exercise of power over their most basic needs by public sector, private sector, and charitable organizations. They too often lack access to effective legal services. This is so despite the fact that they are needier than most for recourse to lawyers' services to vindicate their rights and freedoms."[11]

Persons with disabilities are found living in large Canadian cities, small towns, and villages as well as in remote, rural communities. They are represented in all walks of life and all political sectors in the country. Finally, disabled persons clearly reflect the diversity of Canada's population with respect to their gender; racial, cultural, ethnic origin; religious persuasion; and sexual orientation.[12]

# REASONS FOR THE PROLONGED EXISTENCE OF BARRIERS

The Charter of Rights and Freedoms (amended 1981) states at section 15:

1. Every individual is equal before and under the law and has the right to the equal protection and equal benefit of the law without discrimination and, in particular, without discrimination

---

10  Basbaum, p. 384.

11  Lepofsky, p. 133.

12  Lepofsky, p. 133.

based on race, national or ethnic origin, colour, religion, sex, age, or mental or physical disability. (2) Subsection (1) does not preclude any law, program, or activity that has as its object the amelioration of conditions of disadvantaged individuals or groups including those that are disadvantaged because of race, national or ethnic origin, colour, religion, sex, age, or mental or physical disability.[13]

Further, Article 1 of the United Nations' Convention on the Rights of Persons with Disabilities declares that "the purpose of the present Convention is to promote, protect, and ensure the full and equal enjoyment of all human rights and fundamental freedoms by all persons with disabilities, and to promote respect for their inherent dignity."[14]

After a seven-year period of hard work, the implementation of complex strategies and pressure put upon provincial legislators, a hitherto unknown grassroots disability rights movement in Ontario was able to set in motion a legislative process that resulted in the enactment of the *Ontario Disabilities Act* (ODA), December 13, 2001.[15] The act was distinctive in that it is one of a few Canadian statutes passed as a result of the efforts of a province-wide group of disabled and non-disabled Ontarians called the Ontarians with Disabilities Act Committee. This courageous and tireless group, under the direction of David Lepofsky, pressed forward with a single, determined focus to get new disability rights legislation passed in Ontario. Their goal was to make Ontario a barrier-free province for its 1.9 million disabled citizens.

The ODA was a pioneer venture that brought a great deal of attention to Ontario and Canada. It was a most important first step in achieving legislation to promote the removal and prevention of barriers against persons with disabilities in Ontario. However, the act lacked strength and needed several major amendments to reach the goal of a barrier-free province. For example, it did not extend barriers to the private sector but only to government and the public sector. It did not make barrier removal or prevention mandatory. It did not provide for accessibility standards to be developed or reviewed. It made no call for a new and effective enforcement mechanism to ensure that the removal and prevention of barriers would be carried out.

Although the ODA (2001) was considered a weak and limited law, its passage paved the way for much stronger and more comprehensive legislation enacted, such as the *Accessibility for Ontarians with Disabilities Act*, in 2005. The purpose of this act is to "benefit all Ontarians by

a.  developing, implementing, and enforcing accessibility standards in order to achieve accessibility for Ontarians with disabilities with respect to goods, services, facilities, accommodation, employment, buildings, structures, and premises on or before January 1, 2025; and,

b.  providing for the involvement of persons with disabilities, of the Government of Ontario, and of representatives of industries and of various sectors of the economy in the development of the accessibility standards."[16]

In light of the progress these laws have made in the recognition of disability rights in Ontario, many advocates hope for similar legislation that might in the future advance the rights of all Canadians with disabilities.

---

13  Quoted in Lepofsky, p. 146 note.

14  In a draft resolution of a Convention on the Rights of Persons with Disabilities, Article 1, "purpose," p. 5.

15  Lepofsky, p. 312.

16  *Accessibility for Ontarians with Disabilities Act*, 2005, c. 11, s. 1.

With the Charter of Rights, human rights codes, and the newly crafted United Nations' Convention on the Rights of Persons with Disabilities, as well as new provincial laws protecting disability rights, it may seem to many people that the barriers facing persons with disabilities should soon be eradicated. Further, with greater public awareness of disabilities in Canada, it would be reasonable to imagine that barriers against persons with disabilities are mostly removed by now and that no new ones are being created. Unfortunately, this is far from the reality that is occurring.

Many reasons for barriers are subtle and difficult to eliminate. It makes no sense that people and organizations in the public and private sectors would deliberately put up barriers against persons with disabilities to prevent them from becoming fully integrated into society's mainstream. No one would consciously deny the protection persons with disabilities enjoy and are fully entitled to under the Charter of Rights and other human rights codes.

Why then, do barriers still exist and why are new ones still being created? In order to understand this paradoxical situation, it is useful to consider some of the reasons barriers against persons with disabilities exist and remain in place as well as why new barriers are continuing to emerge.

One major reason is that many people in authority in the public and private sectors simply do not know that they have created barriers. If they have had no encounters with people with disabilities, nor any cause to learn about disabilities, they have never thought about what would constitute barriers for persons with disabilities. Therefore, in spite of requirements of the Charter of Rights, human rights, and other disability legislations, they may be totally unaware of a need to remove barriers or prevent them in the future. Another reason for the existence of barriers is that people in industries and organizations do not believe that it is their duty to remove or prevent them. Some people and organizations reason that if their competitors do not have to remove or prevent barriers, neither should they have to think about or take action to remove them. If their competitors don't "get caught" or are not charged with having erected barriers against persons with disabilities, they will take the same chance and risk doing nothing.

Lepofsky suggests that one reason people don't remove barriers is that they do not understand how. This is reasonable if they have not been provided with methods, standards, blueprints, or models of how to go about barrier removal.

Yet another reason is that organizations, in removing barriers of which they are aware, may create others for persons with different disabilities. For example, cities that have cut curbs to street level to accommodate people who use wheelchairs have obviously eliminated a barrier for mobility-challenged people. Yet, in doing this, they may, in some instances, have created barriers for blind or vision-impaired people who use white canes to find curbs at a different level from the sidewalk. Thus, by not co-ordinating services for all disabled persons, they have created a barrier in their efforts to remove one.[17]

---

17  In Chicago, for example, curbs at street corners have been cut to sidewalk level in order to accommodate persons in wheelchairs crossing streets. However, at the same corners where the curbs have been levelled, a tiled surface, different in texture from the paved sidewalk and street surface, has been installed for the distance that the curb has been made level with the sidewalk. Thus, the needs of blind and vision-impaired people who use white canes have been effectively integrated with the needs of people who use wheelchairs at street crossings.

Also, others fear that the cost of barrier removal and prevention will be too high. They have not considered, or been shown clearly, that their removal costs very little, if anything at all. In fact, the benefits of removal far outweigh any costs incurred. More importantly, removal and prevention of barriers will increase benefits and revenue for businesses. For example, physical barriers at the entry of buildings where stores are located discourage customers with disabilities and their families from buying goods and services there.

As Lepofsky points out: "Society as a whole also loses out because of these barriers. When people with disabilities are impeded from getting an effective education and/or competitive employment, they can end up on social assistance. They must draw from the public purse, when they would rather be earning a salary and paying taxes into the public purse. When governments continue to use tax dollars to create new barriers that could have been avoided, they saddle future generations with the cost of later having to undo the mess they now make. A society full of barriers is a lose-lose proposition."[18]

It can be seen that certain attitudes can drive the reasons for creating barriers and thus, those attitudes in themselves become barriers. They can take the form of impatience: no time to consider persons with disabilities' special needs in constructing a building; frustration: too much effort to bother renovating for the small population of disabled persons who might use the building; annoyance: a sign language interpreter is too costly to retain for a conference attended by only one deaf person. Attitudes of indifference or complacency can be the reason some people do not know what barriers they may be erecting for people with certain disabilities. Designers and architects may believe that if they put a ramp in front of a store they will have done all that is necessary or even possible for people with mobility challenges. However, their attitude of complacency may have prevented them from noticing or acknowledging that inside the door there is a set of steps making it impossible for a person with a mobility challenge to get into the store, the aisles of the store may be too narrow for a wheelchair, or the bathroom door may be too narrow for a large electric wheelchair to go through. If a firm's competitors are taking no action to remove barriers, its owners may feel no urgency to act themselves. Linear attitudes of preoccupation and rigidity with the set budget may cause some people to refrain from removing and preventing barriers because the process will be costly and "unnecessary" for the few potential customers with disabilities.

Even the individuals who truly want to make buildings accessible often do not take the time to consider the accessibility of the building as a whole. For example, without careful planning, a ramp may be too steep for a wheelchair to ascend. Or the bathroom in the building may be completely accessible for people with mobility challenges while the entrance to the building is not accessible at all. Such a building recalls the problem of the palace of Versailles, whose architect forgot to include washrooms until construction was too far advanced to work them in.

Thus, well-meaning planners fail to see the whole picture, believing that if they make some effort toward accessibility it will be sufficient to accommodate physically challenged people. Unfortunately, these erroneous attitudes are held by many people in positions of authority. Often such people suppose that they, without consulting disabled persons or doing any research, understand what is necessary for the people they wish to accommodate.

Removing obvious barriers of wood and stone is infinitely simpler than altering entrenched attitudes.

---

18  Lepofsky, p. 138.

Lepofsky points out with regard to the employment of persons with disabilities that "Some of the most pervasive barriers are those that cannot be seen. They are the result of policies or programs designed without taking into account the needs of people with disabilities. For example, collective agreements, employer policies, and insurance plans may include provisions which create barriers that make it difficult for people with some disabilities to obtain competitive employment or to take advantage of benefit plans used by other employees. Attitudinal barriers and workplace harassment can create impediments that inhibit people with disabilities from trying to enforce their legal rights. They may discourage people from staying at their jobs."[19]

Other attitudes of employers may bar persons with disabilities from obtaining and keeping jobs. If part of the work involves filling out forms or writing in a chart or log, a person with a learning disability or with a physical disability affecting their co-ordination may not be able to write legibly or fast enough. If employers demonstrate an attitude of acceptance and flexibility, they may be able to inquire of such employees what type of arrangements could be made to accommodate their inability to write well on the spot. Employers with an attitude of skepticism and doubt about hiring persons with disabilities may not be able to consider specific accommodations to make for them. They are more likely to be on the look-out for proof that the employee is incapable of doing the job. How much time does he take off for medical reasons? How often is he late for work? Does he make too many mistakes? The employers whose attitudes are more open to differences among workers may be prepared to spend some time with a disabled employee to learn the reasons for their requests for time off, their tardiness, and errors. Such employers may learn a good deal about what employees with various disabilities need to accommodate their disability, and discover that when those needs are met, their disabled employees are as hard working and productive as, if not more than, their non-disabled workers, and true assets to their company.

What will remove and prevent barriers against persons with disabilities?

The question defies a ready answer. Barriers against persons with disabilities have been erected since the beginning of time. Prejudices and discriminatory behaviours directed at persons with any form of difference, including those with disabilities, die hard. Even with the enlightenment of our age of technology and with campaigns for increased public awareness, ingrained stereotypes and myths about disabilities are difficult to change. It will be useful to look more closely at some of the barriers encountered by persons with disabilities in order to understand the underlying attitudes that foster them.

Three of the many attitudes that underlie barriers are tokenism, the degree of willingness to help, and the fear of becoming overwhelmed.

For purposes of this chapter, "tokenism" means the decision on the part of governments, people, and organizations in the public and private sectors to do only the minimum in removing barriers against persons with disabilities. They make such gestures in the hope of being seen as having done something adequate, or all that is, in their view, really necessary. For instance, as Lepofsky asserts: "even buildings that are labelled as 'accessible' are often not in reality fully physically accessible for all people with disabilities."[20]

He offers the striking example of laws that are currently in place called *building codes*: "The reality is that, typically, building codes only require that when a new building

---

**19**   Lepofsky, p. 136.

**20**   Lepofsky, p. 134.

is constructed it must meet certain stipulated accessibility requirements, or that accessibility features must be added to an older building when and if it is renovated. A building that does not comply with an applicable building code need not be retrofitted to comply with that law if it is not renovated. Often these building codes provide that even where an existing building is renovated, accessibility features need only be added to that part of the building that is being renovated."[21]

The solutions to these problems will likely be much clearer to most persons with mobility challenges than to non-disabled designers and architects. Difficult though it is for non-disabled persons to see the whole picture of what persons with particular disabilities require, still, walking in such unfamiliar shoes is essential. Planners of buildings without disabilities must learn what it is like for a person with a particular disability to live, work, or travel on a daily basis. Planners of programs without disabilities must extend their knowledge and understanding to encompass the total life of the disabled person, rather than only a specific part of that person's existence, when removing or preventing barriers. For example, like the ramp that leads to a store with a few steps, to install an elevator in a school where there are a few stairs directly inside its front door obviously will not make the building accessible for persons with mobility challenges. Walking in the disabled person's shoes in order to truly comprehend his or her actual needs ought to expand the imagination of the designers. In this example, looking at the complete picture, the designers and builders of the school will be aware not only that the stairs just inside the door need to be removed or that there needs to be another entrance for students in wheelchairs to get into the school, but also that a ramp at the door must not be too steep for a wheelchair to ascend with ease and comfort. Moreover, they will be aware at the planning stage of the construction that at least two of the bathrooms in the school must be made accessible. Then, there will be no need for future renovations in order to comply with building codes to make the school accessible for students with mobility challenges.

The willingness to help can be a complex problem for some and is accentuated by attitudes that surround the concept. For example, people who are responsible for making buildings accessible often concentrate on only one type of disability at a time, giving no thought to persons otherwise impaired. For example, designers and architects will take great pains to make buildings accessible for persons with mobility challenges, while unknowingly erecting communication and informational barriers. They may not realize that blind persons who must go to specific locations in large office towers are faced with informational barriers when there are no tactile markings (such as raised print or braille numbers) in the elevator or auditory announcements of the floors at which the elevator stops. Those infernally loud bells that are attached to fire alarm systems in large stores or apartment buildings are useless to persons who are deaf or hard-of-hearing. Without a visually displayed alarm to indicate that there is a fire, these individuals could face grave danger of injury or death.

Thus, the willingness to be helpful in knocking down barriers against persons with disabilities must be enhanced with careful planning that considers all types of disabilities. This requires not only knowledge of the needs of persons with disabilities but also co-ordination of resources that can be allocated to meet their needs efficiently and effectively.

Many people willing to help persons with disabilities believe that they will be required not only to break down barriers that block persons with disabilities from getting their needs

---

21   Lepofsky, p. 136

met and achieving their goals, but also to make choices and decisions for them. This arises from the misguided assumption that persons with disabilities will be excessively dependent upon others to the point where they will not be capable of making choices or decisions for themselves. In particular, some people fear that persons with disabilities will be unable to decide when and what type of help they need. This occurs frequently in families of children with disabilities. The genuine concern and willingness to help often causes family members to be overprotective, excessively vigilant, and unnecessarily restrictive towards a child who has a disability. Parents and older siblings take the position that their disabled child is not capable of reasoning or thinking clearly enough to make choices or decisions on his or her own. As a consequence, family members, believing it is their duty, make choices and decisions for him or her. Perhaps without knowing it, they deprive their disabled children of the practical opportunity to solve simple problems on their own. Without the knowledge or experience of trial and error, these children are not equipped to make choices by themselves or to arrive at independent decisions. Thus, many children with disabilities are frequently overprotected and not permitted to take age-appropriate risks or interact freely with non-disabled peers. For children with disabilities, the anxious care and concern of well-meaning parents and siblings becomes a barrier preventing them from learning to make choices, take necessary risks, make decisions, acquire social skills, and complete the developmental tasks of adolescence and youth. (A brilliant portrayal of where this trajectory can lead is created by Tennessee Williams in the character of Laura Wingfield in *The Glass Menagerie*. She has learned to get her needs met by manipulating the people around her. Between fear of the unknown and learned helplessness, many disabled children behave similarly.)

Senior citizens with disabilities often find themselves confronted with the same attitudinal barriers. As well, caregivers and family members tend to overprotect older persons with disabilities for whom they take on total responsibility. This kind of overprotection erects barriers these older persons are forced to overcome in order to maintain their independence and their customary self-reliance. Fortunately, most persons with disabilities function normally in all areas of their lives beyond the limitations of their disability. They are perfectly capable of making decisions and choices that allow them to function in most situations. Many older persons discover compensatory ways of living and coping well with their disability.

In both the public and private sectors, people and organizations may fear that making changes to accommodate the disabled will be too costly, require too much time, consume too many available resources, and benefit only a small number of people for whom accommodations are made. As a result, their fear tends to produce inertia and they do little or nothing about barrier removal or prevention. Although the Charter of Rights and Freedoms and other human rights codes make the removal and prevention of barriers obligatory, to date, there appears to be little incentive for compliance. The fact is that without strong, effective, and mandatory legislation enforced by the courts, neither attitudes nor behaviour will change.

Consider, for example, that the necessity of wearing seat belts in automobiles was not made a law punishable by fines until the mid '70s. Since that time, the wearing of seat belts has become automatic for most adults and young children.

A more recent case in point is the landmark victory achieved by a coalition of disabled groups, including the Council of Canadians with Disabilities, who took a Crown corporation, Via Rail, to court because it had purchased, at a huge discount, 139 railcars that were far below acceptable standards for wheelchair accessibility. The Council of Canadians with Disabilities' spokesperson observed that the corporation spent more in legal fees than it would have cost to make the trains accessible. When this case was resolved, the Supreme Court of Canada ordered Via Rail to spend approximately $50 million to retrofit 30 of the 139 railcars to make them accessible for people in wheelchairs. This case is a striking example of the need for legislation and the justice system to force the breakdown of barriers against people with disabilities.[22]

Encouraging is the passage in 2005 of the *Accessibility for Ontarians with Disabilities Act*. This act provides for the establishment of accessibility standards through regulations,[23] the removal of barriers through a specific process and within certain time-lines.[24] Such accessibility standards are to be made public.[25]

## SELF-CREATED PERSONAL BARRIERS OF PERSONS WITH DISABILITIES: "THE ENEMY WITHIN"

*"The fault, dear Brutus, is not in our stars*

*But in ourselves, that we are underlings."*[26]

In addition to social and other barriers faced by persons with disabilities, there may be some personal barriers to overcome. These barriers have to do with their own attitudes towards their disability, as well as how they feel as individuals with a disability. For many, these feelings and self-evaluations can become barriers that impede them from achieving the maximum of which they are capable. Thus, such persons are hampered in their efforts to become fully integrated into society. Examples of personal barriers are a sense of poor self-worth resulting in feelings of low self-esteem; fear of rejection and/or retaliation by authority figures in particular and non-disabled people in general; lack of knowledge of available techniques and resources; and time constraints needed to acquire special knowledge, skills, and practice to manage a disability.

In light of the many barriers against persons with disabilities, it is easy to understand that some can feel that their disability makes them less worthy than non-disabled persons. They receive confirmation of this in the often unconscious attitudes of the non-disabled toward them. The earlier example of families with children with disabilities is relevant here as well. As indicated earlier, children with disabilities are often overprotected by parents and older siblings from learning to share responsibility and from taking part in family activities in the same way as the non-disabled members do. If steps are not taken to rectify this inequality, the disabled members may feel that their disability makes them less desirable, less valued, and less productive than others without disabilities. Unless they receive positive support from others about their worth, they are likely to develop feelings of low

---

**22**  This case was reported by *The Globe and Mail* over a ten-month period: Kirk Makin, "Court to Rule Whether Via Ignored Accessibility in Purchasing Railcars," *The Globe and Mail*, May 19, 2006, p. A.6; Kirk Makin, "Disabled Win Battle with Via," *The Globe and Mail*, March 24, 2007, p. A12.

**23**  AODA, c.11, s. 7.

**24**  AODA, c.11, s. 6.

**25**  AODA, c. 11, s. 10.

**26**  *Julius Caesar,* Act I, Scene ii.

self-esteem and powerlessness. Out of such feelings emerge issues of bitterness, resentment, self-pity, and fear of isolation and abandonment. These personal barriers are not always removed without therapeutic intervention. Nevertheless, many persons are able to accept their disability and to own it as they own their bodies. Ownership of a disability means transcending it—going beyond or surpassing it to the extent that it is no longer the cardinal point around which all of life's activities revolve. When the disability is not the pivotal focus in the life of its owner, there is room for talents, abilities, and preferences to emerge and take precedence.

To own a disability means to reduce its significance to the point where it almost ceases to be an impairment to normal living. Childhood polio left the world-renowned Canadian soprano, Lois Marshall (1924–1997) unable to walk smoothly. As she came on stage her audiences could not help noticing her jerky gait—until she began to sing! From that moment her movements faded into insignificance. It is a fact that her mobility problem prevented her from singing in opera, but she specialized in concert performances where she was able to sing while standing still. Her disability was relegated to the background of her life. What she could not do became subservient to what she could do superbly.

Taking possession of their own disability allows people to take charge of it in learning the best ways of managing it for themselves, while accepting external assistance only when it is wanted and/or needed. Individuals who are able to transcend their disability refuse to accept the social roles that society assigns to them. Further, taking control of their disability allows them the freedom to choose a lifestyle which accommodates it. In this way, people with disabilities can break down their own personal barriers.

This requires that they strive to cultivate the self-confidence that conveys that they are neither powerless nor helpless victims. They are hampered only by the limitations of their disability, most of which they are able to accommodate. Then they can reach the goals they set for themselves when they are prepared to take the necessary risks to achieve them.

This is elaborated by Hansen and Laub:

> You can also be constrained from taking risks by your feelings. The most common feeling that gets in the way of risk-taking is a weak or even absent sense of self-worth. People who do not believe in themselves do not act because they have come to feel powerless and trapped. They frequently lack motivation, become apathetic and complacent, accepting what is, rather than trying to change. At the core of a weak sense of self-worth is the overriding feeling that the real self is worthless, unacceptable and, therefore, must be covered up and hidden. People who lack self-worth have a tendency to not act on authentic, meaningful motives. That which is most meaningful to them—whether it's a feeling, a goal, or a thought—is not divulged, but instead is hidden away. It is not acted upon and, consequently, is not made a reality in their life. [27]

These elusive emotional barriers are difficult to eradicate. For persons with disabilities who have erected them, it is important to acquire a good, solid support system. If it is not present in their family, persons with disabilities must enlist and develop it from friends and acquaintances. Often, this takes courage, hard work, and the determination to abandon reticence and shyness. Hansen and Laub confirm this view in their declaration that: "You don't have to have a strong sense of self-worth to risk and succeed. However, you must be willing to push through the discomfort and take the risk despite these feelings. This is what

---

**27**   Rick Hansen and Joan Laub, *Going the Distance: Seven Steps to Personal Change* (Vancouver and Toronto: Douglas and McIntyre, 1994), pp. 84–85.

counts, taking action despite how you feel about yourself. It is through the experience of taking risks that you will naturally enhance your self-worth."[28]

The attributes of self-worth and self-confidence, often hard won for persons with disabilities, along with a strong support network, are the key forces to be mustered in the elimination of personal barriers.

## SUMMARY AND CONCLUSION

This chapter has provided a detailed definition of "disability." It has looked at disabilities in the context of the general barriers many people with disabilities face. In particular, it has examined many of the attitudinal barriers that must be removed and prevented in order for persons with disabilities to become fully integrated into society. The reasons for the existence and creation of barriers were examined and some possible solutions were offered. The chapter ended with a discussion of the barriers some persons with disabilities tend to erect themselves, and some comments on how they may be overcome.

Whether we are able-bodied or have a disability, it is this writer's firm conviction that we must be able to show strength in the acceptance of differences that come about because of a disability, through ethnic diversity, or for a host of other reasons. We must not only accept differences in our society but also embrace them and revel in them. When we find joy in our differences from others and we can embrace those differences, we truly enrich our own lives. When the commitment to accept and understand differences among those in our society is acted upon, barriers (especially our attitudinal ones) will, in due course, dissolve.

---

28 Hansen and Laub, p. 85.

# CHAPTER 23

# Corrections

*Donald G. Evans*

## INTRODUCTION

The question of what to do with citizens who offend against the law continues to be a serious matter of public and political debate. The swings in ideological positions regarding the management of offenders have been dramatic in the past century. For example, in the last 55 years we have witnessed the shift from rehabilitation as a major focus for working with offenders to a greater emphasis on strict discipline and punitive approaches. The major focus has been selective incapacitation and, in some instances, a curtailing of conditional-release opportunities for incarcerated offenders. As a result, working in corrections today is a challenging experience.

Changes in community tolerance toward the management of offenders have put new pressures on correctional administrators to develop effective programs and to find ways to lessen the cost of administering correctional services. Although governments have passed legislation that increases the length of sentences, they have not increased significantly the budgets of correctional services.

The last 30 years have seen considerable reform in sentencing, which has led to an increase in the lengths of sentences for violent and sexual offenders and efforts to detain those offenders deemed at risk of re-offending. Accordingly, these offenders are denied statutory release and they are incarcerated until the expiry of their sentences. There has also been a growth in legislative remedies that add to or supplement sentences such as those in recent sex offender legislation and the sex offender registry.

This effort of getting tough on offenders has crowded the prison system and left the community programs woefully short of supervising capacity. As a result, there has been no substantive impact on recidivism, and the return rate of offenders to the system is unacceptably high. In recent years there has been some recognition that the answer to reducing crime is not to toughen the justice system or build more prisons, but to work toward prevention through social development. This effort to convince governments that crime prevention can be achieved by improving social conditions that contribute to criminality is in its infancy. It is one of the hopeful signs we see in the wake of the mass incarceration rates experienced in the United States and the United Kingdom.

## CORRECTIONAL SERVICES: AN HISTORICAL OVERVIEW

The criminal justice system in Canada is composed of three major systems: the police, the courts, and correctional services. Most simply, one can describe their functions as apprehension, adjudication, and containment.

The importance of each of the various elements of the criminal justice system was evident even in the earliest days of the emerging Canadian state. The Royal Canadian Mounted Police's (RCMP) contribution to providing law and order has been widely acclaimed and romanticized. Similarly, courts have been available from our earliest days to adjudicate disputes and to deal with the accused. Early settlers usually saw fit to construct a local jail to contain difficult citizens. In fact, to be recognized as a county, a community had to have a courthouse and a jail. Consequently, throughout the older parts of the country one often finds courthouses and jails, usually formidable structures, in the central part of the county towns.

We owe some of the most humanitarian features of the current prison system to the kind-heartedness of the Quakers (Society of Friends), who believed that capital punishment was being applied in too many cases and covering too many categories of offences. They urged the creation of an environment where offenders could repent of their deeds and reform. The Walnut Street Jail in Philadelphia, opened in 1789, was the product of their efforts. This institution kept each inmate separate from the others, and each inmate was assigned his own cell with a small exercise yard. The Quakers felt that solitude was vital to allow the offender to listen to his own conscience and dwell on the errors he had committed. In 1829, the development of the Auburn system challenged the Pennsylvania system by allowing inmates to work in groups while continuing to provide the majority of the prisoners with solitude during their incarceration. This congregate style of managing offenders would eventually predominate in North America.

Kingston Penitentiary, modelled on the Auburn system, was built in the 1830s. It was only a few years later that Charles Dickens, in his visits to both Kingston and Auburn, recorded his opinion that, while well-intentioned, the isolation enforced in these institutions was causing mental illness in many of their inmates.

Penitentiaries developed rapidly across North America from the early 1800s on and, in Canada, reformatories—usually called industrial farms—for less serious offenders were established.

While local jails were usually comparatively small institutions, penitentiaries and reformatories tended to be considerably larger. The jails were originally designed to hold individuals during the process of their trials as well as those who were incarcerated for very short periods of time. The reformatories, on the other hand, held people for terms ranging from 30 days to two years, and the penitentiaries assumed responsibility for individuals serving terms of imprisonment that exceeded two years.

The jails built since the 1970s, often called detention centres, are more spacious and are usually capable of accommodating offenders for as long as three months, although many accused individuals who are remanded in custody sometimes spend far more than three months there while awaiting completion of their trials. The provision of legal aid in the latter part of the twentieth century has offered offenders the opportunity to provide formal defences and, therefore, requires more time in processing them before judgment is rendered and sentencing commences.

Until the 1950s, reformatories and penitentiaries had programs that involved inmates in mainly agricultural and industrial work. Just as with large psychiatric hospitals and institutions for the mentally handicapped, reformatories and penitentiaries were usually surrounded by large farm acreage, in which the inmates were the principal workers. Within the institutions, the inmates engaged in activities such as performing metal trades, manufacturing licence plates, sewing mailbags, weaving baskets, and manufacturing shoes as well as performing basic maintenance and food services. Almost all of these activities related to goods and services the correctional system itself needed, and in many ways the system was self-sufficient.

The staff-to-inmate ratio in these institutions was quite low, and staff members had little training, let alone any professional consultation, to assist them in dealing with offenders in any manner other than direct supervision. Until the late 1950s, some institutions still required that inmates maintain silence in dining rooms and other institutional areas. Since the 1970s, more attention has been given to the number of staff required as well as to providing staff training and professional staff for consultation. These measures have allowed for a more efficient allocation of security and program space within the institutions.

The conditional release of offenders from prison evolved slowly over the years. Commencing in 1899 with the "ticket-of-leave" legislation, the gradual release was used sparingly. The legislators were interested in shifting the responsibility from the correctional authorities to the offender for earning an early release. The public voiced concerns at the time about separating what today we call high-risk offenders from those who present less of a safety risk to the community. The conditional release is designed to assist this latter group.

In those early days the released offender was required to report to the local police for supervision, but by 1905, the appointment of the first parole officer in Canada augmented this requirement. The duties of the parole officer were to include visiting inmates to assess whether they were ready for release, and to provide supervision, in conjunction with the police, of released inmates.

For the next 50 years this approach continued to develop, and the system slowly took on a more systematic approach to managing the conditional releases that today's modern parole system resembles. The parole system as we know it began in 1959 when the "ticket-of-leave" legislation was repealed and the *Parole Act* came into force. This act established an independent National Parole Board with the authority to grant, deny, terminate, or revoke conditional releases. The board was to be guided in its decision making by three criteria:

- Parole would be granted when the inmate had derived maximum benefit from incarceration.
- Parole would assist the inmates in their rehabilitation.
- The release of the inmate would not constitute a major risk to the community.

With minor amendments this act stood until 1992, when the *Corrections and Conditional Release Act* replaced it. Probation supervision, the most frequently used alternative to imprisonment, had its beginnings in England in 1841. From 1876, the English court missionaries provided a formal supervisory service in the courts. Further evidence of how unevenly the corrections system developed across the world is that Canada's earliest probation supervisory service began in Ontario in 1921 and was expanded into a province-wide service only in the 1950s.

With the development of probation and parole, we see the first recognition that offenders must be managed according to their individual needs. Between 1955 and 1975, Canada saw an exceptional expansion of options for incarcerated offenders. For a brief time therapeutic programming was in vogue; given the predisposition of the corrections system to move from one panacea to another, many people believed that all offenders could and should be treated and that all could be cured of whatever compelled them to offend. This, of course, was folly and led, in the 1970s, to the widespread notion that nothing works in the treating of offenders.

Since 1965, community program alternatives for offenders have expanded markedly. Specifically, there has been an expanded use of probation and associated specialized service programs, such as community service orders and victim–offender reconciliation projects involving the offenders' paying some form of restitution to the victims of their crimes. Supervised community work programs and temporary absence programs for regular employment or school attendance have also been implemented. In the 1970s, correctional services became much more versatile and responsive to the needs of the offender, the victim, and the community.

## MORE RECENT DEVELOPMENTS

To understand the Canadian correctional system one must first appreciate the developments in the current Canadian criminal justice system as a whole, including corrections, the police, the courts, and the government.

The correctional system in Canada underwent considerable review during the mid- to late 1970s. The review was based on an interest in developing an approach that balanced the need for punitive measures, which were viewed as often having limited impact on offenders, with the desire to reintegrate the offenders and assimilate them back into society as productive and contributing members. This led to the expansion of adult-offender skills training and therapeutic programs and a refinement of the probation and parole system with a focus on victim–offender reconciliation and community restitution.

The basic desire was to establish a correctional system that could be flexible and responsive to the needs of both the community and the offender. In fact, corrections was the first sector of the criminal justice system to successfully employ alternative tactics and move towards a community-based model of operations.

A similar examination of traditional police work took place in the late 1980s. This led to the development of community-based policing, a model of policing that balances law enforcement with crime prevention. Community policing identifies factors such as poverty, neglect, unemployment, and abuse as the contributing causes of crime and social order problems. In doing so, it recognizes that only through co-operative efforts on the part of the criminal justice system and the social welfare system are we likely to provide lasting solutions to the problem of crime.

Over the last decade of the twentieth century, public opinion about the criminal justice system shifted toward more concern for law and order. Social protest centred on the alleged leniency of the courts, particularly as they dealt with young offenders, and on the operations of the parole system in relation to cases of violent offenders.

In the field of corrections this shift has manifested itself in higher incarceration rates and longer sentences. This, in turn, has led to prison overcrowding at a time when the public funding needed to build additional long-term facilities is not readily available. The result has been that governments cut back on programs aimed at rehabilitation of offenders and provide stricter regimes in both institutional and community correctional programs. Development of boot camps, intensive supervision of probation, and super-max prisons are examples of this trend. The curtailment of conditional releases for serious offenders and the development of community notification programs for sex offenders who are released from prison at the ends of their sentences are further efforts by government officials to satisfy public opinion.

As a result of their inability to build new jails and prisons quickly, some governments in Canada are flirting with the idea of privatizing some of their prison capacity. This trend is especially noticeable in jurisdictions favouring incapacitating correctional strategies.

Others are coming to a different conclusion, based on the growing awareness that crime and economic and social disadvantages may be linked. These people are reaffirming a commitment to rehabilitation in their prison programs and to the expansion of community programs. This renewed interest in rehabilitation has been fuelled by the desire to develop evidence-based programs, which are based on research and owe a great deal to the "what works" research that has been a major focus of the past decade. Governments and, as a consequence, correctional departments have had to look at other ways of doing business, including working closely with police and the courts in the areas of prevention, information-sharing, and offender supervision.

# CUSTODIAL CORRECTIONS

Convicted offenders serve sentences of two years or more in federal penitentiaries while those sentenced to less than two years serve in provincial correctional centres. Besides the jurisdictional differences between federal and provincial prisons, institutions are categorized differently according to their security classifications.

## Institutional Levels of Security

Most prison systems tend to organize their accommodation into three major types of institutions, classified as maximum, medium, or minimum security.

Maximum-security institutions are for offenders who are considered a risk to the staff, other offenders, or the community. Offenders' movements are restricted, as are their associations with others and other privileges. This classification of institution also includes psychiatric centres and special handling units (super-max facilities).

Medium-security institutions comprise the majority of prison accommodation in most jurisdictions and they are for offenders who pose a risk to the community. It is at these institutions that the majority of correctional programming takes place. Offenders' movements and associations are more flexible, but are regulated and supervised.

Minimum-security institutions are for those offenders who pose little or no risk to the safety of the community. Offenders have minimal restriction on their movements, associations, and privileges, and minimal supervision is provided. Cottage-style facilities or camp-type structures usually indicate a minimum-level institution.

## Industrial Programs

Industrial programs are considered an important part of the programming in adult institutions. In Ontario, for example, outside industries operate commercial ventures within the institutions. In the federal system a special agency, Corcan, provides industrial program opportunities for offenders. This agency expects to recover its costs through the sales of the products offenders make.

Agricultural programs are another mainstay of many prison systems. In the last couple of decades, farming has seen a resurgence as institutions attempt to offset high food costs. This trend towards self-sufficiency is also seen in the manufacturing end of the programs, in that the institutions use some of the products internally.

In some of these programs, offenders are paid regular wages, while in others they are paid an amount that reflects the training aspect of the job. In some programs, an incentive allowance is provided; usually this is available for offenders serving longer sentences. The incentive allowance program allows the offender a spending allowance for use in the institution and provides a compulsory savings allowance. It is a graded system in which an offender's earning depends on his or her conduct, industry, and attitude. The introduction of regular industrial wages for offender employment in the federal system addresses the difficulty in creating work incentives in institutions, especially for long-term offenders. Regular industrial wages are based on the recognition that work training, with its demands and rewards, may be an effective means to prepare offenders for successful reintegration.

## Education and Life Skills

A wide range of academic, vocational, and correspondence (distance-education) programs, as well as on-the-job training, are provided in many correctional facilities. Corrections either employs or contracts with local school boards for highly qualified teachers. Recently, courses available on computer are being used in some institutions and allow teachers to work with a larger number of students while still providing individual assistance when required.

Life-skills programs give offenders opportunities to develop skills that can assist them to function more effectively in the community. This type of training focuses on decision making, family life, sex education, the world of work, consumer education, the use of leisure time, and human relations.

## Treatment Programs

If we are to avoid merely warehousing offenders, our prison systems will need to offer a variety of programs geared to reducing the offenders' prospects of re-offending. These programs should be developed with a perspective that sees the continuation of the program in the community. After-care seems to have become a forgotten concept in corrections and needs to be reintroduced if significant gains are to be made in reducing re-offending. Better case management and supervision in community settings would enhance rather than detract from prison sentences. As a result of adopting this perspective, prison systems will need to address a critical concern that relates to the lack of continuity and consistency in offender programming both in the prison setting and in community supervision efforts. Safe, secure custody is an imperative, but corrections must do more than this if it is to promote public safety. Too often programs supportive of a prisoner's re-socialization are commenced but not continued for a host of reasons including insufficient resources, lack of trained personnel, changes in leadership, or outright failure of leadership. If treatment programs are to fulfill their promise, there will need to be consistency in program efforts.

A treatment program is a structured intervention that addresses the factors directly linked to the offender's criminal behaviour. A major goal of the correctional system is to assist in the re-socialization of offenders and their subsequent resettlement in the community as law-abiding citizens through the provision of programs in prisons and in the community. It is critically important that treatment programs meet the identified needs of offenders and contribute to their successful resettlement in the community. This is essential if the correctional system is to contribute to public safety.

From the work done by Canadian researchers we can distill at least eight minimum characteristics of an effective treatment program in both prison and community settings. They can be summarized as follows:

1. The use of an empirically based model of change which facilitates a change in the offender's attitudes and behaviour and is based on a theory supported by research.
2. The targeting of the criminogenic factors that contribute directly to criminal behaviour.
3. The deployment of effective methods of program delivery, including the statement of qualifications for treatment staff conducting or involved in the program.
4. A strong skills orientation in the program.
5. Attending to the issue of responsivity, this refers to the characteristics of offenders that have direct impact on how much benefit they will derive from the structured intervention.
6. Paying attention to program intensity, which means the scope, sequencing, and duration of treatment related to the seriousness and persistence of the offender's risk and need.
7. Being cognizant of the need for continuity of care issues. This means that treatment gains made during imprisonment are reinforced and strengthened by intervention efforts in the community.
8. Providing for ongoing monitoring and evaluation of the treatment programs.

The legislative purpose of the correctional system in Canada is to assist the rehabilitation of offenders and their reintegration into the community as law-abiding citizens through the provision of programs in penitentiaries and in the community. The Canadian Correctional System is, therefore, responsible for providing programs that will meet the legislative aim of the Parliament of Canada. All of the programs used in the Correctional Service of Canada start with the three basic principles of effective correctional interventions, namely, risk, need, and responsivity (Andrews and Bonta, 2006).

These principles suggest the following:

- Risk: Treat only offenders who are likely to re-offend (moderate risk or higher).
- Need: Target criminogenic needs (needs that are likely to produce criminal behaviour). Examples of criminogenic needs are: antisocial personality, antisocial associates, antisocial cognitions, low attachment to family/lovers, low engagement in education/employment, poor use of leisure time, and abusing drugs or alcohol.
- Responsivity: Matching the treatment regime to the offenders' learning styles and culture.

These themes are repeated and modified in programs that are geared to meeting the specific needs of sexual offenders, substance abusers, and mentally ill offenders.

## Women Offenders

The vast majority of incarcerated offenders are men. Consequently, there are few women's correctional centres in Canada. Until very recently, there was only one facility for federally sentenced women in Canada, and it was situated in Kingston's Prison for Women in

Ontario. That facility is expected to close sometime in the next couple of years. This announced closing is the result of a series of events that include both positive—the task force recommendations of a women's advocate and correctional officials group in their report, *Creating Choices*—and negative—the Arbour Inquiry.

*Creating Choices* recommended an emphasis on women-centred programming, the establishment of five new institutions across Canada, and the closing of the Prison for Women in Kingston. The Arbour Inquiry was established following a disturbance at the Prison for Women and the subsequent problem of strip searches conducted by male guards.

There are now five women's centres for federally sentenced women, one of which is located in each of the regions—Pacific, Western, Ontario, Quebec, and the Atlantic. These facilities are intended to address the special needs of women offenders. Programming for women offenders still lags behind the efforts expended on men, and because of limited resources women offenders' needs are not being adequately met. Efforts to define principles to guide the programming for women have been undertaken. The principles stress that programs should match women's needs rather than merely fit women into existing programs. The programs are more beneficial when they take into account issues of housing, employment, therapy, services, relationships, and the offenders' individual rights as citizens.

In terms of effective programming for women offenders, it appears that the outcomes would be influenced by

- attention to designing a continuum of care and support;
- clarity in the stated expectations of the interventions;
- clarity about the enforcement of rules and sanctions;
- consistent supervision;
- the co-ordination of resources in the community;
- the provision of social and emotional support; and
- a multifaceted approach that deals specifically with the issues in the lives of women offenders.

The current economic situation and the emphasis on law and order have negatively affected the availability of resources for women offenders. However, the majority of programming has been limited to monitoring and surveillance and has not addressed the women's specific needs. The result has been a failure to supply adequate employment and affordable housing opportunities that would assist their re-entry and reintegration into the community. This situation provides an opportunity and a challenge to community corrections.

## First Nations Offenders

First Nations are overrepresented in the criminal justice system, especially in the institutional population. Also, First Nations offenders are less likely to receive full parole and have higher recidivism rates.

Efforts to address the needs of this population have centred on the development of specific programs geared to First Nations and enlist the assistance of traditional cultural and spiritual leaders. The participation of elders in the evaluation process in parole hearings is one effort to improve the parole grant rate for First Nations offenders. In Alberta, the Native Counselling Services created a minimum-security forestry camp as an alternative to incarceration and also manages the operation of a minimum-security correctional institution. As is the case with women offenders, more attention will be given to this segment of the population in the coming years, and a greater involvement of the First Nations community is anticipated.

## Community Corrections

The approach to managing offenders in the community falls to probation, parole, and the voluntary sector. Probation is, after fines, the most frequently used court sanction and is administered by provincial probation services. In recent years probation workers have been dealing with increased workloads that have necessitated a number of innovations.

Given the interest in public safety, some probation services have introduced special programs for the high-risk offender. These include intensive supervision programs that closely monitor offenders and enforce probation conditions strictly. Also, specialized teams, working with the local police, have been formed to deal with violent and/or sexual offenders to supervise them more adequately. Probation continues to provide reports to the courts to assist in the latter's sentencing decisions and to institutions and parole boards to assist in their release planning. The development of improved risk/need assessments and specific programs that address substance abuse issues and violence prevention are also being undertaken. In the future, probation services will be called upon to develop outcome performance measures to justify the resources expended. This will be one of the service's greatest challenges.

Another community correctional approach is the use of parole. The National Parole Board has jurisdiction for all federally sentenced offenders and for those offenders serving time in provincial institutions, with the exception of Ontario and Quebec, which have their own provincial parole boards.

Parole allows an offender to be released into the community under specified conditions and with supervision. There are generally two forms of parole:

- Day parole is used to prepare offenders for full parole or statutory release. The offender must return either to a penitentiary or to a community-based residential facility each night unless specific authorization in writing has been given.
- Full parole is given under the authority of the parole board to allow the offender to live in the community subject to conditions and supervision.

Volunteers back up the supervision of offenders on parole by providing residential facilities for day parole or temporary-absence programs. At a community residential facility, the offender has the opportunity to go out into the community every day to pursue employment or education programs. This training effort, combined with a supervised living experience, has proven effective. Individuals are able to pay rent and taxes and support their families in ways that are not possible in the traditional institutional programs. Another benefit of the voluntary sector's involvement has been the increased contact between the community, offenders, staff, and, in some specialized programs, victims. The John Howard, Elizabeth Fry, and St. Leonard's societies, as well as the Salvation Army, are the primary voluntary organizations in the correctional environment.

# CAN CORRECTIONS BE EFFECTIVE?

Investment in programs for offenders needs to be accompanied by evaluation efforts to ensure that the resources are being used effectively. In the last number of years an emphasis on evidence-based programming has developed. Much of this emphasis results from the work of a number of Canadian researchers. They have suggested some basic factors to consider in the development of effective programs to reduce recidivism (there is some overlap with the effective treatment characteristics of prison and community setting programs):

- Intensive programs that are behavioural are provided to higher-risk offenders, and target the offender's criminogenic needs (needs that increase the likelihood of re-offending) are essential.
- Effective programs ensure responsivity, carefully matching offender, therapist, and program.
- Effective programs involve program contingencies and/or behavioural strategies being enforced in a firm but fair way.
- In effective programs, staff relate to offenders in an interpersonally sensitive and constructive manner. The staff are well-trained and supervised.
- Effective program structure and activities disrupt the criminal associations of offenders by placing them in situations of predominantly pro-social activities.
- Relapse prevention in the community is provided.
- Advocacy and brokerage are provided to community agencies that offer programs that adhere to the principles of effective intervention.

   More programs in correctional environments are attempting to develop procedures and interventions using this research, and Correctional Service of Canada has become a leading advocate for this method of corrections. As we enter this next century of correctional service, it appears that rehabilitative programming, based on solid research, is poised to make a significant contribution to the management of offenders.

# FUTURE TRENDS AND CHALLENGES

In the coming years, corrections in Canada will be faced with a more complex population of offenders and can expect an impact owing to the following factors:

- Increasing numbers of young offenders are becoming adults and entering the adult system.
- The number of women offenders being sentenced to periods of incarceration has increased.
- With the decrease in resources to mental health services, a greater number of people with mental health problems will end up in the corrections system.
- The number of offenders with contagious diseases will increase.
- Owing to longer sentences and an increase in the number of admissions to prison for offences committed 15 to 20 years ago, the system will see an increase in its demands on health care services.
- With the increasing disclosure of sexual offences, the population of sex offenders in the prison population is correspondingly rising.
- An increase in the growth of gangs and gang-related activities will present order problems for prison administrators.

- Correctional services will work more closely with police major crime units and criminal intelligence services to supervise sexual and violent offenders.

We will continue to see an emphasis on cost-containment in corrections, and some jurisdictions will entertain ideas of privatizing parts of the correctional system. The full impact of the private sector's involvement in delivering correctional services cannot be adequately measured at this time, but it is very likely that we will see some privatized efforts. The continued search for technological applications will also dominate the correctional scene, especially in efforts to more effectively manage the system's information requirements, as well as in providing supervision assistance through drug testing or electronic monitoring.

## CONCLUSION

Correctional programming, whether at the custodial or the community level, is attempting to meet the public demand for public safety. By improving their own capacity to assess, classify, and offer appropriate programs to offenders, corrections services are contributing to community safety. Continual evaluation and research are required to continue to improve the system's capacity to manage effectively those who offend against the law.

## References

Andrews, D. A., & Bonta, James. 2006. *Psychology of criminal conduct*, 4th ed. Newark, NJ: Lexus-Nexis Publishing.

Hannah-Moffat, Kelly. 2001. *Punishment in disguise: Penal governance and federal imprisonment of women in Canada*. Toronto: University of Toronto Press.

Jackson, Michael. 2002. *Justice behind the walls: Human rights in Canadian prisons*. Vancouver: Douglas & McIntyre.

# CHAPTER 24

# Social Workers*

*Dennis Kimberley and Louise Osmond*

## INTEGRATION OF PHILOSOPHIES

### Mission

Social work is an action-oriented profession, with its actions and purposes being guided by repeating philosophical themes. Transcending any one of these themes, within the context of globalization (Ferguson, 2006), is a mission to promote, enable, and enhance the well-being and functioning of individuals and social collectives through mutual, reciprocal, co-operative and interdependent action, guided by values that promote social justice and that respect and enhance the dignity and worth of diverse persons and social collectives, and that transcend national interests. Social humanism, social justice, the application of science and art in undertaking social responsibility (sometimes referred to as social care), and the needs and rights of women and children appear as the most common themes in the development of social work practices within the context of social welfare/social care (e.g., welfare of children), social movements (e.g., women's movement), and social action (e.g., challenging female genital mutilation). (See, for example, Payne, 2006.)

Philosophical orientations and ideologies have not been treated as mutually exclusive domains; they have most often been approached as if they converge and relate to one another. While the integration of ideologies may be imperfect, each orientation has given social workers sets of conceptual and value frameworks for undertaking and evaluating professional responsibilities for helping consumers, be they individuals, partnerships, families, groups, organizations, communities, or societies (often termed "client systems"). Social workers have promoted and enabled both personal and social change with special attention to the justice, social well-being, and health of oppressed and marginalized persons and groups (Baines, 2007).

### Social Humanism and Promoting Social Care

Since the emergence of identifiable sets of practices in the late 1800s, social work has undertaken to promote and enable change in social well-being and health (Richmond, 1917), and to support individual and collective strengths, human potential, and diversity (e.g., The Settlement House movement). Assuming the dignity, potential, worth, and relative freedom of each individual and culture within the context of persons and collectives as being fundamentally interdependent, social workers have promoted the value of undertaking to better understand (termed "assessment" or "social diagnosis," Turner, 2002) and mediate between client systems and their social and physical environments (termed "social work intervention" or "practice"), to change and ameliorate personal and collective problems, risks, impacts, and unmet fundamental needs. Also, consistent with the humanist tradition, getting beyond deficits, social workers have emphasized building on strengths and abilities and enabling normative growth and development as well as the development of human capacity and potential (Payne, 2005). The humanist position has typically called for individual and collective social responsibility in the

---

* Note to Readers: The case examples used in this chapter are based on the current work of Canadian social workers in practice.

interest of promoting and enabling biopsychosocial well-being of both the individual and the collective, as well as in preventing and ameliorating health and social problems, including oppression and impeding social forces.

The paradox is that individual freedom and dignity are partially dependent on collective support and sacrifice; the strength of the collective is enhanced by the co-operation and sacrifices made by individuals. The other paradox is that while each individual and collective is unique and diverse, problems, needs, risks, harm, and potentials may be addressed because of much that is common in the human condition (Towle, 1945).

## Social Justice and Anti-oppressive Practice

Since its inception, and especially since the early 1900s, social work has attempted to get beyond the boundaries of a social responsibility perspective, beyond the provision of social services and social care, to include promoting social justice and related rights and freedoms that transcend national constitutions. Social workers have led in the promotion of

- human rights and support for human dignity (e.g., rights of physically disabled to paid employment);
- entitlements and provision (e.g., assistance to persons and groups who face barriers to independence and functioning);
- fairness and equality (e.g., paternity leave opportunity and a social voice for those marginalized);
- equity (e.g., extraordinary supports to overcome barriers faced by women in male-dominated work environments);
- social and intellectual freedoms and self-determination (e.g., freedom of gay men and lesbians to be treated as married couples);
- social inclusion of diverse, minority, and marginalized collectives (e.g., social integration of disabled persons or Aboriginals); and
- reduction or social control of injustice and oppression (e.g., control of economic and sexual exploitation of children and youth).

The social justice perspective advocates for the inclusion of multiple stakeholders in decision making, promotes active participation of those with less powerful voices, and defines social work responsibility as that of enabling multiple voices to be heard— especially marginalized and oppressed persons (Carniol, 2005). The paradox is that the social justice perspective also promotes collective social controls and social responsibilities needed to enable social justice, as well as supporting individual and collective rights and freedoms.

## Science and Art

Social workers are permitted and expected to make independent professional judgments for which they are publicly accountable. Recognizing the limitations of abstract and value-laden philosophies in guiding social workers, the profession, since the early 1900s, has sought to account for the judgments and actions of its members through adopting a "scientific" orientation to inform professional practice. The profession has promoted the application of verifiable knowledge that reflects observable and relatively predictable truths (e.g., many abused women demonstrate predictable patterns, labelled "battered woman syndrome") and realities (e.g., many women return to risky and abusive partners) in guiding professional observations, judgments, predictions, and actions. In accountable practice, to the degree feasible, the social worker is expected to be able to support judgments and decisions and to account for actions with a credible evidence base that includes practice wisdom and best known practices (Roberts and Yeager, 2006).

The lack of complete knowledge, or the presence of incomplete information, has not been an excuse for inaction (Gambrill, 2006), but the profession has defined part of the social worker's responsibilities as that of creating new knowledge through the practice wisdom that comes from case study (e.g., Harper and Lantz, 2007), the collective wisdom of experienced social workers, or the aggregate information from studies with multiple persons (e.g., social work research on children of alcoholics by Cork, 1969).

Empirically based knowledge is expected to be evaluated and applied with, and in the interest of, the client. But social workers historically recognized the dynamic interplay between the relatively common, repeated, and predictable human experience that is uncovered by systematic inquiry (e.g., persons who have been abused are overrepresented among violent offenders) and the personal subjective human experience of a particular person (Graveline, 2007). While recognizing some similarities among clients who experience particular types of problems, risks, needs, and oppression, social workers have promoted the individualization of service, based on each client's unique experience of reality and his or her unique personal life journey (Rothman, 1998). Consistent with the latter is a strong commitment to the importance of social work as art, in the sense of being based on a personal and interpersonal process that involves reflective practice (Knott, 2007) and the effective use of self (Baldwin and Satir, 1987). The dialectic continues in a profession that promotes practice as both art and science. The paradox in this dialectic is that the scientific approach that generates common and generalized knowledge often provides the insight that enables the promotion and enhancement of individual differences and support of collective diversity.

## Women's Movements

Social work practice, as a female-dominated activity, has been impacted by various women's movements, and other social movements, from social action groups such as the women's temperance movement to the more modern feminist movement (Dominelli, 2002). Social workers have been active in promoting equality (e.g., equal pay for work of equal value), advocating for equity (e.g., support for mothers to complete education while undertaking custodial parenting), and challenging barriers and practices that oppress women (e.g., unjust "mother blaming"). In addition, practitioners have been active in promoting values, services, and practices that are consistent with themes espoused by women's groups. Among these have included rights to social assistance, rights to safe contraception, accessible and safe abortion as personal choice, access to affordable daycare, the cessation of sexual exploitation of children and youth, and freedom from fear of violence and assault. Those stakeholder groups advocating on behalf of the rights, needs, and potential of those marginalized and oppressed have partnered with social workers in various ways, in part influenced by relatively congruent value orientations.

# A MANDATE TO PROMOTE AND ENABLE PERSONAL AND SOCIAL CHANGE

## Changing Personal and Social Functioning of Collectives and Individuals

Informed by converging ideologies and knowledge about individuals and collectives operating in dynamic interaction, social workers continue to clarify a focus on change in the biopsychosocial functioning of individuals and collectives. Practices in the interest of personal and social change are influenced by a professional value base, the function of the agency, and the professional mandates supported by the client, agency, government, and/or society. Since social workers began to professionalize in the early 1900s with the development of university-based education and associations of social workers, they have come to be treated more as professionals by society, by the community, under the law, and within the context of private contracts. This means that social workers have the right and responsibility to make independent professional judgments and to take relatively independent action.

The focus of change in professional practice has included persons, dyadic relationships (commonly referred to as couples or partners), families, social and therapeutic groups, local communities, formal organizations, societies, and the "global village" (reflected in work with the International Council on Social Welfare, the International Federation of Social Workers, and the United Nations). The focus of the individual social worker or agency may vary, depending on the situation between personal change and collective change. In either case, social work values the importance of interpersonal relationships in enabling and sustaining meaningful personal and social change.

From the beginning, social workers have been concerned with biological well-being, psychological well-being, and social well-being, as well as the interaction among these fundamental life dimensions. In current practice, with the notion of changing and improving biopsychosocial well-being and building client strengths, the professional social worker and client system may focus on one or more of the following (based on Kimberley and Bohm, 1999):

- changing the *behaviour and actions* of an individual (e.g., challenging wife battering actions), or the collective (e.g., challenging prejudicial actions by the police against Aboriginals) (Gambrill, 2006);

- changing or learning to adjust to intense *feelings* of an individual (such as ameliorating depression and related suicide risk), or collective (such as stress debriefing for communities) (Roberts, 2005);

- changing the *beliefs, attitudes, values, expectations, and other knowledge or awareness dimensions* of an individual (e.g., challenging beliefs that physical "punishment" is evidence of "good" parenting), or collective (e.g., confronting community values and attitudes supporting female genital mutilation) (Ronen and Freeman, 2006);

- *changing or adjusting to a biophysical or biomedical condition or other such realities* of an individual (e.g., promoting an "ability" orientation in persons with physical challenges), or collective (e.g., advocating social policies, legislation, and social action to remove social barriers for those with mental disabilities) (Cox, 2007);

- changing the *person-to-environment transactions* of the individual (e.g., strengthening parenting capacity in an addicted parent), or collective (e.g., enabling a group of survivors of sex abuse to trust mutual aid relationships);[1]

- changing *social environment-to-person transactions* that are part of social reality at the level of the individual (e.g., enabling a youth to assert her needs within a family), the level of the individual in a position of power (e.g., advocating to a financial assistance officer on behalf of a client oppressed by poverty), or the collective with political power(e.g., promoting policies such that a community provides services that are more ethnically sensitive and culturally relevant) (Al-Krenawi and Graham, 2002);

- changing or adjusting to some aspect of *biopsychosocial development* for the individual (e.g., providing assessment, education, counselling, therapy, and foster care support for a child suffering from premature sexualization), or the collective (e.g., social group support for relatives of Alzheimer's patients) (Davies, 2004);

- changing how any or all of the above *factors interact to impact the sense of identity* of an individual (e.g., "I am always the hopeless victim"), a couple (e.g., "We are deviant because we are gay"), a family (e.g., "We are failing to adjust to having a developmenaly delayed daughter/sister"), or a larger collective (e.g., "We are a dying and hopeless community") (Dansky, 1997);

- intervening to *enable change in patterns of interaction of biopsychosocial dimensions and interpersonal relationships* that converge to impact individual and collective well-being and biopsychosocial functioning (e.g., the pattern of efforts by a partner to control a mate that is addicted to pornography) (Stuart, 2003);

- helping client systems to *process existential issues* associated with the realities of their existence (e.g., death and dying), spirituality concerns, and meaning in life issues (Walsh and Lantz, 2007).

By focusing on multiple dimensions that require change to ensure biopsychosocial well-being and functioning of individuals and collectives, social workers define themselves as taking a holistic and integrated approach, sometimes in an interdisciplinary context, to helping client systems (consumers) meet their needs, solve problems, control risks, reduce harm, mobilize strengths, increase resilience, develop capacity, and actualize more of their individual and collective potential.

## Social Worker Mandates

In promoting social responsibility, social care, social justice, anti-oppression, evidence-based practice, the needs and rights of disadvantaged and oppressed or marginalized persons, and biopsychosocial change, social workers (often under the direction of professional associations and/or professionalized service organizations) have been given the right and responsibility, under law, contract, or informal social mandate:

- to make informed professional observations about a client system (e.g., "The incidence of alcohol abuse and spousal violence problems have increased since the closure of the town's plant");

---

1  For an example from the social group work tradition, see Lindsay, Turcotte, and Hopmeyer, 2003.

- to formulate informed professional judgments (e.g., "The stress of added economic hardship has impacted individual and collective coping in this family; without effective support, there is a high risk of family dissolution");

- to make relatively independent professional decisions or recommendations, and at times give binding direction to a client system (e.g., "In the interest of safety of the woman and prevention of violence, it is best if her partner leaves the familial home until he demonstrates effective, sustained, and verifiable anger management; the community also needs increased education-awareness interventions to prevent or intervene early in partner violence");

- to undertake relatively independent professional interventions and related practices that require specialized knowledge, skills, and competent action (from intake to after-care) in enabling individual and collective well-being (e.g., post-trauma counselling with a battered woman, anger management therapy with a battering male, family therapy with children exposed to violence, and community development focus groups to raise community awareness and to prevent partner violence);

- to undertake and provide what society would clearly define as professional services and specialized and expert consultation (e.g., expert testimony to the court and case consultation to a community service, sometimes within independent private practice);

- to partner and team with other stakeholders (e.g., clients), professionals (e.g., public health nurses), administrators, or community leaders in promoting well-being, social welfare, social care, and social justice.

## Professional Ethics in Action

When acting on a professional mandate, social workers cannot be guided solely by law, organizational policy, government policy, or political expedience. Given that people, individually and collectively, make decisions—not organizations—one of the distinguishing features of professionals is that their observations, judgments, decisions, and actions are guided by a set of principles that are reflected in statements of mission, belief, values, ethical decision rules, and standards of practice. The professional responsibility of the social worker may even transcend the wishes of the client, the agency, the law, and societal or cultural practices, and be guided more by a set of values and code of ethics that reflect universal values (e.g., The U.N. Convention on the Rights of the Child) or the collective wisdom of the profession (e.g., The Canadian Association of Social Workers, or CASW). The reader might wish to consider the following examples:

- If the client wishes to have a social worker assist with a suicide plan, the social worker may not assist with self-destruction and would normally have a professional mandate to protect the client against his or her wishes.

- If the agency demands disclosure of confidential client information beyond the ethical principles and standards permitting a breach of confidentiality, then the social worker is justified in refusing and would be able to call on her professional association as external arbiter.

- If a society systematically maltreats or systematically disadvantages some members, then social workers as individuals and the profession as a collective, often partnering with others, have a responsibility to advocate for change in policies, laws, and/or practices—such as those social workers in the 1960s who advocated to ensure access to contraception.

## PROFESSIONAL KNOWLEDGE

When society or the law attributes professional knowledge to an identified group, the assumption is made that included in professional knowledge is a range of uncommon knowledge in the form of relatively specialized information (e.g., impacts of child abuse) and specialized skills knowledge (e.g., how to complete a parenting capacity and child risk-need assessment). Within the context of complex societies with complex problems, needs, and risks, this specialized and sometimes expert knowledge is expected to be derived from a number of sources as well as be created by researchers and professional groups including social work. Professional groups

- borrow and apply knowledge from cognate disciplines (e.g., understanding impacts of the political economy on poverty and labour markets may help social workers address policy and program issues, as well as community patterns of blaming the unemployed for their own situation);

- borrow knowledge from related disciplines (e.g., an understanding of the expected bio-medical course of a disease such as AIDS allows social workers to address their area of expertise, such as permanency planning for children of parents with AIDS);

- co-create, sometimes in conscious partnerships, knowledge associated with problems, risks, needs, harmful impacts, client potential, and best practices for intervention (e.g., social workers, psychiatrists, and psychologists have contributed to the development of solution-focused therapy with addiction problems);

- create new knowledge (e.g., practices to assess and help children who are HIV- infected) and refine existing knowledge (e.g., strategies to empower economically depressed communities) out of practice wisdom from case experience, case and community studies, and larger systematic studies that guide interventions;[2]

- continuously create, improve, and synthesize knowledge, in part to derive best known practices for social workers (e.g., demonstration projects that support the attachment between birth parents and their child in care, in the best interest of the child);

- modify existing practices and construct innovative solutions for unique expressions of problem, need, and potential, for which there are no standard practices (e.g., social policies, community development interventions, and consciousness-raising groups to address female genital mutilation associated with specific cultural-religious practices).

What is important to recognize is that what constitutes professional knowledge is ever-changing. Under conditions of complexity and uncertainty, knowledge is imperfect and subject to challenge.[3] The fact that specialized and professional knowledge is imperfect

---

2  For example, Margaret Cork (1969) in her research on children of parents with alcohol problems confirmed that alcoholism was a family problem and that family problems continued after sobriety was achieved; her findings were instrumental in the creation of services for children of alcoholics.

3  See, for example, social work writing on indicators of childhood trauma and the challenge of "false memory theory" (Coulborn Faller, 2007).

and that expected personal and social change cannot be predicted with absolute assurance has not stopped social workers from constructing innovative solutions related to the personal and social goals of persons, collectives, and societies.

## Skills and Competence

A defining characteristic of a profession is that knowledge is created and adopted not in the interest of the knowledge for the sake of knowledge, but in the interest of informing professional observations, judgments, predictions, decisions, recommendations, actions, and reflective evaluation—with, and on behalf of, client systems. In professional practice, such applied knowledge must be translated into skills through the clarification of abstract theories and concepts, as well as more concrete information that guides applied practices. Additionally, for professionals, it is not sufficient to be knowledgeable and skilled; both must converge to ensure competent application that respects the uniqueness of each situation and each client system. In addition, social workers do not simply apply information and techniques in a contextual vacuum; knowledge and skills must be applied with due respect to the professional mission, values, ethics, and social/political climate in which client systems live.

## Social Worker Independence and Partnerships

One of the defining characteristics of being a professional is that the social worker is individually accountable and liable for judgments, decisions, and actions that presume professional knowledge, skills, and competence. Social workers must be prepared to make independent decisions and take independent actions (e.g., a children's protection social worker may have less than one minute to observe, judge, predict, decide, and act in apprehending a child at imminent risk). The most independent of social work practitioners are typically those who undertake private practice.

While the agency that employs the social worker is liable for the actions of its employees, when it comes to professional employees, each social worker is also independently accountable and liable for his or her professional judgments and actions. It is important for professional social workers to carry independent liability insurance. While social workers often make independent decisions, the level of complexity and uncertainty associated with typical client systems suggests a need for partnering with others in refining observations, judgments, predictions, decisions, and plans.

# CLIENTS, CONSUMERS, AND OTHER PARTNERSHIPS
## Clients as Consumers and Partners

The first level of partnership is with the client, as a large part of social work practice involves arriving at judgments, decisions, and agreed-upon plans with client systems who expect professional services. The responsibility of social workers is to utilize their expertise in conjunction with the clients' expertise in the interest of the clients' unique change goals. Social workers currently utilize the concept of empowerment to refer to person-centred practices that enable client systems to optimize their strengths, develop capacity, and join in creating solutions. These inclusion and empowerment notions assume that the client is sufficiently developed biopsychosocially, is sufficiently reality-based, and is not at imminent personal risk, such that relatively independent or more coercive action by the social worker may be required (e.g., when a client expresses the intent to harm self or others). There are more restrictions to the partnership when clients are not engaged in the partnership on a more voluntary basis (DuBois and Krogsrud Miley, 2005).

## Professional Supervision

Because of the complexity, uncertainty, and uniqueness associated with most client situations, social workers have historically supported the practice of having a more experienced social worker act as a support, mentor, consultant, teacher, supervisor and, at times, the source of final decisions for the more junior or otherwise less experienced practitioners. Supervision may be formalized or informal, but the profession often demands that the professional judgments and actions of a social worker be supervised by another professional social worker (Munson, 2002). In the current climate of multidisciplined practice and managerial expedience, a social worker may provide supervision to another professional or paraprofessional, or another professional may provide supervision to a social worker.

## Case Consultation and Case Conferencing

Social workers have a long history of promoting the consolidation and application of collective wisdom through the use of peer and interdisciplinary groups for case-project consultation and case conferences. Often the aim is to refine observations, judgments, progress evaluation, and case or service decisions. Collective wisdom helps when addressing complex issues under conditions of relative uncertainty, but it also encourages that the service to the client be based on informed and reflective practice versus reactive responses. The guiding principles are often the best interest of the client system and the least harmful or least intrusive interventions. Consistent with a philosophy of inclusion and empowerment, clients of social workers may participate in case conferences and other collective consultations.

**Professional Teams** The current trend in most of the Western world continues to be toward the integration of human services. As part of strategic social planning, it is not uncommon to define education, health, social, and employment related services, and justice and corrections, as part of a dynamic and interdependent system established to meet the needs of student-patient-client-consumer-community in a holistic fashion. The assumption is that team members have an active contribution (of information, specialized knowledge, and skills) to make the co-ordinated and effective effort. In some cases, each discipline has a clear and professionally differentiated role to play in the overall service plan. The social worker is likely to be called upon to address client service needs that have biosocial, psychosocial, socio-economic, socio-legal, or socio-political components. The social worker is also likely to be called upon to be case manager, especially in cases requiring advanced case management (Rapp and Goscha, 2006).

# SOCIAL WORK IS WHAT SOCIAL WORKERS DO: PARTNERSHIPS FOR PERSONAL AND SOCIAL CHANGE

## General Goals for Individual and Collective Change

The guiding philosophy, mission, professional mandate to enable personal and social change, concern with the disadvantaged and the oppressed, professional rights and responsibilities, ethics, knowledge, and skills, as well as agency mandate and partnerships, all converge to support social worker competence and to guide practice. While these dimensions are definers of the practice, social work has such broad boundaries of fields of practice (e.g., genetic counselling), methods of practice (e.g., critical incident debriefing), and goals of intervention (e.g., health promotion and prevention) that it is difficult to articulate in a simple statement what constitutes professional social work practice. This problem of clear and simple definition is also true for other professions such as medicine, law, and engineering. One way to address the problem is to rely on philosophy, mission, and mandate to set some boundaries for action and to conclude that, being an action-oriented profession, social work is what social workers do within a temporal and socio-political context. This approach recognizes that identity, including professional identity, is not fixed; it is fluid and ever-changing as the personal, social, economic, and political contexts of practice and social welfare evolve.

## General Goals

Social workers have made a commitment to help with biopsychosocial change and the interaction among social justice, law, and politics, three overlapping dimensions. While the profession may formulate many *general goals in the best interest of client-consumer systems*, the most common themes in theory, concept, and practice that guide social workers include the following:

1. They undertake to evaluate and enable the *meeting of basic biopsychosocial needs* that are common to most persons (e.g., shelter for the homeless), and to meet special human needs reflected in the life experiences of those disadvantaged by personal or social-structural limitations (e.g., social exclusion of the physically challenged). As well as intervening at the point of interaction between the personal and the social, social workers support action to prevent undue hardship and to empower client systems to advocate for their own needs.

2. They undertake to evaluate and enable the formulation of *solutions to personal and social problems* common to many persons (e.g., adjusting to life-cycle problems), and help address special problems at the level of the person (e.g., loss of income security), and/or the collective (e.g., loss to a small community's economy). Individual and social problems are often reflected in the life experiences of those disadvantaged by personal or social-structural limitations (e.g., exclusion of the illiterate in training programs). As well as intervening at the point of interaction between the personal and the social, social workers also act to prevent problems from developing or getting worse and empower client systems to share in solutions (e.g., social and economic development).

3. They undertake to evaluate and enable avoidance, reduction, and/or *control of personal or social risks* associated with common life experiences (e.g., substance use becoming an addiction) or less commonly surfaced risks (e.g., sibling incest) often reflected in the life experiences of those oppressed by personal or social-structural limitations (e.g., sexually exploited street kids). Social workers support action to prevent risks from developing and empower client systems to share in controlling risks. Some social workers have the power to enforce risk control, such as in children's protection.

4. Social workers undertake to evaluate and enable the reduction and/or *control of personal or collective harm* (e.g., individuals and families adjusting to family dissolution) or less common experiences (e.g., post-trauma effects associated with sexual assault) often reflected in the life experiences of those oppressed by personal or social-structural limitations (e.g., those living in inner-city public housing "ghettos"). They also support action to prevent harm from becoming a repeated cycle or from increasing, and empower client systems to control harm and its impact (e.g., self-help groups for survivors of sexual assault). Some social workers have the power to enforce actions to prevent harm and to ameliorate the impacts (e.g., sex offender assessment and treatment).

5. They undertake to evaluate and promote the *recognition, enhancement, and development of client strengths, capacity, and potential* often overlooked when clients demonstrate individual or collective deficits (e.g., parenting capacity limitations that put children at risk), and experience individual or collective social barriers (e.g., language and cultural differences that reduce personal and collective opportunities). Social workers support action to prevent strengths, capacity, and potential from not being actualized and empower client systems to demonstrate strengths, develop new capacities, and actualize their potential through their own actions, social system support, and mutual aid.

Social workers undertake both social control functions (e.g., reducing the risk and harm of wife battering), and helping-enabling functions (e.g., community and social development with an Aboriginal community trying to manage solvent abuse risks). The preference is to enable individual or collective action from a facilitative frame and in a partnership with the client. Even when some part of the client system is dependent or vulnerable (e.g., aged persons at risk for abuse), the preference is to avoid or reduce more intensive, intrusive, or coercive interventions as is feasible. Consider the following exchange, implying mild coercion but also reflecting a beginning partnership between a single mother and a children's protection social worker:

Social Worker: "I feel relieved that you have agreed to end your relationship with your boyfriend who has been convicted of sex abuse of children; it is an effective way to control immediate risks to you and your children."

Client: "I am going to miss my boyfriend, but it is better to lose him than to take a chance."

Social Worker: "It takes a lot of strength to do what you are doing; I will support you through this transition."

Client: "Thanks! Me and my kids are going to need it; we have no one to be there for us (pause) in this big city."

Social Worker: "I hope that as we put more supports in place for you and your children, you will feel more sure of your decision."

While the goals articulated above are general, and while the social worker may predict many dimensions of need, problem, risk, harm, and potential based on an understanding of the human condition and human growth and development, the profession is also committed to respecting the unique objective experiences of individuals or collectives (e.g., having a parent who is an alcoholic), and subjective experiences (e.g., "We had to take care of dad to take the pressure off mom"). While the professional social worker typically has specialized knowledge and experience that may be generalized from one client to another, the application of that knowledge is normally undertaken with a reasonable understanding of the client's unique life experiences, personal life story, and particular strengths (or lack thereof) with a range of coping strategies. While social workers may have the knowledge and the skills to predict likelihood (e.g., "This child exhibits patterns consistent with sex abuse or early eroticization") or outcome (e.g., "If you return to living together too soon you increase your risk of returning to wife abuse"), the accuracy of prediction is increased if the social worker has an in-depth understanding of the client system and the social context in which the client has lived. As well, culturally and ethnically sensitive practice is defined as a professional responsibility to ensure effective partnerships for change.

Social work interventions in the interest of addressing needs, problems, risk, harmful impacts, and potential or opportunity may be framed within the context of

- preferred ideologies (e.g., helping individuals address their problems and systemic-structural change);
- preferred definitions of problem or need (e.g., children need protection versus the problem is mother blaming);
- preferred practices (e.g., solution-focused therapy versus radical social action);
- preferred units of observation, intervention, and change (e.g., individual, family, community, organization, society); and
- preferred goals (e.g., taking a child into care versus family preservation).

An integrative approach suggests that preferences need not be acted out as either/or conflicts as these may ensure that the client is forced into an ideology versus professional action being tailored to the needs of a specific client system.

## A CONTINUUM OF SOCIAL WORKER INTERVENTIONS

No matter what the ideology, definition of need or problem, preferred practice, preferred unit of intervention, or preferred goals, a *continuum of social worker interventions*, in current practice, involves the following responsibility areas. These areas are not necessarily the exclusive domain of social work or of any one helping profession, but social work brings its own knowledge, skill, and competency base to each sphere of health, social well-being, social security, social justice, and education.

Social workers may take more leadership and have more profile in some fields of practice within various dimensions of the continuum of biopsychosocial intervention. These activity and change dimensions are not mutually exclusive; in practice there is much interaction across dimensions. Also, the worker and client systems may enter at many points.

## Assessment and Social Diagnosis

Social workers focus on one or more levels of client systems and enter into partnerships to assess needs, problems, risks, harm, strengths, potential, and biopsychosocial development. Social workers make direct observations (e.g., observing parenting), engage in interviews, apply standardized instruments (e.g., child risk-need), or consult with collaterals in formulating judgments and arriving at decisions with the client or in the best interest of the client. Since social workers undertook case studies and community studies at the turn of the last century, there has been an assumption that a clear understanding of individuals and collectives in their social situation and context could guide policies and action to improve well-being, justice, and social security. Social workers have emphasized optimal inclusion of the client system in the assessment process, as both the client and the social worker are defined as having expertise to bring to the assessment. (Corcoran and Walsh, 2006). Some observations and judgments may be translated into social diagnoses (Turner, 2003).

## Formulation and Analysis of Social Policy

Social workers have been leaders in promoting, formulating, and analyzing both formal and informal organizational policies and social policies, some of which may be enacted in legislation. They advocate for social and political action in undertaking social responsibility. Policies generally address issues of biopsychosocial well-being, health and social welfare, social security, and social justice. The policies may be directed towards personal health and social services (e.g., addiction assessment and counselling), or towards more generalized social benefits (e.g., universal old age security). Social workers have been actively involved in creating legislation, policies, and agreements provincially, nationally, and internationally. Social policies may be interpreted as being directed at goals of promotion of health, welfare, and capacity building; prevention of problems and need; reduction of individual and collective harm; provision of material and social support; amelioration of needs, problems, risks, and harmful impacts; protection of individuals, families, groups, and the public; and promotion of social justice (Baines, 2007).

## Promotion of Biopsychosocial Health, Welfare, Capacity, and Social Security

Social workers have undertaken to *promote* well-being of individuals and collectives and enable the undertaking of social responsibility by collectives and individuals. Historically, they have promoted social development where the strengths of a society or group are mobilized and further capacity is developed. Through activities such as increasing public awareness and information, as well as consciousness-raising, social workers promote the creation of individual and collective strengths and capacity, as well as biopsychosocial well-being, health, social security, and social justice (Lymbery and Millward, 2001; Fides and Cooper, 2003).

## Prevention

They have developed policies, programs, and intervention methods to prevent unnecessary hardship, loss of security, problems, risks, harmful impacts, and unmet basic needs. Social workers engage in preventive activities such as education (e.g., addiction awareness), dissemination of information (e.g., contraceptive information), raising collective awareness (e.g., risks of sexually transmitted infections), early brief intervention (e.g., re-engaging recent school dropouts), and timely concrete support (e.g., for an abandoned mother and children). Prevention activities may be aimed at individuals or collectives and currently involve the "global village" in such activities as prevention of HIV infection (Bloom, 1996).

## Harm Reduction

There are many differences in individuals, collectives, and their circumstances. Within this context, and respecting personal choices, social workers have also recognized harmful impacts to individuals, families, and society when promotion, prevention, and other measures are less likely to be fully effective. As a result, they have taken the lead to promote harm reduction policies and programs. Historically, among the most notable were programs to control the impacts of prostitution and street drug use. More recently they have promoted activities such as needle exchanges to prevent the spread of HIV infection (Malowaniec and Rowe, 2003).

## Provision of Economic and Material Support

When promotion and prevention are not effective and harm reduction is not sufficient, the situation of any person or collective may result in their becoming dependent on extended family, society, and community groups for economic and material support. Other groups may be systematically disadvantaged and marginalized (e.g., those with physical challenges). Social workers have been instrumental in promoting programs to provide economic and material assistance, managing such programs, and delivering concrete services (Hick, 2007).

## Ensuring Protection and Safety

When promotion, prevention, harm reduction, and social provision are not sufficient, social workers have formulated policies, programs, and legislation to ensure the safety of persons and collectives who are defined as dependent or at significant and imminent risk. Under the authority of law, children's protection activities such as investigation, apprehension, foster placement, and adoption services are often undertaken by social workers. Under the mandate of private not-for-profit agencies, social workers may take a major role in activities such as providing shelter and support for abused women and children exposed to violence (Kurst, Swanger, and Petcosky, 2003).

## Intervening to Stabilize Individual or Collective Crisis and Trauma

Social workers have also undertaken major responsibilities to manage and control crisis situations. Activities include stabilizing the individual or group experiencing a crisis state and post-traumatic stress, and enabling the client to resume self-control and return to a relative state of well-being with the least intrusive intervention possible. Ameliorative interventions may range from individually oriented rape crisis support to collective critical incident debriefing after collective trauma (Roberts, 2005).

## Counselling, Therapy, and Psychosocial Education

For many (individuals, couples, families, and groups), some fundamental aspect of themselves and their life experiences presents a barrier for social supports such as promotion, prevention, harm reduction, prevention, or crisis intervention to be sufficient. Levels of need, problem, risk, and harmful impacts are so extensive and complex that clients may need help to arrive at more substantial personal change (e.g., reduction of depression), or change in their social lives (e.g., being socially marginalized) or their social situation (e.g., being unemployed while having reasonable skills). They may also suffer from the impacts of developmental experiences and trauma that have not been resolved (e.g., being abandoned to die as a disabled child). As well, they may experience systemic disadvantages and oppression. It is under such conditions of complex and multiple problems that social workers have provided counselling, therapy, and psychosocial education since the early 1900s (Gambrill, 2006). The majority of professional counsellor-therapists in North America are social workers. Their practice may overlap with psychology and psychiatry, but social workers have a special commitment to the poor and the oppressed.

Social workers provide counselling, therapy, and psychosocial educational services through various methods designed for intervention with individuals (e.g., solution-focused therapy and assertion training), families (e.g., systemic family therapy and anger management education), partners (e.g., sexuality counselling and communication skills), and groups (e.g., psychodrama or education on breaking patterns of repeated victimization). New directions to which social workers have made contributions include postmodern approaches to counselling and therapy and strengths-based interventions. The needs of most clients are not likely to be met by psychosocial education, counselling, and therapy alone; these methods are most often part of a more complex case or service plan. The general goal is still individual and collective well-being and social justice.

## Self-Help and Mutual Aid

The development of social work practice was associated with a strong recognition of the importance of natural and informal mutual aid (such as extended family or common interest groups). As well, social workers assisted in the creation of social networks that could provide more formal support for personal growth and development (e.g., a YWCA psycho-education group) or for problem solving and strength building (e.g., survivors of incest group). They have also taken an active role in creating self-help and mutual aid opportunities for persons who may come together for mutual support based on common interest, need, or life experience (Kimberley and Osmond, 2003).

## Advocacy and Social Justice

Faced with barriers to individual and social welfare and to co-operative action, traditionally, on behalf of individuals and collectives, social workers have been leaders in advocating for social change and social justice. The target of change may be rights (e.g., rights to access contraception), or to entitlements (e.g., support for the disabled), or opportunity (e.g., social integration of disabled), or social support (e.g., gradual release of offenders into society with social support). While social workers prefer to utilize methods that enable co-operation in change, they are also prepared to improve social situations and to remove social barriers through methods that include publicly challenging the status quo, constructive confrontation, and conflict resolution. In some political contexts, social workers have also engaged in civil protests. From another perspective, social workers act to empower client systems to mobilize their own strengths and capacity for self-advocacy (Baines, 2007).

## Collective Social Action

Social workers promote group and community strength through relationship building, group partnering, and community building. The emphasis is on empowering the collective and facilitating effective action to define problems and needs, decide on priorities, confirm group ownership, plan and commit to action, and promote or establish needed services. Another emphasis is on co-operation in change, but conflict strategies may be used to remove structural and systemic socio-economic or socio-political barriers. The emphasis is on community ownership of solutions with the worker acting as animator, facilitator, and advocate (Carniol, 2005).

## Case Management, Referral, and Liaison

What is defined as case management in current practice was derived out of what social workers called "social casework" in the early 1900s (Richmond, 1917). The practice of managing cases was derived out of concerns that clients would "fall through the cracks" and their needs would not be met, provision of community services would be unco-ordinated and fragmented, services would be duplicated, the clients' situation would change but plans would not be modified, new opportunities for help would be missed, and connections with needed services would not be made (referral and liaison). Social workers have undertaken to ensure co-ordination, integration, and relevance. In advanced case management (a social work practice), counselling and other activities are integrated with the case management function. Whether the client is an individual, family, group, community, or organization, service management activities by a case manager or project manager are needed to ensure continuous, integrated, and quality service.

## After-care and Follow-Up

Social work practice has promoted the provision of after-care and follow-up services

- to enable return to needed service for those who have terminated service prematurely;
- to enable return to service for those who might need additional services to maintain the effects of earlier interventions;
- to monitor clients' maintenance of gains and progress; and
- to ensure clients are satisfied with the results of the services to date.

Under conditions of decades of serious underfunding of health and social services, beginning in the 1980s, follow-up is often one of the required services that is not undertaken or only superficially completed.

## Development of Social, Community, Health, and Other Service Programs

While some social workers are undertaking private practice, for the most part social workers have been instrumental in the development and implementation of health, social, justice, and other service organizations and programs that our communities have come to expect. They may emphasize one or more of promotion, prevention, harm reduction, social provision, protection, crisis intervention, psychosocial education, counselling or therapy, case management and follow-up, advocacy, collective social action, and social justice.

Some social worker contributions have been

- universal benefits such as the Canada Pension Plan and family allowances;
- targeted security benefits such as workers' compensation;
- personal community health services such as addiction programs;
- personal social services such as family services;
- protection services such as children's protection;
- family preservation services such as support for lone parents;
- permanency policies and services such as fostering and adoption;
- crisis and trauma services such as rape crisis and women's shelters;
- community mental health and Canadian Mental Health Association Services;
- community correctional services such as the John Howard Society;
- promotion of HIV and AIDS prevention and support;
- prevention and support programs such as Planned Parenthood programs;
- early intervention services such as school social worker services;
- home support and social centres for the aged and disabled;
- policies and services for the blind and visually impaired;

- national policies and programs supporting rights for the physically challenged;
- promotion of self-help and mutual aid such as victim and survivor groups;
- disaster and emergency services including the international Red Cross;
- post-traumatic stress services such as in military social work;
- United Nations programs for health, education, and welfare; and
- International Council on Social Welfare, International Federation of Social Workers, and International Association of Schools of Social Work programs.

## Team, Community, Societal, and Organizational Capacity

Social workers have undertaken responsibility within the area of mobilization of collective strength and building collective capacity for team development, organizational development, community development, and social development. They have led in creating services (e.g., social centres for the mentally ill) and social development organizations (e.g., Canadian Council on Social Development), as well as improving the performance of existing organizations. The assumption is that effective collective team, community, and organizational action will enhance collective health, social welfare, social justice, and social security. Another assumption is that, fundamentally, decisions and actions are made by persons in interpersonal transactions, not by organizations or "the system."

## Systematic Inquiry

In support of practice, social workers have traditionally conducted systematic inquiries, using a variety of methods to inform professional practice and social development. Among these activities are systematic codification of practice based on case experience; systematic case studies and community studies; evaluation of community needs, strengths, and problems; evaluation of service, client satisfaction, progress, and outcome; demonstration studies; and larger sample studies of biopsychosocial problems, risks, harmful impacts, strengths, and potential. The subject may be an individual or a larger collective, such as a group of organizations who help international refugees. Applied research and other inquiry is often conducted to promote well-being, health, social welfare, social security, and social justice (Neuman and Kreuger, 2002). Other studies may explore leading edge issues such as child sexual exploitation on the Internet.

## Providing Expert Consultation and Opinion

The verified professional knowledge, skills, competence, and experience of social workers may converge and be of such significance that they are called upon for expert opinion and consultation. Formal venues include courts (e.g., child protection cases), judicial hearings (e.g., a provincial inquiry into the death of children in care), case conferences (e.g., an addiction agency dealing with a case of sex addiction), or international advisory bodies (e.g., the United Nations). Such expert consultation and opinion is typically defined as that of an established professional person, provided to the body that needs the opinion. In this context, the professional status of social workers is confirmed provincially, nationally, and internationally (Barker and Branson, 1998).

## Education and Mentoring for New Social Workers and Others

The profession engages in a cycle of renewal and dissemination of knowledge through university-based social work programs. These programs are typically accredited by the Canadian Association of Schools of Social Work (CASSW), which sets the standards for the development and evaluation of knowledge, skills, and competence at the Bachelor of Social Work and Master of Social Work levels. Given that social workers operate under conditions of high complexity and ever-shifting social contexts, most schools of social work also provide continuing education offerings. Social workers are expected to take responsibility for lifelong learning. Some programs may offer specialty diplomas or certificates to social workers. As health and social services move to a more multidisciplinary model, social workers may take more courses with cognate disciplines (such as health education), and cognate disciplines may take more courses in social work (such as family therapy). Specialized studies for Aboriginal social work have been leading edge in Canada.

Doctoral programs may be guided by the spirit of CASSW educational policies and accreditation standards, but they are subject to independent regulations and criteria set by universities.

## Professional Associations and Future-Building

Associations for professional social workers at the provincial level may be members of the Canadian Association of Social Workers (CASW). Mandates include supporting a code of ethics and standards of knowledge and practice. They also promote professional issues related to social work mandates (e.g., liability insurance), as well as advocacy on social issues (e.g., juvenile prostitution). The professional associations also support research (e.g., factors that support effective child welfare practice), as well as professional and scholarly production in the form of presentations, articles, and reports. Some associations have also partnered with women's groups on issues of common concern such as wife abuse. The CASW has also joined coalitions in the interest of promoting social welfare and social justice.

CASW represents social workers internationally in the International Federation of Social Workers, and nationally at the interface of related organizations such as the Canadian Council on Social Development and the Canadian Association of Schools of Social Work, as well as other voluntary association interest groups. At provincial and national levels, the association models independent advocacy, partnerships, client consultation (e.g., some associations have client representatives on the board) and teamwork. Social workers are typically regulated by law, and either the professional association or an independent social work regulatory body controls title ("social worker") and/or practice (especially within areas of assessment, counselling, and therapy). In short, persons who call themselves social workers when they are not, or who practice social work when they are not registered, may be charged and punished.

Some of the initiatives that have been undertaken by social work organizations include

- developing social work capacity among Aboriginal peoples;
- promoting culturally and ethnically sensitive social work practice;
- drafting a labour mobility agreement so social work graduates may move freely between provinces to take on social work positions; and
- studying the impact of globalized economies and trade agreements on social workers and social services.

As advocates for clients, social workers must view the profession, its mission, and its goals as being worthy of continued advocacy. It is important that we assert our strengths as we adapt to new futures and create more opportunities for the voices of social workers and our clientele to be heard, and to actively participate in the new global order. Social workers in the present carry with them the values and strengths of social workers who undertook social responsibility and built a respectable profession in the interest of creating better futures for individuals, communities, society, and the profession.

# References

Al-Krenawi, A. and Graham, J. R., Editors. (2002). *Multicultural social work in Canada*. Toronto, Canada: Oxford University Press.

Baines, D., Editor. (2007). *Doing anti-oppressive practice: Building transformative politicized social work*. Halifax, Canada: Fernwood Publishing.

Baldwin, M. and Satir, V. (1987). *The use of self in therapy*. New York: Haworth Press.

Barker, R. L. and Branson, D. M. (2000). *Forensic social work: Legal aspects of professional practice*. Second Edition. New York: Haworth Press.

Bloom, M. (1996). *Primary prevention practices*. Newbury Park, CA: Sage Publications.

Carniol, B. (2005). *Case critical: Social services and social justice in Canada. Fifth Edition*. Toronto: Between the Lines.

Corcoran, J. and Walsh, J. (2006). *Clinical assessment and diagnosis in social work practice*. New York: Oxford University Press.

Cork, R. Margaret. (1969). *The forgotten children*. Toronto, Ontario: PaperJacks, in association with the Addiction Research Foundation of Ontario.

Coulborn Faller, K. (2007). *Interviewing children about sexual abuse: Controversies and best practice*. New York: Oxford University Press.

Cox, C. B. (2007). *Dementia in social work practice*. New York: Springer Publishing.

Dansky, S. F. (1997). *Nobody's children: orphans of the HIV epidemic*. New York: Haworth Press.

Davies, Douglas. (2004). *Child development: A practitioner's guide. Second Edition*. New York: Guilford Press.

Dominelli, L. (2002). *Feminist social work theory and practice*. Hampshire, England: Palgrave Macmillan.

Dubois, B. and Krogsrud Miley, K. (2005). *Social work: An empowering profession. Fifth Edition*. Boston: Allyn & Bacon.

Ferguson, I. (2006). Globalization and global justice. *International Social Work*, 49 (3): 309–318.

Fides, R. and Cooper, B. (2003). *Preparing for change: Social work and primary health care.* Ottawa: Canadian Association of Social Workers (October 17th, 2003).

Gambrill, E. (2006). *Critical thinking in clinical practice: Improving the quality of judgments and decisions. Second Edition.* New York: John Wiley & Sons.

Graveline, F. J. (2007). *Healing wounded hearts.* Peterborough, Canada: Fernwood Books.

Harper, K. V. and Lantz, J. (2007). *Cross-cultural practice: Social work with diverse populations. Second Edition.* Chicago: Lyceum Books.

Hick, S. (2007). *Social welfare in Canada: Understanding income security.* Toronto: Thompson Educational Publishing.

Kimberley, D. and Bohm, P. (1999). Drug addiction: a BSPI model, in Turner, F. J., Editor, *Adult psychopathology: A social work perspective. Second Edition.* New York: The Free Press.

Kimberley, D. and Osmond, L. (2003). Night of the tortured souls: Integration of group therapy and mutual aid for treated male sex offenders, in Lindsay, J., Turcotte, D., and Hopmeyer, E., Editors, *Crossing boundaries and developing alliances through group work.* New York: Haworth Press: 75–98.

Knott, C. (2007). *Reflective practice in social work.* Exeter: Learning Matters, Ltd.

Kurst Swanger, K. and Petcosky, J. L. (2003). *Violence in the home: Multidisciplinary perspectives.* New York: Oxford University Press.

Lindsay, J., Turcotte, D. and Hopmeyer, E., Editors. (2003). *Crossing boundaries and developing alliances through group work.* New York: Haworth Press.

Lymbery, M. and Millward, A. (2001). Community care in practice: social work in primary health care. *Social Work in Health Care*, 34 (3/4): 241–259.

Malowaniec, L. and Rowe, W. S. (2003). Social workers and safer injection rooms: "We accept them the way they are... ," in Csiernik, R. and Rowe, W. S., Editors, *Responding to the oppression of addiction: Canadian social work perspectives.* Toronto, Canada: Canadian Scholars' Press: 37–54.

Munson, C. E. (2002). *Handbook of clinical social work supervision. Third Edition.* New York: Haworth Press.

Neuman, W. L. and Kreuger, L.W. (2002). *Social work research methods: qualitative and quantitative applications.* Boston: Allyn & Bacon.

Payne, M. (2006). *What is professional social work?* Chicago: Lyceum Books.

Payne, M. (2005). *Modern social work theory. Third Edition.* Chicago: Lyceum Books.

Rapp, C. A. and Goscha, R. J. (2006). *The strengths model—case management with people with psychiatric disabilities. Second Edition.* New York: Oxford University Press.

Richmond, M. E. (1917). *Social Diagnosis.* New York: Russell Sage Foundation.

Roberts, A. R. and Yeager, K. R., Editors. (2006). *Foundations of evidence-based social work practice.* New York: Oxford University Press.

Roberts, A. R., Editor. (2005). *Crisis intervention handbook: Assessment, treatment, and research. Third Edition.* New York: Oxford University Press.

Ronen, T. and Freeman, A. (2006). *Cognitive behaviour therapy in clinical social work practice.* New York: Springer Publishing.

Rothman, J. C. (1998). *The self-awareness workbook for social workers.* Boston: Allyn & Bacon.

Stuart, R. B. (2003). *Helping couples change: A social learning approach to marital therapy.* New York: Guilford Press.

Towle, C. (1945/1987 Revised). *Common human needs.* Washington: National Association of Social Workers.

Turner, F. (2002). *Diagnosis in social work: New imperatives.* New York: The Haworth Press.

Walsh, J. and Lantz, J. (2007). *Short-term existential intervention in clinical practice.* Chicago: Lyceum Books.

# CHAPTER 25

# Social Service Workers

*Sabra Desai and Linda Hill*

## INTRODUCTION

Social service workers (SSWs) assume a critical role in providing services in the system of government programs, allied health, and social and welfare services. The work undertaken by SSWs focuses on building the capacity of individuals, groups, communities, and society. Despite the importance of SSWs to the delivery of programs and services, little is written about this paraprofession and its expanding role within the realm of social work. This chapter will be devoted to briefly describing the historical precursors that resulted in the development of social service work, the scope of practice, definition, college programs, workplace issues, challenges, and tensions.

## HISTORICAL CONTEXT

The 1960s marked the beginning of what has come to be known as the Canadian welfare state with the expansion of a public system of education, health care, and social services. New income security and assistance programs for the unemployed, single parents, and children created a variety of positions that needed to be filled by social workers. The concomitant bureaucratization, inevitable in any public system, provided opportunities for workers to both administer and deliver new programs (Turner & Turner, 2006).

This was also a time when tertiary education in Canada emerged, resulting in the establishment of paraprofessionals[1] intended to fill needed positions in sectors that were in short supply of post-secondary educated workers. Social service worker programs were introduced in 1966 at community colleges to help meet the increased need for trained workers. The social services and welfare area continued growing as population expanded, immigration increased, and social problems related to urban living continued to rise and become more complex. Moreover, professionalization of the helping role meant new expectations of who was qualified to help individuals, groups, and communities facing problems. These trends—expansion of the social safety net, tertiary education, growing social problems, and professionalization—resulted in the creation of a new type of practitioner: techniciens d'assistance sociale and social service workers (Stephenson et al., 2000).

Today, the number of community and social service workers has risen to 78 800 across Canada. College-trained graduates outnumber degree-trained graduates by two to one (Stephenson et al., 2000; Service Canada, 2004). These statistics speak not only to the importance of paraprofessionals in providing social and welfare services, but also to the volume of work provided.

## SCOPE OF PRACTICE

The scope of practice for SSWs is defined in Ontario by the *Social Work and Social Service Work Act* (1998), which established a professional college to oversee standards of ethical practice. The Ontario College of Social Workers and Social Service Workers (OCSWSSW) defines the scope of practice to

---

[1] A social work paraprofessional is someone trained to assist the social worker, but not licensed to practise the profession.

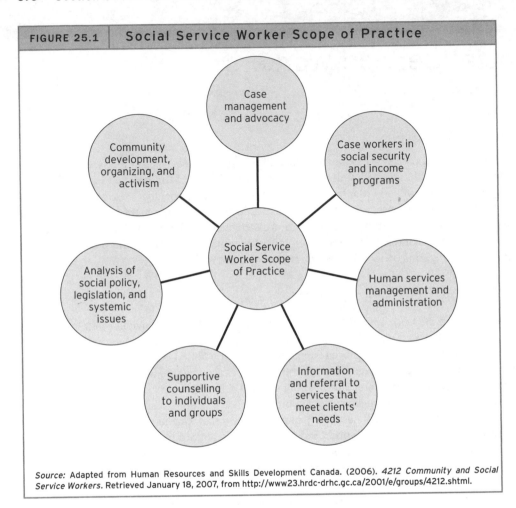

**FIGURE 25.1    Social Service Worker Scope of Practice**

*Source:* Adapted from Human Resources and Skills Development Canada. (2006). *4212 Community and Social Service Workers.* Retrieved January 18, 2007, from http://www23.hrdc-drhc.gc.ca/2001/e/groups/4212.shtml.

be the "assessment, treatment, and evaluation of individual, interpersonal, and societal problems through the use of social service work knowledge, skills, interventions, and strategies, to assist individuals, dyads, families, groups, organizations, and communities to achieve optimum social functioning" (OCSWSSW, 2000, p. 1).

According to the *Standards of Practice Handbook* published by OCSWSSW (2000), the work undertaken by SSWs is similar to that of social workers and there is overlap in functions. However, the defining difference between a social worker and a social service worker centres on the concept of diagnosis. Social service workers, unlike their social worker colleagues, are not able to diagnose, and are limited in their ability to undertake therapeutic counselling. This being said, the social service worker performs a range of skilled duties including (1) assessing client needs and linking them to resources in the community; (2) counselling and providing emotional support to individuals, families, and small groups; (3) case management, advising clients about their rights, and engaging in advocating on their behalf (Chappell, 1997, p. 191).

Figure 25.1 provides examples of the scope and breadth of social service work and the broad range of opportunities available from front-line casework to service administration.

# DEFINING SOCIAL SERVICE WORK

It is difficult to define the term "social service worker" because it means different things to different people in various work settings. There are over 50 college programs across Canada that have not developed uniformly and, therefore, graduates have different competencies and lengths of training from a one-year certificate to two-year diploma (Stephenson et al., 2000). To add to the confusion, many employers use terminology other than social service worker to describe paraprofessional work in social services and welfare. Table 25.1 provides examples of common job titles for SSWs by job setting.

In general, social service work is defined as practical, direct service, and non-counselling tasks. Graduates, however, of two-year diploma programs and those who gain experience in

| TABLE 25.1 | Examples of Common Job Titles for SSWs by Job Setting |
|---|---|
| **Job Setting** | **Common Job Titles** |
| Government Services and Programs | Income Maintenance Officer<br>Welfare and Compensation Worker<br>Social Housing Intake Worker<br>Employment and Vocational Counsellor<br>Veterans Service Officer<br>Victim Services Worker |
| Community-Based Services | Outreach Worker<br>Intake, Information, and Referral Worker<br>Addiction Worker<br>Food Bank Worker<br>Life Skills Instructor<br>Drop-in Centre Worker<br>Crisis Intervention Worker<br>Family Service Worker<br>Mental Health Worker<br>Care Coordinator/Manager<br>Home Support Services Coordinator<br>Volunteer Coordinator<br>Integration and Settlement Worker<br>Community and Neighbourhood Development Worker<br>Program Leader in Recreation, Sports, and Fitness<br>Camp Counsellor<br>Educational Assistant<br>Youth Worker<br>Supportive Counselling and Advocacy Worker |
| Residential Programs | Residential Counsellor<br>Group Home Worker<br>Activation and Support Worker in Long-Term Care Settings<br>Shelter Worker<br>Supportive Housing Worker<br>Social Housing Worker |

*Source:* Adapted from Human Resources and Skills Development Canada. (2006). *4212 Community and Social Service Workers.* Retrieved January 18, 2007, from http://www23.hrdc-drhc.gc.ca/2001/e/groups/4212.shtml.

the workforce may undertake more complex supportive counselling duties (Stephenson et al., 2000). According to early work by Segal (1977), attempts were made to link differing levels of education with task complexity. In spite of these efforts, a consensus was not reached and to this day there is no real agreement among employers and social service worker educators regarding tasks that clearly define social service work. However, it is fair to say that what social service workers do falls well within the definition of social work adopted through an international consensus at the General Meeting of the International Federation of Social Workers (IFSW): "The social work profession promotes social change, problem-solving in human relationships, and empowerment and liberation of people to enhance well-being. Utilizing theories of human behaviour and social systems, social work intervenes at the points where people interact with their environments. Principles of human rights and social justice are fundamental to social work" (see IFSW, July 2000, http://www.ifsw.org).

## COLLEGE PROGRAMS

Here again, a lack of consensus regarding terminology and language adds to confusion in the sector. Twenty-three colleges of applied arts and technology in Ontario and about 46 in total across Canada offer social service worker programs that are recognized by the professional college. Recently, other named programs have been identified as sufficiently equivalent, including Durham's Human Services Counsellor Program and George Brown College's Community Worker Program (OCSWSSW, 2007b). To add further murkiness to the waters, private colleges offering one-year "social service worker" programs are lobbying the Ontario Ministry of Training, Colleges and Universities for inclusion in the professional college.

Fortunately, consistency at some level has occurred in curricula because community colleges are collectively influenced by the needs of the employment market. Presently, course work concentrates on a generalist/empowerment approach to practice with studies in the core areas of (1) human growth and development; (2) social work values and ethical practice; (3) social problems and systemic barriers; (4) personal and social values; (5) social service delivery systems; and (6) basic interventions. Some colleges offer SSW diploma programs with specialization in such areas as gerontology, Aboriginal studies, and mental health/addictions. Different pathways to education have been established to enhance learner access and include full-time day programs, part-time evening and weekend programs, and online coursework. All programs include a practicum component which enables graduates to gain valuable field practice experience in the sector (Lecomte, 2001; Ontario Ministry of Education and Training, 1996).

In Ontario, the Ministry of Training, Colleges and Universities sets out specific vocational learning outcomes for accredited social service worker programs that must be demonstrated in curricula. This regulation further helps to standardize learning. Table 25.2 outlines vocational learning outcomes set by the Ontario Ministry of Training, Colleges and Universities for accredited social service worker programs offered at colleges of applied arts and technology.

## PROFILE OF SOCIAL SERVICE WORKER STUDENTS

SSW students are typically women (75%) although a growing number of men and transgendered individuals have been entering college programs over the past ten years (Service Canada, 2003). The student population tends to be younger with 78 percent under the age of 30 years and the majority entering programs directly from high school. Older learners enter programs as mature students and are often seeking a second career or are interested

| TABLE 25.2 | Core Vocational Learning Outcomes (VLOs) for SSW Programs' Two-Year Diploma from Colleges of Arts and Applied Technology |
|---|---|
| **Outcome** | **Vocational Learning Outcome Description** |
| VLO 1 | Develop and maintain professional relationships which adhere to professional, legal, and ethical standards aligned to social service work. |
| VLO 2 | Identify strengths, resources, and needs of individuals, families, groups, and communities to assist them in achieving their goals. |
| VLO 3 | Respect needs and experiences of individuals, groups, families, organizations, and communities within a diverse and global society. |
| VLO 4 | Work with communities and emerging leaders in the community to advocate for systemic change. |
| VLO 5 | Identify current social policy, relevant legislation, and political, social, and/or cconomic systems to assist in the development of effective plans of action. |
| VLO 6 | Advocate for appropriate access to resources to assist individuals, families, groups, and the community. |
| VLO 7 | Develop and maintain positive working relationships with colleagues, supervisors, and community partners. |
| VLO 8 | Implement ongoing personal and professional development strategies and plans to promote self-care, improve job performance, and enhance work relationships. |
| VLO 9 | Integrate social group work and group facilitation skills across a wide range of environments, promoting growth and development of individuals, families, and communities. |
| VLO 10 | Promote social and economic justice through the application of change strategies that challenge and break patterns of oppression and discrimination. |

*Source:* Ontario Ministry of Education and Training. (1996). *Social Service Worker Program Standard Manual.* College Standards and Accreditation Council. Retrieved March 1, 2007, from http://www.edu.gov.on.ca/eng/general/college/progstan/humserv/soc-serv.html#preamble.

in re-entering the workforce after raising a family. The student population tends to be eth- nically and culturally diverse, particularly in urban areas (Ontario Ministry of Training, Colleges and Universities, KPI data, 2005).

SSW students are often attracted to the field because of personal life experiences that have motivated them to become helpers. Some have experienced personal adversity or crises for which they sought assistance and because of the help received want to give back to others in similar situations. Others are attracted to the field because they are nat- ural helpers and have experienced positive feedback from peers and family that has encouraged them to seek out a profession where they can utilize their interpersonal skills. Some colleges continue to screen applicants applying to programs, seeking recruits who

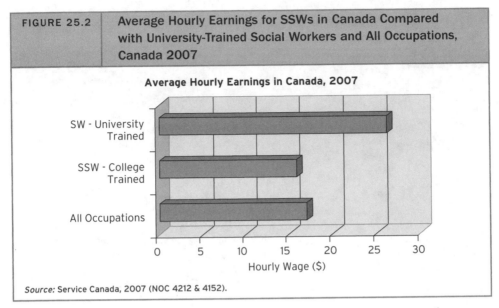

| FIGURE 25.2 | Average Hourly Earnings for SSWs in Canada Compared with University-Trained Social Workers and All Occupations, Canada 2007 |

*Source:* Service Canada, 2007 (NOC 4212 & 4152).

demonstrate core attributes which include the ability to demonstrate empathy, a non-judgmental attitude, and genuine caring. In addition to these criteria, literacy entrance requirements ensure that students are proficient in written English.

## WORKING CONDITIONS

Employment prospects are fair with the number of job seekers matching the number of job openings, and the overall unemployment rate for the field is below average at 3.3 percent. Employment opportunities rose significantly between 1999 and 2001 because of increases in government funding for health and social services. Recent concern over youth and urban violence has produced a new wave of funding and additional jobs. There are regional disparities in employment opportunities. The highest concentration—per 10 000 people—of social service workers is found in the provinces of Alberta, Manitoba, and Prince Edward Island. The lowest concentration is in Newfoundland and Labrador and New Brunswick (Service Canada, 2007).

Despite the positive outlook in employment trends in this sector, a number of jobs are part-time and/or contract positions. As many social service agencies rely on project funding, job uncertainty is the norm (Saunders, 2004). As illustrated in Figure 25.2, the average hourly earnings for a social service worker in Canada is $15.84, which is below the average earnings of other occupations and well below the average earning for university-trained social workers. A relatively high percentage of younger-than-average workers may indicate high burnout in the field due to the stressful nature of direct service work (Service Canada, 2007).

## TENSIONS AND CHALLENGES

Lack of uniformity continues to cast skepticism on the merits of professionalization of social service and welfare work. Employers use different job titles for SSWs and often do not require membership in the professional college or other regulatory associations. Figures from the Ontario College of Social Workers and Social Service Workers confirm this finding with only 1030 SSWs registered, compared with 10 505 degree-trained professionals (Pamela Blake, personal communication, February 2007).

Tensions and challenges in social service work stem from the hierarchy that has developed within the social work profession. Social work has been struggling for recognition as a profession for many years and critiqued for drawing on other disciplines such as psychology and sociology for its knowledge base (Stephenson et al., 2000). The incorporation of a paraprofessional position into the mix has caused dissent among some BSW, MSW, and doctoral practitioners. Elitism has resulted in the alienation of some SSWs whose front-line, direct service work is viewed as "lesser" or "not as skilled." Stories gathered by the authors from the field poignantly illustrate these feelings of being treated as second-class citizens by the profession. The following are just two real-life examples that reflect many more recounted:

> When I expressed an interest in doing intake and one-on-one supportive counselling, I was told that college students are not allowed to even shadow counselling or intake sessions. The agency did, however, allow Bachelor students to become fully engaged in these tasks (SSW student, Humber College).

> I had been working for several years at a crisis centre as a trained volunteer. Before getting accepted into college, I spoke with one of my colleagues who had a Bachelor of Social Work degree. She asked where I was applying and when I told her an SSW program, she responded that I would regret this decision because in this field a diploma is worthless (SSW student, Humber College).

There is a genuine lack of understanding and appreciation among many university-trained social workers regarding the curriculum, education, and training offered through social service worker programs at community colleges. The most common myth to be dispelled is the belief that college education lacks the rigour and theoretical foundation received through university programs. This can result in devaluing the work and role of SSWs in the field, which can have detrimental effects resulting in marginalization and low expectations of what SSWs are capable of providing. Moreover, the risk of de-motivating SSWs is increased and a self-fulfilling prophecy can result, whereby even the most competent are kept down because of hierarchical thinking.

Of even greater impact is the insidious and pervasive "us and them" attitude within the profession of social work which may contribute to alienation resulting in stress, ineffectual interventions, and eventually more and more SSWs leaving the field altogether. In this context, social service workers and social workers view each other as separate groups of people divided by differences instead of being bound together by common foundational training, values, and goals.

In order to foster inclusiveness, an anti-oppression framework must be applied such that the profession begins working towards embracing different levels of education and establishing a "we" attitude. When *Bill 76* was passed in Ontario on December 16, 1998, it marked the beginning of a new way of thinking which embraced social service workers and social workers under one piece of legislation with a common code of ethics and standards for practice. The challenge today is to get to a point of true acceptance recognizing that individuals enter the profession at different levels, but contribute collectively to the overall goals of social work.

Ironically, the very evils social workers seek to overcome in society—systemic barriers, prejudice, and discrimination—are reflected in the structure of the profession. The challenge is to embrace different types and levels of helping work as equally valuable and part of the realm of social work. A critical analysis of how hierarchical structures oppress persons on the frontlines must be incorporated into the evolving structure of social service work in Canada.

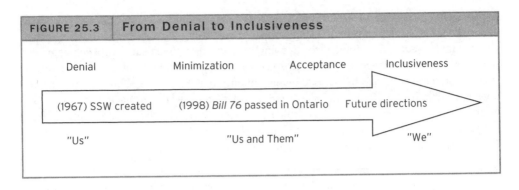

FIGURE 25.3    **From Denial to Inclusiveness**

Figure 25.3 illustrates what seems to be the prevailing dynamic between some social workers with degrees and SSWs. When we examine this dynamic through an equity and inclusive anti-oppression lens, we find that the dynamic can be characterized on a continuum from denial of differences to inclusiveness and integration. Understanding the hierarchy and elitism is critical for practitioners particularly since, according to the IFSW definition, the profession is all about problem solving, social change, and empowerment.

Denial on this continuum refers to the tendency to not acknowledge the differential treatment existing between practitioners who have degrees and those who do not. There is a deliberate repudiation of the hierarchy that exists on the basis of education, additional training, and function. A person at this level of awareness is not able to perceive the differential treatment in how practitioners in the field with different levels of education are socially located and, therefore, is in denial of the privileges accrued to those with degrees and in denial of opportunities and marginalization that SSWs might experience.

The next level on the continuum is minimization, which is beyond denial because differences among levels of social work practitioners are overtly acknowledged but trivialized. This refers to individuals who acknowledge that differences in education can result in differential treatment, but not necessarily with sincerity or political consciousness of the implications of the differences in status. Dismissiveness is often a characteristic associated with minimization and can be seen as a non-confrontational position—"I see, but I don't want to reveal" or "I see, but I don't want to take a position"—as compared to denial, which is "I see, but no, I don't see."

Acceptance represents a major conceptual shift from denial to some form of relativism. It is when a person moves from the denial of educational elitism ("educentrism") to educational relativism (edurelativism). Here educational differences are acknowledged and respected and perceived as fundamentally necessary and integral to the delivery of social services, which is so varied and complex. Differences are not judged and evaluated from the perspective of "us" and "them"; they simply exist. At this stage in the continuum there is a shift in both the cognitive and the behavioural levels in the practitioner. First, there is the acceptance that differences in education and training exist and that they lead to differences in function and interventions. The assumption is that a major shift occurs from educational elitism to educational relativism and differences are necessary for acceptance and inclusiveness to occur.

The last level is inclusiveness and integration, which refers to practitioners' ability to acknowledge, integrate, and work with differences. It is an ability to see how one is different by bringing something unique and yet being a part of a bigger picture or context. A person at this stage can construe differences and see the process and engage in contextual relativism. The differences are acknowledged and respected because they are not perceived as threatening. At this level or stage a person is open and available to others, affirming of others, and does not feel threatened that others are capable and competent since s/he has a healthy sense of self that comes from knowing that s/he belongs to a greater whole. In a sense, this level is about the person having a healthy self-created identity, feeling safe in his or her own zone and being able to adjust to a wide array of professionals with differing levels of education, training, and function.

## CONCLUSION

The profession of social work in Canada faces many challenges, and among these is the ever-increasing threat of cutbacks to social and welfare programs. If the profession is going to fight against this trend, collectivism and cohesiveness among professional categories within the social work field would only help to build a unified front when advocating for systemic changes and lobbying governments against funding cutbacks.

Like many professions with a variety of levels of intervention and educational backgrounds, social work too continues to face struggles internally and externally. It is by acknowledging and facing these challenges that practitioners can continue to individually and collectively as a profession become stronger. To reduce tensions, it is crucial that clear scopes of practice, job descriptions, and boundaries be developed to dissipate the notion of elitism that currently prevails. The ultimate goal is to establish new and innovative ways of organizing the profession into a progressive partnership of practitioners working together for the betterment of individuals, groups, communities, and society.

# References

Chappell, R. (2006). *Social Welfare in Canadian Society.* Toronto: Thomson Nelson.

Crane, J. (1974). *Employment of Social Service Graduates in Canada.* Ottawa: Canadian Association of Schools of Social Work.

Hicks, S. (2006). *Social Work in Canada: An Introduction.* 2nd edition. Toronto: Thompson Educational Publishing Inc.

Human Resources and Skills Development Canada. (2006). *4212 Community and Social Service Workers.* Retrieved January 18, 2007, from http://www23.hrdc-hrhc.gc.ca/2001/e/groups/4212.shtml

Human Resources and Skills Development Canada. (2005). *4212 Community and Social Service Workers.* Retrieved January 18, 2007, from http://www1.on.hrdc-gc.ca/ojf.jsp?lang=e&lang=e&section=Profile&noc=4212

Lecomte, R. (2005). Distinguishing Features of Social Work Education in Canada. In J. C. Turner and F. J. Turner (Eds). *Canadian Social Welfare.* 5th edition. Toronto: Pearson Allyn and Bacon.

Ontario College of Social Workers and Social Service Workers. (2007a). *About Social Service Work.* Retrieved February 1, 2007, from http://www.ocswssw.org/sections/about_ocsw/about_ssw.html

Ontario College of Social Workers and Social Service Workers. (2007b). *Social Service Work Programs in Ontario.* Retrieved February 1, 2007, from http://www.ocswssw.org/sections/info_public/sw_sswprograms.html

Ontario College of Social Workers and Social Service Workers. (2000). *Standards of Practice Handbook.* Retrieved March 15, 2007, from http://www.ocswssw.org/sections/pdf/1. 6B%20code%20of%20ethics%20english.pdf

Ontario Ministry of Training, Colleges and Universities. (1996). *Social Service Worker Standards Manual.* Retrieved March 15, 2007, from http://www.edu.gov.on.ca/eng/general/college/progstan/ humserv/soc-serv.html#preamble

Ontario Ministry of Training, Colleges and Universities. (2005). *Key Performance Indicators.* Retrieved March 15, 2007, from http://www.edu.gov.on.ca/eng/general/postsec/colindicator. html

Saunders, R. (2004). *Passion and Commitment Under Stress: Human Resources Issues in Canada's Non-Profit Sector.* Ottawa: Canadian Policy Research Network. Retrieved September 10, 2006, from http://www.cprn.org

Segal, B. (1977). *Carleton-Algonquin Social Work Education and Manpower Project.* Ottawa: Carleton University of Social Work.

Service Canada. (2003). *Job Futures.* Retrieved March 15, 2007, from http://www.jobfutures.ca

Stephenson, M., G. Rondeau, J.C. Michaud, and S. Fiddler. (2000). *In Critical Demand: Social Work in Canada,* Vol. 1. Social Work Sector Steering Committee. Retrieved February 15, 2007, from www.socialworkincanada.org/pdf/vol1_en/toc/en.pdf

Turner, J.C. and F. J. Turner (Eds). (2005). *Canadian Social Welfare.* 5th edition. Toronto: Pearson Allyn and Bacon.

# CHAPTER 26

# Informal Helping and Mutual Aid

*John Cossom*

## INTRODUCTION

This chapter focuses on various kinds of informal help that people use outside the boundaries of formal social service agencies with employed, professional helpers. It has several objectives.

First, the chapter intends to draw attention to the wide continuum of formal and informal helping resources that people use to deal with personal problems. Second, we examine why informal care and support are now a subject of renewed importance for professional helpers, social science research, and social policy. Third, we consider the concepts of natural helping and social support, the important roles they play in the ecology of helping, and why professional helpers need to understand them. We look at mutual aid groups and, in particular, self-help groups. We deal with the latter at some length because of their ubiquity, their phenomenal growth, and their increasing significance as a source of support and empowerment for so many people. Then we draw a contrast between lay, informal helping with the kinds of help that social service professionals offer.

Because we can look at informal helping according to distinct ideological perspectives, we examine its social policy and political significance. The chapter concludes with a discussion of how professional helpers can understand, establish links with, and champion informal help and mutual aid in their practice.

## THE LEXICON OF INFORMAL HELPING

As various kinds of informal helping have attracted burgeoning interest, a plethora of terms and definitions has sprung up to describe these complex and diverse phenomena. A reader is likely to encounter some of the following terms:

- informal or natural helping
- natural helping network
- natural or lay helper
- caregiver or natural caregiver
- social network
- social support network
- informal support system
- support group
- mutual aid
- self-help

These concepts interest different academics and professionals in the fields of social work, sociology, psychology, nursing, anthropology, psychiatry, pastoral counselling, and so on. As often happens in social science, there is far from universal agreement on the meaning of these terms, and a great deal of overlap and variation in their use. As this chapter progresses, we will offer definitions of some of these terms.

# MUTUAL AID, INFORMAL, AND PROFESSIONAL HELP

*Mutual aid* is a generic term. Historically, it refers to the many ways that human beings care for one another. People sharing resources and taking common action to deal with shared problems are the essence of society (Kropotkin). Throughout recorded time, people in differing cultures have developed their own, natural ways to deal with inevitable but unpredictable personal troubles, social problems, and environmental catastrophes. Humankind's very survival has often depended on social co-operation, for example, in food gathering, mutual protection against invaders, child care, and agriculture. Families, neighbours, and clan members were the significant sources of mutual assistance.

Over time, other more structured approaches to mutual aid arose.

An important twentieth-century Canadian example is the Antigonish Movement. This liberal, Catholic, social, and economic community development movement began in the 1920s and ultimately led to the establishment of credit unions and fishing, agricultural, and consumer co-operatives that dotted the Atlantic provinces in the 1930s and 1940s (MacPherson).

With the emergence of faster moving, urbanizing industrial societies, professional, paid helpers and state social welfare interventions increasingly became a feature of the social structure. In Canada, this was primarily a twentieth-century development, a response to human need that surfaced in increasingly formal, specialized ways. In part, public social welfare programs and professional helpers were necessary to deal with the inordinate demands placed on informal helping systems in a rapidly changing world. Geographic population mobility and the transition to a nuclear family made the extended family support system much less viable.

An industrially driven economy disrupted long-standing natural support systems for many people. When economies crashed, family and friends usually did not have the resources needed to help one other survive the ravages of mass unemployment. They could not generate jobs that no longer existed. Local churches, charities, or benevolent associations also could not cope with the tremendous human need this large-scale dislocation produced. In response to widespread social, health, and economic problems, a national and provincial social welfare system slowly assumed greater responsibility for broad public needs. Specialized professional disciplines evolved to address people's personal troubles. Sometimes grassroots volunteer helping evolved into formal social services organizations that employed professional staff. Many social service agencies emerged from voluntary services and caring.

Society accepts the importance of specialized professional help to assist individuals and groups in dealing effectively with their troubles in complex situations. We also better understand now that both informal and professional kinds of assistance perform important, legitimate, if different, functions and that we usually need them to work in tandem if people are to gain the most help.

Not surprisingly though, in our age of expanding professional specializations, status, control of turf, and the rapid growth of knowledge and helping technologies, paid helpers often overlook, underestimate, or dismiss the significance of mutual aid and natural forms of help. Indeed, professionals are quite capable of treating informal helping as of lesser importance or, worse, as irrelevant to a specialized helping process. Still other professionals may consider mutual aid an "adjunct" or "after-care" to their clinical work and see it as secondary to the "real" work that they do as experts (Humphreys).

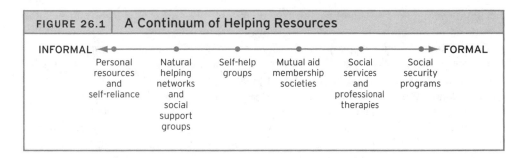

FIGURE 26.1 | **A Continuum of Helping Resources**

It is tempting to assume that with the development of public assistance, social insurance, universal transfer payments, and a wide array of public and voluntary personal social services, the more informal natural helping roles have greatly diminished in importance. Such is not the case. These contrasting cultures of care continue to exist side by side in our communities. All manner of informal, everyday helping continues to play a crucial role in people's lives. Even though we now claim to understand these natural and informal kinds of help better, we still have much to learn about them.

Helping takes multiple forms. It ranges from individual self-reliance—think of the glut of self-improvement and self-healing books on the market today—to sophisticated professional therapies and national social security schemes. Figure 26.1 illustrates the continuum of helping resources.

These different helping systems interact with and affect one another, whether or not this mutual influence is recognized. Unfortunately, they too often operate in rigid isolation from, ignorance or suspicion of, or competition with one another.

## RENEWED AWARENESS OF INFORMAL HELPING

Nowadays, professional helpers are becoming much more knowledgeable about the extent and significance of natural helpers and support systems in people's lives. One striking example comes from research into the care of older people (Brody; Kane & Penrod).

This is an important issue, given Canada's significant and growing population of elderly people. Many think that the public and private institutional health care and social services personnel constitute all the services available for our elderly. The reality is very different. "In Canada, as in comparable Western economic systems, it is estimated that 85 to 90 percent of the care of old people is provided informally, largely in the context of families. The rest, only 10 or 15 percent, is supplied by the formal health and social services" (Aronson).

Informal family care roles are of huge significance. Women provide most of this "family" care. This is true not only in the case of the elderly, but in other areas too, such as the care of disabled children and adults. Knowing such facts aids our understanding of these crucial informal helping patterns.

### Support as Social Buffering

There are a number of reasons why professionals are now less likely to see informal kinds of helping as insignificant, antagonistic, or competitive. The first is that social science and health researchers are paying more attention to informal helping. Patterns of lay help are becoming more visible. Therefore, we take them less for granted as a feature of people's social ecology. A body of knowledge, concepts, and theory is growing about the forms that natural help takes, and how people use various informal resources. As we appreciate more and more the nature, extent, and importance of informal help in society, we also learn what positive effects social connections have on people's individual health and general well-being and how this kind of help is an integral part of a community's health care. "The conclusion that supportive interactions among people are important is hardly new. What is new is the assembling of hard evidence that adequate social support can protect people in crisis from a wide variety of pathological states: from low birth weight to death, from arthritis through tuberculosis to depression, alcoholism, and other psychiatric illness. Furthermore, social support can reduce the amount of medication required and accelerate recovery and facilitate compliance with required regimes" (Cobb, p. 310).

Evidence is mounting strongly in many quarters about the many ways that people benefit from their everyday connections with family, friends, or neighbours; how these relationships support them; and how people's participation in mutual aid groups can help them solve problems and live with challenges.

The social-buffering hypothesis posits that people with strong natural support systems are better able to deal with major life changes and challenges. The corollary is that those with little or no social support are at a greater disadvantage in coping with the demands of everyday living (Cameron & Vanderwoerd; Cohen & Syme; Cohen & Wills; Gottlieb, 1981, 1983). Generally, then, people in stressful situations are likely to suffer less physical, emotional, or social dysfunction if they have good linkage to supportive social networks, compared to those who do not have the advantage of these connections. This research demands that practitioners pay attention to support networks as important health-promoting and health-preserving features in people's lives.

## THE LIMITATIONS OF FORMAL HELPING SYSTEMS

A second reason for increased attention to informal helping is that professional helpers realize there will never be sufficient formal helping systems to answer society's growing demands for health and social services. This realization deepened with compounding cutbacks to health and welfare services, leading to even scarcer resources and more competition for those that are already limited. These factors have pushed professionals toward a greater appreciation of, alliance with, and dependence on natural helping systems.

For example, patients are now discharged from hospital at breathtaking speed after having major medical interventions. It is true that medical knowledge and technology allow many patients to spend far less treatment time in hospital than in the past. However, early discharges also demonstrate the extreme scarcity of hospital and medical resources, and the enormous pressures on health personnel to free up hospital beds. A major implication of such discharge practices is that family and friends are expected or pressured to assume caregiving roles, with or without adequate community health and social services support.

Governments are well aware of the exorbitant human and economic costs of residential care as compared to community living arrangements. In many provinces, large numbers of sick, elderly, and physically and mentally disabled people previously housed in institutions have been returned to live in their communities. At the same time, people are admitted to acute and long-term health care institutions less frequently. These policy shifts force pub-lic attention onto community-based services and supports for people who would formerly have been institutionalized. (Some policy issues related to this development will be dis-cussed later in the chapter.)

Community living policies move informal helpers to the forefront of caregiving and support and into more prominent roles alongside professionals. However, government savings through de-institutionalization are rarely reallocated in kind to support the informal helpers and community services that now exert heavy emotional and physical effort in caregiving (Bullock, p. 74).

## NEW PARADIGMS OF PRACTICE AND POLICY

A third reason for embracing lay helping is that, despite explosions of knowledge and the-ories about human problems, professionals are humbler about the limits of their own expertise to solve them. Major social problems such as poverty, addictions, child abuse and neglect, and violence toward women are not being resolved and diminishing. Professionals and society in general are becoming painfully aware of the limits of professional interven-tions and social policy.

All these factors point to the need for new models for practitioners. We need ways that shine a spotlight on natural helping systems. Social work has always focused on helping people in their own social environments. Early approaches to caring intuitively emphasized working with people in this context and understanding the importance of family, friends, and neighbours. In later decades, however, this central feature of social work did not receive the attention it warranted. Emphasis shifted to office-based therapeutic sessions. Now, there are new ways of thinking about helping to re-assert the importance of this understanding and working with people and their social situations.

A social–ecological paradigm of practice places renewed emphasis on the interaction and relations between people in their social networks and shows a renewed appreciation of and interest in natural helping systems. Social and emotional loneliness and isolation can lead to human vulnerability. Accordingly, practitioners must think about informal support and helping relationships as critical environmental factors in helping their clients cope with stress (Germain & Gitterman, p. 491). Current social work thinking, then, takes the whole of clients' social landscapes into account and concentrates on working with their own social ecology. This entails understanding people's social support networks and rela-tionships, or assessing their absence, depletion, or exhaustion.

What often brings people to the doors of the social agencies is their *lack* of natural supportive relationships, or ones that are frayed, broken, or dysfunctional. Intervention efforts may link these people with new support systems or rebuild and sustain existing ones.

## SOCIAL SUPPORT AND NATURAL HELPING NETWORKS

People belong to *social networks* (Abrams; Attneave; Israel; Maguire; Mitchell). The con-cept conjures up the image of a net or web and what it represents—a set of connections or relationships between people (Collins & Pancoast, p. 18). A network is a set of relationships among family members, friends, co-workers, members of a religious, ethnic, or political group, self-help group, sports or recreational club, or any other interest group.

The term "network" has become a buzzword. Despite the term's everyday use, social networks are relatively invisible to us and are easily taken for granted. To social workers especially, however, the concept of network is very useful for understanding people's social functioning. Social workers can focus more on people's helping and social support networks as key resources in dealing with developmental tasks and particular problems of living.

The generic concept of social network has given rise to subsidiary concepts of the helping network and the social support network. These social science terms describe the natural relationships to which people turn for help with their physical care, emotional support, advice, and material assistance. Whittaker and Garbarino define a *social support network* as "a set of interconnected relationships among a group of people that provides enduring patterns of nurturance (in any or all forms) and provides contingent reinforcement for efforts to cope with life on a day-to-day basis" (p. 5).

Like professionals, informal helpers can listen, empathize, help clarify problems, make referrals to other helpers, and give advice. Lay support is more likely "to involve practical help, reciprocity, friendship-based relationships, altruism, experiential knowledge, solicited and unsolicited advice, self-disclosure on the part of the helper, reassurance, alternative interpretations, minimization of the importance of problems, consensual valida-tion, and self-deprecation" (Ayers, p. 217). On the other hand, professional, consultative relationships "focus on such elements as communication and listening skills ... confronta-tion, goal-directed problem-solving, and behaviour change" (Ayers, p. 217).

We see various patterns of natural helping in Canada's social and cultural mosaic. Peo-ple in different classes and cultural, ethnic, age, and religious groups have different atti-tudes and norms about seeking and giving help. The notion of formal services may actually be anathema to someone not familiar with turning to a professional stranger to deal with a life problem. Those who speak the same language and understand an immigrant's culture may be the most important initial resource for newcomers to Canada. Professionals are slowly becoming aware of these factors affecting the patterns of informal help in various Aboriginal cultures, for example, and how the disregard of these by the majority has led to untold misery for First Nations people.

When they are in difficulty, most people turn first and most frequently to their family members, friends, co-workers, neighbours, and even acquaintances (Gottlieb, 1980, 1982; Cowan). At the same time we must not forget that some people use neither professional help nor informal networks in times of stress, for a variety of reasons (Brown; Veroff, Dou-van & Kulka).

People often seek assistance from *natural helpers*. These people have intuitive helping skills and use them to assist others in their everyday lives. They can be people with sound reputations for wisdom, concern, or empathy in a family, group, or neighbourhood. Peo-ple who fill this role may be experienced foster parents to whom other surrogate parents turn to at times of special need, teachers with whom students can talk comfortably, or neighbours who simply have a natural ability to understand. Natural helpers are found in all kinds of social niches. A number of researchers have studied natural helpers and the informal roles they play (Cowan; Eddy, Paap, & Glad; Gottlieb, 1982; Turner, Kim-brough, & Traynhan). Also, projects have been undertaken to train people in key contact roles with the public—such as taxi drivers, bartenders, and hairdressers—to recognize and help others in crisis.

People in need are likely to contact professionals much later as problems develop, if at all. When a problem has resisted other attempts at resolution, or when the stress it produces becomes intolerable, a person is more prepared to seek out and accept professional help (Gourash). Then clergy, teachers, and physicians are often among the first consulted.

Ironically, people are likely to rank the formal social services quite low on the list of resources to which they turn. This is unfortunate, given the special resources, information, and expertise available to them in this sector. All this research reinforces the importance of professionals' understanding the sociology of help-seeking and how people approach it.

## SELF-HELP AND MUTUAL AID GROUPS

A multiplicity of mutual aid groups exists in our society. These groups form whenever people face common problems and join to tackle them, to seek reciprocal support, or take common action. Such groups can take form spontaneously, as when students discover a difficulty they share and get together to help each other learn challenging material. Groups can also be created formally for specific purposes. For example, a social worker sets up group sessions at a clinic for people coping with a diagnosis of cancer; or single parents in a housing complex organize a co-operative child care pool. Increasingly, the formal social service sector uses these sorts of created mutual aid groups to bring together clients who face similar problems. They represent a blend of professional and informal approaches to support. Gitterman and Shulman (2005) provide an excellent array of examples of formed mutual aid groups that social workers mediate for a wide range of vulnerable populations at all stages of life.

The *self-help group* is one particular form of mutual aid occupying an increasingly prominent place among the means of helping people. According to Katz and Bender,

> Self-help groups are voluntary, small group structures for mutual aid and the accomplishment of a special purpose. They are usually formed by peers who have come together for mutual assistance in satisfying a common need, overcoming a common handicap or life-disrupting problem, or attempting desired social and/or personal change. The initiators and members of such groups perceive that their needs are not, or cannot be, met by or through existing social institutions. Self-help groups emphasize face-to-face social interactions and the assumption of personal responsibility by members. They often provide material assistance as well as emotional support; they are frequently "cause"-oriented, and promulgate an ideology or values through which members may attain an enhanced sense of personal identity (p. 9).

Self-help groups have become extraordinarily numerous in recent times (Reissman, 1982; Katz & Bender). Metropolitan areas such as Toronto, Montreal, or Vancouver boast hundreds of self-help groups. While proportionately fewer exist in smaller communities, some self-help groups exist virtually everywhere in Canada. New groups are constantly emerging to help people cope with common problems they feel are not addressed properly elsewhere, or in response to perceived deficiencies in professional care.

Not surprisingly in an electronic age, all kinds of computer-based self-help groups are also flourishing, made possible by the explosive growth of computers in the home and the workplace (Madara; Finn, 1999). Ready availability and cheap access to commercial and private computer-based email, chat, and bulletin board systems have attracted all kinds of self-help groups to them. For example, a person can now attend an Alcoholics Anonymous meeting in cyberspace at any time, from any location (Finn, 1996).

Different explanations are offered to explain the popularity of self-help groups (Adams). According to one, the growth of self-help extends traditional forms of natural helping in a contemporary way. A functional perspective suggests that self-help fills gaps left by formal services and the state's and professionals' inability or unwillingness to help in certain circumstances. Others see the self-help movement as a natural developmental reaction to the professional view of what people need. A more radical interpretation attributes self-help's popularity to people's alienation due to technological development, dehumanizing institutions, and the increasing professionalization and impersonalization of social welfare services. Gartner and Reissman (1977, p. 3) concur with this latter view and point out that self-help values emphasize "concern for personal autonomy, participation, quality of life, human potential, consumer rights, deprofessionalization and decentralization."

Whatever the explanations for their existence, self-help groups deal with a wide range of human problems and play a significant part in many people's lives. They offer people a recovery strategy for all manner of addictions: therapy; self-fulfillment and personal growth; an avenue to tackle social issues by pursuing social action; raising consciousness and engaging in social and self-advocacy; help dealing with stigma; assistance for the friends, relatives, or caregivers of those facing special problems; support for survivors of traumatic events; and so on. Probably the best-known type of self-help group is one that offers an anonymous membership to those recovering from all kinds of addictions. More than 200 different programs base themselves on the original Alcoholics Anonymous 12-step model—Overspenders, Emotions, Co-dependents, Sexaholics, and even Clutterers Anonymous (Powell; Canadian Broadcasting Corporation).

Self-help groups can offer short-term help to people undergoing a crisis—a bereavement support group—or long-term support for lifestyle change—Overeaters or Gamblers Anonymous. They can focus on members' inner well-being, as Al Anon does, or on some external point in order to change some feature of the social environment, such as a welfare rights group (Katz & Bender, p. 39). This classification is not watertight, as some groups combine these functions. For example, a gay liberation group may support individual members as well as actively espousing larger causes.

Given the tremendous variations in form and substantive concern of these groups, generalizing about their features is hazardous. Nevertheless, themes culled from the extensive literature and research about them help explain how these lay group-helping approaches differ from professionally led groups and what qualities they share:

1. The help provided is not a commodity that is bought and sold. It is a free, shared resource and a voluntary activity. Self-help draws on the often unfulfilled need of people to be helpful, concerned, and involved (Banks; Reissman, 1982; Romeder).

2. The "helper-therapy" principle seems to be important for participants, in which people are greatly helped through assisting others (Reissman, 1965, 1977).

3. Self-help groups are usually small and quite informal and function on a face-to-face basis. The ties between members are horizontal, not vertical or authoritarian. They develop spontaneously and avoid size and bureaucracy (Adams; Banks; Reissman, 1982; Katz & Bender). However, some do develop national and international organizations through their success (Silverman).

4. They are populist in nature and anti-expert. Self-helpers are likely to be critical of professional methods. But not all groups reject such help, and some develop working relationships with professionals (Adams; Reissman, 1982).

5. Self-empowerment is an important theme. Self-helpers seek to control their own lives. People are seen as experts in their own situations rather than as "cases with problems" (Adams; Froland, Pancoast, Chapman, & Kimboko; Reissman, 1982).

6. Self-help groups usually have fluid structures, unlike bureaucratic or professional organizations. Often leadership is shared and shifts easily, or can be diffuse. They emphasize democracy, equality of status, and co-operation in decision making (Adams; Reissman, 1982; Romeder; Silverman).

7. The knowledge base is experiential, indigenous, and rooted in wisdom. Groups build on the strengths and common experiences of members, are based in reality, and look for results (Borkman; Froland, Pancoast, Chapman, & Kimboko; Reissman, 1982).

8. Organization is usually from the bottom-up, not top-down. Ideology holds a self-help group together, not bureaucracy (Reissman, 1982; Silverman).

Self-help groups serve multiple functions for their members. They offer information about problems and practical help and advice. Often a framework and specific strategies may be offered to deal with a problem. Members feel cared about and wanted, and learn that others like themselves share a particular problem, concern, or disability. A new social network can readily emerge for the member offering supportive peer relationships (Silverman).

One fact is clear. Many people belong to such groups and find solace, help, and satisfaction in them. It has been estimated that more than 400 distinct types of mutual aid groups exist, comprising 500 000 groups in the United States (Finn, 1996). Wuthnow (1994) notes that, in 1994, four out of every 10 Americans belonged to a rapidly growing small-group movement, while Kessler (1994) shows through his research that the number of self-help and mutual aid groups and the frequency of their members' meetings are expanding.

Self-help groups are important helping networks, so helping professionals can ill afford to ignore them. At the very least, practitioners need to inform themselves of the range of self-help resources in their communities so that they can apprise consumers of these services, help them decide whether to use them, and make effective referral suggestions.

Beyond this, professionals can sometimes serve in advisory or consultative roles to self-help groups when asked. Several books have been written to help professional practitioners understand these groups and how to offer appropriate support when invited (Gartner & Reissman, 1980; Kurtz; Powell; Silverman, 1980; Hill). Some groups such as La Leche League and the Ostomy Society maintain professional advisory committees to keep on top of new information that members can use to their advantage (Silverman, p. 174).

Practitioners can also play facilitative roles to help establish new self-help groups where unmet client needs can be addressed. They have to do this without co-opting or colonizing the group, and they have to know how to get out at the right time. Perhaps the most important quality a professional can cultivate is an open-minded philosophy about the benefits of both informal and professional helping, and a readiness to lend support to whatever means help people find strength in themselves.

## A Child Welfare Mutual Aid Example

When appropriate, social workers can play an active role in the formation, maintenance, and programming of mutual aid groups. A three-year Ontario child welfare demonstration project provides an excellent example of the innovative professional use of mutual aid groups (Cameron; Cameron, Hayward, & Mamatis).

Researchers have found that informal helping strategies and mutual aid programs, despite their known potential, are seldom used in child welfare practice. So the project investigators set out to discover "whether mutual aid organizations could be designed that would bring informal helping resources within the reach of professional helpers and the high-risk families they are trying to help" (Cameron, Hayward, & Mamatis, p. 26).

Families were referred to the Parent Mutual Aid Organizations (PMAO) project from the open-protection caseloads of three Southern Ontario Children's Aid Societies (CAS). Comparison cases were selected randomly from the same caseloads and not referred to the mutual aid groups, but continued to receive standard child welfare protection services. The families in both groups were similar in that they all faced problems of very limited income, social isolation, family conflict, parenting difficulties, and managing a home. The children in both samples were at risk of neglect and emotional and possible physical abuse (Cameron, p. 40).

The three CASs hosted the PMAOs. Approximately half the parents who were referred participated. The staff offered scheduled as well as informal contact for the participants, a range of supportive and educational activities, and a chance for the members to build their own peer social support network and friendships. In short, they gave the participants the opportunity to benefit from all the known advantages of involvement in mutual aid/self-help groups.

The results showed that the PMAO sample felt significant benefits of social integration and social support, in both making and maintaining friendships. They found the same benefits in the members' more concrete exchanges of help among themselves—babysitting, transportation, clothing, and emergency shelter (Cameron, p. 46).

PMAO members also showed considerably more improvement in self-esteem than the comparison group. Like many self-help group members, they felt the power of helping others (helper-therapy principle) and being helped by peers, rather than receiving assistance from a professional child welfare worker. Many PMAO members described themselves as better equipped to deal with stress and cope with daily challenges, and the research findings supported these conclusions. More mutual-aid group sample members reported positive changes in their parenting than the comparison group did, although the extent of the positive changes in this area was not as great as the changes in social support, self-esteem, and perceived stress measures (Cameron, p. 51). The data from this study showed that about half the referrals to the PMAOs enjoyed the rich, intense involvement the project model anticipated (Cameron, p. 53).

During the study period the PMAO sample was significantly less involved with child protection workers than the comparison group was. They also made significantly less use statistically of child placements than did their counterparts (Cameron, pp. 49, 51). A basic cost analysis for the study showed that families involved in the PMAOs demonstrated a lower per-case cost than the comparison families and that this model of service produced cost savings for the host agencies (Cameron, p. 52).

As you might expect, this mutual aid group model did not suit all child welfare families, just as it would not satisfy everyone facing other life problems. Creating and supporting this model of self-help is difficult, time-consuming work that makes big demands of child welfare personnel. It calls for strong agency commitment and talented personnel who can dramatically shift their child protection patterns (Cameron, p. 53).

Nevertheless, the project proved that a created network could be a "powerful vehicle for support and healing . . . that it is both positive and practical to create mutual aid organizations for families coming to child welfare agencies [and that such networks] should be common and respected parts of what is available to protect children and support families" (Cameron, p. 54).

## THE DIFFERENT STRENGTHS OF FORMAL AND INFORMAL SERVICE SYSTEMS

A number of authors have analyzed the respective advantages and disadvantages of informal approaches to helping and mutual aid as opposed to those services the formal social welfare sector provides (Froland; Froland, Pancoast, Chapman, & Kimboko; Lauffer; Litwak). Informal services may be an effective, non-intrusive first line of defence for those in need, but "voluntarism is no substitute for services that can best be delivered by government, particularly if coverage, equity, and entitlement are valued" (Kramer).

The strengths of the informal sector are considerable. Help is usually available quickly and without complicated qualifying criteria. Often it comes at a time when it can prevent further problems, is highly personalized, and suited to the recipients' particular needs. Natural help is non-stigmatizing and is offered in relationship contexts that are natural and familiar to the people accepting it. It is a far less costly intervention (Humphreys).

But let's avoid romanticizing the capacities of informal helping networks. Those with supportive networks are well served. However, many people are isolated, alone, and vulnerable. Those in greatest need are often those with the fewest natural helping resources at their disposal—people who do not have informal helping networks that can be mobilized for support and care.

For others, the family network is the very reason they need help. They are abused, neglected, abandoned by their kith and kin, or caught up in a web of difficult relationships that complicate their problems. Just as social networks can be a source of support, so can they be sources of conflict. No cure-all necessarily exists in a natural system of relationships, just as professional helpers cannot guarantee successful help. Some people are no more comfortable accepting informal help than formal help.

It is simply not possible to supply enough informal care and support to people in many circumstances. Continuity of care may be a problem, and specialized knowledge and resources are often necessary to support people in community care. The burdens of care can be great for informal helpers. Caregivers frequently need respite themselves, lest they too become casualties and end up needing the same services that they provide (Montgomery).

The formal service sector can offer greater equity, breadth of coverage, continuity of care, diffusion of risk, and public accountability. It can respond to catastrophes and marshal specialized and technical resources that lay people do not have and which most individuals cannot afford, especially when care is required to address chronic and complicated needs.

The weaknesses of formal service systems are well understood. They can be costly and may develop inefficiencies and methods of operation that are hard to change in large bureaucracies. Broad-based services may not respond readily to local, idiosyncratic needs. Large formal services tend to develop "red tape" in standardizing their services, which makes accessing them frustrating for consumers. The stigma attached to seeking their help can act as a significant deterrent or side effect for service recipients, too.

# POLITICS, SOCIAL POLICY, AND THE RESPONSIBILITY FOR CARE

Considerable debate continues about the preferred relationship of state services to more informal approaches to care and support in society. Competing ideologies underlie discussions about the means through which health and social services should be delivered, and by whom.

National and provincial economic problems have led governments to severely curtail their social services. As far back as 1991, the passage of Canada's *Bill C-69* reduced the amount of transfer payments from the federal to the provincial governments for health, education, and social services. It cut monies available for social assistance, child care subsidies, homemaking programs, and child welfare. The spiralling costs of health care have forced us to scrutinize cost-saving alternatives and consider an emphasis shift to community-based health services. As previously noted, these factors mean that our society pays much more attention now to the role of informal helping services. A common assumption and policy stance has been that the other forms of "community care" would automatically take up the slack created by the state's reduction in its services.

The political right calls for a greater reliance on community, family, volunteers, and natural helping. "Pro-family/informal help" advocates interpret state intervention in social services as a force eroding family life and people's taking responsibility for loved ones. Returning care to "community and family ownership" is heralded as a reinstatement of "traditional values" and a strengthening of informal ties. The powerful underlying economic rationale is that this shift saves money and relieves pressure on formal services.

Those on the political left see these rationales as thin rhetoric that disguises a wish to reduce health and social services further, rather than a genuine commitment to strengthen the informal and voluntary sector and community social infrastructure. They interpret the call for more community care as a way of off-loading expensive services from the state to a volunteer, predominantly female constituency that is ill-supported to take on draining assignments. Critics point out that rarely are fiscal resources or support services available to sustain unpaid helpers in the demanding roles they are expected to assume.

The director of the British Carers National Association, speaking at a British Columbia caregivers' conference, cited the example of one overextended caregiver. An 85-year-old woman looked after both her 50-year-old daughter who suffered from Down's syndrome and her double-amputee husband. Only after she broke her own wrist and was unable to lift her husband did she call the association about getting some temporary help (Helm, p. A7). An extreme case? Perhaps, but many caregivers are older women and, like this woman, they desperately need help themselves at times.

A strong feminist criticism of the relationship of organized versus communal and family care has been expressed (Baines, Evans, & Neysmith; Bullock; Hooyman & Gonyea). In this society, women carry out and are assumed to carry out most of the caring roles—as wives, mothers, sisters, and daughters. Aronson (p. 189) points out that women do indeed provide most of the care for older people and that this is well-documented. "Community care" there tends to mean the unpaid care by female family members. Similarly, much of the care of the sick and the severely disabled is likely to fall to women. At the same time, the shrinking of the contemporary family, women's greatly increased participation in the labour force, people's geographic mobility, high divorce rates, and an aging population, all raise the question of what happens to this major source of informal care and what resources women have left to give to demanding caregiving roles. Public policy statements that assert that the family is the best kind of support leave unanswered such key questions as "How do we provide for the needs of all, and not at the expense of women?" (Segal, p. 242).

Two worlds of care exist: the organized and the communal, "the public world of the bureaucrat and the private world of mothers" (Abrams, 1978). These two worlds now seem to be operating in greater proximity to each other and in more complex relations, with neither fully understanding the other or working with the other to their mutual advantage. Yet each of these systems of care is insufficient by itself to meet contemporary human needs in our society. Each can perform successfully only in tandem with the other. Our expanding expectation of informal helping means that we face many policy questions and will find no pat answers in that quarter.

In 2004, the Canadian government took a small but significant step to recognize and support informal caregivers by enacting a new compassionate leave program (www.hrsdc.gc.ca/en/ei/types/compassionate_care.shtml). Through this program, compassionate care benefits can be paid to people who need to be away from their paid work temporarily to care for or support family members who are dying or gravely ill and very near death. After initial success with the program, the definition of "family members" was extended in 2006. Care or support is broadly defined as psychological or emotional support, arranging for care by a third party, or directly providing or participating in that care.

This benefit is part of the national Employment Insurance (EI) program and available to workers with established eligibility through their employment contributions to this social insurance scheme. A maximum of six weeks of compassionate care benefits is payable within a 26-week period. An employee can share the six weeks of benefits with other family members who also qualify for them. The administrative demands made on applicants appear to be reasonable and kept to a minimum. When requesting compassionate care benefits, the applicant provides a medical certificate as proof that the ill family member needs his or her care or support and is at risk of dying within 26 weeks.

This is a social policy breakthrough that recognizes the demands and stress placed on family members when a close relative is gravely ill with a probable life-ending condition. The outcomes from this new national program will be important in assessing informal family caregiving. They may also provide important data for other approaches to support informal caregivers in future. As Canada faces further significant population aging, forward-thinking social policy like this will be required as further demands are placed on natural caregivers. It is essential that significant, creative forms of government aid be available to buttress the private world of caring.

## PROFESSIONALS AND INFORMAL HELPING SYSTEMS

Clearly, formal and informal services are two different cultures operating on different sets of assumptions, values, rules, and norms. Can these cultures co-exist and collaborate, or are they doomed to remain worlds apart?

Besides the larger policy questions already posed, stronger interplay between these two sectors requires that professionals be prepared to adjust their practice paradigms. Most professionals who want to work with the informal sector are likely to find that their training has not sufficiently emphasized this focus of practice. They are more prepared for and skilled in dealing with the organizational culture of the social welfare system, offering expert forms of help, and serving clients on professional turf. Working with informal helping networks is a much more uncertain and unpredictable form of practice than the planned, methodical work of professional intervention.

What are the implications for a practice that actively seeks to relate to natural helping systems rather than ignore or compete with them? Perhaps the single most important factor is the individual practitioner's mindset. To work with natural helping systems, one has to be able to live with and accept the differences between the two helping cultures and discard the baggage of professional imperialism. Natural helping is spontaneous, based on mutual sharing and unspoken rules of operation. These qualities contrast with an agency's emphasis on planned change, efficiency, effectiveness, accountability and monitoring of costs, and its formal rules and procedures.

Since the late 1980s, "People Helping People" in Tacoma, Washington, has pioneered a new practice model using a partnership team of a professional and a natural helper (Kinney & Trent). Families requiring child protective services from the Washington State Division of Child and Family Services receive an initial visit within 24 hours of referral from a paired team. Following an assessment, a primary mentor or coach—which can be the professional or the natural helper—is assigned to work with the family. In this model the natural helpers are not volunteers, but paid indigenous helpers from the community they serve. They have demonstrated their understanding of the neighbourhood and its needs, are positive role models, have basic skills of helping, and are comfortable working with families in the context of their own neighbourhood.

The experience of People Helping People has demonstrated that natural helpers and professionals each have distinctly different and important strengths to offer in serving families facing serious difficulties. However, the evidence is that both partners have to work hard to understand, respect, and capitalize on each other's differential knowledge, strengths, and approaches to helping. Over time, team members learn that they have much more to offer families in combination than they do separately. The experience and practice wisdom from this Washington child welfare model is a valuable resource for professionals who are interested in developing greater competence in working with natural helpers.

Despite knowledge advances about natural helping systems, there are no standard rules, no finely tuned models to apply. This is practice artistry, not science. It is guided as much by the philosophy of the practitioner as by the techniques of practice. Informal relationships are by their very nature unpredictable and lack formality compared to professional ones. A practitioner must be prepared to deal with uncertainty and fluidity in working with this other culture. It is also true that if a social worker is to collaborate with natural helping networks, then practice will be more in the community than in the office.

Such practice demands sensitivity toward informal helpers. One of the great dangers in attempting to work with a natural, unpolished, spontaneous entity is the urge to change it and make it look like the professional version. A student of mine from the Northwest Territories once said, "The trouble with social workers is that they often try to improve people off the face of the earth!" Part of what he was saying, I think, is that sometimes the art of practice entails accepting something for what it is and letting it work in its own sweet way.

Working with informal helpers can mean just this. Avoiding attempts to co-opt and colonize natural helpers is an important professional objective. This fits well with the fundamental philosophy of social work that aims to empower individuals, groups, and communities to take ownership of their own lives.

Sometimes working collaboratively with clients' natural support systems is easier said than done! Conflicts can emerge quickly. For example, suppose you work with a woman who is the victim of assault by her partner. Your priority must be to ensure her safety from further assaults. Her friends and family may urge her to maintain the relationship, despite its high risk. The challenge to creative practice may be to find some common ground between the two. For example, urging help for the abusive partner, developing a sound safety plan with your client if *she* chooses to reconcile, involving her friends and family in a plan to prevent a further assault, or providing crisis support, if the worst happens.

A number of practitioner roles can be useful in relating to informal helping systems. Acting as a referral agent, broker, and link between networks is significant. One must be able to ask good questions and listen with an open mind to what people say about their support systems and helpers. Giving people clear information about mutual aid and self-help groups is another important asset. Not everyone will find a self-help group helpful or to their liking. However, the risks to the clients of referring them to this source of help are slight, but the potential benefits are considerable (Humphreys).

There are ways that professional education programs can better prepare prospective practitioners for these roles. First, the curriculum must include relevant content about the sociology and ecology of natural helping networks and how to recognize, understand, enhance, and support them. This education could include content on mutual aid, self-help groups, and the diverse roles that natural helping relationships play in supporting people. Informal helping can fill important functions at different levels, from working with an individual client to bringing together groups of people who can support one another (building new support systems), to encouraging neighbourhoods and community leadership to take charge in identifying community issues and ways to respond to them.

Disseminating knowledge about informal helping systems is not enough. Students must be encouraged to interact with and use these resources. An undue emphasis on professional methods in a training program may actually prevent beginning practitioners from reaching out to informal helpers. Professional endorsement and support are important to ensure that action follows knowledge (Davenport & Davenport). Many formal organizations are not set up on the assumption that working with natural helping networks is an appropriate strategy. Practitioners who consider this aspect of social work important must be prepared to negotiate their own paths within agencies to support this co-operation, and challenge prevailing philosophies of practice.

## CONCLUSION

Relatives, friends, and neighbours cannot provide the basic safety net of security against events that produce great individual vulnerability, illness, accident, unemployment, and loss of income. Informal helping cannot replace the public provision and support for basic human needs. Natural support was all that was available to people who needed help in less complicated times. However, by itself, it is inappropriate, unacceptable, and unworkable in our contemporary, complex, capitalist society.

Nevertheless, people helping people continues to be an integral part of everyday life, even in post-industrial societies. Informal helping takes many forms. It is an important first line of defence and antidote for most of us when we face inevitable troubles and catastrophes in our lives. Although a chasm exists between natural and formal systems of help, a challenge is to find ways to bridge that gap to the advantage of both individuals and society.

It is not a question of which is better. They are different and both essential for our well-being (Humphreys).

Informal helping can co-exist with the fabric of formal public social services. The natural concern and involvement of individuals, groups, and communities must be supported as an indispensable part of human caring that cannot be replicated by formal mechanisms. This is an essential ingredient in the health and lives of people, a vital aspect of our social well-being. Our great challenge is to find new ways for formal and informal social support systems to co-exist, collaborate, and support each other in responding to human need.

## References

Abrams, P. (1978). Community care: Some research problems and priorities. In J. Barnes & N. Connelly (Eds.), *Social care research* (pp. 18–99). London: Bedford Square Press.

Adams, R. (1990). *Self-help, social work, and empowerment*. London: Macmillan.

Aronson, J. (1991). Dutiful daughters and undemanding mothers: Contrasting images of giving and receiving care in middle and later life. In C. T. Baines, P. T. Evans, & S. M. Neysmith (Eds.), *Women's caring: Feminist perspectives on social welfare* (pp. 138–168). Toronto: McClelland & Stewart.

Attneave, C. L. (1976). Social networks as the unit of intervention. In P. J. Guerin, Jr. (Ed.), *Family therapy, theory and practice* (pp. 220–231). New York: Gardner Press.

Ayers, T. D. (1989). Dimensions and characteristics of lay helping. *American Journal of Orthopsychiatry, 59,* 215–225.

Baines, C. T., Evans, P. T., & Neysmith, S. M. (Eds.). (1991). *Women's caring: Feminist perspectives on social welfare*. Toronto: McClelland & Stewart.

Banks, E. (Fall 1997). The social capital of self-help groups. *Social Policy, 28,* 30–38.

Borkman, T. (1976). Experiential knowledge: A new concept for the analysis of self-help groups. *Social Service Review, 50,* 445–456.

Borman, L. (1982). Introduction: Helping people to help themselves: Self-help and prevention. *Prevention in Human Services, 1,* 3–15.

Brody, E. M. (1995). Prospects for family caregiving: Response to change, continuity, and diversity. In R. A. Kane & J. D. Penrod (Eds.), *Family caregiving in an aging society: Policy perspectives* (pp. 15–28). Thousand Oaks, CA: Sage.

Brown, B. B. (1978). Social and psychological correlates of help-seeking behavior among urban adults. *American Journal of Community Psychology, 6,* 425–439.

Bullock, A. (1990). Community care: Ideology and lived experience. In R. Ng, G. Walker, & J. Muller (Eds.), *Community organization and the Canadian state* (pp. 65–82). Toronto: Garamond Press.

Cameron, G. (2002). Motivation to join and benefits from participation in parent mutual aid organizations. *Child Welfare, 81.1,* 33–57.

Cameron, G., Hayward, K., & Mamatis, D. (1992). *Mutual aid and child welfare: The parent mutual aid organizations in child welfare demonstration project*. Waterloo, ON: Wilfrid Laurier Press.

Cameron, G., & Vanderwoerd, J. (1997). *Protecting children and supporting families: Promising programs and institutional realities*. New York: Aldine de Gruyter.

Canadian Broadcasting Corporation. (April 29, 1991). *Addicted to addiction.* Transcript of radio program *"Ideas."* Toronto: CBC *Ideas* Transcripts.

Cobb, S. (1976). Social support as a moderator of life stress. *Psychosomatic Medicine, 38,* 300–314.

Cohen, S., & Syme, L. (1985). *Social support and health.* New York: Academic Press.

Cohen, S., & Wills, T. A. (1985). Stress, social support, and the buffering hypothesis. *Psychological Bulletin, 98.2,* 310–357.

Collins, A. H., & Pancoast, D. L. (1976). *Natural helping networks.* Washington, DC: National Association of Social Workers.

Cowan, E. L. (1982). Help is where you find it: Four informal helping groups. *American Psychologist, 37,* 385–395.

Davenport, J., & Davenport III, J. (1982). Utilizing the social network in rural communities. *Social Casework, 63,* 106–113.

Eddy, W., Paap, S., & Glad, D. (1970). Solving problems of living: The citizen's viewpoint. *Mental Hygiene, 54,* 64–72.

Finn, J. (1996). Computer-based self-help groups: Online recovery for addictions. *Computers in Human Services, 13.1,* 21–41.

Finn, J. (1999). An exploration of helping processes in an online self-help group focusing on issues of disability. *Health and Social Work, 24.3,* 220 231.

Froland, C. (1980). Formal and informal care: Discontinuities on a continuum. *Social Service Review, 54,* 572–587.

Froland, C., Pancoast, D. L., Chapman, N., & Kimboko, P. (1981). *Helping networks and human services.* Beverly Hills, CA: Sage Publications.

Gartner, A., & Reissman, F. (1977). *Self-help in the human services.* San Francisco: Jossey-Bass.

Gartner, A., & Reissman, F. (1980). *A working guide to self-help groups.* New York: Franklin Watts.

Germain, C. B., & Gitterman, A. (1987). Ecological perspective. In *Encyclopedia of social work* (pp. 488–499). Silver Spring, MD: National Association of Social Workers.

Gitterman, A., & Shulman, L. (Eds.). (2005). *Mutual aid groups, vulnerable and resistant populations, and the life cycle* (3rd ed.). New York: Columbia University Press.

Gottlieb, B. H. (1980). The role of individual and social support in preventing child maltreatment. In J. Garbarino, H. Stocking and Associates (Eds.), *Protecting children from abuse and neglect* (pp. 37–60). San Francisco: Jossey-Bass.

Gottlieb, B. H. (1981). *Social networks and social support.* Beverly Hills, CA: Sage.

Gottlieb, B. H. (June 1982). Social networks and the gestalt of help-seeking. Keynote address presented at the national conference of the Canadian Counselling and Guidance Association. Victoria, B.C.

Gottlieb, B. H. (1983). *Social support strategies.* Beverly Hills, CA: Sage.

Gourash, N. (1978). Help seeking: A review of the literature. *American Journal of Community Psychology, 6,* 413–425.

Helm, D. (November 13, 1991). Caregivers need recognition, says director of British group. *Victoria Times-Colonist,* p. A7.

Hill, K. (1987). *Helping you helps me: A guide for self-help groups* (H. Balthazar, Rev. & updated). Ottawa: Canadian Council on Social Development.

Hooyman, N. R., & Gonyea, J. G. (1995). *Feminist perspectives on family care: Policies for gender justice.* Thousand Oaks, CA: Sage.

Humphreys, K. (Winter 1998). Can addiction-related self-help/mutual aid groups lower demand for professional substance abuse treatment? *Social Policy, 29.2,* 13–17.

Israel, B. A. (1982). Social networks and health status: Linking theory, research, and practice. *Patient Counselling and Health Education, 4.2,* 65–79.

Kane, R. A., & Penrod, J. D. (Eds.). (1995). *Family caregiving in an aging society: Policy perspectives.* Thousand Oaks, CA: Sage.

Katz, A. H. (2003). Self-help and mutual aid groups as factors in prevention. *International Journal of Self-Help and Self-Care, 2 (1),* 5–20.

Katz, A. H., & Bender, E. I. (Eds.). (1976). *The strength in us.* New York: Franklin Watts.

Kessler, R., et al. (1994). *Midlife development inventory (MIDI).* Chicago: John D. and Catherine T. MacArthur Foundation.

Kinney, J., & Trent, M. (2003). Walking our talk in the neighborhoods: Building professional/natural helper partnerships. *Family Preservation Journal, 7(7),* 57–77.

Kramer, R. (1981). *Voluntary agencies in the welfare state.* Berkeley: University of California Press.

Kropotkin, P. (1955). *Mutual aid: A factor of evolution.* Boston: Extending Horizons Books.

Kurtz, L. F. (1997). *Self-help and support groups: A handbook for practitioners.* Thousand Oaks, CA: Sage.

Lauffer, A. (1978). Natural and "extra-professional" helping systems. In A. Lauffer (Ed.), *Social planning at the community level* (pp. 241–258). Englewood Cliffs, NJ: Prentice-Hall.

Litwak, E. (1978). Organizational constructs and mega bureaucracy. In R. Sarri & Y. Hasenfeld (Eds.), *The management of human services* (pp. 123–162). New York: Columbia University Press.

MacPherson, I. (1987). Antigonish movement. In *Canadian encyclopedia.* (2nd ed., p. 84). Edmonton: Hurtig Publishers.

Madara, E. J. (Spring 1997). Computer-mediated communication: Internet self-help groups. *Social Policy, 27,* 20–26.

Maguire, L. (1983). *Understanding social networks.* Beverly Hills, CA: Sage Publications.

Mitchell, J. C. (1969). The concept and use of social networks. In J. C. Mitchell (Ed.), *Social networks in urban situations* (pp. 1–50). Manchester: University of Manchester Press.

Montgomery, R. J. V. (1995). Examining respite care. In R. A. Kane & J. D. Penrod (Eds.), *Family caregiving in an aging society: Policy perspectives* (pp. 29–45). Thousand Oaks, CA: Sage.

Powell, T. J. (Ed.). (1990). *Working with self-help.* Silver Spring, MD: NASW Press.

Reissman, F. (1965). The "helper" therapy principle. *Social Work, 10,* 27–32.

Reissman, F. (1977). The helper-therapy principle. In A. Gartner & F. Reissman (Eds.) *Self-help in the human services* (pp. 99–103). San Francisco: Jossey-Bass.

Reissman, F. (1982). The self-help ethos. *Social Policy, 13,* 42–43.

Romeder, J. (1990). *The self-help way: Mutual aid and health*. Ottawa: Canadian Council on Social Development.

Segal, L. (1987). *Is the future female? Troubled thoughts on contemporary feminism*. London: Virago Press.

Silverman, P. R. (1987). Mutual help groups. In *Encyclopedia of social work* (pp. 171–176). Silver Spring, MD: National Association of Social Workers.

Turner, J. T., Kimbrough, W. W., & Traynhan, R. N. (1977). A survey of community perceptions of critical life situations and community helping sources as a tool for mental health development. *Journal of Community Psychology, 5,* 225–230.

Veroff, J., Douvan, E., & Kulka, R. A. (1981). *The inner American: A self-portrait*. New York: Basic Books.

Whittaker, J. K., & Garbarino, J. (Eds.). (1983). *Social support networks: Informal helping in the human services*. Hawthorne, NY: Aldine Publishing Co.

Wuthnow, R. (1994). *Sharing the journey: Support groups and America's new quest for community*. New York: Basic Books.

# CHAPTER 27

# Regulation: Challenges and Opportunities for the Social Work Profession in Canada

*Dan Andreae*

## INTRODUCTION

Regulation marks an evolutionary step in the ongoing development of a profession in which a governmental legislative body sanctions a code of conduct in law for that group. According to Allison Mac-Donald and Rod Adachi in *Regulation of Social Work Practice in Canada*, "When a government makes a decision to impose regulation on the practice of a profession, it does so in recognition of the fact that practitioners regulated are providing a service that may involve some risk to the public."[1] A group of trained and competent university-educated individuals may possess a body of knowledge, scope of practice, and specialized skills, but until the state legally sanctions a profession in statutory legislation they are practising without being members of a recognized and defined profession.

The achievement of regulatory legislation enhances credibility and confers upon a profession and its members accountability to their peers for their delivery of services. And more importantly, the members demonstrate their commitment and obligation to the public at large for whom regulations are crafted. Indeed, the vast majority of social workers are highly trained and university educated, holding either a Bachelor (BSW), Master (MSW), or Doctoral (PhD/DSW) degree. According to the Canadian Association of Social Workers' (CASW) *Scope of Practice Statement* published in March 2000, "In Canada, the profession of social work constitutes a community of post-secondary educated social workers. They are guided in their work by international ethical principles; a national code of ethics; provincial statutes governing registration, regulations and standards of practice; common curriculum requirements in schools of social work; and an expanding repertoire of evidence-based methods of practice."[2] Many have received further specialized training in areas such as child welfare, mediation, crisis management, various methodologies of short-term and long-term therapy, gerontology, or hospital-trained social work. They keep abreast of emerging developments through participation in continuing education programs including conferences, seminars, and workshops.

Yet, as within any professional group, there are occasionally breaches of professional conduct by those who abuse their power and privilege and thus need to be held to account. Regulation of a profession can provide the legally sanctioned structures, means, and processes that allow clients to redress any indiscretions or complaints in a formally recognized manner. This process is of benefit to any client, but especially to those who may lack the means or access to funds or expertise to engage in court challenges that can be costly, time-consuming, and a potential invasion of privacy. Regulation recognizes for the public who can and cannot call him- or herself a social worker and allows clients to realize that they are entitled to a certain level of service and that the practitioner is accountable to a legal body

---

1 MacDonald, A. & Adachi, R. (2001). "Regulation of Social Work Practice in Canada," Canadian Association of Social Workers, Social Work Summit, p. 7.

2 Canadian Association of Social Workers. (2000). *CASW National Scope of Practice Statement*, p. 2.

(i.e., a college), that is empowered to carry out actions. Using the Ontario College of Social Workers and Social Service Workers' (OCSWSSW) mission statement as a template, the following are key activities, which encompass the scope for regulatory frameworks:

- Establishing and enforcing professional and ethical standards;
- Regulating the practice of social work and the practice of social service work and governing its members;
- Developing, establishing, and maintaining qualifications for membership in the College;
- Approving ongoing education programs for the purpose of continuing education for members of the College;
- Providing for the ongoing education of members of the College;
- Issuing certificates of registration to members of the College as well as renews, amends, suspends, cancels, revokes, and reinstatements;
- Receiving and investigating complaints against members of the College and dealing with the issues of discipline, professional misconduct, incompetence, and incapacity; and
- Promoting high standards and quality assurance with respect to the social work and social service work and communicating with the public on behalf of the members.[3]

## CONFLICTING VIEWS RELATED TO SOCIAL WORK PRACTICE AND THE NEED FOR PROFESSIONAL REGULATION

It has been raised by opponents to social work regulation that, at best, it may be appropriate for those in the field working directly with clients in a clinically oriented setting, but is not necessary or relevant for those engaged in macro or systemic social work in areas such as community development, policy, education, or administration. This situation is made more complex by the fact that social work is, in some respects, such a broad-based profession that it is considered problematic by some to define the glue that binds these diverse sectors together. Indeed, the scope of practice is more easily defined in a profession such as nursing or medicine where there are actual physical interventions (i.e., administration of a needle), that are amenable to exacting rigorous measurements and standards of practice. Social workers are employed in a plethora of settings including mental health clinics, counselling agencies, hospitals, not-for-profit organizations, Children's Aid societies, seniors' centres, non-profit housing, government and academic institutions, industry think-tanks such as the Caledon Institute, and private practice. They are involved in such diverse issues as poverty, homelessness, environmental issues, custody and access, and competency assessment. They work with individuals and groups through every phase of lifespan development, utilizing a biopsychosocial approach to understanding contextual human behaviour. According to the Canadian Association of Social Workers, social workers employ a diverse range of methodologies while working in a variety of settings, which exacerbates the task of arriving at national consensus around practice and regulatory issues. Table 27.1 shows a partial list.[4]

---

3   Ontario College of Social Workers and Social Service Workers. (2003). *Annual Report 2003*, p. 2.

4   Canadian Association of Social Workers. (2000). *CASW National Scope of Practice Statement*, p. 4.

| TABLE 27.1 | Examples of Employment Tasks, Methodologies, and Settings | |
|---|---|---|
| Case management | Psychosocial therapy | Community resource co-ordination |
| Child protection assessments | Psychotherapy | Developmental social welfare |
| Client-centred therapy | Psychotherapy | Grassroots mobilization/locality development |
| Clinical social work | Social casework | |
| Crisis management | Social group work | Program evaluation |
| Discharge planning | Client advocacy | Neighbourhood and community organizing |
| Family and marital therapy | Network facilitation | |
| Family mediation | Network skills training | Political and social action |
| Group therapy | Structural social work | Social planning |
| | Class action social work | Social policy analysis and development |
| | | Structural change |

Social workers recognize the importance of the synergy of micro stresses and macro presses on behavioural and systemic functioning. Uniquely among professions, social workers practise what Dr. Frank Turner has termed the "person in situation." According to the Canadian Association of Social Workers (CASW), its national scope of practice statement states: "The person-in-environment domain gives social work a common organizing framework and a holistic context for its mission and vision. The global vision of social work is a world consistently working toward social justice and well-being for all citizens. The central mission is to have social workers engaged in activities that will improve social well-being structures and enhance individual, family and community social functioning at local, national, and international levels."[5] This reality forms one of the bedrocks of social work theory and intervention that encompasses all facets of professional practice regardless of specialization or focus. This binds the profession together at its core and helps and assists in fostering a sense of professional cohesion and identity.

Others have objected to the concept of regulation because it is seen as supporting an elitist philosophy. According to Globerman, "Carniol and Kitchen elucidate the arguments against legislation. They suggest that the profession is motivated by a desire for greater power and privilege." However, Turner counters this argument by stating that regulation is motivated by an interest in the public welfare, particularly "guaranteeing adequate protection for the public."[6]

Yet statutory regulation can also provide secondary benefits to the social work profession, one of whose key tenets is to advocate for social change to benefit clients at all levels, especially the most vulnerable. How can regulation potentially assist toward its objective? The fact is that to be included in key pieces of government-sponsored legislation, a profession often has to be regulated by an appropriate government ministry. Although an unregulated profession *might be included or added* to

---

**5**   Canadian Association of Social Workers. (2000). *CASW National Scope of Practice Statement*, Appendix 1.

**6**   Cited in Globerman, J. "Regulating Social Work, Illuminating Motives," in *Canadian Social Work Review*, Volume 9, Number 2 (Summer 1992), p. 230.

a list of professions authorized to provide specific services or to engage in particular tasks, *not being included or added* could be problematic. For example, in the province of Ontario, social workers are often responsible for carrying out capacity assessments that determine who is *compos mentis* and thus capable of making rational decisions. However, social work was originally excluded from a list of professions empowered to conduct these assessments and was added only because of a concerted effort by the profession to educate government about the role of social work and the fact that the provincial government was seriously contemplating professional regulation for social workers at the time.

In terms of the role of the social worker in hospital settings, it might be tempting for a physician as the leader of a multidisciplinary team to delegate certain tasks and functions to regulated professional colleagues. Therefore, he or she might refer the patient to a psychologist for counselling and to a nurse for discharge planning, thus circumventing the social worker and depriving the patient of a potentially valuable social work approach. As hospitals increasingly move to models of program management as opposed to individual departments (medicine, nursing, occupational therapy, social work), it becomes increasingly problematic for a profession not to be a regulated body. Individual departments are being phased out or closed down and programs are being staffed by allied multidisciplinary professionals. Additionally, when interacting with regulated colleagues it is advantageous to be on a level playing field not only in terms of self-respect and recognition of professional training, but also because of increased professional accredibility accorded to those professions under government legislation. According to Barbara Chisholm, renowned child advocate and expert witness, being regulated greatly enhances the legitimacy of testimony before a judge. This, of course, will not change what the professional social worker may say or recount in, for example, child custody cases. However, it cannot be denied that perception becomes reality and a recognized profession is more likely to be treated as such. This arguably may not be fair or just but it is a reality that should be acknowledged, and being legally accountable to peers and the public through a statutorily based body lends credence to a social worker's assessment. Indeed, Chisholm argues that regulation represents a natural evolutionary step in the maturing of a profession.

## CRITERIA FOR SOCIAL WORK REGULATION

In Canada, the form and scope of regulation differs from province to province as regulation falls under the jurisdiction of the provincial government. However, regardless of the structure, McCorquodale outlines key criteria that are shared by regulated professions. These include

1. A governing body with representatives of the public as well as the profession.
2. Registration that identifies the standards and procedures for evaluating applicants.
3. A complaint review process wherein structure and procedures are identified and by which complaints may be received and investigated and a review conducted.
4. Discipline wherein a hearing of the complaint can be conducted. This stage of the complaint review process requires a more formal structure, legal representation of the parties, examination and cross-examination, and witnesses and expert witnesses.
5. Appeal process wherein decisions of the regulatory body may be appealed. The form of the

appeal process is dependent upon the legislation of the provincial setting of the regulatory body. There may be appeal procedures for each of the regulatory decisions.

6. "Continuing competency" is the element requiring professionals to maintain their professional knowledge and skills, and to meet specified standards for maintaining the relevance of their professional knowledge.

7. "Standards" is the responsibility to develop and publish standards, and the provision of consultation with regard to the interpretation of those standards.[7]

McCorquodale provides Table 27.2 that outlines an analysis of social work legislation throughout the country. Ontario is regulated under the *Social Work and Social Service Work Act, Bill 76*, 1998, Ministry of Community and Social Services.

As McCorquodale points out, the goal of professional regulation is to advance the public interest and not the interests of the profession, although there may be secondary benefits thus derived. She points out, "Regulation is aimed at advancing the public interest in four ways: (1) protecting the public to the extent possible from unqualified, incompetent and unfit social workers; (2) developing mechanisms to encourage the provision of high quality social work services; (3) permitting the public to exercise freedom of choice of a social work service provider within a range of self options; (4) promoting evolution in the roles played by individual professionals and flexibility in how individual professionals can be utilized so that social work services are delivered with maximum efficiency."[8] The government in each provincial jurisdiction has the purview of deciding whom to regulate and which ministry or system provides for the most appropriate mechanisms of professional accountability given already existing structures and the culture of a particular jurisdiction. In Ontario, for example, the provincial government in 1998 chose the Ministry of Community and Social Services, thus making social work the first profession to be regulated under this particular ministry. The government chose this particular ministry as opposed to the Ministry of Health which oversees the *Regulated Health Professions Act* (RHPA), which provides a framework for self-regulation of 23 health professions. According to Robert England of the law firm Miller Thompson

> The statutory model employed for the regulated health professions is predicated upon all the regulated health professions being subject to two separate statutes: the RHPA and the individual statute that governs each such profession. The policy objectives sought to be achieved by this statutory regime include, in the public interest, definition of those potentially hazardous or [intrusive] acts performed by health care professionals, and the allocation amongst health care professions of the authority to perform such acts. Thus, the RHPA defines 'controlled acts' and prohibits the performance of such acts save by those authorized to perform the controlled act.[9]

---

7  Samuels, M. and Tanner, E. (2003). *Managing a Legal and Ethical Social Work Practice,* p. 20.

8  McCorquodale, S. (1999). "The Role of Regulators in Practice," in Turner, F. J., *Social Work Practice: A Canadian Perspective.*

9  Correspondence written to the Ontario Association of Social Workers from Robert W. England from Miller Thompson Barristers and Solicitors, November 1998.

| TABLE 27.2 | Analysis of Social Work Legislation throughout the Country[10] | | | | | | |
|---|---|---|---|---|---|---|---|
| Province | Title of Act | Year | Jurisdiction | Title Protection | Licensing | Scope of Practice | Academic Requirement |
| Newfoundland/ Labrador | *An Act Respecting the Newfound-land and Labrador Association of Social Workers, Chapter S-18.1* | 1993 | Department of Social Services | ✓ | ✓ | X | ✓ |
| Prince Edward Island | *Bill # 55 – Social Work Act, 1988* | 1988 | Health and Social Services | ✓ | ✓ | ✓ | ✓ |
| Nova Scotia | *An Act to Regulate the Practice of Social Work, Chapter 12* | 1993 | None | ✓ | ✓ | ✓ | ✓ |
| New Brunswick | *An Act to Incorporate the New Brunswick Associations of Social Workers, 1988, Chapter 78* | 1988 | None | ✓ | ✓ | ✓ | ✓ |
| Quebec | *The Professional Code Revised Regulations of Québec, 1981, C.26 r.1 – C.60 r.12* | 1994 | Offices des Professions du Québec | ✓ | X | ✓ | ✓ |
| Manitoba | *An Act to Incorporate the Manitoba Institute of Registered Social Workers, Chapter 104, 1966, Statutes of Manitoba, 1966* | 1966 | Ministry of Family Services | ✓ | X | X | ✓ |
| Saskatchewan | *An Act Respecting Social Workers, Chapter S-52.1, 1993* | 1993 | Social Services | ✓ | X | X | ✓ |
| Alberta | *Social Work Profession Act, Ch. S-16.5, 1991* | 1991 | Labour | ✓ | X | X | ✓ |
| British Columbia | *The Social Workers Act, R.S.B.C. 1979, c.389, Revised Statutes of B.C. 1996* | First enacted 1968 | Ministry of Children and Families | ✓ | X | X | ✓ |

*Source:* McCorquodale, S. (1999). "The Role of Regulators in Practice," in Turner, F. J., *Social Work Practice: A Canadian Perspective, p. 466.* Legislation may have changed since original publication. Reprinted with kind permission from Pearson Education Canada.

---

**10** Data from original 1999 source has been updated as of 2007.

As social work does not practise "controlled acts" in the manner of certain health professions, and given the fact that social work is a broadly based profession with an expertise in the psychosocial functioning of individuals, the government decided that the Ministry of Community and Social Services was more appropriate. Thus, social work regulation became a template for other social service-based professions should the government decide to expand the scope of public protection into other domains by setting up similar incorporated bodies such as the OCSWSSW. As a result of legislation enacted by the Ontario government in June 2007 (*Bill 171*), the profession of social work is now linked for the first time to the Ministry of Health through an amendment, which allows for social workers to practise psychotherapy along with the allied professions of medicine, psychology, nursing, and occupational therapy. The Ontario government is planning to implement a College of Psychotherapy which will set standards and criteria for membership within the next three years.

# DIFFERENCES BETWEEN AN ASSOCIATION AND REGULATORY BODY—THE ONTARIO EXAMPLE

It is important for the public to recognize the separateness of the college from the professional association. Table 27.3 delineates separate responsibilities as well as some overlapping spheres utilizing the model as it exists in Ontario.

The traditional professional model in Ontario has been to separate the profession from the regulatory body (i.e., college), which is responsible for protecting the public. Other provinces, such as Alberta, have a different system whereby the college and the association are combined into one body.

| **TABLE 27.3** | **Distinct Mandates of Professional Membership Association (OASW) and Regulatory College[11]** | |
|---|---|---|
| | **OASW** | **REGULATORY COLLEGE** |
| Mandate | To advocate for the interests and concerns of professional social workers and to contribute to social justice | To protect the public |
| How mandate is fulfilled | 1. Advocating for social and professional issues<br>2. Promoting the social work profession<br>3. Providing a wide range of tangible and intangible membership services | 1. Setting professional standards<br>2. Registering individuals who meet its requirements<br>3. Investigating complaints<br>4. Disciplining members for failing to comply with standards |
| Areas of overlapping mandates | Promote professional social work code of ethics<br>Develop guidelines of professional practice as resource to members | Promote professional social work code of ethics<br>Develop standards of professional practice |

11 Produced by the Ontario Association of Social Workers (December 1998). Reproduced with kind permission.

# MANDATE OF A REGULATORY BODY

Should a client wish to lodge a complaint against a social work practitioner for professional misconduct, or one practitioner against a colleague, there are appropriate channels and processes to follow in relation to the regulatory body. These involve specific committees, including a Complaints Committee. According to the OCSWSSW, the mandate of the Complaints Committee states that "the College is required to have a formal complaints process, which gives anyone (clients, colleagues, other regulated professionals, etc.) the ability to have their complaint about a College member's conduct or actions submitted to the College's Complaints Committee. This complaints process is designed to identify and address concerns about professional misconduct, incompetence, or incapacity of College members. The process is also designed to ensure fairness to both the individual making the complaint and the member who is the subject of the complaint."[12] According to the Ministry of Community and Social Services, "in response to a written complaint relating to professional misconduct, competence, or incapacity, the Complaints Committee would take one of the following courses or action:

- Dismiss the complaint;
- Determine that the matter be referred to the Discipline Committee or the Fitness of Practice Committee;
- Caution the member;
- Refer the matter for alternate dispute resolution; or
- Take other action considered appropriate.[13]

Another key committee is the Discipline Committee whose mandate includes "to hear and determine allegations of professional misconduct or incompetence on the part of the member of the College directed or referred to it by the Complaints Committee, the Council, or the Executive Committee; and perform any other duties assigned to it by the Council. Hearings of the Discipline Committee are usually open to the public."[14]

According to the Ministry of Community and Social Services, after hearing a matter, the Discipline Committee could

- Dismiss the complaint;
- Revoke a certificate;
- Suspend a certificate;
- Impose terms, conditions, or limitations on a certificate; or
- Postpone a penalty in certain circumstances.

In the case of professional misconduct, the Discipline Committee could, in addition,

- Reprimand, admonish, or counsel the member;
- Impose a fine on the member payable to the Minister of Finance;

---

12 Ontario College of Social Workers and Social Service Workers, *Annual Report 2003*, p. 5.

13 Compendium. *Social Work and Social Service Work Act*, 1998, p. 4.

14 Ontario College of Social Workers and Social Service Workers, *Annual Report 2003*, p. 6.

- Direct that the finding be published in the official publication of the College; or
- Fix costs to be paid by the member.

It also states that "a member could appeal a decision of either the Discipline Committee or the Fitness to Practise Committee to Divisional Court. The filing of an appeal would not stay an order of the committee."[15]

The Fitness to Practise Committee has a mandate "to hear and determine allegations of incapacity on the part of a College member and to perform other duties as assigned by Council. Hearings of this committee are usually closed to the public due to their confidential nature."[16]

According to McCorquodale, "social workers are asked to articulate reasons for the judgments they have made through demonstrating (1) adherence to professional standards; (2) the ability to form judgments that adhere to those standards; and (3) the ability to defend the rationale for these judgments."[17]

Following are examples of situations in which actions or non-actions of social work services could result in negative consequences to clients:

1. Making an error in judgment by leaving an infant in, or returning an infant to, a situation where abuse, either sexual or physical, might occur, leading to serious injury or death.

2. Placing a child in a foster home with persons unsuitable to be foster parents, resulting in serious, long-term adjustment difficulties for the child.

3. Making an incorrect assessment of an adoptive home that leads to an adoption breakdown with permanent personality scars for the child involved.

4. Misdiagnosing the seriousness of an adolescent's depression, which could lead to suicide.

5. Misdiagnosing the intensity of a young adult's suppressed rage, which could lead to lethal acts.

6. Misdiagnosing a person's readiness for probation, which could lead to further antisocial and possibly injurious behaviour to self and others.

7. Under-evaluating the potential of further assault by a violence-prone partner in supporting a person's decision to remain in a highly dangerous domestic situation.

8. Failing to recognize the intensity of a person's highly controlled crisis response to a situation of high stress that results in the failure to provide the needed intervention.

9. Failing to diagnose adequately the operative factors in a family system that are causing serious family disruption and possibly leading to a situation of total disintegration of a family that could have been helped.

10. Inadequately assessing a home, leading to a decision to leave a highly dysfunctional person in a situation where he or she is at grave risk to himself or herself and others.

---

**15** Compendium. *Social Work and Social Service Work Act*, 1998, pp. 4–5.

**16** Ontario College of Social Workers and Social Service Workers, *Annual Report 2003*, p. 7.

**17** McCorquodale, S. (1999). "The Role of Regulators in Practice," in Turner, F. J., *Social Work Practice: A Canadian Perspective*, p. 472.

11. Employing a particular treatment modality where it is inappropriate to do so, causing further trauma to the client.

12. Further traumatizing a client by violating boundaries and breaching fiduciary duty such as in the case of breach of confidentiality or sexual abuse.[18]

The *Social Work and Social Service Work Act* incorporates the college as a legal entity and establishes a council to oversee its operations. An Executive Committee of the college is responsible for approving the strategic plan, striking additional task groups to assist in accomplishing the strategic priorities identified in the plan, and monitoring their progress against projected timelines. The composition of the governing council consists of 21 persons with equal representation from social workers, social service workers, and members of the public appointed by the government. There are seven representatives from each sector comprising a council of 21 members. As the profession has been conferred the status of self-regulation, it was considered important by the government to include significant public representation in order to provide an additional perspective, thus potentially augmenting professional accountability. The public members are appointed for a set term of office. These public appointees may enter into this position without knowledge of social work practice or legislation, but learn these specifics once they assume their duties.

A key feature of the legislation is to identify who can and who cannot call himself or herself a social worker. A social worker in Ontario must be a graduate from an accredited social work program and hold a Bachelor (BSW), Master (MSW), or Doctoral (PhD/DSW) degree in social work in order to qualify for membership. They receive the designation of RSW (registered social worker). Also included in the legislation are persons who possess a community college diploma from an accredited educational institution (usually a two-year program) and hold the designation RSSW (registered social service worker). The regulation allows for title protection and does not include other groups with similar educational backgrounds such as development service workers. Other provinces are structured differently and may allow both social workers and social service workers to hold the designation of social work. There has been considerable discussion and debate across Canada as to who should be included in any legislation, proposed act, or changes in existing acts, and the differences often focus on the level of educational depth, perspective, and complexity. There are those who believe that an education at the university level is more theoretically based than at community college and builds upon the community college applied focus. Indeed, several universities now offer what are termed "articulation agreements," whereby a community college graduate can achieve a certain number of credits toward a Bachelor of Social Work degree. Others argue that some community college graduates, for example, have completed clinical placements which a BSW graduate may never have experienced, especially if he or she focuses on specialization in policy and is not exposed to clinical training. However, there is general consensus that there are discernible differences in the comprehensiveness and rigour of methodology between community college- and university-based programs.

---

18 McCorquodale, S. (1999). "The Role of Regulators in Practice," in Turner, F. J., *Social Work Practice: A Canadian Perspective*, pp. 472–473.

## TYPES OF REGULATION

According to MacDonald and Adachi, "Within the Canadian federal system, regulation of the professions is a provincial matter. In each province, that authority has been further delegated to a regulatory board with specific statutory provisions and regulations. The oldest social work legislation still in use is the *Act to Incorporate the Manitoba Institute of Registered Social Workers*, Statutes of Manitoba, 1966. Most other jurisdictions have legislation proclaimed sometime in the 1990s."[19]

According to their research, greater numbers of discrepancies than commonalities exist among the ten provincial statutes, each province enacting legislation within different timeframes, according to different agendas and provincial pressures. As a result, reaching common national consensus on such matters as a code of ethics, promotion of the profession, or the Agreement on Internal Trade has proved to be challenging. Drawing on the work of Graeme Roderick in *The Social Worker*, 1990,[20] they outline different interpretations applied to the term "regulation," a term utilized across the country for regulated practice. This includes regulation, which is simply a listing of all individuals who have met a set of criteria within a registration framework. This person may or may not hold a social work degree, hold a position within the scope of social work practice, or use the term "social worker" without holding a certificate of registration. Although no province in Canada reflects a pure registration approach, Manitoba and Quebec most closely adhere to this model.

The next type of regulation that Roderick classes is "certification."[21] This is based on a model defining eligibility which indicates that the practitioner has achieved a specific level of competence (e.g., attainment of specific knowledge and professional skills). Legislation in Nova Scotia and British Columbia incorporate components of a certification model.

Finally, the last model includes "licensure." This extends beyond the concept of eligibility into the sphere of public accountability. A licensed practitioner is granted permission and authority to work with the public, and that privilege may be revoked by the licensing body if standards are not maintained or adhered to. Such a jurisdiction practising a form of licensing will probably have mandatory regulation of practice based on a widely defined scope of practice. This model encompasses the largest number of practitioners and holds them accountable within a system that is transparent to the public. According to Roderick, the province most closely linked to this approach is Alberta.[22] All of these models strive to protect the public to various degrees, but licensure represents a stronger approach than simple "credentialism," which accomplishes the goal of offering credentials to members.

## SCOPE OF PRACTICE

The issue of scope of practice has been problematic in Canada due in part to the broad and complex range of social work interventions. According to MacDonald and Adachi, the province of Nova Scotia has attempted to define a scope of practice in its *Social Work Act,*

---

19 MacDonald, A. & Adachi, R. (2001)."Regulation of Social Work Practice in Canada," Canadian Association of Social Workers, Social Work Summit, p. 1.

20 Ibid.

21 Ibid., p. 2.

22 Ibid.

which states that "social work practice requires the application of specialized knowledge, values, and skills within the field of social work."[23] However, there is not national consensus for an agreed upon definition of scope of practice. Nova Scotia's approach to define criteria for a scope of practice has resulted in further examination of the values, knowledge, and skills paramount to an accredited social work education program. MacDonald and Adachi continue by noting that the registrars of regulatory bodies in Canada have indicated that a national consensus on this definition is required, especially as the profession in Canada will be affected by discussions around issues such as the Agreement on Internal Trade.

According to MacDonald and Adachi, a trend gaining favour in North America is legislation that protects both a title and scope of practice without granting any profession an exclusive scope of practice. Within this model, if a practitioner qualifies for registration within a profession and works within the scope of practice of that profession, the person will still be required to be registered regardless of title. Practitioners are prevented from using the professional title if they do not qualify for registration but may be able to practise, nonetheless, implementing some of the tasks within the scope of the profession. According to this approach, restrictions are instituted on specific procedures that require a high level of specialization and are considered to be a high risk to the public.[24]

As previously mentioned, the act in Ontario does not offer a scope of practice provision that delineates certain acts to be the exclusive or shared domain of social work. In other words, it does not restrict practice and, therefore, should not be confused with licensing, which it is not. In addition, the act does not differentiate between university and community college functions. Indeed, it has been argued that one potential deficiency of the act is that individuals who do not wish, for whatever reason, to be accountable to the regulatory body may opt out and call themselves another title, such as psychotherapist or addictions counsellor. Indeed, at the time of introduction it was considered politically problematic and challenging to introduce the restriction of acts, such as counselling, which would involve an overlapping plethora of professions from social work to nursing to lay counsellors to the clergy. Yet the act does restrict the use of title and offers clients and potential clients the assurance that the social worker is accountable to the regulatory body and practises according to a code of ethics. The government has included a built-in review process of the act which took place in 2005, at which time the effectiveness of the legislation was evaluated.

## CONCLUSION

The evolution toward social work statutory regulation has progressed significantly in Canada over the past decade, yet many challenges remain. Primary among these is the need to develop a national consensus around key definitions such as the development of an acceptable scope of practice. This is important as federal initiatives, such as the Agreement on Internal Trade, require a homogeneous front for social work to benefit from its implementation. If the various regulatory bodies across Canada are not able to reach a

---

23 Ibid., p. 3

24 Ibid.

national agreement around complex regulatory and practice issues, then it is ultimately the clients served who will be placed in jeopardy around issues of service delivery.

It is important to note that self-regulation of social work, although representing an advance in professional maturity and accountability, does not solve all problems but simply closes one important door. It would be faulty to interpret regulation as an end unto itself and the answer to the profession's problems. According to McCorquodale, it does provide public protection in two main aspects: "(1) compensating for the client's lack of knowledge about the services they are receiving; and (2) providing equitable treatment by obliging all members of the profession to meet common standards."[25] Indeed, the achievement of regulation can potentially assist in the future quest for additional legislation benefiting clients but, in and of itself, will not resolve longstanding societal problems which have long been the purview of the social work profession: the battle for justice, equality, fairness, and tolerance in society. It has not resulted in improved salaries or compensation for social workers, and this is not the goal of regulation. It has heightened the profile of the profession among the public by showcasing the valuable work that social workers do to improve the quality of life and the social fabric of the community. In the quest for legislation in Ontario, a public opinion poll commissioned by the Ontario Association of Social Workers indicated that the vast majority of Ontarians believed that social work was already regulated and were surprised to learn that no such regulation yet existed at that time. Models of regulation are constantly being developed and refined and this represents an ongoing process that will continue into the future. Social workers must remain vigilant not to allow regulatory status in whatever form to create or exacerbate gaps between values and practice. Indeed, regulations should strengthen the bond between ethical practice and the pursuit of a more equitable society.

# References

Canadian Association of Social Workers. (2000). CASW National Scope of Practice Statement. Available at http://www/casw-acts.ca/practice/recpubsart1.htm (accessed 12 July 2007).

Compendium. *Social Work and Social Service Work Act*, 1998.

Conversation with Barbara Chisholm, 1992.

Conversation with Dr. Frank Turner, 1998.

Globerman, J. *"Regulating Social Work, Illuminating Motives,"* in *Canadian Social Work Review*, Volume 9, Number 2 (Summer 1992).

MacDonald, A. & Adachi, R. *Regulation of Social Work Practice in Canada*. Available at http://www.casw-acts.ca/SW-Forum/CdnSWForum-Regulation.htm (accessed 12 July 2007).

McCorquodale, S. (1999). *"The Role of Regulators in Practice,"* in Turner, F. J., *Social Work Practice: A Canadian Perspective*, Prentice Hall Allyn and Bacon Canada, Scarborough, ON.

Miller Thompson Barristers and Solicitors. (1998). *Correspondence written to the Ontario Association of Social Workers* from Robert W. England, Toronto, ON.

---

25 McCorquodale, S. (1999). "The Role of Regulators in Practice," in Turner, F. J., *Social Work Practice: A Canadian Perspective*, p. 463

Ontario Association of Social Workers. (1998). *Distinct Mandates of Professional Membership Association and Regulatory College*, Toronto, ON.

Ontario College of Social Workers and Social Service Workers. (2003). *Annual Report 2003*. Toronto, ON.

Ontario College of Social Workers and Social Service Workers. (2003). General information. Available at http://www.ocswssw.org/sections/about_ocsw/generalinfo.html (accessed 12 July 2007).

Samuels, M. & Tanner, E. (2003). *Managing a Legal and Ethical Social Work Practice.* Irwin Law Inc., Toronto, ON.

# CHAPTER 28

# Evaluation as Control

*Grant Macdonald*

## INTRODUCTION

Social welfare in Canada is entering a new era of accountability, in which everyone, including politicians, planners, program managers, and front-line social workers, is being held accountable and responsible for his or her actions. The public is asking whether a reasonable return on its investment of monies spent on social welfare programs is being achieved. Also, fundamental questions are being asked: *Are those who need these programs the ones actually using them? Are they run efficiently?* Perhaps most important, *do the programs achieve their intended objectives and, if not, how can they be improved? Are programs having unanticipated negative impacts?* These kinds of critical questions about the value of our social programs are addressed through the process of evaluation.

Simply stated, *evaluation* in social welfare can be defined as the process by which services and programs are examined to determine whether they are needed and used, how well they are run, whether they meet their stated objectives, and whether they are worth the costs. Evaluations serve a variety of target audiences, each with its own stake in the service or program being examined. Some of these stakeholders include governments at all levels, actual and potential funders, the general public, the media, policy-makers, planners, academics, professional program staff, and, of course, clients. Each target audience has different information needs and its own reasons for wanting evidence of effective and efficient service delivery. No single evaluation could possibly serve the needs of all these constituencies.

## SERVICE–OUTCOME EFFICIENCY

We can examine the elements and context of evaluation using a schematic overview of social welfare activities. Figure 28.1 illustrates the RSO cycle (Resources–Services–Outcomes), or the key elements in the development and delivery of social welfare programs. While social welfare programs are often talked about as important in enriching a society's or a community's quality of life, or that of a specific subgroup of individuals, in reality, most if not all programs evolve from a general perception of a "social problem" and a belief that something should be done to either alleviate or prevent the problem. Unemployment insurance was developed as a response to the plight of unemployed individuals and the problems their families experienced. Addiction treatment programs have been established across Canada and have grown out of a concern for the millions of dollars lost to business and industry through alcohol and drug abuse. Of course, these programs arise as well from the untold misery of the families of those addicted. Similarly, Children's Aid Societies developed to protect children at risk, programs for unwed mothers are intended to help resolve their problems and support them, and specialized programs are planned to help new immigrants adjust to Canadian society.

Social welfare programs and services evolve from a collective sense that there is a social problem that must be dealt with. Figure 28.1 illustrates that, in response to this perception of a social problem, funds collected either through our tax system or through voluntary donations are dedicated toward social programs designed to deal with those perceived problems. These financial "resources" are

| FIGURE 28.1 | Schematic Overview of Evaluation Activities in Relation to Human Services |

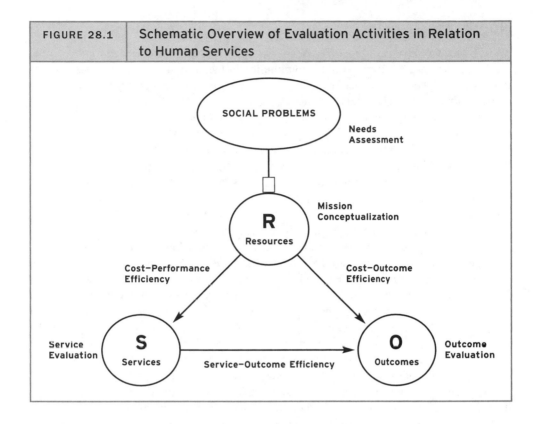

managed ideally in accordance with the programs' stated mandate or purpose. Typically controlled by boards, executive directors, managers, and/or planners, this sector makes decisions about how to allocate these resources responsibly to achieve the programs' stated objectives.

Frequently, most of these funds support "services" delivered to clients, often by social workers or other helping professionals, as in the case of a social agency. These social workers, governed in part by their professional codes of ethics, seek to achieve specific "outcomes" with their clients. They monitor these outcomes either routinely or as part of a formal evaluation to determine the degree to which the agency has achieved its mandate for the service. Is the service doing what it is supposed to do? Finally, based on the results of these assessments, the boards, managers, or planners complete the cycle by refining future allocations of resources either to improve the delivery of their services or attain the intended outcomes. This process of allocating resources to services to achieve desired outcomes will be referred to as the RSO cycle.

At various points in the RSO cycle, different types of evaluation activities can be carried out. These activities and their relation to the stages of the RSO cycle are also illustrated in Figure 28.1. The major categories of evaluation activities are: (1) needs assessment; (2) mission conceptualization; (3) service evaluation; (4) outcome evaluation; and (5) cost–outcome efficiency.

## Needs Assessment

The first level of analysis is a *needs assessment*. This level explores the need for a potential or already existing program within a community. In the case of such an assessment conducted before the establishment of a proposed program, one would want to conduct it to confirm that a particular social problem does indeed exist in that community and that existing community resources are inadequate to meet that need. This type of needs assessment might involve a survey to determine the extent and seriousness of the perceived problem, as well as a review of the community resources that might deal with various aspects of the problem. When examining the delivery of services, it is often helpful to examine the degree to which services are integrated, continuous, accessible, and accountable (Gilbert and Terrell, 2002).

In examining an existing program, a needs assessment should consider who the proposed clients are, compared to who is really being served by the program. Are services that are offered in any way discriminatory based on age, disability, gender, race, ethnicity, religion, sexual orientation, or socio-economic background? Sometimes a program developed to help one group in need ends up serving another. Those in need may not be aware of the program, or perhaps the service lacks accessibility owing to its location, hours of operation, lack of wheelchair access, and so on. Other factors might include other agencies' or services' reluctance to refer their clients, or possibly the reluctance of a "gatekeeper" of the service to admit these clients for whatever reason.

For example, in the early 1970s in Ontario, a network of detoxification centres was set up to serve the needs of "skid-row" alcoholics. It was felt that these programs would serve as an alternative to jail and would be a more humane and treatment-oriented way of dealing with "revolving-door skid-row" alcoholics. However, an evaluation study found that in fact only two out of every five admissions to the detoxification centres were made by police, and almost half of the clients had not been arrested for public drunkenness in the past year (Annis, Giesbrecht, Ogborne, and Smart, 1979). Many of the clients had intact marriages and nearly half had stable accommodation and steady employment records. In short, the detoxification centres were not serving their intended clients.

Thus, needs assessments are helpful in establishing whether existing programs are indeed meeting the needs of those people they are intended to serve. They are also used to determine whether there is an appropriate blend of human services for a given community and to identify important areas where there are gaps in services. Needs assessments are central elements of program planning and are frequently used to justify requests for new funding or continued funding of programs.

## Mission Conceptualization

The activities associated with resource allocation are guided by one's perception of the "mission" or goals of a given human service program. Goals are simply a statement, usually in quite general terms, about the desired qualities that a program seeks to achieve in the welfare of the individuals it serves (Rossi, Lipsey, and Freeman, 2004).

For example, one of a child welfare agency's goals might be to protect children from physical, emotional, and sexual abuse, and neglect. Having stated goals is important since they help to begin to answer the question *What is this program or service supposed to do?* (Chambers and Wedel, 2004). All aspects of any program, including its personnel, structure, process, and outcome, can be examined and evaluated to determine whether these elements serve the program's goals. However, while goals are necessary and helpful in articulating desired ends, they are inadequate in evaluating whether or not these ends have been achieved.

Program objectives must be used in conjunction with program goals. Objectives differ from goals in that they constitute specific statements about desired outcomes expressed in measurable terms (Chambers and Wedel, 2004). Ideally, objectives relate to goals and are stated in such a manner that efforts made to implement them can be measured objectively. For example, a school program might have as an objective "to reduce the incidence of reported pregnancy of students in west-end schools."

Chambers and Wedel (2004) recommend four criteria that might be useful in assessing the merits of objectives: (1) clarity; (2) measurability; (3) manipulability; and (4) concern with ends, not means to ends.

By *clarity* he means that there is consensus about the meaning of the terms used in the stated objectives. Terms such as child abuse, family violence, or racism can be defined in dozens of ways, and they mean different things to different people. Thus, terms used in statements of objectives must be clearly defined.

Objectives must also be *measurable*. They enable evaluators and administrators to know when in fact they are achieving objectives.

*Manipulability* refers to the achievability of objectives. Objectives should be expressed in ways that convey the belief that they can be achieved.

Finally, according to Chambers and Wedel (2004), objectives should be conceived in terms of *ends*, *rather than means to ends*. Here is an objective expressed in terms of means, rather than ends: "The objective of the program is to provide 10 sessions of supportive counselling to single adolescent mothers." Compare this with this objective expressed in terms of ends: "The objective of the program is to increase the self-esteem of single adolescent mothers who have been identified as 'high risk' by Children's Aid and increase the parenting skills of these mothers."

In summary, the process of allocating resources to programs and services is done in order to achieve or meet certain goals and objectives. Questions to ask are: *How well are these goals and more specific program objectives articulated? Is the mission of the organization or social program conceived clearly enough and operationalized so that the program itself can be evaluated?* Part of any evaluator's responsibility is to analyze how the mission of the service is conceptualized. Evaluators first need to know what results an organization is trying to achieve, if they are going to try to determine how well the organization has achieved them. As part of this mission evaluation, an evaluator will want to examine the program's objectives to assess their clarity, measurability, manipulability, and their concern with ends, rather than means.

## Service Evaluation

*Service evaluation* involves the monitoring, measurement, and evaluation of services delivered to the intended targets of social programs. It is an examination of the service delivery process as distinct from its outcome, or as an examination of the means as opposed to the ends. Essentially, service evaluation examines three things: *What services were delivered by whom to whom? How well were those services delivered? Were the services delivered consistently in a standardized manner and according to predetermined standards and procedures?*

Evaluators often examine records in order to establish a profile of who receives services. This may involve obtaining an understanding of the types of clients a program or service serves in terms of socio-demographic characteristics and the nature of presenting problems. Typical variables that would be of interest are age, sex, marital status, ethno-cultural background, and the nature and severity of problems. An analysis of the distribution of these characteristics among the general population in the catchment area of the service will help identify who receives service and who does not.

Workload analysis can be part of service evaluation. It evaluates the allocation of workers' time to various activities. These analyses help program administrators monitor and assess the proportion of time devoted to the different categories of work, such as direct service, indirect service, community work, and operations/administration. These types of analyses can then lead to the development of standards or guidelines to help the workers allocate their time to best serve the organization's goals and objectives.

The monitoring of exactly what services are being delivered is increasingly done with the aid of computerized information systems. New software programs permit an analysis of staff workloads to help their managers picture how employees' time is being used.

The question of how well services are delivered is often dealt with by formal means that are articulated in a quality assurance program. *Quality assurance* is the process by which quality can be demonstrated through the development and articulation of desired, obtainable, and measurable standards; the assessment of the degree to which these standards have been achieved; and plans of action that are designed to correct any situations found to be substandard. A quality assurance committee generally oversees this process, composed of different stakeholders within the program.

One of the common methods of assessing the quality of interventions is *peer review* or *case review*. When the evaluation focuses on how well a service is delivered and the evaluation is conducted by other members of the same profession, it is generally referred to as a peer review process (Osman and Shueman, 1988). Typically, it includes designating standards or criteria for the evaluation of workers' performance, monitoring on a regular or occasional basis the degree to which program workers adhere to standards, and delineating a set of procedures to remedy substandard performance. When the quality review focuses on cases as opposed to workers, it is generally called a case review.

Another important data source for assessing service delivery is *client feedback*. Clients can provide helpful information about which therapeutic techniques they believe enhance or hinder their progress so that practitioners can refine and improve their techniques. This kind of feedback can be obtained either informally as part of the client/worker therapeutic relationship or formally through the systematic administration of client feedback questionnaires. Client feedback should look at both the clients' perceptions of the service itself and their personal subjective assessments of how interventions have helped them. This kind of feedback helps practitioners evaluate their own behaviours, attitudes, and attributes as their clients see them.

## Outcome Evaluation

*Outcome evaluation* involves a large variety of research activities that address the question *Does the program produce its intended outcome?* So, outcome evaluations focus on the clients and on the impact services have on them.

There is a vast array of methods for assessing outcomes, and three general approaches are typical. The first compares those who receive services with those who do not. Here, of course, one hopes to find that those who received services are "better off" than those who did not. This *comparison method* may involve using a comparison group that may be waiting for help or may be receiving a different intervention or no intervention at all.

The second general approach is a *group method*, which involves monitoring only those who receive service. Most often this would involve gathering information before and after interventions. This broad approach uses a group of clients as its own control and monitors changes in key indicators that the interventions target. Often data are collected at a number of points in the process, such as just before treatment, sometime during an intervention, at the completion of an intervention, and ideally at one or more follow-up occasions.

The third approach monitors treatment evaluation as an integral part of the intervention itself. Referred to as *case-level evaluations*, these obtain continuous feedback on the effects of interventions over time, through the repeated application of assessment measures (Unrau, Gabor, and Grinnell, 2006). The feedback gained from these assessments in turn helps shape the intervention strategy itself. Software programs have been developed that increase the efficiency, convenience, and accuracy of this kind of practitioner/researcher evaluation (Nurius and Hudson, 1999).

Regardless of the broad approach one takes in conducting outcome evaluations, a number of alternative factors can account for the observed changes. Evaluations are not highly controlled experiments and they cannot be conducted in a laboratory. The severity of a problem that an intervention aims to address is influenced by many other factors besides the program itself.

Evaluators must concern themselves with a number of possible confounding variables or possible alternative explanations for the changes they observe. Simply because one group of clients improves does not necessarily mean evaluators can conclude that the program works or is effective. Other explanations for improvement or confounding factors are said to be threats to the internal validity of evaluations. By *internal validity* we mean the degree to which an evaluation design allows us to make causal conclusions about the impact of a program or intervention on client outcome. Possible threats to this internal validity come from many sources, and almost any social work research textbook discusses these in detail, as in Grinnell and Unrau's (2005) *Social Work Research and Evaluation: Quantitative and Qualitative Approaches*.

## Cost–Outcome Evaluation

Funders are concerned not only with the effectiveness of programs but also with their efficiency. Efficiency in the human services may be broadly defined as a program's ability to produce desired services or outcomes at the minimum cost or effort, according to a *cost–outcome evaluation*. In short, programs seek to achieve desired benefits for minimal costs. Evaluators, therefore, are concerned as much with efficiency as with effectiveness.

Cost–benefit evaluations can address three kinds of efficiency: cost–performance efficiency, service–outcome efficiency, and cost–outcome efficiency. These types of efficiencies involve different sectors of the RSO cycle depicted in Figure 28.1. Cost–performance efficiency concerns the relation between resources and services; it focuses on those costs associated with producing the services. Cost–performance measures might include the average cost per interview or the per diem cost of services to clients. Analysis of the costs across a range of services can lead to a better understanding of the factors that influence unit costs of services.

Service–outcome efficiency deals with the relations between the amounts and the types of services in relation to the outcomes. This kind of evaluation allows for comparisons of amounts of service to achieve outcome objectives. For example, such an evaluation might look at the average number of interviews required to treat a drug addict successfully, or the optimum length of time unemployed people use a program designed to help them develop skills to find work. Thus, service–outcome efficiency analysis involves examining service activities as they relate to outcome.

Finally, cost–outcome efficiency examines various kinds of costs in relation to outcomes. For example, how much does it cost to treat a cocaine abuser successfully on an in-patient basis compared to the cost to treat a similar case on an out-patient basis?

Cost–benefit analysis, then, allows the evaluator to examine the degree to which a program or service achieves its desired ends and at what cost.

## QUALITATIVE VERSUS QUANTITATIVE APPROACHES TO EVALUATIONS

While it is important to determine whether or not programs are achieving their desired results, evaluation should go beyond simple verification and include elements of exploration and discovery. Programs may have unanticipated side effects that could have powerful negative impacts on clients or other stakeholders. *Qualitative approaches* to evaluation help to uncover the unexpected, unplanned factors that the more formal, structured *quantitative methods* focused on verification of desired outcomes can miss. While there has been a vigorous debate on the pros and cons of quantitative versus qualitative methods of evaluation, it is clear that each plays a distinctive role (Macdonald, 2002).

Quantitative approaches are generally most appropriate when we want to determine whether a particular program achieves a clearly specified outcome. The approach focuses on key variables and typically watches for changes that can be attributed to the intervention. As noted earlier, internal validity is a strong concern here. Careful measurement is also critical. Standardized tests that can be used to measure changes in the attributes associated with positive and negative outcomes are often employed. In any event, quantitative approaches, although sometimes criticized for being used inappropriately, are valuable methods for establishing both the effectiveness and efficiencies of programs.

Evaluations should not be limited to examining outcomes, but should also embrace process. *Process evaluations* examine the internal dynamics of a program and determine whether it is operating on schedule and doing what it is supposed to do (Yegidis and Weinbach, 2006). They explore the "sequence of activities that a program undertakes to achieve its objectives, including all the decisions made, who made them, and on what criteria they were based" (Gabor and Grinnell, 1994, 24). Process evaluations get at how and why interventions work or do not work. These evaluations examine how well programs actually conform to their plans or designs and help point the way to adjustments. The focus is on how an outcome is achieved or how a program gets the results it does. This type of evaluation is far more flexible, developmental, and inductive than the more formal structured-outcome evaluations. These kinds of evaluation can explore the complex dynamics of how a program operates day-to-day and seek an understanding of how the program works, and its strengths and weaknesses.

Process evaluations typically call for the use of qualitative methodologies that can respond to the complex internal dynamics of an operating program. This approach calls for the researcher to get close to the issues at hand. Sometimes this includes face-to-face interviews with clients (past, present, or potential), program administrators and staff, board members, and even funders. The evaluator seeks to understand how the people and the situations influence the ways decisions are made and how the program operates. Sometimes participant observation is employed. Observational data can also help complement or confirm the conclusions obtained through the analysis of interview data.

Thus, both quantitative and qualitative approaches are important to successful evaluations. Each offers its own strengths and limitations, and each helps answer the questions *Does the program work?* and *How does the program work?*

## CONCLUSION

The field of evaluation, as we have seen here, encompasses many kinds of activities and involves a wide range of stakeholders. It is a rapidly expanding field today, fuelled by new computer technologies that manage information and driven by demands for increased accountability in a time of fiscal restraint. The time has come when social welfare programs must produce evidence that their services are needed and used, that they are effective, that they are well run, that they achieve their stated objectives, and that they are worth their costs. These are the challenges that confront the evaluators of social welfare programs.

## References

Annis, H., Giesbrecht, N., Ogborne, A., & Smart, R. 1979. *The Ontario detoxification system*. Toronto: Addiction Research Foundation of Ontario.

Chambers, D. E., & Wedel, K. R. 2004. *Social policy and social programs: A method for the practical public policy analyst* (4th edn.). Needham Heights, MA: Allyn and Bacon.

Gabor, P. A., & Grinnell, R. M. 1994. *Evaluation and quality improvement in the human services*. Needham Heights, MA: Allyn and Bacon.

Gilbert, N., & Terrell, P. 2002. *Dimensions of social welfare policy*. Boston: Allyn and Bacon.

Grinnell, R., & Unrau, Y. A. M. 2005. *Social work research and evaluation: Quantitative and qualitative approaches* (7th edn). Itasca, IL: F. E. Peacock.

Macdonald, J. G. 2002. The practitioner as researcher. In F. J. Turner (Ed.), *Social work practice: A Canadian perspective* (pp. 579–587). Scarborough, ON: Prentice-Hall of Canada.

Nurius, P. S., & Hudson, W. W. 1999. *Human services: Practice, evaluation, and computers: A practical guide for today and beyond*. Pacific Grove, CA: Brooks/Cole Publishing.

Osman, S., & Shueman, S. A. July–August 1988. A guide to the peer review process for clinicians. *Social Work*, 345–348.

Rossi, P., Lipsey, M. W., & Freeman, H. E. 2004. *Evaluation: A systematic approach* (7th edn.). Newbury Park, CA: Sage Publishing.

Unrau, Y. A., Gabor, P. A., & Grinnell, R. M. 2006. *Evaluation in social work: The art and science of practice* (4th edn.). USA: Oxford University Press.

Yegidis, B. L., & Weinbach, R. W. 2006. *Research methods for social workers* (5th edn.). Toronto: Allyn and Bacon.

# CHAPTER 29

# The Code of Ethics as a Means of Control: Is It?

*Rachel Birnbaum*

## INTRODUCTION

In 2005, the Canadian Association of Social Workers' (CASW) Code of Ethics replaced the 1994 Code of Ethics.[1] The 1994 code was viewed as too prescriptive to the profession as it set standards for ethical behaviour. The 2005 code recognizes the individual and personal diversity of the profession and is based on situational ethics. That is, the social worker can work to determine what *may be* right in a specific situation rather than *what is* always right. In addition, the 2005 code explicitly highlights the importance of the client's ethno-cultural background and belief systems when examining ethical questions. The code is accompanied by a companion document, *Guidelines for Ethical Responsibilities in Common Practice Situations.*[2] The companion document details ethical responsibilities for social workers in various roles and practice areas of their profession.

In the Preamble to the Code, it states that "the social work profession is dedicated to the welfare and self-realization of all people; the development and disciplined use of scientific and professional knowledge; the development of resources and skills to meet individual, group, national, and international changing needs and aspirations, and the achievement of social justice for all."[3] The 2005 code lists the six core social work values and practice principles:

Value 1: Respect for inherent dignity and worth
Value 2: Pursuit of social justice
Value 3: Service to humanity
Value 4: Integrity to professional practice
Value 5: Confidentiality in professional practice
Value 6: Competence in professional practice

The CASW Code of Ethics, which includes standards of practice in some jurisdictions, is a document that serves three main purposes: (1) to articulate minimum standards of professional practice and conduct; (2) to provide assistance to social workers to guide and assess their professional behaviour; and (3) to provide a means by which a regulatory body can adjudicate issues of professional practice. In Alberta, Saskatchewan, Manitoba, New Brunswick, Nova Scotia, Newfoundland & Labrador, Quebec, and the Association of Social Workers of Northern Canada, the responsibility for regulation of the social work profession has been delegated to the professional social work associations. In Prince Edward Island, Ontario, and British Columbia, the responsibility has been delegated to the profession

---

1 Dr. Beverley Antle was instrumental in the development of the revised *Code of Ethics* (2005) until her untimely death on November 11, 2006.

2 CASW-ACTS, Companion document to the *Social Work Code of Ethics* (2005).

3 Ibid., p. 2.

through the establishment of a social work regulatory body that is separate from and independent of the provincial social work association.[4] The code of ethics and standards to which members will be held accountable is typically set out in the provincial statute that determines the regulatory framework for the social work members of the regulatory body in their respective province. Although the regulatory bodies may have different codes of ethics and standards of practice to which their members are accountable, there is significant similarity in the code of ethics and standards of practice across jurisdictions.

The purpose of this chapter is to explore the role of the code of ethics and examine whether or not the code is being used as a means of controlling the behaviour of the social worker. To place this discussion in context it would be helpful to review discipline decisions across Canada to identify some fact patterns and principles that highlight breaches of professional misconduct in regards to the standards of practice and code of ethics. It is hoped that by doing so social workers would: (1) appreciate some of the practice dilemmas that arise across the country regarding professional misconduct and ethical dilemmas[5] ; (2) understand how the standards of practice and code of ethics are being applied in the different provinces; (3) understand what the courts have to say regarding the authority and the jurisdiction of the Discipline Committees; and (4) examine what lessons can be learned with respect to implications for practitioners and schools of social work. Underlying these fact situations is the larger question that is being explored: that is, is the code of ethics being used as a means of controlling the behaviour of social workers, or not?

All the associations and colleges across Canada were contacted for information about discipline decisions since 2000. All decisions are based on the CASW (1994) Code of Ethics unless otherwise specified. It was not possible to obtain all the written decisions in each province because: (1) not all Discipline Committees direct that decisions be made public; (2) some provinces did not have any Discipline Committee hearings take place and/or the matter was resolved during the complaint process stage[6] ; (3) some provinces publish only the findings made by a Discipline Committee and do not go into detail regarding the process; and (4) some provinces still have matters before their Discipline Committee. Additional searches were conducted in legal search engines including: (1) WestlawCarswell; (2) Hein Online; (3) LexisNexis; and (4) Quicklaw™ for decisions that were appealed.[7] These latter decisions help situate the nexus between law and social work practice. Additionally, they provide useful information about how the court interprets the role and authority of the Discipline Committees.

---

4   The role of the regulatory colleges is to protect the public. The role of the provincial associations is to support and be a voice for the profession of social work. The regulatory colleges and the associations have clear and distinctly different mandates.

5   There is very little Canadian literature available regarding the types of ethical breaches in social work and resulting discipline decisions. Regehr & Kanani (2006) report that disciplinary hearings across Canada do not occur often. Much of the literature addresses American data and/or other disciplines such as law and psychology (Strom-Gottfried, 2000; Ogloff & Olley, 1998). Antle (2002) also found that there was a paucity of peer-reviewed literature on ethics by Canadian social workers.

6   For purposes of this discussion only, discipline decisions are being examined as they are public records.

7   As Discipline Committee decisions are legal proceedings, they can be appealed to a court for review.

As Jones (2002) aptly points out,

> It is important that the social worker be clear as to how the law and ethical codes interrelate. It is also important that the social worker understand how to balance conflicting ethical standards and legal considerations and how at times the law may override (p. 420).

Kerry Boman, a well-known bio-ethicist at the Hospital for Sick Children, Toronto, Ontario, addressed the topic of ethics in *Newsmagazine,*[8] *The Journal of the Ontario Association of Social Workers*. He suggested that most people believe that ethical behaviour in social work practice is common sense, while unethical violations represent uncommon breaches of conduct and behaviour. He cautioned social workers not to rely on our collective belief systems, as they can be rife with personal bias and misinformation. He maintained that the code of ethics serves to address the human side of our collective professional behaviours. Given the complex and often challenging work that social workers face in all areas of practice, policy, research, and education, the code of ethics, at minimum, serves as a guide for ethical decision-making based on our core values and beliefs of the profession.[9]

What does it mean to be ethical? Barker (2003) defines ethics for social workers as "a system of moral principles and perceptions about right versus wrong and the resulting philosophy of conduct that is practiced by an individual, group, profession, or culture."[10] Garner (2006) defines ethical practice from a legal perspective as "of or relating to moral obligations that one person owes another; esp. in law, of or relating to legal ethics."[11] Does adherence to ethical codes necessarily make one more ethical and right? Who determines what is ethical and what is not? These are long-standing questions that continue to confound the social work profession. There has never been a more hotly debated and polarized discussion in the literature about social work (Irving, 2007; Mullaly, 2007; Reamer, 1998, 2002; Rossiter, 2007; Strom-Gottfried & D'Aprix, 2006) or in any other professional discipline (i.e, law, medicine, nursing, psychology, teaching, business) than the topic of ethics[12] (Dodek, 2000; Lindsay, Lindsay, & Irvine, 1996; Ogloff & Oley, 1998; Weaver, Trevino, & Cochran, 1999).

Freud & Krug (2002) argue that most ethical dilemmas do not fall into neatly categorized areas but often combine ethical, legal, and clinical issues. The discipline decisions reviewed represent a variety of clinical practice situations where social workers find themselves in breach of their ethical and legal responsibilities.

---

**8** *Newsmagazine, The Journal of the Ontario Association of Social Workers*, 2004.

**9** Throughout this chapter, I refer to both the *Canadian Association of Social Work Code of Ethics* (CASW, 2005) and the *Ontario College of Social Workers and Social Service Workers Code of Ethics* (OCSWSSW, 2000). In Ontario, social workers who are members of the OCSWSSW are governed by the *Ontario College of Social Workers and Social Service Workers Code of Ethics* (2000). Social workers across Canada should be familiar with their respective standards of practice and codes of ethics in each jurisdiction, as well as the CASW (2005).

**10** Barker, R.L. (2003). *The Social Work Dictionary* (5th Edition). National Association of Social Workers, Washington, D.C. NASW Press, p. 147.

**11** Garner, B.A. (2006). *Black's Law Dictionary* (3rd Edition). Thomson/West, p. 254.

**12** One could also include the topic of regulation of social workers across Canada. However, it is not the purpose of this chapter to debate the regulation of the profession. Please see Chapter 27 for more information re: regulation.

## ETHICAL ISSUES

The Code of Ethics (1994) under "Ethical Duties and Obligations" states that "a social worker shall maintain the best interest of the client as the primary professional obligation" (p. 9). Under "Limit on Professional Relationship," the code states that, "a social worker shall not exploit the relationship with a client for personal benefit, gain, or gratification, the social worker shall not have a sexual relationship with a client, and the social worker shall not sexually harass any person" (p. 13).

## Boundaries (Sexual Abuse)

In 2000, Ms. G provided private practice counselling to the public and operated a social work agency in Alberta. She treated Mr. X in individual counselling for issues related to sexual abuse, anger, and depression. Immediately after therapy ended, Ms. G began a personal and intimate relationship with Mr. X that included living together. The Discipline Committee found that Ms. G was in breach of professional boundaries and trust (Code of Ethics, s. 2.6, 5.6). The Discipline Committee and Ms. G agreed to the following sanctions: (1) that she be suspended from the practice of social work for a period of eight months; (2) that she undergo an assessment to determine whether she understands the consequences of her behaviour and the issues of boundaries; (3) that the assessment has to be satisfactory to the college and that Ms. G undergo counselling in relation to the concerns raised by the assessment; (4) that she be reprimanded and a copy of the reprimand be in her discipline file for 10 years; (5) that should Ms. G return to the province to practice she would be under supervision for sixteen months by a supervisor agreed upon by the college; (6) that Ms. G pay for the costs of the hearing; and (7) that the contents of the consent order be made public by being published in the college newsletter.

In 2001, Mr. V was involved in a client/therapist relationship in Alberta. He attended a client's home and engaged in sexual touching and a sexual relationship, among other allegations made against him. The Discipline Committee found that Mr. V. violated professional boundaries (breached Code of Ethics, s.1, 2.2, 2.5, 2.6, 5.6, 5.7) and abused the client's trust by entering into a sexual relationship (breached Code of Ethics, s.5.2, 5.3, 5.6, 5.7). The sanctions imposed on Mr. V included: (1) that he obtain an assessment by a qualified individual approved by the college in assessing sexual offending behaviour; (2) that he comply with the recommendations made by the assessment; (3) that he cover all costs of the assessment; (4) that he provide proof that the assessment was to take place within three months; (5) that he successfully complete a course on professional ethics, standards of practice, and professional boundaries; (6) that he assume costs associated with it; and (6) that a letter of reprimand be made available on a permanent basis in his file. If the requirements were met, Mr. V could apply to have his suspension lifted providing that he practice under the supervision of an approved college social worker for one year. Mr. V was also ordered to pay the costs associated with the discipline hearing and his name, a description of his conduct, and the findings made were published in the local newspaper.

In 2003, Ms. A was alleged to have sexually exploited a former client at an agency she was employed at in Ontario. Ms. A did not attend the discipline hearing although she was served. The college did prove that Ms. A engaged in behaviour that, "having regard to all circumstances, would reasonably be regarded by members as disgraceful, dishonourable, or unprofessional" (subsection 2.36 of the Professional Misconduct Regulation [O.Reg.-384/00]. The Discipline Committee found that: "(1) the member established a personal and/or sexual relationship with a client to whom she provided counselling services and/or psychotherapy services and who remained a client of her employer, an agency in Orangeville; and (2) the member behaved in a manner that showed patent disregard and indifference to the well-being of her client while she satisfied her own sexual curiosity at the expense of her client, who had already suffered childhood sexual assault and rape."

Prior to the hearing, Ms. A's certificate of registration was suspended and subsequently cancelled further with her resigning from the college. Counsel for the college sought an order that: (1) the member be reprimanded, in writing and in person, and that the fact of the reprimand be recorded on the College Registrar for an unlimited period; (2) the Discipline Committee's findings and order be published with the member's name in the college's newsletter, on the College's Web site, and in the Orangeville area on the newswire; and (3) that the Discipline Committee's findings and order be made known to social work regulators in other provinces and to the American Association of Marriage and Family Therapists.[13]

In reaching its decision, the Discipline Committee heard independent expert evidence about sexual abuse, found that Ms. A showed no remorse for the conduct, had told the client to keep their relationship a secret, and fulfilled her needs without regard to the impact on the client. All of these factors seriously impacted the former client.

In 2004, a social worker in Ontario was providing treatment to youths and young adults. The social worker admitted to allegations of professional misconduct. Specifically, the social worker acknowledged abusing a client physically, sexually, verbally, and psychologically. The social worker also failed to maintain clear and appropriate boundaries in the member's professional relationship with the client. The member and the college jointly submitted an agreement on penalty having regard to the member co-operating with the College by agreeing to the facts and proposed penalty. Moreover, the member accepted personal responsibility and expressed regret for the conduct. The member was reprimanded and the reprimand was recorded on the register, the Registrar was directed to impose terms and conditions on the member's practice, the findings of the Discipline Committee were published without the member's name in the college newsletter, the member obtained psychotherapy for a period of two years, and the therapy was monitored at the college's discretion. In 2006, the member applied for removal of the terms, conditions, and limitations imposed on the member's certificate of registration. The Discipline Committee reviewed all the documentation provided by the member and directed the Registrar to remove the terms, conditions, and limitations that were previously imposed.[14]

In 2005, a social work member employed by a hospital in Ontario admitted to allegations of professional misconduct. The misconduct included, but was not limited to, abusing a client physically, sexually, verbally, and psychological. In addition, the social worker used information obtained during a professional relationship with the client to harass or exploit the former client; engaged in conduct that would be considered disgraceful, dishonourable, and

---

13 Made under the *Social Work and Social Service Work Act*. See the OCSWSSW Web site: www.ocswssw.org/sections/council_info/disciplinedecisions.html. Accessed on May 8, 2007.

14 See the OCSWSSW Web site: www.ocswssw.org/sections/council_info/disciplinedecisions.html. Accessed on May 8, 2007, for the discipline decision summary.

unprofessional; and failed to regard the well-being of the client. The social worker and the college entered into a joint submission on penalty. Amongst other penalties, the member was reprimanded and the reprimand placed on the register; the Registrar was directed to impose terms and conditions; the member was not permitted to provide social work services to female clients, students, or supervisors for two years; and the member's certificate of registration was suspended for 24 months.[15]

In 2007, a social work member employed as a therapist in adult mental health at a community hospital admitted to allegations of professional misconduct. The member acknowledged that she engaged in conduct that would be disgraceful, dishonourable, and unprofessional when she established a personal and/or sexual relationship with the client. The following facts were agreed upon: (1) the member abused the client physically, sexually, verbally, psychologically, or emotionally when the member engaged in a personal and/or sexual relationship with a client; (2) the member used her professional position of authority to improperly influence or exploit a client or former client when the member provided counselling services; and (3) the member failed to distinguish her own needs from those of her client and failed to appreciate how her own needs might impact on her professional relationship with the client.[16] The Discipline Committee accepted a joint submission on penalty. The Registrar was directed to revoke the member's certificate of registration and the revocation was noted in the Registrar. The findings and Order of the Discipline Committee were made public, and the member was not allowed to apply to the Registrar or the college for a new certificate of registration for a period of four years.

Boundary violations can also involve a conflict of interest. The Code of Ethics (1994) states, "the social worker shall not have a business relationship with a client, borrow money from a client, or loan money to a client."[17] In 2006, Ms. MG was an employee of a children's agency in Alberta. After a Discipline Committee hearing, Ms. MG was charged with the following breaches: (1) asking a foster parent for money; (2) accepting money from a foster parent; (3) asking a foster parent to co-sign a loan; (4) making friendships with foster parents; (5) caring for children on her professional caseload in her own home; (6) entering into a written agreement to use a client's bank debit card while the client was in treatment; and (7) blurring boundaries with numerous clients including self-disclosure (Code of Ethics, s.1, 3.6.18, 5.3, 5.6, 6.7.1, 6.5.1). Some of Ms. MG's breaches were also considered violations of standards of practice including (1) asking a foster parent for money; (2) accepting money from a foster parent; (3) asking a foster parent to co-sign a loan; (4) making friendships with foster parents; and (5) blurring boundaries with clients including inappropriate self-disclosure (Standards of Practice, s.21, 25, 29(3)).

The Discipline Committee suspended her certificate until she: (1) completed a workshop on social work ethics; (2) completed a program on personal/professional boundaries; (3) completed a workshop on social work record keeping; (4) obtained a period of supervision (this was removed as she was already suspended); (5) completed an anger management course; and (6) completed a physical and mental assessment and follow-up.

---

15  Ibid.

16  Ibid. Accessed on September 18, 2007.

17  "When a social worker does keep money or assets belonging to a client, the social worker should hold this money or asset in a trust account or hold the money or asset in conjunction with an additional professional person" (p. 13, footnote 16).

## Integrity and Objectivity/Confidential Information (Recording Information)

In the Code of Ethics (1994), the code states: "a social worker shall carry out his or her professional duties and obligations with integrity and objectivity" (p. 11); "the social worker shall maintain only one master file on each client"; and "the social worker shall record all relevant information and keep all relevant documents in the file" (p. 15).

In 2002, Ms. M claimed reimbursement for travel expenses incurred while on business for a mental health agency in Alberta. On five separate occasions Ms. M claimed reimbursement for mileage. In fact, Ms. M did not incur the expenses as stated on her expense form. The college charged Ms. M with having breached the Code of Ethics by engaging in (1) dishonesty by filing expense claims to her employer; (2) failing to maintain professional standards for record keeping; and (3) dishonesty (Code of Ethics, s. 2.0, 2.1, 8.6, 6.5, 6.8. 3.2, 2.1, 8.1). The Discipline Committee found Ms. M guilty of the allegations and ordered: (1) that a letter of reprimand be sent to her and placed on file with the college; (2) that her certificate of registration be suspended for two years with conditions that must be met before the suspension is lifted; (3) that she complete a course on social work ethics as approved by the college; (4) that she pay part of the costs of the hearing; and (5) that the order be made public.

In Saskatchewan in 2006, Ms. H was found to be unfit to continue as a member of the association.[18] Section 31 of the *Social Workers Act* states: "The Discipline Committee may, by resolution, expel the member from the Association where: (a) a member has been convicted of an indictable offence pursuant to the Criminal Code; (b) a report of the professional conduct committee is made to the Discipline Committee respecting the conviction mentioned in Clause A; (c) the Discipline Committee has given the member mentioned in Clause A an opportunity to be heard; and (d) the Discipline Committee finds that the conduct of the member giving rise to the conviction makes the member unfit to continue to be a member" (p. 3).[19] The Discipline Committee ordered: (1) that Ms. H be expelled from the Saskatchewan Association of Social Workers (SASW); (2) that pursuant to section 29(3) of the act, Ms. H be served with a copy of the decision; (3) that the executive director of the SASW prepare a synopsis of the decision and publish the findings in the SASW newsletter identifying Ms. H; (4) that the executive director publish Ms. H's name and decision in two local newspapers; and (5) that the executive director send a copy of the decision to member associations of the CASW.

## SOCIAL WORK ETHICS AND THE LAW
## COURT DECISIONS

While not many cases have been appealed, the following examples highlight some practice issues.

---

18   The social worker was criminally charged with fraud over $5000. She was found guilty and sentenced to four years in jail. See *R* v. *Hynes* [2006] S.J. No. 515, (Sask Prov Crt).

19   Notice of Decision of the Discipline Committee of the Saskatchewan Association of Social Workers. (2007), Vol. 18(1). *Saskatchewan Social Worker.*

In *Penny* v. *New Brunswick Association of Social Workers*[20] Mr. Penny appealed the New Brunswick Association of Social Workers' Discipline Committee's decision. Mr. Penny was a social worker employed by the province of New Brunswick. In 1999, he had an affair with one of the department's clients. He signed an affidavit that was used in court by the client in a custody dispute with her husband. The affidavit stated that he (Mr. Penny) was employed with the Department of Health and Community Services in child protection and child care. He stated that if he (Mr. Penny) were involved in the family dispute as a child protection worker he would not recommend that the child be returned to live with his father. The father of the child complained to the association. The matter was referred to the Discipline Committee of the association and Mr. Penny was found guilty of digressing from recognized professional standards of the profession with respect to the Social Work Code of Ethics.[21] The Discipline Committee ordered: (1) that Mr. Penny attend a presentation on the Code of Ethics and submit a written report to the Dossier Journal on a specified date; (2) that Mr. Penny receive a reprimand and that the reprimand be recorded on the register; (3) that Mr. Penny be fined $1500.00 to be paid in three equal installments; (4) that Mr. Penny's name be published in the Dossier in summary and in the local *Times Globe*; and (5) that the matter remain under the jurisdiction of the Discipline Committee until all the requirements are met. Mr. Penny appealed to the New Brunswick Court of Queen's Bench. The judge agreed with some of Mr. Penny's appeal. The judge found that: (1) Mr. Penny did not have to submit a written report to the Dossier Journal; (2) that the fine be paid after the award became final; (3) that his name was not to be published in the local newspaper; and (4) that once a decision was made by the Discipline Committee, it (the committee) could not continue to have jurisdiction. The judge gave deference to the committee's decisions on all the other matters.

Mr. Penny appealed the court's decision to the New Brunswick Court of Appeal. Mr. Penny argued that his affidavit was made for use in court and that it was protected by absolute immunity at common law. That is, the affidavit Mr. Penny filed in court to support his partner should not have been used by the association in a subsequent discipline matter. The Justices of the Court of Appeal dismissed Mr. Penny's appeal and stated at paragraph 20: "what was being inquired into by the Discipline Committee was, however, the appellant's use of the weight of his office to influence the Court by giving advice or opinions as an expert at a time when he was in an alleged conflict of interest, and in failing to clearly distinguish his statements as a private citizen from those of a social worker employed in the Child Protection Program."[22]

Another interesting case was in Quebec in 2003. Mr. B was employed as a social worker and an officer with the Canadian Armed Forces. Mr. B engaged in counselling with Mr. X. Mr. X requested information on the boundaries of confidentiality and under what circumstances he (Mr. B) would need to disclose information, Mr. B provided a description of the types of information that would need to be disclosed to the military,

**20**  *Penny* v. *New Brunswick Association of Social Workers,* 2002 CarswellNB 109, 2002 NBCA 28, 249 N.B.R. (2d) 185, 648 A.P.R. 185, 47 Admin. L.R. (3d) 258 (C.A.).

**21**  *New Brunswick Association of Social Workers Act,* S.N.B. (1988), c. 78, s. 23 (2)(d).

**22**  *Penny* v. *New Brunswick Association of Social Workers,* 2002 CarswellNB 109, 2002 NBCA 28, 249 N.B.R. (2d) 185, 648 A.P.R. 185, 47 Admin. L.R. (3d) 258 (C.A.), para.20.

but did not mention the need to disclose if the individual was using alcohol or drugs. During counselling, Mr. X did disclose his use of alcohol and drugs. Mr. B later disclosed this information to the military as it was a reportable offence and contrary to the military code of conduct. Mr. X reported Mr. B to the Professional Order of Social Workers of Quebec with the following breaches of ethics: (1) Mr. B falsified documents with dates that were wrong, indicating that he (Mr. B) advised him (Mr. X) of the obligations for disclosure; (2) Mr. B failed to adequately inform Mr. X of this; and (3) Mr. B breached two counts of confidentiality. However, before the Discipline Committee could deal with the allegations, Mr. B and the army appealed to the court. They argued that the Order's Discipline Committee did not have jurisdiction to hear the case.

The Quebec Court of Appeal rejected the argument from the Attorney General of Canada that the obligation to adhere to military regulations superseded the Code of Ethics of the Professional Order of Social Workers of Quebec.[23] The court also noted that Mr. B voluntarily joined the Professional Order of Social Workers and agreed to respect its code of ethics. The judge rejected the claim for Crown immunity simply because the social worker was a member of the armed forces. Furthermore, the court concluded that caution must be used when extending immunity to individual Crown servants and it must not be applied simply because a Crown servant is acting in the course of his employment. Immunity should be enjoyed only if it can be established that compliance with the statute would otherwise prejudice the Crown. The argument of Mr. B and the Attorney General of Canada that a federal statute (to disclose the use of drugs and alcohol) should be paramount was also rejected because Mr. B became subject to the code of ethics when he joined the Professional Order of Social Workers of Quebec. Moreover, the court noted that, as a military social worker, Mr. B also had to abide by a code of ethics of the Canadian Association of Social Workers. In effect, the Quebec Court of Appeal's decision in this case required the professional to respect his code of ethics rather than follow the directives of the armed forces.[24]

In *Silverthorne* v. *Ontario College of Social Workers and Social Service Workers*[25] a member sought a judicial review of a complaint decision. The issue for the court was to review whether the Complaints Committee breached a duty of procedural fairness in failing to provide certain documents to the member before a decision was disposed of concerning her. The complaint related to social work services provided by the member while employed by the Children's Aid Society of Brant, with respect to the complainant's 15-year-old daughter, who was made a Crown ward. The complaint to the college by the child's father alleged that the member was directly and negligently responsible for allowing his daughter to live at-risk for a period of weeks in the community. The father also alleged that the member had attempted to conceal the negligence and lied in affidavits filed in court proceedings. The Complaints Committee

---

23  *Breton c. Comité de discipline de l'Ordre professionnel des travailleurs sociaux du Québec*, [2005] QCCCA 195.

24  Every social worker should be aware when his or her ethical obligations are in conflict with his or her employer's expectation of ethical behaviour, and consult with his or her respective associations and/or colleges for clarification and advice.

25  *Silverthorne* v. *Ontario College of Social Workers and Social Service Workers* (Ontario), 2006 CarswellOnt 279, 206 O.A.C. 375, 264 D.L.R. (4th) 175 (S.C.J.).

concluded that none of the allegations warranted a referral to the Discipline Committee. However, the Complaints Committee decided to issue a verbal caution to the member. The member refused to attend the caution and brought an application for a judicial review in Divisional Court challenging the decision. A three-person panel of the Divisional Court met in 2005 and the majority of the panel dismissed the application. The court concluded that the Complaints Committee's investigation and decision-making procedure did not breach any obligation of fairness to the member. The court went on to consider whether the decision to caution the member was unreasonable. The court's findings on this point are important because the court analyzed the standard of review applicable to the decisions of the college's Complaints Committee. The Divisional Court in this case determined that the appropriate standard of review for the college's Complaints Committee on this type of decision was that of "reasonableness." That is the most common standard of review for tribunals of professional regulatory colleges and reflects a level of deference by the courts to the special expertise of such tribunals.

## LESSONS LEARNED

### Implications for Practitioners

The number of discipline hearings across Canada remains relatively low. Strom-Gottfried (2000) analyzed more than a decade's worth of American data based on the National Association of Social Workers (NASW) between 1986 and 1997 and found similar results. To date, breaches of professional conduct in Canada have been based on difficulties with dual relationships, issues of confidentiality, boundary violations (usually sexual in nature), dishonesty in billing practices, and fraud. Dual relationships and boundary violations (sexual) tend to be the most reported ethical complaints made against social workers in the U.S. (Aguilar, Williams, & Akin, 2004; Mittendorf & Schroeder, 2004).

An examination of the penalties reached by the committees indicates that they all order, at minimum, that the social worker must complete a clinical assessment, attend a course on professional ethics and boundaries, and be supervised for a period of time. From a practice point of view, the penalties reached are directly related to the ethical breaches of conduct. That is, the penalties are proportionate to the offence.

As stated previously, discipline decisions are legal proceedings and the social worker may seek a judicial review of a discipline decision. However, the social worker who pursues a review of a discipline decision has a high bar to overcome in order to be successful. For example, the social worker has to demonstrate to the court that the Discipline Committee's decision was unreasonable and that the procedures in place were not conducted in a fair manner.[26] It has now been established in case law that immunity[27] is not a defence for professional misconduct.

---

26   *Silverthorne* v. *Ontario College of Social Workers and Social Service Workers* (Ontario), 2006 CarswellOnt 279, 206 O.A.C. 375, 264 D.L.R. (4th) 175 (S.C.J.).

27   *Penny* v. *New Brunswick Assn. of Social Workers,* 2002 CarswellNB 109 (C.A.); *Breton c. Comite de discipline de l'Ordre professional des travailleurs sociaux du Quebec* [2005] QCCCA 195. Every social worker should be aware when their ethical obligations are in conflict with their employer's and discuss these issues as soon as possible.

## Implications for Schools of Social Work

If social work students are to understand the code of ethics and standards of practice, it would seem that the responsibility should start with the schools of social work. After all, it is the schools that graduate social workers. The Canadian Association of Schools of Social Work (CASSW) requires that schools across the country implement policy and procedures for their students that focus on suitability to practice.[28] In addition, the field education component of the programs must also reflect the social work values of the CASW Code of Ethics.[29] However, there does not appear to be a link between these two important policies and what is often taught in schools of social work.

The practice of social work is fraught with complexity, ambiguity, multiple meanings, and, more importantly, intersects with the law. Issues such as confidentiality and privilege, disclosure, reporting obligations and the duty to warn, record keeping, and boundaries are important practice components that social work students will confront in every practice area (community, clinical, policy, and research) on a daily basis. While most social work students will go out and practice ethically, it is incumbent that a mandatory course for students on ethics and the legal implications of practice be included as part of their training and education.

## CONCLUSION

I now return to where I started. Does the code of ethics control social work behaviour? After reviewing the decisions reached across the country it would seem that the majority of social workers practice ethically and professionally. The frequency with which social workers face disciplinary action remains relatively low. I have tried to highlight the most common ethical dilemmas in which social workers find themselves based on discipline decisions. Many of these examples involve the most serious breaches of professional misconduct. That is, social workers are being disciplined for behaviours that the average citizen (public) and professional would consider unethical conduct at the very least.

At the end of the day, social workers must continuously seek ways to translate their practice and behaviour into what is ethical in all its multiple meanings. I would argue that the code of ethics provides a template to *begin* this process, rather than arguing about whether the code of ethics *controls* social work behaviour or not.

# References

Aguillar, G., Williams, C., & Akin, J. (2004). A comparative study of practitioners and students in the understanding of sexual ethics. *Journal of Social Work Values and Ethics, 1,* 10–19.

Antle, B. (2002). CASW-ACTS project to research and develop a national statement of ethical principles: Phase 1: Critical appraisal of the literature, September, 2002.

Barker, R.L. (2003). *The Social Work Dictionary* (5th Edition). National Association of Social Workers. Washington, D.C.: NASW Press.

---

28  CASSW, B3d, Standards related to students (SB 4.3.2, 6.10).

29  CASSW, B3f, Standards related to field education (SB 6.4).

Barlow, C., & Coleman, H. (2003). Suitability for practice guidelines for students: A survey of Canadian social work programs. *Social Work Education, 22(2),* 151–164.

Dodek, A.M. (2000). Canadian legal ethics: A subject in search of scholarship. *University of Toronto Law Journal, 50,* 115–134.

Freud, S., & Krug, S. (2002). Beyond the Code of Ethics, Part 1: Complexities of ethical decision-making in social work practice. *Families in Society, 83(5/6),* 474–482.

Garner, B.A. (2006). *Black's Law Dictionary* (3rd Edition). Thomson/West.

Irving, A. (2007). "Being is not syntactical": Ethics as intensities. *Canadian Social Work Review, 23(1–2),* 131–137.

Jones, K. (2002). Ethical issues. In Frank Turner (Ed.), *Social work practice: A Canadian perspective* (pp. 417–429). Prentice Hall, Toronto.

Lindsay, R.M., Lindsay, L.M., & Irvine, V.B. (1996). Instilling ethical behaviour in organizations: A survey of Canadian companies. *Journal of Business Ethics, 15(4),* 393–407.

Mittendorf, S., & Schroeder, J. (2004). Boundaries in social work: The ethical dilemma of social worker-client sexual relationships. *Journal of Social Work Values and Ethics, 1,* 2–9.

Mullaly, B. (2007). Forward to the past: The 2005 CASW Code of Ethics. *Canadian Social Work Review, 23(1–2),* 145–150.

Ogloff, J.R., & Oley, M.C. (1998). The interaction between ethics and the law: The ongoing refinement of ethical standards for psychologists in Canada. *Canadian Psychology, 39(3),* 221–239.

Reamer, F.G. (1998). *Ethical standards in social work.* NASW Press, Washington, D.C.

Reamer, F.G. (2002). "Ethical issues in social work," in *Social Worker's Desk Reference,* (Eds.) Albert R. Roberts & Gilbert J. Greene, Oxford University Press, New York (pp. 65–69).

Regehr, C., & Kanani, K. (2006). *Essential law for social work practice in Canada.* Oxford University Press.

Rossiter, A. (2007). The "beyond" of ethics in social work. *Canadian Social Work Review, 23(1–2),* 139–144.

Strom-Gottfried, K. (2000). Ensuring ethical practice: An examination of NASW code violations, 1986–97. *Social Work, 45(3),* 251–261.

Strom-Gottfried, K., & D'Aprix, A. (2006). Ethics for academics. *Social Workers' Education, 25(3),* 225–244.

Weaver, G.R., Trevino, L.K., & Cochran, P.L. (1999). Corporate ethics programs as control systems: Influences of executive commitment and environmental factors. *Academy of Management Journal, 42,* 41–57.

# CHAPTER 30

# Globalization and Social Welfare

*Glenn Drover*

## INTRODUCTION

Proponents and opponents of globalization are agreed on one issue: it has a profound impact on human and social welfare. Proponents highlight the benefits of economic growth, improvements in average income, enhanced participation of women in the labour force, improvements in food supply, increased life expectancy, combatting terrorism, and countering fundamentalism. Opponents, on the other hand, stress the disadvantages of globalization including uneven economic development, increasing income inequality, the de-unionization of workers, the deterioration of agricultural land, the increasing influence of corporations, the weakening of the nation-state, and the loss of cultural diversity.

In parts of the world (for example, East and South Asia), globalization has been associated with rapid expansion and economic growth. In other parts (Africa), there has been limited or no growth and increasing instability. In countries throughout the world (including Canada), globalization has been accompanied by a redistribution of income. Within and between countries (particularly between countries of the north and the south), there has been a widening disparity in incomes. In Northern Europe, market income has been distributed more and more unequally, but governments have intervened to offset the disparities through transfer payments (Hyde & Dixon, 2002; Hyde, Dixon, & Drover, 2006). North America has seen some increase in income inequality, but it is not clear to what extent the inequality in our society is owing to globalization or to changing demographics, employment, and technology (Mishra, 2002; Bhagwati, 2004).

In some ways, the recent movement of capital and labour between countries is similar to earlier cycles of globalization. Historically, there have been four such cycles (Coatsworth, 2004). The first, in the sixteenth century, was associated with the early colonization of the Americas by the Europeans. The second, in the seventeenth and eighteenth centuries, included the establishment of the slave colonies of the Americas and the extension of European conquest into Asia. The third, during the nineteenth and early twentieth centuries, was fueled by the industrial revolution and mass migrations from Europe and Asia to the Americas. The recent cycle began with the rebuilding of Europe after World War II, the liberalization of trade in Asia, and the gradual demolition of protectionist strategies of economic growth. It accelerated toward the end of the twentieth century after the end of the Cold War.

Coatsworth also describes how each cycle of globalization has been associated with massive population movements. The first cycle precipitated the decimation of the Aboriginal populations through slaughter and exposure to disease, the second led to the massive displacement of Africans through slavery, the third to the migration of poor European labourers to the colonies, and the fourth to a worldwide displacement of immigrants and refugees both within and between countries. The social costs in terms of human mortality, disease, extensive deforestation, coercive systems of labour, income disparities, the depletion of resources, environmental degradation, and the eventual proliferation of unhealthy urban settlements were equally problematic.

It is in this historical context, during a slowdown in globalization at the beginning of the twentieth century, that the rise of the welfare state and modern welfare services can be considered. Until the nineteenth century, the state played a minor role in welfare during the French and British colonial periods except insofar as it encouraged immigration and land settlement. By the time of Confederation in the late nineteenth century, the role of the state began to change in order to accommodate industrialization and emerging national markets. At the same time Canadian governments were pushed by reform movements to expand basic civil and political rights, to build a sense of national identity, and to ensure an informed electorate. Education and public health became state obligations.

In the twentieth century, Canadian governments, under pressure from organized labour and radicalized politics, further expanded public services to provide benefits for the disabled, the unemployed, the sick, and the elderly. In doing so, they extended the notion of entitlement to include social and economic rights as well as civil and political rights (Banting, 1982: Guest, 1997). At the beginning of the twenty-first century, however, Canadians are faced once again with the transformation of social welfare provision because of the pressure of globalization. As in earlier cycles of globalization, the most recent cycle affects more than trade and labour markets, finance, and communications; it also influences the way the state functions and public services are provided.

Globalization requires us to think beyond the welfare state, to develop new concepts of social welfare entitlement, and to identify new ways of meeting human need. This chapter, therefore, describes the impact of the globalization process on the welfare state, the security state, governance, social movements, information technology, and welfare pluralism. Before turning to these six issues, however, it will be useful to clarify the use of the term *globalization* in this chapter.

## GLOBALIZATION

Globalization can be defined narrowly to refer to the movement of goods and services across countries, or broadly to include global interdependence in all spheres of life. The first circumscribes globalization in economic terms, the latter is closer to the vision of world federalism. As used in this chapter, the term refers to a series of exchanges which fall mid-way between these two positions.

George and Wilding (2002) suggest that our understanding of globalization depends on our way of looking at it. Technological enthusiasts emphasize the impact of technology. Nationalists focus on the driving logic of capitalism and the decline of the nation-state. Pluralists stress the multifaceted nature of globalization. Internationalists acknowledge a trend toward greater trade and financial integration.

Steger (2002) defines globalization as a multiplicity and intensification of interconnections that transcend the nation-state. Giddens (1991, 2006) suggests that it is a complex set of forces reconfiguring the relationship between time and space, interlocking the local and the universal. Overbeek (1993) claims that it represents a new world order in which a neo-liberalist ideology dominates. Sklair (1991) describes globalization as a system based on transnational practices. The Organization for Economic Co-operation and Development (OECD) (1994) associates it with an expanded trading system.

Part of the difficulty in defining globalization is that the term is also associated with multilateralism and regionalism (Sampson & Woolcock, 2002). As multilateralism, it is primarily a global trading system fostered by four major determinants: technology, finance, production, and trade. As regionalism, it is a concerted effort by corporations and states to integrate regional economies that are bound by political alliances, geography, culture, and language. Both forces are at work and both challenge the nation-state.

In the Canadian context, multilateralism is manifested through a rapidly expanding information infrastructure and an international financial system that have essentially no national boundaries. Competition is international in its scope. Similarly, multilateralism forces changes in the Canadian labour market, creating greater flexibility in the face of international competition, challenging structural barriers, undermining commitments to full employment, substituting non-unionized labour for unionized labour, and fostering export markets (Workman, 2003; Scott, Salas, & Campbell, 2001).

But globalization is more than multilateralism. It is also a form of regionalism (Schirm, 2002; Drover, Johnson, & Tao, 2001). The world is being divided into major regional trading blocs dominated by Europe, the Americas, and East and South Asia. Canada is profoundly influenced by developments within the Americas, particularly through free trade agreements and cross-border concerns about trade and security in a post-9/11 world. Hence, Canadian companies and labour markets are under pressure to meet international norms, and they are also being pressured to integrate within a continental economy.

Since the introduction of the Canada–United States Free Trade Agreement (FTA) in 1989 and the North American Free Trade Agreement (NAFTA) in 1992, American ownership of the Canadian economy has intensified, public procurement is open to American competition (the purchase of goods by governments), Canadian culture is threatened, and Canadian environmental standards are challenged. Equally important, American corporate interests aim to extend their influence through a Free Trade Agreement of the Americas (FTAA) and possibly a multilateral agreement on investment (Clark & Barlow, 1997; Council of Canadians, 1999). To offset American dominance, Canada's governments promote multilateral and bilateral agreements with other countries.

## Welfare State

Welfare states have responded in roughly three ways to globalization (Deacon, 2000; Timonen, 2003). In social democratic welfare states like Sweden, in which the majority of the population still shares a common set of welfare values, changes have been minor and cautious, promoted more by fiscal restraint than by any shift in political priorities (Timonen, 2003). In Bismarkian states like Germany or France, the basic challenge is the existence of a two-tiered system of social insurance; insiders, mainly white non-immigrant males, enjoy comprehensive coverage and other workers are excluded entirely. Finally, in liberal welfare states like Canada, which contain a diverse population and equally diverse welfare values, state policies have been more in tune with liberalizing globalization, fed in part by right-wing politics and in part by resistance from sectors of society that do not benefit, or benefit only marginally, from established social welfare practices. The policy response in recent years has been to cut social welfare expenditures, to limit people's accessibility to some social services, to deregulate the labour market, and to stimulate economic growth through lower taxes.

Jessop (1993, 2007) claims that global pressures are fundamentally changing the welfare state to a workfare state. In the original welfare state, welfare provision was based on national interests. In the workfare state, it is increasingly aligned with the needs of a global labour market, the redistribution of income toward capital, a growing reliance on welfare technology, and an increasing surveillance of individuals to see how they perform. In North America, workfare has been an integral part of welfare provision for some time. A recent extension of workfare is asset-based provision. The basic idea behind this approach to provision is that the poor are short in assets and need an assist to encourage their acquisition through savings, housing, and work training skills. One negative consequence of the approach is that it downplays "the need to act collectively through the state to counteract the commodifying practices of the market that leave out so many low income individuals in the rush to find the greater sources of profit. In such a market-centred society, the relatively less attractive personal assets of the poor will go begging, while others with more attractive homes or brighter, shinier credentials will see their assets appreciate." (Schram, 2006).

To make national economies like Canada more competitive globally, social programs have been restricted for two reasons. Governments reduce taxes to become more competitive, and this in turn limits their capacity to spend money on a variety of social initiatives (Brawley, 2003, Chapter 5). Canadians have also become acutely aware of these dual pressures through the debates surrounding NAFTA. Opponents argue strongly that the impact of free trade has been anything but good for working people, public services, and the environment (Workman, 2002; Barlow, 2004).

While NAFTA ostensibly protects social services and social security because such services are not involved directly in international trade (Jackson & Sanger, 2003), critics of the deals argue that pressure toward their inclusion will likely increase with the expansion of the agreement on services and investment. Furthermore, since the agreement currently requires that professional standards be harmonized to eliminate cross-border barriers to trade in services and also opens government procurement to American and Mexican companies, it is clear that NAFTA is about far more than trade in the conventional sense. It establishes a regulatory environment that safeguards corporate interests while constraining governments. Deep down, therefore, globalization and free trade raise fundamental questions, not only about the future of the Canadian state but also about the future of established welfare practices.

Still, as the experience of countries like Sweden and Denmark demonstrate, the future of the welfare state may depend as much on political will as trade agreements (Sodersten, 2004). Globalization does not necessarily threaten the well-being of citizens of welfare states since more trade seems to be associated, in many countries, with more social expenditures. Part of the reason for this relationship may be the necessity for governments of different political stripes to obtain the support of citizens for trade openness by insuring some degree of protection and training to face the competition. Resistance to retrenchment, according to Cynthia Kite (2004), depends largely on the institutions and political alignments of each country more than it does on globalization and free trade.

Whether political forces in Canada collaborate in the future to protect social programs remains to be seen. One option may be for Ottawa to strengthen a common economic space while disengaging from social programs, which can be left to the provinces (Gibbins, 2007). Another may be the development of a new social architecture through the use of negative income taxes to promote income redistribution, incentives to work, and human capital development as well as family-friendly initiatives (Scott, 2004). Townson (2004) is a critic of the new architecture approach and doubts that such an initiative will strengthen the welfare state. Rather, she thinks that it will lead to its replacement by a post-welfare state in which individual, rather than societal, responsibility becomes the basis of welfare policy.

## Security State

While globalization has, in some respects, challenged the viability of the welfare state, it has conversely reinforced the importance of the state for purposes of security. Economic liberalization creates global instability because people are affected very differently by the transformation of economic and social structures which fall in its wake. Globalization seems to generate enormous opportunities for some people and some regions while leaving others out or relegating them to poverty. In other cases, it leads to cultural and religious clashes (Huntington, 1996; Barber, 1995). Huntington argues that ideologies of the Cold War between left and right have been replaced or overtaken by longstanding cultural/religious beliefs. Hence, he thinks that international conflicts in the future will be fed less by economic liberalism than by clashes of civilization, the most influential of which are Western-Christian, Arabic-Islamic, Hindu-Buddhist, and Confucian-Sinic.

While Huntington's theory is contested and questionable in many respects (Berman, 2003), it almost seems prophetic in light of the events of September 11, 2001, when small cell groups associated with Islamic fundamentals struck in New York, Washington, and Pennsylvania. The impact of the attacks on the World Trade Center and the Pentagon not only highlighted the vulnerability of the United States in the face of small-scale counter insurgency, but also drew attention to the symbolic victory of personal commitment and sacrifice over military might. At the same time, the attack, which was immediately labelled as terrorist, reinforced the significance of the state as an instrument of security and protection in a world of openness and risk.

On the other hand, while the terrorist attacks valorized the state, it cancelled its historic form, the nation-state (Beck, 2005). The old nation-state assured security inside the state and relied on inter-state alliances to secure security outside. After 9/11, transnational co-operation has become essential to assure internal as well as external security. The search for security seems to be creating the potential for realignments within, as well as between, existing states. And this, in turn, may serve to tame ethnic tensions which cross established borders or address borderless issues such as poverty, financial crises, environmental degradation, and human migration. It may also serve to generate institutional mechanisms for building trust in order to overcome suspicion in international conflict (Hoffman, 2006).

That, however, is a positive view of the new security state. There is also a negative side; the potential to compromise human rights. While the United States uses the language of human rights to justify its new security measures, a gap between practice and rhetoric has led to violent rejection of American interventionism abroad and internal resistance at home (Ishay, 2005). In Canada, tension exists around a concern to protect citizens from external threats and support for basic rights and freedoms, particularly privacy rights. In addition, as Adelman (2002) notes, there is tension between Canadians' practice of taking shelter under the American security umbrella, Canadians' desire to be a lead player in the human security agenda, and Canadians' desire to maintain sovereignty, while at the same time assuring that the U.S./Canadian border does not interfere with the free movement of goods and services under NAFTA.

Recently, security measures have been used in Canada and the United States to clamp down on the movement of people. While there has not been a total harmonization of immigration and refugee policy between the two countries (Adelman, 2002), Canada has faced considerable pressure since 9/11 to restrict border and immigration policies. A Smart Border Accord was signed between the two countries in December 2001. Canada and the United States have separated the administration of the enforcement and entry of immigrants and refugees. Canada also took the initiative in negotiating a Safe Third Country border agreement, which forces refugees in North America to seek asylum in the country of first arrival (which has considerably reduced the flow of refugees into Canada from Central and South America). At the same time, the country has been opened to temporary workers. Hence, while we continue to provide relatively easy access to cheap labour, new laws and measures are increasingly selective about who is granted access as an immigrant or a refugee (Chute, 2005).

## Governance

Governance is about more than government. In a global context, governance refers to the increasing role of international institutions and sources of power which serve, in fact, to constrain the capacity of the nation-state to act independently (Schram, 2006). In the mid-1990s, Kenichi Ohmae (1995) wrote about the importance of emerging forms of economic and political governance that transcend national boundaries and replace national governments. The reality of global interdependence is that welfare policies, like economic and foreign policies, are increasingly subject to multiple mechanisms and strategies of co-ordination that involve international, national, and sub-national institutions. Among the most influential of these are transnational corporations (Greider, 1997). Few would disagree that they are powerful, that they have contributed to a weakening of the nation-state, and that international trade and investment agreements enhance their operational autonomy. The dominance of corporations and various institutions that seem to be aligned with them, such as the World Trade Organization, the World Bank, and the International Monetary Fund, have led opponents of globalization to feel that the whole process must be reversed or at least slowed down (Pauly, 1997; Cox, 2000).

Other commentators, however, present an optimistic view of new governance mechanisms and their implications for social welfare. Heraldo Muñoz (2006, p. 1) claims that globalization "can be credited with a growing awareness of the value of democracy and respect for human rights." According to John Naisbitt (1994), one paradox of globalization is that the bigger the economy, the more human welfare shifts into the hands of the small players. The breakdown of national boundaries liberates the forces of the free market. According to this perspective, the new information technology allows the small to compete with the large. The more one moves to a free-market democracy, the more each individual takes control of his or her own destiny. On a similarly optimistic note, some claim that globalization is pushing us toward a world marked by openness, diversity, and cohesion in which the wealthy nations can no longer use their domestic policies to exclude the products of poorer nations or gain unfair advantage (Lawrence, Bressand, & Ito, 1996). In addition, they suggest that globalization is leading to new forms of governance by which national governments remain players that assure minimum standards and the redistribution of resources while other players establish rights and duties for their members according to shared values and benefits.

While we must consider these differing views of world governance with caution, we can see that they emphasize the changing complexity of a new world order and, within it, the growth of welfare pluralism and experimentation. Given challenges to established welfare provision inside and outside national boundaries, more and more observers agree that multiple bodies must meet basic welfare needs, not just the state. To equate welfare with the state, therefore, is to ignore other forms of protection and benefit, forms as diverse as the family, social networks, voluntary associations, and the market. Mishra (1990) notes one implication of welfare pluralism, that not only can there be state equivalents to welfare provision, but also that human welfare entails more than state intervention.

In Canada, as in other countries throughout the world (Rieger & Leibfried, 2003; Timonen, 2003), there is a growing and contested trend toward experimentation with public and private partnerships. Initially, public–private partnerships were developed in response to concerns about the public debt but increasingly they are seen as an avenue for a wide spectrum of service provision from contracting out to publicly administered, privately financed ventures (Canadian Council for Public-Private Partnerships, 2007). *Privatization* extends well beyond the sale of government assets or even Crown corporations. In its common usage, the term covers general efforts to reduce the scope of government. More restrictively, it includes "efforts to replace policies based on ownership or control by policies based on information or incentives" (Howlett & Ramesh, 1993, p. 19). It embraces denationalization, contracting out, de-monopolization, partnering, user fees, and mandatory private provision (Aulich & Reynolds, 1993).

An important area of public provision that is partially privatized in Canada is retirement income protection and the Canada Pension Plan Investment Board. Contracting out is also growing in the provision of personal social services and health care. A critical examination of its impact on health support workers and their families, as well as the health care system, is documented in B.C. by a recent study of the Canadian Centre for Policy Alternatives (Stinson, Pollack, & Cohen, 2005). User fees are growing in social welfare programs like day care, retirement homes, and long-term care. Partnering is encouraged in community economic development.

## Social Movements

New forms of governance also raise questions about the role of social movements in civil society. Through civil society, people come together in geographic, occupational, voluntary, and political communities to articulate their view of the good life and to persuade others of its merits. Through civil society, organizations are formed to address social concerns and social problems. Through civil society, citizenship is furthered through democratic means. Through civil society, people develop caring communities, promote economic security, and foster social investment. Our ability to make claims that are recognized in civil society, however, depends ultimately on the legitimacy of our representation (Jenson, 1993; Jenson & Phillips, 2002).

Not all actors in civil society are equal; they represent different constellations of power. Nor are they necessarily making claims against the nation-state. In fact, their claims may transcend the state. Some struggle to maintain their place in society while others want to change it. Many actors in the politics of globalization act as forces of opposition and resistance to the liberalization of trade and corporate dominance (Veltmeyer, 2004, p. 7).

In the twentieth century, the labour movement profoundly influenced the development of the Canadian welfare state. Because of that influence, we based the early construction of social services and social security on a pan-Canadian vision of welfare in which all citizens of the country were to have common provision. The Quebec nationalist movement challenged the idea of pan-Canadian welfare by highlighting the right to a distinct society and by making welfare claims and social provision without reference to the federal state. Recently, Alberta has also challenged federalist claims of dominance in the welfare field.

In a similar fashion, Aboriginal movements have made identity claims that transcend the nation-state. As Canada continues to confront globalization pressures to restructure its economy, other sectors of society are increasing their own demands for change. The plight of women, visible minorities, disabled persons, environmentalists, prisoners, and children has reconfigured our thinking about welfare entitlement and citizenship rights. Social movements spotlight the fragility and the limits of the Canadian state to meet the growing insistence that our society accommodate differences.

In a sense, therefore, the central dilemma Canadian social movements face is whether they function simply to articulate welfare claims or whether they also serve to resolve them, whether they are simply a part of the civil society or whether they can transform state and economic relations. Lustiger-Thaler and Shragge (1993) argue that two kinds of social movements exist: those that try to influence political processes by framing their demands in terms of basic rights and those that try to alter existing political and economic decision-making processes by articulating counter rights. This distinction stresses that social movements not only make claims for resources, they also make demands to participate and exercise their own self-determination. Hence, in dealing with global realities, Canadian social movements play an important role in redefining our welfare expectations and basic rights.

Social movements have also stood at the forefront of the resistance to corporate globalization. Environmental groups like Greenpeace, Friends of the Earth, and the Sierra Club were among the first to sound the alarm about this growing influence of corporations. Recently, a groundswell of reaction to international free trade agreements has united traditional social movements such as labour, women, and students with citizen organizations that represent the marginalized and the powerless. While this new loose alliance of social movements does not represent the kind of threat to established authority that the labour movement represented in the early part of the twentieth century, it nevertheless challenges the legitimacy of corporate-dominated globalization (Mitzman, 2003, p. 160; Veltmeyer, 2004). The new movements demand greater consideration of the rights of labour, women, children, and minorities. They also pose a challenge to those national governments that try to dismantle their welfare states. In Canada, the Council of Canadians and the Polaris Institute are actively involved in activities to enable social movements to combat the corporate dominance of globalization.

## Information Technology

Globalization has also shaped welfare through the increasing use of information technology (Resnick & Anderson, 2002). Information technology has affected at least four aspects of social welfare: management, education, professional practice, and professional ethics. The debate regarding global development in these four areas covers more than concerns about the speed of information technology or the diffusion of technological applications. It deals fundamentally with whether information technology is transforming society, building on the technologies of the past, or transforming some aspects of society while retaining others.

Kellner (2007) suggests the new information technology is so powerful that it is transforming capitalism itself. It is creating what he calls a new "infotainment society," part and parcel of global restructuring. He also suggests that it can be used to foster globalization from above (an elite) or from below (social movements). The former he associates with "Microsoftcapitalism" and the latter with "cyberdemocracy." Within the former, he sees little chance of a reinvigorated welfare state. Through the latter, he is more optimistic.

Some authors also elaborate on how information technology can be employed to further social action and social change. Recently, non-governmental organizations (NGOs) in many countries used the Internet to facilitate communication around the globe and to successfully oppose the implementation of the proposed Multilateral Agreement on Investment (MAI) (Jackson & Sanger, 1998). They were concerned that the agreement, if approved, would dramatically and negatively affect national governments' capacity to control multinational corporations operating within their borders and their power to raise revenues to pay for social welfare programs. The debate swirling around trade and investment agreements reflects a growing conviction among NGOs that Canada's federal and provincial governments are accommodating free trade, investment, and international financial transactions in the name of economic growth and at the price of a sense of community and solidarity. This collective feeling forms the basis for facilitating society's participation in and commitment to public institutions. One strategy rapidly developing to meet the challenge, both in Canada and the United States, is the use of computer networks to link individuals around the globe as well as local organizations (Schuler, 1997). According to "OneWorld.net," information communication technologies form the basis of development, giving people the opportunity to participate in even the most marginalized communities.

In general, it seems that companies and organizations which make greater use of technology create more jobs. Job forecasters also believe that it will affect hiring practices (O'Reilly, 2007). Peter Drucker (1989) claims that social and health services lend themselves to the use of information technology in order to accommodate innovation and to integrate people with shared values in common ventures. In spite of this potential power, however, it seems that social welfare organizations have been slow to take advantage of the technology because of a concern about the impact on human communication and interaction as well as power struggles among staff and management (Neugeboren, 1995: Benbenishty & Oyserman, 1995).

Perhaps the greatest future application of information technology, however, lies in education (Garrison & Anderson, 2003). Distance learning (online) is transforming university and college education. The virtual university and the virtual library are signs of the present, not the future. They offer choices never before available for linking work and study, for professional studies, and continuing education. They encourage lifelong learning, and link the local and the global, the urban and the rural, the north and the south. In response to demands from students as well as faculties, university and college programs in Canada—including social work education programs—are turning to computers to test the benefits of information technology, assessing the impact of cyberspace, communicating by email and listservs, engaging in WebBoard conferencing, and reframing pedagogic issues. Computers in professional education can be viewed from two perspectives (MacFadden, 1995). As a tool, they calculate as well as identify new tasks and needs. As a mechanism for developing knowledge, they frame the way human service professionals learn and the way they practise.

## Rethinking Welfare

In a global society, how will groups and individuals articulate their welfare claims? How will they engage in making those claims? And how will institutions be structured to respond to claims? During the heyday of the welfare state, the answers to such questions seemed deceptively simple. For the greater part of the twentieth century, there was a consensus that the state should and could act to satisfy basic human needs. Human welfare, regardless of class, was maximized through the provision of comprehensive services and income security. Professionals allocated scarce resources to those in need. Society came to view universal services as rights of citizenship, available to all who qualified. As noted earlier, however, one major difficulty with this interpretation of welfare provision is that it excludes or marginalizes many in society (minorities in particular), and it also presupposes a highly centralized welfare state that is capable of responding to all human needs.

An alternative view of future welfare provision is associated with neo-liberalism (Mitzman, 2003). It has been a driving ideological force in the opening up of global markets through international free trade agreements. But it is much more than a theory of markets. It is also a theory of well-being or welfare. Neo-liberalism affirms the primacy of individual choice as an arbiter of human worth. Each individual, rather than the state or the community, is in the best position to decide his or her welfare. Hence, each person, from this perspective, should be free to maximize that right with only one restraint—the necessity to respect others so that they can do the same.

The maximization of human welfare, therefore, is the maximization of free choice through the market. Obeying the dictates of the market, however, creates a basic problem in that it leads to a society in which human values are wrapped around lifestyles. Through the commercialization of lifestyles, corporations help to shape the society of the future. They define appropriate forms of behaviour and codes of conduct. Among youth, they do this by shaping mass culture and sporting events—what Naomi Klein (2000) calls the branding of lifestyles. For other observers, the process may appear more gradual but people's emulation of consumption is no less pervasive as the values of consumerism are inculcated into all strata of society. As a vision of a welfare future, this is not one that many are willing to accept.

Another perspective on welfare, which rejects the fundamentals of neo-liberalism while accepting the multiplicity of human difference, is post-structuralism or postmodernism. Post-structuralism is closely associated with those who reject the universalizing principles on which either the welfare state or markets are built. It promotes an emancipatory project of welfare that frees people from the grand narratives of the past. It problematizes welfare assumptions and social practices that are taken for granted (Chambon, Irving, & Epstein, 1999).

An advantage of post-structural theories is that they serve as an intellectual force for minorities, the forgotten, and the neglected. They remind us of the stigmatizing ideas that shape our way of thinking, speaking, and acting. They challenge the idea that universal institutions can respond to the multiple needs of different people throughout the world. They affirm the need for the freedom to deconstruct "dominant ideologies and phony universalism" (Ferguson, Lavalette, & Mooney, 2002, p. 179). A difficulty, however, is the negating or downplaying of commonalities, such as universal rights, that are integral to people's sense of well-being. In addition, they contribute to a process of fragmentation between and within oppressed groups that, in turn, weakens their capacity to be heard in a global world (Ferguson, Lavalette, & Mooney, 2002, Chapter 10).

Faced with a highly influential notion of neo-liberal welfare and a fragmented notion of welfare inherent in post-structuralism, it is imperative to think about a way of balancing, or linking, the welfare bonds between the individual and the community. In *A Theory of Human Need*, Doyal and Gough (1991) attempt to come to terms with globalization through the articulation of a universal concept of basic needs. They claim that all people share two basic needs regardless of culture or background—autonomy and health. Needs, in this sense, are more than drives, goals, or strategies; they are fundamental to human functioning. They transcend classism, racism, ageism, sexism, and other forms of oppression. For their realization, they presuppose a concept of global citizenship in which individuals are bearers of minimal rights and duties under international law and an institutional context in which some of the present attributes of national rights are transferred to a world state (Carter, 2001, p. 193; Drover, 2003).

There is, in addition, one other element that is central to a concept of welfare in a global village, and that is the potential of people to participate in the process of making claims. None of us is fully autonomous; all of us are interdependent. Drover and Kerans (1993) argue that without the freedom of people to name their claims, and without an institutional framework in which those claims can be legitimately recognized, a theory of need risks being either a subjective assessment grounded in individual experience or an objective assessment based on the judgment of experts. To avoid both extremes, they suggest that welfare has to be rooted in social action that presupposes a duality of claims-making between the individual and community. Welfare is a dynamic process, which they call "well-seeking" (rather than well-being), because it involves "increasing levels of personal and institutional complexity within which bonds of attachment and affection are integral parts of relationships" (Drover & Kerans, 1993, p. 7).

They focus on the dynamic nature of welfare in a global context for three reasons. First, welfare claims-making involves a creative use of language. Need may be universal, as Doyal and Gough suggest, yet its expression is culturally specific. Second, to have meaning and value, those claims must be acknowledged by others. Without the encouragement of others, individuals rarely, if ever, find their claims are accepted. Third, claims-making is fundamentally moral as it requires the claims-makers to assume the perspective of others. In a global society, therefore, the claims of welfare which take into account the needs of people only within one nation-state are necessarily selective. To move beyond particular states, we must reconstruct welfare provision on a global basis in the context of global citizenship.

## CONCLUSION

Throughout much of the twentieth century, it was largely assumed that welfare policy was determined by each nation. This chapter implies that such an assumption no longer holds true because of the dynamics of globalization. While we must be cautious about attributing too much to globalization, we would be equally imprudent to attribute too little to its forces. Whether we like it or not, globalization is an intractable and irreversible process that affects us all in some measure. So is security.

In welfare terms, the fundamental impact of the global process is the limitations it places on nation-states. Fiscal and monetary policies that governments once invoked to garner and redistribute resources are increasingly counteracted by the flexibility of international labour markets and the mobility of international capital. In addition, the welfare state frequently cannot satisfy the multiplicity and diversity of claims made on it at a national level. Faced with this dilemma, people look increasingly to other forms of governance to make certain that their voices are heard in the political process. While national governments remain important, they have become only one source of legitimacy.

Other institutions are implicated in the welfare agenda. Deep down, globalization raises fundamental questions about that agenda. Since the global process concerns the compression of time and space, welfare too must bridge the local and the global, the particular and the universal, the individual and the collective. First and foremost, welfare has to do with people's sense of themselves, their aspirations, their sense of security, and their identity. At the same time, it also has to do with mutual respect and taking into account other people's welfare as well as institutional reliability and stability. Without mutual respect, there is little sense of self-worth. Without both of those, there is little trust. Globalization's great advantage is that it makes us more aware of the interdependency of the three aspects of welfare. Its great disadvantage is that it challenges many of our current assumptions.

# References

Adelman, Howard. (2002). *Governance, Globalization, and Security*. Toronto: York University. http://www.iigr.ca/conferences/archive/pdfs1/adelman.pdf

Aulich, C., & Reynolds, M. (1993). Competitive Tendering and Contracting Out. *Australian Journal of Public Administration, 52.4.*

Banting, Keith. (1982). *The Welfare State and Canadian Federalism*. Kingston: McGill-Queen's University Press.

Barber, Benjamin. (1995). *Jihad versus McWorld*. New York: Times Books.

Barlow, Maude. (2004). *The Free Trade Area of the Americas and the Threat to Social Programs, Environmental Sustainability, and Social Justice in Canada and the Americas*. www.attac.org/fra/list/doc/barlow.htm.

Beck, Ulrich. (2005). The Silence of Words and Political Dynamics in the World Risk Society. In Bronner, Stephen Eric (Ed.). *Planetary Politics: Human Rights, Terror and Global Security*. Lanham: Rowman & Littlefield Publishers, Inc.

Benbenishty, R., & Oyserman, D. (1995). Integrated Information Systems for Human Services: A Conceptual Framework, Methodology, and Technology. In J. Rafferty, J. Steyaert, & D. Colombi (Eds.). *Human Services in the Information Age*. New York: Haworth Press.

Berman, Paul. (2003). *Terror and Liberalism*. New York: Norton.

Bhagwati, Jagdish. (2004). *In Defense of Globalization*. New York: Oxford University Press.

Brawley, Mark. (2003). *The Politics of Globalization: Gaining Perspective, Assessing Consequences*. Peterborough, ON: Broadview Press.

Canadian Council for Public-Private Partnerships. (2007). *About PPP, Definitions*. http://www.pppcouncil.ca/aboutPPP_definition.asp

Carter, April. (2001). *The Political Theory of Global Citizenship*. London: Routledge.

Chambon, Adrienne, Irving, Alan, & Epstein, Laura. (1999). *Reading Foucault for Social Work*. New York: Columbia University Press.

Chute, Tanya. (2005). *Globalization, Security, and Exclusion*. Toronto: York University, Centre for Refugee Studies Working Paper Series. No. 3.

Clark, Tony, & Barlow, Maude. (1997). *MAI: The Multilateral Agreement on Investment and the Threat to Canadian sovereignty*. Toronto: Stoddart.

Coatsworth, John. (2004). "Globalization, Growth, and Welfare in History," in Suárez, Marcello and Baolian Qin-Hilliard, Desirée (Eds.), *Globalization*. Berkeley: University of California Press.

Council of Canadians. (1999). *The MAI Inquiry: Confronting Globalization and Reclaiming Democracy*. Ottawa.

Cox, Robert. (2000). Political Economy and World Governance: Problems of Power and Knowledge at the Turn of the Millennium. In Richard Stubbs & Geoffrey Underhill (Eds.), *Political Economy and the Changing Global Order*. Don Mills, ON: Oxford University Press.

Doyal, L., & Gough, I. (1991). *A Theory of Human Need*. London: Macmillan.

Drover, Glenn. (2003). Poverty Alleviation: A Rights-Based Approach. In Tang, Kwong-Leung & Wong, Chack-kie (Eds.), *Poverty Monitoring and Alleviation in East Asia*. New York: Nova Science Publishers.

Drover, G., & Kerans, P. (1993). *New Approaches to Welfare Theory*. Aldershot: Edgar Elgar.

Drover, Glenn, Johnson, Graham, & Tao, Julia (Eds.). (2001). *Regionalism and Subregionalism in East Asia: The Dynamics of China*. New York: Nova Science Publishers.

Drucker, P. (1989). *The New Realities*. New York. Harper and Row.

Ferguson, Iain, Lavalette, Michael, & Mooney, Gerry. (2002). *Rethinking Welfare: A Critical Perspective*. London: Sage Publications.

Garrison, D. R., & Anderson, T. (2003). *E-learning in the 21st Century: A Framework for Research and Practice*. London: Rutledge Falmer.

George, Vic, & Wilding, Paul. (2002). *Globalization and Human Welfare*. Basingstoke, Hampshire: Palgrave.

Gibbins, Roger. (2007). Federalism in the 21st Century: Defining the Common Economic Space. *Policy Options*, March.

Giddens, A. (1991). *Modernity and Self-identity*. Stanford: Stanford University Press.

Giddens, A. (2006). Globalisation. In Eitzen, D. Stanely, & Maxine Baca Zinn (Eds.), *Globalization: The Transformation of Social Worlds*. Belmont: Thomson Wadsworth.

Greider, W. (1997). *One World, Ready or Not*. New York: Simon & Schuster.

Guest, Dennis. (1997). *The Emergence of Social Security in Canada*. Vancouver: University of British Columbia Press.

Hile, M. G. (1998). (Guest Ed.). The History and Function of the Target Cities Management Information Systems. *Computers in Human Services, 14*, 3–4.

Hoffman, Aaron. (2006). *Building Trust*. Albany: State University of New York Press.

Howlett, M., & Ramesh, M. (1993). Patterns of Policy Instrument Choice: Policy Styles, Policy Learning, and the Privatization Experiences. *Policy Studies Review, 12*, 1–2.

Huntington, Samuel. (1996). *The Clash of Civilizations and the Remaking of World Order*. New York: Simon and Schuster.

Hyde, Mark, & Dixon, John. (2002). Globalization, Poverty, Ideology, and the Privatization of Social Protections in Western Europe. *New Global Development: Journal of International and Comparative Social Welfare, 18, 1 & 2*.

Hyde, Mark, Dixon, John, & Drover, Glenn. (2006). *The Privatization of Mandatory Retirement Income Protection*. Lewiston: The Edwin Mellon Press.

Ishay, Micheline. (2005). Human Rights in the Age of Empire. In Bronner, Stephen Eric (Ed.), *Planetary Politics: Human Rights, Terror and Global Security*. Lanham: Rowman & Littlefield Publishers, Inc.

Jackson, Andrew, & Sanger, Matthew. (1998). *Dismantling Democracy: The Multilateral Agreement on Investment*. Ottawa: Canadian Centre for Policy Alternatives.

Jackson, Andrew, & Sanger, Matthew. (2003). *When Worlds Collide*. Ottawa: Canadian Centre for Policy Alternatives.

Jenson, Jane. (1993). De-constructing Dualities: Making Rights Claims in Political Institutions. In G. Drover & P. Kerans (Eds.), *New Approaches to Welfare Theory*. Aldershot, UK: Edward Elgar, 113–126.

Jenson, Jane, & Phillips, Susan. (2002). Redesigning the Canadian Citizenship Regime: Remaking the Institutions of Representation. In C. Crouch, K. Eder, & D. Tambini (Eds.), *Citizenship, Markets and the State*. London, UK: Oxford University Press.

Jessop, B. (1993). Towards a Schumpeterian Workfare State? Preliminary Remarks on Post-Fordist Political Economy. *Studies in Political Economy, 40,* 7–39.

Jessop, B. (2007). The Transition to Post-Fordism and the Schumpeterian Workfare State. In Vij, Ritu (Ed.), *Globalization and Welfare: A Critical Reader*. Basingstoke: Palgrave Macmillan.

Kellner, Douglas. (2007). New Technologies, the Welfare State, and the Prospects for Democratization. http://www.gseis.ucla.edu/rcscarch/kellner/ntd.wd.html

Kite, Cynthia. (2004). The Stability of the Globalized Welfare State. In Bo Sodersten (Ed.), *Globalization and the Welfare State*. Basingstoke: Palgrave Macmillan.

Klein, Naomi. (2000). *No Logo*. London, UK: Flamingo.

Korten, D. C. (1995). *When Corporations Rule the World*. West Hartford, CT: Kamarian Press.

Lawrence, R., Bressand, A., & Takatoshi, I. (1996). *A Vision for the World Economy: Openness, Diversity, and Cohesion*. Washington, D.C.: Brookings Institute.

Lustiger-Thaler, H., & Shragge, E. (1993). Social Movements and Social Welfare: The Political Problems of Need. In G. Drover & P. Kerans (Eds.), *New Approaches to Welfare Theory*. Aldershot, UK: Edward Elgar, pp. 161–176.

MacFadden, R. J. (1995). IT and Knowledge Development in Human Services: Tool, Paradigm, and Promise. In J. Rafferty, J. Steyaert, & D. Colombi (Eds.), *Human Services in the Information Age*. New York: Haworth Press.

Michael, J. (1994). *Privacy and Human Rights*. Dartmouth, NS: UNESCO.

Miles, I., Rush, H., Turner, K., & Bessant, J. (1998). *Information Horizons: The Long-Term Social Implications of New Information Technologies*. Aldershot, UK: Edward Elgar.

Mishra. R. (1990). *The Welfare State in Capitalist Society*. Toronto: University of Toronto Press.

Mishra, R. (2002). Globalization and Poverty in the Americas. *New Global Development: Journal of International and Comparative Social Welfare, 18.1 & 2.*

Mitzman, Arthur. (2003). *Prometheus Revisited: The Quest for Global Justice in the Twenty-First Century*. Amherst, MA: University of Massachusetts Press.

Muñoz, Heraldo, Ed. (2006). *Democracy Rising: Assessing the Global Challenges*. Boulder: Lynne Rienner Publishers.

Naisbitt, J. (1994). *Global Paradox: The Bigger the World Economy, the More Powerful Its Smaller Players*. New York: William Morrow.

Neugeboren, B. (1995). Organizational Influences on Management Information Systems in the Human Services. In J. Rafferty, J. Steyaert, & D. Colombi (Eds.), *Human Services in the Information Age*. New York: Haworth Press.

Organization for Economic Co-operation and Development, OECD. (1994). *The New World Trading System*. Paris: OECD.

Ohmae, K. (1995). *The End of the Nation State: The Rise of Regional Economics*. New York: Free Press.

O'Reilly, Elaine. (2007). M*aking Career Sense of Labour Market Information*. Ottawa/Victoria. Human Resources Development Canada and the BC Ministry of Advanced Education. http://makingcareersense.org/

Overbeek, H. (Ed.). (1993). *Restructuring Hegemony in the Global Political Economy: The Rise of Transnational Neo-liberalism in the 1980s*. London, UK: Routledge.

Pauly, Louis. (1997). *Who Elected the Gankers?* Ithaca, NY: Cornell University Press.

Rieger, Elmar, & Leibried, Stephan. (2003). *Limits to Globalization: Welfare States and the World Economy*. Cambridge, UK: Polity Press.

Resnick, Hy, & Anderson, Phoebe Sadie (Eds.). (2002). Innovations in Technology and Human Services: Practice and Education. *Journal of Technology in Human Services*, *Special Issue, 20*.

Sampson, Gary, & Woolcock, Stephen. (2003). *Regionalism, Multilateralism and Economic Integration: The Recent Experience*. New York: United Nations University Press.

Schirm, Stefan. (2002). *Globalization and the New Regionalism*. Cambridge: Polity Press.

Schram, Sanford F. (2006). *Welfare Discourse: Discourse, Governance and Globalization*. Philadelphia: Temple University Press.

Schuler, D. (1997). *The New Community Networks: Wired for Change*. Reading, MA: Addison.

Scott, A. (1993). On Lustiger-Thaler and Shragge. In G. Drover & P. Kerans (Eds.), *New Approaches to Welfare Theory*. Aldershot, UK: Edward Elgar, pp. 281–283.

Scott, Katherine. (2004). *The World We Have: Toward a New Social Architecture*. Ottawa: Canadian Council on Social Development.

Scott, Robert, Salas, Carlos, & Campbell, Bruce. (2001). *NAFTA at Seven: Its Impact on Workers in All Three Nations*. Ottawa: Canadian Centre for Policy Alternatives.

Shragge, E. (1995). *Community Economic Development: In Search of Empowerment and Alternatives*. Montreal: Black Rose Press.

Singh, N., & Titi, V. (1995). *Empowerment for Sustainable Development: Toward Operational Strategies*. Halifax: Fernwood.

Sklair, L. (1991). *Sociology of the Global System*. Baltimore: Johns Hopkins University Press.

Sodersten, Bo. (2004). *Globalization and the Welfare State*. Basingstoke: Palgrave Macmillan.

Steger, Manfred. (2002). *Globalism: The New Market Ideology*. Lanham: Rowman & Littlefield.

Stinson, Jane, Pollack, Nancy, & Cohen, Marcy. (2005). *The Pains of Privatization*. Vancouver: Canadian Centre for Policy Alternatives, BC Office.

Strange, S. (1996). *The Retreat of the State: The Diffusion of Power in the World Economy.* Cambridge: Cambridge University Press.

Timonen, Virpi. (2003). *Restructuring the Welfare State: Globalization and Social Policy Reform in Finland and Sweden.* Cheltenham, UK: Edward Elgar.

Townson, Monica. (2004). A New "Social Architecture" for Canada?: Planned Redesign of Programs Could Lead to Privatization. *The CCPA Monitor.* Canadian Centre for Policy Alternatives. September.

United Nations Research Institute for Social Development. (1995). *States of Disarray: The Social Effects of Globalization.* London: Banson Productions.

Veltmeyer, Henry (Ed.). (2004). *Globalization and Anti-globalization: Dynamics of Change in the New World Order.* Aldershot: Ashgate Publishing.

Workman, Thom. (2002). *Social Torment: Globalization in Atlantic Canada.* Halifax: Fernwood Press.

# CHAPTER 31

# International Social Work

*Linda Snyder*

## INTRODUCTION

Many social work practitioners, academics, and students are drawn to international social work because of the compelling needs of people within and beyond our local boundaries and the connectedness we experience through our sense of common humanity. The realities in our globalized world bring us to a professional practice that works toward well-being for all: "The social work profession promotes social change, problem-solving in human relationships, and the empowerment and liberation of people to enhance well-being. Utilizing theories of human behaviour and social systems, social work intervenes at the points where people interact with their environments. Principles of human rights and social justice are fundamental to social work" (IFSW & IASSW, 2001).

## GLOBAL CONTEXT

Poverty levels that cannot support life, growing inequality within and between nations, health issues including the AIDS pandemic, migration and refugee conditions, conflicts resulting in war and human rights abuses, and environmental degradation are aspects of our global circumstance that demand attention. The United Nations *Report on the World Social Situation* (UNESA, 2005) tells us that "eighty percent of the world's gross domestic product is held by the one billion people living in the developed world; the remaining 20% is shared by the five billion people living in developing countries" (Executive Summary, paragraph 1). Also, we know from the UN (2006) *Millennium Goals Report* that nearly 20 percent of the developing world's population live on less than $1 US per day and that this often means they lack sufficient food to meet their basic daily requirements. Within our own country of Canada we are also experiencing a widening gap between the rich and the poor (Yalnizyan, 2007). Disproportionate levels of poverty among female-headed single parent families as well as the desperate conditions of many Aboriginal communities, some of whom are without safe drinking water, have resulted in criticism of Canada by the United Nations Economic and Social Council (2006).

Nearly 40 million people are living with HIV (64 percent of them in sub-Saharan Africa where 12 million children are orphans), and nearly 3 million people die of AIDS each year (UN, 2006). Infant mortality and maternal deaths in childbirth, child deaths before age five, as well as other diseases including malaria and vaccine-preventable illnesses are all more prevalent in the most impoverished areas of the world (UN, 2006).

Migration occurs for economic reasons, requiring many people to learn to live in new environments—sometimes in congested urban settings, sometimes in cultures where they are not respected, and often sending meagre earnings home to family as remittances. Even harsher conditions often face the over 20 million refugees, internally displaced persons, and other people of concern to the United Nations High Commission for Refugees (UNHCR, 2007). The atrocities of war and conflict in distant places like Iraq, Israel, Uganda, and Darfur (to name a few), as well as terrorist actions like the bombing of the Air India flight, which originated in Canada, also command our attention. The media keep us well apprised of the loss of life, human rights abuses, and displacement, even if thoughtful analyses of underlying issues are more difficult to find. Global warming and other serious environmental problems must also concern us as people who share a common ecosystem with real limits. It is this global context which motivates many people holding the fundamental social work ideals of humanitarianism and egalitarianism to look to international social work as a field of professional practice from which to make a contribution toward a better world.

## DEFINITIONS, TERMINOLOGY, AND OVERVIEW

What is meant by *international social work*? Unfortunately, there isn't a definition that is widely agreed upon, but a very useful one is provided by Healy (2001): "International social work is defined as international professional action and the capacity for international action by the social work profession and its members. International action has four dimensions: internationally related domestic practice and advocacy, professional exchange, international practice, and international policy development and advocacy" (p. 7).

International social work is inextricably linked to the concept of social development—the promotion of "improvement in the total human condition" (Huene, 1991, p. 8). Social development recognizes that both social welfare and economic stability are required for human well-being (Midgley & Livermore, 2004). Clearly, increases in gross domestic product (GDP) per capita do not ensure an equitable distribution of wealth, and there are limits to the planet's ability to absorb the negative ecological consequences of economic growth.

Social workers are not the only actors in the field of international social development. Members of other human service professions (e.g., faith-based workers like Mother Teresa) and people from other academic disciplines (e.g., economists like Dr. Muhammad Yunus who founded the Grameen Bank) have made enormous contributions to international social development. However, the social work profession—with its dedication to "the welfare and self-realization of all people ... and the achievement of social justice for all" (CASW, 2005, p. 3); its theoretical frameworks, including systems theory and structural and empowerment approaches; as well as its methods, including practice at individual, community, and societal levels with skills in empathy, advocacy, and community organizing—is particularly well-suited to participation in social development (Wilson & Whitmore, 2000).

Related to definitional understanding is the need for clarity in the use of terminology in this chapter. First, the differentiation between *global* and *international*: *global* will be used to connote matters related to the entire world; *international* generally will refer to matters involving two or more nations. Second, the challenge is choosing terms to differentiate between rich and poor countries—which is a false dichotomy at the outset since pockets of poverty exist in rich countries like Canada, and there is often a small, but very wealthy, elite in many poor countries. During the Cold War era, it was common to hear references to industrialized capitalist democracies as the First World, industrialized communist countries as the Second World, and others as the Third World, but this terminology is less relevant politically today and contains potential interpretations of first class versus third rate. More neutral terms of North/South or West/East are used by many writers; however, they are problematic in the lack of "fit" for many countries such as Australia and Japan. This chapter will use the terminology "developed" and "developing," which is not without shortcomings, but is most commonly used in United Nations publications and the international social work and social development literature.

The chapter will continue with background material about the history of international social work as well as an overview of models of social development organizations. A typology of international social work practice will follow along with a presentation of contributions from social work theory and practice.

## BRIEF HISTORY

The history of international social work is evident in the development of social welfare and social work. The Canadian social welfare system acknowledges the British influences of the *Poor Laws*, which were adopted in the maritime provinces in the eighteenth century, and the Beveridge Report, which was first to suggest, in 1942, that the state should ensure a comprehensive range of income security programs for its citizens (Guest, 1997). Similarly, the potential of the early Charity Organization Society and Settlement House movement in England was observed by Jane Addams who established Hull House in Chicago, from whence the concept of educated members of society working with the poor to develop neighbourhood services and to promote social reform spread in North America (Hokenstad & Midgley, 2004).

After the Second World War, assistance from industrialized countries was provided to the newly independent countries (often in the form of aid which was "tied" to the economic and political objectives of the donor country) and much social work knowledge was transferred to the developing world—often without attention to its appropriateness to a distinct cultural, social, economic, or political reality. In reaction to the dominance of "Western" social work knowledge, many developing countries (with those in Latin America initiating the process) began a reconceptualization process to develop a critical, alternative method of social work more relevant to their contexts (Healy, 2001; Quiroz, n.d.). The outcome has been described succinctly by Hokenstad and Midgley (2004): "The need for a more discerning attitude to the diffusion of innovations was emphasized [and] ... it is today generally accepted that mutuality and the reciprocal sharing of social work knowledge and practice approaches should characterize exchanges in social work." (p. ix). Hence, we are now able to see the transfer of social work and social development knowledge from developing to developed countries. The collective kitchens and community gardens that were formed during the 1970s in urban shantytowns in Latin America (such as Villa El Salvador in Peru) and are now a key element of urban food security programs in Canada (Fairholm, 1999) are a striking example of this.

## MODELS OF SOCIAL DEVELOPMENT

International social work action occurs within models of social development. The models are based on theories about the factors underlying problems and about likely solutions. The theories, in turn, are consistent with the core values and ideologies upon which they are founded. Since social work is a value-anchored profession (Stalwick, 1997), practitioners must critically assess program models before taking action. Hence, an overview of models of social development is offered.

Nederveen Pieterse (2001) provides a useful classification distinguishing between the "growth" model and the "social transformation" model. The growth model, which is sometimes referred to as the modernization model, is based on classic "laissez-faire" economic theory which holds that the free market, unfettered by the state, is the best means to bring economic well-being to all. It is within this model that Rostow (1960) postulated five stages to development from traditional agricultural societies through a "take off" phase to an end goal of high mass consumption. Since the 1970s, we have witnessed a strong revival of the growth model under the rubric of "neo-liberal" economics (the new free market approach) which prioritizes economic growth and advocates a reduced role for the state and cutbacks to social programs. Ferguson, Lavalette, and Whitmore (2005) provide a succinct description of its recipe and its promise:

> Over the past two decades the world has been dramatically shaped by the development of neo-liberal globalization. Neo-liberal advocates argue that economic and social liberalism will benefit everyone: wealth will trickle down from the wealthiest nations and individuals to the very poorest across the globe. The solution to debt and poverty, so they would have us believe, is structural adjustment: lowering trade barriers and opening economies up to multinational companies, encouraging direct foreign investments, welfare retrenchment and privatization of state-owned enterprises, abolition of subsidies and price controls, and the withdrawal of controls on capital movements. By following these simple measures, economic growth and expansion is sure to follow and the lives of the poor vastly improved. (p. 1)

In contrast, the social transformation model described by Nederveen Pieterse (2001) prioritizes social objectives over economic objectives. It is consistent with the critiques of structures such as colonialism and imperialism which, according to this model, have created underdevelopment and continue to maintain inequality (Frank, 1978). Emerging from this analysis are beliefs in the need for vigorous participatory processes to transform the exploitative and oppressive structures. Feminist scholars have added to the conceptualization the importance of incorporating strategies to address the oppression of women (Sen & Grown, 1987).

Midgley (2001) advocates a developmental model that could be positioned between the two extremes illuminated by Nederveen Pieterse. Midgley is critical of excessive emphasis on remedial social welfare approaches and cautious of activist social work perspectives. He acknowledges the wisdom of the "developmentistas" in Latin America who incorporated an important role for the state (not a laissez-faire approach) and, in contrast with the assumptions of the growth model, "rejects the idea that relentless pursuit of profits will somehow result in tangible improvements for all" (Midgley & Livermore, 2004, p. 132). He advocates a balanced role for the market, state, and civil society and calls for productivist strategies to enhance human capital (the employability of individuals) and social capital (mutual support systems in communities) (Hall & Midgley, 2004). The focus is on bringing social objectives to the current economic structures rather than transforming the structures themselves. Facilitating the development of microenterprises exemplifies the productivist strategy within Midgley's developmental model.

The notion of a continuum of social development models is found in liberation theology. The Boff brothers (1987/92) describe a continuum from aid, through reformism, to liberation. In the aid approach, the poor are recipients of charity and there is no examination of the structural roots of their circumstances. Reformism attempts to improve the situation of the poor, but within the existing structures which favour the elite. In the liberation model, which they espouse, the objectives are raising consciousness, claiming rights, and transforming society. A parallelism with the growth, developmental, and social transformation models described above is apparent. One can also envision similarities in a continuum that addresses different levels of needs/change: moving from physical survival (emergency relief), through economic and social needs (developmental programs of sustainable development including ecological objectives), to political change (liberation and transformation).

While social workers may align themselves with reform or transformational models of social development, there are few who would find any congruence between the neo-liberal economic theories of the growth model and social work's core values (Mullaly, 1997). The dire consequences of neo-liberal policies have been witnessed in developed and less developed countries alike. Teeple (2000) has chronicled the assaults to Canada's social safety net and even the former chief economist of the World Bank, Joseph Stiglitz (2006), speaks about the devastation wreaked by the structural adjustment programs required of low income countries that needed to borrow from the World Bank or the International Monetary Fund (IMF). Wilson and Whitmore (2000) provide numerous examples of how the neo-liberal approach is responsible for making this era of globalism the "age of disposable humanity" (p. 13). A movement for social justice has involved many social activists in demonstrating their opposition to the excesses of the free market and its power imbalances (George, 2004). Some social work academics have proposed a "new social work of resistance" (Ferguson & Lavalette, 2006) and, in concert with this stance, others suggest that in our current globalized context, all social work is really international social work (Ife & Tessoriero, 2006; Dudziak, 2005).

Also related to models of social development is concern with human rights. Social work, with its fundamental belief in the dignity and worth of every human being, will not condone actions which ignore or violate human rights, as stated in the Preamble to the CASW (2005) *Code of Ethics*: "Social workers are committed to human rights as enshrined in Canadian law, as well as in international conventions on human rights created or supported by the United Nations" (p. 3). The *Universal Declaration of Human Rights* proclaimed by the United Nations in 1948, along with several subsequent specific conventions and declarations (e.g., rights of children, elimination of discrimination) constitute international instruments that governments and organizations use as foundational reference points for the development of legislation and programs to protect and promote human rights.

Similarly, ecological sustainability must be included in any comprehensive model of social development. The report of the World Commission on Environment and Development in 1987 (also know as the Brundtland Commission because it was headed by Gro Harlem Brundtland, the Prime Minister of Norway) identified sustainable development as "meeting the needs of the present without compromising the ability of future generations to meet their own needs" (p. 43). Its title, *Our Common Future*, conveys the sense of collective responsibility for connected humanity that compels social workers and others to work toward social development in ways that are sustainable in the long term.

## ORGANIZATIONS IN INTERNATIONAL SOCIAL DEVELOPMENT

Work in the area of international social development is most often carried out within organizations. Some of these organizations pertain specifically to social work and others relate more broadly to international development. The social work organizations will be described after the presentation of the organizations with broader mandates.

## International Organizations

No doubt the largest and most important international organization concerned with social development is the United Nations. After World War II, the countries of the world created a charter to form this organization in order to promote international peace and social progress. As already noted, its *Universal Declaration of Human Rights* and related covenants and declarations provide the foundation for the promotion and protection of important rights around the world. Many of its related bodies such as the United Nations Children's Fund (UNICEF), the United Nations High Commission for Refugees (UNHCR), the World Health Organization (WHO), and the International Labour Organization (ILO) are well known for their work in areas fundamental to social development. The United Nations also establishes specific times to draw attention to important issues, such as International Women's Day (March 8), International Year of Planet Earth (2008), and the Second International Decade of the World's Indigenous People (2005–2014). It organizes special commissions and summits such as the Earth Summit, which produced the accord on cutting carbon dioxide emissions in 1997 at Kyoto. It conducts research and publishes findings such as the UN Department of Economic and Social Affairs' biennial *Report on the World Social Situation*. It also establishes and monitors goals, as it has done with the Millennium Development Goals in order to galvanize "efforts to meet the needs of the world's poorest" (UN, n.d., p. 1). Canada has played a key role in the United Nations from the drafting of the *Universal Declaration of Human Rights* by Canadian John Peters Humphrey, and the ratification of most of the conventions of rights (in contrast to the United States' failure to do so), to the important role of Stephen Lewis as the UN special envoy for HIV/AIDS in Africa. However, Canada's participation in the bombing of Kosovo in 1999 without the approval of the UN Security Council was a break from this otherwise positive record (Gilchrist, 2001).

International financial institutions also have a significant role in international social development because of the impact of their loans and policies. The 1944 agreement that emerged from an international conference in Bretton Woods, New Hampshire, created the International Monetary Fund to promote stability in international exchange, including lending to correct nations' balance of payments maladjustments (IMF, 1944), the World Bank to provide loans for reconstruction and development (World Bank, n.d.), and the antecedents to the World Trade Organization (WTO) to establish the rules of trade between nations (WTO, n.d.). These three organizations have followed the neo-liberal economic paradigm and have been strongly criticized for worsening the circumstances of many poor countries. The structural adjustment programs required of borrowing nations stipulated that they cut health, education, and social programs as well as open their borders to imports and orient their economies toward export rather than domestic consumption (Green, 1996). Worsened poverty and inequality resulted in many developing countries. The World Trade Organization's rules have similarly wreaked havoc on poor countries that are unable to protect their agricultural and industrial sectors from cheaper imports that frequently come from rich countries that subsidize their own producers (Oxfam, 2004). The undemocratic structure of the three organizations and the inordinate power the United States wields within them also warrant the loud cries for reform (Ferguson & Lavalette, 2005; Stiglitz, 2006).

In addition to these supranational bodies, there are international non-governmental organizations (INGOs) engaged in social development activities. The Red Cross and Red

Crescent societies, who are often first responders in disasters and conflict zones, are a well-known example. Others include Amnesty International, which brings international awareness and advocacy to stop human rights violations around the world; Oxfam International, which is involved in emergency relief, community development, research, and advocacy; as well as many faith-based organizations such as Mennonite Central Committee, which is engaged in relief, development, and peace activities. Also of note is the International Consortium for Social Development (ICSD) which links academics and practitioners in capacity building and developing conceptual frameworks for effective strategies through conferences, its technical assistance roster, and its journal *Social Development Issues*.

## National Organizations

National organizations involved in social development, both governmental and non-governmental, are found in developed countries. Our government program, the Canadian International Development Agency (CIDA), was formed to administer official development assistance (ODA) through bilateral (nation to nation) aid. Now it also works in partnership with Canadian and international non-governmental organizations to contribute toward social development. Although it was a Canadian prime minister, Lester B. Pearson, who chaired the commission in 1969, that recommended that developed countries provide 0.7% of gross national product as ODA, Canada has never reached this target; in 2006, our commitment was only 0.3% in comparison with Nordic countries which exceeded the 0.7% target (UNICEF, 2007). Collective awareness of the inadequate contributions by developed countries has risen through the Make Poverty History campaign and actions such as the Live 8 concert, organized by high-profile rock musicians Bob Geldof and Bono, to coincide with the G8 summit in Scotland in July 2005 (Make Poverty History, n.d.).

Non-governmental organizations (NGOs) in Canada are involved in direct community development work as well as advocacy and activism. CUSO, originally known as Canadian University Services Overseas and a volunteer placement service, is one such NGO that now has a large development program working in partnership with organizations in many developing countries (CUSO, n.d.). The Council of Canadians is an example of an NGO that engages in advocacy work. Although its focus is primarily on Canadian independence, it is very active in opposing free trade and was a leader in the 1998 defeat of the Multinational Agreement on Investment (Council of Canadians, n.d.). The Canadian social work organizations will be identified in the next section; however, a related academic institution is the Canadian Association for the Study of International Development (CASID), which publishes the *Canadian Journal of Development Studies*.

Developing countries also have both governmental and non-governmental organizations that are engaged in activities to foster social development within their own country. In Chile, for example, the national women's service (SERNAM) promotes women's rights and participation in the transition to democracy; an NGO, the Christian churches' social assistance foundation (FASIC), provided support to human rights victims during the Pinochet dictatorship. In Mexico, the government's social development secretariat (SEDESOL) administers a program for the very poor entitled "Oportunidades"; an NGO, the women's council of the San Cristóbal diocese in Chiapas (CODIMUJ), uses liberation theology methods to strengthen the women's recognition of their dignity and worth.

## International Social Work Organizations

There are three international social work organizations, sometimes referred to as "the three sisters": the International Federation of Social Workers (IFSW), the International Association of Schools of Social Work (IASSW), and the International Council on Social Welfare (ICSW). The three organizations were founded at an international social work conference held in Paris in 1928—although their original names were slightly different (Healy, 2001). The International Federation of Social Workers, whose national counterpart is the Canadian Association of Social Workers (CASW), promotes the profession and represents it at the international level. The International Association of Schools of Social Work, whose counterpart is the Canadian Association of Schools of Social Work (CASSW), promotes excellence in social work education throughout the world and the engagement of educators in exchange of knowledge and expertise. Canadian Ralph Garber is a past-president of IASSW and was responsible for the 2000 World Census of Social Work Education. The International Council on Social Welfare, whose national counterpart is the Canadian Council on Social Development (CCSD), works to advance social welfare and social development. All three of the organizations have consultative status at the United Nations and together they sponsor the journal *International Social Work*, which was edited for many years by another Canadian (and the editor of this textbook), Frank Turner. A very important accomplishment in the past few years has been the development of joint documents by the IFSW and the IASSW: the *International Definition of Social Work* adopted June 2001 in Copenhagen, and the *Ethics in Social Work* and *Global Standards for Social Work Education and Training* adopted October 2004 in Adelaide.

## INTERNATIONAL SOCIAL WORK PRACTICE

This section on international social work practice describes a typology of practice, frameworks for international practice, and methods for practice. Healy's (2001) definition of international social work, quoted earlier, includes a typology differentiating four dimensions of practice. *Internationally related domestic practice and advocacy* encompasses work with immigrants in one's own country, which includes refugee resettlement and family reunification, assisting families whose members may be responding differently to mainstream cultural practices, as well as advocating with government and professional associations to remove barriers to employment for new Canadians. *Professional exchange* relates to sharing of knowledge and experience across borders and includes comparative research on social policy and programs, faculty and student exchange programs (which can be part of supporting the development of new professional education programs), and adapting innovations from other countries. *International practice* refers to the direct intervention of foreign social workers in host countries, such as helping communities develop programs to respond to trauma from war or disaster. The fourth dimension of practice identified by Healy is *international policy and advocacy* which encompasses the consultative work with the United Nations done by the international social work organizations and the participation of social workers in the global justice movement, such as the involvement of faculty and students from the School of Social Work at St. Thomas University in the protest at the Summit of the Americas in Quebec City (Dudziak, 2005). Beyond the fundamental description of what international social workers do, Healy and others provide important thoughts about the framework for how they practise.

# Frameworks for International Social Work Practice

Some initial suggestions for practice frameworks are drawn from the broader literature regarding social development. Midgley and Livermore (2004) stipulate that social development can be effective in enhancing widespread well-being, "provided that it is people-centred, sustainable, inclusive and egalitarian, and … harmonized with social welfare policies that foster economic participation" (p. 117). Adopting practice ideas from another country requires "careful examination of both the innovation and the context in which it is to be implemented" (Hokenstad & Midgley, 2004, p. 7).

The social work literature also has much to offer in terms of framing international practice. From the reconceptualization of social work in Latin America comes the emancipatory perspective that positions social workers side by side with the masses based on an analysis of the exploitative processes underlying their current dependent and excluded circumstances (Mendoza, 2005). Liberation theology's teachings about the priority for the poor and the scriptural foundations for liberation from oppression through bringing about the kingdom of God on earth are central to this framework. Paulo Freire's pedagogy of raising critical consciousness and learning through a cyclical process of action followed by reflection (praxis) is also one of its fundamental tenets.

Social work academics in developed countries write about the importance of caution and humility in suggesting relevant knowledge for developing countries, lest we repeat the arrogance of colonial imperialism (Payne, 2006; Razack, 2002; Wilson & Whitmore, 2000). Midgley (2001) describes the criticism from social workers in developing countries that "the profession's individualized, therapeutic approach is unsuited to the pressing problems of poverty, unemployment, hunger, homelessness, and ill-health that characterize the global South" (p. 28) and suggests that macro-level approaches of social policy, planning, social action, and community development are more relevant to the context (Hokenstad, Khinduka, & Midgley, 1992). Wilson and Whitmore (2000) assert that international practice has greater potential for effectiveness when it is based on structural and conjunctural analysis—structural analysis of the societal underpinnings of oppressive conditions and conjunctural analysis of the power relations and possibilities for change at the particular time. They also suggest that, rather than uncritically applying theories from developed countries, it is more conducive to local capacity building to seek out local experience and understanding and to facilitate the sharing of this indigenous knowledge.

Another framework with much potential in international social work is an inclusive, anti-oppressive practice model coupled with an empowerment perspective. International social work, in domestic settings and beyond our borders, often involves working with people whose race, ethnicity, culture, and/or religion are different from those of the Canadian mainstream. Thus, international practice requires taking these differences into account and being aware of our own position in relation to privilege (Dominelli, 2002). Tsang and George (1998) have described the evolution of social work practice from early Eurocentric models infused with colonial notions of superiority, to "colour-blind" approaches in which everyone was to be treated "the same," through multicultural models that celebrate difference, to anti-oppressive models that include an analysis of power and a recognition of the role of oppression in people's realities. A framework that includes an understanding of oppression must include commitment to work toward inclusion and empowerment (Gutiérrez, Parsons, & Cox, 2003).

# METHODS FOR INTERNATIONAL SOCIAL WORK PRACTICE

Many useful ideas about effective methods for international social work practice have been shared in the literature. A brief selection of these will be described, beginning with things learned from developing countries, then methods that have been developed jointly, and, finally, a method that is of particular relevance when social workers from developed countries are working in developing countries.

Midgley and Livermore (2004) provide three concrete examples of practice methods (congruent with their notion of productivist social development) learned from "the global south." A child welfare program was established in India through community-based preschool centres that incorporated education, nutrition, health, women's well-being, and community solidarity. Beginning in South Africa, community development has focused on building social capital to "help build social networks ... to enhance people's participation and mobilize communities to advocate for improved services [and] to promote local economic development" (p. 124). Asian countries and the Philippines pioneered microenterprise development and microfinance programs which have been useful in helping poor people with barriers to employment to generate their own income. Adaptations of these methods have been applied in other developing countries and in developed countries. Microenterprise development programs for women in Chile and Canada were a substantial focus of my dissertation research (Snyder, 2004). In these later applications I similarly found that collective approaches (more common in Latin America) rather than individualistic approaches (more typical in Canada's Western culture) contributed to a sense of solidarity conducive to further community achievements.

Latin America has been the source of innovative methods in popular education that are very effective in raising awareness and critical consciousness. Liam Kane (2001) provides a collection of illustrations, from poor neighbourhoods in Mexico, Brazil, and Central America, of the captivating visual and vocal means of engaging people in critical thinking about their reality and how to change it. A specific example of popular education is radical drama, developed by Brazilian Augusto Boal, that has been used to help oppressed people sculpt their image of their present situation, their vision of their ideal situation, and a transformative image to suggest how change might be achieved (Spratt, 2005).

Campfens (1997) has written with practitioners and academics from six countries: Canada, the Netherlands, Israel, Ghana, Bangladesh, and Chile to describe community development practice (as well as theory, research, and training) around the world. A particularly striking case illustration is provided by Ameyaw about an action research methodology used in Ghana called "appreciative inquiry." Leadership was drawn from the local community to facilitate community discussions in which members made the key decisions about the focus and process of the research, thereby becoming invested in its outcomes. In the book's conclusion (see References), Campfens identifies some of the common factors in effective practice, for example, the organization of self-managing groups of the poor. Castelloe, Watson, and White (2002) draw from the strengths of popular education and participatory action research and integrate them with the capacity of Alinsky-style community organizing to accomplish tangible social objectives in a methodology they call "participatory action." They provide a very practical, phased method beginning with research, outreach, and forming an idea, and moving through project implementation and organizational capacity building to creating a grassroots network.

Methodological contributions have emerged concurrently and often jointly from developed and developing countries in the broader social justice movement that is challenging neo-liberal economic globalization. Ferguson, Lavalette, and Whitmore (2005) have produced a collection of case examples from Mexico, Argentina, India, Senegal, France, Australia, the UK, and Canada describing methods that have been used to contest the dominance of the economic growth model. They write about a new, robust, engaged, and critical social work of resistance. Brecher, Costello, and Smith (2002) present a similar methodology in the practice of "withdrawal of consent" and building social movements through questioning the status quo in isolated locations of oppression, linking the marginalized and their allies, building a common project, and changing the balance of power. They provide several examples of how disenfranchised groups have linked to larger networks which were ultimately able to tie up the powerful in the same way the allegorical Lilliputians were able to capture the gigantic Gulliver. The larger networks now are often making use of electronic communication and advocacy—from the messages of the Zapatista movement in Chiapas since their uprising at the implementation of the NAFTA agreement, to the messages from the Make Poverty History coalition encouraging its constituents to forward messages to members of the federal government in advance of G8 summit meetings.

A practice methodology that is specifically intended for social workers from developed countries working with people in developing countries has been suggested by Canadian social work academics Wilson and Whitmore (2000). They have elaborated a method of "accompaniment" through their reflection on their collaboration with a Nicaraguan school of social work to integrate gender awareness into the curriculum. The approach, initially put forward by Bill Clinton (1991), is predicated on a true partnership based on common commitment and solidarity and utilizes "sympathetic listening, engaged questioning, non-directive suggesting, and solidarity in the face of setbacks" (p. 64). Wilson and Whitmore add the following principles for social workers from developed countries who are accompanying a process "owned by" their developing country partners: non-intrusiveness, mutual trust, a common analysis of the problem, a sincere solidarity and stake in the outcome, a relationship of equality, an explicit focus on process, and usage of the host country's language. Accompaniment, in their view, is the combination of the structural and conjectural analysis described earlier, a feminist approach, and our social work principles, knowledge, and skills.

## CONCLUSION

International social work is a field of practice that addresses the critical issues of poverty and injustice facing our interconnected world. The dominant neo-liberal economic paradigm has worsened conditions for the poor in developed and developing countries alike. Development models that emphasize social objectives, equality, and sustainability are required. A principled and engaged social work practice has much to contribute given egalitarian ideals and commitment to working in true partnership and solidarity with the poor and oppressed, theoretical frameworks that encourage critically thinking about structural causes and conjunctural possibilities, and practice models employing participatory and empowering methods. This holds much promise for contributing to the social change needed to bring us closer to a world in which all humankind can enjoy their fair share of the earth's resources and live in conditions of harmony and justice.

# References

Ameyaw, S. (1997). Ghana: Research in community development. In H. Campfens (Ed.), *Community development around the world: Practice, theory, research, training* (pp. 306–312). Toronto: University of Toronto Press.

Boff, L. & Boff, C. (1987/92). *Introducing liberation theology*. Maryknoll, NY: Orbis Books.

Brecher, J., Costello, T., & Smith, B. (2002). *Globalization from below: The power of solidarity*. Cambridge, MA: South End Press.

Campfens, H. (Ed.). (1997). *Community development around the world: Practice, theory, research, training*. Toronto: University of Toronto Press.

Canadian Association of Social Workers (CASW). (2005). *Code of Ethics*. Ottawa: CASW.

Castelloe, P., Watson, T., & White, C. (2002). Participatory change: An integrative approach to community practice. *Journal of Community Practice, 10*(4), 7–31.

Clinton, R. (1991). Grassroots development where no grass grows: Small-scale development efforts on the Peruvian coast. *Studies in Comparative International Development, 26*(2).

Dominelli, L. (2002). Oppression, social division and identity. In L. Dominelli, *Anti-oppressive social work theory and practice* (pp. 37–58). New York: Palgrave Macmillan.

Dudziak, S. (2005). Educating for justice. Challenges and openings in the context of globalisation. In I. Ferguson, M. Lavalette, & E. Whitmore (Eds.), *Globalisation, global justice, and social work* (pp. 141–153). New York: Routledge.

Fairholm, J. (1999). *Urban agriculture and food security initiatives in Canada* (Cities Feeding People Series). Ottawa: International Development Research Centre.

Ferguson I. & Lavalette, M. (2006). Globalization and social justice: Towards a social work of resistance. *International Social Work, 49*(3), 309–318.

Ferguson, I., Lavalette, M., & Whitmore, E. (Eds.). (2005). *Globalisation, global justice, and social work*. New York: Routledge.

Frank, A. G. (1978). *Dependent accumulation and underdevelopment*. London: Macmillan.

George, S. (2004). *Another world is possible if...*. New York: Verso.

Gilchrist Jones, G. (2001). International social welfare. In J. Turner & F. Turner (Eds.), *Canadian social welfare* (4th ed.; pp. 485–502). Toronto: Pearson Education.

Green, D. (1996). Latin America: Neoliberal failure and the search for alternatives. *Third World Quarterly, 17*(1), 109–122.

Guest, D. (1997). *The emergence of social security in Canada* (3rd ed.). Vancouver: UBC Press.

Gutiérrez, L., Parsons, R., & Cox, E. (Eds.). (2003). *Empowerment in social work practice*. Belmont CA: Wadsworth/Thomson.

Hall, A. & Midgley, J. (2004). *Social policy for development*. London: Sage.

Healy, L. (2001). *International social work*. New York: Oxford University Press.

Hokenstad, M. C., Khinduka, S., & Midgley, J. (Eds.). (1992). *Profiles in international social work*. Washington, DC: NASW Press.

Hokenstad, M. C. & Midgley, J. (Eds.). (2004). *Lessons from abroad: Adapting international social welfare innovations*. Washington, DC: NASW Press.

Huene, C. (1991). Ama llulla, ama sua, ama kella. *Participatory Development Review*, *2*(1).

Ife, J. & Tessoriero, F. (2006). The local and the global. In J. Ife & F. Tessoriero, *Community development: Community-based alternatives in an age of globalisation* (3rd ed., pp. 186–208). Frenchs Forest, NSW, Australia: Pearson.

International Federation of Social Workers (IFSW) & International Association of Schools of Social Work (IASSW). (2001). *International Definition of Social Work*. Retrieved June 15, 2007, from http://www.ifsw.org/en/p38000208.html

International Monetary Fund (IMF). (1944). *Articles of agreement of the International Monetary Fund*. Retrieved June 24, 2007, from http://www.imf.org/external/pubs/ft/aa/aa01.htm

Kane, L. (2001). *Popular education and social change in Latin America*. London, UK: Latin American Bureau.

Make Poverty History. (n.d.). *What has happened?* Retrieved June 25, 2007, from http://www.makepovertyhistory.org/2005/index.shtml

Mendoza Rangel, M. (2005). *Social work in Mexico: Towards a different practice*. In I. Ferguson, M. Lavalette, & E. Whitmore (Eds.), *Globalisation, global justice, and social work* (pp. 11–22). New York: Routledge.

Midgley, J. (2001). Issues in international social work: Resolving critical debates in the profession. *Journal of Social Work*, *1*, 21–35.

Midgley, J. & Livermore, M. (2004). Social development: Lessons from the global south. In M. C. Hokenstad & J. Midgley (Eds.), *Lessons from abroad: Adapting international social welfare innovations* (pp. 117–135). Washington, DC: NASW Press.

Mullaly, B. (1997). *Structural social work: Ideology, theory, and practice*. Toronto: Oxford University Press.

Nederveen Pieterse, J. (2001). Development models: Growth & transformation. In J. N. Pieterse, *Development theory: Deconstructions/reconstructions*. London: Sage Publications.

Oxfam. (2004). *The rural poverty trap: Why agricultural trade rules need to change and what UNCTAD XI could do about it*. Retrieved October 8, 2004, from http://www.oxfam.org.uk/what_we_do/issues/trade/bp_unctad.htm

Payne, M. (2006). *What is professional social work?* Bristol, UK: Policy Press.

Quiroz, T. (n.d.). *Reconceptualizacion*. Retrieved June 22, 2007, from http://reconceptualizacion.googlepages.com/teresaquirozmartin

Razack, N. (2002). *Transforming the field*. Halifax: Fernwood Publishing.

Rostow, W. (1960). *The stages of economic growth: A non-communist manifesto*. New York: Cambridge University Press.

Sen, G. & Grown, C. (1987). *Development, crises and alternative visions: Third World women's perspectives*. New York: Monthly Review Press.

Snyder, L. (2004). Collective outcomes and social mobilization in Chilean employment initiatives for women. *International Social Work, 47*(3), 321–335.

Spratt, T. (2005). Radical drama with children: Working with children using critical social work methods. In S. Hick, J. Fook, R. Pozzuto (Eds.), *Social work: A critical turn* (pp. 105–117). Toronto: Thompson.

Stalwick, H. (1997). Theory. In Hubert Campfens (Ed.), *Community development around the world: Practice, theory, research, training* (pp. 116–123). Toronto: University of Toronto Press.

Stiglitz, J. (2006). *Making globalization work.* New York: Norton & Company.

Teeple, G. (2000). *Globalization and the decline of social reform: Into the twenty-first century.* Aurora, ON: Garamond Press.

Tsang, A. K. T. & George, U. (1998). Towards an integrated framework for cross-cultural social work practice. *Canadian Social Work Review, 15*(1), 73–93.

United Nations (UN). (1948). *Universal Declaration of Human Rights.* Retrieved June 20, 2007, from: http://www.un.org/Overview/rights.html

United Nations (UN). (2006). *Millennium development goals report 2006.* Retrieved November 21, 2006, from http://unstats.un.org/unsd/mdg/Resources/Static/Products/Progress2006/MDG-Report2006.pdf

United Nations (UN). (n.d.). *UN millennium development goals.* Retrieved June 24, 2007, from http://www.un.org/millenniumgoals

United Nations Children's Fund (UNICEF). (2007). *0.7% Background.* Retrieved June 25, 2007, from http://www.unicef.ca/portal/Secure/Community/502/WCM/HELP/take_action/G8/Point7_EN2.pdf

United Nations Department of Economic and Social Affairs (UNESA). (2005). *Report on the World Social Situation, 2005.* Retrieved June 20, 2007, from http://www.un.org/esa/socdev/rwss/docs/Executivesummary.pdf

United Nations Economic and Social Council (ECOSOC). (19 May 2006). *Consideration of reports submitted by state parties: Canada.* Retrieved June 20, 2007, from http://www.ohchr.org/english/bodies/cescr/docs/E.C.12.CAN.CO.5.pdf

United Nations High Commission on Refugees (UNHCR). (2007). *Statistics.* Retrieved June 20, 2007, from http://www.unhcr.org/statistics.html

Wilson, M. G. & Whitmore, E. (2000). *Seeds of fire: Social development in an era of globalism.* Halifax: Fernwood.

World Bank (n.d.). *About: History.* Retrieved June 24, 2007, from http://web.worldbank.org/

World Commission on Environment and Development. (1987). *Our common future.* New York: Oxford University Press.

World Trade Organization. (n.d.). *What is the World Trade Organization?* (Section: Born in 1995, but not so young). Retrieved June 24, 2007, from http://www.wto.org/english/thewto_e/whatis_e/tif_e/fact1_e.htm

Yalnizyan, A. (2007). *The rich and the rest of us: The changing face of Canada's growing gap.* Toronto: Canadian Centre for Policy Alternatives.

# Epilogue

*Joanne and Francis Turner*

The dictionary tells us that an epilogue serves to round out and complete a non-dramatic literary work. Now that we have completed the task of assembling these 31 viewpoints on Canadian social welfare as perceived by a highly experienced cadre of senior colleagues in our field, we need to bring the task to some form of conclusion or completion.

In so doing, it is not our purpose to summarize each contribution, as such an exercise would contribute little. Rather, we will attempt to pick up on some of the major ideas that emerge—ideas that serve to unite the various contributions.

Clearly, in this sweep of our welfare system in Canada, one of the oft reflected themes has been that of the complexity of our country. A complexity of history, geography, language, environment, culture, size, ideologies, political structures, beliefs, attitudes, and values. As each of these differences interacts in the complex social welfare configuration of jurisdictions, policies, programs, and resources, surprisingly, the result is a reasonably efficient, yet highly diverse, structure. In addition, overshadowing our own Canadian complexity, we realize daily that we are very much influenced by events outside of the country. Questions regarding resources, politics, the environment, refugees, terrorism, and warfare have become our daily reality. These factors, all of which influence the emergence and functioning of a social welfare network, result in the need for a highly flexible system that can respond quickly to a broad range of changing needs and situations both within and without the country.

Over the decades, Canada has had a good track record of response to international need following disaster situations around the globe. This readiness to respond has greatly expanded given the reality of the present day. This openness to need is also reflected in our attitude to immigration and our eagerness to adopt children from other countries, as well as our promptness to send help of all kinds wherever it is needed. Indeed, at times we seem more ready to help people far from our shores than to respond to need here at home.

One of the many criticisms of our social welfare network (one mentioned by several of our authors) is the need for greater flexibility between and among the multifaceted system that exists within the country. More practitioners in the social welfare system need to be able to make decisions and allot resources that fit the needs of clients, rather than having to fit the client to the system. Because of the plurality of programs, restrictive legislation, varying jurisdictions, and resources, too much of practitioners' time is spent on bureaucratic issues and challenges. As mentioned in Chapter 17, a high degree of professional autonomy is built into the health care system, but not nearly as much into the social welfare system. In many instances, it is much easier to get a prescription for an expensive medication than it would be to obtain emergency financial aid to permit a person to travel to a job that becomes available.

We have become more aware across the country that few of the problems facing the people we meet in our various practices are the result of some moral weakness. We are learning that most of the challenges we face are systemic and are minimizing the influence of the Elizabethan view of the "undeserving poor."

We are also learning that professionals practising in this field need considerable academic preparation and ongoing continuing education to remain effective. Advances in the field will come from a strong commitment to top-level research. We know that new, flexible, and imaginative social policies, as well as legislation and services at all levels of government, are going to be needed to help address the many systemic issues that limit the effectiveness of our existing system. We need to learn from our own store of knowledge, but as well from that of other countries.

Poverty as it exists in Canada needs to be addressed much more aggressively. We know, for example, that adequate minimum wage can have a profound effect on poverty. Here in Canada, although some progress has been made, we still resist a commitment to increase the minimum wage to a living wage.

A further theme that emerges in several of the chapters is oppression and the many forms it can take in Canadian society. Most of this oppression is hidden, indeed, often unrecognized by many. Thus, an important component of the practice of social work and social welfare work involves confronting and attempting to bring some modification to these various forms of oppression. This will enhance the human dignity of all citizens and ensure that individuals in various oppressed groups can have equal access to needed services, resources, opportunities, and policies. The reality of many First Nations people underscores the importance of this goal.

Overall, Canada's social welfare network, like its health care system, is something about which we can be pleased but not complacent. There is much that can be done to improve it. There are many excellent ideas to be tried; there are many problems to be solved. The professionals in the field cannot rest. We must continue the advance of knowledge on all fronts, being aware that knowledge and its application are built on a step-by-step process of intelligent, concerned, and well-educated professionals committed to the enhancement of human potential for the good of all.

# Index

**Notes:** All references are to Canada unless otherwise noted. "(t)" stands for a table; "(f)," for a figure; "n" for a footnote; "CCSD," for Canadian Council on Social Development; "CIC," for Citizenship and Immigration Canada.